Contents

In this guide we have adopted the name Netherlands when speaking of the country as a whole, to avoid confusion with the two provinces called Holland.

PRINCIPAL SIGHTS

TOURING PROGRAMMES

WADDENEILANDEN
NOORDZEE
IJSSELMEER
GRONINGEN
BREMEN
Ems
A 7
Winschoterdiep
N 355
★ Leeuwarden
Harlingen
A 31
Bolsward ★
N 354
Sneek
A 7
N 359
N 32
A 7
Assen
Friese meren ★
★★ Afsluitdijk
Den Helder
A 7
Sloten ★
A 32
A 28
N 9
Noordhollandskanaal
Medemblik
Enkhuizen ★
A 50
★★ Giethoorn
Hoogeveense vaart

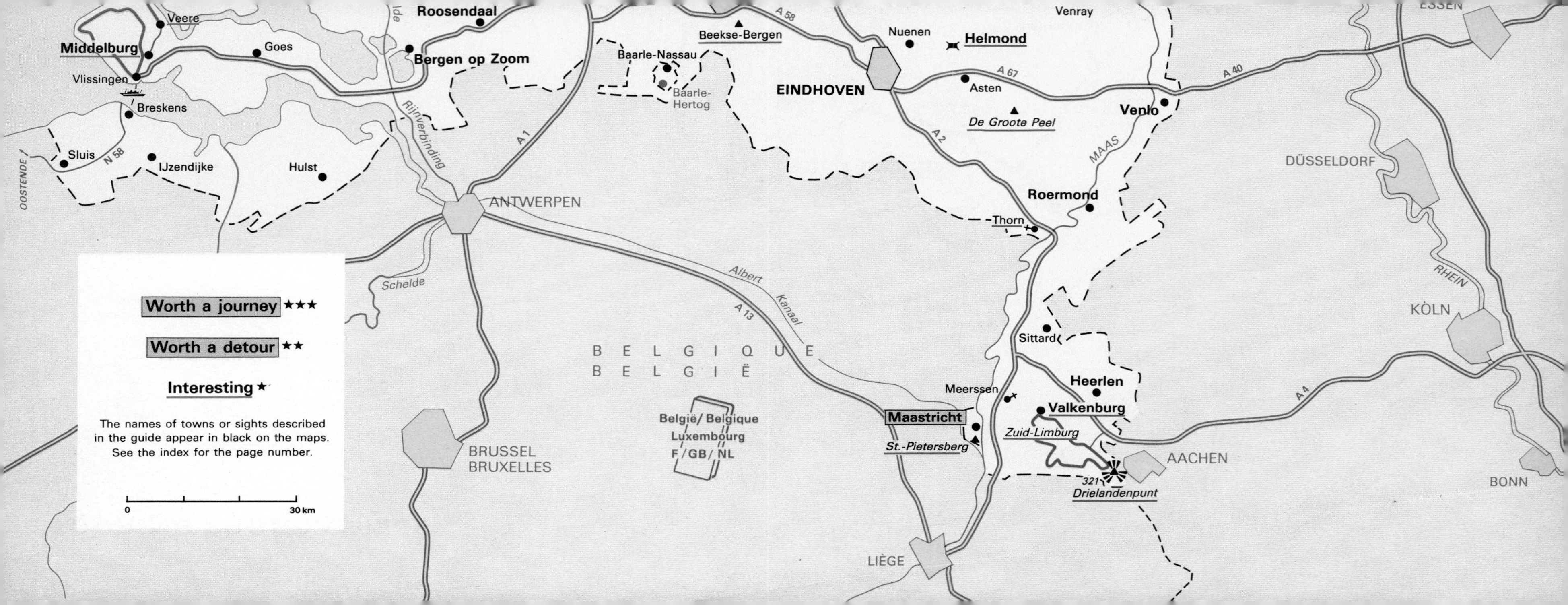

Worth a journey ★★★
Worth a detour ★★
Interesting ★
The names of towns or sights described in the guide appear in black on the maps. See the index for the page number.
0
30 km
Middelburg
Veere
Goes
Vlissingen
Breskens
Sluis
N 58
IJzendijke
Hulst
OOSTENDE
Roosendaal
Bergen op Zoom
Rijnverbinding
Scheldе
A 1
ANTWERPEN
BRUSSEL
BRUXELLES
Baarle-Nassau
Baarle-Hertog
Beekse-Bergen
A 58
EINDHOVEN
Nuenen
Helmond
A 67
Asten
De Groote Peel
A 2
Venray
Venlo
MAAS
Roermond
Thorn
A 40
DÜSSELDORF
RHEIN
KÖLN
BONN
ESSEN
Albert Kanaal
A 13
B E L G I Q U E
B E L G I Ë
België/ Belgique
Luxembourg
F / GB / NL
Sittard
Meerssen
Heerlen
Valkenburg
Zuid-Limburg
Maastricht
St.-Pietersberg
321
Drielandenpunt
AACHEN
A 4
LIÈGE

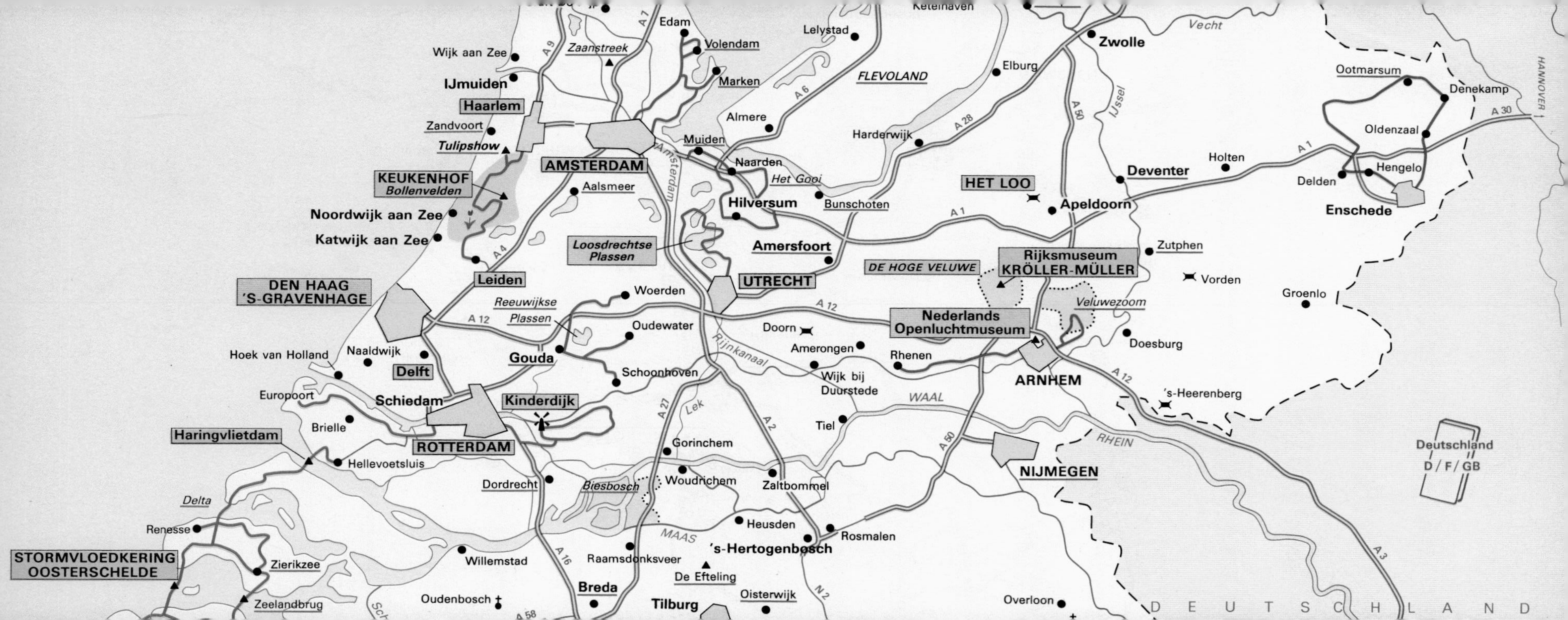

Edam
Volendam
Marken
Lelystad
Keteinaven
Zwolle
Vecht
Wijk aan Zee
Zaanstreek
IJmuiden
Haarlem
Zandvoort
Tulipshow
KEUKENHOF
Bollenvelden
AMSTERDAM
Amsterdam
Aalsmeer
Noordwijk aan Zee
Katwijk aan Zee
Loosdrechtse
Plassen
Leiden
DEN HAAG
'S-GRAVENHAGE
FLEVOLAND
Almere
Muiden
Naarden
Het Gooi
Hilversum
Bunschoten
Amersfoort
UTRECHT
Harderwijk
Elburg
IJssel
HET LOO
Apeldoorn
Deventer
Holten
Ootmarsum
Denekamp
HANNOVER
Oldenzaal
Hengelo
Delden
Enschede
Zutphen
Vorden
Groenlo
Rijksmuseum
KRÖLLER-MÜLLER
DE HOGE VELUWE
Veluwezoom
Nederlands
Openluchtmuseum
Doesburg
ARNHEM
's-Heerenberg
Woerden
Reeuwijkse
Plassen
Oudewater
Doorn
Amerongen
Rhenen
Gouda
Schoonhoven
Rijnkanaal
Wijk bij
Duurstede
Hoek van Holland
Naaldwijk
Delft
Europoort
Schiedam
Kinderdijk
WAAL
Tiel
Brielle
Haringvlietdam
ROTTERDAM
Lek
Gorinchem
RHEIN
NIJMEGEN
Deutschland
D / F / GB
Hellevoetsluis
Dordrecht
Biesbosch
Woudrichem
Zaltbommel
Delta
Renesse
MAAS
Heusden
Rosmalen
STORMVLOEDKERING
OOSTERSCHELDE
Zierikzee
Willemstad
Raamsdonksveer
's-Hertogenbosch
De Efteling
Breda
Tilburg
Oisterwijk
Oudenbosch
Zeelandbrug
Overloon
D E U T S C H L A N D
A 7
A 9
A 4
A 12
A 6
A 28
A 50
A 1
A 30
A 27
A 2
A 16
A 58
N 2
A 3

★ Hoorn
★ Urk
Schokland
Staphorst ★
Ketelhaven
N 50
A 28
★ Kampen
Vecht
Edam
Lelystad
Zwolle
Volendam ★
Marken ★
N 247
A 7
A 9
A 6
★★ Haarlem
AMSTERDAM ★★★
IJssel
A 30
HANNOVER
A 5
Muiden ★
A 28
A 50
A 1
Zandvoort
Het Gooi ★
★★★ HET LOO
Apeldoorn
Aalsmeer ★
Enschede
★★★ KEUKENHOF
Bollenvelden
Amsterdam
A 4
Hilversum
A 1
A 44
Amersfoort ★
Leiden ★★
★★ UTRECHT
★★★ Rijksmuseum
KRÖLLER-MÜLLER
★★ DEN HAAG
('s-GRAVENHAGE)
★★★ DE HOGE VELUWE
A 12
ARNHEM
A 12
Delft ★★
Gouda ★
Rijnkanaal
A 13
A 52
A 12
Lek
Schiedam
ROTTERDAM ★★
A 15
A 27
A 2
WAAL
★★ Haringvlietdam
A 15
Gorinchem
A 50
RHEIN
★★ Kinderdijk
N 57
NIJMEGEN ★
★ Dordrecht
Biesbosch ★
MAAS
★ Delta
A 27
A 59
's-Hertogenbosch
A 3

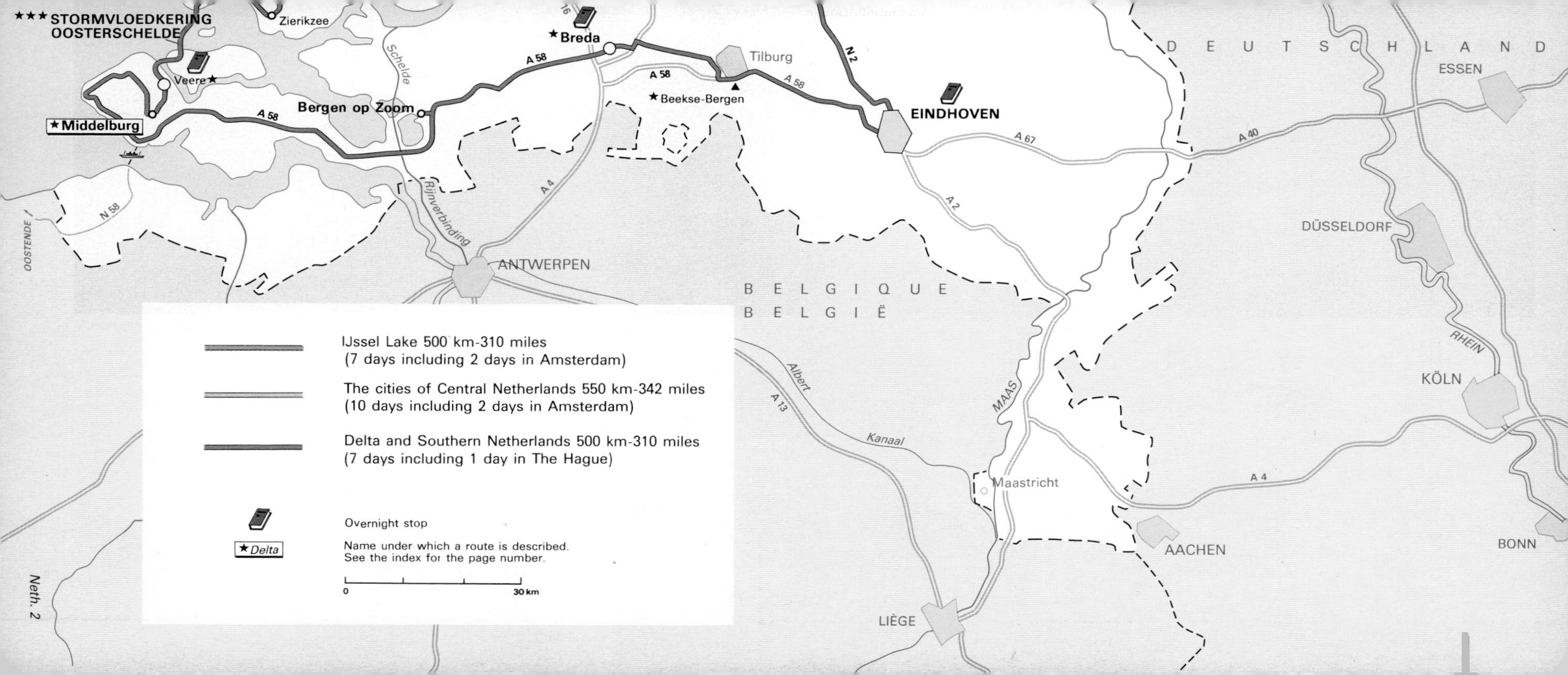
★★★ STORMVLOEDKERING OOSTERSCHELDE
Zierikzee
Veere ★
★ Middelburg
Bergen op Zoom
★ Breda
Tilburg
★ Beekse-Bergen
EINDHOVEN
A 58
N 2
A 67
A 2
A 4
A 40
A 13
N 58
OOSTENDE
Schelde
Rijnverbinding
ANTWERPEN
BELGIQUE
BELGIË
Albert Kanaal
MAAS
Maastricht
LIÈGE
AACHEN
DEUTSCHLAND
ESSEN
DÜSSELDORF
RHEIN
KÖLN
BONN
IJssel Lake 500 km-310 miles
(7 days including 2 days in Amsterdam)
The cities of Central Netherlands 550 km-342 miles
(10 days including 2 days in Amsterdam)
Delta and Southern Netherlands 500 km-310 miles
(7 days including 1 day in The Hague)
Overnight stop
★ Delta
Name under which a route is described.
See the index for the page number.
0
30 km

Windmill in Kinderdijk

Introduction

PICTOR

DESCRIPTION OF THE COUNTRY

The territory of the Netherlands, which has immense stretches of water such as IJsselmeer and the Waddenzee extends over 41 863sq km – 16 163sq miles, of which 9 896sq km – 3 820sq miles are reclaimed land. The longest distance from one end of the country to the other is 310km - 193 miles, ie from Rottum Island in the north of the province of Groningen to the south of Limburg.

The Netherlands has a total population of 15 239 182 (1993 census). With a density of 449 persons per sq km or 1 162 per sq mile it is one of the most densely populated countries in the world (United Kingdom 236 per sq km or 612 per sq mile). The population distribution is very uneven and the highest densities are to be found in the provinces of Noord- and Zuid- Holland. Together with the province of Utrecht they form the **Randstad** a large conurbation encompassing the country's four main cities: Amsterdam, The Hague, Rotterdam and Utrecht.

Agriculture in the Netherlands is highly intensive and highly productive but only represents a small percentage of the gross national product. Stock raising is well suited to the fertile reclaimed areas. Industry, especially chemicals, metallurgy and food processing, is concentrated within the Randstad area, the Twente, Noord-Brabant and Limburg. The Netherlands relies heavily on imported raw materials and the exportation of its manufactured goods. Because of its privileged geographical location trade, especially goods in transit between Europe and the rest of the world, plays an important role in the Dutch economy.

Holland and the Netherlands – Over the years the name **Holland** has come to designate all the Netherlands. In fact, this old province – separated since 1840 into Noord-Holland and Zuid-Holland supplanted the other regions of the United Provinces in the 17C due to its economic prosperity and political supremacy. Napoleon I ratified the primacy of Holland by creating the short-lived kingdom of Holland in 1810.

In fact as early as the late Middle Ages, the plains stretching from Friesland to Flanders were called **Lage Landen** or Nederlanden (Low Countries). In 1581 the United Provinces of the Netherlands (Verenigde Provinciën der Nederlanden) came into being. In 1815 this was still the name used when William I became ruler of the kingdom which included part of Belgium. The name has remained unchanged – Netherlands – despite the secession of Belgium in 1830, and Queen Beatrix has the title of Queen of the Netherlands (Koningin der Nederlanden).

On 1 January 1986 a new province was created: Flevoland *(qv)* consisting of the two polders of this name (Oostelijk Flevoland and Zuidelijk Flevoland Polders), the Noordoostpolder *(qv)*, as well as the old island of Urk. The Netherlands, together with the Netherlands Antilles *(qv)* form the Kingdom of the Netherlands.

A "LOW COUNTRY"

The name Netherlands is very apt (*land* = country, *neder* = low). The sea offers a constant threat as more than one third of the country is below sea level *(see The Fight Against the Sea)*. Without the protection of dunes and dikes more than half the country would be under water during surge tides or when the rivers are in spate. The lowest point, 6.5m - 21ft below sea level, is at Alexanderpolder, near Rotterdam. There is a marked difference between east and west. The west of the country is a low-lying plain with an altitude of less than 5m - 16ft. This is the most densely populated area. In the east, on the other hand, the Veluwe Hills rise to a height of 100m - 328ft (106m - 348ft at Zijpenberg to the north-east of Arnhem) and **Drielandenpunt** (321m - 1 053ft), at the junction of the Belgian and German frontiers, is the highest point.

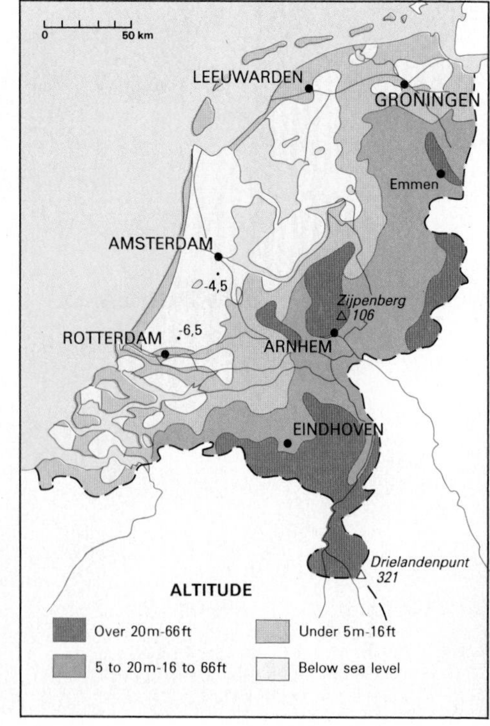

The Netherlands represents a depressed area of the earth's crust which has subsequently been infilled by depositions of sands and morainic material during the Quaternary Era and then by alluvial deposits from the rivers Rhine and Maas. Water level in the Netherlands is calculated from the Amsterdam Ordnance Datum (NAP or Normaal Amsterdams Peil).

A land of water – The land above sea level represents only five sixths of the total area. The country is criss-crossed by a network of rivers, whose estuaries form an immense delta *(qv)*. In addition, the large freshwater lake, IJsselmeer, created by the Zuiderzee Project still covers an area of 120 000ha - 296 400 acres. Elsewhere ponds, small lakes, canals, streams and ditches abound, especially in Friesland where the local flag has water lily leaves as its emblem. The percentage of land above sea level increases with the altitude from west to east. In the east the land is relatively well drained while water tends to accumulate in the low-lying plains and polders of the west.

LANDSCAPE

Apart from a few hilly regions the Netherlands consists of an immense plain with little diversity of soil, resulting in a corresponding lack of variety in the landscapes.
The polder lands *(qv)* are the heritage of man's determined intervention throughout the ages, but they also give a somewhat monotonous appearance to the countryside. However, they are one of the quintessential aspects of the country and by their peacefulness, light and colour give the landscape a poetic dimension.

Vast sandy tracts – Sand covers 43 % of the territory with the main areas in the south and the east, notably the **Kempenland** of Noord-Brabant, which is a continuation of the Belgian Kempenland, the **Veluwe** and the north of the provinces of Overijssel and Drenthe. In addition to agricultural land there are moorlands of heather, broom and gorse and forests (in the vicinity of Breda and the pines of the Veluwe).
The great Scandinavian glaciers of the Quaternary left tracts of **morainic material** with their tell-tale erratics in the undulating Utrechtse Heuvelrug *(qv)* and the Veluwe. The glaciers were also responsible for deflecting the course of the Rhine and Maas rivers westwards.
There are several areas of **marshland** (De Peel and Biesbosch) or lakes as in the south of Friesland *(qv)*. Unlike those in the province of Holland, these have not been reclaimed due to the infertility of their sandy soil.

Dunes – Coastal currents have caused offshore sand bars to form along the coast. The coastal sand dunes are of the utmost importance as they provide protection against the high tides. Marram grass is planted to stabilise the dunes which are carefully monitored by local authorities.
Public access is restricted in certain sectors to prevent further erosion and damage to this fragile ecosystem.
In some cases the chain of dunes is strengthened by a dike. The dunes also act as reservoirs for the rainwater which then filters down to the watertable.
The vast sandy beaches beyond the dunes and dikes are a valuable asset for the local seaside resorts.
In the north the Wadden Islands *(qv)* form an important offshore barrier. They are lashed on the north and west by the waves of the North Sea with the calmer waters of the Waddenzee on the landward side.

Alluvial deposits – **Marine deposited clays** cover 28 % of the territory especially in the Delta area, around the great coastal estuaries and bays and in those which have been reclaimed as polders such as the Lauwerszee and the Middelzee, which once reached as far inland as Leeuwarden.
The **fluvial clays** which cover 10 % of the territory are associated with the many rivers in the centre of the country and the Maas Valley, to the south of Venlo.

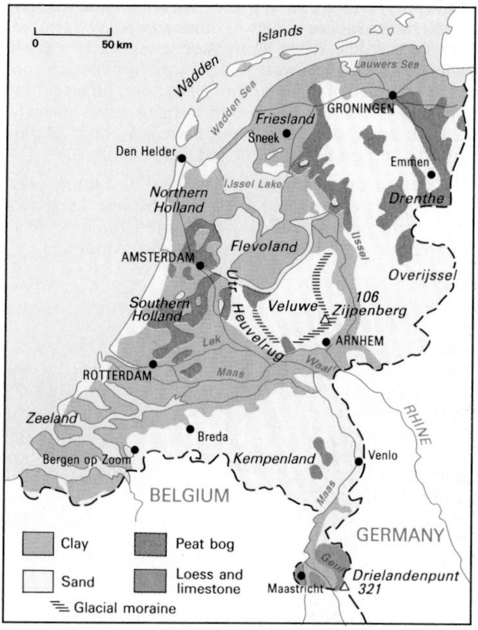

Peat bogs – In the Netherlands there are two types of peat bog. The first kind or "low peat" formed below the water table in the lagoons on top of the marine sediments. Once the peat was extracted lakes then formed which were drained and used for agricultural purposes.
In the upland region "high peat" formed in the marshy areas; once again it was used for fuel and the land was then given over to agriculture. The provinces of Groningen and Drenthe were known for the peat colonies *(veenkoloniën)* which flourished from the 16C to 19C.

Limestone plateau – The limestone landscapes of southern Limburg provide a sharp contrast to the rest of the country. Some parts of the bedrock are silt-covered (loess) as in the Hesbaye region of Belgium while others appear as rocky outcrops more akin to the ancient (hercynian) Ardennes Massif, again in Belgium.
All mining activity has now ceased in the Limburg coalfields which are a continuation of the Belgian Kempenland coal seams.

CLIMATE

A cloudy sky pierced by a few timid rays of sunshine or a misty horizon are typical of the climate and were beautifully captured by the landscape artists of the 17C.
The oceanic climate is humid and cool. An average of 750mm - 30in of rain falls each year, spread over more than 200 days. The temperature is fairly cool in summer without being too harsh in winter. Winters are warmer than in the past as proved by Avercamp's delightful skating scenes. The westerly winds are often strong and many of the farmhouses are protected by a screen of poplar trees.

THE FIGHT AGAINST THE SEA

The history of the Netherlands tells of man's continuous struggle with the elements, against the sea, storm surges and rivers in spate.
The first dunes were formed to the south of Haarlem around 5BC and by 1000AD a sand bar stretched from the Scheldt to the Eems. The bar was breached at several points creating the chain of islands now known as the Wadden Islands and the sea inundated the peat bogs lying inland to form the **Waddenzee**.

First steps: terps and dikes – Around 500BC the **Frisians**, the earliest inhabitants of the coastal areas, were already engaged in their struggle with the sea. They built artificial mounds or **terps** *(qv)* to protect their settlements from the encroaching sea. As early as 1200AD they were already building dikes and had drained a few parcels of land – the very first polders – between Leeuwarden and Sneek.
During the 13C there were at least 35 great floods and large tracts of land were flooded creating the Dollard and **Lauwerszee** in the north and the **Zuiderzee**, now IJsselmeer, in 1287.

Windmills: the first polders – In the 14C **windmills** *(qv)* were being used to drain lakes and marshes. By the 15C the rivers of Zeeland had already carved out an intricate network of peninsulas and islands and the coastal dunes were crumbling under the assaults of the waves. The overall lack of protection was responsible for the catastrophic **St Elisabeth Flood** *(qv)*. Following this disaster windmills were increasingly used in the threatened low-lying areas. Thus in Noord-Holland small **polders** appeared in Schagen in 1456 and in Alkmaar in 1564. Many of the coastal dikes of the time were the work of **Andries Vierlingh** (1507-79).

Creation of a polder – By definition a polder is land reclaimed from the sea, a lake or marshland. The area is enclosed with dikes and then pumping begins to regulate the water level. The method has been the same since earliest times despite various technological developments (windmills have been replaced by steam, diesel engine or electrically operated pumps).
The coastal or riverside peat-bogs, lying above sea level, necessitate the creation of a simple polder where all the surplus water is returned directly to the sea or the river via locks at low tide. However when the polder lies below sea level then pumping is necessary to evacuate the water into diversion canals (lodes) and thence to the sea.
A more complex type of polder is required when draining a lake. The lake is surrounded by a dike and then a canal, which also encircles the ring dikes of neighbouring polders. The polder itself is crisscrossed with small canals linked to each other by collector canals. When the water level reaches a set height the pump (formerly the windmill) forces the water back into the collector canals towards the peripheral canal and a network of lakes or canals serving as a temporary reservoir. The water is then discharged into the rivers and the sea either directly or by pumping. When the lake to be drained was fairly deep then a number of windmills (known as a gang) were required to pump the water out of the polder.

17C: a series of polders – In the 17C a name was associated with the drainage of inland tracts of water, that of **Jan Adriaensz. Leeghwater** (his name means low water). Leeghwater supervised the successful draining of the **Beemstermeer** to the north of Amsterdam in 1612 with the help of 40 windmills.

Landscape in the vicinity of Utrecht

The success of this initial project encouraged the Dutch to continue reclamation work and they built the polders of **Purmer** in 1622 and **Wormer** in 1626.

In 1631 the town of Alkmaar started reclaiming the **Schermermeer** following instructions from Leeghwater. This time 50 windmills were used and the work was completed in 1635. Another of Leeghwater's projects was the draining of Haarlemmermeer.

As early as 1667 Hendrick Stevin *(qv)* proposed a project to drain the Zuiderzee "to evacuate the violence and poison of the North Sea". The project was only completed in the 20C.

In the 18C autonomous water boards **(waterschappen)** were invested with the responsibility for building, maintaining and monitoring the country's dikes, canals and locks. These bodies still exist but since 1798 they are assisted by the Ministry of Public Works **(Waterstaat).**

Steam power was introduced just before 1800 and it proved capable of pumping water over high dikes thus replacing several rows or gangs of windmills. Pumping operations no longer depended on the vagaries of wind power.

The daring projects of the 19C and 20C – The most spectacular period of land reclamation began in 1848 with the draining of **Haarlemmermeer** *(qv)* which was completed four years later. Three large pumping stations were built such as Cruquius's which has now been converted into a museum.

After the great floods of 1916 it was the turn of the Zuiderzee itself. This great arm of the sea was closed off by the barrier dam, **Afsluitdijk**, in 1932 creating the outer Waddenzee and an inland freshwater lake now known as the **IJsselmeer** *(qv).*

Once enclosed, work began on draining several polders around the edge (Wieringermeer, Noordoost, Zuidelijk Flevoland and Oostelijk Flevoland). Originally a fifth polder (Markerwaard) was to have been reclaimed but the project was abandoned in 1986.

Other polders reclaimed in the 19C and 20C were the Prins Alexander Polder (1872) near Rotterdam and the Lauwersmeer Polder *(qv).*

The most recent disaster occurred during the night of 31 January 1953 when gale force winds swept landwards at high tide. 1 865 people died and 260 000ha - 642 200 acres were inundated. The success of the Zuiderzee Project encouraged engineers to find a similar way of protecting the islands of Noord- and Zuid-Holland. The outcome was the **Delta Plan** *(qv).*

The water levels in the canals crisscrossing the polders are constantly monitored and regulated. The same is also true for the many rivers and waterways which have been canalised by the building of dikes and locks.

Since the 13C about 7 050sq km - 2 745sq miles have been reclaimed from the sea. Coastal dikes have been responsible for creating 4 000sq km - 2 400sq miles, the IJsselmeer for another 1 650sq km - 644sq miles and a further 1 400sq km - 546sq miles by other means. These figures do not include territory which was flooded during military operations and which was subsequently reclaimed.

However, at the dawn of the 21C, some parts of the Dutch landscape may undergo a radical change. New EC farming regulations, the surplus of floral and market garden products, and the critical level of pollution – partly caused by large-scale pig breeding – led the Dutch government to vote a bill (1993) that stipulates that one tenth of arable land should be left fallow.

NATURE CONSERVATION

In this highly industrialised and densely populated country certain groups are very active in the protection of the environment. The Nature Conservation Society (Vereniging tot Behoud van Natuurmonumenten) is a private organisation which acquires unspoilt coastline and countryside properties for their preservation.

The Society currently manages 250 sites **(natuurmonumenten)** covering a total area of 67 000ha - 163 010 acres of varied habitats (woodlands, moors, dunes and marshes). In general visitors are welcome to the reserves (visitor centres, nature trails and bird hides), but there are usually restrictions.

State-owned forests and woodlands are managed by the Forestry Commission, Staatsbosbeheer, *(qv)*. Recreation is encouraged and the facilities include picnic sites, trails, camp sites...

Lapwing

Dessin S. Nicolle/Extrait de l'Inventaire de la faune

Birds

The great variety of habitats provided by the Netherlands' seasides, hillsides, watersides and woodsides attracts many bird species, both native and migratory. One of the most common species is the **lapwing** with its plaintif "pee-wit" cry, which is almost considered the national bird.

This plump little bird (with a wingspan of 30cm - 12in long) with its lustrous bronze plumage prefers grassy areas, especially in Friesland. Its eggs are considered a delicacy *(see Food and Drink)*.

S. Cordier/JACANA

Black-headed gull

The seashores are home to **terns, seagulls** and other **gulls**, particularly the black-headed gulls, which often nest inland. Colonies of **oystercatchers**, a small back and white wader, nest along the shores while the **grey heron** can be seen along the canals. The **spoonbill** *(photograph see Waddeneilanden)* is rarer but can be seen in shallow estuaries while the **white stork** is protected to prevent its extinction.

All sorts of **ducks** abound in the canals, ponds and marshes: the mallard and the sheldrake with multicoloured plumage are the most common.

The country's numerous **nature reserves** provide protection for a variety of species and their coastal and inland habitats. The reserves provide safe breeding and feeding grounds and facilities for scientific study. Public access is limited and usually prohibited during the breeding season (April to August).

F./Ph. Schreider/JACANA

Grey Heron

HISTORICAL TABLE AND NOTES

Prehistory

BC	
30 000	Earliest traces of human settlement in the east of the country.
4500	Agriculturalists settle in Limburg; their pottery belongs to the Spiral Meander Ware culture.
3000-2000	The megalithic Hunebed culture flourishes in the Drenthe area.
2200	A nomadic people settles to the north of the great rivers; stroke ornamented pottery ware.
2000	Bell-Beaker civilisation, notably in the Drenthe. New settlements in the alluvial areas of the delta.
1900	Bronze Age. The dead are buried in burial mounds.
800	In the east the people incinerate their dead and bury them in urnfields.
750-400	First Iron Age: Hallstatt Period.
500	First **terps** are built in Friesland and the Groningen area.
450	South of the great rivers, Second Iron Age: La Tene Period.
300	Arrival of Germanic and Celtic tribes to the area south of the Rhine.

Romans - Vikings

57-1	South of the Rhine **Caesar** defeats the Menapii and Eburones Celtic tribes belonging to the Roman province of Gallia Belgica.
12	The Germanic tribe the **Batavi** settles the banks of the great rivers.
AD	
69-70	Batavian uprising against the Roman garrisons.
3C	Incursions by Germanic tribes: the **Franks** settle the banks of the Rhine. At this time the main tribes occupying the territory are the Franks, **Saxons** and **Frisians**.
Late 3C	The area south of the Rhine belongs to the Roman province of Germania Secunda (capital: Colonia now Cologne).
4C	Power struggle between the Salian Franks and the Romans.
382	St Servatius transfers his bishopric from Tongeren to Maastricht, marking the christianisation of the region.
Early 6C	The Merovingian kingdom under Clovis (465-511) extends from the north of Gaul to the Rhine.
561	The Merovingian kingdom is divided into Neustria (west of the river Scheldt) and Austrasia (east of the Scheldt; the present Netherlands).
Late 7C	The Northumbrian missionary **Willibrord** evangelises Friesland.
800	**Charlemagne** is crowned Emperor of the West, a territory which covers the whole of the country and is centred on Aachen.
834	First of the **Viking** raids at Dorestad.
843	**Treaty of Verdun.** The Carolingian Empire is divided into three kingdoms: Germania, Francia and between the two, a Middle Kingdom stretching from the North Sea to the Mediterranean and including the present-day Netherlands. The Middle Kingdom (Lotharingia) was short-lived and Lothair II received only the northern part.
879-882	Viking invasions: from their base in Utrecht they make raids into the surrounding countryside.
925	Henry I, the Fowler unites **Lotharingia** to Germany.
959	Lotharingia is divided into Upper Lotharingia (Lorraine) and Lower Lotharingia covering nearly all the present country.

Counties and Dukedoms

10C	Bishop Balderic (919-976) extends the see of **Utrecht**.
Early 11C	The **Brabant** Dukedom is founded by Lambert, Count of Louvain.
11C	Creation of the countship of Geldern.
Late 11C	The county of **Holland** is extended at the expense of the county of Flanders (in Zeeland) and the See of Utrecht.
Early 13C	Zutphen and Veluwe become part of the county of Geldern.
Late 13C	**Floris V**, Count of Holland conquers West Friesland.
1323	Zeeland passes from Flanders to Holland.
1350	Start of the civil war between the **Hooks** (*Hoeken* - backed by Margaret of Bavaria) and the **Cods** (*Kabbeljauwen* - backed by her son William V).

Consolidation of Burgundian power

Late 14C	The Duchy of Burgundy is extended northwards when **Philip the Bold** acquires Limburg and certain rights over Brabant.
1421	St Elisabeth Floods.
1428	Philip the Good deposes **Jacoba** *(qv)* and makes himself master of Holland and Zeeland.
1473	**Charles the Bold** acquires Geldern; the only territory not in Burgundian hands is Friesland.

The Habsburgs

1477	Death of Charles the Bold; his daughter and heir Mary of Burgundy marries Maximilian of Austria (House of Habsburg). Mary is forced to sign the Great Privilege, a charter conferring far-reaching local powers.

1494 Philip the Fair, their son, inherits the Low Countries when Maximilian is elected Holy Roman Emperor.

1515 Charles I of Spain, son of Philip the Fair, inherits the Low Countries. In 1516 he becomes King of Spain then in 1519 Emperor of Germany as **Charles V**. He adds **Friesland** to the Low Countries in 1523; the see of Utrecht in 1527; Overijssel in 1528; and takes Groningen and Drenthe by force in 1536.

1543 The Duke of Geldern cedes his dukedom to Charles V who thus rules over nearly the whole of Europe.

1548 Charles V groups the 17 provinces of the Low Countries and the Franche-Comté into the independent Burgundian Kreis.

The Spanish Netherlands

1555 Charles V abdicates his claim to the Low Countries in favour of his son Philip II, soon to become King of Spain.

1555-1579 The **Revolt of the Netherlands**; the rise of Protestantism.

1566 The **Breda Compromise** *(qv)* also known as the Compromise of the Nobility; the Beggars protest against the Inquisition.
Iconoclastic Fury *(qv)* with rioting and destruction of Church property.

1567 The Duke of Alva is appointed governor of the Low Countries.

1568 **William the Silent** *(qv)* raises an army; beginning of the Eighty Years War.

Ph. Gajic/MICHELIN

William the Silent (detail of a stained glass window in St.-Janskerk), Gouda

1572 **Capture of Brielle** by the Sea Beggars; Vlissingen and Enkhuizen follow.

1579 **Union of Arras** is signed by Catholic Hainaut, Artois and Douai pledging allegiance to Philip; in reply the northern Protestant provinces form an essentially military alliance and sign the **Union of Utrecht** *(qv)*.

The United Provinces

1581 Creation of the **Republic of the United Provinces**, a federation of seven provinces, independent of Spanish rule: Philip II is deposed.

1584 William the Silent is assassinated in Delft.

1585 The second son, Maurice of Nassau, succeeds his father as Stadtholder of Holland and Zeeland. He becomes undisputed leader of the United Provinces in 1618 on the death of his elder brother.

1596 Cornelis de Houtman establishes trading relations with Java.

1598 Edict of Nantes.

1602 **Dutch East India Company** founded to trade with Asia.

1609-21 **Twelve Years Truce** with Spain. Henry Hudson sails up the river which bears his name, in his ship the *Half Moon* while on a voyage for the Dutch East India Company.

1614 The name New Netherland is first used for the colony founded in the New World.

1618 **Synod of Dort** *(qv)*. Reprobation of the Remonstrants.

1619 Founding of Batavia (Jakarta) in the Dutch East Indies.

1620 The Pilgrim Fathers arrive on the *Mayflower* and establish Plymouth Colony.

1621 Founding of the **Dutch West India Company** to trade with America. Renewal of hostilities with Spain.

1624-54 Colonisation of northeast Brazil.

1625 The Dutch trading post on Manhattan is called Nieuw Amsterdam.

1626 Peter Minuit of the Dutch West India Company buys Manhattan from the Indians for the equivalent of $24.

1634 | Dutch West India Company establishes a trading post in Curaçao in the Antilles.
1648 | Treaty of Westphalia ends the Thirty Years War, also called the Eighty Years War. By the **Peace of Munster** Philip IV of Spain recognises the independence of the United Provinces.
1651 | The English Navigation Act augurs ill for Dutch trade.
1652 | Jan van Riebeeck *(qv)* founds the Cape colony.
1652-54 | **First Anglo-Dutch War**: commercial and colonial rivalry lead to what is essentially a war at sea; the Dutch fleet is commanded by Admiral Tromp *(qv)*.
1653-72 | Stadtholderless Period: the statesman **Johan de Witt** *(qv)* Grand Pensionary runs the State.
1658-1795 | Colonisation of Ceylon (Sri Lanka).
1664 | The English seize New Netherlands and rename its capital New York for the Duke of York, later James II.
1665-7 | **Second Anglo-Dutch War**, Admiral de Ruyter distinguishes himself. Under the **Treaty of Breda** Dutch Guiana (Suriname) is ceded to the Dutch in exchange for control of New Netherland.
1667-8 | War of Devolution led by Louis XIV; Treaty of Aachen.
1672 | **William III**, Stadtholder of Holland and Zeeland.
1677 | William marries Mary the daughter of James II.
1672-8 | Louis XIV wages war against the United Provinces.
Peace of Nijmegen *(qv)*.
1685 | Revocation of the Edict of Nantes.
1688 | Glorious Revolution: British crown offered jointly to William and Mary on the flight of James II.
1689 | William becomes King of England.
1701-13 | Spanish War of Succession: alliance of several countries, including the United Provinces, against Louis XIV. **Peace of Utrecht**.
1702 | The Stadtholder William III dies without an heir. The title of Prince of Orange passes to the Frisian stadtholder Jan Willem Friso.
1701-13 | War of the Spanish Succession.
1702-47 | Stadtholderless Period.
1714-27 | Reign of George I.
1747 | **William IV**, son of the latter, is the first elected Stadtholder of the United Provinces.
1751-95 | **William V**, son of the former Stadtholder.

French domination

1795 | A French army under General Pichegru overruns the country; William V flees to England; the United Provinces become the **Batavian Republic** (1795-1806).
1806 | **Louis Bonaparte** becomes king of the **Kingdom of Holland** with Amsterdam as the capital.
1810-13 | Louis Bonaparte abdicates; the country becomes part of the **French Empire** under Napoleon.

Union with Belgium

Dec. 1813 | William VI of Orange, son of William V, last Stadtholder of the United Provinces, becomes sovereign of the Kingdom of the Netherlands.
1815 | Battle of Waterloo and the fall of Napoleon. The Congress of Vienna recognises William VI Prince of Orange as the King of the Netherlands (including Belgium), under the name **William I**. In addition he becomes Grand Duke of Luxembourg.
The western seaboard of New Guinea is colonised.
1830 | Brussels Revolution leads to Belgium's independence.

Kingdom of the Netherlands: an independent kingdom

1831 | Parts of Limburg and Brabant are ceded to Belgium but William I only ratifies the treaty in 1839.
1890-1948 | Reign of **Queen Wilhelmina** (b 1880).
1932 | Zuiderzee Project.
May 1940 | The country is invaded by the German army. The Queen and her family leave for London.
5 May 1945 | Surrender of the German army *(see Arnhem: Excursions)*. Return of the Queen.
1948 | Queen Wilhelmina abdicates in favour of her daughter **Juliana** (b 1909). Economic Union of Benelux.
Dec. 1949 | Independence of the Dutch East Indies which become the Republic of **Indonesia**.
1954 | Autonomy of Dutch Guiana or Suriname and the archipelago of the Dutch Antilles.
1957 | The Netherlands joins the EC.
1960 | The **Benelux** economic union comes into effect.
Nov. 1975 | Independence of Dutch Guiana which becomes the Republic of **Suriname**.
30 April 1980 | Queen Juliana abdicates in favour of her daughter **Beatrix**.
1986 | Flevoland becomes the 12th province.
1987 | Inauguration of the Oosterschelde storm-surge barrier.
Dec. 1991 | **Treaty of Maastricht** signed by the twelve EC members advocating commercial, monetary and political union.
23 Jan. 1993 | Dutch is recognised by law as the official national language; Frisian in Friesland is accorded the status of second governmental language.

THE HOUSES OF ORANGE AND STUART

This chart is selective; it shows the association between the two houses.
For monarchs after William V see Historical Table and Notes.

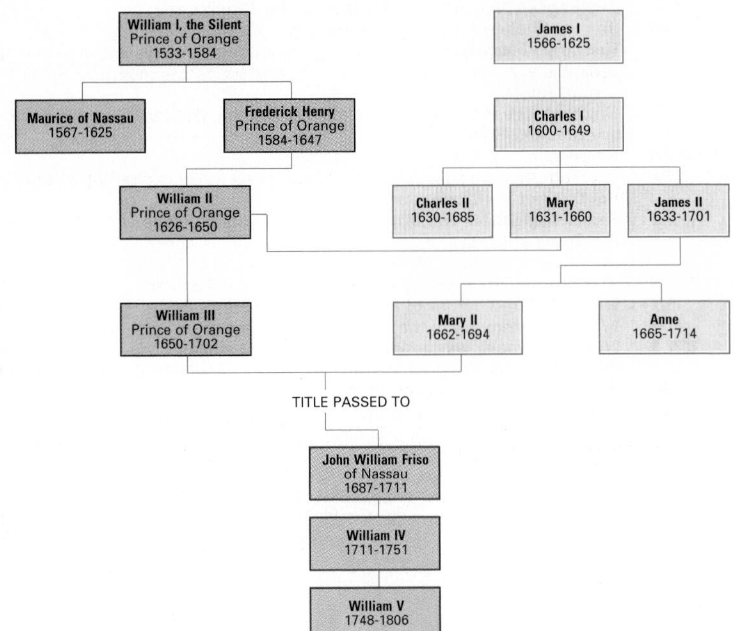

THE BRITISH AND DUTCH TIES

Two small sea-faring nations with a strong protestant voice, in an otherwise predominantly Catholic world, were the Netherlands and Britain. They were linked politically, religiously, commercially, intellectually and artistically long before William III's reign and yet it was during his reign that their friendship reached its peak.

William III, Prince of Orange, nephew and son-in-law to King James II (1685-8) of England was Stadtholder of the United Provinces. He had married Mary, James's daughter in 1677. In England King James set about establishing Catholicism creating unrest and dissent throughout the nation. The British wrote to William in June 1688 asking him to restore peace and unity to the country. William landed in October 1688, James abdicated; the throne being vacant, Mary, the nearest Protestant claimant, with her husband William were jointly crowned in April 1689; with their reign (1689-1702) a vogue for all things Dutch developed.

Political decisions were closely linked to commercial interests (Dutch Wars) and the Dutch, English and Scots had been exchanging naval techniques and trading together for years (Dutch trading English wool, weavers invited to England to teach their craft, with Scotland exchange of luxury goods existed, shipbuilding...).

Once commercial relationships had been established between the two countries, Dutch goods and influence began appearing in Britain (bricks and gables, sash windows, Dutch-style gardens, marinescapes and portraits, interior decorative detail...). Dutch influence reached its peak during William and Mary's reign with the transformation of Hampton Court and Kensington Palace: the influence of their Dutch residence, Het Loo, is apparent. They employed Grinling Gibbons (carvings), Daniel Marot (architect and interior decorator) and Sir Godfrey Kneller (portraitist) all in some way related to the Netherlands. Attention to interior decoration (carvings, tulip-vases, laquerware cabinets, upholstered cabriole-legged chairs...), Mary's obvious love of porcelain and William's for gardens were duplicated in many stately homes (Belton, Ashdown, Easton, Neston, Breamore...) of that time.

The Dutch tradition of religious tolerance and freedom of expression attracted thinkers (Erasmus, Spinoza, Grotius, Voetius...), printers (English books printed and translated into Dutch) and scholars (Jonson, Boswell...) and enabled the English Bill of Rights to exist. Political (mid-17C Royalists, 1st Earl of Shaftesbury, Bishop Burnet...) and religious (Presbyterians, Separatists, Congregationalists...) refugees were welcomed.

With the reign of William and Mary, a wave of tolerance spread through Britain rendering exile to the Netherlands unnecessary.

Origins of the House of Orange

In the 13C the small principality of Orange in southern France belonged to a branch of the Baux family, who were also heirs to the German principality of Nassau. In the 16C it came into the possession of William the Silent, ruler of the German principality of Nassau and stadtholder of the United Provinces. William was the founder of the royal house. By the Treaty of Utrecht in 1713 the tiny Dutch enclave of Orange was ceded to France. However the title of Prince or Princess of Orange has remained the preferred title of the royal dynasty of the Netherlands.

OVERSEAS EXPANSION

In the middle of the 16C Amsterdam traders went to Antwerp to obtain goods brought back from the Indies by Portuguese ships. The mouth of the Scheldt being cut off by the Sea Beggars the traders started sailing to Lisbon in 1580, the same year that Philip II of Spain invaded Portugal. In 1585 he put an embargo on Dutch trade in Spain and Portugal. The Dutch merchants, forced to take care of shipments themselves, clashed with the Spanish, Portuguese and above all the English, fearsome competitors in overseas markets.

On the spice route – When looking for access to India from the north of Europe, **Willem Barents** *(qv)* discovered Spitsbergen in 1596. The same year **Cornelis de Houtman** *(qv)* landed in **Java**.
To coordinate the ever increasing trading companies, in 1602 Johan van Oldenbarnevelt founded the **Dutch East India Company** *(qv)*. This institution which obtained a monopoly over shipping and trade to the east of the Cape of Good Hope kept going until 1798.
In 1619 the foundation of **Batavia** by **Jan Pieterszoon Coen** *(qv)* marks the beginning of the colonisation of Java. **Malacca** was taken from the Portuguese in 1641. The following yeard Tasman discovered **Tasmania** and **New Zealand**, then Australia (1644) but did not reside there. In 1652 **Jan Anthonisz. van Riebeeck** *(qv)* founded the **Cape Colony**. Originally a stopping point on the way to India, it grew into a rambling but vigorous community which subsequently became an independent settlement, expanding and spreading inland. Finally **Ceylon** was occupied from 1658.

The Americas – At the same time Dutch trade turned towards the New World.
In 1609 the **Hudson** *(qv)* expedition took place. In 1613 the **Guiana** coast was occupied by traders. **Willem Schouten** *(qv)* discovered Cape Horn in 1616.
The **Dutch West India Company**, created in 1621, covered both Africa and the Americas. In **Brazil**, **John Maurice of Nassau** (1604-79) was appointed governor general (1636-44). Patron of arts and science, he surrounded himself with a team of scientists, painters and draftsmen who assembled abundant documentation on the country.
The settlement called **Nieuw Amsterdam** (New Amsterdam) was founded in 1625 on the eastern coast of North America. **Peter Stuyvesant** *(qv)* soon became its Governor. In the Antilles, the Dutch West India Company founded the colony of **Curaçao** in 1634.
Many of these conquests were only temporary. However, the Dutch succeeded in making lasting settlements in Java, Guiana and in the Antilles; the **Netherlands Antilles** (capital: Willemstad), still belong to the Kingdom of the Netherlands.

RELIGIONS

The Protestant proverb which says: "One Dutchman, a theologian; two Dutchmen, a Church; three Dutchmen, a schism" has been borne out over the years. Dutch interest in doctrines and theology, linked to a certain taste for tolerance, explains the proliferation in the country of different beliefs and the most diverse movements.

A mystic trend – In the 14C the mystical writings of the Flemish **Jan van Ruysbroeck** are the origin of a spiritual movement, the **Devotio Moderna**, which developed within the Order of the **Brethren of the Common Life** *(qv)* due to the theologian **Gerhard Groote**.

The Reformation – The Lutheran doctrine, born in 1517 and condemned by the Diet of Worms in 1521, spread quickly over the Low Countries.
In 1530 the **Anabaptist** movement appeared. A few fanatics joined up with **John of Leiden** *(qv)* and formed a community of a slightly revolutionary type in Munster, in Germany. In Friesland, **Menno Simonsz.** *(qv)*, a Catholic priest, founded in 1536, the Anabaptist sect, the **doopsgezinden** (Mennonites), which gathered together the faithful remaining in the country. The Anabaptists were persecuted for nearly a century.
However, it was **Calvinism** which obtained the upper hand in the Low Countries. This doctrine spread over the country from 1550 through France.
In the 16 and 17C Protestant refugees coming from Belgium and France established the **Walloon Churches** *(qv)* using the French language.
Quite early, the religious convictions of the Calvinists became the symbol of the struggle against the Spanish Catholics. Soon after the Breda Compromise *(qv)*, the iconoclastic Fury broke out in 1566.

Clandestine Catholicism – After the fight for independence, Calvinist fanaticism grew stronger. Holland and Zeeland considering the Calvinist religion as official, forbade other religions in 1579 *(p 202)* and Catholics, in particular, were obliged to practise their cult in **clandestine churches** up to 1798, however, they were not persecuted.

From the 17C to today – The Synod of Dort from 1618-9 gave a new cohesion to the Dutch Reformed Church (successor to the Dutch Reformed Church; changed to the Reformed Church of the Netherlands in 1816 by King William I). And yet its unity was established to the detriment of the Arminians or **Remonstrants** *(qv)*. They were the object of persecution for several years, as can be seen by the arrest of Oldenbarnevelt *(qv)*.
Towards the end of the 17C the **Labadist** *(qv)* movement was born.
Persecuted in France, the Jansenists took refuge in Utrecht where they contributed to the establishment of an independent Catholic church, the **Old Catholics Church** *(qv)*.
In the beginning of the 18C the **Moravian Brothers** *(qv)* sect was created.
Presently the **Protestants** of the Netherlands belong either to the Reformed Church of the Netherlands (Nederlands Hervormde Kerk) which dates from the 1619 Synod of Dort and has nearly 2.5 million members, or to the group of Reformed Churches in the Netherlands (Gereformeerde Kerken in Nederland) founded in 1892 and which counts about 820 000 members.
The **Catholics**, numerous in the south of the country, represented 38 % of the population in 1985.

THE ARTS

ABC OF ARCHITECTURE

To assist readers unfamiliar with the terminology employed in architecture, we describe below the most commonly used terms.

Ecclesiastical architecture

illustration I ▶

NAVE

CHEVET

Ground plan – The more usual Catholic form is based on the outline of a cross with the two arms of the cross forming the transept: ① Porch – ② Narthex – ③ Side aisles (sometimes double) – ④ Bay (transverse section of the nave between 2 pillars) – ⑤ Side chapel (often predates the church) – ⑥ Transept crossing – ⑦ Arms of the transept, sometimes with a side doorway – ⑧ Chancel, nearly always facing east towards Jerusalem; the chancel often vast in size was reserved for the monks in abbatial churches – ⑨ High altar – ⑩ Ambulatory: in pilgrimage churches the aisles were extended round the chancel, forming the ambulatory, to allow the faithful to file past the relics – ⑪ Radiating or apsidal chapel – ⑫ Axial chapel. In churches which are not dedicated to the Virgin this chapel, in the main axis of the building is often consecrated to the Virgin (Lady Chapel) – ⑬ Transept chapel.

romanesque　　gothic

◀ illustration II

Cross-section: ① Nave – ② Aisle – ③ Tribune or Gallery – ④ Triforium – ⑤ Barrel vault – ⑥ Half-Barrel vault – ⑦ Pointed vault – ⑧ Buttress – ⑨ Flying buttress – ⑩ Pier of a flying buttress – ⑪ Pinnacle – ⑫ Clerestory window.

illustration III ▶

Gothic cathedral: ① Bell tower or belfry – ② Spire – ③ Flying buttress – ④ Buttress – ⑤ Side chapel – ⑥ Transept crossing tower with cupola – ⑦ Gable – ⑧ Side doorway – ⑨ Radiating or apsidal chapel – ⑩ Pinnacle.

◀ illustration IV

Quadripartite vaulting: ① Diagonal – ② Transverse – ③ Stringer – ④ Flying buttress – ⑤ Keystone.

illustration V ▶

Arches and pillars: ① Ribs or ribbed vaulting – ② Abacus – ③ Capital – ④ Shaft – ⑤ Base – ⑥ Engaged column – ⑦ Pier of arch wall – ⑧ Lintel – ⑨ Discharging or relieving arch – ⑩ Frieze.

GLOSSARY OF ART AND ARCHITECTURAL TERMS USED IN THIS GUIDE

Aisle: illustration I.

Ambulatory: illustration I.

Apse: semicircular or semi-polygonal east end of a church.

Atlante: male figure used as a support.

Avant-corps: the part of a building which projects obviously from the main body or façade.

Barrel vaulting: illustration II.

Bas-relief: carved or sculpted figures which are slightly proud of their background; low-relief.

Bay: illustration I.

Bracket: piece of projecting stone or timber supporting a beam or cornice.

Capital: illustration V.

Caryatid: female figure used as a support.

Chevet: French term for the exterior of the apse (the east end); illustration I.

Corbel: see bracket.

Crowstepped gable: triangular upper part of a wall which supports two slopes of the roof and which has stepped edges.

Consistory: place where church officers meet to conduct church affairs.

Crypt: underground chamber or chapel.

Doric order: Greek architectural order.

Dormer: vertically set window on a sloping roof.

Festoon: carved, moulded or painted garland of fruit, flowers or leaves.

Fluted: vertical grooves in column shafts.

Gable: triangular part of an end wall carrying a sloping roof; illustrations see Amsterdam: Herengracht.

Hatchment: wooden panel adorned with the armorial bearings of the deceased.

Hipped roof: roof with four uniformly pitched sides.

Keystone: illustration IV.

Misericord: illustration VII.

Perron: a landing or platform, usually approached by a single or double flight of steps, outside the main entrance of a building.

Pilaster: engaged rectangular column.

Pinnacle: illustrations II and II.

Quoin: stones or bricks used to emphasise the corners of buildings.

Rood-screen: carved screen separating chancel and nave, generally bearing a large crucifix (rood) and sometimes representations of other figures present at the Crucifixion.

Stalls: illustration VII.

Transept: illustration I.

Triforium: small arcaded gallery above the aisles; illustration II.

Twinned or paired: applied to columns or pilasters grouped in twos.

Westwork: tall tower adjoining the west front.

▼ illustration VI

Doorway: ① Archivolt. Depending on the architectural style of the building this can be rounded, pointed, basket-handled, ogee or even adorned by a gable – ② Arching, covings (with string courses, mouldings, carvings or adorned with statues). Recessed arches or orders form the archivolt – ③ Tympanum – ④ Lintel – ⑤ Archshafts – ⑥ Embrasures. Arch shafts, splaying sometimes adorned with statues or columns – ⑦ Pier (often adorned by a statue) – ⑧ Hinges and other ironwork.

illustration VII ▼

Stalls ① High back – ② Elbowrest – ③ Cheek piece – ④ Misericord.

In the domain of the arts, the Netherlands has made a first-rate contribution to Western civilisation.
Sculpture, most likely due to lack of material more or less up to the 20C, and music occupy a relatively modest place in the Dutch artistic heritage. But architecture, at certain epochs very remarkable, and above all paintings, make the Netherlands a place of pilgrimage and inspiration.

Romanesque Art

It can be seen in several regions far apart from each other.

Rhenish-Mosan Art – This developed in the Maas Valley and in particular at Maastricht, (which belonged to the Diocese of Liège). The style is very similar to the Rhine Valley style, hence its name.

Architecture – Maastricht was an important town in the Roman era and then a place of pilgrimage – the relics of St Servatius, who died in 384, are venerated there. It has magnificent buildings such as St Servaasbasiliek and the Onze Lieve Vrouwebasiliek.
In its early days Mosan art borrowed a lot from **Carolingian architecture**. Apart from St Nicolaaskapel at Nijmegen, whose shape imitated the octagonal basilica of Charlemagne in the cathedral at Aachen, Carolingian churches usually have two chancels, an imposing westwork, and a chapel called the emperor's room, Keizerszaal, situated upstairs on the west side. Inside the wooden ceiling is flat, the pillars square.
Towards 1000AD the construction of **St Servaasbasiliek** was started, with a westwork with two large towers decorated with Lombard arcading. The **Onze Lieve Vrouwebasiliek**, of the same period, also has a massive westwork, flanked by round turrets *(photograph: see Maastricht)*. St-Amelbergakerk at **Susteren** *(qv)* built in the second half of the 11C is still very plain.
In the 12C Mosan architecture mellowed and decoration increased. Sculpture started appearing on the capitals, low reliefs and portals. It was the period when St-Servaasbasiliek was altered, as well as the Onze Lieve Vrouwebasiliek (both in Maastricht), where the chancel, seen from the nave, is one of the most beautiful Romanesque achievements of the country. **Rolduc Abbey** in Kerkrade, shows by its original trefoiled plan, Rhenish influence.
The Onze Lieve Vrouwe Munsterkerk at **Roermond**, although restored, has kept Rhenish-Mosan characteristics. The crypts of these edifices are often very beautiful.

Gold and silversmith's work – As in the rest of the Diocese of Liège, in Belgium, Mosan art has produced masterpieces of gold and silversmith's work. Thus, St.-Servaasbasiliek in Maastricht has preserved the gilded copper **shrine** of the saint, with richly decorated enamel work, cabochons, and: Christ and St Servatius (on each end), and the Apostles (on the sides) *(photograph; see Maastricht)*.
It should also be mentioned that there is a lovely 11C Mosan Christ in bronze which belongs to the Rijksmuseum Het Catharijneconvent in Utrecht.

Other regions – It was normal that **Utrecht**, an important bishopric in the Middle Ages, was embellished with religious buildings in the Romanesque period. However, apart from Pieterskerk, a good example of the local style (1148), there are only a few remains of the lovely Romanesque series conceived by Bishop Bernulphus.
Among the edifices built in the Diocese of Utrecht, the Grote Kerk at **Deventer** has preserved the remains of a double transept and a westwork (*c*1040) which links it to Mosan churches.
At **Oldenzaal**, the great St-Plechelmusbasiliek is later (early 12C) and has a nave with vaulting supported by strong pillars.
Utrecht keeps **gold and silverware** objects in its museums which are witness to the prosperity of its bishops from the Romanesque period: monstrances, pyxes, shrines, processional crosses and gospel books with engraved bindings.
Beginning in the mid-12C the Romanesque style appeared in a particular regional manner in **Friesland** and in the **province of Groningen** in the village churches where the outside walls were enlivened by **brick decoration** *(see the Excursions of Groningen and Leeuwarden)* and inside there are often fresco remains.

Gothic Art

Gothic art appeared only in the 14C and mainly in the 15C under Burgundian rule. Many religious buildings, as well as a few town halls date from this period.

Churches – Noord-Brabant, a province where the majority of the inhabitants are Catholic, has most of the large churches and **cathedrals** in the country. These buildings were built in the **Brabant Gothic style** similar to a number of edifices in Belgium and similar to Flamboyant Gothic: exterior – many openwork gables and crocket spires, tall windows, flying buttresses, tall belfry porch on the west side; interior – a slender central nave with pointed vaulting resting on round columns with crocket capitals and a triforium.
The Grote Kerk in **Breda** *(photograph: see Breda)* is a typical example of Brabant Gothic as is St-Janskathedraal in **'s Hertogenbosch** *(photograph: see 's-Hertogenbosch)*, started in the 14C and one of the most beautiful and greatest achievements in the country. Contrary to other edifices, the vaults of the latter do not rest on columns but on a cluster of small columns without capitals.
The Brabant Gothic style influenced the construction of many other churches in the country. In Holland, the stone vault was rare and the church was covered with a wooden ceiling, flat or barrel vaulted. The only exception is the Grote Kerk in Dordrecht. A number of lovely Gothic buildings worth noting include: in Leyden Hooglandse- of St-Pancraskerk, in Alkmaar the Grote Kerk, in Amsterdam the Nieuwe Kerk, in Gouda St-Janskerk and in Haarlem St-Bavokerk. The cathedral in Utrecht, unfortu-

nately, did not survive the great storm of 1672. There still exists, however, a harmonious bell tower, the **Domtoren**, similar in outline to many bell towers which can be seen in the country, as at Amersfoort.

In the same diocese, the St.-Nicolaaskerk in Kampen is also interesting.

Town Halls (Stadhuizen) – Two town halls in the Flamboyant Gothic style are particularly remarkable. That of **Gouda** *(photograph: see Gouda)* is delightful with its façade where a multitude of pinnacles and slender spires rear up. That of **Middelburg** *(photograph: see Middelburg)*, more sumptuous, built by Belgian architects shows the influence of the Brussels town hall.

Domtoren, Utrecht

C. Sappa/CEDRI

Sculpture – Not as abundant as in Belgium, church furnishings have, however, some interesting 15C and early 16C wood carvings. The groups by **Adriaen van Wesel** (late 15C) shown in the Rijksmuseum in Amsterdam *(qv)* are carved with a remarkable sense of composition and a great strength of expression.

The **Brabant altarpieces** are triptyches in the Flamboyant style, with a central panel in wood, carved on several levels, showing very animated scenes with comical details and flanked by two painted panels (altarpieces of St-Janskathedraal in s-Hertogenbosch and Onze Lieve Vrouwe Munsterkerk in Roermond).

The **stalls**, often carved with satirical themes are a pleasure to see in several churches in the country, as in Martinikerk or the Grote Kerk in Breda.

The Renaissance

The Renaissance reached the Netherlands late.

Architecture – This influence only appears in the mid-16C. Brought by Italian artists such as **Thomas Vincidor of Bologna** who designed Breda castle (as from 1536); it was then taken up by local architects.

In fact, Renaissance elements were used without important architectural change and the traditional plan was often retained. It was especially through the details that a new contribution was made: shell-shaped window tympana, dormer windows overburdened with pinnacles and blind arcading, octagonal turrets...

Hans Vredeman de Vries (1527-*c*1603), a great adept of Renaissance decoration applied to architecture, did not remain long in his country.

Lieven de Key *(qv)* worked a great deal in Haarlem, his native town. The old meat market, Vleeshal, (1603) is his most complete work.

Hendrick de Keyser (1565-1621) is at the same time sculptor and architect. He built notably in Amsterdam several churches (Zuiderkerk, Westerkerk), large town houses (Huis Bartolotti) and, in Hoorn, the weigh house (waag). His style already forecasts the baroque; more monumental and heavier, the buildings became severe and imposing.

The Renaissance manifested itself particularly in **Friesland** where the taste for geometric decoration, for cheerful and picturesque details, already appearing in Romanesque churches, can once again be found in many buildings.

The town halls (Franeker, Bolsward), the Law Courts (Leeuwarden s Chancellery), fortified gateways (Sneek s Waterpoort: *illustration see Sneek*), all have the imprint of the new style; the east and south of the country remain a little apart from these influences, though the weigh house in Nijmegen is a good example of the Renaissance.

Sculpture – **Mausoleums** in the Italian Renaissance style multiply.

Thomas Vincidor of Bologna designed the tomb of Count Englebert II of Nassau in Breda; the four Romanesque figures at the corners and the contrasts of colour in material convey a new contribution.

Hendrick de Keyser continued this style in the early 17C with the tomb of William the Silent in Delft. He is also responsible for the sober statue of Erasmus in Rotterdam.

In **Friesland** the Renaissance style is expressed in woodwork. The **pulpits**, finely decorated, have symbolic panels (carved and added on Martinikerk in Bolsward, Grote Kerk in Dokkum).

The remarkable 17C stalls of Dordrecht s Grote Kerk are also inspired by the Renaissance.

Finally, the magnificent stained glass of St.-Janskerk in Gouda *(photograph see the Historical Table)* is one of the finest examples of Renaissance art.

The Golden Age: 17C

Beginning in the middle of the century the grace and lightness of the Renaissance style is over. The style called baroque, which reigns in architecture of exceptional sobriety in comparison with other countries, is sometimes called classic.

Architecture and Sculpture – One of the most famous architects of the Golden Age is **Jacob van Campen** (1595-1657), designer of **Amsterdam s town hall** (1648) which subsequently became the royal palace. Quadrilateral in shape, with its slightly severe lines, it is barely restrained by the slight projection of the forepart, its sculptured pediments and bell tower. It is a majestic work which greatly influenced architecture throughout the country. **Pieter Post** (1608-69) who built the royal palace (Huis ten Bosch) and the Mauritshuis in The Hague after the plans of Van Campen, and the town hall in Maastricht, follows this trend. **Jacob Roman**, also in the same style, built Het Loo Palace (1685) in Apeldoorn *(qv)*.
This art which reveals undoubted prosperity can be found in the **town houses** which are built along Amsterdam s main canals *(illustration: see Amsterdam)*. One of the most representative models of this solemn style is the Trippen Huis built by **Juste Vingboons** (*c*1620-98) who worked a great deal with his brother Philip.
Many of the Protestant **churches** of this period are built on a central plan, and are sometimes topped by a dome (Nieuwe of Ronde Lutherse Kerk of Amsterdam, 1671).
The Antwerp sculptor **Artus I Quellin the Elder** (1609-68) decorated in a particularly baroque style, the pediments and the interior of Amsterdam s town hall.

Gold and silversmiths work, pottery – Beginning in the 16C, but mainly in the 17C, the guilds and the bourgeois had magnificent silver objects made for their banquets and reunions, finely engraved and chased, most of which are in museum collections: hanaps (a metal standing drinking vessel), goblets, large dishes, ewers, **nautilus shell cup** (a cup made with a nautilus shell mounted on a silver stem), chains of office *(illustration: see Nijmegen)*. The most famous gold and silversmiths were the **Van Vianen** brothers.
Protestant churches also have their silver goblets which are filled with wine when celebrating the Last Supper.
Frisian silverware is particularly remarkable. Beautiful **brandy bowls**, oval in shape with two flat handles and highly decorated, held brandy; to drink one dipped a silver chased spoon. The 17C is also an important period for pottery *(see Delft)* and above all earthenware tiles.

Fries Museum

Brandy bowl (1726) by J van der Lely, Fries Museum, Leeuwarden

18-19C

Daniel Marot (*c*1663-1752) from France, builder in The Hague of patrician residences (Lange Voorhout 34, 1736) continued the Golden Age trend. However, he allowed the rococo style to make a timid appearance in the sculptures of façades (porch pediments, statues) and in the grilles and imposts which, above the gateways, usually formed an elegant decoration. William III commissioned Marot to redecorate the interior of Het Loo *(qv)*, where he was also responsible for designing the gardens in the formal Dutch style.
In the 19C architecture declined. **P.J.H. Cuypers** (1827-1921) introduced a certain form of neo-Gothic in a number of monuments (Rijksmuseum, central railway station in Amsterdam) and effected daring restoration work on medieval buildings.

20C

This century has seen the renewal of architecture in the Netherlands, as well as a passion for sculpture.

Architecture – At the end of the 19C **Berlage** (1856-1934), in building Amsterdam s Stock Exchange, became the precursor of an architectural movement where importance is given to material and the use of space for a determined function. **De Bazel** (1869-1923) used the same formula (Algemene Bank Nederland in Vijzelstraat in Amsterdam).

The **Amsterdam School** (*c*1912-23) *(qv)* reacting against Berlage, turned towards a less austere architecture and **Michel de Klerk**, **Peter Kramer** and **J.M. van der Mey** were the enlightened craftsmen in the renovation of the town.
At the same time, the **De Stijl movement** *(qv)* was founded by **Mondrian**, **Theo van Doesburg** (1883-1931) and **J.J.P. Oud** (1890-1963). Architects like **G. Rietveld** drew their theories from it; their concrete buildings consist of cubic spaces which are superimposed or juxtaposed forming a whole (Rietveld Schröderhuis in Utrecht, 1924); he was also interested in furnishings and designed armchairs with very original shapes.
A little on the fringe of these movements, **Dudok** (b 1884), influenced by the American Frank Lloyd Wright, is above all known for designing the town hall in Hilversum *(qv)*; he is also responsible for the theatre in Utrecht.
After 1950, during the reconstruction of **Rotterdam**, the town planners set out to enhance the quality of urban life: the Lijnbaan (1952-4) by **J.B. Bakema** (1914-81) was the first pedestrian precinct in Europe.
The present trend is to integrate architecture with nature by giving a very important role to openings as well as gardens and lakes.

Sculpture – In most of the towns in the Netherlands the pedestrian precincts and parks are embellished with structures in bronze, ceramic, concrete or plastic, and the modern façades with geometric lines are enhanced with mosaics, coloured elements or bronze indentations.
Often figurative, the sculptures depict people *(illustration of Bartje see Assen)* or animals *(illustration see Rotterdam)*.
Mari Andriessen (1897-1979) one of the most remarkable 20C sculptors, is responsible for the statue of a Docker near the Portuguese Synagogue in Amsterdam, the Volkspark monument in Enschede, as well as the statue of Queen Wilhelmina in Wilhelmina Park in Utrecht.
Other leading contemporary sculptors are **Fortuyn** and **O'Brien** whose light, elegant compositions feature wooden slats wrapped in paper or silk. The works of **Carel Visser** (b 1928) are noted for their extreme diversity. After having pioneered metal sculptures in the late forties, he later chose to work with steel bands, often associated with leather (during the sixties). In 1975 he produced collages-sculptures, while his subsequent creations consisted of discarded objects. His recent work is more fragile and shows a high degree of precision.

PAINTING

In the beginning, very similar to Flemish painting, then for a while influenced by Italy, Dutch painting had its Golden Age in the 17C with the country's new found freedom from the Spanish yoke; painting flourished alongside the booming mercantile economy which brought wealth and prosperity to the nation.

Primitives – Amongst the greatest, a fantastic painter appeared in the 15C in 's-Hertogenbosch, **Hieronymus Bosch** *(qv)*. His work, original for his country and epoch, remains mysterious and is subject to many interpretations. Still medieval in the portrayal of a world haunted by sin, Bosch by his realism is, however, a forerunner of 17C painting, and by his imagination, Surrealism.
The other painters are closer to the Flemish Primitives, such as **Geertgen tot Sint Jans** *(qv)* the delicate and serene painter of *The Adoration of the Magi* (in the Rijksmuseum) which has a beautiful and skilfully painted landscape in the background; **Cornelis Engebrechtsz.** *(qv)*, a painter of turbulent scenes with numerous people, and a remarkable colourist, whose work can be seen in the Stedelijk Museum De Lakenhal in Leyden, and finally **Jan Mostaert** *(qv)*.

The Prodigal Son by Hieronymus Bosch, Museum Boymans-van Beuningen, Rotterdam

Museum Boymans-van Beuningen

Renaissance – **Jan van Scorel** *(qv)* a pupil of **Jacob Cornelisz. van Oostsanen** (*c*1470-1533) on his return from Rome in 1524 introduced the Renaissance in the northern Netherlands. He is the first of the Romanist painters (northern artists who went to Italy and were greatly influenced by Italian Renaissance art). He painted portraits of great sensitivity (*Portrait of a Young Scholar*, in the Museum Boymans-van Beuningen in Rotterdam), as well as religious works, rather Mannerist in style. **Maarten van Heemskerck** *(qv)* his pupil was also a painter of refined portraits and religious scenes.
Lucas van Leyden *(qv)*, pupil of Cornelis Engebrechtsz., was also influenced by the Renaissance. He painted notably large harmonious compositions such as the *The Last Judgment* in the Stedelijk Museum De Lakenhal in Leyden, and the *Adoration of the Golden Calf* (c1525) in the Rijksmuseum in Amsterdam.
Pieter Aertsen (*c*1509-75) was not at all affected by the Romanist influence. This great Amsterdam artist, who lived for a time in Antwerp, painted rustic or interior scenes with a certain subtlety and embellished the scenery with still lifes.

A Black Squall by Willem van de Velde the Younger, Rijksmuseum, Amsterdam

Antoon Mor acquired fame under the Spanish name of **Antonio Moro** *(qv)* by becoming Charles V's official painter and then Philip II's. He went to England as Sir Anthony More to paint the portrait of Queen Mary (exhibited in the Prado, Madrid) for her bridegroom Philip II. He died in Antwerp in 1575.

The Golden Age – Dominated by great figures such as Rembrandt, Frans Hals, Vermeer and Jacob van Ruisdael, the 17C also includes a plethora of painters with very diverse talents. Whereas the Flemish still painted many religious scenes (due to the Spanish-Catholic influence), a large part of Dutch art was destined to decorate rich bourgeois interiors, consequently the subjects were more profane and of great variety. They are, at the same time, a remarkable record of the daily life of the period.

Guild portraits – Civic guards, syndics, surgeons, almshouse regents, wished to immortalise their features, therefore, group portraits were tremendously in vogue.
Bartholomeus van der Helst *(qv)*, apart from portraits of the bourgeois or members of the House of Orange, painted numerous group portraits, severe and classic. Less conformist, **Frans Hals** *(qv)* had the ease of genius. Most of his large guild paintings are in the Frans Hals Museum, in Haarlem, where he lived. He also painted striking portraits full of life *(Jolly Toper,* Rijksmuseum in Amsterdam).

Rembrandt and his pupils – **Rembrandt** *(qv)* also painted guild portraits such as the famous *The Anatomy Lesson of Doctor Tulp* which is in the Mauritshuis in The Hague, but the best known example is the *Night Watch,* in the Rijksmuseum in Amsterdam. This museum, furthermore, has an excellent collection of this master's work, notably Biblical scenes, portraits and self-portraits, where the light shines on solemn people looming up from a mysterious darkness.
Rembrandt had a number of pupils: **Gerrit Dou** *(qv)* who did chiaroscuro genre paintings; **Ferdinand Bol** *(qv)*, one of the closest to the master in style; **Nicolaes Maes** *(qv)* who used warm colours to paint calm interior scenes; **Samuel van Hoogstraten** *(qv)*; **Aert van Gelder** *(qv)*; **Carel Fabritius** (1622-54) who died young, was the most gifted of all; and **Philips Koninck** *(qv)* who was mainly a landscape painter.

Landscape and seascape painters – Although Rembrandt drew and etched admirable landscapes, he painted few. Numerous artists, on the other hand, specialised in this genre. in the early 17C **Hercules Seghers** (1589/90-1638) and **Salomon van Ruysdael** *(qv)* are painters of nature, as well as **Van Goyen** *(qv)*. Wide horizons, peaceful rivers, clouds filtering through the sun's brightness, silhouettes of trees, churches, windmills, fill their luminous and serene compositions. The greatest landscape painter of the time, **Jacob van Ruisdael** *(qv)*, nephew of Salomon, depicts slightly romantic sites.
Meindert Hobbema *(qv)* is the painter of large trees with vivid green foliage where the light plays. **Cornelis van Poelenburgh** *(qv)* had a preference for Italian-like landscapes with the setting sun.
Sometimes landscapes are only a pretext to bring in people as with **Aelbert Cuyp** *(qv)*, shepherds and their flocks with **Nicolaes Berchem** *(qv)*, or cows and horses as with **Paulus Potter** *(qv)*; horses (and their riders) with **Philips Wouwerman** *(qv)*.
Hendrick Avercamp *(qv)* is slightly different: with an art which is similar to that of miniatures and with subtle colours he brings back to life the picturesque world of ice skaters. **Aert van der Neer** (1603/4-77) also paints winter scenes and rivers in moonlight.

Willem van de Velde the Elder and above all his son **Willem van de Velde the Younger** *(qv)* who ended their lives in the English court, were remarkable marine painters, as was **Ludolf Bakhuizen** (1631-1708), **Jan van de Cappelle** (1626-79) and the Ghent painter **Jan Porcellis** (1584-1632).
Pieter Saenredam (1597-1665) and **Emanuel de Witte** (*c*1617-92) whose work was highly appreciated during their lifetime, depict church interiors with much studied composition. **Job** (1630-93) and his younger brother **Gerrit** (1638-98) **Berckheyde** are known as painters of architecture.

Genre scenes – Apart from certain of Rembrandt s pupils a number of painters specialised in interior scenes. **Gerard Terborch** *(qv)*, **Frans van Mieris the Elder** *(qv)*, **Gabriel Metsu** *(qv)* recreate domestic scenes with delicate brushwork. **Pieter de Hooch** *(qv)*, a remarkable colourist and virtuoso of perspective depicts the daily occupations of rich bourgeois.
Vermeer *(qv)*, a painter long neglected, is today considered as one of the greatest. He painted mainly interior scenes, realistic but tinged with a surprising poetry, simple in appearance but revealing a subtle research for colours, composition and light effects.
Country scenes, more popular and animated, are the speciality of **Adriaen van Ostade** *(qv)*, painter of rustic life influenced by the Flemish painter Adriaen Brouwer, and his pupil **Jan Steen** *(qv)* whose cheerfulness and humour show a certain moralising intention.
In Utrecht where the Italian influence was widespread in the 16C, **Abraham Bloemaert** continued this trend. One of his pupils, **Hendrick Terbrugghen** introduced Caravaggesque motifs and elements into the country, as did **Gerrit van Honthorst**: the contrast between light and shadow, half-length portraits of common folk, and musical scenes characterise their work. A pupil of Frans Hals, **Judith Leyster** *(qv)*, wife of the painter Jan Molenaer, is also influenced by the Caravaggists.

Still lifes – The tradition of still life painting of Flemish origin (Fyt, Snyders) is resumed in Haarlem by **Pieter Claesz.** and **Willem Claesz. Heda** *(qv)*. Their favourite subject was a table covered with the remains of a meal, and glasses and dishes brought into light. Less exaggerated than those of the Flemish paintings, more monochrome, their compositions follow a skilful geometry.
The works of **Willem Kalff** (1619-93), **Abraham van Beyeren** (1620/1-90) and **Jan Davidsz. de Heem** *(qv)* are more colourful and baroque.

Drawings and engravings – The numerous drawings and engravings, notably etchings, by 17C painters were much sought after by contemporary collectors. Rembrandt, himself, excelled in this genre.

From the 18 to 20C – In the 18C a decline set in. **Cornelis Troost** (1697-1750), however, stands out, a painter from Amsterdam who inspired by the theatre, evokes Watteau and Hogarth. **Jacob de Wit** (1695-1754) is known for his *grisailles* (in Dutch: *witjes*) which decorate a number of bourgeois homes. **Wouter Joannes van Troostwijk** who died young (1782-1810) is the painter of Amsterdam.
In the 19C, with **The Hague School** *(qv)* directed by **Jozef Israëls** (1824-1911) there is a rebirth of Dutch art. Nature, the beaches, dunes and fishermen s life constitute countless subjects for paintings by artists of this school.
Living mainly in France, **J.B. Jongkind** (1819-1891) a partisan of Impressionism gives importance to light and a certain atmosphere in his paintings, as does **George Hendrick Breitner** (1857-1923), known also as a painter of horsemen and of old Amsterdam.
Isaac Israëls (1865-1934), son of Jozef, painted beach scenes and numerous portraits.
At the end of the 19C **Vincent van Gogh** *(qv)* first painted in a sombre manner, but under the influence of Impressionism, which he discovered in Paris, his canvas became lighter and more colourful. Starting in 1886 he worked mainly in France – in Paris and in Provence near Arles – but his masterpieces can be seen in the Rijksmuseum Kröller-Müller or the Rijksmuseum Van Gogh in Amsterdam.
Jan Theodoor Toorcop, called **Jan Toorop** (1858-1928) born in Java, was first an Impressionist, before turning to Symbolism, a movement in which he held an important place in Europe as did **Johan Thorn Prikker** (1868-1932). Later Toorop went through a pointillist and divisionist period and also took an interest in the Art Nouveau movement, doing a number of posters in this style.
Mondrian *(qv)* was one of the greatest innovators of his time. A staunch defender of the De Stijl movement, he regularly contributed to the magazine that voiced its ideas. Together with **Theo van Doesburg** and **J.J.P. Oud**, he founded a new artistic trend: Constructivism.
One of the most interesting artists of the interwar period was **Herman Kruyder** (1881-1935), whose work is seeped in mystery.

Haags Gemeentemuseum

Counter-composition in Dissonance XVI (1925) by Theo van Doesburg, Collectie Haags Gemeentemuseum, The Hague

Jan Wiegers (1893-1953) was the leader of the Expressionist movement **De Ploeg** (The Plough), characterised by contrasting colours; despite their personal touch, Wiegers' paintings are clearly influenced by the German Kirchner. More recently, **Hendrik Werkman** (1882-1945) is seen as the main representative of the group; he introduced radical changes in wood engraving and typography.
After a brief incursion into Expressionism, **Charley Toorop** (1891-1955), son of Jan, subsequently opted for Realism.
Kees van Dongen became famous in Paris *(qv)*.
The **Magic Realism** or Neo-Realism theorists **Raoul Hynckes** (1893-1973), **Pyke Koch** (1901-1991) and **Carel Willink** (1900-1983) influenced many young artists by their near-photographic work tinged with Surrealism and the fantastic.
Founded by an international group led by the Dane Asger Jorn, the Belgian Dotremont and three Dutchmen **Karel Appel** (b 1921), **Constant** (b 1920) and **Corneille** (b 1922), the **CoBrA** movement (a contraction of Copenhagen, Brussels and Amsterdam) advocated free, spontaneous creation, often inspired by children's drawings. Constant is also known for his plans of a futuristic town: New Babylon (1956).
The year 1961 saw the creation of the Dutch group **Nul** (Zero) whose three principles were impersonality, detachment and objectivity. Its most fervent spokesman was **Jan Schoonhoven** (b 1941), best known for his white relief compositions.
During the seventies, **Jan Dibbets** (b 1944) and **Ger van Elk** (b 1941) chose to express their creativity through photography; Dibbets turned reality into abstraction by creating trick montages characterised by a strong sense of perspective.
Rob van Koningsbruggen (b 1948) resorted to unconventional techniques to execute his quasi-monochrome creations: he took one or several canvases and made them slide or turn over other canvases painted in black, white or primary colours.
The leading artistic figures of the eighties are **Rob Scholte** (b 1955) and **Marlene Dumas** (b 1953) who, despite their different styles, both draw inspiration from the visual imagery generated by the mass media.

Art in the Netherlands

The Netherlands is known for its "art mountain" and for its large number of museums and art galleries. The following list gives some idea of where to find the leading collections period by period.

Primitives	Rijksmuseum, Amsterdam; Museum Boymans-van Beuningen, Rotterdam; Stedelijk Museum De Lakenhal, Leyden.
Renaissance	Rijksmuseum, Amsterdam; Rijksmuseum Het Catharijneconvent, Utrecht; Stedelijk Museum De Lakenhal, Leyden.
The Golden Age	Rijksmuseum, Amsterdam; Frans Halsmuseum, Haarlem; Museum Bredius, The Hague; Mauritshuis, The Hague; Schilderijengalerij Prins Willem V, The Hague; Stedelijk Museum De Lakenhal, Leyden.
19C and 20C	Rijksmuseum, Amsterdam; Van Gogh Museum, Amsterdam; Gemeentemuseum, Arnhem; Rijksmuseum Kröller-Müller, near Arnhem; Stedelijk Van Abbemuseum, Eindhoven; Frans Halsmuseum, Haarlem; Museum Mesdag, The Hague; Haags Gemeentemuseum, The Hague; Centraal Museum, Utrecht.

FURNITURE

With each epoch there is a style which spreads over the whole country and yet, certain local products are interesting for their uniqueness. The Late Gothic period produced carved oak chests, credence tables, a sort of small side-table with shelves, and dressers decorated with pointed arches and fan-tailed motifs.

Renaissance wardrobe

Naar foto Rijksmuseum, Amsterdam

Beginning in 1550 the Italian Renaissance inspired a few credence tables with carved panels depicting medallions and grotesques; heavy tables in the Flemish style *(bolpoottafels)* with turned feet widening into vase-like shapes appear.

These tables first had rectangular struts but later were characterised by their H-shaped cross-bars, then beginning in 1650 the cross-bars were shaped like two forks.

Elegant stools with highly decorated backs and divergent legs belong to the Renaissance period.

The dutch chandelier of voluted copper *(kaarsenkroon)* is part of the 17C interior; it is also frequently found in churches, as seen in several of the church interiors painted by Saenredam and De Witte. In fact 17C Dutch painting in general gives a good insight to the interior decoration and furniture styles of the period.

Kussenkast wardrobe

Naar foto Rijksmuseum, Amsterdam

Wardrobes in the Golden Age – The most beautiful Dutch productions at the end of the 16C and the Golden Age are linen wardrobes.

The **Dutch Renaissance wardrobe** *(Hollandse kast)* is perhaps the wardrobe seen the most often. It has very varied decoration: lion muzzles, caryatids, friezes of foliated scrolls and grotesques, and flat panels later replaced by geometric embossed designs. It has a wide plinth, four doors (those below usually divided into two panels) and a heavy cornice decorated with a frieze of plants. Its uprights consist of fluted pilasters, and subsequently columns: it is then called a columned wardrobe *(kolommenkast)*.

By the second half of the 17C magnificent and imposing wardrobes in various kinds of wood were made called **kussenkast wardrobes** because of the bulging shape (*kussen* means cushion) of their panels, usually veneered with ebony. The wardrobe rests on enormous ball feet. Five Delft vases often potbellied were frequently placed on the cornice.

The **Zeeland wardrobe** *(Zeeuwse kast)* wider than it was high, with four or five doors, is low and has few raised designs, but its Renaissance decoration, which is like that of the Dutch wardrobe, is very finely worked.

Zeeland wardrobe

Naar foto Gemeente-Archief, Middelburg

Frisian wardrobe

Naar foto Fries Museum, Leeuwarden

Frisian wardrobes have two doors. The panels are enhanced by engraved decorations between the uprights, formed by engaged columns similar to the columned wardrobes. The cornice is very thick and decorated with a finely engraved frieze.

In the **Gelderland**, wardrobes have two large doors with relief designs on the panels and fluted uprights, precious wood inlays, and a projecting cornice, simply decorated with gadrooning (convex curves). The **Utrecht wardrobe**, which, in fact, is made in the province of Holland, is like that of the Gelderland: the panels are topped by an arch outlined with ebony inlay.

In town as well as in the country, at that time, people usually slept in box beds, the wooden panels matching the style of the room.

Marquetry and inlaid work – Beginning in the 17C and particularly in the 18C, there is a vogue for marquetry and above all inlaying with ebony, tortoise-shell, brass and ivory. As in Flanders writing-desks and cabinets, with numerous drawers intended to hold precious objects are decorated in this manner. The **sterrekabinet** is inlaid with ivory motifs or with marquetry depicting stars *(sterren)* enclosed in circles or ovals.

18 and 19C wardrobes – The Louis XV style, imported by the French Huguenots after the Revocation of the Edict of Nantes (1685), was very much in vogue in the 18C, but interpreted with a certain liberty. The **18C wardrobe** with two doors has a base with drawers, which in the middle of the century, had a characteristic bulge *(buikkabinet).* It is topped with an undulating cornice. Inlaid work and marquetry were also appreciated.
Finally, the English influence was quite important due to intensive commercial relations with England *(p 20).*
At the end of the 18C furniture was influenced by the Louis XVI style, more austere, which was very faithfully reproduced.
In the 19C, influence of the Empire style was felt (under Napoleonic domination), due to the presence in the country of Louis Bonaparte and Queen Hortense, very attached to Parisian fashions.

18C wardrobe

Naar foto Rijksmuseum, Amsterdam

Painted furniture – Several localities in the north of the country specialised in the production of painted furniture in the 18C. It was mainly in the old ports of the Zuiderzee, during the months of forced inactivity, that the fishermen worked and painted wood according to the methods seen during their journeys in the Baltic or in the East.
This furniture has particularly indented outlines; the wood is covered with very crowded paintings in a more or less popular and naive style. In the Zuiderzee ports (Hindeloopen, Enkhuizen), in the Zaanstreek, in the Wadden Islands, painting covers, wardrobes, fold-away tables, box beds, chairs, etc.

Longcase and pendulum clocks – After the discovery in 1656 by Christiaan Huygens of the pendulum principle (pendulum serves to control the time in clocks) a **longcase clock** (also known as a grandfather clock) can be found in all wealthy looking interiors. Its tall clockcase has a fair amount of decoration and is topped by a rectangular head with an arched cornice. The clockface is often painted with an astral representation below with people or boats on the sea moving about. Amsterdam was a great longcase clockmaking centre in the 18C. However, clocks in the Louis XV style or cartels (hanging wall-clocks) were also appreciated.
In the provinces of Friesland, Groningen and Drenthe, the **clocks** called *stoeltjesklokken* are adorned with fanciful open-worked decoration, similar to that of the painted furniture *(see above)* and have a special mechanism installed on a small console. The clocks in the Zaanstreek are of a more precious type.
Several museums have lovely clock collections: in particular the Gold, Silver and Clock Museum in Schoonhoven and the Clock Museum in the Zaan Quarter.
A number of Dutch museums have a decorative arts section where rooms, *stijlkamers,* have assembled furniture belonging to a particular style, period or region. Furthermore the **doll houses**, which can be seen in certain museums, are detailed reproductions, making it possible to visualise the bourgeois interior in Holland during the Golden Age.

DUTCH FURNISHINGS

Dutch furnishings can be admired throughout the country. Listed below is a selection of museums with good furniture collections:

Assen – Drents Museum: Ontvangershuis
Enkhuizen – Zuiderzeemuseum
Hindeloopen – Museum Hidde Nijland Stichting
Leeuwarden – Fries Museum
Middelburg – Zeeuws Museum
Rotterdam – Historisch Museum Het Schielandshuis
Utrecht – Centraal Museum
Zwolle – Provinciaal Overijssels Museum

FARMHOUSES

The lovely farmhouses which are scattered over the countryside are part of the country's familiar landscape. It is in the polder areas that they are largest in size.

Frisian farmhouses – These have surprisingly large roofs and they can be seen all over Friesland or in the territories which formerly belonged to it (north of the province of Noord-Holland) and in the province of Groningen.

D'après photo Ch. Cuzol/MICHELIN

Pyramid-shaped Frisian farmhouse

Pyramid-shaped farmhouses – There are many in the north of the province of Noord-Holland (beyond the North Sea canal) where they are called *stolp;* they can also be seen in the south of Friesland, where they are called *stelp.* Their enormous four-sided pyramid-shaped roofs, bring to mind that of a haystack. Grouped under the same roof are the stables, a barn and living quarters. On one side of the roof, thatch takes the place of tiles forming a decorative pattern resembling a mirror, called *spiegel.* Sometimes in more substantial farmhouses the front of the house is embellished with a richly decorated brick pediment.

Naar foto Hr. Buis/MICHELIN

Frisian head-neck-trunk farmhouse

Head-neck-trunk farmhouses – They are called *kop-hals-rompboerderij,* a farmhouse with head-neck-trunk. They can be seen in the north of Friesland and a few in the province of Groningen.
Made up of three parts (thus head-neck-trunk), they consist of the living quarters (head), linked by a narrow part (neck), to a large building (trunk). The latter includes the cowshed, stable and barn.
The living quarters are covered with tiles whereas the barn is roofed traditionally with reeds. They are often built on a *terp* *(See Leeuwarden: Excursions).*
At the top of the roof over the trunk part – shed, barn... – is a **uilebord**, a wooden triangular panel pierced with holes for owls *(uil)* to pass through and nest in the hay. It is often decorated with carved wooden motifs depicting two swans.

Kop-romp farmhouses – In Friesland, as in the province of Groningen, there is also a type of farmhouse, which is a combination of the others (*kop* = head; *romp* = trunk): a tiled roof covers the living quarters as in the head-neck-trunk farmhouse, but as in the pyramid-shaped farmhouse a few rooms remain in the barn, under the large thatched roof. The house is also sometimes joined to the barn by a series of projections characteristic of the Oldambt farmhouse.

D'après photo Ch. Cuzol

Kop-romp farmhouse

Oldambt farmhouses – From the Oldambt area, to the east of the province of Groningen, they can be seen all over the province. They are linked to the barn by a progressive widening at right angles to the house. Sometimes too, this model is combined with the head-neck-trunk type.
The house, high and wide, often has a main entrance surrounded by stucco mouldings. A floor with low windows serves as a granary. The living quarters, covered in tiles can be distinguished from the barn, which is usually thatched.

Hall-farmhouses – They are the most widespread type found in the Netherlands and particularly in the provinces of Drenthe, Overijssel, Gelderland and Utrecht; they can also be seen in Zuid-Holland and in the Gooi (Noord-Holland). Inside, as in hall-churches, the timberwork is supported by wooden pillars. They are arranged to form two rows delimiting a wide central nave and two narrower side aisles.

Twente farmhouses – In the Twenthe (Overijssel) and east of Gelderland towards Winterswijk, the walls, formerly of cob are now of brick, sometimes keeping the check-pattern half-timbering. The roof is wide, with two sides, and a wooden gable.

Los hoes farmhouses – They can still be found in Twente, but rarely. Originally all the hall-farmhouses were like this one.

Los hoes means open house: inside, to begin with, there were no partitions. the farmers and cattle shared the same space, the hay being heaped up on to planks halfway up. There was an open fire on the ground.

The parents' house, called *eendskamer,* sometimes consisted of a small independent building joined to the façade. A *los hoes* farmhouse has been reconstructed in the Rijksmuseum Twenthe in Enschede

D'après photo A. van Iterson

Drenthe farmhouse

Drenthe farmhouses – It has an elongated shape. Today it is still very often covered with thatch. The same roof, with four sides, covers two distinct parts: the living quarters with high windows, and the barn-stable where the carts entered at the back through a carriage entrance whose opening was cut into the thatched roof. Beginning in the 18C in certain farmhouses in the southwest of Drenthe and to the north of Overijssel, the carriage entrance at the back had been replaced by side doors in order to increase the space in the barn. It is like this in Wanneperveen *(qv)* where however, because the houses were set too close together, the doors were placed at the corners.

D'après photo Ch. Cuzol MICHELIN

T-shaped farmhouse

T-shaped farmhouses – In Gelderland and notably in the region of Achterhoek, in the region of IJssel (province of Overijssel), in the provinces of Utrecht and Zuid-Holland, and in Gooi (Noord-Holland), the house is set at right angles to the barn, hence its name *T-huis,* that is to say: t-shaped house. Prosperity brought about this type of farmhouse which lies on fertile river banks. The farmer enlarged his living quarters by adding two living rooms *(pronkkamer* and *royale opkamer)* overlooking the road; this formed a transept-like extension. The carriage entrance to the farmhouse was at the back.

In the Veluwe (Gelderland) farmhouses are complemented by a separate hay shed and sheep pen. In Gooi, the hay was formerly heaped up at the back of the house, the doors being on the side; subsequently, in the 19C, it was also stored in an annexe. In the provinces of Utrecht and Zuid-Holland (near Woerden), cheese-making farms had a dairy and cheese dairy in the basement of the dwelling.

Hall-type farmhouses can also be seen in Staphorst *(qv),* Giethoorn *(qv)* Lopikerwaard (province of Utrecht); and in the province of Zuid-Holland, the farmhouses of Krimpenerwaard and Alblasserwaard *(qv)* possess the distinctive feature of having the living quarters on raised ground, due to the risk of floods.

D'après photo Off. Nat. Néerl. du Tourisme,

Southern Limburg farmhouse

Transversal farmhouses

Transversal farmhouses – These farmhouses, where the longest side was the façade, consist of juxtaposed rooms, the living quarters set at right angles to the work area. They can be seen in Limburg and in the east part of Noord-Brabant.

Limburg farmhouses – Today, the farmhouses stand out by their closed-in layout, unique in Holland. The buildings often form a square round a courtyard which only opens to the outside by a large carriage gateway. Near this stands the dwelling house. This layout came about progressively: originally there was only a barn at right angles to the house.

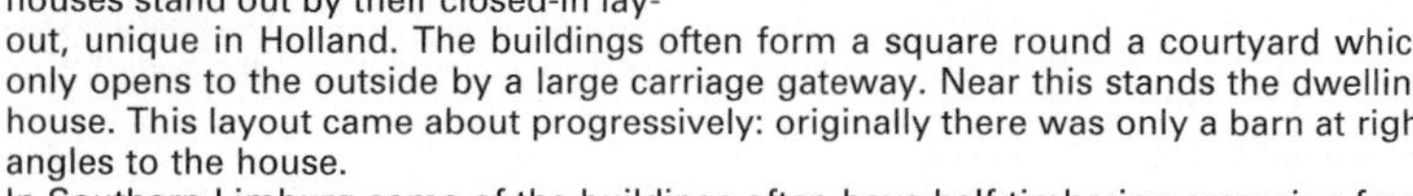

In Southern Limburg some of the buildings often have half-timbering emerging from white roughcast.

D'après photo Ch. Cuzol MICHELIN

Brabant farmhouse

Brabant farmhouses – They present a very long façade facing the road, with a line of doors, hence their name long façade farmhouses.

Their long roof is covered in part by tiles and in part by thatch.

These farmhouses were often quite small. They were usually enlarged by adding a barn in Flemish style, with wooden partitions and a thatched roof, set in the place of the door.

Zeeland farmhouses

Zeeland farmhouses – They consist of isolated buildings where the wooden barn is the most typical construction, with its tarred partitions and its doors and windows emphasised by a frame of white paint.

WINDMILLS

Perched high on the old ramparts of the town or on the dikes of polders or rivers, or else erected at the entrance to villages or along waterways, the numerous windmills (about 950) which still exist in the Netherlands are a characteristic feature of the Dutch landscape.
The best known and greatest concentration of windmills are those of Kinderdijk *(qv)*.

Windmill language – The sails turn counter clockwise. When stationary, their position means something. The windmill speaks and sends its message afar:
– two vertical sails (+): rest for a short time during a working period.
– two diagonal sails (x): rest for a longer period, if it is a polder windmill.
– upper sail just to the right of vertical (x): celebration.
– upper sail just to the left of vertical (x): mourning.
On the occasion of a marriage, the windmill sails are abundantly decorated with garlands and symbolic motifs.
During the last war the windmills were used to send signals to the Allied pilots and maintain the population's morale.

D'après photo Ch. Cuzol/MICHELIN
Post mill, Asten

Windmill decorations – Many wooden windmills are painted green, with white frames. Where the sail crosses, there is usually a star motif painted, yellow and red, or else blue and white. Below, on a carved panel, there is often the windmill's name and the date of its construction.

Main types of windmills – There are two kinds of windmills, the polder windmills and industrial windmills.
The **polder mill** serves, or served to pump water *(see The Fight Against the Sea)*. There are none to be found in the east of the country where the height above sea level ensures natural drainage of water.

Industrial mills – about 500 – mill wheat, extract oil, hull rice and pepper, saw wood, etc. Several are still in use.

D'après photo Jos P. Faure
Wip mill, Hellouw, Gelderland

Percursor - the post mill – To begin with the only mills known in the Netherlands were the watermill and the cattle power mill. Similar to those in Persia or Arabia, where they are used to mill grain, the first windmills appeared in the middle of the 13C (their existence is vouched for in 1274). Contrary to oriental mills, built of stone, these are of wood. Called *standerdmolen* or *standaardmolen,* they are post mills where the body turns with the sails round a heavy wooden pillar post made out of a tree trunk. Inside, the millstone moves when the sails move. Outside, on the side opposite the sails, a tail pole joined to the post and operated by a wheel made it possible to turn the windmill round on itself. The ladder fixed to the main body of the windmill is also drawn by the movement. Few windmills of this type remain in the country.

First polder mills – The first windmill used for drainage, in about 1350, was the post windmill *(see above)*. Converted for this use, the central pillar post was replaced by a hollow post where the axis of the sails pivoted, it became the **hollow post mill** or **wip mill**, the first known dating from 1513. The upper part was reduced, but the base was larger, making it possible to install a scoop wheel to circulate the water. However, quite often this remained outside and the base was used as living accommodation, particularly in Zuid-Holland. The **sleeve windmill** *(kokermolen)* is easier to position, the pillar post having been replaced by a heavy hollow post about which the top can turn with the sails.
A miniature variant of the wip mill is the **spinnekop** or spinbol which looks like a spider *(spin)*. They are many in Friesland. In Noord-Holland, the small meadow mill, **weidemolentje** is even smaller. In Friesland and Overijssel, the **tjasker**, very rare, has a primitive system where the sails are fixed directly to the device drawing up water.

Mills with rotating caps – The **bovenkruier** (literally cap winder) in Zuid-Holland is a large windmill topped by a small cap which pivots alone. If the winding gear, which makes the cap and sails move, is outside, the windmill belongs to the **buitenkruier** type (the outside winder type). It is the most usual type, but in Noord-Holland, there is also the **binnenkruier** (the inside winder type) which differs with the winding gear placed inside, giving it a more massive silhouette. The mills with rotating caps are always built of wood, often **thatch** covered and octagonal; in this case the base is of brick. Sometimes the framework is also covered with **brick** and has a truncated shape.

D'après photo Ch. Cuzol/MICHELIN
Octagonal-shaped polder mill, Amstelveen

Industrial mills – In the 16C the windmill was adapted for industrial purposes.
In 1582 the first oil windmill worked in Alkmaar. In 1592 Cornelis Corneliszoon of Uitgeest (Noord-Holland) built the first **saw mill**. Improved, it became the first **paltrok saw mill** which has a mobile base *(illustration: see Zaan)*.
Then **husking mills** were made to husk grain (barley, then rice after journeys to the Orient): the first was built in 1639 in Koog aan de Zaan.
Paper mills (invented *c*1600), developed in 1673, when French manufacturers withdrew to the Zaanstreek. Up to the 19C the greatest concentration could be found in the **Zaan region** *(qv)*, specialising in making paper and sawing wood for boat building. Most of the different types of windmills developed there, such as snuff mills (for tobacco snuff), hemp mills for ropes, tan mills for leather, spice mills mainly for mustard, fulling mills for textiles. Many of them, which included a workshop, were very tall with a handrail.

Tall windmills – Industrial windmills, often built in towns, had to be tall to catch the wind and were, therefore, several storeys high. The sails were operated from a circular stage with a handrail called *stelling* or *balie,* placed halfway up. It is the *stellingmolen,* tower mill with a stage often called a **stage mill**.
When it was built on a rampart *(wal)*, it was called *walmolen* or **wall mill**. The miller s living quarters and the granary are usually located under the handrail.
Other tall windmills stand on an artifical mound and are surrounded by an embankment (*bergmolen* or *beltmolen*) which facilitates the operation and avoids the need to build a handrail.
The stage mill is usually of brick and truncated, but in the province of Groningen it is built on a octagonal brick base, and in the Zaan over a workshop made of wood.

D après photo A. van Iterson/MICHELIN

Stage mill,
Kromme Zandweg in Rotterdam

E. Luider/RAPHO

Kinderdijk on a winter s day

A few proverbs relating to windmills:

Hij heeft een klap van de molen gehad: ***he was struck by a mill (he is a bit mad).***
Hij loopt met molentjes: ***he functions with small mills (he is a little simple-minded).***
Dat is koren op zijn molen: ***it is grain for his mill: (it brings water to his mill).***

MUSIC

Music has always held a very important place in the life of the Dutch whether it is played at home, in churches or even in the street.

Musicians – The most famous musician is **J.P. Sweelinck** (1562-1621), organist of the Oude Kerk in Amsterdam, composer, percursor of J.S. Bach. During the same period **Constantijn Huygens** (1596-1687), statesman and poet, took an active interest in musical composition.

In the 19C, **Johannes Verhulst** (1816-91) was a composer and conductor, and **Richard Hol** (1825-1904), conductor, pianist and composer of cantatas and symphonies.

A student of Hol's, **Johan Wagenaar** (1862-1941), organist and unusual composer taught **Willem Pijper** (1894-1947) composer, who was also known for his essays on music.

Presently, the Dutch with the Royal Concertgebouw Orchestra in Amsterdam and the Residentie Orchestra in The Hague, have two of the greatest orchestras in the world.

The first conductor of the Concertgebouw Orchestra was **Willem Mengelberg** (1871-1951) who took an active interest in many composers of his time, such as Mahler.

The Holland Festival *(see the Practical Information)* is host to important musical events.

Organs – Created in Byzantium, imported into Western Europe in the 9C, the organ took a large place in Catholic liturgy as from the 12C. The instrument was originally made by monks. Soon spreading into private houses, the organ was spared the Iconoclastic Fury.

However, organ music was at first despised by the Calvanist religion. It was only in the middle of the 17C that it spread into Protestant churches.

Numerous instruments were made at this period and the following century. In the 18C the sons of the famous German organ builder **Arp Schnitger**, living in Groningen, perfected the instrument in the Netherlands and built the great organ in **Zwolle's** Grote Kerk. The great organ of St-Bavokerk in **Haarlem** (18C) built by **Christiaen Müller** is one of the best known in the country.

Most of the organ cases dating from the baroque era are sumptuous achievements: crowning the pipes are statues and carvings.

A few organ concerts are indicated under the locality's heading.

B. Lipnitzki/EXPLORER

The organ case, Grote Kerk, Haarlem

Barrel organ – In the Netherlands the streets often resound with a cheerful and familiar music, that of barrel organs as well as carillons. Whereas the barrel organ has practically disappeared in other European countries, a number of Dutch towns still have theirs – with its picturesque name, painted and carved case – which can be heard Saturdays in the shopping streets as well as on feast days.

The barrel organ, which appeared in the 18C, invented by an Italian, is a **cylinder-type organ**. A pinned barrel, turned by a handle, raises levers which admits wind to a set of organ pipes. Mounted on wheels, this organ became widespread in 19C Europe. In 1892 Gavioli built the first **book organ** *(pierement)* which took the place of the cylinder-type organ. The handle works a perforated music book which releases a mechanism. Use of a music roll made it possible to have an unlimited repertoire, and when linked to the use of a pneumatic system which improved it, thus its distribution increased.

A builder of barrel organs, **Carl Frei** set up in Breda in 1920, but most of the instruments were imported from abroad, from Belgium (Mortier) and France (Gasparini and the Limonaire Brothers).

At the end of the 19C, the dance-hall organ became popular, a magnificent, very large sculptured instrument. At the beginning of the 20C fair organs produced loud music intended to be heard above the hubbub. Finally, after 1945 an electronic dance-hall organ appeared, a real animated orchestra with all sorts of instruments.

In Utrecht, the Nationaal Museum "from the musical clock to the barrel organ" contains an interesting series of barrel organs.

Carillons – There are countless churches and town halls in the Netherlands which have a carillon (bronze bells in fixed suspension).

The carillon, which has probably existed since the 15C in Belgium is activated, like the organ, by a cylinder driven originally by the movement of a clock.

In the 17C **François** and **Pierre Hemony** from Lorraine, the famous bell founders, played a primordial role in their development in the Netherlands. There still exist, amongst many others of theirs, the carillons of the Onze Lieve Vrouwe Toren in Amersfoort, the Martinitoren in Groningen and the Domtoren in Utrecht.

A little on the decline in the 18 and 19C, there is a renewed interest in carillon music today. In 1941 a bell founder in Heiligerlee (province of Groningen) invented an **electromagnetic system**, replacing the cylinder. This is used in several towns.
Since 1953 there is the Netherlands School for Bellringers at Amersfoort.
Finally, Asten has an interesting National Carillon Museum *(see Eindhoven: Excursions).*
In the text of localities and at the end of the guide we indicate some of the carillon concerts.

DUTCH LITERATURE

Language – The Dutch language is the official language for about 20 million people throughout the world. Dutch is not only spoken in the Netherlands, but in places as diverse as the Antilles, Suriname, South Africa (Afrikaans) and parts of Belgium. Dutch is one of the western branches of the Germanic language and resembles both German and English. Frisian is not a dialect of Dutch but an autonomous sister language. It was only on 29 January 1993 that Dutch was recognised by law as being the official national language and that Frisian in Friesland was accorded the status of second governmental language.
Dutch literature developed in Flanders from the 12C, but disappeared entirely after the break with the Netherlands at the end of the 16C.
Printing activities developed at a great pace following Gutenberg's invention (1455) alongside flourishing workshops of copyists and illustrators (William Caxton printed his *Recuyell of the historyes of Troye* in 1474 in Bruges). The printing press was used by the humanists as a weapon in the battle of ideas in which the University of Leuven (f 1425, now Belgium) played a leading role.

16C-17C – In the 16C and 17C **Erasmus** *(qv)* the great humanist from Rotterdam, **Jansenius** (1585-1638) *(qv)* the theologian, Hugo de Groot or **Grotius** *(qv)* the jurist and the great Jewish philosopher **Spinoza** (1634-1677) all wrote in Latin. The country and especially Amsterdam became known for its liberal attitude and many foreign philosophers (John Locke) and men of wisdom (Descartes, Pierre Bayle) sought shelter in the country and found freedom to publish. Dutch literature of the period is marked by the poet and historian **P C Hooft** (1581-1647) *(qv)* and the poet and dramatist **Joost van den Vondel** (1587-1679) who belonged to the **Muiderkring** *(qv)*, a circle of artists, writers and musicians, founded by Hooft.

18C - Age of Enlightenment – The Dutch presses continued to print the uncensored works of great foreigners including such prophets of enlightenment as Voltaire and Diderot but for Dutch literature this was a period of decline.

19C – **Eduard Douwes Dekker**, known under the pseudonym of **Multatuli** (1820-87), became an international name with his novel *Max Havelaar* (1860), a satire on colonial life in the Dutch East Indies. **Louis Couperus** (1863-1923) was an important novelist of the 1880 literary revival and he is best known for *Eline vere* (1889) dealing with contemporary life in The Hague and *Old People and the Things That Pass* (1906).

20C – Other writers of the early 20C include the historian **Johan Huizinga** (1872-1945) known for his lively style in *The Waning of the Middle Ages*, the prolific novelist **Simon Vestdijk** *(qv)* who wrote several works on middle-class provincial life and **Simon Carmiggelt** (1913-87).
The postwar generation included Willem Frederik Hermans, **Gerard Reve** (b 1923), Cees Nooteboom and **Harry Mulisch** (b 1927). The prevalence of the war theme in postwar Dutch literature is evident in Jeroen Brouwer's *Sunken Road* (1981), Willem Frederik Hermans' controversial novels (*The Tears of the Acacia's* and *The Dark Room of Damocles*), Gerrit Kouwenaar's *I was not a Soldier* (1951) and Mulisch's *The Assault.* This period was also known for the work of the poetess **Ida Gerhardt** (b 1905) and **Hella Haasse** (b 1918), renowned for her historical novels.
The new vanguard or *Revisor* writers reacted against realism: Dirk Ayelt Kooiman *(A Romance)*, Doeschka Meijsing *(Tiger, Tiger!)*, Frans Kellendonk (1951-1990) *(Letter and Spirit)* and Nicholas Matsier *(The Eternal City)*.
The *Raster* writers formed an even more influential group named after the literary magazine of the same name. These representatives of "the alternative prose" formed a less homogeneous group and represented several generations. The Flemish writers Louis Paul Boon and Hugo Claus influenced their younger compatriots.
Other writers remained outside the mainstream of Dutch literature. The *Revisor* opponent and traditional realist storyteller Maarten' t Haart, Jeroen Brouwers, Joost Zwagerman *(Gimmick)* who portrayed a tarnished image of the Amsterdam art world and Willem Jan Otten. A F T van der Heijden's *Toothless Tiger* is a chronicle of the seventies and eighties.
It was the old guard who triumphed with bestsellers: Hugo Claus with his much acclaimed *The Sorrow of Belgium* (1983) and Harry Mulisch *(The Discovery of Heaven)*. Kellendonk's very topical *Mystic Body* in 1986 caused considerable consternation on publication.

Join us in our constant task of keeping up-to-date
Please send us your comments and suggestions

Michelin Tyre PLC
Tourism Department
The Edward Hyde Building
38 Clarendon Road
WATFORD - Herts WD1 1SX
Tel: (0923) 41 50 00

TRADITIONS AND FOLKLORE

COLOURFUL COSTUMES

In the past the variety of costumes in the Netherlands was remarkable.
Apart from Marken and Volendam where, in season, all the population wears the traditional costume for the tourists' pleasure, costumes today, are only worn in very few areas regularly and mainly by women.
However, by their variety, originality and the way they are assembled, which is slightly ritual in colour and motif, the costumes and headdresses still worn in the Netherlands are of exceptional interest.

Fabrics – Women's jackets and shawls, and also men's shirts worn under their black jackets are made out of traditional, brightly coloured textiles striped with checks, or flowers. In the latter case it is most often of **chintz**.
Starting in the 17C the Dutch East India Company imported enormous quantities of chintz from the East. This fabric, whose dutch name *sits* come from the Indian word *chint*, which means multi-coloured, is cotton decorated with a coloured pattern done by hand, using a special technique. Greatly appreciated not only for its suppleness and lightness but for its colours and designs, this material was soon the rage in the Netherlands. Interiors are decorated with it (bedspreads, curtains, wall hangings) and it is used to make all kinds of clothes. The women of Hindeloopen even make their traditional coat called *wentke* and other women happily replace their plain jacket by one in *sits* with shimmering colours.
At the end of the 17C chintz was made in the Twente *(qv)* and printed mechanically.

The female costume – In spite of its variety, it retains certain unchanging features. It consists of a skirt, an apron and a jacket done up in front, often with short sleeves. Over the jacket some women wear a stiff bodice as in bunschoten-Spakenburg, or a shawl as in Staphorst.
The costume worn on Sundays is always more elegant than that on other days. Whit Sunday is particularly honoured: that day the women usually dress up in their most beautiful attire.

C. Sappa/CEDRI

Lace caps and shawls from Middelburg

Headdress – Although a young girl in wooden shoes wearing a cap with wings, typical in Volendam often symbolises Dutch folklore for foreigners, there exists a wide variety of headdresses through out the country.
The most spectacular are those worn on the island of South Beveland, particularly in Goes *(qv)* on weekly market days.
Many headdresses have the distinctive feature of including golden ornaments: they conceal a head band ending in rings (Scheveningen), by animal heads (Urk) or by amusing types of spiral-shaped antennae raised up in front (Walcheren, Axel, Arnemuiden). Pins with a golden head or ending in a pearl are sometimes put into the headdress above the ears.
The magnificent lace work of these headdresses is admirable.

The male costume – It only exists now in a few ports, such as Urk, Volendam and in South Beveland. Today it is nearly always black, whereas in the past brighter colours were worn. It consists of a jacket, often double breasted and wide or baggy trousers (Zuiderzee). The shirt, rarely visible, is made of brightly coloured cotton with a striped or checked pattern. Its straight collar closes with two gold buttons. They are the costume's only ornaments, except in Zeeland (Zuid-Beveland) where two lovely silver chased buckles hold up the trousers.
The man wears a small cotton scarf round his neck. On his head he wears black headgear: a round hat in Zeeland, a sort of military cap in Urk, or a plain cap. He often wears wooden clogs.

Where to see the costumes? – The main centres where local costumes are worn by the population (men, women and children) daily are **Volendam** and **Marken**, but the custom is less respected in winter than in summer. In **Staphorst** and in the neighbouring village of **Rouveen**, women and young girls wear a very unique costume as do a few inhabitants of **Bunschoten** and **Spakenburg**.
In the Zeeland islands of **Walcheren** and **South Beveland**, a number of women still remain faithful to their costume and headdress to such a point that in 1975 they revolted against the wearing of a crash helmet when riding a motorcycle.
Other places which should be mentioned are **Scheveningen**, **Urk** and a few towns in the Overijssel (Rijssen, Dalfsen, Raalte).
In a few cities women wear the traditional costume mainly for the Sunday church service or the weekly market. Sometimes during the festivals and folklore markets, there is the possibility of seeing the Dutch decked out in their regional costumes *(see Practical Information)*. The costumes are described in the guide under the locality's heading. Several museums make it possible to admire the detail.

CUSTOMS

St Nicholas Day – Today in the Netherlands Christmas remains essentially religious and St Nicholas Day (6 December) plays a particularly important role, above all for children to whom the saint is supposed to bring presents. Coming from Spain by boat, **Saint Nicholas** (Sinterklaas) landed in Amsterdam where he made his official entry *(see Calender of Events)*. Riding a white horse and dressed as a bishop, he is always attended by one or two black devils or **Zwarte Piet** (Black Peter) who, armed with canes, must punish all naughty children. In the houses, the scattering of small cakes called **pepernoten**, indicate that Zwarte Piet has called.
The day before St Nicholas Day, 5 December, families meet in the evening and place shoes by the fireplace, which are filled with presents during the night. Adults give short humorous poems as well as anonymous presents.
It is also the occasion to eat a number of specialities like the **borstplaat**, sweets that melt in the mouth, **speculaas** (speculos), brown sugar girdle cakes, **taai-taai**, aniseed biscuits in the shape of different figures, **vrijer**, equally with aniseed, and also initials in almond paste *(boterletters)* or chocolate *(chocoladeletters)*.

A far cry from the modern Father Christmas – Recent excavations on the island of Gemile have uncovered an important pilgrimage centre which was in all probability the original shrine of St Nicholas the 4C Bishop of Myra. When the island was under threat of an Arab invasion the relics may have been translated to the saint's episcopal seat, Myra, where it was originally thought he died. Then when Myra was taken by the Muslims in 1097, Nicholas's relics were carried across the Adriatic to Bari. A new church was built to house the relics and it became an important pilgrimage centre.
The Bishop of Myra was in all probability a far cry from the jovial Father Christmas we know today. He was probably an emaciated Levantine swarthy in appearance and definitely argumentative and fanatical. He is seen as a thaumaturge (a worker of miracles) especially among children. The best known miracles were when he saved three small boys who had been dismembered and left in a barrel or the three girls, who for a lack of a dowry, were to be turned into prostitutes. He is the patron saint of children, sailors in peril on the high seas, prisoners in certain countries and perfumiers.

From St Nicholas to Father Christmas – It was as patron saint of small children that people in the Low Countries started giving presents to children on his feast day, 6 December. During the 17C the Dutch introduced the Feast of St Nicholas and its attendant traditions to America. During the 19C this giver of presents became known as Santa Claus a deformation of Sinter Klaas the Dutch for St Nicholas.

Traditional sports – Some sports, particularly the older or more unusual ones, are derived from regional traditions.
Archery or **shooting with an arquebus** is very popular in Limburg. This pastime dates from the time when citizens deemed it necessary to arm themselves against possible troubles. Members of these societies or guilds congregate at an annual gathering, when the marksmen *(schutters)* parade resplendent in their colourful uniforms.
In Friesland **kaatsen** is a ball game with six players divided into two teams and the **skûtsjesilen** are popular regattas with the traditional *skûtsjes (see Sneek)*. Pole vaulting (polsstokspringen; ljeppen in Frisian) is another traditional activity. Originally bird's egg hunters used to cross the canals with the help of a long pole.
In the Zeeland town of Middelburg the **ringrijderljen** has been revived. This is a tournament where riders on horseback gallop past and try to unhook a ring with their lance.
Skating was not only a traditional sport and pastime but it was a practical means of transport in difficult weather conditions. The delightful winter scenes by the 17C Dutch master Hendrick Avercamp show how popular skating was at the time. Sleighs were also used on the ice.
Another activity that Avercamp portrayed in his paintings is **kolfspel**. This game was also played on ice with a club *(kolf)* and a ball or puck and the aim was to hit a pole stuck into the ice. This game has been a subject of controversy between the Dutch and the Scots for centuries. The former claim that it was the origins of the game of golf. The Scots however claim that the early ball and stick version of golf was already being played on the sandy links of Scotland in 1457 when an Act of the Scottish Parliament was passed requiring that "futeball and the golfe be utterly cryit down" in favour of church attendance and archery practice *(see Green Guide Scotland)*.

The Elfstedentocht – Eleven Towns Race – links 11 Frisian towns in a 210km - 131 mile skating race held only when it is cold enough for the waterways that link them to be rock solid. 400 qualify as competitors but hundreds of other skaters are allowed to follow the competitors as touring skaters.
The race begins at 0500 and the course may take 7 punishing hours to complete.

FOOD AND DRINK

An enticing breakfast – Breakfast (*ontbijt,* pronounced ontbeyt) in the Netherlands is similar to an English or American breakfast: in most hotels, coffee, tea or chocolate is served with a boiled egg, thin slices of cheese, ham, sometimes salami, paté, and always *boterhammen* (literally slices of bread) of different kinds (rye bread, sandwich loaf, raisin bread, gingerbread) with butter and jam.

A quick lunck – For lunch the Dutch often content themselves with a cold meal (without a cooked dish) or a very light meal and a cup of coffee. It is the time for a sandwich which is made of a soft roll or **broodje**. They also like the **uitsmijter** which consists of slices of buttered sandwich loaf, covered with ham or roast beef and two fried eggs, served with a sweet gherkin. As to **koffietafel**, mentioned on many menus, it is a kind of breakfast eaten for lunch, with coffee (*koffie,* hence its name) or tea.

A copious dinner – The main meal is in the evening (between 6 and 7pm) and fairly plentiful. Soup is liked and notably, in winter, the traditional green pea soup, **erwtensoep** which must be sufficiently thick so that a spoon can stand up in it...
Oysters and mussels from Zeeland (Yerseke) are served in some restaurants.
Smoked eel *(gerookte paling)* and **red herring** *(bokking)* or a herring *(haring)* marinated in vinegar are eaten as starters. In the streets of Zuiderzee's old ports, they are sold on bread rolls. "Green" herring, **maatje** (or *groene haring,* or *nieuwe haring*) is eaten in May-June, raw and flavoured with chopped onions. It is also sold (in Amsterdam) by peddlers: it is then eaten by holding it by the tail and throwing one's head back. The first cask of herrings is offered each year to the Queen, who conforms to the tradition.
From 15 March to 10 April (a week later in Friesland) **lapwing's eggs** *(kievitseieren)* served in jelly on a bed of watercress with pink radishes make a choice starter.
Limburg asparagus (Venlo), in season *(May-June)*, are popular starters. Limburg mushrooms are eaten fried, or with snails.

A. Saucez/EXPLORER

A tasty herring

The main course – meat, poultry or fish – is served with vegetables, generally covered with plenty of sauce, and with a salad. The **vegetables** are varied: potatoes, cauliflower, green beans *(snijbonen)* cut into long strips, carrots or peas. Greenhouse cultivation makes it possible to have fresh vegetables all year long. Salads (lettuce, tomatoes, cucumbers, etc) are usually served with mayonnaise. As in Great Britain some meat dishes are served with apple or rhubarb compote.
Fish is a rare dish, and varies little: the menu usually offers fried **sole** *(tong)*, sometimes plaice *(schol)* or turbot *(tarbot)*.
A few family dishes are rarely found on restaurant menus: the **boerenkool**, mashed potatoes and green cabbage, often served with sausages *(worst)*; **hutspot**, a sort of beef stew with mincemeat (or rib of beef), potatoes, carrots, turnips and onions, the origin of which dates back to 1573.
Ham (*ham* in Dutch) and **sausages** *(worsten)* from the Veluwe are well-known.

Indonesian cooking – In most towns, it is possible to satisfy an urge for exoticism by eating in an Indonesian restaurant, often called *chinees-indisch restaurant.*

Cheese – Rarely served at the end of the meal, cheese on the contrary is the main ingredient of breakfasts and cold meals. Creamy when they are fresh *(jonge)*, they subsequently become dry and pungent when they are ripe *(oude)*: **Gouda cheese** *(qv)* is cylindrical and flat, **Edam cheese** *(qv)* is ball-shaped with a yellow skin which is given a red covering when exported. They are the two cheeses found in the Alkmaar market *(qv)*. The **Leyden cheese** *(Leidse kaas)* has caraway seeds which makes it a tasty cheese with drinks. That of **Friesland** *(Friese kaas)* is flavoured with cloves.

Desserts – The Dutch are very fond of ice-cream and pastries, abundantly covered with whipped cream *(slagroom)*. The **vlaaien** are delicious tarts with Limburg fruit (Weert, Venlo). All over the country small doughnuts called **poffertjes** and shortbread called **spritsen** are made. In Friesland, the **suikerbrood** is a tasty bread roll with sugar. Finally, amongst the numerous sweets, there are the **kletskoppen** a round crunchy cake with almonds (Gouda, Leyden); the **Haagse hopjes** coffee caramels, a speciality of The Hague and the **Zeeuwse babbelaars,** hard caramels of salted butter, made in Zeeland.

Drinks – **Coffee** *(koffie)* is the preferred drink, with milk *(melk)*. Black coffee made in a percolator is called "espresso". Beer is also enjoyed. The usual aperitif is sherry, but there are local specialities such as **advocaat**, a thick type of egg-nog, or **gin** *(jenever)*, a small glass *(borrel)* of it is usually drunk before meals. Liqueurs such as kummel with a caraway seed base, anisette, apricot brandy, and above all **curaçao** made with alcohol and bitter orange peel, are also appreciated.

Amsterdam – Prinsengracht

Sights

M.J. Jarry – J.F. Tripelou/TOP

★ AALSMEER Noord-Holland

Pop 22 196

Michelin map 408 F5

Aalsmeer, a centre for growing flowers in greenhouses, is on the edge of Haarlemmermeerpolder *(qv)* reclaimed land criss-crossed with canals and the larger Westeinder Plassen. The town is mainly known for its flower auction where most Dutch florists buy their flowers and, thanks to the proximity of Schiphol airport *(qv)*, foreign buyers, as well. About 80% of sales are exported.
Around 9 milliard cut flowers were sold in the Netherlands in 1990, amongst which 1 milliard carnations and 2 milliard roses, added to which were 750 million potted plants.
The procession of floral floats which takes place from Aalsmeer to Amsterdam is renowned *(see Calendar of Events)*.

SIGHTS

★★ **Bloemenveiling (Flower Auction)** ⏲ – It takes place in a large building decorated with a tulip, the headquarters of the Aalsmeer Flower Auction, the **V.B.A.** (Verenigde Bloemenveilingen Aalsmeer), whose estate extends over 63ha-156 acres.
Inside **footbridges** make it possible to watch the activity in the market and the auctioneering.
Part of the hall is reserved for the arrival of cut flowers, which takes place the day before or early in the morning. Packing and loading onto trucks is carried out further away.
In the centre of the hall, four amphitheatres have been designed for the selling of cut flowers. The retail buyers are installed in tiers facing dials linked to a computer. A cart carrying flowers in bunches is brought to the foot of each dial.
On the dial a number indicates the price in units *(above)*, the number of the cart and the quantity of flowers it contains. The first buyer who, by pushing a button in front of him, interrupts the countdown from 100 to 0, stops the auction and thus fixes the price.
His number then appears on the dial as well as the number of bunches bought. The selling of potted plants takes place in another part of the building which is not visible from the visitors' footbridge.

Westeinder Plassen – This vast lake is one of the most frequented water sports centres near Amsterdam. The road which goes round it by Kudelstaart provides lovely **views**.

★ ALKMAAR Noord-Holland

Pop 90 778

Michelin map 408 F4

A historic town, Alkmaar owes its present reputation to its picturesque weekly cheese market.
Inside its surrounding moat, occupied partly by the canal, Noordhollandskanaal, the old town has more or less preserved its 17C plan and a number of old façades. The old fortifications have been transformed into a garden. Alkmaar is now the centre for the agricultural regions of the Noord-Holland peninsula.

HISTORICAL NOTES

Alkmaar was founded in the 10C in the middle of marshes and lakes. Its name means "all lake" or "auk lake" from the name of a bird, a kind of penguin which lived in the marshes.

A heroic siege – During the Eighty Years' War, which began in 1568, Alkmaar was besieged in August 1573 by 16 000 Spaniards commanded by Dom Frederico of Toledo, son of the Duke of Alba.
Heavy autumn rain, flooding the surrounding countryside, obliged the assailants to withdraw on 8 October, after a seven-week siege. Alkmaar was, thus, the first town to resist the Spanish: "It was in Alkmaar that victory started" has been said for centuries.

Boat trips ⏲ – Tours on offer include Alkmaar's canals as well as excursions to Amsterdam and the Zaanstreek *(qv)*.

J.P. Lescourret/EXPLORER

Cheese porters

★★ KAASMARKT (CHEESE MARKET) (BYZ) ⏲ *1/2 hour*

This traditional market, known since the early 17C, is held on Waagplein.
Early in the morning loads of cheese from Edam *(qv)* or Gouda *(qv)* are carefully piled up. At 1000 the buyers start tasting and comparing the different cheeses and bargain, then they make a deal with a vigorous gesture of the hand, to seal their agreement with the seller.
Then the famous **cheese porters** *(kaasdragers)* take over, wearing the traditional white clothes and straw hats; the porters belong to an ancient guild, which is divided into four companies each identified by a different colour (green, blue, red and yellow) and consisting of six porters and a weigher or stacker *(tasman)*.
Once a batch of cheese is sold, it is placed on a stretcher with the company's colour. The porters then run with the load (weighing up to 160kg-353lbs) to the weigh house where the *tasman* officiates. Finally the cheese is taken to the trucks.

ADDITIONAL SIGHTS

Waag (BZ) – It is the former Chapel of the Holy Ghost, built at the end of the 14C and transformed in 1582 into a weigh house: on the east side, the chancel has been replaced by a Renaissance building with a finely worked gable, which since the 19C, is decorated with a painting, on Auvergne lava, depicting trade and industry.
The tower, which was built at the end of the 16C, modelled on that of the Oude Kerk in Amsterdam *(qv)*, has a **carillon** and automata of knights jousting every hour.
The Waag contains a Museum of Dutch Cheese, **Hollands Kaasmuseum** ⏲. The tour starts on the 2nd floor, which is devoted to the history and making of cheese and butter. Note the lovely decorated wooden cheese moulds. Documentation on the 1st floor shows present cheese-making procedures, on the farm, in the dairy, as well as the importance of dairy products to the Dutch economy. Cheese tasting sessions are held on the ground floor.

Huis met de Kogel (BZ **D**) – Overlooking the canal the house has a corbelled wooden façade. Embedded in the gable there is a Spanish cannonball from the battle of 1573.
From the neighbouring bridge there is a fine **view** of the weigh house.

Mient (BZ 22) – On this square and along the canal, one can see numerous old façades. To the south there is the fish market, Vismarkt.

Langestraat (AY) – This pedestrian precinct is the town's main shopping street.

Stadhuis (AYZ **H**) ⏲ – The town hall's charming Gothic façade with its flight of steps is flanked by an elegant octagonal tower with streaks of white limestone. The adjoining building is 17C. The town hall has a collection of porcelain.

Grote of St.-Laurenskerk (AY) ⏲ – A Protestant church, it is a beautiful edifice with three naves, transept, and ambulatory dating from the end of the 15C and beginning of the 16C. It was built by members of the Keldermans family, famous architects from Mechelen in Belgium.
The imposing interior is roofed with wooden vaults from which hang beautiful 17C chandeliers. A plain triforium runs above the large arcades. Under the chancel vault there is a painting, the *Last Judgment*, by Cornelis Buys (15-16C), known as the Master of Alkmaar.
The case of the **great organ**★ made in 1645 by Jacob van Campen *(qv)* is decorated with panels depicting the Triumph of David. The **small organ**★, on the north side of the ambulatory, dates from 1511: it is one of the country's oldest instruments.
The consistory, the room where the ministers met to discuss church affairs, has kept its original aspect.

ALKMAAR

Boterstraat	BZ 3	Canadaplein	AY 4	Koorstraat	AYZ 19
Huigbrouwerstr.	BZ 16	Dijk	BY 6	Luttik Oudorp	BZ 21
Laat	ABZ	Doelenstraat	AY 7	Mient	BZ 22
Langestraat	AYZ	Gasthuisstraat	AY 9	Nieuwe Schermerweg	BZ 24
Payglop	AZ 27	Gedempte Nieuwesloot	ABY 10	Paternosterstr.	AY 25
Schoutenstraat	AYZ 30	Hofstraat	ABZ 12	Ridderstraat	AZ 28
		Hoogstraat	AY 13	Waagplein	BYZ 31
		Houttil	BZ 15	Zevenhuizen	AY 33
		Kooltuin	BZ 18	Zilverstraat	AZ 34

On the south side of the transept there is a memorial brass to Pieter Palinck and his wife. Numerous stone slabs can be seen embedded in the floor. There is also the tomb built in memory of Count Floris V, assassinated in 1296.

Stedelijk Museum (AY **M**) ⊙ – The municipal museum occupies the Nieuwe Doelen, a 17C building which used to house the Archers' Guild. It presents several interesting collections related to the history of the town: 16 and 17C paintings, including a great many portraying civic guards and works by M. van Heemskerk, Pieter Saenredam, G. van Honthorst, W. van de Velde the Elder and Van Everdingen, together with various sculptures, ancient façade stones and items made of pewter, silver and gold plate. Note the display of 19C toys. The museum also hosts exhibitions on modern art.

EXCURSIONS

The dunes – *Round tour of 35km - 21 1/2 miles - about 1 1/2 hours. Leave by* Scharlo (AY).

Bergen – Pop 14 056. Called also Bergen-Binnen (*binnen:* inner) as opposed to the neighbouring seaside resort, Bergen is an agreeable holiday resort where substantial villas stand in rows along tree-lined avenues. It has a popular university installed in the former manor-house of the lords of Bergen.

Towards 1915 the **Bergen School** was formed; its members (Leo Gestel, the Wiegman brothers) were influenced by the French painters, Cézanne and Le Fauconnier. Bergen still attracts numerous artists, whose work is exhibited in the Noordhollands Kunstcentrum *(on Plein)* or in the summer in open-air markets.

The battle of Bergen took place in September 1799, with the Anglo-Russians (British soldiers under the command of Abercromby) against the troops of the Batavian Republic commanded by Brune. Subsequently, the Alkmaar convention was signed by which the invaders left the country.

At the crossroads with the road to Egmond, is the entrance to the **Noordhollands Duinreservaat** ⊙ a private nature reserve of 4 760ha-11 757 acres. A large number of bird species nest in the dunes.

Bergen aan Zee – The seaside resort is located on a coast lined with high dunes dotted with villas. From the boulevard there is an extensive view over the desolate landscape of dunes, with trees lining the horizon. The **Zee-Aquarium** ⊙ has a collection of exotic fish and a small seal pool.

Egmond aan de Hoef – The village is set in the bulbfield area to the south of Alkmaar. To the east, on the Alkmaar road, beyond the church, the ruins of the moated **Slot van Egmond** can be seen. One of its better known owners was the famous count executed in 1568 in Brussels *(see Delft).*

Egmond aan Zee – This small seaside resort is in the middle of the dunes. At the foot of the lighthouse a statue of a lion symbolises the heroism of **Lieutenant Van Speijk**, who on 5 February 1831 near Antwerp, blew up his gunboat with all on board rather than surrender to the Belgians.

Return to Egmond aan de Hoef.

Egmond-Binnen – In 1639 Descartes stayed here. The famous **abbey** of Egmond destroyed by the Beggars *(qv)* in 1572, was rebuilt in 1935.

Return to Alkmaar.

Graft - De Rijp – Pop 5 500. *17km - 10 1/2 miles to the southeast by Nieuwe Schermerveg* (BZ **24**)
These two localities merged in 1970. **Graft** has kept its beautiful raadhuis built in 1613, with crow-stepped gables. **De Rijp**, an important centre for herring fishing and whaling in the 16 and 17C also has a town hall (1630) and houses built in the regional style with wooden gables and a church, **Hervormde Kerk** ⏲, decorated with 17C stained glass windows. It was the birthplace of **Jan Adriaensz. Leeghwater** (1575-1650) *(qv).*

★ AMERSFOORT Utrecht — Pop 101 974

Michelin map 408 H5
Plan of the conurbation in the current Michelin Red Guide Benelux

Amersfoort stands at the confluence of two waterways which form the navigable River Eem in the Gelderse Valley. It is a quiet town with a certain melancholy charm. In the surrounding area woodland and moorland cover the poor glacial soils while the hills to the south, **Utrechtse Heuvelrug**, are moraines deposited by a Scandinavian ice sheet.
Amersfoort is a delightful medieval town encircled by a double ring of canals.

Historical notes – The town grew up around its 12C castle and in 1259 it was granted civic rights. The first town wall with its girdle of canals dated from the 13C.
Amersfoort prospered in the 15C and 16C thanks to its thriving trade in wool and cloth and to a growing brewing industry. A second town wall was built *c*1400 and reinforced by a ring of canals, now partially replaced by the wide circular boulevard, the Stadsring. The Koppelpoort and other foundations at the far end of the main street Kamp (BY) are all that remain of the second city wall.
The town's main activities are metallurgy (engineering), chemicals, food processing, graphics, the building industry and the service sector. The town has expanded far beyond its medieval centre.
Amersfoort is home to the Netherlands School for Bellringers.

Two Celebrities – Amersfoort was the birthplace of **Johan van Oldenbarnevelt** (1547-1619). **Grand Pensionary** (top civil servant) of Holland, the most important province in the United Provinces; he was at the origin of the country's power, by his will to ensure its development in all spheres (Twelve Year Truce in 1609, founding of the Dutch East India Company in 1602, etc). Unfortunately, he clashed with Maurice of Nassau, son of William the Silent and stadtholder as from 1584, who had him imprisoned in 1618; he was executed in the Hague in May 1619.
The painter Pieter Mondriaan, called **Piet Mondrian**, was born in Amsterdam in 1872. After attempting all kinds of painting and a stay in Paris (1911-4) where he experimented with Cubism, Mondrian founded the abstract art movement called **De Stijl** (meaning style) with **Theo van Doesburg** *(p 29)* and **J.P.P. Oud**. He passionately expounded his theories in the art periodical *De Stijl,* first published by Van Doesburg. Abandoning all subjectivity, his painting, thereafter, only had vertical and horizontal lines and primary colours – red, blue, yellow – to which he added neutral – black, white and grey. Mondrian unremittingly pursued his research in this method, called Neo-Plasticism. In 1940 he moved to New York where he died in 1944. he is considered one of the founders of geometric abstraction. His influence can also be seen in architecture. Buildings designed by **G. Rietveld** (1888-1964), like the **Zonnehof** (AZ) of 1959, or the Rietveld Schröder Huis in Utrecht *(qv)* are directly inspired by his theories.

★ MEDIEVAL CITY *4 hours*

The recommended itinerary follows the alignment of the first town wall. It was on or against this wall that the famous **Muurhuizen★** (BYZ) were built in the 15C.

De Amersfoortse Kei (AZ **A**) – A grassy patch on the Stadsring is the final resting place of this enormous **glacial boulder** weighing 9 metric tons. It was originally found in a nearby wood, where it had been deposited by the Scandinavian ice sheet. In 1661 it was moved to Varkensmarkt in the centre of town before it was finally transferred to its present-day site.

Varkensmarkt (AZ **27**) – This was the site of the pig market. From the bridge over the canal there is a lovely view to the left over the tree-shaded canal to the tower, Onze Lieve Vrouwe Toren.

AMERSFOORT

Arnhemsestr. .... AZ 5
Krommestr. .... AY 20
Langestr. .... ABZ
Utrechtsestr. .... AZ 26

Appelmarkt .... BY 2
Arnhemseweg .... AZ 3
Bloemendalse Binnenpoort ABY 6
Groenmarkt .... BY 12
Grote Spui .... AY 14
Herenstr. .... BZ 15

Kleine Spui .... AY 17
Krankeledenstr. .... AZ 18
Lieve Vrouwekerkhof .... AZ 23
Lieve Vrouwestr. .... AY 24
Varkensmarkt .... AZ 27
Windsteeg .... BY 30

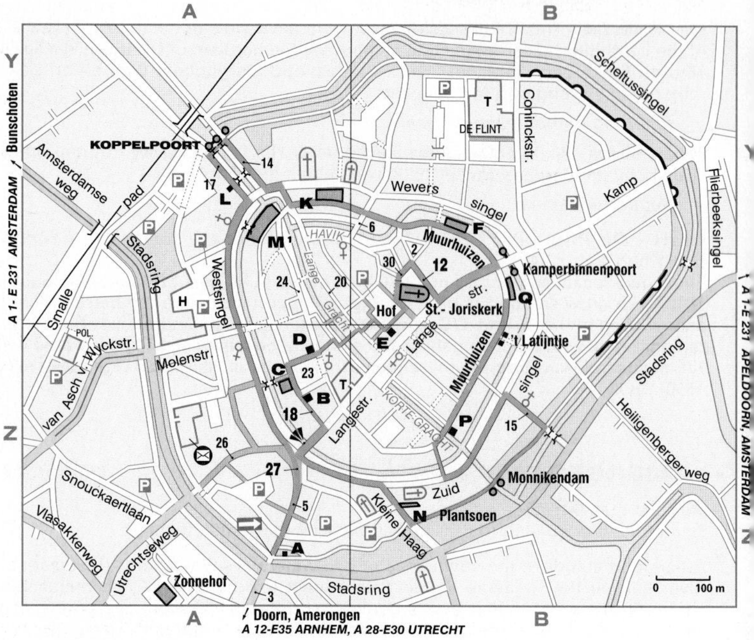

Krankeledenstraat (AZ **18**) – There are numerous old houses in this street. Note in particular the late Gothic **Kapelhuis** (**B**)

★ **Onze Lieve Vrouwe Toren** (AZ **C**) ⊙ – This beautiful 15C Gothic tower dedicated to Our Lady stands 100m - 328ft high in a large, peaceful square, Lieve Vrouwekerkhof. The brick tower has an octagonal upper storey crowned by an onion-shaped dome and is all that remains of a church destroyed in 1787 by the explosion of a gunpowder mill. The carillon was by François Hemony *(qv)*.
At the corner with Lieve Vrouwestraat there is an attractive house (AZ **D**).

Take the small footbridge to cross the canal which divides Amersfoort in two, the Lange Gracht.

Hof (BYZ) – This spacious square is still bordered by some old houses (no 24, **E**) and is the scene of a lively market on Friday mornings and Saturdays.

St.-Joriskerk (BY) ⊙ – The Romanesque **church** of St Georges, dating from 1243, was destroyed by fire in 1370. The church was rebuilt and then extended in 1534. The porch tower, a few superimposed arcades and traces of a fresco (west wall) depicting St George, are all that remain of the original building.
A finely sculpted sandstone **rood screen**, in the late 15C Gothic style, separates the naves from the chancel. The capital and consoles in the chancel depict people (monks and angels) and animals (lions and stags). Against the wall, not far from the rood screen, is the funerary monument of **Jacob van Campen** (1595-1657), the architect of Amsterdam's old Stadhuis, now the Royal Palace. Other items worthy of attention include the 14C baptismal font beside the pulpit and a jack o'the clock (Klockman) dated 1724 now associated with a 15C clock.
In an annexe is a 17C surgeons' room (Chirurgijnskamer).

Groenmarkt (BY **12**) – Several of the lovely old houses have been restored, in particular those near the adjoining square, Appelmarkt. This is the site of an **antiques market** ⊙.

Take Langestraat to reach Kamperbinnenpoort.

Kamperbinnenpoort (BY) – This 13C brick gateway with its octagonal turrets stood just outside the inner town wall on the road to Kampen. A pewter foundry, **tinnegieterij** ⊙ occupies the first floor of the west turret.
In the street to the west are some of the smaller Muurhuizen (BY **F**) which have been well restored.

Bloemendalse Binnenpoort to the left leads to Havik.

Havik (AY) – This is Amersfoort's old port situated near the ford where the town was founded (Amersfoort means ford on the Amer). The waterfront is lined with lovely houses. The flower market is held here every Friday morning.

Return to Bloemendalse Binnenpoort.

There are some interesting and quite impressive **Muurhuizen**★ (AY **K**) to be seen between nos 217 and 243.

★ **Koppelpoort** (AY) ⊙ – This beautiful double gate built *c*1400 includes a fortified bridge or watergate over the Eem, a fulling mill for cloth in the centre and the gateway proper, flanked by polygonal towers. The Boatmen's Guild used this as their meeting place and today it is occupied by a puppet theatre, **poppentheater** ⏲. In **Kleine Spui**, almost level with the lock, no 8 (AY **L**) sports two façades stones, one of which depicts a sailing ship.

Museum Flehite (AY **M**[1]) ⏲ – The collections cover the history, archaeology and decorative arts of the town and the Flehite area (eastern part of the province of Utrecht). There is also a section devoted to the local dignitary, Johan van Oldenbarnevelt *(see above)*.

Take Westsingel back to Varkensmarkt then continue to Zuid singel turning right into Kleine Haag.

Kleine Haag leads past a former Ursuline convent, **Mariënhof** (BZ **N**). This lovely 16C building has recently been restored.

Plantsoen (BZ) – A garden has been laid out on the site of the ramparts. Erratics and monoliths from various countries are scattered on the lawns.

Monnikendam (BZ) – This graceful water-gate (1430) overlooks the outer ring canal on one side and the leafy gardens of patrician houses on the other.

Take Herenstraat back to Zuid singel and turn left.

The lovely shaded **canal**, Zuid singel, runs along the foot of the Muurhuizen gardens. Cross the canal then turn right and admire some more Muurhuizen. The bridge over the **Korte Gracht** (BZ) is an attractive site, overlooked by the **Tinnenburg** (BZ **P**), another impressive wall house.

Ph. Gajic/MICHELIN

Monnikendam

't Latijntje (BZ) – Also known as the Dieventoren or the Pompetoren, the 13C tower on the right is a relic of the first town wall. It houses the exercise keyboard of the Netherlands School for Bellringers.
There is a remarkable succession of **Muurhuizen**★ (BY **Q**) further along on the right.

EXCURSIONS

★ **Bunschoten** – Pop 18 674. *12km - 7 1/2 miles to the north. Leave by Amsterdamseweg* (AY).
Bunschoten forms a single built-up area with **Spakenburg**, a small port on the edge of the freshwater Eemmeer (eel fishing).
The two villages run along a street for more than 2km - 1 mile, which divides in the north to form the quays of a canal. The canal then widens into a dock where old boats, typical of the Zuiderzee, sometimes moor.
Opposite the church in Bunschoten, there is a charming house with side crow-stepped gables and a door decorated with a shell.
The two villages are famous for their traditions. Some women, as well as little girls still wear a very unusual **costume**★. The skirt is long, black and covered with a black apron. The distinctive feature of the costume is the stiff, flowered panels, often of chintz *(qv)* on either side of the tartan band which marks the centre of the bodice. Widows wear a violet or black bodice for the rest of their lives, if they do not marry again. It covers a black shirt with short check sleeves. In the winter some women wear a cotton overblouse with long sleeves.
A small white crocheted bonnet is perched on the back of the head.
These costumes can be seen on Saturday afternoons, during the market, as well as during the last two Wednesdays of July and the first two Wednesdays of August (Spakenburgse Dagen), when handicrafts are on sale on the market place and around the port.

A heathland area – *41km - 25 1/2 miles to the south - about 3 1/2 hours. Leave to the south by Arnhemseweg* (AZ **3**).
The road crosses the forest and heathland called **Leusder Heide**, which developed on the edges of terminal moraines.

At the Utrecht-Woudenberg crossroads turn right.

Piramide van Austerlitz (Austerlitz Pyramid) – During a period of inactivity Napoleon's soldiers built a sand pyramid here in 1804. Hidden under vegetation, it was discovered in 1894, restored, equipped with a staircase and topped by a small memorial.

Doorn – *See Doorn.*

Wijk bij Duurstede – Pop 16 419. This town, near the Lek, is former **Dorestad**, a great trading centre which was abandoned after its destruction by the Vikings in 863. The city developed again in the 15C through the Bishop of Utrecht's influence, who chose it as his place of residence.

Marktplein, the great square, is overlooked by the church with its uncompleted square tower and the town hall (1662).

In an adjoining street *(Volderstraat 15-17)* a small museum, **Kantonnaal en Stedelijk Museum** ⊙ has been opened, which retraces the history of the town and recalls, notably, the excavations undertaken on the site of ancient Dorestad.

Near the Lek, a **stage mill** (Molen Rijn en Lek), where the base forms an arch, bears a striking resemblance to the one which Jacob van Ruysdael painted in one of his works exhibited in the Rijksmuseum in Amsterdam.

On the outskirts of town, the ruined and moated castle, **Kasteel Duurstede**, still has the remains of a square keep and a 15C round tower.

Amerongen – Pop 6 801. A peaceful place in the Lower Rhine (Neder Rijn) region, where tobacco was formerly cultivated; typical wood tobacco drying sheds can be seen. Its Gothic **church** is overlooked by a tall 16C tower of sandstone with limestone courses. On the square, with lovely rustic houses, an oak tree was planted in 1898 in honour of Queen Wilhelmina's coming of age.

Not far away, in Drotestraat, stands the famous castle, **Kasteel Amerongen** ⊙. A first castle was built on the foundations of a medieval stronghold erected in 1286.

After it was destroyed by fire in 1673, its owner Godard van Reede commissioned a new castle to be built on the same site. It was finished in 1684: an oblong brick construction circled by double moats, a marvel of simplicity and elegance. Kaiser Wilhelm II of Germany lived there from 1918 to 1920, before abdicating and moving to Doorn.

The rooms inside feature splendid furniture, tapestries and paintings (17-19C).

North of **Leersum**, on the Maarsbergen road, the Het Leersumse Veld Nature Reserve is situated on the heathlands of an old glacial moraine. The lakes, **Leersumse Plassen**, ⊙ are favourite breeding grounds with seagulls.

★★★ AMSTERDAM Noord-Holland

Pop 702 444

Michelin map 408 F4 folds 27 and 28 (inset) – Local map see IJSSELMEER
Plan of the conurbation in the current Michelin Red Guide Benelux

Capital of the Netherlands, Amsterdam is not the seat of the government. The sovereigns are enthroned here but do not live here.
The town is built on the banks of the IJ and the Amstel. Its network of canals like a spider's web, its tall and narrow brick houses with stepped or voluted façades, its port, its intense commercial and cultural activity, its museums, give Amsterdam a pronounced and very fascinating charm.

P. van Riel/EXPLORER

Amsterdam in winter

Practical information – For the young there are several brochures on sale with all sorts of useful information.

Transportation – Due to the narrow quays and parking problems, traffic is difficult in Amsterdam and congestion is frequent.

Public transport – The visitor to Amsterdam is well advised to use the city's integrated public transport system (buses, tramways and the underground). The **strip card** *(strippenkaart)* is valid for buses, trams and underground, nationwide. The card can be purchased from all stations, newsagents, tobacconists and VVV offices. The card is fed into a punch-machine to cancel one strip per trip and per zone covered. The stamp is valid for one hour and it is possible to change the mode of transport and route within the hour. A leaflet on public transport is available from the VVV offices.

Illuminations ⏲ – In the summer many of Amsterdam's public and historic buildings and bridges are illuminated. An evening canal boat cruise is one of the more relaxing ways to admire the marvellous variety and decoration of all those canalside houses.
Taxi-boats, ⏲ maximum 7 passengers, are a pleasant and quick way to get around the city.
The **hiring of bicycles** ⏲ allows you to choose your own itinerary without having to cope with parking.

Entertainment – In cinemas, films are shown in the original version, with sub-titles in Dutch. The ballet companies (Het Nationale Ballet), the Netherlands National Opera (Nederlandse Opera) and the Koninklijk Concertgebouworkest give excellent performances for those who do not know the language.
The VVV edits a small magazine *(What's on in Amsterdam)*, in English only, where the city's entertainment, and where it takes place, is indicated.

Eating out – All Dutch and international specialities are served in Amsterdam. The town also has a large number of Indonesian restaurants *(see Introduction: Food and Drink)*.

Markets – Apart from the various markets mentioned in the text, there is a stamp market which takes places once a week *(Saturday afternoons)* to the south of Nieuwezijds Voorburgwal.

Festivals – Among the most important are the Holland Festival, the floral float procession, and the official entry of Saint Nicholas, a national event *(see Calendar of Events)*.

HISTORICAL NOTES

Legend has it that Amsterdam was founded by two Frisian fishermen who had landed on the shores of the Amstel in their small boat. They had a dog with them. The boat and the animal are depicted on the town seals (15C).
In fact the city's existence was only known from 1275: Count Floris V of Holland granted trading privileges to this herring fishing village situated on a jetty or dike *(dam)*, at the mouth of the Amstel. Amsterdam developed in stages round the original village centre, now Dam. Towards 1300 it was awarded its city charter, then in 1317 it was annexed by William III, to the county of Holland.
In 1345, following a miracle (an Eucharistic host was found intact in a brazier), Amsterdam became a place of pilgrimage. In 1428 the town, with the county of Holland, passed into the hands of the Duke of Burgundy, Philip the Good.
The imperial crown shown on its coat of arms was granted in 1489 by Emperor Maximilian, widower of Mary of Burgundy, the daughter of Charles the Bold, for the support given by the city to the Burgundian-Austrian monarchs.

The beginning of prosperity – The end of the 16C marked the beginning of a brilliant period for Amsterdam. After the town had been pillaged by the Spanish in 1576, the rich merchants from Antwerp took refuge in Amsterdam; they brought their diamond industry with them.
Once freed from Spanish dominance by the Union of Utrecht (1579) the town became very prosperous; the new immigrants actively contributed.
Then at the end of the 16C, the Marranos arrived from Spain and Portugal; they were Jews, who had been converted by force to Catholicism but continued to practice their own religion in secret. To encourage the trading activities of the latter, the authorities granted them extensive privileges.

The Golden Age (17C) – This century marked the height of Amsterdam's glory. Following in the wake of the Portuguese, the Dutch undertook their overseas expansion. In a few years their sailing ships plied all over the Far East. In 1602 they founded the East India Company (Verenigde Oostindische Compagnie, or V.O.C.), then in 1621 the West India Company. It is the Englishman Henry Hudson *(qv)*, who was sailing for the Dutch India Company, who is credited with discovering Manhattan in 1609.
The Bank of Amsterdam, created in 1609, became one of the first European credit establishments. The Stock Exchange was built 1608-11 by Hendrick de Keyser.
In 1610 it was decided to build the three main canals, Herengracht *(illustration opposite)*, Keizersgracht and Prinsengracht. They were soon lined with the mansions of the rich merchant burghers.
The town was surrounded with a high wall on which windmills were placed.
Rembrandt, born in Leyden *(qv)* went to live in Amsterdam in 1630 (d 1669). He was buried in Westerkerk (KX).
In 1648, with the Treaty of Munster ending the Eighty Years' War with Spain, the independence of the United Provinces was officially recognised.
The development of navigation led to the making of maps and globes; it became Amsterdam's speciality.
The Revocation of the Edict of Nantes in France in 1685 brought about the immigration of a large number of Huguenots who joined in the town's commercial activity.
At the end of the 17C, however, Dutch maritime power was on the decline and so was textile manufacturing.

French occupation – The accumulated wealth was such that Amsterdam for a long time resisted the effects of the economic decline which occurred in the 18C. Although in 1672 Amsterdam had been able to repel the attack of Louis XIV's troops by opening the locks which protected it, it could do nothing in 1795 against Pichegru's army. In 1806 Napoleon made his brother Louis Bonaparte, King of Holland. He settled in Amsterdam, which became the capital of the kingdom.
Reunited to France in 1810, decreed by Napoleon as the third town of the French Empire and seat of the local government of the Zuiderzee *département*, Amsterdam was then hit by the Continental System which ruined its trade.
In November 1813, the population revolted and recognised the Prince of Orange, William I, as sovereign on 2 December.

Economic reawakening – It is only in the second half of the 19C that the town emerged from a long period of economic lethargy. The bastioned ramparts which, by Singelgracht, demarcated the inner town, were razed in the 19C.
In 1876 a new canal was opened linking it to the North Sea (Noordzeekanaal) which facilitated the shipping trade.
The Central Station (MX) in the neo-Renaissance style was built in 1889 on 8 657 wooden piles laid on the IJ islands.
Thanks to foreign and government aid the diamond industry rapidly redeveloped. Here, in the City of Diamonds, such diamonds as the Cullinan and Koh-i-Nohr were cut. A number of **diamond cutting workshops** ⊙ are open to visitors.

A house-boat

Amsterdam in the 20C – In 1903 the new Stock Exchange by **Berlage** was completed, inaugurating a modern era in architecture.

A little before the First World War, the town started expanding and new quarters were built. Several architects grouped together into the **Amsterdam School** which spread an original style of building (Navigation House) and developed mainly after the First World War, with **Michel de Klerk**. Until his death in 1923 he built, together with **Peter Kramer** and **J.M. van der Mey** a good deal of local authority housing, particularly to the south of Sarphatipark (GV) and to the west of Spaarndammerstraat (FT). They show a desire to break the monotony of façades by asymmetry and differences in levels and reduce the severity of straight lines with sections of curving walls.

The last war hit the town badly. Under the German occupation which lasted five years nearly 80 000 Jews were deported (only 5 000 survived). In February 1941 the heroic dockers' strike, protesting against the massive deportations, had no effect. A statue commemorating this event was sculpted by Mari Andriessen. *(qv).*

Post-war period – Amsterdam rose magnificently from its ordeals.

The large industrial city, which is part of the Randstad Holland *(qv)*, is now devoted to medical technology, metallurgical, graphic and food industries, and tourism – it hosts many international congresses.

On Europaplein the RAI (FV) is a large congress and exhibition centre. The World Trade Centre, near the Station Zuid was inaugurated in 1985.

The canal from Amsterdam to the Rhine (Amsterdam-Rijnkanaal), completed in 1952, has contributed to the development of the port which has increased its trade with countries to the east.

A road tunnel for cars built under the IJ in 1968 has made communication easier between the old town and the area situated to the north of the port. An underground was opened in 1976. Schiphol airport, which can be reached by rail has furthered Amsterdam's activity.

The town has grown with the development of such modern suburbs as Buitenveldert to the south, and Bijlmermeer to the southeast. However, the housing problem remains acute and this has led to an increasing number of new urban districts.

Another typical feature of the city are the 2 400 picturesque house-boats lining 36km – 22 miles of quays.

As tolerant as it was in the 17C and readily avant garde, Amsterdam with two universities totalling 39 000 students and also numerous higher educational institutions, is very open to new ideas and allows freedom of expression to the young who represent 30% of the population. There is a continual feeling of optimism in the air drawing the young from all over the world.

★★★ OLD AMSTERDAM *allow a day*

★★★ **Grachten (Canals)** – Most of the town houses which stand behind the trees, lining the canals in the centre of the town, were built in the 17 and 18C by wealthy merchants. Somewhat similar in appearance with their narrow façades and front steps, and yet they differ by the colour of their brick – pink, blue, violet or grey – and by the gable decoration. Beams with pulleys project over the pediments: the narrow staircases make it impossible to bring in furniture, so it is not unusual to see a piano, a wardrobe or a sideboard being hoisted upwards.

Gables and façade stones – *See illustration below.* Gables have the most varied shapes. The oldest ones, concealing a two-pitched roof, are plain (a legacy from wooden houses), with pinnacles or crow-steps *(see Huis Leeuwenburg, p 64).*

Then the gable becomes taller. It is sometimes in the shape of a bell *(klokgevel)* (A), or else that of a neck *(halsgevel)* (B): it is then topped by a triangular or curved pediment and often framed with fine sculptures.

The finest houses stand out by the width of their façade. The roof is then hidden by a large pilaster gable ending in a triangular pediment (C) or if the roofing is parallel to the street, by an emblazoned balustrade crowned with statues.

Herengracht

Finally a large type of house developed with pilasters and topped with a triangular carved pediment (D) where the façade, sometimes in stone, is often decorated with garlands.

On some façades there is a small sculptured stone: it is the emblem of the owner or the symbol of his trade, for example a bunch of grapes indicated the location of a wine merchant. The **façade stones** in Amsterdam outdo each other in extravagance. Many have disappeared but some have been recuperated and regrouped on the walls throughout the city.

To the north, near the port, there is a long line of **warehouses**, with the characteristic wooden shutters.

★ **Boat trip** (Rondvaart) ⊙ – The boat trip gives an excellent view of the most important canals as well as part of the port (the evening trip is recommended). The route varies according to the opening of the locks. They make it possible to regulate the water level in the canals and ensure their cleanliness (canals are pumped clean every couple of days) due to the circulation of water pumped from IJsselmeer.

Leave from Dam.

Dam (LY) – The Dam, Amsterdam's main square, is at the junction of the two large central thoroughfares: Damrak and Rokin, on the site of the dike (dam) on the Amstel. Overlooking this very animated square, there is the Royal Palace and the Nieuwe Kerk.

The National Liberation Monument, **Nationaal Monument**, (LY **A**) (1956) by the sculptor Raedeker, symbolising suffering humanity bent under the scourge of war, is the rendez-vous of strollers.

The café at no 11 (LY) is the oldest house, **De Wildeman** (the wild man) in the square; it has a charming red brick façade, dating from 1632.

★ **Koninklijk Paleis** (Royal Palace) (LY) ⊙ – The old town hall (burned down in 1652), known thanks to the painting by Saenredam in the Rijksmuseum, had become too small and was in disrepair, therefore, Jacob van Campen was called in to design a new town hall, whose construction began in 1648. It became the Royal Palace in 1808 under the reign of Louis Bonaparte.

It is a heavy classical construction, quadrilateral in shape, and built on 13 659 wooden piles. The east and west façades are topped by tympana carved by Artus I Quellin the Elder from Antwerp, who also did the building's interior decoration.

On the ground floor is the Hall of Justice (Vierschaar) where the death sentence was pronounced. The judges sat on a marble bench, above which were marble reliefs depicting Misericordia, Wisdom and Justice, and they sat facing statues of Prudence and Justice. This lay-out shows, symbolically, the cross-examiner and the judges. The people could follow the case through grilles. In the citizens' gallery (1st floor), the flooring illustrates the two hemispheres east and west and the northern firmament. There is also the famous sculpture by Artus I Quellin the Elder of Atlas holding up the celestial globe. It was in the Aldermans' Gallery that Queen Juliana abdicated in 1980. Above the chimney admire the painting by Ferdinand Bol *(qv)*, one of Rembrandt's pupils, of Moses coming down from Mount Sinai.

★ **Nieuwe Kerk** (LX) ⊙ – A Protestant church, the New Church or St Catherine's is to the Dutch what Westminster Abbey is to the English. It is here, in fact, that sovereigns are enthroned: Queen Wilhelmina was enthroned here on 6 September 1898, her daughter Queen Juliana 50 years later, day for day, her grand-daughter Queen Beatrix on 30 April 1980.

This lovely Late Gothic church was several times pillaged and gutted by fire. After a fire in 1645, its tower, designed by Jacob van Campen, remained unfinished.

It has a wooden vault, a **pulpit**★ in mahogany carved by Vinckenbrink in the 17C and a copper chancel screen, which is one of the masterpieces of Johannes Lutma, Amsterdam's famous gold and silversmith. The main organ case (*c*1650) was built from Van Campen's drawings; the whole has been greatly restored.

Dutch Admirals have their mausoleums here, in particular that of De Ruyter by Rombout Verhulst of Mechelen (Belgium).

★ **Madame Tussaud Scenerama** (LY **M**[1]) ⊙ – Revolutionary techniques and the use of Audio-Animatronics have led to the creation of an amazing museum. Visitors first discover 17C Holland, in particular Amsterdam. During that period the city was fighting against Spain – a war that lasted eighty years – but it also saw the Golden Age, an epoch of intense artistic activity and economic prosperity, as demonstrated by the scenes depicting Rembrandt, Vermeer and Jan Steen. The section devoted to the 20C presents many well-known public figures from the Netherlands and abroad (members of the Dutch royal family, politicians, sportsmen, etc.).

Kalverstraat (LY) – A very busy and picturesque pedestrian precinct, this is the most important shopping street in Amsterdam.

★★ **Amsterdams Historisch Museum** (LY) ⊙ – In this modern museum, housed in a former orphanage (Burgerweeshuis), Amsterdam's history unfolds before the visitor's eye in the form of paintings, sculptures, objects and archive documents displayed in a series of 21 rooms. The main entrance is off **St-Luciënsteeg** (St Lucy's alleyway) (LY **99**), named after the convent that preceded the orphanage. Access to the courtyard is through a low porchway surmounted by the town's coat of arms. On the left is the boys' playground with the cubby-holes where they used to keep their belongings. Opposite, a building of classical proportions hosts temporary exhibitions. On one wall are gathered a great many picturesque **façade stones** from the city's old houses. In the glass **gallery** are hung portraits of civic guards who united to defend the town in 1580. The entrance to the museum is through the second courtyard, formerly reserved for the girl orphans.

One follows in order the 21 rooms, spread over several levels.

In the first room, an amusing illuminated map shows the remarkable expansion of the city while a mobile column indicates the corresponding population growth. The city built on sand endowed itself with a town hall (**room 2**) and turned towards trade (**room 3**). In 1345 a miracle made it a pilgrimage centre (**room 3**). Then Amsterdam was subjected to Spanish domination (**room 4**). During this period it began to extend its influence to the rest of the world (**room 5**). At its peak, it built a new town hall, the present Royal Palace (**room 6**). The city began attracting many artists (**room 9**). Many other buildings were commissioned, including several churches (**room 10**). Although the town had become wealthy, it did not forget those living in poverty: charity institutions abounded and their Regents had their portraits painted (**room 11**). In the 18C, despite strong competition from foreign countries, Amsterdam still occupied a prominent position in the world of the arts (**room 12**). The actual number of painters was in decline but the standard of their work nonetheless remained high (**room 13**). In 1795 the French arrived; the towns lost their independence but the country acquired national unity (**room 16**). During the 20C Amsterdam has remained extremely dynamic (**room 17**). The last rooms house a collection of engravings and various artefacts salvaged from excavation sites. On leaving, on your left, visit the **Regents' Room** (Regentenkamer) where the directors of the orphanage sat and which has retained its original appearance.

By a passage in the courtyard, reach the Beguinage.

★★ **Begijnhof** (Beguinage) (LY) – It appears as a haven of peace in the heart of the town. Founded in the 14C, it is one of the rare enclosures of this type which remain in the Netherlands, together with the one in Breda *(qv)*. Beguines are women belonging to a lay sisterhood; although they take no vows, they do devote themselves to religious life and wear a uniform. Its tall 17 and 18C façades, preceded by a small flowered garden, are arranged round a meadow where the ancient church of the Beguines stands. It belongs to the Presbyterian Reformed Church, which has been using the English language since 1607.

Lovely sculptured façade stones can be seen at nos 11, 19, 23 and 24. No 26, a tall and elegant house was for the Mother Superior of the Beguinage. At no 31 there is a hidden Catholic chapel, built by the Beguines in 1665. Not far is the town's oldest house (15C) with its wooden façade; note in the left courtyard the façade stones.

Muntplein (LY 72) – This square, called Mint Square, is an animated crossroads dominated by the Mint Tower, **Munttoren**. The tower, the remains of a 17C gateway, is crowned with a spire, which was added by Hendrick de Keyser and has a **carillon** ⊙. In 1672 during the war against France money was minted here.

★ **Bloemenmarkt (Flower Market)** (LY) ⊙ – There are many flower sellers in Amsterdam and the sight of the shop windows and carts is a pleasure to the eye, but without doubt the most picturesque sight is that of the open-air stalls, supplied by barges which ride along the Singel. Some of the stalls are installed on the barge itself, transforming the barge into a floating greenhouse.

Singel (KY) – On this canal, at no 423, there is the university library, **Universiteitsbibliotheek**, (LY **U**[1]) and a 17C Lutheran church, Oude Lutherse Kerk (LY **B**).

Herengracht (KY) – It is one of the main 17C canals where wealthy merchants came to live. Their houses rival in richness and decoration, and most of all in the height of their gables.

Starting at no 364: Cromhouthuizen★ (KY **C**): built by Philip Vingboons in 1662 they form a harmonious whole. The classical style façades are enhanced by a more baroque decoration (note the *œil-de-bœuf* windows). One of them houses the Bible Museum.

Valdin/DIAF

Flower market

Nos 386 to 394 (KY): a lovely series of façades *(illustration p 53)*. At no 394, below a graceful gable, a charming façade stone depicts the four Aymon sons, legendary heroes of the Ardennes, mounted on their horse Bayard.

Further on the right Leidsestraat begins.

At the 2nd bend formed by the canal, vast solemn residences form the Golden Curve, **Bocht** (LZ **O**). It was the opulent quarter inhabited in the 17C by the elite society who could afford to have "double houses" built; they are now occupied by banks and consulates. When façades widened, the pediments leveled out and adopted the classical style while still keeping their decorative exuberance: the balustrades which crowned them, topped by flame ornaments or statues, surrounded the armorial bearings or allegorical scenes.

No 475 (LY) *(opposite bank)*: residence with a stone façade, built by Daniel Marot and Jacob Husley and decorated by Jan van Logteren; note the sumptuous roof

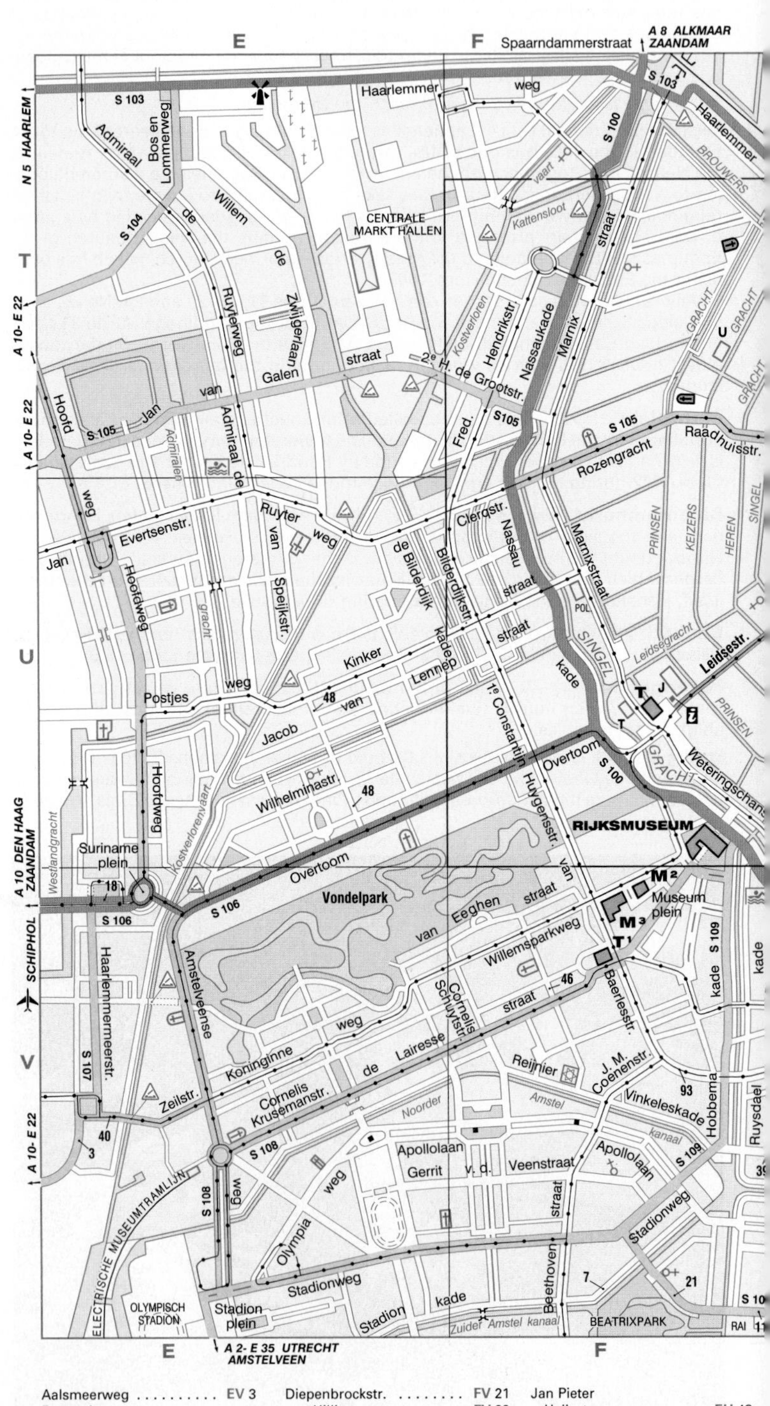

Aalsmeerweg .... EV 3
Bernard Zweerskade .... FV 7
Cornelis Lelylaan ...... EUV 18
Diepenbrockstr. .... FV 21
van Hilligaertstr. .... FV 39
Hoofddorpweg .... EV 40
Jacob Obrechtstr. .... FV 46
Jan Pieter Heijestr. .... EU 48
Kattenburgergracht ...... HU 54
Maritzstr. .... HV 63

ridge. At the corner of Vijzelstraat, the Algemene Bank Nederland building is the work of the architect De Bazel, Berlage's *(qv)* contemporary.

No 502: Huis met de Kolommen (LZ **E**): the Burgomaster's House was built in 1672 for a rich merchant of the Dutch India Company and altered in the 18C (the balcony supported by columns dates from this period). In 1927 it became the burgomaster's *(burgemeester)* official residence where he received distinguished guests.

Reguliersgracht (LZ) – From the bridge which crosses this canal, there is a lovely **view★** to the right over it and the some seven bridges spanning it.
Going a little further up to Keizersgracht, there is another agreable **viewpoint★**: note the picturesque group of old houses (LZ **F**). The **Keizersgracht** or Emperor's Canal takes its name from Emperor Maximilian's crown on the crown spire of Westerkerk.

Return to Herengracht.

From the bridge which crosses it, there is a lovely **view★** to the left and right.

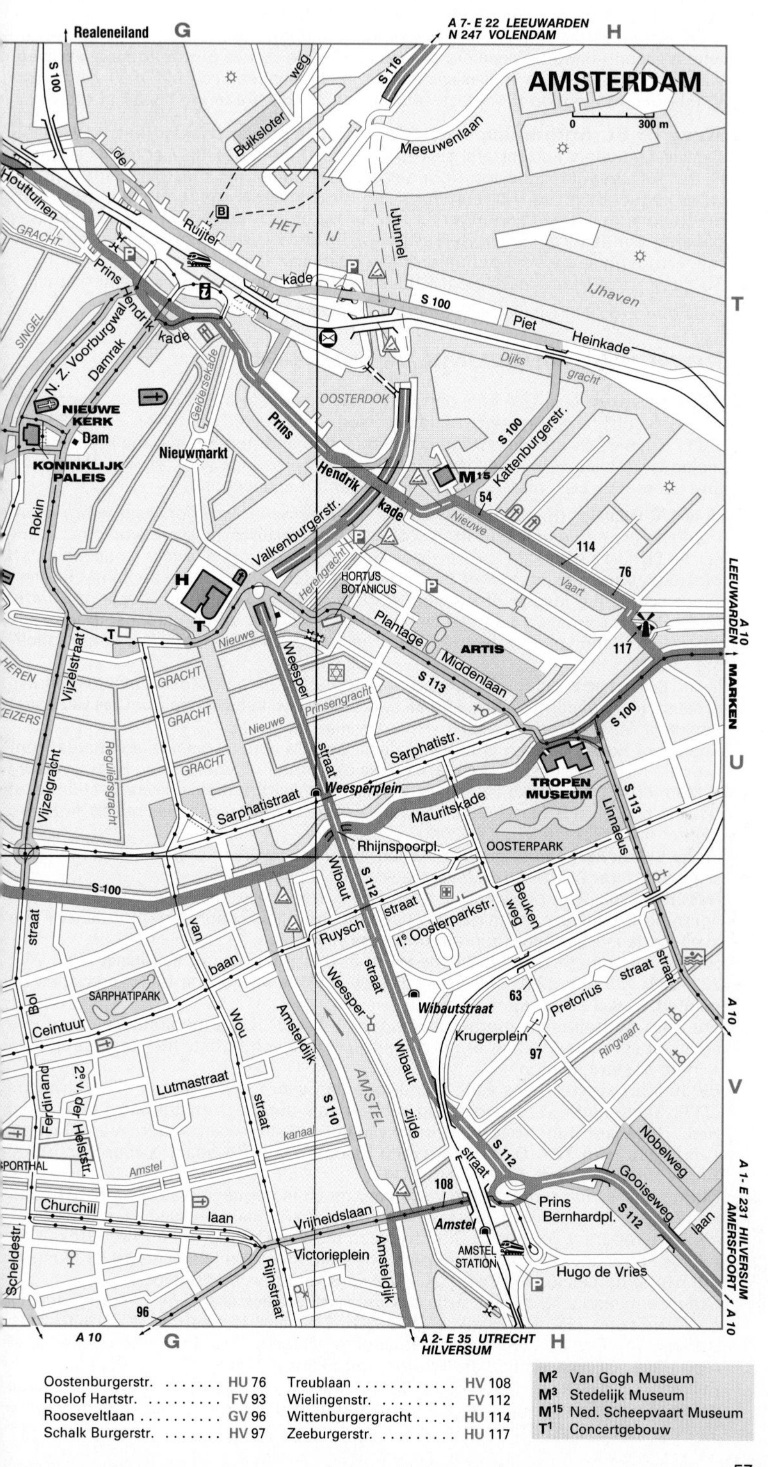

Oostenburgerstr.	HU 76	Treublaan	HV 108	**M²** Van Gogh Museum
Roelof Hartstr.	FV 93	Wielingenstr.	FV 112	**M³** Stedelijk Museum
Rooseveltlaan	GV 96	Wittenburgergracht	HU 114	**M¹⁵** Ned. Scheepvaart Museum
Schalk Burgerstr.	HV 97	Zeeburgerstr.	HU 117	**T¹** Concertgebouw

Thorbeckeplein (LYZ **105**) – With its string of nightclubs, this square is one of the livliest spots in the evening.

Rembrandtsplein (LYZ) – It is one of the Amsterdamers favourite squares for their evening stroll. Round the square, with its statue of the painter by Royer (1852), there are several large brasseries.

Rokin (LY) – This dock is situated at the far end of the Amstel, the continuation having been filled in. At the far end of the dock stands the equestian statue of Queen Wilhelmina (LY **K**) by Theresia van der Pant.
Langebrugsteeg leads into Amsterdam's oldest quarter around which the town developed.
Crossing Oudezijds Voorburgwal, one sees the old houses and warehouses which line this canal.

University (LY **U**[2]) – The **Agnietenpoort** (LY **L**) is the former entrance to the **Atheneum Illustre** a college which, founded in 1632, became a university in 1877. The chapel and the nearby buildings still belong to the university.
Walk alongside the university and its inner courtyard by the vaulted passageway, where second-hand booksellers are installed. One comes out on to **Kloveniersburgwal.** At no 29 (MY), the **Trippenhuis** is a large classical edifice built 1660-4 by Juste Vingboons for cannon manufacturers: the chimneys are in the shape of mortars.

Waag or St.-Anthoniespoort (MY) – This imposing fortified gateway (1488) flanked by towers and turrets, served as a weigh house in 1617 and was restored in the 19C. In winter the top floor served as an anatomy theatre where lectures were frequently given. The surgeons and their students could attend public demonstrations of a dissection often on the corpse of a criminal. Rembrandt's famous painting entitled *The Anatomy Lesson of Dr Joan Deyman* records for posterity the lecture given by Dr Deyman on the 29 January 1656.
To the west of Nieuwmarkt near Oudezijds Voorburgwal is the red light district.

Return to Dam by Oude Hoogstraat and Damstraat.

PRINCIPAL MUSEUMS *allow 1 day minimum*

★★★ **Rijksmuseum** (KZ) ⏲ – This national museum was founded by Louis Bonaparte in 1808 but the present building was constructed between 1876-85 by P.J.H. Cuypers in a style combining neo-Gothic and neo-Renaissance features. It includes an exceptional collection of 15 to 17C paintings with, as well, sculpture and decorative arts, history, prints and Asian art collections.

15 to 17C Paintings (Schilderkunst 15de - 17de eeuw) – *1st floor, east wing; room numbers appear in brackets.* In the collection of **Primitives** there are works by: **Geertgen tot Sint-Jans** (room 201), *The Adoration of the Magi* in a lovely landscape; Jan Mostaert, whose *Adoration of the Three Wise Men* (202) is set in an Italian Renaissance scene; the Master of Alkmaar *(qv)*, famous for his *Seven Works of Charity* (202); Jacob Cornelisz. van Oostsanen shows elegant draughtsmanship with his *Adoration of the Magi triptych* (203); Cornelis Engebrechtsz. (204) is a rather touching painter.
In the **Renaissance, Lucas van Leyden** in his *Adoration of the Golden Calf* (204) shows great mastery of composition and an expressive and lively technique; **Jan van Scorel** depicts a *Mary Magdalene* (205) of very Italian elegance.
The art of Pieter Aertsen is more realistic while a certain reserve emanates from Antonio Moro's portraits. There are works by Cornelis Cornelisz. van Haarlem (206) a Mannerist painter like Abraham Bloemaert. Visitors may admire a still-life of flowers by Velvet Bruegel (206) as well as some lovely landscapes by the Antwerp painter, Momper (all in room 206).
In the **Golden Age,** painting styles varied. Hendrick Avercamp specialised in winter scenes: *Winter Landscape* (IJsvermaak) (207).
Frans Hals (209, 210) produced outstanding portraits like *The Couple*; the vivid and lightning brushwork technique he used in *The Jolly Toper* is reminiscent of the lively surface treatment found in Impressionism.
Several rooms are devoted to the work of the great master **Rembrandt** (211, 215, 222, 224, 229 and 230). *The Stone Bridge* (211) is one of the few landscapes he painted; it was executed in 1638.
The 1631 portrait of his mother reading the Bible (211) in a meditative atmosphere could be compared to that of his pupil Gerrit Dou, who treats the same subject in a more austere fashion.
By Judith Leyster, Frans Hals' pupil, one can see a genre scene, *The Serenade* (213). Saenredam liked portraying monuments such as Amsterdam's Old Town Hall. There are numerous landscape painters. Visitors can admire Van Goyen's *Landscape with Two Oaks* (214) while Salomon van Ruysdael is represented by *River Landscape with Cattle Ferry* (214).
During this period portraits too were very much in vogue: it was around 1640 that Rembrandt immortalised *Maria Trip* (215), a luxuriously-dressed young woman; his contemporary Ferdinand Bol produced the fine *Portrait of Elisabeth Bas* (215).
Paulus Potter chose to depict animals while Jan Steen exercised his art by illustrating happy domestic life in the 17C (*The Feast of St Nicholas,* 216).
Other remarkable landscape artists were **Jacob van Ruysdael** *(The Windmill at Wijk bij Duurstede,* 217, and *View of Haarlem,* 218) and Hobbema (*Watermill,* 217).
Adriaen van Ostade was more interested in villagers, catching them in scenes of their daily life (*Peasants in an Interior: The Skaters,* 218).
Philippe Wouwerman (220) and Adam Pynacker (221) were two fine landscape painters. On display are also some outstanding naval battles by Willem van de Velde the Younger (220).

The Feast of St Nicholas by Jan Steen

The four works (221a) signed by the extraordinary colourist **Vermeer** are truly masterpieces: *The Little Street* (c1658), painted from the windows of his house, *The Kitchen Maid* (c1658), pouring milk with a measured gesture, *Young Woman Reading a Letter* (c1662), in luminous blue tones, and finally *The Letter* (*c*1666).

Room 222a presents portraits by Terborch, a *Self-portrait with Pipe* by Gerrit Dou and a sentimental scene by Metsu, *The Sick Child*.

Pieter de Hooch is an intimist painter famous for his sober, geometric settings (*The Pantry*, 222). In the same room you can appreciate *Girl at a Window: The Daydreamer* by Nicolaes Maes.

One room (224) is devoted to the Company of Captain Frans Banning Cocq called **The Night Watch** (Nachtwacht) (224). Commissioned by the arquebusiers, this enormous painting was completed by Rembrandt in 1642 and throned in the guild headquarters, the Doelen, in Kloveniersburgwal until it was transferred to Amsterdam's town hall in 1715. At that time, it was made smaller by cutting off 60cm – 23 1/2in on the left, 10cm – 4in on the right, 20cm – 8in from top and bottom. Owned by the Amsterdam Municipality, the painting was lent to the museum as soon as it was founded, but hidden during the Second World War in caves near Maastricht *(qv)*. It owes its name (night) to the layers of varnish which darkened it until 1947, but it in fact depicts the civic guards coming out in full daylight.

The guards, shown in great agitation, in a very disorderly group, are taken by surprise: the captain is giving the departure signal and the guards, some of whom have their faces half hidden, make a very original group portrait.

A few details add to the spontaneity of the whole: the little girl who is crossing the group a bird attached to her belt, the barking dog, the dwarf running, the man with a helmet covered with leaves. Spots of bright colour enhance the rather grey tones of the guards' uniforms: bright yellow dress of the small child and the lieutenant's costume, red outfit of the guard who is reloading his gun, red scarf of the captain.

One room (225) is reserved for the **foreign paintings' collection**.

From the Italian School, amongst numerous Primitives, there is a *Virgin and Child* by Fra Angelico as well as a *Mary Magdalene* by Crivelli (225). Portraits by the Florentine painter Piero di Cosimo are interesting, as are the views of Venice by Guardi. From Spain there is a lovely *Virgin and Child* by Murillo. The portrait of *Ramon Satue* by **Goya**, the only painting by this artist in the Netherlands, is exhibited in room 143 (ground floor).

The Flemish are present with two works by **Rubens**. The great gallery (229-236) contains paintings by the Dutch masters from the second half on the 17C; note Rembrandt's late works.

It was towards 1660 that the master produced *Portrait of Titus,* portraying his son in a monk's hood. Rembrandt as St-Paul (1661) comes across as a disillusioned old man (229). The portrait of a couple titled *The Jewish Bride* (1668-1669) radiates light and is bathed in tenderness (229).

The Sampling Officials of the Drapers' Guild of 1662, grouped behind a table highlighted by a red carpet, have serious expressions but are very much alive (230).

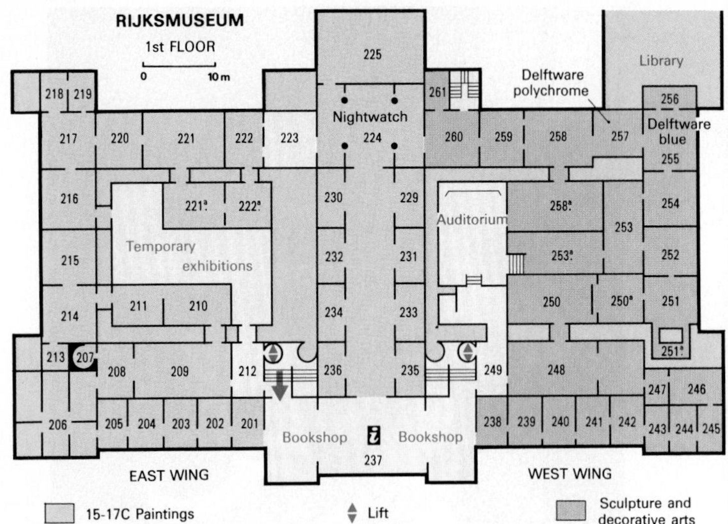

Room 231 presents a work by Nicolaas Maes, a contemporary of Rembrandt: *Old Woman in Prayer.*
Greatly influenced by the master was his pupil Aert de Gelder, represented here by *Portrait of Ernst van Beveren* (232).
Aelbert Cuyp was more of a landscape painter whose compositions featured shepherds, cattle and small human figures (234).

Sculpture and Decorative Arts (Beeldhouwkunst en Kunstnijverheid) – *1st floor, ground floor and basement, west wing.* This extensive section takes up numerous rooms, which are richly furnished and decorated with *objets d'art* (sculpture, paintings, gold and silversmith's work, glassware and tapestries) dating from the 15C to the 1900s. As regards local production, amongst the sculptures there are: **The Meeting of Saints Joachim and Anne**, a moving, late 15C work in wood, anonymous (241); the groups by **Adriaen van Wesel** of the same period, full of life and elegance, such as the *Music Making Angels* (241) and the *Death of the Virgin* (242) there is also a rood screen executed *c*1500 (248).
Also notable, from the 17C, are tapestries by the Flemish, Spiering, from his Delft workshops (rooms 250[a] and 253), a terracotta bust by **Hendrick de Keyser** (250[a]) a Renaissance oak wardrobe, a type widespread in the country (252) *(illustration p 31)*, a lovely bouquet painted by Velvet Bruegel (253), engraved glassware (253), a Ceylanese colonial bed (253[a]), gold and silversmith work by the Van Vianen brothers and Johannes Lutma (254), Delftware both blue (255) and polychrome (257) and a *kussenkast* cupboard (260) *(illustration p 31).* On the ground floor and in the basement, there is 18 to 20C furniture and lovely collections of pottery, glassware, materials, doll's houses, etc.

Dutch history (Nederlandse Geschiedenis) – *Ground floor, east wing.* The history of the country, from the Middle Ages, is pleasantly illustrated, notably by *objets d'art.* The large room is devoted to the Golden Age, its wars, sea battles and daily life. There is a portrait by Van Dyck of the young Prince William II and his wife Mary Stuart, daughter of Charles I; he was 15 and she was 9 when they were married in 1641. The Stadtholders, in particular, are evoked in a series of portraits, as well as the Batavian Republic, the domination of Napoleon, the Battle of Waterloo and the monarchy.

Print Room (Rijksprentenkabinet) – *Ground floor, west wing.* The museum possesses a large number of drawings and engravings, from the 15C to the present, which are exhibited in rotation. **Temporary exhibitions** of drawings and prints of foreign origin also take place.

18 and 19C Paintings (Schilderkunst 18[de] en 19[de] eeuw) – *Ground floor, southwest wing.* This section has paintings and a few ceramic collections.

Cornelis Troost *(An Amsterdam Town Garden)* is the best of the 18C Dutch painters (room 136).
At the beginning of the 19C, Wouter Johannes van Troostwijk (143) painted Amsterdam with much poetry while artists of **The Hague School** (Jacob Maris, Anton Mauve, Jozef Israëls) observed the country and the sea in their landscape paintings. George H. Breitner and Isaac Israëls were two fine Impressionist painters.

Asian Art (Aziatische Kunst) – *Basement, southwest wing. Direct access by 19 Hobbemastraat or else by the 18 and 19C Paintings section.* This section houses some works of art from the Far East (China, Japan, Korea), India, Ceylon, Southeast Asia and Indonesia. Chinese and Japanese art are beautifully exhibited.
Rooms 20 to 22 give a good overall view of Chinese porcelain. In room 15 a polychrome wooden sculpture, of the Sung dynasty (960-1279), depicting the Chinese bodhisattva (future Buddha), Kuan-Yin, bears witness to the skill and craftsmanship of Chinese sculpture of this period. Amongst the Japanese collections, note the ceramic objects used for the tea ceremony (rooms 14 and 23) and the lacquer-work (room 13).

Two fragments from a series of stone low reliefs from eastern Java show a curious landscape. The 12C bronze sculpture showing **Śiva** in a cosmic dance (room 17) comes from Southern India.

From Java there is a small carved Buddha (room 18), which either comes from Southern India or Ceylon, and dates from the 8C.

★★★ **Van Gogh Museum** (FV M^2) ⊙ – A modern building houses the collections of this museum: over 200 paintings and nearly 600 drawings by Vincent Van Gogh (1853-1890), the letters he wrote to his brother Theo and works by contemporary artists such as Toulouse-Lautrec, Gauguin and Odilon Redon. A display of almost 100 paintings on the first floor, enables visitors to follow the artist's development, from the sombre canvases of his early career to the violent tonalities of his last years.

Born in Zundert, south of Breda, Van Gogh sketched right from childhood, but he only became conscious of his vocation at the age of 27; he then drew with passion before taking up oil painting the following year in The Hague.

He started with dark landscapes of the Drenthe with its thatched cottages. Then came the Nuenen period, the village where Vincent lived in his parents' presbytery *(see Nuenen)*. A series of portraits of peasants, striking by the intensity of their expression, served as studies for *The Potato Eaters* (1885).

After staying in Antwerp he went to Paris in February 1886. His palette became more luminous (1887-8) under the Impressionist influence with the *View over Paris* from Vincent's atelier *Rue Lepic*, the *Grande Jatte Bridge*, the *Seine at Asnières*, and numerous self-portraits including the *Self-Portrait in Front of an Easel*.

He also worked on painting landscapes in the style of Japanese prints. *Orchards* in Provence, the *Zouave*, the *Drawbridge*, and *Sunflowers* emphasise his determination to depict the violence of colour contrasts under the Arles sky (February 1888 - May 1889).

Frenzied wheat fields, tormented olive trees, cypress trees twisted by the *mistral*, and more subdued tonalities reveal the troubles which caused his hospitalisation in Arles and then to the asylum in St-Rémy-de-Provence (May 1889 - May 1890), from where he painted from memory his room in Arles. Finally, after a calm spell in Auvers-sur-Oise, near Paris, he painted in 1890 the dramatic composition, *Wheat Fields with Crows*.

The same year, in which, on 27 July, he wounded himself in a despairing gesture, which two days later ended his brilliant but short-lived career.

Van Gogh Museum

Van Gogh,
Self-portrait with a straw hat (1887)

The museum also hosts temporary exhibitions on art in the second half of the 19C.

ADDITIONAL SIGHTS

Vondelpark Quarter

★★ **Stedelijk Museum** (FV M^3) ⊙ – Built in 1895 and enlarged in 1954, this modern art museum is continually being renewed with works of art covering the period from 1850 to the present.

There are also paintings by Cézanne, Monet, Picasso, Léger, Malevitch, Chagall as well as Mondrian and Van Doesburg, who represent the De Stijl *(qv)* movement. The most recent trends in European and American art are well represented.

Concertgebouw (FV T^1) – The name of this building, completed in 1888, evokes a famous concert hall and a prestigious symphony orchestra. In 1988, when the centennial of the orchestra was celebrated, Queen Beatrix graced it with the designation "Royal".

Leidseplein (KZ) – It is a very lively square with a shaded terrace, very busy in the summer and lined on the north side by a row of old gabled houses (KZ **N**). All around there are theatres, including the well-known municipal theatre, **Stadsschouwburg** (KZ T^2), restaurants and discos: this quarter specialises in pop music. To the east on Weteringschans (no 6), the Paradiso (KZ), a secularised church, has been converted, by the municipality, into a youth centre and is a well-known meeting place for music lovers.

Leidsestraat (KYZ) – In this long and pleasant pedestrian street linking Leidseplein to the centre, a barrel organ *(qv)* plays popular tunes daily.

Vondelpark (EUV) – Vondel Park, named after the great 17C Dutch poet, Joost van den Vondel (1587-1679), stretches from the large Singelgracht to Amstelveenseweg. There is an open-air theatre in summer.

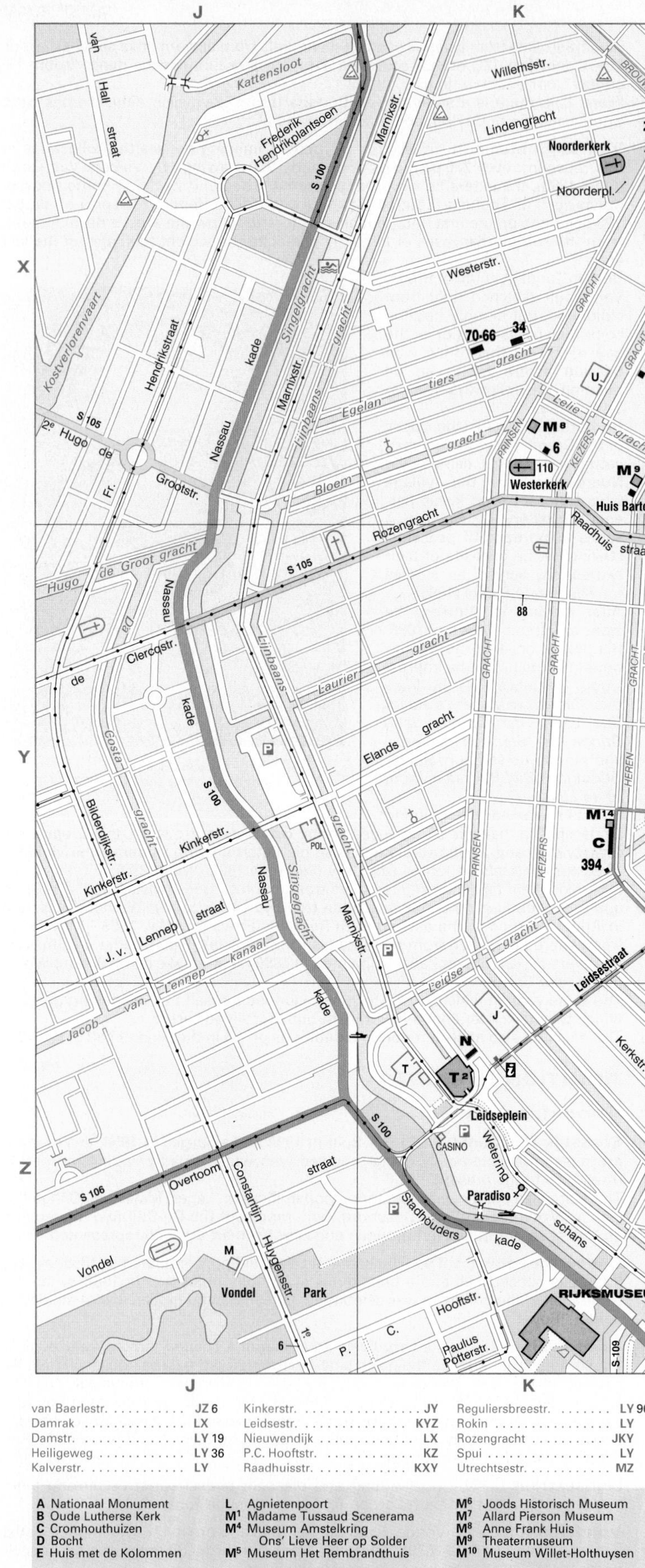

van Baerlestr.	JZ 6	Kinkerstr.	JY	Reguliersbreestr.	LY 90
Damrak	LX	Leidsestr.	KYZ	Rokin	LY
Damstr.	LY 19	Nieuwendijk	LX	Rozengracht	JKY
Heiligeweg	LY 36	P.C. Hooftstr.	KZ	Spui	LY
Kalverstr.	LY	Raadhuisstr.	KXY	Utrechtsestr.	MZ

A Nationaal Monument
B Oude Lutherse Kerk
C Cromhouthuizen
D Bocht
E Huis met de Kolommen

L Agnietenpoort
M1 Madame Tussaud Scenerama
M4 Museum Amstelkring Ons' Lieve Heer op Solder
M5 Museum Het Rembrandthuis

M6 Joods Historisch Museum
M7 Allard Pierson Museum
M8 Anne Frank Huis
M9 Theatermuseum
M10 Museum Willet-Holthuysen

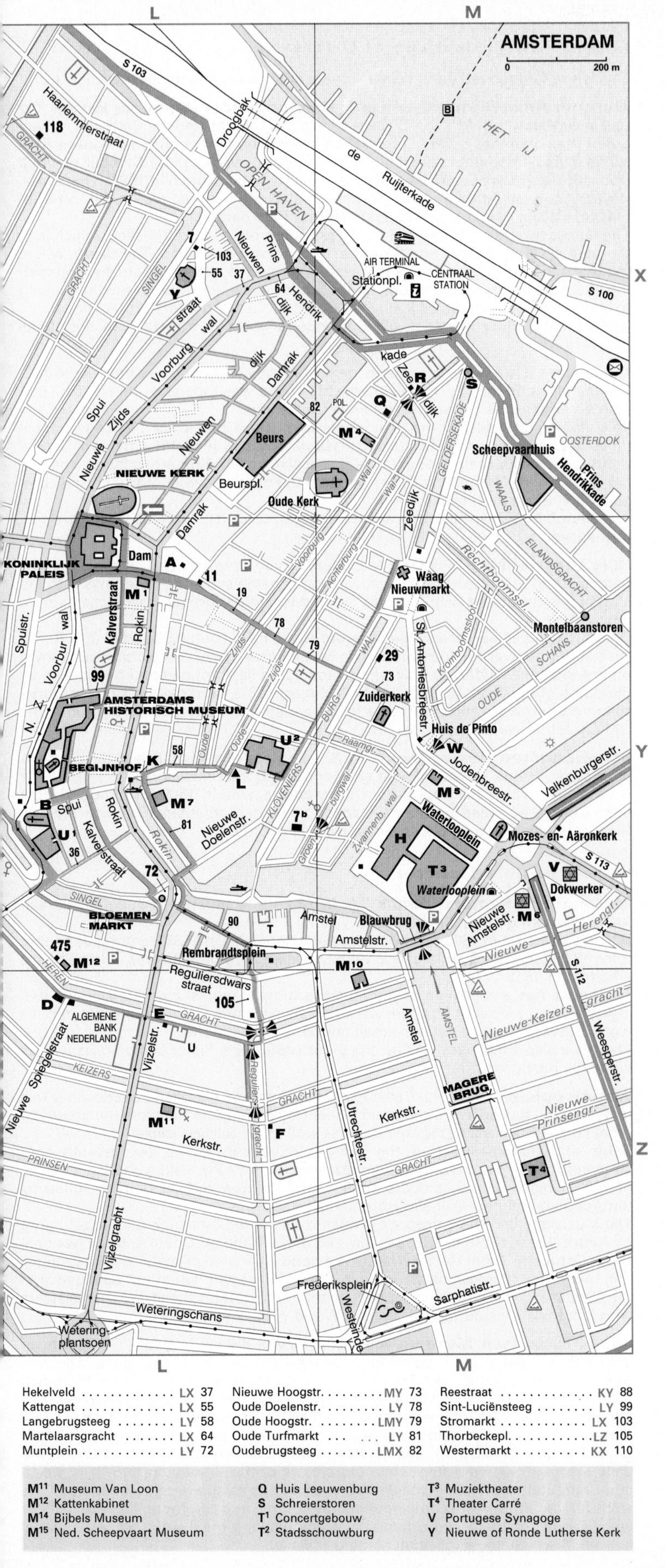

Hekelveld	LX	37
Kattengat	LX	55
Langebrugsteeg	LY	58
Martelaarsgracht	LX	64
Muntplein	LY	72
Nieuwe Hoogstr.	MY	73
Oude Doelenstr.	LY	78
Oude Hoogstr.	LMY	79
Oude Turfmarkt	LY	81
Oudebrugsteeg	LMX	82
Reestraat	KY	88
Sint-Luciënsteeg	LY	99
Stromarkt	LX	103
Thorbeckepl.	LZ	105
Westermarkt	KX	110

M[11] Museum Van Loon
M[12] Kattenkabinet
M[14] Bijbels Museum
M[15] Ned. Scheepvaart Museum
Q Huis Leeuwenburg
S Schreierstoren
T[1] Concertgebouw
T[2] Stadsschouwburg
T[3] Muziektheater
T[4] Theater Carré
V Portugese Synagoge
Y Nieuwe of Ronde Lutherse Kerk

Oudezijds Voorburgwal Quarter

This is the famous red light district. Lovely old houses line its narrow canals.

★ **Museum Amstelkring Ons' Lieve Heer op Solder** (**Amstelkring Museum "Our Lord in the Attic"**) (MX **M**[4]) ⊙ – Since the Union of Utrecht *(qv)* the Catholics, driven out of their churches by the Reformation, celebrated mass in private houses. This secret chapel fitted out in the attics of three houses was used for Catholic worship from 1663 until the construction of the new St Nicholas Church in 1887, whereupon it was converted into a museum for the Amstelkring Foundation. Certain ceremonies take place here; concerts are sometimes held here.
The staircase leading to the 2nd floor passes in front of the hall (sael), which is in the pure 17C Dutch style, and the abbot's room with a box bed. The **church**, where the two superimposed galleries correspond to the 3rd and 4th floors, has interesting 18C furnishings. In one room, on the confessional floor, there is an interesting exhibition of liturgical objects in silver, some of them from this secret chapel.
Opposite the museum, at no 19, the house's gable is framed with enormous dolphins.

Oude Kerk (LMX) ⊙ – This church, dedicated to St Nicholas, was built in the 14C. It is the oldest in the city. In the 16C the bell tower was topped by an elegant spire whose carillon was in part cast by François Hemony.
Very damaged inside by the Iconoclasts *(qv)*, it still has in its 16C Lady Chapel three elegantly designed 16C stained glass windows. In 1642 the remains of Saskia, Rembrandt's wife, were brought here (stone slab no 29). Numerous famous people are buried here (the painter Pieter Aertsen, the writer Roemer Visscher, the composer J.P. Sweelinck, etc.).
The church hosts various cultural events: organ concerts, exhibitions, theatre performances...

Huis Leeuwenburg (MX **Q**) – *14 Oudezijds Voorburgwal.* This picturesque 17C rust coloured brick façade with a crow-stepped gable and lattice windows with red shutters, is decorated with a carved stone depicting a fortified castle sheltering a lion.
On a nearby wall some very lovely **façade stones** have been embedded (MX **R**).
On the bridge over the lock where two canals meet, there is a picturesque **view**★: on one side, the Oudezijds Kolk where old houses lie shrouded and overlooked by the dome of the Catholic church of St Nicholas (1887), on the other side the Oudezijds Voorburgwal, which frames a lovely series of old façades, further on is the Old Church tower.

Schreierstoren (**Weeping Tower**) (MX **S**) – Folklore relates that near the old rampart tower, sailors' wives came to say goodbye to their husbands.
A low relief evokes the Englishman, **Henry Hudson**, who in 1609 for the Dutch East India Company, sailed up the river which now bears his name, Hudson River in New York *(see Michelin Green Guide New York City)*.

Rembrandt's Quarter

★ **Museum Het Rembrandthuis** (MY **M**[5]) ⊙ – It is situated in Jodenbreestraat, the old Jewish quarter's main street.
When it was built in 1606 this house had one floor less. In 1639 Rembrandt bought it for 13 000 florins payable over 6 years; he lived here until he was evicted by his creditors in 1659.
The house has a collection of the master's graphic works. Exhibited beside two lovely ancient pieces of furniture are about 250 etchings, giving an insight into his work. Drawings can be seen in small temporary exhibitions.
There are also a few canvases by one of his professors, Pieter Lastman, as well as works by his pupils.

Waterlooplein (MY) – The Catholic church **Mozes- en Aäronkerk**, overlooking this large square, is used in the summer as a centre for entertainment and metaphysical reflection. A **flea market** ⊙ is held here, as well as an **antiques market** ⊙.
South of Jodenbreestraat, on the former Vlooyenburg Island, two recently constructed buildings are worth noting: **Muziektheater** (MY **T**[3]), with a seating capacity of 1600, which opened its doors in 1986, and the new **stadhuis** both designed by the Austrian architect Wilhelm Holzbauer.
The Muziektheater, the entrance of which is decorated by a pink granite sculpture by André Volten (born in 1925), is the seat of the National Opera and the National Ballet Company. From the foyer there is a good view of the Amstel and its bridges.
The black marble **monument** standing in front of the town hall at the confluence of the Amstel and the Zwanenburgwal canals commemorates those Jewish resistants who lost their lives during the Second World War.

★ **Joods Historisch Museum** (**Museum of Jewish History**) (MY **M**[6]) ⊙ – South of Jonas Daniel Meijerplein stand four restored Ashkenazic synagogues. The first one, Great Synagogue, was built in 1671 by D. Stalpaert; as it became too small the Obbene (1686), Dritt (1700) and New Synagogue (1752) were successively added. The New Synagogue is easily identified by its Ionic columned entrance and dome. The exhibition inside covers different aspects of the Jewish identity: religion, Zionism, persecution and survival, culture, environment and history. In the **Grote Synagoge**, where a fine white marble ark of the Convenant (1671) is worth admiring, Judaic themes – the Jewish year and its religious celebrations and the steps into adulthood are complemented by cultural and ceremonial objects (silverware, lamps, clothing and ornaments accompanying the Torah, drapes...). Note, as well, the receptacle for ritual bathing *(mikwe)*.

Portugese Synagogue (MY V) ⊙ – This massive building, lit by tall windows, was built in 1675 by Elias Bouman as a place of worship for the three Portuguese Jewish congregations which had just united. It is presently undergoing restoration. The interior remains as shown in the painting by Emmanuel de Witte (can be viewed in the Rijksmuseum) with wide wood barrel vaults supported by very high columns, galleries for the women, the ark of the Covenant, and large copper chandeliers as the only decoration. Note the absence of curtains (Parochet), a feature unknown in Jewish Hispano-Portuguese tradition.
Near the Portuguese Synagogue, the **statue of a Docker** (Dokwerker) by Mari Andriessen commemorates the strike launched by the dockers on 25 February 1941 in protest against the deportation of Amsterdam's Jewish population.

Bridge to the south of Oude Schans (MY W) – From this bridge there is a fine **view** over the Oude Schans basin and tower, **Montelbaanstoren.**
This tower, as well as St.-Anthoniespoort was part of the town's curtain wall in the 16C.

Zuiderkerk (MY) ⊙ – The first church built in Amsterdam after the Reformation was built between 1603 and 1611 from a plan by Hendrick de Keyser; it is flanked by a **tower** (1614). At present it is used to house temporary exhibitions.
Further along, at 69 St-Antoniesbreestraat, there is the **Huis de Pinto** (MY) which was built *c*1600 and once belonged to a rich Portuguese Jew. It is now a public library.

Groenburgwal (LMY) – In a picturesque site, a wooden **lever bridge** crosses this shaded canal which in earlier days went through what used to be the dyers' district. There is a lovely **view**★ of the Zuiderkerk tower from here.
Near the bridge, at 7b Staalstraat, is the former seat of the Drapers' Guild, immortalised by Rembrandt.

Damrak, Rokin and Amstel

Beurs (Stock Exchange) (LX) – Built by Berlage between 1897 and 1903, this is the principal work of this Amsterdam architect enamoured by functionalism and pioneer of modern architecture in the Netherlands. This brick building has a sober exterior. Inside, the open steel framework supports a glass roof.
Since 1987, this former Commodity Exchange (stock market is located in a neighbouring building) serves as a cultural centre (exhibitions, concerts) and is home to the Netherlands Philharmonic and Chamber Orchestras.

★ **Allard Pierson Museum** (LY M[7]) ⊙ – It is the archaeological museum of Amsterdam University and contains a remarkable collection of antiquities from Egypt, the Near East, Cyprus, Greece, Etruria and the Roman world.

1st floor – This section is concerned with Egypt (coffins with mummies, sculptures, Coptic textiles), the Near East (Iranian pottery and jewellery) and archaeological artefacts excavated from Syria, Anatolia and Mesopotamia (cylinder-seals, cuneiform scriptures).

2nd floor – It is devoted to Mycenae, Crete, Greece, Etruria and the Roman world: a stone head, Greek archaic art, statues from the Classical period (Aphrodite, *c*400BC), a funerary stele from Attica (*c*400BC), ceramics, a Roman sarcophagus (*c*300AD) and various Etruscan exhibits (sculptures and fragments of pottery).

Blauwbrug (MY) – It is a copy of the Alexandre III Bridge in Paris *(see Michelin Green Guide Paris).*
It commands nice views of the Magere Brug to the south and on the other side, the canalside façades of the controversial Stopera development with the rounded form of the Muziektheater adjoining the massive new Stadhuis.

★ **Magere Brug** (MZ) – This fragile 18C wooden bridge (*magere* means thin) crossing the wide Amstel canal evokes the bridges dear to Van Gogh.
The large building to the east is the **Theater Carré** (MZ T[4]), dating from 1887 (circus, opera, musicals, variety shows). Standing beside the bridge one can see several bell towers, including that of Zuiderkerk.
At the corner of Prinsengracht and Amstel quay, a former wine shop has a bunch of grapes over the door.

Westerkerk Quarter

★ **Anne Frank Huis (Anne Frank's House)** (KX M[8]) ⊙ – This narrow building erected in 1635 stretches well back and has a house behind, which was enlarged in 1740. It is here that Anne Frank's father, a German Jew who emigrated in 1933, hid his family and friends in July 1942. Betrayed and deported in August 1944 with the other refugees, he alone returned from Auschwitz. The moving diary *(Diary of Anne Frank)* kept by his 13 year old daughter was found in the house, and reveals a rare sensitivity. The Anne Frank Foundation spreads her message of peace throughout the world.
A revolving bookcase reveals a secret passage which leads to the bare rooms where they all lived in clandestinity. As well as standing exhibitions on Anne's life, war and antisemitism, temporary displays are also organised on the same subject.

★ **Westerkerk** (KX) ⊙ – This church was built between 1619 and 1631 by Pieter de Keyser, after the plans of his father Hendrick. An important programme of restoration was carried out between 1985 and 1990 and has given this building of brick and stone – building materials typical of the Renaissance period in the Netherlands – a good as new look.

The **bell tower** dating from 1638 is topped by the Imperial Crown commemorating Maximilian of Austria. The emperor also gave the town permission to add the Imperial Crown to the city's coat of arms, above the three crosses of St Andrew. The remarkable carillon was the work of the Hemony brothers. The pleasant view from the top of the tower takes in the central canals and the Jordaan district.

The church interior is very plain; the nave has wooden barrel vaulting and the 12 candle chandeliers are copies of the original ones. In 1727 new stops were added to the splendid 1686 organ and its musical capacity can be appreciated during concerts. The painted panels are the work of Gerard de Lairesse (1641-1721). The painter Rembrandt was buried here, one year after his son Titus. The exact location of the tomb is not known.

On the adjoining square, called **Westermarkt** (KX), at no 6, stands the house where **Descartes** lived in 1634 (commemorative plaque).

V.C.L./PIX

Westerkerk bell tower

Theatermuseum (Theatre Museum) (KX M⁹) ⊙ – Belonging to the Netherlands Theatre Institute, the museum is installed in a house, which was built in 1618 and converted in 1638 by Philip Vingboons. It has a fine stone façade decorated with the coat of arms of its earlier owner, Michel de Pauw.

The interior, fitted up *c*1730 in Louis XIV style, preserves a valuable decoration of stuccos, mural frescoes and ceilings painted notably by Jacob de Wit.

The museum presents the famous miniature stage created by Hieronymus van Slingelandt, stage costumes, theatre posters, etc. The museum library is set up next door in the **Huis Bartolotti** (no 170) (KX), built by Hendrick de Keyser around 1617. Its wide brick façade, topped by a highly ornate gable, is further embellished by a multitude of ornamental compositions carved in white stone.

Huis met de Hoofden (House of Heads) (KX X) – It is a lovely brick house dating from 1624, and where the façade, a little like that of the Huis Bartolotti *(see above)* is decorated with six sculptured heads representing the gods of Roman mythology.

The Central Canals

Museum Willet-Holthuysen (MYZ M¹⁰) ⊙ – This patrician house built *c*1687 has a series of elegantly furnished rooms, evoking the life-style of rich merchants. There are also collections of pottery, glassware and gold and silversmiths' work.

Museum Van Loon (LZ M¹¹) ⊙ – Built in 1671-2 (altered in the 18C) on the edge of Keizersgracht by Adriaan Dorstman, this fine mansion belonged to the painter Ferdinand Bol (1616-80). The refined interior contains numerous portraits.

At the bottom of the garden, there is a Renaissance style coach house.

Kattenkabinet (Cat Gallery) (LYZ M¹²) ⊙ – The sumptuous hotel which stands at no 497 Herengracht, is the temporary setting for a collection in honour of the cat, and more specifically, the cat in the history of art. A wide selection of exhibits demonstrates the strong influence cats have had over society through the ages.

Bijbels Museum (Bible Museum) (KY M¹⁴) ⊙ – Installed in the **Cromhouthuizen** *(p 55)*, this museum gives information on Judaic religious life, history of the Bible in the Netherlands, and life in Palestine in Biblical times.

Nieuwe of Ronde Lutherse Kerk (LX Y) – Built in 1668-71, the New Lutheran Church with its high dome stands on the edge of the Singel. This deconsecrated church has been refurbished as a **concert hall★** ⊙ and conference centre.

Nearby, no 7, is the narrowest house in Amsterdam.

The Jordaan

Efforts are being made to enhance this popular area which dates from the 17C. At that time it was inhabited by French immigrants, whence its name which is a deformation of the French word *jardin* (garden). Most of its canals bear the names of flowers.

Brouwersgracht (KLX) – The Brewers' Canal lies perpendicular to the three main canals and is lined with picturesque quays and old houses and warehouses.
The **De Kroon warehouse** (no 118) has been nicely restored. On its façade, it has a carved stone depicting a crown *(kroon).*
Near the bridge at the confluence of Prinsengracht there are many old façades (KX **Z**), two with crow-stepped gables are notable.

Noorderkerk (KX) – Built in 1623 by Hendrick de Keyser, this church is in the shape of a Greek cross. On Noorderplein there is a **bird market** (vogelmarkt) on Saturday mornings. In the neighbouring Westerstraat a large second-hand market is held (Monday mornings). In the summer the **fruit and vegetable market** (boerenmarkt) ⊙ specialises in organically grown products.

Egelantiersgracht (KX) – At no 34, the **Claes Claesz. Hofje** is an old 17C almshouse (KX) *(enter by Eerste Egelantiersdwarsstraat)* surrounding a picturesque little courtyard. At nos 66-70, near a bridge, there are three trim houses, lit on the ground floor by numerous windows, and with a gable in the shape of a neck.

Quarters to the East

★ **Artis** (HU) ⊙ – This is Amsterdam's **zoological garden**, named after the acronym of the company that founded it in 1838: Natura Artis Magistra (Nature, Mistress of Art). In a large, well-tended park, more than 6 000 animals can be seen, featuring around 1 200 species. The building for small mammals houses lemur, fennec, otters... There is also a reptile pavilion and a new enclosure for gorillas. The successive stages of the hatching of a chick are shown to visitors by means of an artificial incubator *(1 April to 1 October).*
The domed **Zeis Planetarium Artis** ⊙ has a 630m^2 – 6 780ft^2 screen onto which the cosmic projector Zeiss faithfully recreates the movements of the planets. Special effects are ensured by ultra-sophisticated audio-visual equipment. The exhibition around the room is devoted to astronomy and the exploration of space.

★ **Tropenmuseum** (HU) ⊙ – Life in the tropical and subtropical regions of Africa, Asia, Middle East, Oceania and Latin America is shown with the help of *objets d'art* and a wide variety of everyday objects, reconstructed dwellings and primitive shops. Photographs and slide shows complete the exhibit.
Temporary exhibits and gamelan (Indonesian orchestra) concerts are held.

The Quays of the Port

★ **Nederlands Scheepvaart Museum** (HU M[15]) ⊙ – This large maritime warehouse installed in the old arsenal was built in 1656 on 18 000 piles in the waters of the Ossterdok. It has interesting collections concerning navigation in Holland: maps and globes, ship models, nautical instruments, paintings and prints.
Among the boats moored along the quays is the **Amsterdam**, a replica of the 18C merchant ship belonging to the Dutch East India Company (VOC). The goods on board and the activity of the crew suggest that it was returning from a trip to Asia.

Prins Hendrikkade (MX) – On the quay running alongside the Oosterdok at the corner of Binnenkant, there are the immense buildings of Navigation House, **Scheepvaarthuis**. Built in 1913 by the principal architects of the Amsterdam School – Van der Mey, Michel de Klerk and P.L. Kramer – it is representative of their style. From the bridge to the east, there is a fine **view** of Montelbaanstoren *(p 65).*

Realeneiland (GT) – This is one of the islands in the west quarter of the port, lined with warehouses. On **Zandhoek**, a row of 17C houses have been restored, whose façades, decorated with sculptured stones, overlook the Westerdok.

EXCURSIONS

South of Amsterdam – *24km – 15 miles to the south – about 1 hour. Follow Amsteldijk* (HV) *and the west bank of the Amstel.*

Rieker Molen – *See Introduction: Windmills.* Formerly located in the Rieker Polder, this lovely thatched polder mill *(p 35)* with a rotating cap has been transferred to the banks of the Amstel.
The bronze statue depicting Rembrandt drawing, reminds one that the artist often walked along the Amstel seeking inspiration.

K. Russel/EXPLORER
Zandhoek

M. Trigalou/PIX

Durgerdam

Ouderkerk aan de Amstel – This picturesque village is popular with Amsterdamers on Sundays. To the north is a **stage mill.**

Amsterdamse Bos – This is Amsterdam's main woodland area, an immense park strewn with lakes (boating, fishing with permit).

Amstelveen – Pop 70 340. A modern residential city which contains several **botanical gardens** (heemparken) devoted to the country's flora. The most well known is **Dr. J.P. Thijssepark** *(between Amsterdamseweg and Amsterdamse Bos).* One can also visit a cheese dairy **Kaasboerderij Clara Maria** *(Bovenkerkerweg 106).*

Schiphol – Amsterdam's international airport lies 4.5m - 14ft below sea level in an old cove of Haarlemmermeer *(qv).* It is one of the continent's great stop-overs.
Not far from the runways is the **Aviodome,** ⊙ a strange parachute in mat aluminium, honeycombed with stars, which houses the National Aviation Museum's collection. Various airplane models, some of them old, showing technical evolution can be seen as well as space-craft and an exhibition on civil aviation.
There is a film theatre in the basement

Round tour of 65km - 40 miles – *About 4 hours. Leave Amsterdam by Mauritskade* (HU). *After the second bridge (Schellingwouderbrug) near the locks (Oranjesluizen), turn towards Schellingwoude then pass under the road and go towards Durgerdam.*
Just before reaching **Durgerdam** there is a lovely **view★** of the village.
The houses painted in different colours sometimes with a wooden gable, and an amusing square building with a pyramid-shaped roof topped with a pinnacle, hug the shore of a small cove. Beyond Durgerdam, the dike road, very narrow and winding, which follows the former Zuiderzee coast, offers lovely views.

★ **Marken** – *See Marken.*

Monnickendam – This small pleasure boat harbour was renowned in the past for its eels. Like several ports on IJsselmeer, smoked herrings are eaten here. The town is overlooked by the 16C brick tower, **Speeltoren.** Opposite, the town hall, **Stadhuis,** is an 18C patrician house with a decorated pediment; note the entrance ramps shaped like a serpent. In the same street (Noordeinde) and in Kerkstraat, several houses have picturesque gables and façade stones. Not far, in Middendam, stands the weigh house, **Waag,** a small building *c*1600, which is decorated with pilasters and a heavily carved gable. To the south, the Gothic **Grote of St.-Nicolaaskerk,** a three-naved hall-type church, contains a lovely 16C chancel screen of carved wood.

★ **Volendam** – *See Volendam.*

Edam – *See Edam.*

Broek in Waterland – Near a lake, the Havenrak, this flowery village with freshly painted houses has always been known for its cleanliness: in the past was it not necessary to take off one's wooden shoes before entering? It is said that Napoleon took off his boots when he came here for a friendly meeting with the burgomaster on 15 October 1811. Several 17 and 18C wooden houses can be seen in the village. Some of the 17C ones are U-shaped. Some have two doors, the one on the façade being used only for marriages and funerals. On the edge of the lake is the pavilion where Napoleon was received (Napoleon-huisje). Dating from 1656 it is a small white pagoda-shaped wood construction.
Near the canal, the church, **kerk,** ⊙ set on fire by the Spaniards in 1573 was rebuilt between 1585 and 1639. In the north aisle, there is an interesting stained glass window (*c*1640) in harmonious and original colours, which recalls the tragic event and the church's reconstruction. A model cheese dairy, **Kaasmakerij De Domme Dirk** *(Roomeinde 17)* allows one to taste and buy Edam cheese.

Return to Amsterdam by S116 (HT).

APELDOORN Gelderland

Pop 148 204

Michelin map 408 I5
Town plan in the current Michelin Red Guide Benelux

A real garden-city, Apeldoorn is situated in the heart of the Veluwe *(qv)* which seems to continue right into the city; it is cut by wide avenues lined with great trees and endowed with numerous parks. Apeldoorn has a few industries; in addition, due to the very pure spring water it has become a laundering centre.
A **steam train** (De Veluwsche Stoomtrein) ⊙ runs between Apeldoorn and Dieren *(23km - 14 miles).*

Historisch Museum Marialust ⊙ – *Raadhuisplein 8.*
The Marialust mansion overlooks a pleasant park and now serves as an appropriate setting for a local history museum, with exhibits ranging from prehistoric times to the present.

EXCURSION

★★★ **Het Loo Palace and Museum** – *See Het Loo.*

ARNHEM Gelderland Ⓟ

Pop 131 703

Michelin map 408 I6
Plan of the conurbation in the current Michelin Red Guide Benelux

Arnhem is the capital of Gelderland province, a former duchy. Situated on the Neder Rijn or Lower Rhine, one of the branches of the Rhine which separated from the IJssel, Arnhem is an important road junction near one of the country's major trunk roads.

Boat trips ⊙ – On the Gelderland rivers.

HISTORICAL NOTES

A coveted duchy – Residence of the Counts of Geldern, who fortified it in the beginning of the 13C and granted it city rights, Arnhem, in the Middle Ages, was a prosperous town dealing in the trade of goods along the Rhine and the IJssel; it belonged to the Hanseatic League *(qv).* Geldern became a duchy in 1339.
Arnhem was taken by Charles the Bold in 1473, then by the Emperor Maximilian (Charles the Bold's son-in-law) in 1505. Invaded by Emperor Charles V, the duchy was defended by Charles of Egmont, who was killed in battle in 1538. His successor ceded his rights to the duchy to Charles V in the Treaty of Venlo (1543). In 1585 under the reign of Philip II (Charles V's son), the town was taken from the Spanish. It passed to the French during the 1672-4 war, then between 1795-1813 the Austrians possessed it.
Arnhem is the birthplace of Professor Lorentz (1853-1928), who, with his former pupil Zeeman, received the Nobel Prize for Physics in 1902 for his work on electromagnetic radiation.

The garden-city – Arnhem, with its many parks and gardens and its attractive setting on the foothills of the Veluwe *(qv)*, is a very pleasant open and green city. Before the last war, it was one of the favourite retirement places for colonials returning from the Dutch Indies (Indonesia): their lovely residences are dispersed throughout the woods.

The Battle of Arnhem (17-27 September 1944) – The name Arnhem is linked to one of the most tragic episodes in the liberation of the Netherlands. **Operation Market Garden** was intended to open a corridor north from the Belgian border across the three great rivers and give access to the Ruhr.
On 17 September 1944 more than 10 000 men of the 1st British Airborne Division were parachuted into **Oosterbeek**, west of Arnhem. They were to march on Arnhem to secure a bridgehead on the Neder Rijn and hold it until the 20 000 Americans (18th, 101st and 82nd US Airborne Divisions) and the 3 000 Poles parachuted to the south, could ensure the movement of troops over two important canals to the north of Eindhoven, then the Maas at Grave and the Waal at Nijmegen. General Montgomery, who directed this operation, called Market Garden, counted on a surprise attack to disorganise the enemy. In this way he hoped to reach IJsselmeer, cut the country in two and isolate the German troops located to the west (preventing them from retreating to Germany), then reach the Ruhr. It was a failure.
On the 18th a thick fog enveloped Arnhem making help impossible. Only a few batallions of parachutists from Oosterbeek had reached the town. After 9 days of very hard fighting the **Red Devils**, who had not managed to capture the bridge, left 2 000 dead and more than 5 000 wounded or missing in the ruins of the town. On the other hand 500 soldiers were hidden by the inhabitants and 2 300 were evacuated towards the south during the night of 25-26 September.
In the meantime the progress of armoured divisions effecting a junction had been held up by several German attacks. The crossing of the Maas at **Grave** (on 19 September) and the Waal at **Nijmegen** (the 20th) made it possible for the Allies to come within sight of Arnhem, but it was too late. The bridge over the Neder Rijn was, according to General Browning "a bridge too far". For more details read *A Bridge Too Far* by Cornelius Ryan.
If the operation had been successful, the terrible famine which occurred during the winter of 1944-5 in the country's western provinces could have been avoided. Arnhem was liberated by the Allies on 8 April 1945, shortly before the German capitulation.

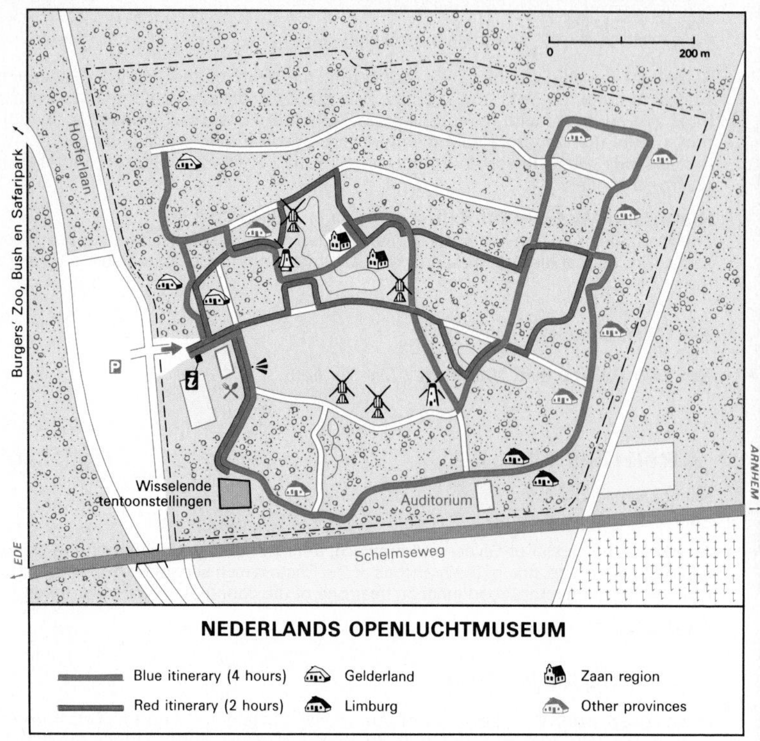

NEDERLANDS OPENLUCHTMUSEUM

Arnhem today – The town is an active city which lives by its textile manufacturing (synthetic fibres) and its metallurgical industries. The tertiary sector occupies a major position with, notably, technological research institutions and research consultancies. It also plays an important administrative role in the east of the Netherlands. A speciality of the town are *Arnhemse meisjes*, small puff-pastry biscuits.

★★ HET NEDERLANDS OPENLUCHTMUSEUM

(NETHERLANDS OPEN-AIR MUSEUM) ⏲ *4 hours*

The museum is set in 44ha - 109 acres of undulating parkland (AV). Around 100 farmhouses, cottages, barns, windmills and workshops from all the Dutch provinces have been assembled here to illustrate rural architecture and life in the past. Each building has been decorated and furnished appropriately and special exhibitions (carts, implements and pottery) and demonstrations (bread and paper making as well as a variety of handicrafts) add interest to the visit.

From the road in front of the restaurant there is a delightful view of several **windmills** grouped around a clearing. The taller ones are grain mills while the smaller ones are polder mills *(see the section on windmills in the Introduction).*

The buildings from some of the provinces are grouped together, as in the case of the handsome half-timbered farmsteads from Limburg (nos 100 to 104) or the farmhouses from Gelderland (nos 1 to 19). However the most picturesque corner is without doubt the one representing **Zaanstreek** *(qv)* with its very characteristic houses. The green-painted buildings with variously shaped gables are attractively decorated with white trims. The calm waters of the nearby pool are reminiscent of the Zaan and are spanned by a wooden lever-bridge. Of the three windmills standing at the water's edge two are for milling grain and the third is a saw mill. In the building reserved for **temporary exhibitions** (no 125) traditional costumes and other items are shown in rotation. Tableaux illustrate scenes from daily life set against a background of typical interiors peopled with models wearing traditional dress, some of which are still worn.

ADDITIONAL SIGHTS

Markt (BZ) – This long square is bordered by the Law Courts, **Paleis van Justitie** (BZ **J**) and, at the end, by the Gelderland government seat, **Het Huis der Provincie** (BZ **P**). Destroyed during the war, this building was reconstructed in 1954 by the architect J.J.M. Vegter. In rather severe style, it encloses an interior courtyard. Adjoining this building is the **Sabelspoort** (BZ), a 14C fortified gateway (altered in 1645), which is all that remains of the town's ramparts.

Grote- of Eusebiuskerk (BZ) ⏲ – Near Markt, this church was erected in the 15C on the site of an old Romanesque church.

Destroyed during the Battle of Arnhem, it, as well as its tower (93m - 305ft), was rebuilt in the Gothic style; the upper part was reconstructed in a more modern style. The church has an organ (1793) which came from an Amsterdam church.

The mausoleum of Charles of Egmont *(qv)*, Duke of Geldern, was built in 1538. The tower has a modern **carillon** with 49 bells. It also has a carillon of seven bells, four of which were cast by the Hemony brothers.

ARNHEM

Jansbinnensingel .... BY 28
Jansstraat .... ABY 31
Ketelstraat .... BY 34
Looierstraat .... BY 39
Rijnstraat .... AY
Roggestraat .... BY 55
Vijzelstraat .... ABY 63

Apeldoornstr. .... BY 3
Arnhemsestraatweg ..... BV 4
Beekhuizenseweg .... BV 6
Beukenweg .... BV 7
Bouriciusstraat .... AY 9
Bronbeeklaan .... BV 10
Burg. Matsersingel ...... AX 12
Cattepoelsweg .... AV 13
Eusebiusbinnensingel .... BZ 16
van Heemstralaan .... AV 18
Heijenoordseweg .... AV 19
Heuvelink BD. .... BZ 21
Hulkesteinseweg .... AX 22
Huygenslaan .... BV 24
Ir. J. P. van Muylwijkstr. .. BY 25
Jacob Marislaan .... AV 27
Jansplein .... ABY 230
Johan de Witlaan .... AX 33
Koppelstraat .... AX 36
Lerensteinselaan .... BV 37
Nijmeegeseweg .... AX 42
Nordlaan .... BV 43
van Oldenbarneveldstr. ... AX 45
Onderlangs .... AX 46
Oranjewachtstr. .... BZ 48
Parkweg .... AV 49
President Kennedylaan ... BV 52
Ringallee .... BV 54
Rosendaalseweg .... BV 57
Thomas a Kempislaan ... AV 58
Velperbinnensingel ..... BY 60
Velperbuitensingel ...... BY 61
Voetiuslaan .... ABX 64
Walburgstraat .... BZ 66
Weg achter het Bos ..... AV 67
Zijpendaalseweg .... AV 69
Zutphensestraatweg ..... BV 70

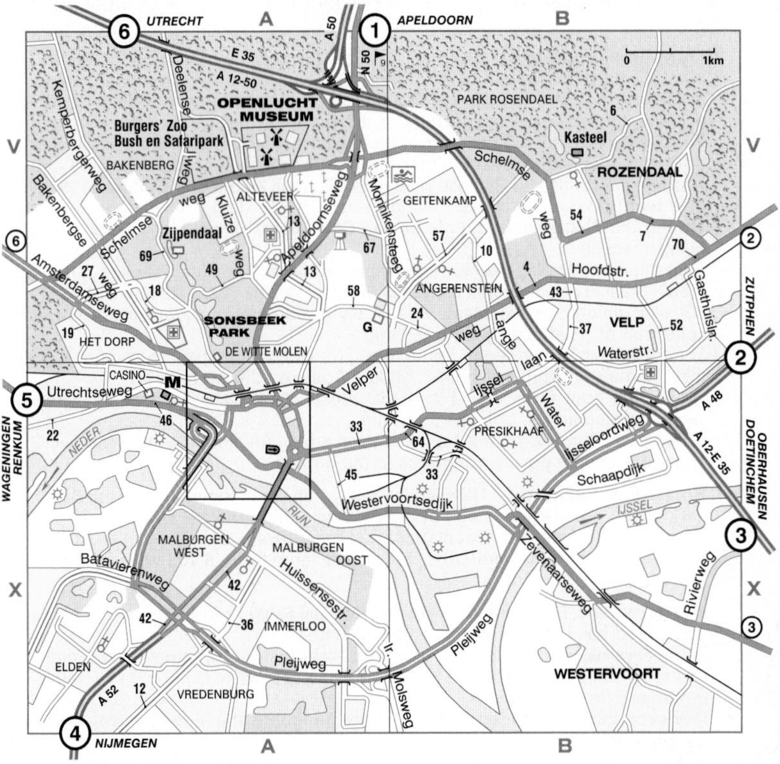

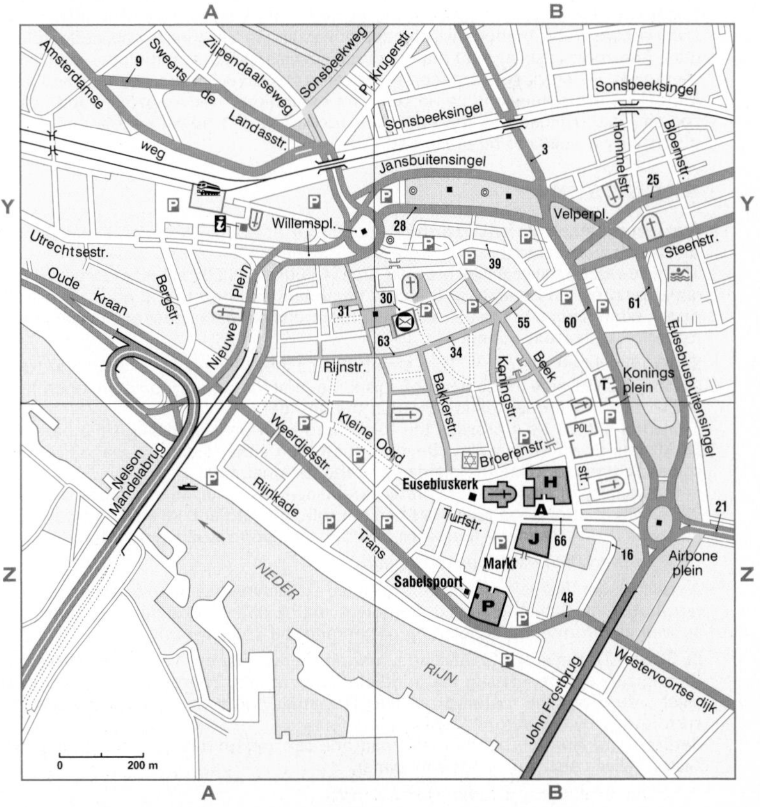

Duivelshuis (Devil's House) (BZ **A**) – This fine Renaissance edifice, built in 1645 and much restored in 1829 was spared during the war. It takes its name from the strange statues and grotesque heads which decorate its walls. It was the last dwelling place of the blood thirsty general **Maarten van Rossum**, chief of the armies of the Duke of Gelderland, Charles of Egmont, and adversary of Emperor Charles V. According to legend, Van Rossum had these demons carved to offend the magistrates of Arnhem, who refused to allow him to pave the steps of his perron with gold.
Formerly the town hall, this house is still occupied by certain municipal services. Behind is the new **stadhuis** (BZ **H**) built in 1964 to plans by the architect J.J. Konijnenburg.

★ **Gemeentemuseum** (AVX **M**) ⊙ – Situated on a hill overlooking the Rhine, in an old 19C mansion, topped by a rotunda, and with a modern new wing added, this museum contains interesting collections on the art and history of Gelderland. Modern and contemporary art exhibitions are organised regularly.
The rooms with 15-18C decorative arts are particularly rich: wardrobes and clocks, gold and silversmiths' work either liturgical or of guild corporations, 18 and 19C Arnhem ceramics and Chinese porcelain. There is also a doll's house in the shape of a wardrobe, a fine carved wood group (*c*1500) depicting St John the Baptist among the Pharisees, a still life by Jan Davidsz. de Heem and a *View of Arnhem* by Van Goyen.
This museum displays some remarkable works by the Dutch painter Jan Mankes (1880-1920); it also presents canvases by Carel Willink (1900-83) and Dick Ket (1902-40) who painted in the Magic Realist style. Contemporary art is present with a collection of paintings and engravings.
The basement is devoted to items of regional archaeological excavations: prehistory, Roman times (glass, coins), Middle Ages (earthenware).
On the 1st floor there are 17 and 18C *objets d'art:* glass, gold and silversmiths' work, Delft ceramics, Chinese porcelain.
A large bay window on the 1st floor gives a magnificent view over the river.
There are contemporary sculptures in the garden.

★ **Sonsbeek Park** (AV) – This park of 75ha - 185 acres together with the Zijpendaal Park which prolongs it, is one of the most beautiful parks in the Netherlands. It is an undulating area with woodlands, vast meadows and a string of lakes.
A castle is part of the landscape, and near a large farm, a 16C watermill (De Witte Molen).

Burgers' Zoo Bush en Safaripark (Zoo and Safari Park) (AV) ⊙ – This 25ha - 62 acre wood has been divided into four parks.
In the **Savannah**, a vast clearing, giraffes, zebras, ostriches, rhinoceroses, antelopes and crowned cranes stroll freely. The **Wild Beast Enclosure** is peopled by many lions together with their females.
However, the zoo's star attractions are the penguins, the birds, the wolves and the pongidae.
The vast hall (90m - 96yd by 200m - 218yd) known as **Burgers' Bush** houses a tropical forest with various plants and trees imported from Asia, Africa and South America (rice, rubber trees, mahogany, pineapple, vanilla plants, sugar cane, coffee plants, etc.). The zoo boasts a great many animal species: birds, amphibians, reptiles and mammals. When visitors are scarse, the sea cows, dwarf otters, caimans and pretty butterflies are bolder and come out. The exhibition "Het Amazonewoud" (Amazonian Forest) illustrates the abundant resources of tropical vegetation and explains why it needs to be preserved.

EXCURSIONS

★ **Nationaal Park Veluwezoom** – *Round tour of 20km – 12 miles. Leave Arnhem by Beekhuizenseweg* (BV).
The **Veluwezoom National Park** is a vast area (4 600ha - 11 362 acres) of forests (pines, silver birches) and deeply undulating heathland situated to the north of Arnhem on the edge *(zoom)* of the Veluwe *(qv)*. Numerous car parks, foot and cycling paths, make for a pleasant outing.

Kasteel Rosendael (BV) ⊙ – This small 18C castle, flanked by a medieval tower, stands at a lakeside in the heart of a **park**. Several furnished rooms are open to the public and in summer tea is served in the orangery.
The road climbs as it crosses the forest and then passes through the hamlet of **Beekhuizen** down in its valley. Beyond, roads run either side of a magnificent row of beech trees to reach the plateau and the national park.
In the vicinity of **Posbank** there are several viewing points, at an altitude of 100m - 328ft, which offer good **panoramas**★ of the rolling heathland stretching away to the horizon. There are many footpaths and it makes good walking country.

The road then descends to Rhedan.

A **visitor centre** (Bezoekerscentrum) ⊙ called De Hewne has been installed in an old farmhouse on Schietberseweg. Ramblers will be able to find detailed maps here, as well as information concerning nature and the environment.

De Steeg – To the east of the village, among the woods, the 17C **Kasteel Middachten** ⊙ raises its severe walls in the middle of wide moats. There is a fine view on the west side, from the restored garden. The inner courtyard *(access forbidden)* is surrounded by the outbuildings.
Returning to Arnhem by the main road one can see on the left, on entering Velp, **Kasteel Biljoen** also surrounded by water.

Enter Arnhem by Zutphensestraat (BV).

The southern edge of the Veluwe – *25km - 15 1/2 miles to the west – about 2 1/2 hours. Leave by ⑤ on the town plan.*
The route follows the north bank of the Neder Rijn where the last hills of the Veluwe are dotted with numerous villages.

Oosterbeek – To the north of this small town, on the road to Warnsborn, a little beyond the railway, the war cemetery, **Airborne Kerkhof**, of Allied troops who fell during the battle of Arnhem, has more than 1 700 gravestones (1 667 British and 79 Polish).
The **Huize Hartenstein** *(Utrechtseweg 232)* was General Urquhart's (Commander of 1st British Airborne Division) headquarters in September 1944. It houses the **Airborne Museum** ⊙, previously at Doorwerth.
Devoted to the Operation Market Garden and the Battle of Arnhem *(qv)*, this museum contains memorabilia of the parachuting of the airborne troops, notably in the Oosterbeek area. General Urquhart's headquarters have been reconstructed in a cellar.
To the south, on the banks of the Rhine, the terraces of **Westerbouwing** (restaurant) offer a fine **view** over the river and the Betuwe with its orchards.

Drive towards the north bank of the Rhine.

Doorwerth – Near a wood, Doorwerthse Bos, on the river's edge, Doorwerth was badly hit in 1944 during the Battle of Arnhem.
Situated in the meadows near the river, **Kasteel Doorwerth** ⊙, built in 1260, was enlarged *c*1600 and consists of a high square building and outbuildings, the whole surrounded by moats. The fortified walls open by a fine door with armorial bearings. Several furnished rooms in the north and east wings are open to visitors. The south wing houses the Netherlands Hunting Museum, **Het Nederlands Jachtmuseum**, which contains information on hunting and the way of life of animals which interest hunters. Fine collections of weapons, stuffed animals, pictures and photographs are attractively displayed.

Go towards Renkum and pass under the motorway to take the road to Wageningen.

Wageningen – Pop 32 818. This industrial town is known for its Agricultural School (Landbouwuniversiteit); in the surrounding country there are orchards and nurseries. In the De Wereld building *(Gen. Foulkesweg 1)*, the Germans signed their capitulation on 5 May 1945 in the presence of General Foulkes, commander of the Canadian troops.
In the Belmonte Arboretum *(Gen. Foulkesweg 94)*, the Higher School of Agriculture cares for a fine collection of shrubs.

5km - 3 miles from Wageningen, opposite a Netherlands military cemetery, situated on the Grebbeberg, a path leads to the **Koningstafel** or king's tableland; view over the Rhine and the Betuwe. It was one of King Frederick V of Bohemia's favourite walks; he took refuge in the Netherlands after having been defeated by the Austrians in 1620.

Rhenen – Pop 16 639. This locality contains the **Ouwehands Dierenpark Zoological Garden** ⊙, which houses nearly 800 animals in a park of 15ha - 37 acres. An enormous aviary of exotic birds, an exhibition of parrots and dolphins, and an aquarium add to the interest of the visit. A monorail takes visitors round the park. It is also a recreation centre with a lake and attractions for children.
Cunerakerk ⊙ with its lovely tower has been restored since it was bombed in 1945.

Book well in advance
vacant hotel rooms are often scarce in the high season

ASSEN Drenthe Ⓟ — Pop 50 357

Michelin map 408 K2 – Town plan in the current Michelin Red Guide Benelux

Assen owes its existence to a nunnery, founded in the 13C, of which one can see the chapel, the old town hall, on the main square or Brink. Today, this modern and spacious town is laid out beside **Asserbos**, a pleasant woodland area to the south. It is an area rich in megalithic monuments *(see Hunebedden)*.
Until 1602 members of the States, or Provincial Assembly of Drenthe met out of doors, in the Germanic style, at the Balloërkuil *(see below)* where they dispensed justice. Due to its central location Assen was chosen as capital of the Drenthe in 1809 during the reign of Louis Bonaparte.
To the south of town, a motorcycle **racing circuit** (Tourist Trophy Circuit or T.T.C) is used for the Dutch Grand Prix.

Drenthe – For a long time this province was ill-favoured. The Scandinavian glaciers, which lingered in the north of the Netherlands, left a sandy and not very fertile soil. In places it is covered with **heathland** with a few clumps of oak or pine. In the wetter areas, **peat** covered the surfaces left by the glaciers. Drenthe was the largest peat-producing region. Its extraction has left traces on the land, which remains criss-crossed by a multitude of canals which were dug out in order to transport the peat.
Today much clearing and the use of fertilisers has modified the landscape. The sheep moors are rarer, giving way to pastures or plantations of conifers. The peat bogs, with the help of fertilisers, sand and the upper layer of peat can make a good arable soil (potatoes, cereals, market garden produce); colonials have settled here.

The farmhouses in Drenthe are very picturesque with their vast thatched roofs and are for the most part hall farmhouses *(p 33)*.
Many villages have kept their original Saxon layout: in the centre is the **Brink**, the tree-lined main square, often with a church.

Bartje

D'après photo A. van Iterson/MICHELIN

★ **Drents Museum** ⓥ – *Brink 1.* The old Provincial House (1885) contains this regional museum. On the 1st floor, it has a particularly interesting **archaeological section**★. It displays excellent documentation on prehistoric times: geology, population, *hunebeds (qv)* and has assembled a large number of objects discovered in the province, either in the *hunebeds*, burial mounds, fields of funeral urns, or in the peat-bogs which lends to the preservation of these objects.
Apart from tools, instruments and pottery, there are also a great variety of other pieces: a small boat of 6300BC (discovered in Pesse, 23km - 14 miles south of Assen), mummies of the 3 and 5C, Celtic and Merovingian jewellery, Roman and Merovingian coins.
On the ground floor there is regional silversmiths' work, as well as drawings and prints (views of Drenthe villages), along with *objets d'art* dating from the early 20C.
The adjoining abbey church is used to house temporary exhibitions.
Belonging to the same museum, the **Ontvangershuis**★ *(Brink 7)* former residence of the general tax collector, has been turned into a decorative arts museum. One goes through elegant rooms decorated with beautiful 17 and 18C furniture, a regional kitchen with box beds as well as a delivery room.
Behind the garden of the Ontvangershuis, there is a charming statuette of the young **Bartje**, famous local hero of the regional novelist Anne de Vries (1904-64). The statue was the work of Suze Berkhout (the original is in the town hall).

EXCURSIONS

Rolde – Pop 6 131. *6km - 3 1/2 miles by ② on the town plan, local map see Hunebedden.* To the west of Rolde, in a wood, one can see the **Balloërkuil** *(see above)*, a sort of vast terrace dug into the ground.
Beyond the church, turn left into a paved path indicating *hunebeds (qv)*. In a wood there are two **hunebeds** (D 17/18); one of them is covered with seven slabs.

Norg, Leek and Midwolde – *27km - 16 1/2 miles to the northwest by ⑤ on the town plan; then turn right.*

Norg – Pop 6 726. This charming Drenthe village with numerous thatched roofed cottages is a holiday centre. It is built round a Brink, a large shady square on which stands a small Gothic church, preceded by a bell tower with a saddleback roof.

Leek – Pop 17 414. To the north of town in a vast park surrounded by a moat stands the manor, **Huis Nienoord**. Rebuilt in 1886, it houses the National Carriage Museum, **Nationaal Rijtuigmuseum** ⓥ.
Inside exquisite small vehicles are exhibited: small carriages pulled by goats, royal children's carriages, and 17 and 18C sledges. In the outbuildings, in season, there are carriages with dummies wearing period costumes.
Further on in the park, near a pavilion built *c*1700, whose walls are covered with shells, a modern building contains a collection of stage coaches.

Nationaal Rijtuigmuseum, Kasteel Nienoord

Nationaal Rijtuigmuseum, Kasteel Nienoord

Midwolde – The small brick **kerk** ⓥ with a saddleback roofed bell tower has the fine marble **funerary monument**★ made by Rombout Verhulst in 1669 at the request of Anna van Ewsum.
The young woman is leaning with a gracious gesture over the mortal remains of her husband.
The cherubs in white marble, symbolise the family's children. In the place of the seventh cherub there is now a statue of Anna van Ewsum's second husband, which was made by Bartholomeus Eggers in 1714.
Note the carved pulpit (1711), the tall stalls (*c*1660-70) and the small organ (1630) with lead pipes.

BERGEN OP ZOOM Noord-Brabant Pop 46 900

Michelin map 408 D7 or 212 fold 14 – Local map see DELTA
Town plan in the current Michelin Red Guide Benelux

Already the centre of two important annual fairs in the Middle Ages, Bergen op Zoom, starting in 1287, was the main town of an independent lordship. The old port, today partially filled in, was linked to the Oosterschelde *(qv)*. In 1533 the lordship of Bergen op Zoom was changed into a marquisate.

The town has remained famous for its invincibility as it victoriously withstood two sieges against the Spanish, in 1588 by the Duke of Parma, Alessandro Farnese, then in 1622 when it was invested by troops commanded by Spinola.

Its fortifications were reinforced *c*1700 by **Menno van Coehoorn** (1641-1704), an engineer who designed numerous strongholds throughout the country. However, Bergen could not hold out against the French army in 1747 during the Austrian War of Succession. The ramparts were demolished in 1868 but the boulevards' location recalls the layout.

Bergen op Zoom, set in the middle of woods, is renowned for its carnival *(see Calendar of Events)*. The sandy land around the town is used for growing asparagus.

SIGHTS

Stadhuis ⏲ – It is on Grote Markt and consists of three houses: the one in the middle and the one on the right have been decorated, since 1611, with a lovely stone façade preceded by a perron bearing the **town's arms**; two savages stand on either side of a shield, topped by the marquis's crown; the shield bears three of St Andrew's crosses and a mountain with three peaks (*berg:* mount).

Near Grote Markt, there is a massive stone **bell tower** (14C). Familiarly called De Peperbus (the Pepperpot), due to the shape of its 18C lantern turret, it is the remains of **St.-Geertruidskerk** which was destroyed in 1747 by the French *(see above)*; after being rebuilt it burned down in 1972. The outside walls of the nave, the transept and chancel (15C), as well as a second transept (16C) were all spared by the catastrophes.

★ **Markiezenhof** ⏲ – *Steenbergsestraat 8.*

This is the former palace *(hof)* of the marquisate of Bergen op Zoom. Dating from the 15 and 16C, the work of Anthonis Keldermans, architect from Mechelen (Belgium), it was inhabited by the marquises until 1795 and has been restored. Its façade, decorated with bands of stone, forming an elegant effect, has a stone base ornamented with large latticed windows and topped with brick crow-stepped gables and dormer windows.

The inside has been turned into a cultural centre, with, notably, the **Museum**. The small arcaded courtyard is picturesque. The large palace hall or **Hofzaal** *(concerts)* is particularly remarkable with its carved stone chimney-piece (St Christopher) of 1522, its portraits of Bergen's marquises, a 16C Brussels tapestry *(Charlemagne in Rome)*, paintings and gold and silversmiths' work.

In the wing, renovated in the 18C, there are lovely rooms with **decorative arts** (Louis XIV, Louis XV and Louis XVI styles). The 2nd floor is devoted to fortifications, a scale model of the town in 1747, a copy of the one made for Louis XV. One room has ancient art objects. One can also see objects and banners for processions, as well as ceramics made in Bergen op Zoom.

The museum also holds temporary exhibitions.

Gevangenpoort or Lieve Vrouwepoort – *Access by Lieve Vrouwestraat leaving from Markiezenhof*

This 14C gateway is all that remains of the medieval town's ring of ramparts. Facing the town its brick façade is flanked with bartizans; facing out it has two large stone towers.

Ravelijn "Op den Zoom" – *To the northeast of town.*

Near the lovely **park** (A. van Duinkerken Park) surrounding a lake, there is a small fortified moated outwork, witness to the fortifications built by Coehoorn.

EXCURSION

Wouw and Roosendaal – *15km - 9 miles to the northeast by ② on the town plan – local map under Delta.*

Wouw – Pop 8 539. In the Gothic **kerk** ⏲, rebuilt after the Second World War, there are some lovely statues. The 17C baroque **statues** belonged to the stalls, which disappeared during the war. They are placed in the chancel (on consoles) and in the aisles where they surround the confessional boxes. The figures are shown in very lively attitudes.

The stained glass window on the west side of the tower, depicting the Resurrection, is a work by Joep Nicolas (1937).

Roosendaal – Pop 60 725. It is an important railway junction and industrial city with a modern commercial quarter, De Rozelaar.

Nearby there are several nature reserves, notably the **Visdonk** and **De Rucphense Bossen** (1 200ha - 2 964 acres).

The Golden Rose Museum, **De Ghulden Roos** ⏲, is a regional museum installed in an 18C presbytery *(Molenstraat 2)* called **Tongerlohuys**.

It houses an interesting artistic collection, notably gold and silversmiths' work belonging to the guilds (corporations), pottery, Chinese porcelain, silverware as well as various objects such as Brabant bonnets, agricultural tools, toys, a velocipede of the Michaux type. The interior of an old sweet shop has been reconstructed.

★ BOLSWARD Friesland — Pop 9 716

Michelin map 408 H2 – Local map see SNEEK

Bolsward, or Boalsert in Frisian, is one of the eleven cities of Friesland. The date of its foundation is inscribed on a façade stone of the stadhuis: 713. Its name is believed to mean "the land of Bodel, surrounded by water"; the ending "ward" or "werd" refers to a small mound *(p 163)*.

Formerly linked to the Zuiderzee, Bolsward was a rich and powerful city. In the 11C it was granted the privilege of minting coins and became a Hanseatic town.

Today it is a peaceful city which livens up every three years when it awards the first prize for Frisian literature, which bears the name of **Gysbert Japicx** (1603-1666). Written Frisian had become obsolete for many years and Japicx was the very first author to use it in fiction.

Situated in the centre of a rich pastoral region, Bolsward is also the seat of a school specialised in nutrition technology.

SIGHTS

★ **Stadhuis** ⊙ – This is an elegant Renaissance construction dating back to the years 1614-1717. In the centre of its harmonious façade, a projecting central block and its gable surmount a fine 18C perron decorated with two lions bearing the town's coat of arms. At the top there is a tall octagonal pinnacle with a **carillon**.

In the **Council and Marriage Hall**, you can admire a splendid carved door attributed to Gysbert Japicx, who also undertook the decoration of the lovely wooden chimneypiece framed by stone telamones.

A room on the first floor, with enormous beams supporting the weight of the tower, houses the Museum of Antiquities, **Oudheidkamer**: Frisian silverwork, traditional costumes, artefacts from archaeological excavations, etc.

Martinikerk ⊙ – This large Gothic church, today Protestant, was built in the middle of the 15C. It is preceded by a tower capped with a saddleback roof, like most Frisian bell towers.

Inside, the vaults of the three naves rest on thick cylindrical pillars.

In the chancel, the **stalls**★ (late 15C) are remarkable for their sculptures full of truth and naïvety. The scenes which are shown on the lateral partitions are admirable:

bench against the south wall:

- Manna, a saint; on the other side: St Catherine and the philosophers, St Barbara;
- St Christopher; on the other side: St George and the dragon;
- Moses and the Jews, baptism of Christ, spies and the bunch of grapes.

against the north wall, bench near the nave:

- Judgment of Salomon, St Martin, Abraham's sacrifice; above the lectern: an alchemist;
- St Peter and St Paul, heaven and hell; on the other side: God and angel musicians, the Last Judgment.

G. Biollay/DIAF

Church stalls (detail), Martinikerk

against the north wall, bench near the apse:

- the Virgin crushing the dragon; on the other side: Judith beheading Holofernes;
- dragon, Bolsward's coat of arms, Temptation of Christ.

Equally interesting are the figures on the high backs, the picturesque illustrations of parables shown on the misericords, the figures on the cheekpieces, and the grotesque figures of the lecterns.

The **pulpit**★ (17C), crowned with a tiered canopy, is decorated in the Frisian manner with elegant motifs added on.

The central panel depicts a Bible and the signs of the zodiac; the other panels depict the seasons. Above there is a frieze of fruit and vegetables; below a series of shells.

The ground is strewn with tombstones.

The organ was made in 1775 by Hinsz of Groningen. The church's remarkable acoustics have made it possible to record concerts.

EXCURSION

Witmarsum – *10km - 6 miles to the northwest.*
Near the main road there is the statue of **Menno Simonsz.** (1496-1561). Born in Witmarsum, he became vicar of Pingjum, then the parish priest of his native town and, finally, in 1536, broke away from the Catholics and turned towards the Anabaptist doctrine, founding the *doopsgezinden* brotherhood or **Mennonites.** In 1539, a work summarised his doctrine, more pacific than that of John of Leiden *(qv)*; belief in the Bible, rejection of the baptism of children, accent on personal piety, refusal to obey all the established Church's dogma. The Mennonite religion spread to Germany, Switzerland and North America (the largest groups are in the United States and Canada) where it still has its followers.
The Mennonites of Witmarsum meet in a small church, **Menno-Simonskerkje** *(located on Menno-Simonsstraat)* ⊙, rebuilt in 1961.
One can see the prayer room with the portrait of Menno Simonsz. and the sacristy. Further on, in the same street, set in a small wood, is a monument in memory of Menno Simonsz., on the site of his first church.

★ BREDA Noord-Brabant

Pop 124 794

Michelin map 408 or 212 fold 6
Plan of conurbation in the current Michelin Red Guide Benelux

At the confluence of the Mark and the Aa, Breda was formerly one of the country's main fortified towns and the centre of an important barony. Today it is a dynamic city and a great commercial and industrial centre. Benefiting from its position on one of the main access routes into the country, it is a welcoming stopping place with large pedestrian precincts.
With numerous parks, Breda also has very attractive suburbs where large woods like the **Liesbos** to the west and the **Mastbos** *(qv)* to the south have been laid out for recreation. To the east, **Surae** is a recreational park with a swimming area.
In February *(see Calendar of Events)*, Breda holds its well-known **carnival★**. Around Easter there is the Antiques Fair and in May the International Classical Jazz Festival. At the end of August there is the Taptoe, a military music festival *(see Calendar of Events)*. The month of October marks the Breda Flower Show, held in the Great Church.

HISTORICAL NOTES

The Nassau fief – Breda obtained its city rights in *c*1252. It became part of the Breda barony, but in 1404, this passed to the Nassau family, who made the town its seat. The 13C fortifications were rebuilt (*c*1535) by Count Henry III of Nassau, and the ring canals still show the location of the walls, which were destroyed a little after 1870.

The Compromise of Breda – Decided in September at Spa in Belgium, the Compromise of the Nobility or of Breda was signed in Breda Castle in 1566. Its aim: to abolish the Inquisition.
Following this reunion about 300 nobles went in delegation to Brussels to see the Governor Margaret of Parma to ask her for a convocation of the States General in order to change the edicts against heretics (i.e. Protestants). Whereupon, she burst into tears; her counsellor, the Count of Berlaymont responded in jest with the phrase: "What, Madam, afraid of these *gueux* (beggars)?" This statement did not displease the Calvinists, who from then on took the name **beggars** for their movement and the beggars bowl as the symbol of their fight against Spanish rule. The Calvinists' actions then knew no bounds: in the month of August the **Iconoclastic Fury** started: churches were pillaged and statues destroyed, the direct consequence of which was the arrival in 1567 of the terrible Duke of Alba.

An ardently disputed stronghold – In 1581 Breda was pillaged by the Spanish, who occupied the castle belonging to William the Silent.
In 1590, Maurice of Nassau took the town by surprise, 70 of his men having been able to enter by hiding under a load of peat in a barge belonging to Adriaan van Bergen. In 1625, Breda, after a long siege surrendered to the Spanish commanded by the Marquis of Spinola. This episode was immortalised by Velázquez in *The Surrender of Breda-Las Lanzas* (1634-5). The town was recaptured in 1637 by the Prince-Stadtholder Frederick-Henry.
Upon the Treaty of Breda which, in 1667, put an end to the Second Dutch War the Dutch gave New Amsterdam, which became New York, to the English. They, in exchange, were given Guiana (now Suriname). The negotiations and the signature of the treaty took place in the castle.
During the French Revolutionary Wars, the town was taken by Dumouriez in 1793. He had to evacuate it after the defeat of Neerwinden (Belgium), which obliged him to withdraw from the Netherlands.
Besieged again in 1794 by Pichegru, Breda surrendered only when the whole country was occupied. It became part of the Deux-Nethes *département* (county town Antwerp) until 1813: that year, at the approach of the Russian vanguard, the French garrison sallied out but the population of Breda prevented their return.
On 11 and 12 May 1940 Breda marked the furthest point of the Allied advance in the Netherlands: the Dyle Manœuvre, an operation where the Franco-British forces tried to make a breakthrough to the north to protect Amsterdam, failed.

A scholarly soldier – During the siege of Breda by Spinola, a young mercenary belonging to Maurice of Nassau's army passed through the town's Grote Markt. There he saw a group gathered around a poster written in Dutch. His neighbour, head of Dordrecht College, translated the text for him. Since it was a question of finding the solution to a geometry problem, he asked the soldier if he was going to bring him the solution; the latter promised and kept his word. It was René Descartes *(qv)*.

Charles II's restoration – With the death of Cromwell (d 1658), the Protectorate (1653-9) weakened under his son's rule, and in May 1660 Charles II was recalled. It was here, in Breda, that Charles II issued the Declaration of Breda which set the terms upon which he would accept the throne, re-establishing the English monarchy.

★ GROTE- OF ONZE LIEVE VROUWEKERK

GREAT CHURCH OR CHURCH OF OUR LADY (C B) ⏲ *45 min*

It is an imposing 15-16C edifice in the Gothic Brabant style. With three naves, it was enlarged in the 16C by a few chapels and an ambulatory. Its tall **bell tower★** of 97m - 318ft with a square base and octagonal top is surmounted by an onion-shaped dome. The **carillon** ⏲ has 49 bells.

The interior with typical Gothic Brabant style columns – their capitals decorated with crockets – and with a triforium, contains numerous tombs. The most striking one is the **tomb★** of Engelbert II of Nassau (1451-1504) and his wife in the Chapel of Our Lady, to the north of the ambulatory. This Renaissance alabaster monument was carved in the Michelangelo style, probably from a project by Thomas Vincidor of Bologna. The recumbent statues are placed under a slab held up by fine figures at each corner; they depict Julius Caesar (military courage), Regulus (magnanimity), Hannibal (perseverance) and Philip of Macedonia (prudence). Above the slab the armour of Engelbert II is shown. In the vault under the tomb, René de Chalon *(qv)*, Henry III of Nassau and Anna van Buren, William of Orange's first wife, are buried. In the ambulatory is the 15C tomb of Engelbert I and John IV of Nassau. Note some of the Renaissance epitaphs as well as the memorial slabs covering the floor. The 15C wooden chancel stalls are carved with satirical motifs illustrating vices, proverbs, etc. Other unusual reliefs were added after 1945.

Grote Kerk, Breda

Paul C. Pet/BENELUX PRESS B.V.

In the north transept there is a triptych by Jan van Scorel where the central panel illustrates the Finding of the Holy Cross. At the end of the south aisle there is a bronze baptismal font (1540) made in Mechelen (Belgium) of Gothic construction with Renaissance motifs. The organ case is decorated with a 17C painting depicting David and Goliath and the Ark of the Covenant. The organ, a fine instrument, with its oldest parts dating from the 16C, can be heard during **concerts** ⏲.

ADDITIONAL SIGHTS

Leave from the crossroads of Nieuwe Prinsenkade and Prinsenkade.

From here you have a lovely view of the Grote Kerk's bell tower.

Het Spanjaardsgat (C) – The remains of the fortifications, known as the Spanish Gap, consist of two large towers with small onion-shaped domes flanking a watergate, which was used for the evacuation of water round the castle.

Hidden behind these walls is the castle, **kasteel** (C) ⏲. It is an immense building with numerous windows, surrounded by a moat, and where the north façade (visible from the Academiesingel) is flanked by octagonal turrets. Since 1828 it is occupied by the Netherlands Military Academy. An old fortified castle, it was altered, as from 1536, to the plans of **Thomas Vincidor of Bologna**, and was William the Silent's favourite retreat until his departure for the revolt which was declared in 1567. It was here that the Compromise of Breda *(qv)* was signed by the nobles.

The castle's present aspect dates from between 1686 and 1695, under Stadtholder William III of Orange who continued Vincidor's original plan.

Havermarkt (C 30) – This charming little square at the foot of the Grote Kerk formerly 'hay market', is now invaded by the clients of its numerous cafés.

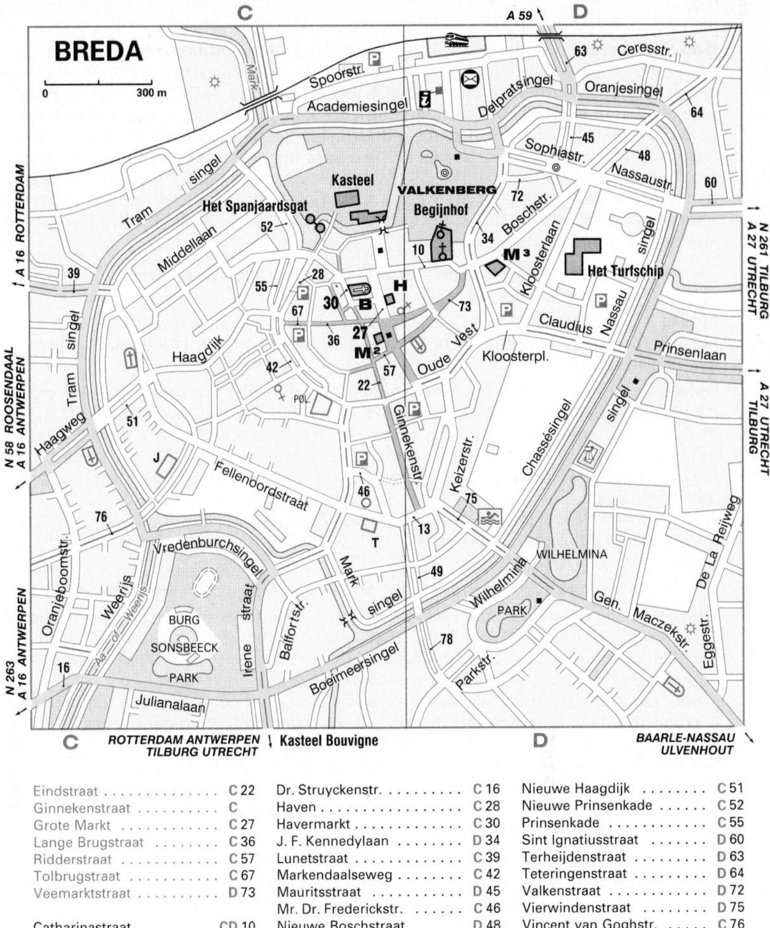

Eindstraat	C 22	Dr. Struyckenstr.	C 16	Nieuwe Haagdijk	C 51
Ginnekenstraat	C	Haven	C 28	Nieuwe Prinsenkade	C 52
Grote Markt	C 27	Havermarkt	C 30	Prinsenkade	C 55
Lange Brugstraat	C 36	J. F. Kennedylaan	D 34	Sint Ignatiusstraat	D 60
Ridderstraat	C 57	Lunetstraat	C 39	Terheijdenstraat	D 63
Tolbrugstraat	C 67	Markendaalseweg	C 42	Teteringenstraat	D 64
Veemarktstraat	D 73	Mauritsstraat	D 45	Valkenstraat	D 72
		Mr. Dr. Frederickstr.	C 46	Vierwindenstraat	D 75
Catharinastraat	CD 10	Nieuwe Boschstraat	D 48	Vincent van Goghstr.	C 76
van Coothplein	CD 13	Nieuwe Ginnekenstraat	CD 49	Wilhelminastraat	D 78

★ **Valkenburg** (D) – This pleasant park, shaded by lovely trees was part of the castle grounds. Nearby is the Beguinage, **Begijnhof**. Founded in 1267 the Beguinage was transferred here in 1531 and groups 29 houses of sobre aspect, arranged round a courtyard with a medicinal plant garden and a chapel.

At the entrance to the Beguine convent is their old chapel, which has become a Walloon Church, **Waalse Kerk**. The Frisian, **Peter Stuyvesant** (1592-1672) was married here; it was he who became the last Dutch governor of Nieuw Amsterdam (New York) from 1647-64 *(see Michelin Green Guide New York City)*.

Grote Markt (C 27) – From the middle of this large square there is a fine **view** of the Grote Kerk.

Stadhuis (CD H) ⊙ – Dating from the 17C, the town hall was altered in 1767. It contains a reproduction of the **Surrender of Breda - Las Lanzas**, the historical composition by Velázquez, the original being in the Prado Museum in Madrid *(see Michelin Green Guide Spain)*. Opposite, at the corner of Reigerstraat, there is a lovely house with a crow-stepped gable. To the south of the square, at no 19, is **Het Wit Lam**, former meat hall and premises of the crossbowmen's guild, where the Municipal and Episcopal Museum is installed *(see below)*. On the façade's (1772) pediment St George is slaying the dragon. Grote Markt, where pedestrian precincts converge, has a food market on Tuesday and Friday mornings and a flea market on Wednesdays.

Breda's Museum (C M²) ⊙ – The collections illustrate the history of Breda: religious art, gold and silversmithing, guilds and daily life.

Het Turfschip (D) – This congress and exhibition hall is called after the "peat boat" *(turfschip)* which freed Breda in 1590.

De Beyerd (D M³) ⊙ – This building, a former almshouse, has been transformed into a centre for plastic arts (Centrum voor beeldende kunst).

The centre also organises temporary exhibitions on international contemporary art, architecture, ceramics, photography and design.

EXCURSIONS

Kasteel Bouvigne ⊙ – *4km - 2 1/2 miles. Leave by the south on the town plan then Duivelsbruglaan and turn right.*

The castle stands on the edge of the **Mastbos** *(qv)*, a lovely wood of pines and beech crisscrossed with cycling paths and rides; the name derives from the word *boeverije* meaning low meadow. Built in 1612 it is flanked with a high octagonal turret with an onion-shaped dome and surrounded by a wide moat.

Baarle-Nassau – Pop 5 888. *37km - 23 miles to the southeast by Gen. Maczekstraat* (**D**). This locality shares its territory with a Belgian district (Baarle-Hertog) consisting of several enclaves in Dutch territory. In the 12C the village of Baerle was divided into two. The south part came back to the Duke of Brabant (Baarle-Duc or Baarle-Hertog). The north part, united to the Breda barony, was called Baarle-Nassau from the time when Breda, in the beginning of the 15C, became the Nassau family fief. The boundary of the districts is very complicated. Presently, each one has its own town hall, church, police, school and post office. Houses of different nationalities are mixed together: their nationality is identified by the numbered sign with the national flag.

From Hoeven to Willemstad – *50km - 31 miles to the west. Leave by Haagweg* (**C**) *and turn right at Etten-Leur.*

Hoeven – Pop 8 235. The Simon Stevin Observatory, **Volkssterrenwacht** ⊙, is located here. It is named after the Flemish scientist, Simon Stevin (1548-1620). There is also a **planetarium.**

Oudenbosch – Pop 12 717. The town is overlooked by the enormous **Basiliek van de H.H. Agatha en Barbara.** It was built by P.J.H. Cuypers in 1867-80, a replica of St Peter's in Rome, but smaller in size. The dome, however, reaches 48m - 157ft (St Paul's in London apex of internal dome: 66m - 218ft). The façade (1892) is a copy of the façade of the Basilica of St John Lateran in Rome. The interior was decorated by an Antwerp sculptor.
A Museum of Pontifical Zouaves, **Nederlands Zouavenmuseum** ⊙, has been set up to honour the 3 000 Dutch, who, in the 19C, contributed to the defence of the Papal States in Italy.

By Standdaarbuiten, then by the A 59 and the A 29, reach Willemstad.

Willemstad – *Local map under Delta.* Pop 3 370. This fortified town in the shape of a seven-pointed star, dating from 1583, owes its name to its founder: William the Silent. Today it has a marina which is very popular with holidaymakers, and commands the lock giving access to the Volkerak.
The octagonal-shaped **church** surrounded by a shaded cemetery and encircled by a small moat was completed in 1607; it was the first Protestant church in the Netherlands. Near the port the **old raadhuis** (17C) is topped by an octagonal tower. **D'Orangemolen** is a white walled mill, truncated in shape, dating from 1734.
Standing in a park of its own within the town walls, the town hall (gemeentehuis) is in the **Mauritshuis** ⊙, built in the 17C for Prince Maurice of Orange. It houses a small historical collection.

★ **From Raamsdonksveer to Biesbosch** – *50km - 31 miles to the north by St Ignatiusstraat and then the A 27. Leave the motorway at the Geertruidenberg exit and follow the signposts "Automuseum".*

Raamsdonksveer – With over 200 vehicles on display the National Motor Museum, **Nationaal Automobielmuseum★** ⊙, traces the history of the car from its origins. Some carriages, 18C sledges, racing trophies, posters and other car accessories add to the interest of the main collection.
The hall to the left of the entrance regroups cars by the Dutch manufacturer Spijker. The company was operational from 1899 to 1925 and its vehicles were popular with the Dutch royal family in the early years of the 20C. The American-built Ahrens-Fox fire engine belonged to the Rotterdam city fire brigade. Elvis Presley owned the bright red Cadillac Fleetwood Brougham (1976).
In the area to the right of the entrance admire the condition of such pioneers of the road as the Peugeot Double Phaeton (1894), the Benz Victoria (1899) and the Panhard-Levassor (1895). Note the Bikkers (1907) steam operated street-sweeping machine which belonged to Amsterdam.
Amidst the serried ranks of the models and racing cars in the other halls look for the magnificent **Auburns, Duesenbergs** and **Cords★★★** of the 1920s and 1930s by the American manufacturer and advocate of front-wheel drive, Errett Lobban Cord. The superb 1932 Bugatti Type 50 is one of only two remaining models.
There is a comprehensive section on Japanese car manufacturers especially Toyota.

Nationaal Automobielmuseum

Nationaal Automobielmuseum, Raamsdonksveer

Geertruidenberg – Pop 6 615. An old fortification on the Amer, this small town is organised round a triangular **square** overlooked by the massive tower of St.-Geertruidskerk. The **stadhuis** has a lovely 18C façade overlooking the square. Nearby a baroque fountain splashes.

Drimmelen – Well situated on the banks of the Amer, excellent for water sports since the completion of the Delta Plan *(qv)*, Drimmelen has become a tourist centre. Its **pleasure boat harbour** can accommodate 1 400 boats; it is also frequented by anglers.

★ **Biesbosch** – The Biesbosch (or Biesbos) consists of four parts, three of which are criss-crossed by roads. The fourth (Zuidwaard) is entirely surrounded by water. The **boat trip★** ⏱ gives a good overall view of the region.
This region of 40 000ha - 98 000 acres suffered in the St Elizabeth Flood in 1421. Due to important diking work undertaken during the last five and a half centuries, the submerged parts now cover no more than 6 000ha - 14 820 acres. Although very busy with pleasure boats, the Biesbosch has an abundant aquatic wild-life. One sees not only coots, godwits and redshanks, but also plovers, herons and pheasants. On the islets, reeds, rushes and grassland are the main vegetation, but numerous other species grow there as well: willows, ash, loosestrife, willow for wickerwork, hogweed, arrowhead, valerian and cress.
The closing of the Haringvliet estuary *(qv)* led to the disappearance of tides in this part, as well as the appearance of a transistory phase in the growth of willow. Recreational facilities in the Biesbosch include rowing, sailing and canoeing.
There is a project underway to make the Biesbosch a national park. Several recreation areas have been developed, as well as a bird santuary and three water reservoirs (spaarbekkens) which supply the Rotterdam and Dordrecht regions.

BRIELLE Zuid-Holland — Pop 14 916

Michelin map 408 D6 and fold 23 (inset) or 212 fold 4 – Local map see ROTTERDAM

An old fortified town on Voorne Island, Brielle, generally known as Den Briel (pronounced bril), was an active port at the mouth of the Maas.
On 1 April 1572 the Sea Beggars (*Gueux de Mer* or *Watergeuzen*), mercenaries, backed by William the Silent left England and landed at Brielle. This was the signal for the uprising of Holland and Zeeland against the Spanish occupation. In July, 19 priests were executed in Brielle of which 16 had just been made prisoners by the Sea Beggars at Gorinchem. Known as the "martyrs of Gorkum", they have been canonised.
Each year, on 1 April, Brielle commemorates the taking of the town by the Sea Beggars by historical sketches.
Brielle is the birthplace of Admiral **Maarten Tromp** (1598-1653).
Today, Brielle is a tourist centre benefiting from the proximity of **Brielse Meer** to which it is linked by a ferry for pedestrians and cyclists.
Reminders of the past include fortifications, laid out as an esplanade, and peaceful quays bordered with old houses, like **Maarland** to the north of the town. At the far eastern end of Maarland, beyond a bridge, there is a fine **view** over the docks and the tower of the Gothic church of St.-Catharijnekerk.

Trompmuseum ⏱ – Behind the 18C stadhuis, on the **Wellerondom**, a picturesque square with its old façades, fountain and canon, this small museum, installed in the weigh house, is devoted to the town's history and its famous son, Admiral Tromp. Admiral Tromp is famous for his victory against the Spanish during the Thirty Years War at the Battle of Downs in 1639, which ended Spanish supremacy at sea. He was knighted in 1642 by Charles I. He died in battle (near Scheveningen) in August 1653 and was buried in the Oude Kerk in Delft *(qv)*.

Grote- of St.-Catharijnekerk ⏱ – Built in the 15C, it remains unfinished. In Brabant Gothic style, it is preceded by a massive stone belfry porch 57m - 187ft high. The carillon cast in 1660 by one of the Hemonys has been enlarged and now has 48 bells.

★★★ BULBFIELDS See KEUKENHOF

★★ DELFT Zuid-Holland — Pop 89 365

Michelin map 408 E5, fold 24 (inset)
Plan of the conurbation in the current Michelin Red Guide Benelux

Delft earthenware has given to the city its worldwide renown.
Its shaded canals, monuments and museums have made Delft one of the country's cities which has retained the most character.
A refined city inspiring daydreaming... It is the homeland of the jurist Grotius *(qv)*, as well as Vermeer *(qv)* and the naturalist **Antonie van Leeuwenhoek** (1632-1723) who, thanks to the microscopes, which he himself perfected, made a multitude of discoveries in microscopic plant and animal life.

★ **Boat trip on the canals** ⏱ – *Landing stage: Wijnhaven 6* (**CZ**).
The boat follows Nieuwe Delft formed by Hippolytusbuurt and Voorstraat. It passes near the Oude Kerk then returns by Oude Delft and Koornmarkt.

HISTORICAL NOTES

A prosperous city – Delft, which means moat, was probably founded by Godefroy the Hunchback, Duke of Lower Lothringen in 1074. It obtained its city rights from Count William II of Holland in 1246; and reached its peak in the 13 and 14C due to the cloth trade and its breweries. At the end of the 14C, in order to export its products, it established a waterway link with the mouth of the Maas, where it soon established a port, Delfshaven, which in 1886 became part of Rotterdam.
In 1428 Jacoba or Jacqueline of Hainaut *(qv)* signed the Treaty of Delft here; she gave all her possessions (Holland, Zeeland, Hainaut) to Philip the Good and kept the title of countess.
In the 15C fortifications gave the town the layout which it was to keep until the 19C.
Extensively damaged by the large fire of 1536, it has few edifices dating from before the 16C. In 1654, the explosion of a powder magazine completed the destruction.
Today Delft is an intellectual centre, due to its schools of Natural Sciences, its hydraulic laboratory and its Technical University. A nuclear reactor to be used for research was installed in 1963. The modern university buildings are in the new quarters to the southwest of the town.
Amongst its industries there is the manufacture of leaven.

William the Silent (Willem de Zwijger) – Son of Count William of Nassau and Juliana of Stolberg, William was born, in Dillenburg Castle, in Germany, in 1533. On the death of his cousin **René de Chalon** (1544) he took his motto *Je maintiendrai* (I shall maintain), his title of **Prince of Orange** and inherited his possessions in France and in the Low Countries. In 1559, Philip II of Spain named him **Stadtholder** of the provinces of Holland, Zeeland and Utrecht.
The measures taken by Philip II to reinforce the repression against the Calvinists created an opposition movement, which William of Orange and the **Counts of Egmont and Hornes** headed. In 1566 the Iconoclastic Fury began *(qv)*. William feeling threatened fled to Dillenburg (1567) but the Counts of Egmont and Hornes were executed in Brussels in 1568. In 1570 William, who had been brought up as a Catholic, became a Calvinist. With his support the struggle of the Beggars *(qv)* was organised, both on land and sea. The capture of Brielle by the Sea Beggars on 1 April 1572 marked the beginning of a merciless fight. The States of Holland meeting in Dordrecht *(qv)* in July, approved of the revolts and acknowledged William of Orange as Stadtholder.
From 1572 onwards the prince often lived in Delft. In 1579 several provinces (Holland, Zeeland, Utrecht, Gelderland and Zutphen) joined forces in the fight with the famous Union of Utrecht *(qv)* followed closely by the other provinces.
A reward for his assassination was offered by Philip II in 1581; William of Orange defended himself with the well-known *Apologie*. He sought support and asked François of Anjou, brother of King Henri II of France, but the latter died (1584) shortly after.
On 10 July 1584 William the Silent was assassinated in the Prinsenhof in Delft.

The father of international law – Born in Delft, Hugo de Groot or **Grotius** (1583-1645) was one of the greatest minds of his time. At the same time theologian, philosopher and occasionally poet, he is best known for his legal writings and notably his *De Jure Belli ac Pacis* (*On the Law of War and Peace* – 1625) which was an accepted authority on matters of civil rights and earned its author the right to be considered as "father of the people's rights".
After the Synod of Dort, Grotius, of Remonstrant religion and follower of Oldenbarnevelt *(qv)*, was imprisoned in Slot Loevestein *(qv)*. He managed to escape and went to live in Paris, then in 1634 he became the Swedish Ambassador to France.

Vermeer of Delft (1632-75) – Delft and its inhabitants were this painter's universe who, born in Delft and dying there practically unknown, is one of the great masters of the Netherlands.
Applying himself to painting scenes of daily life, he is one of those who, without breaking with tradition and without giving up realism practised at the time, revolutionised pictorial art.
With Vermeer the anecdote disappeared, the subject would be banal and everyday if it were not developed by an extraordinary science of composition, geometry, the use of unctuous matter, vivid tones (lemon yellow, sky blue) remarkably blended, and above all, by the marvellous light effects for which Vermeer is the great virtuoso.
This play of light is particularly fine in the famous *View of Delft* as seen from Hooikade (**CZ**) or in the portraits of women suffused with light and grace like the *Young Girl with a Turban* and *The Lacemaker*.
The Mauritshuis in The Hague and the Rijksmuseum in Amsterdam are the two museums in the Netherlands with the greatest number of works by Vermeer, who was not in fact very prolific.
His contemporary, **Pieter de Hooch** or **Hoogh** (1629-84) born in Rotterdam, spent a long time in Delft before going to Amsterdam. He depicts the life of the well-to-do bourgeois seen in interiors with doors and windows open, creating clever perspectives and light effects on the floor.

A serious pretender – It being impossible to substantiate the death of the Dauphin, son of Louis XVI and Marie-Antoinette in the Temple prison in 1795 in Paris, numerous candidates to the throne of France under the reign of Louis XVIII, tried to pass as the young prince.
Amongst them, the clockmaker **Naundorff** gathered round him a circle of followers who, impressed by the precision of his declarations about the Court and the royal family, recognised him as the legitimate sovereign until his death in 1845. His descendant kept, by privilege, the title of Duke of Normandy.

Delftware – In the Netherlands, at the end of the 16C, the vogue for Rhineland stoneware was superseded by majolica, from Italy. The main centres, Haarlem and Amsterdam, made domestic objects then, together with Makkum *(qv)* and Harlingen, started to produce earthenware tiles for wall decoration. In the 17C contacts with the Orient (via the Dutch East India Company) brought new sources of inspiration, in both form and colours taken from Chinese porcelain.

In the second half of the 17C Delft acquired a reputation which soon spread over all of Europe.

Heir to the Italian majolica techniques, Delftware is tin-glazed earthenware and characterised by its remarkable lightness and its particularly shiny aspect, due to the application of a translucent coating.

Firstly, Delft is known for its monochrome painting of blues on a white background; this is still one of the characteristics of Delftware today.

At the end of the 17C, the production became more varied, polychromy appeared, and there was not a design or shape, coming from China or Japan, which the Delft artists did not try out in order to satisfy the tastes of European clients fascinated by the Orient.

Decorating Delftware

V.C.L./PIX

In the 18C the influence of Sèvres and Meissen porcelain expressed itself in objects with mannered outlines and decoration, while some of the pieces remained faithful to traditional Dutch scenes where one sees small boats sailing on the canals spanned by humpback bridges.

In the beginning of the 18C, Delftware reached its peak. But a decline set in rapidly, caused mainly by English competition; production continues today in several local factories.

★★ HISTORICAL CENTRE AND THE CANALS

allow half a day – town plan overleaf

Markt (CY 27) – This vast esplanade where the market takes place (Thursdays) stretches between the Nieuwe Kerk and the Stadhuis.

★ **Nieuwe Kerk** (CDY) ⏲ – This Gothic church (1381) has a brick tower crowned with a lovely stone spire. The carillon has bells cast by one of the Hemonys. The church contains the crypt of the princes of the House of Orange. Only a few members of this family were not buried here: Stadtholder and King of England, William III lies in Westminster Abbey, John William Friso in Leeuwarden, Philip-William, eldest son of William the Silent, in Diest (Belgium).

The interior with three naves is plain. The squat columns support pointed arches, more acute in the chancel.

Under the vault of dark wood, the clerestorey windows of the nave rise above a tier of blind lancet windows which is replaced by a triforium in the chancel.

The light of the nave contrasts with the rich stained glass windows of the transept and the wide ambulatory. Put in between 1927-36, they depict figurative motifs in warm colours. Only the stained glass window of Grotius, in the north transept, by the master **Joep Nicolas** (1897-1972) stands out by its muted grey and blue tones.

The **mausoleum of William the Silent★** stands in the chancel, above the royal crypt. This imposing Renaissance edifice in marble and black stone was made by Hendrick de Keyser from 1614-21. In the middle of a peristyle quartered with great allegorical figures, the prince lies in full-dress uniform, under the eyes of a bronze Fame. At his feet lies his ever faithful dog. At the head of the marble recumbent statue, a bronze statue depicts William the Silent in armour.

In the centre of the chancel, the entrance to the House of Orange's crypt is indicated by a large emblazoned slab.

In the ambulatory, paved with tombstones, there is the mausoleum of King William I by William Geefs (1847) and in the north aisle that of Grotius (1781).

Access to the tower ⏲ – From the penultimate platform there is a **panorama★** over the new town, beyond the ring canal, with the Technical University and the nuclear reactor, and on the horizon, Rotterdam and The Hague.

Stadhuis (CY H) – Burnt down in 1618 it was rebuilt in 1620 by Hendrick de Keyser. Restored in 1965 it has recovered its 17C aspect with its mullioned windows set in lead and its low shutters. The façade overlooking the square, decorated with shells, is dwarfed from behind by the old 15C keep, all that remains of the original stadhuis.

Turn round, there is a fine view of the Nieuwe Kerk's tower.

DELFT

Choorstraat .... CY 7
Hippolytusbuurt .... CY 15
Jacob Gerritstr. .... CYZ 19
Markt .... CY 27
Oude Langendijk ...... CYZ 40
Voldersgracht .... CY 51
Wijnhaven .... CYZ 58

Brabantse Turfmarkt ..... DZ 3
Breestraat .... CZ 4
Camaretten .... CY 6
Doelenstraat .... CY 12
Havenstraat .... CZ 13
Jorisweg .... DY 21
Koornmarkt .... CZ 22
Lange Geer .... CDZ 25
Nassaulaan .... DZ 30
Nieuwe Langendijk ...... DY 33

Nieuwstraat .... CY 34
Noordeinde .... CY 36
oostpoortweg .... DZ 37
Oude Kerkstraat .... CY 39
Schoenmakerstraat ...... DZ 45
Schoolstraat .... CY 46
Sint Agathaplein .... CY 48
Stalpaert v. d. Wieleweg .. DY 49
Voorstraat .... CY 54
Westlandseweg .... CZ 55

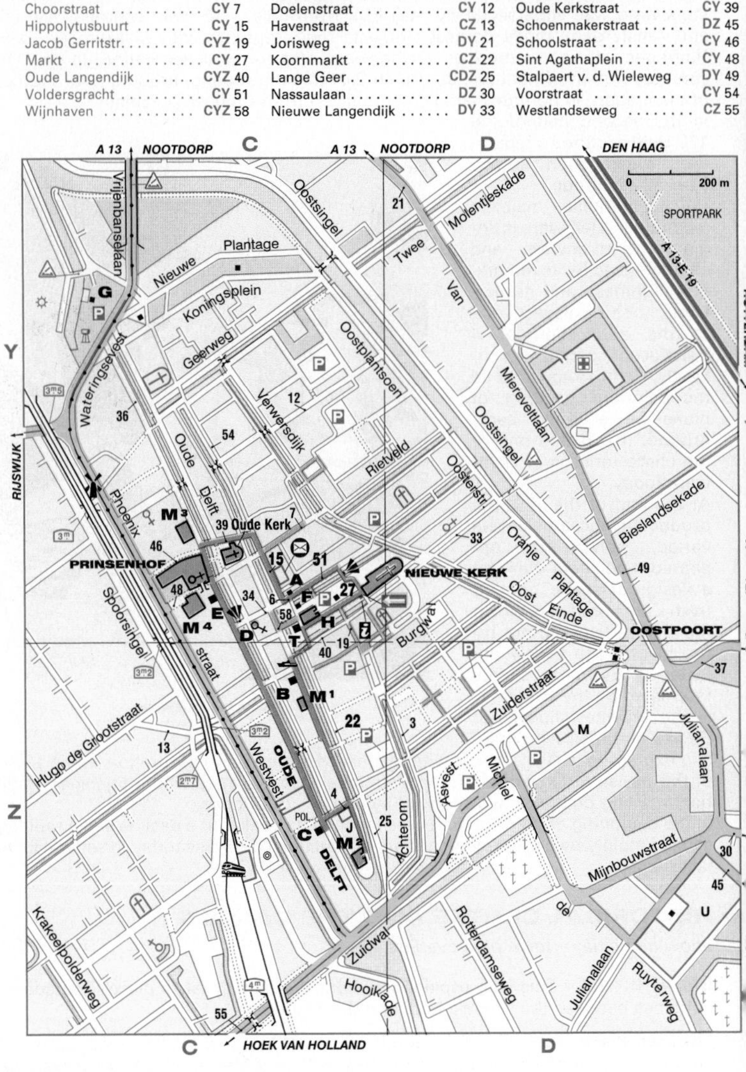

Waag (CYZ **T**) – This building (1770) has been transformed into a theatre. From here one can see the meat market, **vleeshal** (CY **A**), the façade of which is appropriately endowed with two ox heads (1660).

Koornmarkt (CZ **22**) – *Cross the canal.* This is the landing stage for the boat trips. At no 81 (CZ **B**) there is a lovely Renaissance house with medallions, called De Handboog (the bow). At no 67 (CZ **M**[1]), the 18C patrician house, where the painter **Paul Tetar van Elven** lived (1823-96), is now a museum *(qv)*.

★ **Koninklijk Nederlands Leger- en Wapenmuseum** (CZ **M**[2]) ⊙ – *Enter through Korte Geer, the continuation of Koornmarkt.* The two former depots housing the Royal Netherlands Army Museum date from 1602 and 1692; they used to belong to the States of Holland and Western Friesland. The third building was used as a warehouse by the Dutch East India Company. The historical exhibition in the "gebouw 1692" building retraces the evolution of the Dutch army through the ages. Impressive collections illustrate the different stages of development of national military history: weapons (pistols, rifles, cannons), armour, uniforms, headgear (helmets, shakos), banners and trappings, not to mention means of transport, paintings and scale models. Major landmarks in army history were the Eighty Years' War, in which the army reformer Maurice of Orange and his half-brother Frederick Henry distinguished themselves, the French domination (1795-1813) and its upheavals, the Belgian Revolution (1830), and during the 20C, the two World Wars. The post-war events relative to Indonesia, Korea, Suriname and the foundation of NATO are also represented. The 1602 building focuses more specifically on military and technological themes, while the former warehouse organises the screening of films.

★ **Oude Delft** (CZ) – The somber water of the canal shaded by lime trees, the humpbacked bridges and the elegant façades make an attractive picture.
At no 39 the lovely house of the Dutch East India Company, **Oostindisch Huis**, (CZ **C**) has been restored. The façade carries the company's coat of arms and its initials: VOC.

Turn back and follow the quay.

One soon sees the slightly leaning spire of the Oude Kerk. In sombre brick, it is flanked by four pinnacles. On the opposite quay there is the charming Gothic chapel, Kapel van het H. Geestzusterhuis (CY D). From Nieuwstraat Bridge there is a fine **view★** over the canal. At no 167 the Delft Water Board, **Hoogheemraadschap van Delfland** (CY E), an old patrician house (*c*1520), displays a sumptuous Renaissance stone façade decorated with sculptured tympana. The portal is topped with polychrome armorial bearings.
No 169 has a fine façade emblazoned with the arms of the House of Savoy and contains the local archives.

★ **Prinsenhof** (CY) ⊙ – *No 183. Access by St Agathaplein, a small square situated beyond the porch.*
The sculptured stone above the porch is a reminder that in the 17C the Prinsenhof was converted into a cloth hall. It was originally a convent (St Agatha) before becoming, in 1572, the residence of William the Silent, who was assassinated here in 1584.
The palace (Prinsenhof: the Prince's Court) now houses a **museum**. It contains souvenirs of the Eighty Years' War and collections concerning the House of Orange-Nassau, notably numerous historical portraits. The buildings in the 15C Flamboyant Gothic style are arranged round two courtyards. One is flanked by the chapterhouse (room II), the other by the refectory (room IV), opposite the chapel (room XIV). The latter is now used as a Walloon church *(qv)*. Each year the Prinsenhof is the venue for an Antiques Fair *(see Calendar of Events)*.

Oude Kerk (CY) ⊙ – Dedicated to St Hippolytus, this 13C church, which is reflected in the waters of Oude Delft was enlarged four times. Since the 16C it has three chancels and the beginning of a transept. The tower, which leans, embedded in the main nave, is built on the foundations of a watch tower. It has the biggest bell in the Netherlands (9 metric tons).
Numerous memorial slabs (16-18C) are set in the pavement. The finely carved Renaissance pulpit resembles the one in the Grote Kerk in The Hague.
The stained glass windows (1972) in the chancel, the transept and at the end of the side aisles, made by Joep Nicolas have lovely figurative compositions.
Famous people are buried in this church. In the main chancel Admiral Piet Hein *(qv)* is shown lying in full armour: it is the work of Pieter de Keyser, son of Hendrick. In the chapel near the north chancel, the mausoleum of Admiral Tromp *(qv)* by Rombout Verhulst is baroque. The low relief depicts the naval battle of Terheyde, where the admiral was killed in 1653.
To the north of the tower, near the stained glass window depicting William the Silent (no 25), there is the monument to van Leeuwenhoek *(qv)*.

Hippolytusbuurt (CY 15) – This shaded canal is one of the oldest in Delft. Along the quays florists display their wares (Thursdays). On the corner of Hippolytusbuurt and Camaretten is the fish market, next to which stands the former meat market. Opposite this is a lovely 16C house (Kaaskop) (CY F) with crow-stepped gables.

Voldersgracht (CY 51) – This is a picturesque canal, edged on the south by a few corbelled houses.
From the second bridge, there is a fine view of the Nieuw Kerk's tower.

ADDITIONAL SIGHTS

★ **Oostpoort** (DYZ) – Formerly called St Catherine's Gate, it is the only one remaining from the town walls. It is a lovely dark brick construction, flanked with two slender octagonal turrets dating from the 15 and 16C. There is a fine view from the picturesque white lever bridge in front of it. A canal passes under the annexe.

Museum Lambert van Meerten (CY M[3]) ⊙ – This 19C mansion has a magnificent collection of **earthenware tiles★** from the 16 to 19C. Note on the staircase a naval battle against the English and a panel of tulips; upstairs, a series of birds, flowers and a long panel illustrating the various stages in boat building.

Volkenkundig Museum "Nusantara" (CY M[4]) – This museum is devoted to the history and culture of Indonesia. In one of the rooms there is a southeast Asian gong ensemble *(gamelan)*. The museum also hosts temporary exhibitions.

Museum Paul Tetar van Elven (CZ M[1]) ⊙ – The collections include furniture, ceramics and paintings by the local artist Paul Tetar van Elven and his contemporaries.

Graf van Naundorff (CY G) – At the end of Noordeinde canal, the continuation of Oude Delft, there is a shaded square where Naundorff *(qv)* the so-called son of Louis XVI lies. Railings decorated with fleur-de-lis surround a simple engraved slab.

Join us in our constant task of keeping up-to-date
Please send us your comments and suggestions

Michelin Tyre PLC
Tourism Department
The Edward Hyde Building
38 Clarendon Road
WATFORD - Herts WD1 1SX
Tel: (0923) 415000

★ DELTA Zuid-Holland - Zeeland

Michelin map 408 B C D 67 and 8 or 212 folds 2 to 5 and 12 to 14

In the coastal provinces of Zuid-Holland and Zeeland the estuaries of the Rhine, Maas and Scheldt form a complicated network of islands, headlands and channels known as the Delta.

HISTORICAL AND GEOGRAPHICAL NOTES

At the mouth of three great rivers – The **Rijn** (Rhine) divides into two branches as it crosses the Netherlands, the Neder Rijn and the Waal. The **Neder Rijn** (Lower Rhine) becomes the Lek, then the Nieuwe Maas before entering the Nieuwe Waterweg. The **Waal**, the main arm of the Rhine, flows into the Lek and the Maas. The **Maas**, which also has several names (Bergse Maas, Amer) flows into the Hollands Diep.

The Oosterschelde is a former estuary of the **Schelde** (Scheldt), which presently flows into the Westerschelde.

The rivers thread their way between the islands which sometimes become peninsulas.

A region under constant threat – The islands built up slowly towards the end of the Middle Ages as the rivers deposited sediments. They are generally very low-lying, many below Amsterdam Reference Level and most under 5m - 16ft. The coastline is protected by high dunes while the banks of the rivers are strengthened by dikes. Several times throughout history these have proved vulnerable when the great surge tides swept inland.

On the feast day of St Elisabeth (19 November) 1941 the flood waters inundated the entire Delta and swept as far inland as Dordrecht *(qv)* and the Biesbosch area. Six villages were under water and 10 000 lost their lives.

There was another great disaster on the night of the 31 January 1953 when under the combined effects of low atmospheric pressure and high tides a tidal wave breached the dikes in several places. Once again the islands (260 000ha - 642 200 acres in all) were inundated by flood waters, 1 835 died and a further 500 000 were victims of serious flood damage. The effects were felt as far inland as the Hollandse IJssel.

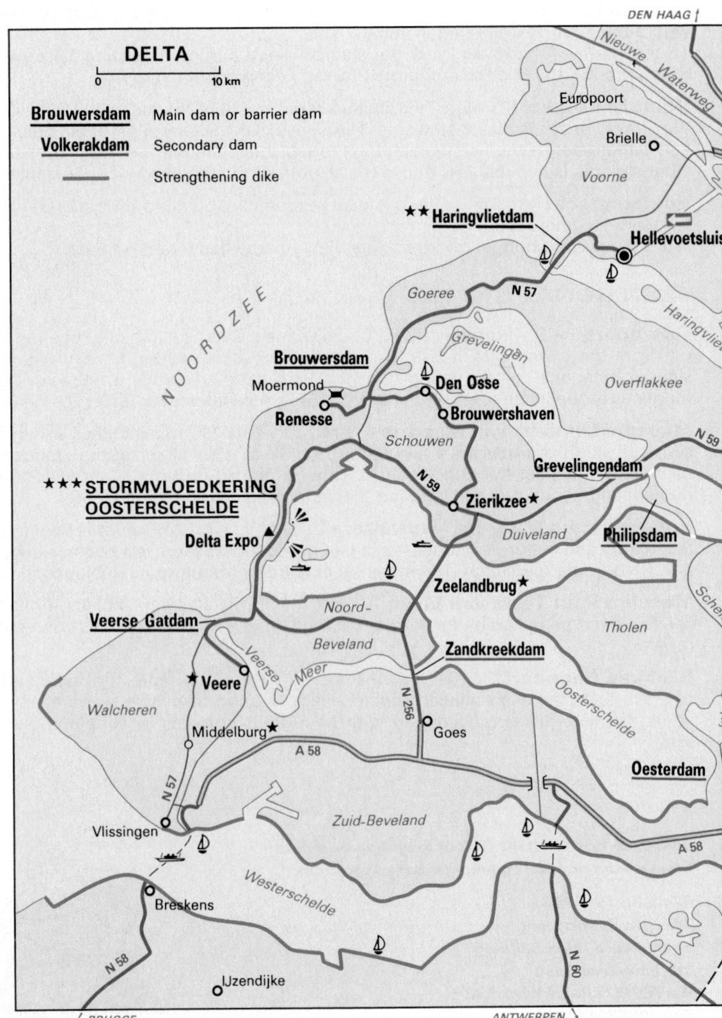

The Delta Plan – Three years after the tidal wave of 1953, two options were under discussion to prevent the recurrence of similar tragedies: heighten the existing dikes or dam the major estuaries and inlets of the Delta. In 1958 the Delta Plan was incorporated in an Act of Parliament.
Four main dams, two with locks, closed off the inlets of the North Sea and several secondary dams closed off the estuaries further inland. The secondary dams afforded initial protection from high tides during the construction of the main dams. Once the main dams were finished the importance of the secondary dams diminished although they proved a considerable asset to the road network. It was decided not to dam the Westerschelde nor the Nieuwe Waterweg to leave free access to the sea ports of Antwerp and Rotterdam. However a new dam, specially designed for stormy weather, is planned for 1997, when it will be possible to seal off the Nieuwe Waterweg which flows through Rotterdam. The dams have many advantages: they shorten the coast by approximately 700km - 435 miles, they form freshwater lakes inland (ie Haringvlietdam and further to the east two auxiliary dams, Philipsdam and Oesterdam, built, once the storm surge barrier project was adopted), they reduce the seeping of saltwater into the water table, they reduce the risk of floods, they form ideal stretches of water for recreational purposes, they improve the road network and encourage the development of the region.
The Delta Plan also included the raising and strengthening of existing dikes along navigable waterways and the development of the Biesbosch area.
The Scheldt-Rhine Canal (Schelde-Rijnverbinding) to the east of the Delta, was completed in 1975 and links Antwerp to Volkerak, a distance of 37km - 23 miles.

Dams and bridges – Already by 1950 the Brielse Maas, downstream from Rotterdam, had been transformed into a lake called the Brielse Meer *(qv)*. Since it was necessary to leave the New Waterway open for navigation a storm surge barrier, **Stormvloedkering Hollandse IJssel**, was built between 1954 and 1958 on the Hollandse IJssel near Krimpen aan de IJssel in the eastern suburbs of Rotterdam. A mobile gate is raised to allow ships through. The lock (120x24m - 394-79ft) alongside is for larger vessels and ships in general when the main barrier gate is closed.
The Haringvliet estuary was closed by the **Haringvlietdam** *(qv)* while further inland the secondary **Volkerakdam** linked Overflakkee to the province of Noord-Brabant. Built between 1957 and 1969 the dam has three large sluice caissons and is itself liked to **Haringvlietbrug** which spans the waterway to the north towards Beijerland.

To the south, the Brouwershavense Gat Channel is closed by the **Brouwersdam** *(qv)* with inland the **Grevelingendam** on the waterway of the same name. The latter links Duiveland and Overflakkee and when it was built in 1958-65, 170 000 tons of rubble were tipped as infill from the gondolas of a cableway. The **Philipsdam** is a prolongation to the southeast.
The year 1986 saw the completion of the Oosterschelde Storm Surge Barrier, **Stormvloedkering in de Oosterschelde**. In the event of a bad storm or when the water level reaches a critical point, it is now possible to close off this estuary, the widest (9km - 6 miles) and the deepest (40m - 130ft) in the Delta. Two dams east of the estuary, **Oesterdam** (1986) and Philipsdam *(see above)* protect the Scheldt-Rhine Canal from tidal flow. The Oosterschelde is also spanned by the **Zeelandbrug** *(qv)*. The saltwater channel, Veerse Meer, to the south of Noord-Beveland is closed off by **Veerse Gatdam**, which is backed up by a secondary dam **Zandkreekdam** on the saltwater Zandreek channel between Noord- and Zuid-Beveland. Built between 1956 and 1960 the 800m - 2 625ft long dam has a lock (140x20m - 459-65ft) spanned by a swing bridge for traffic. The Westerschelde remains open for navigation to the port of Antwerp. Two companies provide regular boat services across the estuary. There is a project under discussion to bridge the crossing.

Boat trips in the Delta ⏲ – *In the north boats leave from Rotterdam and Willemstad; Zierikzee (qv) is the departure point for the Oosterschelde.*

"The Lord made Heaven and Earth but the Dutch made Holland."
The Dutch have more than proved this saying by their tenacity in their struggle against the sea and their expertise in the worlds of hydraulic engineering and land reclamation. The following museums give some insight into Dutch supremacy in these specialised domains:
Delta Expo – see overleaf Museum
De Cruquius – see Haarlem: Excursions.

HELLEVOETSLUIS TO VEERE

99km - 62 miles – allow a day – local map on the previous pages

Northern section

Hellevoetsluis – This small port on an arm of the sea, Haringvliet, has several marinas.

★★ **Haringvlietdam** – This major civil engineering project was undertaken from 1955 to 1971.

Initially an artificial construction site was built in the middle of the estuary and surrounded by an encircling dike. A cableway was used in the final stages, a method that had already been used on the Grevelingendam *(qv)*. Concrete blocks were tipped from the gondolas into the final channel to be dammed.

5km - 3 miles long the Haringvlietdam has 17 drainage sluices of 56.50m - 185ft. Their gates take 20 minutes to open using a hydraulic press system with 68 presses set within the 16 pillars and the abutment piers. Normally these sluice gates are closed and the water is forced back to the Nieuwe Waterweg. The drainage locks help to achieve a balance between fresh and saltwater. A shipping lock has been made near the small port to the south.

Brouwersdam – The dam was built from 1963 to 1972 between the islands of Goeree and Schouwen; there is no lock. To complete the north channel, Springerdiep, sluice caissons were made, the same system which had been used, for the first time when building the Veerse Gatdam *(see opposite)*. The south channel, Brouwershavense Gat, was filled in using the cableway system whereby 15 ton loads of concrete blocks were dropped each time by the gondola.

Between the Brouwerdam and Grevelingendam is the saltwater but tideless lake, Grevelingenmeer.

Renesse – This small village on the north coast of the island of Schouwen has a lovely sandy beach. Just to the east is the 16-17C manor, **Slot Moermond** ⏲. This fine brick manorhouse has a 14C porch.

Den Osse – This recent marina is well hidden by the dikes.

Brouwershaven – Pop 3 650. This was originally a prosperous port trading in beer from Delft (*brouwer:* brewer) however life today revolves around its small pleasure boat harbour.

Brouwershaven suffered during the 1953 floods. This is the home town of the statesman, **Jacob Cats** (1577-1660), nicknamed Father Cats, who was Grand Pensionary of Holland and West Friesland from 1635-51. He was also known for his poetry. Brouwershaven has a lovely 15C Gothic church, **St.-Nicolaaskerk** ⏲ with a transept and ambulatory. Inside the pulpit and chancel screen are in the rococo style. The town hall, **stadhuis**, of 1599 has a Renaissance façade in stone, highly decorated, and topped by a pinnacle.

★ **Zierikzee** – *See Zierikzee.*

The Storm Surge Barrier

★★★ **Stormvloedkering in de Oosterschelde** – The Oosterschelde barrier was originally planned as a dam but in 1973 ecological arguments prevailed and the decision was taken to go for a movable barrier. Engineering work started in 1976 and the barrier was inaugurated ten years later; the road running along the dam was opened in 1987. This imposing 3km - 2 mile long hydraulic engineering project was at the time of construction unique in the world: it was built across the estuary mouth spanning three tidal channels and two artificial islands which had served as construction bases.

Oosterschelde storm-surge barrier

The storm-surge barrier with its 65 prefabricated concrete piers and 62 sliding steel gates is designed to stay open under normal tidal conditions and only be closed in the event of stormy weather.
Each pier is 30 to 38m - 99 to 125ft high and can weigh up to 18 000 metric tons. The sliding gates are 40m - 131ft wide and their height varies from 6 to 12m - 20 to 40ft. In the event of a storm, or when the water level becomes dangerously high, one hour is required to lower the gates.
This new project not only succeeds in preserving 75% of the tidal flow in the Oosterschelde but also preserves much of the unique estuary habitat saving the oyster and mussel beds from destruction as well as the fishing activities.
The Ir. Topshuis in the former artificial island of Neeltje Jans houses the central control room and the **Delta Expo** ⏲, which gives some idea of the importance of the Delta Project to the area as a whole. The history of land reclamation and the development of hydraulic engineering in the Netherlands are illustrated by a selection of objects, scale models and slide presentations. A working model reproduces the 1953 floods and explains the safety measures implemented since then. The film *Delta Finale* recounts the successive stages of development of the dam: the making of the different prefabricated elements, the preparation of foundations in the sandy channel bed, the floating and sinking into position of the concrete piers and finally the fitting of the computer controlled sluice gates.
On a clear day, the roof of the building commands a sweeping view of the whole Delta region. A visit to the barrier is highly interesting. Access to the pillars is through the control room, equipped with oil pumps and electrical controls. Note the powerful current: in the Oosterschelde each tide displaces 800 million cubic metres of water. **Boat trips** ⏲ and visits to oyster and mussel beds are organised in summer.

Southern section

★ **Zeelandbrug** – In 1955 the bridge was built to link Zierikzee to the former island of Noord-Beveland. The crossing was paralleled with the opening of the road along the Oosterschelde Barrier. This impressive feat of engineering bridges the 5 022m - 16 476ft waterway in 50 arches at a height of 17m - 56ft above water level.
The swing bridge on the Schouwen-Duiveland side gives passage to boats with tall masts.

Veerse Gatdam – The dam was built (1958-61) from a point west of Veere on the island of Walcheren to the former island of Noord-Beveland. This enclosing dike 2 700m - 8 858ft long, in spite of protection from a sandbank is very exposed to storms, due to its northwesterly orientation. It was the first dam to use sluice caissons; these were placed on the bed of the channel and the sluice gates were then closed at slack water and this prevented the formation of a destructive current. Another small saltwater and tideless lake, the Veerse Meer, lies between this dam and the Zandkreekdam to the east.

★ **Veere** – *See Veere.*

The Thames Barrier: the other storm barrier
The distinctive silhouette of the barrier's shell-roofs has become a landmark of the London skyline. The barrier, which took ten years to build (1872-82), spans one third of a mile across the Thames in Woolwich Reach. The ten movable steel gates are placed end to end across the river and are pivoted between nine piers and two abutments. The 13-storey concrete piers are capped with distinctive stainless steel roofs which house the hydraulic machinery. In threatening conditions the gates can be shut in 30 minutes. In the last ten years the barrier has been raised around 11 times, largely as precautionary measures.

★ DEVENTER Overijssel

Pop 67 471

Michelin map 408 J5
Plan of the conurbation in the current Michelin Red Guide Benelux

Right in the south of the Overijssel province and the Salland region, Deventer, formerly a Hanseatic town on the east bank of the IJssel, has kept its old character, witness to a rich past.

HISTORICAL NOTES

As early as the 9C it was a prosperous port. At the end of the 9C, the city became the residence of the Utrecht bishops, who fled from their town threatened by the Northmen. On Nieuwe Markt, the remains of an 11C episcopal palace have been found. The town soon played an important religious role. The theologian **Gerhard Groote** (1340-84), born in Deventer, was the innovator of a spiritual movement, the **Devotio Moderna** (modern devotion). One of his pupils, Florentius Radewyns, following the wishes of his master, founded in Deventer *c*1384 the first monastery for the **Order of the Brethren of the Common Life**, a community devoted to the education and care of the poor, which had a large intellectual influence in Europe. Those who passed through his school were Thomas à Kempis *(qv)*, Pope Adrian VI *(qv)*, Erasmus in 1475-6 and Descartes in 1632-3.
In the 16C Hendrick Terbrugghen *(qv)* was born in Deventer. At the end of the 17C, Gerard Terborch, born in Zwolle *(qv)*, came to work here, dying in 1681.
In the 16 and 17C printing was an important enterprise in the town: already in the 15C numerous incunabula were produced.

Today the metallurgical industry, as well as chemical, graphic and foodstuff industries are amongst the main activities of this town; a well-known gingerbread *(Deventer koek)* is made here.
In the heart of the city, in the pedestrian shopping precinct, a very large barrel organ, called the Turk, plays old tunes on Saturdays.
Deventer is an Old Catholic *(qv)* Episcopal See.

Boat trips ⊙ – Tours on the IJssel offer fine views of the city.

TOWN CENTRE *2 hours*

Brink (Z 12) – It is the main square of the town, so named, as in all localities of Saxon origin. A market is held here (Friday mornings and Saturdays). At nos 11 and 12, there is an early 17C façade decorated with shells. The richly decorated **Penninckhuis** (Z D) dates from 1590.

Waag (Z) – This is a large, slightly sloping weigh house built in 1528 in the late Gothic style and complemented in 1643 by the addition of a tall perron resting on arcades. The roofing is flanked by four turrets and topped by a wooden pinnacle. On the north façade hangs a huge cauldron in which, it is purported, counterfeiters used to be boiled. The building contains a **Museum De Waag** ⊙ displaying several collections related to the town's history: archaeological findings, paintings, drawings and miscellaneous objects. Note the splendid 17C majolica oven and the bicycles, believed to be the oldest in the Netherlands.

De Drie Haringen (House of the Three Herrings) (Z E) – Dating from 1575, this merchant's house has a fine Renaissance façade decorated with a façade stone depicting three herrings. It is used by the VVV *(i on the town plan)*.
On the other side of the street no 69 (public library) has an elegant façade.

Speelgoed en Blikmuseum (Z M[1]) ⊙ – The biggest public collection of toys in the country has been set up in two houses dating from the Middle Ages. Most of the exhibits were made after 1860: construction sets, trains, dolls, games, mechanical toys and miniature tea sets. One section presents a range of tins designed for packaging manufactured in the Netherlands between 1800 and 1980.

Retrace your steps and turn right into Bergstraat.

Bergstraat (Z 7) – In this street of Bergkwartier or hill quarter, which has been restored, there are several fine old façades; lovely view over the two towers of the Bergkerk.

DEVENTER

Street	Ref	Street	Ref	Street	Ref
Brink	Z 12	Bergstraat	Z 7	Menstraat	Z 52
Broederenstraat	Z 16	Binnensingel	Y 9	Mr. H. F. de Boerlaan	Z 54
Engestraat	Z 19	Bokkingshang	Z 10	Noordenbergstr.	Z 57
Grote Poot	Z 28	Brinkpoortstr.	Y 15	Ossenweerdstraat	Y 61
Klein Poot	Z 42	Gedempte Gracht	Y 22	Pontsteeg	Z 63
Korte Bisschopstr.	Z 45	Graven	Z 24	Roggestraat	Z 64
Lange Bisschopstr.	Z 46	Grote Kerkhof	Z 25	Snipperlingsdijk	Z 66
Nieuwstraat	YZ 55	Grote Overstraat	Z 27	Spijkerboorsteeg	Z 67
Bagijnenstraat	Y 4	Hofstraat	Z 33	Stromarkt	Z 69
Bergkerkplein	Z 6	Hoge Hondstraat	Y 34	T. G. Gibsonstraat	Y 70
		Industrieweg	Z 36	van Twickelostraat	Y 72
		Kapjeswelle	Y 39	Verlengde Kazernestr.	Z 73
		Kerksteeg	Z 40	Verzetslaan	Y 75
		Leeuwenbrug	Y 49	Zandpoort	Z 78

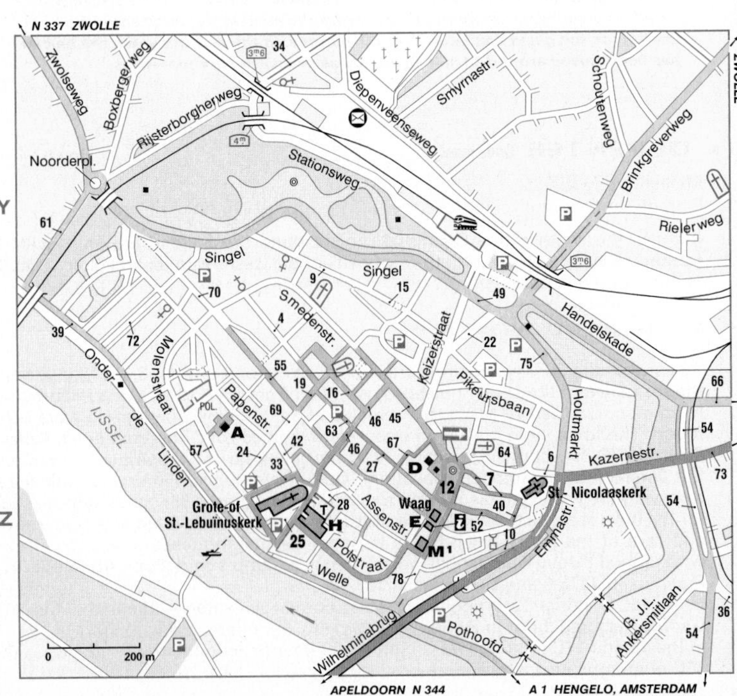

Deventer

St.-Nicolaas or Bergkerk (Z) – It was started *c*1200 AD in the Romanesque style and has kept from that time the two square towers of the façade, topped by spires. The rest was modified in the Gothic style in the 15C.

One returns to Brink via Kerksteeg and Menstraat. The Polstraat leads to Grote Kerkhof.

Grote Kerkhof (Z 25) – The Grote Kerk and Stadhuis are on this square.

Stadhuis (Z H) ⊙ – This complex (greatly restored) is in three parts: the actual Raadhuis, the Wanthuis (also giving on to Polstraat), and the Landshuis. The joint façade of the Raadhuis and the Wanthuis dates from the 17C; its architect Jacob Roman also designed Het Loo Palace in Apeldoorn.
The **Landshuis**, former headquarters of the Overijssel States has a lovely brick façade (1632) punctuated by pilasters and topped by a pinnacled gable.
In the hall of the Raadhuis several 17 and 18C group portraits of guilds are exhibited. A room on the 1st floor of the Raadhuis has a lovely canvas by Terborch: The **Aldermen's Council** (in the koffiekamer) painted in 1657.

Grote- of St.-Lebuïnuskerk (Z) ⊙ – It bears the name of Lebuin, Saxon apostle, who built a church here in the 8C. The Romanesque church founded *c*1040 by Bernulphus, Bishop of Utrecht, was converted after 1235 and then again in the 15C in the Gothic style. It is a vast building flanked to the west by a tower topped with an octagonal lantern in wood designed by Hendrick de Keyser.
Its carillon, which was cast by one of the Hemonys, can be heard during **concerts** ⊙. The hall-type interior has kept the remains of a double transept. The stellar vaulting has paintings round the keystones (16C). Other paintings can be seen, notably under the porch near the tower; the *Bearing of the Cross* dates from the 16C. The 19C great organ has 3 000 pipes; **organ concerts** ⊙ are held.
Under the chancel, the Romanesque crypt (1040) is remarkable with its six short pillars, cabled or decorated with geometric motifs.

Access to the tower ⊙ – From the top there is a lovely view of the city.

ADDITIONAL SIGHT

Buiskensklooster (Z A) – This early 15C building has recovered its brickwork walls. It is the former convent of St Agnes where the Sisters of the Common Life lived, following the rules set forth by Gerhard Groote *(qv)*. It contains the **town archives** (no 3) and a library, **Stads- of Athenaeumbibliotheek** ⊙, where there are interesting exhibitions of books and manuscripts.

EXCURSION

Holten and Markelo – *26km - 16 miles to the east by Snipperlingsdijk* (Z).

Holten – Pop 8 714. This town, situated in the Salland region, attracts many tourists, drawn by the wooded and sandy heights of the **Holterberg** (alt 50m - 164ft), which marks the southern limit of the Scandinavian glaciers.
On the Holterberg, there is the **Bos Museum**★ ⊙. About ten large **dioramas** bring to life various European animals, which are to be found locally; some are shown with their winter coats. Note the diorama showing a group of Scandinavian elks being attacked by wolves.
In a nearby clearing is a beautifully landscaped Canadian cemetery, **Canadese Militaire Begraafplaats**, with 1 496 tombs of Canadians killed in the Second World War.

Markelo – Pop 6 971. At the beginning of the century an important field of funeral urns was found north of Markelo. Markelo has an open-air theatre, **De Kösterskoele**.

DOESBURG Gelderland — Pop 10 589

Michelin map 408 J5.

At the confluence of the IJssel and the Oude IJssel, Doesburg, an old stronghold of the Zutphen earldom, was a prosperous commercial town in the Middle Ages; and a member of the Hanseatic League in 1447. This lovely city of the Achterhoek *(qv)* has kept numerous vestiges of its past, notably the remains of ramparts dating from 1630 *(to the south)* and several Gothic and Renaissance façades.

Boat trips ⏲ – Excursions are organised on the IJssel.

SIGHTS

Grote- of Martinikerk ⏲ – This Gothic church dedicated to St Martin (15C) is lit by tall Flamboyant windows. Its high **tower** ⏲ destroyed in 1945, has been rebuilt and has a carillon. Organ concerts are held inside in summer.

Waag – Now a restaurant, this graceful building (*c*1500), under a gable decorated with pinnacles, has tall picture windows with painted shutters, topped by tympana. Inside, in a typical setting, the weigh house scales can be seen.
There are other interesting houses in the same street, notably the **Baerkenhuizen** (nos 29-31), two Renaissance buildings of 1649 with voluted gables.

Stadhuis – It stands opposite the Waag. Dating from the 14C, it has an interesting façade on Roggestraat.
Next to it is a **museum** ⏲ of local history and handicrafts ("De Roode Tooren" Museum voor Stad en Ambt Doesborgh). Reconstitutions include a clog-maker's workshop, a room where a cigar-maker chopped tobacco and an old grocer's shop *(1st floor)*. Note the scale model of a pontoon bridge: near Doesburg the banks of the IJssel were linked by this type of bridge until 1952.

Doesburgsche Mosterdfabriek ⏲ – *Boekholtstraat 22.*
In this factory, founded in 1457, mustard is prepared according to old techniques using wooden mills.

EXCURSION

Doetinchem and 's-Heerenberg – *22km - 14 miles to the southeast.*

Doetinchem – Pop 42 060. On the banks of the Oude IJssel, this town, situated in the heart of the Achterhoek *(qv)* formerly belonged to the Zutphen earldom. It was badly damaged by a bombardment in 1945. Today, it is a modern industrial and commercial city with numerous pedestrian precincts. The traditional manufacturing of wooden clogs is still one of the specialities of the city and its vicinity.
Doetinchem has a large **wall mill** (1850) near the Oude IJssel (now the VVV).
6km - 3 1/2 miles to the east of the town stands the large **Kasteel Slangenburg**, surrounded by moats and a beautiful **park**; it belongs to the Benedictine Order.

's-Heerenberg – The imposing **Huis Bergh** ⏲ dominates this locality. Built in the 13C by the Van den Berghs, it was altered in the 17C. In 1946 its last owner bequeathed the castle and its contents to the State. The interior is embellished with antique furniture, paintings and carvings on wood and ivory. Nearby, the Gothic castle chapel, has become the parish church.

DOKKUM Friesland

Michelin map 408 J2 – Local map see LEEUWARDEN

Formerly a flourishing port, this small town in the north of Friesland, is hidden behind the remains of its shaded ramparts, from which emerge a few bell towers and tall mills. Built on a mound, it has several slightly sloping streets.
St Boniface, often called the Apostle of Germany, was executed here in 754 with his 52 companions. An Englishman, born in *c*675 of a Wessex family he came to convert the Frisians in 716 and then met St Willibrord *(qv)* in Utrecht. It was during his second mission to Friesland in 754 that he was put to the sword in Dokkum. He is buried in Fulda, Germany, where he had founded a monastery.

SIGHTS

Zijl – From this wide bridge, there is a fine **view** over Klein Diep (meaning small canal) bordered by a mill and the Groot Diep (large canal). The 18C **Stadhuis** is topped by a white pinnacle. Opposite, three lovely houses with crow-stepped gables dating from the early 17C have been restored.

Follow Diepswal to reach the museum.

Museum Het Admiraliteitshuis ⏲ – This regional museum is in the former Admiralty House (1618 - restored) and in the neighbouring 18C mansion; note the Admiralty House's small Renaissance portal.
The collections are very varied: Dokkum silverwork, a Frisian sledge of carved wood, paintings, ancient commodes, Frisian folk art (19C toys), regional costumes and various exhibits excavated from mounds; note the black Carolingian headdress found in a mound.

Waag – This small weigh house with two decorated pediments, one of which has the town's coat of arms (a cresent moon and three stars) stands on Grote Breedstraat.

Grote- of St.-Martinuskerk ⏲ – In commemoration of St Boniface's murder, a mound and a church were erected here. The present building, a Protestant church, is Gothic: the chancel dates from the 15C. Inside there is a very high gallery added above the aisle.
A great number of tombstones are embedded in the floor; note the Frisian pulpit with elegant carved panels (a lion, a pelican, a falcon).

Bonifatiuskapel – *Leave Dokkum to the south in the direction of Leeuwarden and once beyond the lever bridge take the second road on the left.*
In the middle of the square stands the statue (1962) of the bearded monk, St Boniface, shielding his head with his Bible from his Saxon attackers.
Bonifatiuskapel (1934) in the small park is the centre for a popular annual pilgrimage *(see Calendar of Events).*

DOORN Utrecht — Pop 10 439

Michelin map 408 H5

Situated on the edge of a wooded region, Doorn has a castle on the south side.

Huis Doorn ⏲ – Surrounded by moats, set in the middle of a lovely park, this castle was the home of the ex-Kaiser of Germany **Wilhelm II**, from 1920 to his death in 1941. Forced into exile after he refused to abdicate in November 1918, he was first given refuge in Kasteel Amerongen. Then, in May 1920, he and the Empress Augusta Victoria moved into the castle which he had acquired in Doorn. His wife died the following year. In 1922 he married Hermine, Princess of Reuss.
The original castle was built in the 14C by the Bishop of Utrecht to defend his territory (altered in 1780) and the tower on the southwest side is part of the medieval castle.
Now a **museum**, the castle contains souvenirs of Wilhelm II, who had brought his **collections★** (paintings, tapestries) from the imperial palaces. These are shown in a setting which has remained unchanged since the Kaiser's death.
One room is devoted to Frederick the Great (Frederick II of Prussia, 1712-86), the most famous representative of the Hohenzollern family, who was a great art lover and collected paintings and pastels of the French School (Nicolas Lancret, Watteau's emulator) as well as snuff-boxes.
There is also a fine collection of silver, mainly consisting of presents received by the Hohenzollerns in the 19 and 20C as well as a good collection of uniforms, helmets, boots and ceremonial sabres which belonged to Wilhelm II.
Kaiser Wilhelm's mausoleum stands in the park.

★ DORDRECHT Zuid-Holland — Pop 110 473

Michelin map 408 F6 or 212 folds 5 and 6
Plan of the conurbation in the current Michelin Red Guide Benelux

In the south of the province of Zuid-Holland, Dordrecht, which the Dutch familiarly call Dordt, is an important river centre between the Beneden Merwede, branch of the Rhine, the Noord, which links it to Rotterdam and the Nieuwe Maas, the Dordtse Kil, which links it to the Maas and the Oude Maas. It is also a great pleasure boat harbour and yachts are anchored at most of the town's quaysides, and more to the east, in the Wantij. The old town has kept its colourful quays, its canals and its old façades, while the southern quarters rival with their bolder constructions.
It inspired many painters including Van Goyen (1596-1656); a number of 17 and 18C artists were born here *(see below)*. **Ary Scheffer** (1795-1858), painter of biblical and religious scenes, was Louis-Philippe's court painter.

Boat trips ⏲ – Dordrecht is the departure point for boat trips through the Biesbosch *(qv)*.

HISTORICAL NOTES

According to the chronicles, the town was destroyed by the Vikings in 837.
In 1220 it acquired city rights from the Count of Holland, William I, and because of this, it is considered the oldest town in the earldom. It was fortified at the end of the 13C. The 14C was a period of great prosperity for Dordrecht due to the privilege of applying stop-over tolls, which beginning in 1299, were levied on goods coming from the Rhine. The 15C, on the contrary, was disastrous; there was the unsuccessful siege in 1418 by Count John of Brabant as part of the fight between the Hooks and Cods *(qv)*, the St Elisabeth tidal wave *(qv)* of 1421 which isolated the town making it an island, the big fire of 1457 and then its capture in 1480 by John of Egmont. In the 16C the town recovered its splendour.

The cradle of independence – In the Dordrecht Court of Justice (Het Hof), the first free assembly of the Holland and Zeeland States was held in July 1572, brought about by the capture of Brielle by the Sea Beggars in April of that same year *(qv)*.
In Dordrecht the delegates of the twelve confederate states of Holland and the nobility decided to deliver the country from the Duke of Alba's armies, and proclaimed William the Silent as Stadtholder representing Philip II of Spain. In this way they laid the foundation for the future United Provinces *(qv)*.

Synod of Dort – Dordrecht was also the meeting place in 1618-19 of the great synod of Protestant theologians who came to settle the controversy that had arisen between the moderate **Remonstrants** or Arminians, supporters of Arminius *(qv)* who upheld that the blessings of grace were open to all, and the **Gomarists**, supporters of **Gomarus**, a strict Calvinist who defended the principle of predestination. The latter group won, with the help of Maurice of Orange, and carried out bloody persecutions on their opponents, such as Oldenbarnevelt *(qv)* and Grotius *(qv)*.
At this synod (attended by English representatives and a Scotsman sent by James I as well as Germans and Swiss), the union of all Protestant churches in the country took place, except for the Remonstrants, and a joint doctrine (canons of Dort) was established. The theologian **Episcopius**, who had pleaded the cause of the Remonstrants, then founded a Remonstrant Church in Antwerp (1619).

A 17C painters' breeding-ground – A number of 17C painters were born in Dordrecht. Some of them were Rembrandt's students.
Ferdinand Bol (1616-80) went to live in Amsterdam where he worked in Rembrandt's studio. His works, notably the numerous portraits tinged with seriousness, are very like those of his master, by the chiaroscuro, the abundance of impasting and the harmony between warm colours.
He also did the famous guild painting: *The Governors of the Leper Hospital* (1649), exhibited in the Amsterdams Historisch Museum *(qv)*. One of his students, Sir Godfrey Kneller, became court painter to Charles II and subsequent Stuart kings and queens.
Nicolaes Maes (1634-93) was also influenced by Rembrandt, whose pupil he was from 1648-52, in Amsterdam. More realist than the latter, he chose simple people, modest subjects, scenes which he made somewhat touching and which he enriched by his science of chiaroscuro and reddish tones. The best known of his works is *Girl at a Window: the Daydreamer* in the Rijksmuseum in Amsterdam. At the end of his life, on the contrary, he painted fashionable portraits.
Samuel van Hoogstraten (1627-78) studied with Rembrandt, then after having travelled a great deal in Europe, returned to his birthplace. He mainly painted portraits and interior scenes which, by their effects of light and perspective can be compared to those of Pieter de Hooch *(qv)*. **Godfried Schalcken** (1643-1706) was his pupil.
Aert van Gelder (1645-1727) was first a pupil of Van Hoogstraten, then of the ageing Rembrandt, in Amsterdam. His biblical scenes owe a lot to the technique of the great master, notably the sumptuous clothes and the slightly theatrical composition.
Aelbert Cuyp (1620-91) influenced by Jan van Goyen *(qv)* painted landscapes of very studied composition with luminous backgrounds, immense skies and in the foreground horsemen or peaceful herds of cattle.

The De Witt brothers – Dordrecht is the birthplace of the De Witt brothers, distinguished 17C statesmen.
Johan de Witt (1625-72) became the Grand Pensionary of Holland in 1653. An excellent administrator, he failed in international politics. He was unable to avoid the defeat of the Dutch fleet by England in 1654, the end of the First Dutch War. In addition, hostile to the predominance of the House of Orange, he had to confront popular opposition which supported the family.
After having won the Second Dutch War (1665-7) and withstood the War of Devolution led by Louis XIV (1667-8), Johan de Witt managed to get the **Perpetual Edict** of 1667 voted, which abolished the Stadtholdership and thus the Orangist power in the province of Holland.
However, the same year (1672) that Louis XIV and Charles II united against the United Provinces in the Third Dutch War, the people, feeling threatened, repealed the Perpetual Edict electing William of Orange, Stadtholder (under the name of William III) and army commander. Finally, **Cornelis**, brother of Johan de Witt and burgomaster of Dordrecht in 1666, was wrongly accused of conspiring against William III and was imprisoned in the Prison Gate in The Hague *(qv)*. While visiting him, Johan de Witt was the victim of an uprising and murdered with his brother near the prison.

From the 17C to the present – In the early 17C Dordrecht was supplanted by Amsterdam, then above all by Rotterdam. The town became French in 1795.
Presently it is an expanding city due to its advantageous position which attracts numerous firms.
Industry is very varied: chemical, metallurgical (shipbuilding, aeronautics, electronics) and the building industry. The tertiary sector is highly developed.

★ OLD TOWN *half a day*

★ **Grote- of O.L. Vrouwekerk** (CV B) ⊙ – Legend has it that the church was started by a young girl, St Sura, who, wishing to build a chapel to the Virgin and possessing only three *daalders,* saw, each time she prayed that three new coins were miraculously added to her treasure. In fact a chapel existed in the Middle Ages. It was enlarged in the 13C, then in the 14C, but a fire destroyed the building in 1457. The present church, which is Protestant, was built between 1460-1502 in Brabant Gothic style *(qv)*.
The massive **tower** has remained unfinished because it sags on the north side: it ends in a terrace with four clock faces outlining its square shape. The **carillon** ⊙ (1949) consists of 49 bells.

Interior – It is very large (108m - 354ft long) and imposing with its 56 pillars topped in Brabant Gothic style with crocket capitals. The oak choir **stalls**★ are finely carved by the Fleming Jan Terwen between 1538 and 1542 in the Renaissance style, and are amongst the most beautiful in the country.

Grote Kerk, Dordrecht

The low reliefs on top of the backs of the last row, north side, depict secular triumphs notably those of emperor Charles V; south side, religious triumphs. There are also lovely cheek-pieces and misericords carved with fantastic subjects.
The baroque chancel screen (1744) is elegant. In a chapel of the ambulatory on the east side, three stained glass windows depict episodes in the town's history: flood of 1421, fire of 1457 and capture of the town in 1480.
The pulpit (1756) with a marble base is in the rococo style. The **organ** ⊙ was built in 1671 by Nicolaas van Hagen of Antwerp. 17 and 18C stone slabs pave the church floor.

Access to the tower ⊙ – 279 steps. On the way up there is a view of a 1626 clock.
From the top terrace, there is a superb **view★★** over the old town where the houses huddle together along the canals and docks; note the length of the roofs: on the banks of the canals space was so costly that one preferred to build houses in depth. One can also see the rivers which circle round the town, spanned by large bridges, and modern Dordrecht.
To the right of the tower, the Leuvebrug over the Voorstraathaven has four **low reliefs** sculptured in stone in 1937 by **Hildo Krop** (1884-1970); in naive style they depict a prisoner, a baker, a dairywoman and an apothecary-surgeon.

Blauwpoort or Catharijnepoort (CV) – Near this very simple gateway, dating from 1652, there are warehouses and a beautiful patrician house with a perron, the 18C **Beverschaep** (CV E): its door is topped by a naiad and a triton embracing; on the pediment a sheep *(schaap)* and a beaver *(bever)* frame the coat of arms.

Nieuwehaven (CV) – Pleasure boats find shelter in this dock with shaded quays.

★ **Museum Mr. Simon van Gijn** (CV M[1]) ⊙ – This lovely residence (1729) was bequeathed to the town, with its contents, by the banker Simon van Gijn (1836-1922), a great art collector. Inside one can admire an elegant decor, lovely fireplaces, rich furnishings, tapestries, paintings, silver, glass and porcelain show cases. In the music room, on the ground floor, an **organ** (1785) has been restored. The kitchen (*c*1800) is at the end of the corridor on the left: it features copper utensils and a fine fireplace adorned with glazed earthenware tiling.
On the 2nd floor, are scale models of ships (note the Bleiswijk, belonging to the Dutch India Company), and toys, including dolls' shops and houses.

From the north bank of Nieuwehaven, there is a fine **view** over the dock overlooked by the Great Church with its clerestory, its transept and its massive tower. The view is also lovely over the Kuipershaven lined with warehouses.

Kuipershaven (CDV) – Numerous barges are crammed into this old quay of coopers formerly devoted to the wine trade.
At nos 41-42, a barrel is shown on the grill forming a transom window above the door. In the transom window of no 48 a basket is depicted.

Groothoofdspoort (DV) – It was the main gate (1618) to the town. Topped by a dome it is covered on both sides with ornaments and low reliefs in sandstone. From the quay, situated on the north side, there is a fine **view★** over the wide confluence of the Merwede, the Noord and the Oude Maas Rivers. Boat traffic increases as dusk falls.
On the other side of the gate near the lever bridge, the **Wijnhaven** (wine port) a dock for pleasure boats, and the chapel pinnacle make a colourful picture.

Wijnstraat (CDV) – Another evocation of the wine *(wijn)* trade, this unevenly paved street is lined with picturesque houses, all lop-sided. Some are Renaissance, still with crow-stepped gables (nos 73-75; with the emblem of a cock: no 85), others in Louis XIV style (no 87).

Cross the canal.

Around this central canal are the city's oldest residences.

Voorstraat (CDV) – Very commercial, this is the town's main street. There are some interesting façades: at no 178 the façade has a lovely rococo decor; at no 188 is **Muntpoort** (DV) of 1955.

DORDRECHT

Bagijnhof .... DV 6
Groenmarkt .... CV 16
Grote Spuistr. .... CV 21
Spuiweg CX
Visstr. .... CV 57
Voorstr. .... CDV
Vriesestr. .... DV

Achterhakkers .... CX 3
Aert de Gelderstr. .... CX 4
Blauwpoortspl. .... CV 7
Bleijenhoek .... DV 9
Dubbeldamse .... DX 13
Groothoofd .... DV 18
Grote Kerksbuurt .... CV 19
Hoogstratensingel ..... DVX 22
Johan de Wittstr. .... DX 25
Museumsstr. .... DV 54

Oranjelaan .... DX 36
Papeterspad .... CX 39
Prinsenstr. .... CV 42
Riedijk .... DV 46
Schefferspl. .... CDV 48
Stationsweg .... DX 51
Steegoversloot .... DV 52
Twintighuizen .... CX 55
Wilgenbos .... CX 60
Wolwevershaven .... CV 61

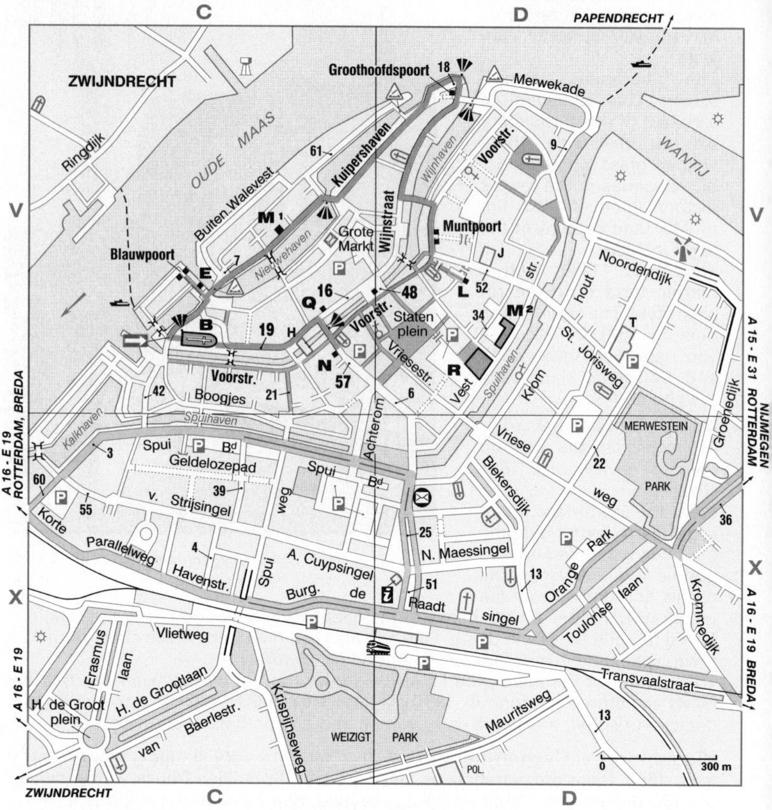

At the beginning of the pedestrian precinct, on the left, near the Augustijnenkerk, at no 214 a porch gives on to **Het Hof** (DV **L**), the former Court of Justice where the States General met in 1572.

Opposite the Het Hof, at the corner of an alley leading to a bridge, there is a fine Renaissance façade with two-coloured tympana decorated with sculptured heads.

Scheffersplein (CDV **48**) – This is the market place; in the middle there is a 19C statue of the painter Ary Scheffer *(qv)*.

Visstraat (CV **57**) – This street which means Fish Street, leads to Dordrecht's very modern commercial quarter. At no 7 there is a lovely small Renaissance house, **De Crimpert Salm** (CV **N**) (1608). Very elaborate, it has a façade stone depicting a salmon *(zalm)* and is topped by a lion. As is usual in Dordrecht, the windows are framed with mouldings coming down to corbels.

Cross the bridge towards Groenmarkt.

Views over the canal, which is narrow here, and the old town hall, a white neo-classical building. On the bridge there is a monument (1922) to the De Witt brothers.

Groenmarkt (CV **16**) – Former vegetable market. On the right, at no 39, the **De Sleutel** house (CV **Q**) has a façade decorated with a key *(sleutel)* and tympana with recessed orders. Dating from 1540, it is the oldest in the town.

At no 53, there is a fine façade with ogee-shaped tympana.

Grote Kerksbuurt (CV **19**) – The house at no 56 has a charming façade.

ADDITIONAL SIGHTS

Dordrechts Museum (DV **M**[2]) ⊙ – This museum contains an interesting collection of paintings. Many were the work of 17C artists born in the town, namely Aelbert Cuyp, Nicolaes Maes and Samuel van Hoogstraten. Dutch Romanticism is present, as well as pictures illustrating The Hague School and the Amsterdam School. In the section on 18 and 19C art, special attention should be given to the biblical scenes and portraits of **Ary Scheffer** *(qv)*: *Self-portrait at the Age of 43* (1883) and especially *Frédéric Chopin,* a remarkable portrayal of the great composer (1847). Scheffer's illustrations for *Histoire de la Révolution française,* a book written by the French politician Adolphe Thiers (1797-1877), are also on display.

Arend Maartenshof (DV **R**) – This old almshouse (1625) has kept its original character with small low houses surrounding a courtyard.

EDAM North Holland — Pop 24 839 (with Volendam)

Michelin map 408 G4

An important cheese centre, Edam is a small, quiet and charming town, crossed by canals still lined with a few fine 17C houses.
It is overlooked by **Speeltoren**, a tall tower with a carillon, the remains of a church demolished in the 19C.
In fact, it was formerly a busy port of the Zuiderzee, known for its shipyards.

Edam chesse – Originally made in Edam, it is now made in several regions. Prepared with slightly skimmed milk, it is similar to Gouda *(qv)* with its smooth texture, but it differs by its easily identifiable shape: a ball with a yellow crust, covered with a thin red coating if it is for export.

SIGHTS

Dam – In the centre of town, and crossed by Voorhaven Canal, this, the main square, is overlooked by the 18C **stadhuis**, topped by a pinnacle.
A lovely house (*c*1530) contains the small local, **Edams Museum** ⏲.

Kaasmarkt – On this square stands the **Kaaswaag** ⏲ where the famous Edam cheese was weighed. The building is decorated with painted panels and now appropriately houses an **exhibition** on cheese making.

Grote- of St-Nicolaaskerk ⏲ – Dating from the 15C, the church has lovely early 17C stained glass windows and a fine organ.

EINDHOVEN Noord-Brabant — Pop 192 895

Michelin map 408 H7 or 212 fold 18
Plan of the conurbation and town plan in the current Michelin Red Guide Benelux

A very important industrial centre, and in constant development, Eindhoven had hardly 5 000 inhabitants in 1900.
Since then the town and its suburbs have developed into an important industrial centre: there are now tobacco factories (cigars), paper making and textile industries, the largest factory for dairy products in the country, the large DAF Trucks automobile factories and electrical industries.

The "city of light" – It is mainly to the Philips Company that the town owes its spectacular expansion. Founded in 1891, this family firm's main activity was the manufacture of electric lights bulbs; it then employed 26 workers. Today, in Eindhoven alone, it employs more than 20 000 people, approximately 13% of the company's workforce throughout the world.
It has considerably diversified its international activities: apart from electric bulbs, it manufactures audio-visual equipment, medical apparatus, small domestic appliances, spare parts for the electronics industry, etc.
On the edge of the town, **Evoluon**, a huge building (1966) supported by 12 V-shaped concrete pillars, resembles a large flying saucer. It was designed for Philips by the two architects, Kalff and De Bever.
Eindhoven also has a well-known engineering school, the Technische Universiteit.

A modern city – Although industrial and laid out to a modern urban plan, Eindhoven is a pleasant city. Bustling commercial activity prevails, notably in the pedestrian precincts such as Demer. The city is well provided with recreational activities, parks and green spaces, like the **De IJzeren Man**, to the east, and has a municipal theatre (built in 1964).
The surrounding wooded areas of Kempenland *(qv)* offer numerous walks.
The Eindhoven carnival is always a lively and popular event *(see Calendar of Events)*.

Stedelijk van Abbemuseum

Horse and Flautist (1951) by Karel Appel, Collectie Stedelijk van Abbemuseum, Eindhoven

★ STEDELIJK VAN ABBEMUSEUM (VAN ABBE MUSEUM) ⊙

1 hour 30min

Separated from the town hall by the Dommel, which runs through its lovely gardens, this building was bequeathed to the town in 1936 by the industrialist H.J. van Abbe. Enlarged in 1978 the museum exhibits, in rotation, a rich collection of paintings and sculpture from 1900 to the present, concentrating especially on contemporary, as from 1945. The museum also has temporary exhibitions of contemporary art.

The permanent collection, which is never all on show at once, consists of the whole evolution of modern art through: the Cubism of Picasso, Braque, Juan Gris; Orphism or poetic interpretation of the real with Delaunay, Chagall, Fernand Léger; the De Stijl movement *(qv)* with Mondrian, Van Doesburg; Constructivism with a great number of works by El Lissitzky, Expressionism of Kokoschka, Kandinsky, Permeke; Surrealism with Miró, Ernst, Pieter Ouborg, Francis Bacon.

After the war the young Paris School was marked by abstract painters such as Bazaine, Sam Francis (born in California), Poliakoff. The CoBrA movement *(qv)* is represented by Karel Appel, Asger Jorn, Corneille. Apart from subject-matter painters such as Dubuffet, Tàpies, there are also works by Vasarely, Lucio Fontana, Klein, the Zero group (Mack, Piene and Uecker), the Americans of Pop Art including Morris Louis, Robert Indiana, Frank Stella.

Conceptual Art (Kosuth, Barry, Brouwn, Kawara), Minimal Art (Judd, Andre, Sol LeWitt) and contemporary German sculpture (Kiefer, Baselitz, Penck) are also represented.

ADDITIONAL SIGHTS

Stadhuis – Not far from the old stadhuis, rebuilt in 1865 in the neo-Gothic style, this modern building, designed by the architect J. van de Laan, dates from 1965-9.

On the square stands a **monument** in memory of the Liberation carved by the Dutchman Paul Grégoire in 1954. It depicts three men leaping towards the sky in pursuit of a dove.

Animali ⊙ – *Roostenlaan 303.*

This flower garden has, apart from numerous swans and pink flamingos, a large collection of rare birds, as well as packs of monkeys.

Museum Kempenland ⊙ – *St-Antoniusstraat 5-7.*

Installed in the old church of St Anthony of Padua, this museum evokes the history and customs of the town and its hinterland, Kempenland *(qv)*. The collections concern archaeology, beliefs, textile industry, handicrafts: note the clocks made in Eindhoven *c*1800.

Temporary exhibitions concerning history and art are organised.

EXCURSION

★ **Helmond, Asten and De Groote Peel** – *38km – 23 1/2 miles. Leave to the northeast by Eisenhowerlaan.*

Helmond – Pop 69 967. Helmond is an active textile manuacturing centre and a busy commercial centre, especially in the pedestrian precincts near the main square, Markt.

Standing in its own parkland the medieval **Kasteel★** ⊙ is an imposing quadrilateral building with an inner courtyard, corner towers and an encircling moat. The building is home to the municipal museum.

Asten – Pop 15 307. To the northwest, a modern building houses two museums.

The National Carillon Museum, **Nationaal Beiaardmuseum** ⊙, has information on bell making, a collection of small bells from all over the world, a series of weight-driven clocks and striking clocks, and a large drum carillon with visible mechanism.

The Nature Museum, **Natuurstudiecentrum en Museum Jan Vriends** ⊙, houses a series of stuffed animals, butterflies, insects, a reproduction of the land and fauna of De Peel marshes and an aquarium with species found in the Peel lakes.

To the southeast of Asten stretches a large marshy zone called **De Peel** (*peel* means marsh). The lakes mark the site of former peat bogs.

★ **De Groote Peel** – *Access to the south by Moostdijk, near Meijelse Dijk.* It is a **national park** ⊙ of about 1 300 ha - 3 211 acres consisting of peat bogs, moors and large stretches of water. This environment which is water-logged and not very fertile attracts numerous birds. Hundreds of **black-headed gulls** *(kokmeeuwen)* come to breed here from mid-March to mid-July. This gull is about 40cm - 16in long and is white but in summer, its head becomes completely black. It can be found on the coasts in winter, but it often comes to nest inland, notably near the lakes. In early spring, black-headed gulls come in thousands to make very neat nests between the clumps of reeds which cover the submerged roots. Males and females share the task of sitting on the eggs and jealously defending their nest. They make an unceasing noise with their strident and not very harmonious call.

A small museum, **Bezoekerscentrum Mijl op Zeven** ⊙, installed in a typical farmhouse in the Peel has documention on the nature reserve, which became a national park in 1985, and the local flora and fauna.

Three signposted nature trails make it possible to discover this strange universe stirred by the shrill cries of the gulls.

EMMEN Drenthe — Pop 92 895

Michelin map 408 L3 – Local map see HUNEBEDDEN

A prosperous market centre, Emmen is a pleasant town bordered to the north and the east by fine forests.
The southern end of the Hondsrug *(qv)* has numerous *hunebeds (qv)*, prehistoric funerary monuments.

SIGHTS

★ **Hunebed of Emmerdennen** (D 45) – *Access by Boslaan, direction Emmer Compascuum. It is situated near a large crossroads and is well sign-posted.*
This remarkable *hunebed,* an alleyway covered with six enormous slabs encircled by uprights, was erected on a mound right in the middle of the forest. Its overall beauty attracts painters.

Hunebeds along the Odoorn road – There is a succession of megaliths as one drives northwards. *After the last farm bear left on a path signposted "hunebed".* Between the trees there is a **hunebed★** (D 43); the shape of the burial mound has been reconstructed and two covered alleyways are hidden.
The whole is surrounded by uprights between which are piles of rocks which hold up the earth.
A few hundred yards further to the north, on the left side of the road, there is a small *hunebed* (D 4) covered with capstones.
On leaving Emmen, on the right, a lane marked *hunebedden* goes through the forest to a large clearing of heather. Three *hunebeds* (D 38/40) stand in this lovely setting: one is half buried, the second, also buried, was given the shape of a square, while the third is covered with fallen stones.

★ **Noorder Dierenpark (Zoo)** ⏲ – This zoo is interesting for the abundance and variety of the species shown. Several exhibit areas are particularly interesting. In a enormous aviary there are birds from South American tropical forests. A tropical garden houses more than a thousand butterflies. The seal pool and the "Africanium", which incorporates a series of greenhouses, a natural history museum, and an ethnographical museum, are other attractions. Finally, on a vast strip of land (1.5ha - 4 acres) giraffes, zebras, antilopes, rhinoceroses, cranes, and impalas all live together.

EXCURSIONS

Noorsleen, Schoonoord and Orvelte★ – *40km – 25 miles to the west – local map see Hunebedden.*

Noordsleen – This charming village of the Drenthe, with a restored mill, has two **hunebeds.**
Access by the small road from Zweeloo and a lane on the right marked hunebedden (**D 51**).
On the left, is a small covered alleyway still topped by three capstones (four have disappeared). Further on the right, the **hunebed★ (D 50)** shaded by a large oak which grows in its centre, is better preserved. Five slabs are still in place as well as the oval crown of upright stones. The entry pillars to the south, which have been leveled, are still visible.

Schoonoord – 3.5km – 2 1/4 miles to the south of the locality, in the woods near a riding centre, a *hunebed* (**D 49**) has been partially reconstructed. Between the uprights there are pebbles. Above, the heather-covered ground forms a mound and hides the large slabs which form the *hunebed's* roof. This *hunebed* is called **De Papeloze Kerk** (church without a priest); congregations met here at the beginning of the Reformation.

G. Morand/CEDRI

Museum village, Orvelte

★ **Orvelte** – This museum-village situated in the heart of the Drenthe consists of a group of farmhouses, barns with thatched roofs, which, due to restoration, have kept their regional character. *No cars allowed.*
With traditional agricultural activities (cattle and sheep breeding, growing of maize), handicraft work has developed: blacksmiths, potters...

Coevorden – Pop 14 369. *21km – 13 miles to the southwest.* An old fortified town, Coevorden has kept several interesting monuments.
The **kasteel** is a fine building flanked by a corner turret, with walls of rose-coloured roughcast and pierced in the left part of the façade (15C) by tall narrow windows. Part of it is occupied by the town hall; in the basement there is a restaurant. Near Markt *(Friesestraat no 9)*, there is a picturesque late Renaissance **house** with voluted gables and ornamentation: bright red shells, heads of women, cherubs, Moors, and inscriptions.
On Markt, facing the docks are the three 17C roofs of the Arsenal (restored), which contains the **Museum "Drenthe's Veste"** ⊙.
To the east, beyond Weyerswold *(6km - 3 1/2 miles)* typical thatched cottages of the Drenthe stand beside innumerable small oil wells. In this respect the **Schoonebeek** region is in fact very rich.

★ ENKHUIZEN Noord-Holland — Pop 16 039

Michelin map 408 G3

Enkhuizen was the main Frisian settlement and seat of their chiefs until 1289 when West Friesland passed to the counts of Holland. The town had one of the largest herring fishing fleets which brought great prosperity; three herrings figure on the town's coat of arms. The port continued to flourish until it silted up in the 18C. Then the building of the Barrier Dam in 1932 put an end to its maritime activities. Enkhuizen was fortified in the mid-16C and it was one of the first towns to revolt against the Spanish in 1672. Around 1600 the city walls were rebuilt. When its maritime activities ceased in the 20C the town then looked to its rich agricultural hinterland for a living and today it is an important market town and centre for bulb growing. The walls are now a pleasant promenade. Enkhuizen is linked to Lelystad, the main town of Flevoland, by the dike road *(31km - 19 miles)*. This was originally to have enclosed the fifth and last polder around the edge of the IJsselmeer *(see local map under IJsselmeer)* but the Markerwaard project was abandoned in 1986. Enkhuizen was the birthplace of **Paulus Potter** (1625-54), the famous animal painter, whose best known painting, *The Bull Calf,* hangs in the Mauritshuis in The Hague.

Boat trips ⊙– *The boats leave from Spoorhaven.* Ferries leave for other ports around IJsselmeer, Stavoren *(qv)* in Friesland, Urk *(qv)* in the Noordoost polder and Medemblik *(qv)*, from where a tourist train runs down to Hoorn.

ENKHUIZEN

Street	Ref	Street	Ref	Street	Ref
Westerstraat	AB	Karnemelksluis	B 9	Staeleversgracht	B 22
Bocht	B 3	Klopperstraat	A 10	Sijbrandspl.	B 24
Driebanen	B 4	Melkmarkt	B 12	Venedie	B 25
Hoornseveer	A 6	Nieuwstraat	B 13	Waagstraat	B 27
Kaasmarkt	B 7	noorder Havendijk	B 15	Wegjes	B 28
		Oosterhavenstr.	B 16	Zuider Boerenvaart	A 30
		Piet Smitstraat	A 18	Zuider Havendijk	B 31
		St. Janstraat	B 19	Zuiderspui	B 33
		Spijtbroeksburgwal	A 21	Zwaanstraat	B 34

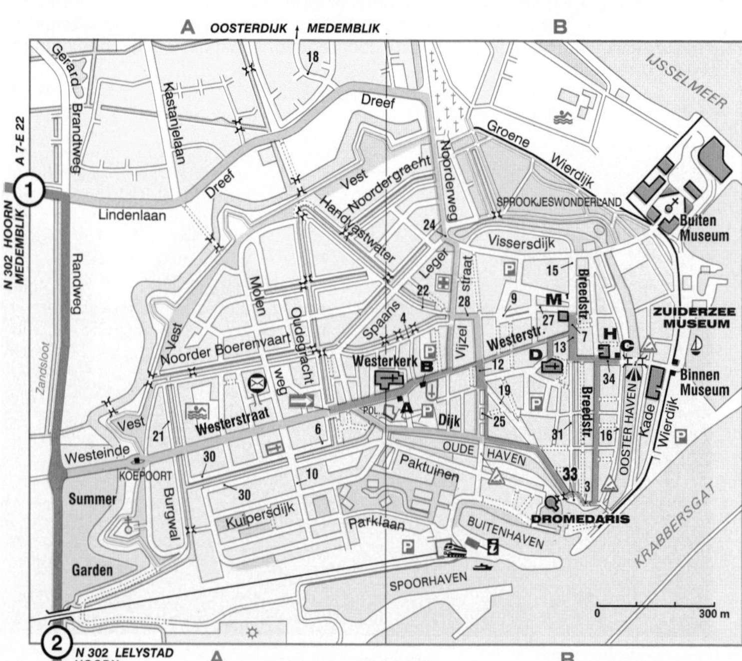

★ OLD TOWN *5 hours*

It has kept numerous 17C façades in Renaissance style, their fine decoration bearing witness to its former prosperity.

Westerstraat (AB) – It is the town's main street. There are lovely façades, notably that of no 158 to the north, dating from 1617 with the town emblem on a gable: a young girl bearing a coat of arms depicting three herrings.

Westerkerk of St.-Gomaruskerk (AB) ⊙ – It is a 15 and 16C building. Its free-standing wooden tower built in the 16C on a stone base was rebuilt in the 19C in the neo-classical style. The hall-interior has three naves of equal height, covered with a wooden vault. There is also a fine wooden **rood-screen**★ with six richly carved panels (16C), tympana, pulpit (both 16C), a replica of the one found in the Grote Kerk in The Hague, and a 1547 organ case. Opposite the church is the former Mint of West Friesland, **West-Friese Munt** (B **A**) with a lovely, finely decorated 15C façade. Further on at no 109 the façade of the Orphanage, **Weeshuis** (B **B**) has been rebuilt after the original façade (1616).

Turn right to take Melkmarkt and Venedie.

Dijk (B) – This quay runs alongside the old port (Oude Haven). At no 32, a house (1625) displays the motto: "Contentement passe rychesse" (happiness is worth more than riches).

★ **Dromedaris** (B) ⊙ – This imposing and well-known building (now a restaurant) which was part of the town's enclosure was, like that of Hoorn *(qv)*, intended for keeping watch over the entrance to the port. It consists of a circular tower with an usually shaped extension. Note the decoration above the doorway. It has a carillon cast by Hemony, which is one of the best in the country.
From the top there is a vast **panorama**★ of Enkhuizen, its port, IJsselmeer and in the distance Friesland.
From the quay to the south of the tower, there is a fine **view**★ to the east over the docks (Zuiderspui) and the backs of houses with picturesque wooden galleries overlooking flowered gardens.
To the south is Buitenhaven, the pleasure boat harbour.

Zuiderspui (B **33**) – This short street is lined with interesting façades: no 1 has five polychrome coats of arms, from left to right can be seen those of Hoorn (a horn), the House of Orange, West Friesland (two lions), Enkhuizen and Medemblik.

Breedstraat (B) – Several houses have interesting façade stones notably: no 81, called Den Kuiser Maegt (the young girl from Enkhuizen), depicting the town's coat of arms, no 60 an old boat and no 59 a young girl also holding the town's coat of arms.

Stadhuis (B **H**) – It is an imposing building dating from the end of the 17C. Above the door there is an excerpt from a poem by Joost van den Vondel *(qv)*.
The interior is decorated with paintings, painted ceilings, tapestries and murals.

On the corner of Zwaanstraat stands the old prison, **gevangenis** (B **C**) a small building, whose picturesque façade dates from 1612.

★ **Zuiderzeemuseum (Zuiderzee Museum)** (B) ⊙ – It is made up of two museums. One is the indoor museum; it is located on Wierdijk (*wier* = seaweed) and faces IJsselmeer.
It occupies several houses and warehouses formerly belonging to the Dutch East India company. The other one is the open-air museum.

★ **Indoor Museum** (Binnenmuseum) – On the corner, the house with a double crow-stepped gable has kept its sculptured stone façade in the shape of a ship and the motto: Spend first to gain later *(De kost gaet voor de baet uyt)*.
The museum hosts four standing exhibitions. In the **main hall** (Schepenhal) there are many old **ships**, mostly sailing boats which used to cruise along the Zuiderzee; note the *botter*, fishing dories with a flat bottom, and the *ijsvlet* from Urk, which slid along the ice. Further along, a display of maps, paintings, tools and various objects evoke the whaling industry (Walvisvaart), highly active in the region from the 17 to the 19C. **Fishing** (Visserij) too played an important role during the last five centuries; from 1550 to 1850 Enkhuizen was the home base for the Dutch fishermen who left for the Zuiderzee and the North Sea in search of herring. The fourth exhibition is devoted to man's long-standing **struggle against water**.

★★ **Open-air Museum** (Buitenmuseum) – *Access by the ferry leaving the car park near the entrance to the dike linking Enkhuizen to Lelystad, or by the entrance facing the Indoor Museum.* This open-air museum is reminiscent of daily life in the old Zuiderzee fishing ports between 1880 and 1932, completion date of the Barrier Dam (Afsluitdijk) *(qv)*. More than 130 shops, houses and workshops from around thirty localities have been reconstructed to make up the charming districts of this village-museum. Although one may find, concentrated in the same quarter, houses coming from different towns or villages, the plans of each district are based on reality and each structure is made to scale. Everything in the museum conspires to evoke life in bygone days: the furniture, the tools, the layout of the gardens, the church from old Wierengen Island and the reconstruction of Marken port in 1830, with the smell of tannin floating in the air. Visitors may buy old-fashioned candy, go for a ride on an old boat, or see the sailmaker and the fish curer at work. Children can have the pleasure of sporting a traditional costume during their visit.

Stedelijk Waagmuseum (B **M**[1]) ⊙ – On Kaasmarkt, or cheese market, this fine building (1559) with curved gables, painted shutters and polychrome coats of arms, is the old weigh house where cheese and butter trading took place. It is now the municipal museum.

Zuiderzeemuseum, Enkhuizen

Zuiderzee Museum, Enkhuizen

There is a dental surgery of 1920 *(in the basement)* and an 18C delivery room. A spiral staircase leads to the **surgeons room** installed in 1636; the members of this guild used this fine room for their meetings. Note the painted panelling, the rostrum and the small room where the students waited before taking their exams. The attic is used for temporary art exhibitions.

Return to Westerstraat.

In the eastern section of the street there are also lovely gables, shop signs and façade stones (a cooking-pot, a bull's head, etc.).

Zuider of St.-Pancraskerk (B **D**) ⏲ – It is flanked by a fine Gothic tower, the wooden cap of which was added in the 16C. Its carillon was cast by the Hemony brothers.

ADDITIONAL SIGHT

Summer Garden (A) ⏲ – Near the old ramparts, this lovely garden with attractive flowerbeds reminds one that the region is one of the country's main flower growing areas.

DUTCH FURNISHINGS

Dutch furnishings can be admired throughout the country. Listed below is a selection of museums with good furniture collections:

Assen - Drents Museum: Ontvangershuis
Enkhuizen - Zuiderzeemuseum
Hindeloopen - Museum Hidde Nijland Stichting
Leeuwarden - Fries Museum
Middelburg - Zeeuws Museum
Rotterdam - Historisch Museum Het Schielandshuis
Utrecht - Centraal Museum
Zwolle - Provinciaal Overijssels Museum

Michelin map 408

Enschede, situated in Twente, a verdant area, is the largest town in Overijssel province. An important industrial centre, it specialises mainly in textiles.

Its rapid expansion due to the development of industry only started at the beginning of the century. Severely damaged by fire in 1862 and bombarded in 1944, it is, today, a modern city. The vast campus of **Twente Technical University** (Universiteit Twente), established in 1964, lies to the northwest of the town.

Twente and the textile industry – Rich in running water which made it possible to wash the fibres and work the looms, Twente, formerly specialised in the processing of linen, which they cultivated, retted, spun and wove on the spot. **Almelo** was the centre of this activity. Twente linen was exported to Norway and to Russia where the Vriezenfveen *(7km - 4 miles to the north of Almelo)* merchants had founded a colony near St Petersburg.

In the 18C, linen was replaced by cotton, less costly; at the same time they produced in large quantities a twill of linen and cotton called bombasine *(bombazijn)*.

In the early 19C weaving and spinning production were industrialised with the development of looms driven by steam-power.

The metallurgical industry also developed greatly at this time; in 1960, together with the textile industry, it represented 86% of industrial activity. Since then, the expansion in the production of artificial fibres, foreign competition and economic recession have caused the decline of the textile industry.

Presently, alongside heavy metallurgy and that of processing, the building industry and the tertiary sector are developing.

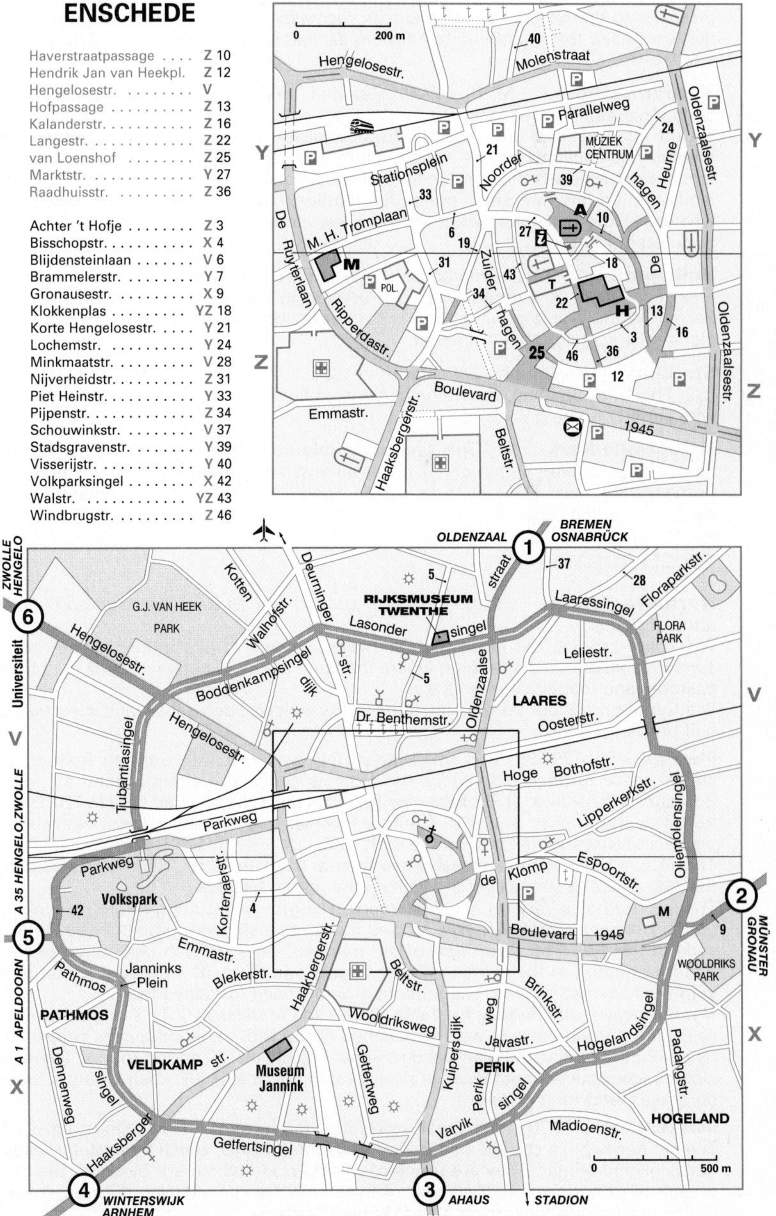

★ RIJKSMUSEUM TWENTHE (TWENTE MUSEUM) (V) ⊙ *1 hour*

The building erected in 1930 after plans by Muller and Beudt was radically converted during the eighties. The museum boasts an impressive collection of works representing ancient art, the decorative arts, as well as modern and contemporary art.
The section on ancient art is largely devoted to painting – in particular works dating back to the late Middle Ages – portraits (Van Cleve, Cranach, Holbein the Younger), 16 and 17C landscapes (Bruegel the Younger, Van Goyen, Ruysdael), still lifes, Romanticism, and the Schools of Barbizon and The Hague.
The museum also displays medieval manuscripts, incunabula, sculptures, tapestries, furniture, silver and gold plate and Delftware tiles.
The collection on modern art covers Expressionism, the CoBrA group and the new Figurative movement: most of the artists here are Dutch. Contemporary painters from the Netherlands include Armando, Sjoerd Buisman, Marlene Dumas, Cornelis Rogge and Henk Visch.
The Twente Museum also stages temporary exhibitions on ancient, modern and contemporary art.

ADDITIONAL SIGHTS

Museum Jannink (X) ⊙ – Located in an old textile mill – opened in 1900 and closed in the 1960s – the museum's collections illustrate the evolution of the textile industry encountered in the Twente *(qv)* over the past 150 years.
Workers' interiors, which have been recreated, show the results of this evolution on living conditions (cottage industry and rural life; then the move to the city to be closer to the factory with all it entails, increased comfort...). Also displayed are the tools used through the different periods: spinning wheels, winding machines and looms.

Natuurmuseum (YZ **M**) ⊙ – Well presented, this natural history museum contains remarkable collections.
On the ground floor are minerals, fossils, mostly discovered in the region; the invertebrate section features insects, shells and coral. The 1st floor is devoted to fauna: **dioramas** show the main species of mammals and birds found in the Netherlands, aquariums and small ponds for reptiles; one room has an exhibition on whales. In the basement there are precious stones as well as radio-active and fluorescent minerals.

Volkspark (X) – To the southeast of this park, one of the many green areas of Enschede, there is a monument (Z **D**) erected to the memory of victims of the Second World War: a group of bronze statues (a hostage, people in the Resistance, etc) by the sculptor **Mari Andriessen**.

Stadhuis (Z **H**) – Built by G. Friedhoff in 1933, it is inspired by Stockholm's town hall. This brick building, somewhat austere, is flanked by a high square bell tower with slightly bulging walls.

Hervormde Kerk (Y **A**) – This sandstone Reformed Church stands on Markt, the town's main square. Begun *c*1200, it was enlarged in the 15C but has kept its great Romanesque **tower** (13C), with its paired openings. The spire was added in the beginning of the century.

EXCURSION

Northern Twente – *80km – 50 miles. Leave by ④ on the town plan and allow about 5 hours.*
The route crosses the north part of **Twente**. Known for its industrial activities, Twente is also a verdant region where the land, cut by waterways, is divided into pastures and magnificent forests.
Scattered throughout the area are large farms with wooden gables and sometimes half-timbered walls.

Oldenzaal – Pop. 29 835. This small industrial town, near the German frontier, is an old, once fortified city, which has kept its concentric streets round a lovely Romanesque basilica, **St-Plechelmusbasiliek** ⊙. A sanctuary existed here in 770. Dedicated to the English and Irish saint, St Plecheln the present edifice, with three naves and transept, dates from the early 12C.
The square bell tower, its massive aspect characteristic of the region, was built in the 13C. Since 1950 the church has held the title of basilica.
The interior has a very robust appearance. The groined vaulting of the nave rests on thick square pillars. The chancel and the south aisle were rebuilt in the Gothic style in the 15C. The south arm of the transept has a triptych (Adoration of the Magi) attributed to the Fleming, Pieter Coecke van Aelst. The baroque pulpit has vigorously carved figures. The modern organ is used for concerts.
Not far away is the **Museum Het Palthe Huis** ⊙ *(on Marktstraat)*. This house with its charming baroque façade was bequeathed to the Oldenzaal antiquities collection by the Palthe family and displays traditional objects in 17C period rooms. There is also a reconstructed apothecary's shop, and in the attic a 17C chair where a murderer was held for 110 days.

Denekamp – Pop 12 307. This small town, situated in one of the loveliest parts of Twente has kept its strange tradition of *midwinterhorens,* which translated means horns of mid-winter. They are horns of carved wood which are blown at the approach of Christmas *(see Calender of Events)* in Twente villages; their origin remains mysterious. Near town stands **Kasteel Singraven** ⊙.

A lovely road runs alongside the Dinkel, a small shaded and calm waterway where there is the lovely 15C watermill, **Watermolen van Singraven** ⊙; grain is still ground here and wood is sawn; the building on the left houses a restaurant. The 17C **mansion** flanked by a square tower is reflected in the Dinkel, one of whose branches waters the magnificent park. The furniture, tapestries (Beauvais, Aubusson), porcelain collections, paintings (Salomon van Ruysdael, Van de Capelle) all add to the refined atmosphere of the 18C interior.

★ **Ootmarsum** – Pop 4 305. Built on a mound, round a Gothic church, this charming village with concentric streets has been restored; lovely, elaborately decorated Renaissance façades and wooden gables can be admired.
On Kerkplein stands **kerk van de HH. Simon en Judas** ⊙. This church is in the Romanesque-Gothic transitional style, which is reminiscent of Westphalian churches by the use of stone and by its thick square tower to the west (partly demolished). The apse is Gothic as well as the fourth bay. Inside, the polychrome colours highlight the lines of the pointed arches, the small columns and ribs. At the end of the north side aisle, there is a lovely statue in wood of the Virgin (*c*1500); in the aisles the modern stained glass windows depict saints; in the chancel there is a silver lamp. The organ in Westphalian style, has been restored *(concerts)*. In the display cabinets are gold and silver liturgical plate and a lovely chasuble (1749) embroidered with the effigy of the church patrons. On the south side aisle a tomb is used as a columbarium.

Take to road to Almelo.

Kuiperberg – From the belvedere on top of the Kuiperberg (alt 65m - 213ft) there is a **view** over Ootmarsum and the wooded countryside. Next to it stands an old Jewish cemetery.

Via Almelo and Borne, go to Delden.

Delden – Delden is an important agricultural market centre. Former residence of the Counts of Wassenaar, **Kasteel Twickel** ⊙ stands to the north of town. Founded in the 14C, it was altered in the 16C (main door) and the 17C. it is surrounded by moats and lovely **gardens**.
Grote- of St-Blasiuskerk, a Gothic style stone hall-church, has a heavy square tower in front.
The old town hall *(Langestraat 21)* houses both the VVV and a salt museum, **Het Zoutmuseum** ⊙. Located not far from the country's main rock salt deposits, the museum explains salt's origin, extraction and use, as well as its importance to men, animals and plants.

Hengelo – Pop 76 371. Town plan in the current Michelin Red Guide Benelux. This commercial and industrial town (metallurgy, electricity, electronics, chemicals) has modern buildings, in particular the **stadhuis**, the work of Berghoef (1963). Since 1972, to the east of town, a new experimental residential quarter is being built by the architect Piet Blom.

Return to Enschede by ③ on the town plan.

★ FLEVOLAND Flevoland

Michelin map 408 G4, 5, H4, 5, I4 – Local map see IJSSELMEER

Flevoland is in fact two polders which form the most recent achievements in the Zuiderzee reclamation project *(see under IJsselmeer)*; that of Oostelijk Flevoland and Zuidelijk Flevoland.

Oostelijk Flevoland – It is the third polder created on IJsselmeer, after Wieringermeer Polder *(qv)* and the Noordoost polder *(qv)*. An area of 54 000ha - 133 380 acres, it was diked and drained between 1950-7. The main part of this polder is destined for agriculture (75% of the area) while 10% of the land has been turned into meadows and woods, 8% for dwellings and the rest alloted to canals, roads and dikes. Before being exploited, the land was first sown with reeds. Farmhouses hidden behind curtains of poplars and enormous barns are scattered over this flat country, criss-crossed by clusters of young trees. Tall trees indicate an already old dwelling-place. In the fields, drained by ditches, sheep, cattle and ponies graze. There are numerous lapwings, golden pheasants and water birds such as the coot, a small dark wader whose black head has a white spot.
Since 1960 towns and villages have sprung up: Lelystad, Dronten, Swifterbant, Biddinghuizen; piles placed on a sand bed ensure the stability of the construction. Large straight roads cut across the polder. Some have been built on the ring dikes. Lakes such as the **Veluwe**, separating the polder from the Zuiderzee's former coast, act as regulators and have become recreation lakes with beaches.

Zuidelijk Flevoland – It is separated from the Oostelijk Flevoland Polder by a security dike, the Knardijk, parts of the road being forbidden to traffic. It is surrounded by a dike built between 1959-67. In 1968 this polder of 43 000ha - 106 210 acres had largely been drained. Half the area is devoted to agriculture, 25% to dwelling areas, 18% for meadows and woods. The rest is taken up by canals, dikes and roads.
To the north, near Oostvaarders dike, there is a nature reserve **De Oostvaardersplassen**. Very marshy, it is a refuge for birds including some very rare species.
Since 1975, **Almere**, a town with a pleasure boat harbour, is being built to the south on Gooi Lake; it should accommodate 150 000 inhabitants. Its lay-out has been carefully studied.
Another residential area, Zeewolde, is being built level with Harderwijk; it already has a large pleasure boat harbour.

SIGHTS

The tour – allow 1 day – is recommended in May-June, at the time when rape is in flower; the countryside is then tinted with spots of very vivid yellow.

Ketelhaven – Near this pleasure boat harbour, a Museum of Maritime Archaeology, **Museum voor Scheepsarcheologie** ⊙ houses remains of ship wrecks found at the bottom of the Zuiderzee, together with their contents: cargoes of goods, pottery, weapons, coins, shoes, pipes.
The oldest wreck exhibited goes back to Roman times (2C).
In the middle of the museum there is the skeleton of a large 17C merchant ship.

Walibi-Flevo ⊙ – *Spijkweg 30, biddinghuizen. Follow the signposts "Walibi-Flevo".* This new amusement park replaces a previous one with an agricultural theme. The present site covers an area of 104ha - 257 acres and includes Veluwemeer. The 24 attractions offer plenty of choice for the thrill-seekers: old-fashioned merry-go-rounds, the big wheel and several big dippers including the El Condor Suspended Looping Coaster. A tropical glasshouse has an important collection of cacti. Within the park there is a 60ha - 148 acre showground for special events, an open-air theatre with a seating capacity of 40 000 and a conference centre.

Lelystad – Lelystad, capital of Flevoland, bears the name of the engineer Lely *(qv)*. This new town built to accommodate 80 000 inhabitants by the year 2000 consists mainly of low buildings. The **Agora**, a community building constructed in 1976 marks the centre of town.
Lelystad is linked to Enkhuizen by a dike, Markerwaarddijk *(31km - 19 miles)* with a road running along the top. The Oostvaardersdiep, a canal 300m - 985ft wide, forms a waterway stretching between Amsterdam and the northern part of the country. Not far from the Houtribsluizen, two large locks spanning the Oostvaardersdiep, stands a **visitor centre** (Informatiecentrum Nieuw Land) ⊙. It contains documentation about the reclamation work carried out on the Zuiderzee, as well as about the creation and exploitation of polders in the area (farming policies, green spaces, new towns like Lelystad and Almere).
Set up next to the information centre is the **Batavia** ⊙, the replica of a merchant ship belonging to the Dutch East India Company. It was built in Amsterdam in 1628. During her first trip, she ran aground on some reefs off the Australian West Coast; some of the crew managed to survive the disaster and the massacre that took place on the islands nearby. The reconstruction of the ship is the work of a group of young people undergoing specialised training; it has now entered its final phase. The guided tour allows you to visit the boat and the workshops where the pulleys, sails and carved wooden sculptures are made. The **Mark Twain**, a one-hundred-year old paddle boat moored opposite the shipyard, houses a restaurant.

Scheepswrak (Ship wreck) – *To the south of Lelystad. Access by the Oostranddreef; at the roundabout (Rotonde) turn left, then the first road on the right, right again at the next crossroads. Nearby a narrow lane leads to the wreck.*
In the middle of cultivated land the skeleton of a 23m - 75ft long ship has been left where it was found during drainage of the polder in 1967. Called *De Zeehond* (the seal), dating from 1878, it transported bricks, a pile of which can be seen nearby. Some of the ship's contents are exhibited in Ketelhaven's Museum of Maritime Archaeology *(see above)*

Dronten – In the heart of the polder this new town extends mainly round a church with an openwork tower, and a community centre, **De Meerpaal.**
This immense glass hall, built in 1967 by Frank van Klingeren *(see Lelystad's Agora)*, is a closed agora, a prolongation of the main square. Built for collective cultural and sporting activities, it also houses, a weekly market in winter.

FLUSHING See VLISSINGEN

Join us in our constant task of keeping up-to-date
Please send us your comments and suggestions

Michelin Tyre PLC
Tourism Department
The Edward Hyde Building
38 Clarendon Road
WATFORD - Herts WD1 1SX
Tel: (0923) 415000

★ FRANEKER Friesland

Michelin map 408 H2

This small Frisian town (Frjentsjer) had a famous university founded in 1585, where Descartes became a student in 1629. It was closed in 1811 under the reign of Louis Bonaparte.

SIGHTS

★ **Stadhuis** ⊙ – A splendid building in the Dutch Renaissance style, dating from 1591, with a double gable, it is topped by an elegant octagonal tower.
The Council Chamber *(Raadzaal; ground floor at the end of the corridor)* and the Registrar's Office (Trouwzaal; *1st floor*) are hung with 18C painted leather, in rich colours.

★ **Planetarium** ⊙ – At the time when a number of his contemporaries feared the end of the world due to the exceptional position of the stars, the Frisian **Eise Eisinga** decided to show that the situation was not dangerous. This wool-comber, who had been interested in astronomy since childhood, built 1774-81, an ingenious system where the movement of stars was depicted on his living room ceiling. Eisinga represented with surprising precision the celestial vault as known by 18C astronomers.
This planetarium, whose movement can be seen in the attic, is the oldest one in working order in Europe.
At the end of Eisingastraat, a charming House of Corn Porters, **Korendragershuisje**, can be seen.

Planetarium Eisinga

Planetarium Eisinga

Museum 't Coopmanshûs ⊙ – *Voorstraat.*
Set up in the Waag and the large adjoining 17 and 18C houses, this museum pays tribute to **Anna Maria van Schurman** (1606-1678). A celebrated entomologist and draugtsman, who belonged to the Labadist sect founded by the French émigré **Jean de Labadie** (1610-1674), she advocated bringing Protestantism back to Primitive Christianity.
The history of the town and its university is illustrated by portraits of professors and a "xylotheque" – an outstanding collection of wood samples presented in the form of books, presented to Franeker University by Louis Bonaparte in 1811. The museum also displays several splendid collections of silver and gold plate from Friesland, ceramics and textiles. Note the miniature charity fête by J. Kooistra. The building is also used to stage exhibitions on modern art.
In the same street, at no 35, the **Martenahuis** was built in 1498.

Martinikerk – Gothic, the church has 15C paintings, and figures of saints on the pillars.
The ground is strewn with finely sculptured tombstones in the Frisian style.

Weeshuis – The former orphanage's door is topped with 17C inscriptions. Nearby, the **Cammingha-Stins** is a lovely residence of the 15-16C, now used by a bank (on the 1st floor, exhibition room of coins and medals).

★★ GIETHOORN Overijssel

Michelin map 408 J3

The small town of Giethoorn stands in a waterlogged fenland area. It owes its name to the great number of wild goats *(geitenhoorns)* found in the area by the peat-workers. In Giethoorn the houses border the canals, dug in the past by the peat workers to transport the peat. The many lakes found locally are the flooded hollows created by peat digging on a massive scale.

Tour ⊙ – *No cars are allowed into the village and it must be visited on foot (a path runs alongside the main canal) or by boat. Visitors can choose to hire a rowing boat, a punt, a motor boat or a yacht or take a boat trip.*

A lakeside village – The pretty thatched cottages of Giethoorn face onto the canals spanned by hump-backed bridges or simple footbridges. Well-tended lawns and gaily planted flowerbeds slope down to the water's edge.
The bicycle is the most popular form of transport although many locals use flat-bottomed punts (punters). Even bridal processions can be seen punting along the canals.

Giethoorn

Kameeldak roofs – The hall-type farmhouses *(see Introduction: Farmhouses)* are remarkable for their thatched hump-backed roofs. When more and more land was reclaimed the quantity of grain harvested increased and the farmers had to extend their storage space. Since land was at a premium they extended upwards and as a consequence the farm buildings became taller than the farmhouse. Roofs with this change in level were called camel-backed *(kameeldak)*. Another characteristic of these farms is that they have no carriage entrance as everything was transported by water. Hay was stored in the barn above the boat house.

The lakes – The broads which stretch to the east and south of the village are vast stretches of water scattered with small reed-covered islands. The entire area is a unique ecological habitat rich in birdlife.

EXCURSION

Giethoorn's Fenlands – *A round tour of 26km - 16 miles*

Wanneperveen – In this small town which, like many peat-bog villages has a name which ends in *veen* (peat-bog or fen), thatched cottages run for several miles alongside a road planted with pear trees. Not far from the village's west entrance, one can see the **cemetery** with its free-standing bell tower scantily built with a few beams, characteristic of Southern Friesland; note in the main street, at no 94, a lovely house with a crow-stepped gable, the **old town hall** (vroegere stadhuis).

Vollenhove – It was another of the historic ports on the Zuiderzee, before the Noordoostpolder was reclaimed. On **Kerkplein** stand a few fine monuments: **St-Nicolaaskerk**, a late Gothic church with two naves and its free-standing bell tower, the **Klokketoren** which was used as a prison; adjoining the bell tower is the **old raadhuis**, a 17C brick and sandstone porticoed building converted into a restaurant; finally the lovely façade with crow-stepped gables of the **Latin School** (1627) (now used by the VVV and a bank) has an entrance with two carved stelae in front. From the church's east end one can see the bastions of the old rampart where pleasure boats are moored. The new town hall is housed in **Oldruitenborgh** manor-house, set in a park near a church (Kleine Kerk).

Blokzijl – This was also one of the prosperous old ports on the Zuiderzee and a member of the Hanseatic League. The Dutch East India Company used the port as a haven for its East Indiamen when storms arose. The lovely 17C houses along the now deserted waterfronts are witness to past prosperity. Kerkstraat, which leads to the 17C church, is also picturesque.

GOES Zeeland

Pop 32 244

Michelin map 408 C7 or 212 fold 13 – Local map see DELTA
Town plan in the current Michelin Red Guide Benelux

Former small port, which owed its prosperity to the salt trade and the madder industry, Goes, today, is the main centre of Zuid Beveland. The town is surrounded by meadows and orchards.
A canal links it to the estuary of the Oosterschelde.
Goes has preserved, through the location of its canals, the layout of its 15C ramparts. A small **steam tramway** (stoomtram) ⊙ runs between Goes and Oudelande.

Jacqueline of Hainaut or Jacoba – Goes was one of the ancestral seats of the Counts of Zeeland and the town is closely associated with the turbulent Jacoba, daughter of William VI, Duke of Bavaria. On his death in 1417 she inherited the

earldoms of Hainaut, Holland and Zeeland, and was envied by many. She had a bone to pick with the **Cods** *(qv)*. in 1421 she left her second husband John IV, Duke of Brabant, who had dispossessed her of the Holland earldom giving it to John of Bavaria, Jacoba's uncle and supporter of the Cods. The following year she married Humphrey, Duke of Gloucester, fourth son of King Henry IV, brother to King Henry V of England.
Later, to escape from the intrigues of Philip the Good, who had invaded her territories, she took refuge in Goes. She was forced by Philip to sign an agreement in Delft in 1428, the Treaty of Delft, in which she recognised him as heir and promised never to remarry. The promise was soon broken (1432) and Jacqueline lost her title of countess (1433); three years later she died in Slot Teilingen, near Sassenheim.

Market day – The weekly market on Goes's Grote Markt (Tuesdays) gives the occasional opportunity of seeing the Zeeland costumes of Zuid-Beveland *(qv)*. The headdresses, above all, are very beautiful, square for Catholics and in the shape of a vast aureola for Protestants.

SIGHTS

Grote Markt – This, the town's main square, is overlooked by the 15C **stadhuis** which was altered in the 18C and has a rococo façade.

Grote- of Maria Magdalenakerk ⊙ – Part of it was built in the 15C, and rebuilt in 1621 after a fire. The main nave is very high. Similar to the two transept portals of the Hooglandse Church in Leyden, the **north portal** is finely decorated in the Flamboyant style, and has a wide window topped by an openwork gable.
Inside, the church has a remarkable 17C **organ** ⊙, crowned with an 18C canopy.

Turfkade – *To the north of Grote Markt.* This "peat" quay is lined with lovely crow-stepped gabled façades.

EXCURSION

Kapelle and Yerseke – *15km - 9 miles east - local map under Delta.*

Kapelle – Pop 10 012. The **Hervormde Kerk** ⊙ with its imposing 14C bell tower and corner pinnacles is visible from afar across the low-lying polderland.
In the nave note the decorated balusters and heads of satyrs. The main chancel, decorated with Gothic blind arcading in red brick contains a 17C tomb.
Nex to the village cemetery, to the west, there is a **French military cemetery** where French soldiers killed in the Netherlands in 1940 are buried.

Yerseke (or Ierseke) – This small port on Oosterschelde specialises in oyster and mussel beds and lobster catching. The Oosterschelde Storm - surge Barrier *(p 88)* has floodgates which make it possible for Yerseke to benefit from tides and continue its activities.

GORINCHEM Zuid-Holland — Pop 28 911

Michelin map 408 F6 or 212 folds 6 and 7

On the borders of three provinces (Zuid-Holland, Noord Brabant and Gelderland) Gorinchem, often called **Gorkum** is an important waterway junction, at the confluence of two large rivers, the Waal (branch of the Rhine) and the Maas, as well as the Merwedekanaal and a small river, the Linge.
It has a large marina to the west.

Hooks and Cods – Gorkum dates from the 13C and because of its strategic position it has suffered numerous sieges.
In 1417 it was the stake of a ferocious fight between the Hooks (Hoeken), supporters of **Jacoba** *(qv)* who had inherited the town, and **William of Arkel**, on the side of the Cods (Kabeljauwen). The latter wished to reconquer the town, which had belonged to his father. He lost his life during a skirmish in the city.
Gorkum was one of the first strongholds wrested from the Spanish by the Beggars in 1572. Amongst the prisoners taken by the Beggars, there were sixteen priests who were executed at Brielle *(qv)* the same year; they are the martyrs of Gorkum.
It was the birthplace of the 16C painter, Abraham Bloemaert *(qv)* who lived mainly in Utrecht.

OLD QUARTER *3/4 hour – town plan see overleaf*

The historic core is girdled by the star-shaped outline of the bastions and ramparts which have been transformed into an esplanade. It is crossed by the Linge, which forms a picturesque harbour, the **Lingehaven**.

Grote Markt and Groenmarkt – On the first of these squares stands the town hall; on the other stands the **Grote- of St.-Maartenskerk**. Dating from the 15C, it is mainly remarkable for its tall early 16C Gothic tower, **St-Janstoren** ⊙, which is slightly curved in shape; as a matter of fact while being built it was noticed that the edifice was collapsing so the upper walls were straightened; these are the only vertical ones.
On Grote Markt, at no 23, a small baroque **door** called Hugo de Grootpoortje (**A**) is the place where the illustrious Grotius took refuge after having escaped from Slot Loevestein *(qv)*.

GORINCHEM

Street	No.
Gasthuisstraat	12
Hoogstraat	16
Langendijk	21
Appeldijk	3
Blauwe Torenstr.	4
Boerenstraat	6
Bornsteeg	7
Burgstraat	9
Dalembolwerk	10
Groenmarkt	13
Hoge Torenstraat	15
Kelenstraat	18
Kruisstraat	19
Lombardstraat	22
Molenstraat	24
Nieuwe Waalsteeg	25
Peterburg	27
Pompstraat	28
Robberstraat	30
Tolsteeg	31
Torenstraat	33
Vijfde Uitgang	34
Visbrug	36
Walstraat	37
Westwagenstraat	39
Zusterhuis	40

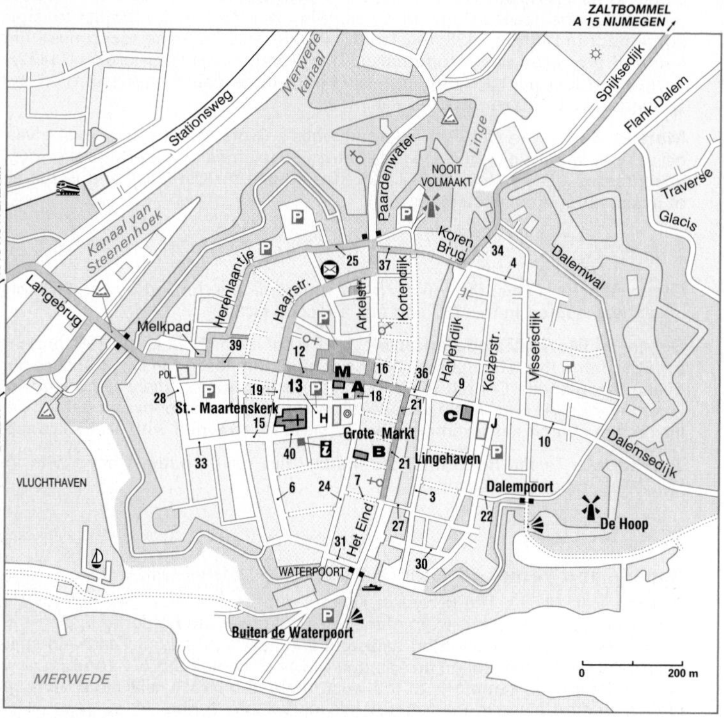

Dit is in Bethlehem (**Bethlehem Museum**) (**M**) ⊙ – Formerly a shop, this house has a lovely façade with decorated window tympana, topped with a voluted gable dating back to 1566. The museum presents collections related to the history of Gorkum: paintings, sculptures, scale models, toys, objects in silver and gold plate. The ground floor houses temporary exhibitions.

Burgerkinderenweeshuis (**B**) – On the 18C façade of the old orphanage, also called **Huize Matthijs-Marijke**, a carved stone depicts Christ and children, between the founders of the orphanage.

Huis of "'t Coemt al van God" (**C**) – Lovely narrow façade with a crow-stepped gable, decorated with Renaissance medallions (1563).

Dalempoort – This lovely, small rampart gateway, square with a high roof topped by a pinnacle, dates from 1597; it was enlarged in 1770. It is the only gateway, which remains of the town's four entrances.
From here, one can see the tall wall mill called **De Hoop**, Hope (1764).

Buiten de Waterpoort – This vast shaded esplanade stretches from the south of the old water-gate (Waterpoort), closed in 1894 to enlarge the road. The landing stage for boat tours is here.
There is a fine **view** over Dalem Gate, the mill and the river; to the southeast, on the opposite bank, one can see, amongst the greenery, the tall bell tower of Woudrichem Church and the pink brick Slot Loevestein.

EXCURSIONS

Leerdam – Pop 19 381. *17km – 10 1/2 miles to the northeast. Leave by Spijksedijk, take the motorway to Nijmegen and turn left towards Leerdam.*
This town, situated on the Linge, is the main glass-making centre in the Netherlands since the creation of its factory in 1878.
To the southwest, on the Oosterwijk road *(Lingedijk 28)*, a small National Glasswork Museum, **Nationaal Glasmuseum** ⊙ is installed in a private home. This museum displays interesting collections of glass and crystal from different countries, notably from Leerdam (19 and 20C) but also from Scandinavia and Italy (since the 18C).

Woudrichem and Slot Loevestein – *21km – 13 miles to the south. Leave by Westwagenstraat, turn left after the first bridge and return to the motorway towards Breda then a road to the left.*

Woudrichem – Pop 13 581. At the confluence of the Rhine (Waal) and the Maas, this small town, commonly called **Workum**, is still enclosed in its encircling bastioned ramparts which have been turned into an esplanade. Formerly it belonged to the region of Heusden and Altena. It obtained its city charter in 1356. By the Peace of

Woudrichem in 1419, John of Bavaria obtained important rights over his niece Jacoba's *(qv)* territories. Workum has a small pleasure boat harbour with a ferry for pedestrians to Slot Loevestein.
To the south one enters the town by **Koepoort**. On the right is the squat **tower** of the Gothic church, the walls of which are decorated with medallions.
To the north near the 15C prison gate, **Gevangenpoort**, the **Oude Raadhuis** *(Hoogstraat 47)* now a restaurant, has a graceful Renaissance façade with a crow-stepped gable and a flight of steps in front topped by two heraldic lions.
In the same street, at no 37, note a façade stone depicting an axe chopping wood, and opposite, two twin houses of 1593 and 1606, whose façade stones evoke by their sculpture a golden angel and a salamander, and by their inscription: To the Golden Angel and To the Salamander, their respective names.

B & U International Picture Service Amsterdam/Herman Scholten, Huizen

Slot Loevestein

Slot Loevestein ⏲ – All that can be seen through the greenery are the high slate roofs of this solid fortress in pink brick, flanked with four square towers and surrounded by moats and ramparts. Slot Loevestein was built between 1357 and 1368 by Dirk Loef van Horne, lord of Altena. The Count of Holland, Albrecht van Beieren (of Bavaria), seized it in 1385 and surrounded it with an enclosure. In the 15C the castle was transformed into a prison by Jacoba who had just seized Gorkum *(qv)*. In 1619 Grotius *(qv)*, who had been taken prisoner the previous year, was imprisoned in Loevestein. There he devoted himself to the preparation of legal and theologicial works. His escape remains famous. He managed to escape in March 1621 by hiding in a chest which had been used to bring him books, and was then given shelter in Gorkum temporarily, before reaching France. Inside the castle one can visit large rooms with lovely chimneypieces. In one of them is the chest used by Grotius for his escape.

★ GOUDA Zuid-Holland — Pop 65 926

Michelin map 408 F5

Gouda (pronounced how-dah) owes its fame to the stained glass in the church, its cheese and its pipes. Situated at the confluence of the Hollandse IJssel and the Gouwe, this peaceful town is criss-crossed by several canals.
In the Middle Ages, Gouda, then called Ter Gouwe, developed under the protection of its castle, which was destroyed in 1577. It had received its city charter in 1272. In the 15C, brewing and trading brought great prosperity to Gouda, while the 16C marked a decline. The town picked up again in the 17C due to the cheese trade and the manufacture of pipes introduced by English potters. Today there is also the production of candles, Gouda having the biggest factory in the country, and pottery.
Gouda is the homeland of **Cornelis de Houtman** (*c*1565-99), who was in charge of an expedition to the East (1595-7) and founded the first Dutch trading post in East India (Indonesia) on the island of Java.

Gouda cheese – Gouda, together with Edam, is one of the most famous cheeses in the Netherlands. Marketed in Gouda, it is a product either from a factory or from farms (its name then becomes *boerenkaas* meaning farm cheese). Gouda is made with cow's milk either straight from the cow or pasturized (when it is made in a factory). It is either young, medium or old. The indication *volvet 48+* means that its fat content is at least 48%. It is usually in the shape of a millstone with a diameter of 35cm - 14in. Other specialities of the town are the *stroopwafels*, wafers filled with treacle.

Boat Trips ⏲ – Tours are organised towards the Reeuwijk Lakes *(p 114)*.

★ HEART OF THE TOWN *3 hours*

Markt (Z) – In the centre of the main square stands the stadhuis with its characteristic tall silhouette. Several markets take place in this square, particularly the **cheese market** and **handicraft market** ⊙.

At no 27, the Arti Legi, houses the tourist information centre.

★ **Stadhuis** (Z H) ⊙ – This lovely mid-15C Gothic building, restored in the 19 and 20C, has a very decorative sandstone façade on the south side with a gable, flanked by turrets and adorned with a small balcony. The staircase in front is in the Renaissance style (1603).

On the east side is a **carillon,** whose small figures come to life every half hour; it depicts the scene of Count Floris V of Holland granting the city charter to Gouda in 1272.

Inside the Registrar's Office (Trouwzaal) is worth visiting; it is decorated with tapestries woven in Gouda in the 17C.

Ch. Sappa/CEDRI

Stadhuis, Gouda

Waag (YZ A) – It is a classical construction of 1668 built by Pieter Post. The façade is decorated with a low relief depicting the weighing of cheese which formerly took place here.

Behind the Waag the lovely **Agnietenkapel** (Y B) has been restored.

★ **St.-Janskerk** (Z) ⊙ – Founded in the 13C, St John's was rebuilt three times after the great fires of 1361, 1438 and 1552. Fronted by a small tower – the remains of the original church – St-John's is surrounded by numerous pointed gables enhanced by large stained-glass windows.

The interior is very light, and sober in the extreme. Architecturally speaking, it is a late Gothic basilica with prominent side aisles, surmounted by wooden barrel vaulting.

★★★ **Stained glass** (Goudse Glazen) – *Photograph p 18.* St John's is renowned for its magnificent collection of 70 stained-glass windows. 40 were spared by the Iconoclasts *(qv)*, the others were made after the Reformation. The largest, of which there are 27, were donated by the king, princes, prelates or rich bourgeois.

The 13 most remarkable stained-glass windows, in both the eastern and the central parts of the church, are attributed to the **Crabeth brothers** (Dirck and Wouter) who made them between 1555 and 1571 when the church was Catholic. They illustrate biblical subjects. The works of the Crabeth brothers are numbered:

- 5: The Queen of Sheba pays a visit to Solomon
- 6: Judith beheading Holofernes
- 7: Dedication of Solomon's temple and the Last Supper (a present from Philip II, King of Spain)
- 8: Heliodorus, temple thief, chastened by the angels
- 12: Nativity
- 14: Sermon of St John the Baptist (patron of the church)
- 15: Baptism of Jesus (the oldest window, 1555)
- 16: First sermon of Jesus
- 18: Jesus replying to St John's disciples
- 22: Jesus driving the money-changers from the Temple (window donated by William the Silent and symbolising the Church's fight for purification)
- 23: Elijah's sacrifice and the Ablutions donated by Margaret of Parma *(qv)*, governor of the Low Countries at the time of the revolt.
- 24: St Philip preaching and baptising
- 30: Jonah cast up by the whale *(tall window above the ambulatory, to the left of the chancel).*

More recent stained-glass windows which date from the Protestant period were put in between 1594 and 1603 on the western side. Donated by the free towns of Holland, they depict armorial bearings, historical events, allegories and a few biblical scenes.

Note numbers:
25: the raising of the siege of Leyden (in 1547) in the middle of floo William the Silent; silhouette of Delft
27: the Pharisee in the temple
28: the adultress in a monumental decor with its exaggerated perspec
28A *(right aisle)*: Stained-glass window by Charles Eyck placed in 1947 and evoking the Second World War and the Liberation.

The seven stained-glass windows in the **chapel** (door under window 14 in the chancel) depict the Capture of Jesus, Christ Mocked, the Scourging, the *Ecce Homo* at Pontius Pilate's House, the Bearing of the Cross, the Resurrection, Ascension and the feast of Pentecost; they are attributed to Dirck Crabeth or his pupils and come from a nearby convent.

The organ at the end of the church *(west side)* dates from 1736. The new organ in the chancel dates from 1974. Interesting tombstones are strewn over the floor of the building.

★ **Stedelijk Museum Het Catharina Gasthuis** (Z M^1) ⊙ – Installed in the governor's old mansion and St Catherine's Hospital (Gasthuis), this municipal museum is a decorative arts museum (fine furnishings) and a regional art museum.

To the north of the museum, there is a garden entered by a **portal** (1609) (Lazaruspoortje), which has a polychrome low relief depicting Lazarus the leper.

Near the hospital governors' former offices, the kitchen and 17 to 19C rooms, the **Great hall** (Ruim) is devoted to the civic guards: there are paintings of groups (one by Ferdinand Bol). A small cellar contains torture instruments of the 16 and 17C.

On the upper floor there are collections of toys, the reconstitution of the surgeons' Guild Room, paintings by the Barbizon School and The Hague School (Mauve, Jacob Maris) as well as Isaac Israëls and Jan Toorop.

In the old part (1542) one can see the former hospital rooms devoted to **religious art**: the *Annunciation,* the *Baptism of St Eustace* by Pourbus the Elder (16C), a collection of pewterware and a chalice presented by Jacoba in the 15C. In a nearby room there is the reconstitution of a 17C town dispensary.

The neigbouring chapel has temporary exhibitions.

ADDITIONAL SIGHTS

Stedelijk Museum de Moriaan (Z M^2) ⊙ – Under the sign of the Blackamoor *(moriaan)* evoking a tobacco shop, this Renaissance style house built *c*1625 has a lovely façade overlooking the picturesque Gouda canal. It has been converted into a **Museum of Pipes and Pottery**. The tobacco shop of 1680 has been reconstructed. Fine collections of pipes, pottery, earthenware tiles 1600-1850 and pictures made of earthenware tiles are displayed in elegant settings. One can also see the reconstructed potter's and a pipe maker' workshops.

Jeruzalemstraat (Z 15) – At the corner of Patersteeg is the **Jeruzalemkapel**, a 15C chapel. Opposite, on the other corner is the former orphanage, **Weeshuis** (Z F) of 1642, now a library, with a lovely façade with a voluted gable, and beside it a doorway topped by a low relief depicting two orphans.

On the opposite pavement, at no 2, an old people's home, **Oude Mannenhuis** (Z K) opens by a door (1614), altered in the 18C.

At the far end of Spieringstraat is the **municipal park** with an 1832 **Walmolen 't Slot** (Z), which was formerly used for milling grain. In the park there is a tree which was planted when Queen Wilhelmina reached majority.

GOUDA

Street	Grid
Agnietenstr.	Y 4
Dubbele Buurt	Z 9
Hoogstr.	Y 12
Kleiweg	Y
Korte Groenendaal	Z 19
Korte Tiendeweg	Z 21
Lange Tiendeweg	YZ 25
Walestr.	Z 39
Wijdstr.	Z 40
Achter de Vismarkt	Z 3
Bogen	Z 6
Burg. Martensstr.	Z 7
Groeneweg	Z 10
Houtmansgracht	Y 13
Jeruzalemstr.	Z 15
Karnemelksloot	Y 16
Kerkhoflaan	Z 18
Lange Groenendaal	Z 22
Lange Noodgodstr.	Z 24
Nieuwe Markt	Y 27
Nieuwe Veerstal	Z 28
Patersteeg	Z 30
Peperstr.	Z 31
Spoorstr.	Y 33
Tuinstr.	Z 34
Vlamingstr.	Z 36
Vredebest	Y 37
Wilhelminastr.	Y 42
Zeedijk	Z 43
Zeugstr.	YZ 45

★ **Reeuwijkse Plassen and Woerden** – *30km – 18 1/2 miles to the north. Leave by Karnemelksloot. After the canal, take the 2nd road on the left in the direction of Platteweg.*

★ **Reeuwijkse Plassen** – Even though these vast stretches of water are much appreciated by water sports enthusiasts, the road winding between the lakes goes through a captivating landscape.

After Sluipwijk, go in the direction of Bodegraven then Woerden.

Woerden – Pop 35 003. Former important stronghold on the Oude Rijn, Woerden was considered for a long time as "the key to Holland": strategically, occupying Woerden meant access to the country. In 1672 Louis XIV's armies commanded by the Duke of Montmorency-Luxembourg defeated William III's Dutch army. The town is still surrounded by a moat which edged its bastioned enclosure. A 15C **castle**, since 1872 turned into a quartermaster's store, stands near the southern gateway to the town. There are imitation machicolations running along the façade.
In the old town hall there is municipal museum, **stadsmuseum** ⊙.
Flanked by a turret it is a delightful small building (1501) with voluted gables and the 1st floor is completely glazed. An old pillory takes up the right part of the façade. Woerden also has a stage mill (1755), De Windhond (The Greyhound).

Oudewater and Schoonhoven – *34km – 21 miles. Leave by Nieuwe Veerstal and follow the verry narrow dike road; passing is difficult.*
This road, which follows the Hollandse IJssel, offers picturesque **views**★ of the river with its marshy banks and thatched farmhouses.

Oudewater – Pop 9 462. Homeland of Jacob **Arminius** (*c*1560-1609) *(qv)*, and the Primitive painter **Gerard David** (*c*1460-1523), who moved to Bruges in 1483, Oudewater is one of the Netherlands' oldest small towns.
Oudewater owes its fame to its **witches' scales**, installed in the **Heksenwaag** ⊙, which houses a small Witch Museum (in the attic: the history of witchcraft is retraced via engravings and documents).
This fine Renaissance building with crow-stepped gables and brick mosaic tympana is near Markt, which spans a canal.
In the 16C women accused of witchcraft came from afar to be weighed at Oudewater in the presence of the burgomaster of the town. If the woman's weight was not too light with respect to her size she was too heavy to ride a broomstick, so she was not a witch. They were then given a certificate of acquittal. All the people weighed in Oudewater were acquitted. The last certificate was issued in 1729.
Next to the weigh house, at no 14, note the Renaissance façade (1601) of Arminius's birthplace: the tympana are decorated with shells; a niche contains the statue of Fortune.
Dating from the town's prosperous era (end 16C) other façades are spread along the quiet streets like Wijdstraat. At no 3 Donkere Gaard, near Markt, there is a fine house. Near Markt, the Renaissance **stadhuis** has a side façade preceded by a flight of steps and topped with a crow-stepped gable.

By the Gouda road, go to Haasrecht, then follow the valley of the Vlist towards Schoonhoven.

It is a picturesque **route**★. The road, shaded by willows, runs alongside the river with banks covered in abundant vegetation. Beautiful reed-covered roofed farmhouses with a conical haystack topped with a small roof, line the road.

Vlist – Pop 9 385. Lovely wooden post mill.

On leaving Vlist, cross the river.

Schoonhoven – Pop 11 487. This charming, small town at the confluence of the Vlist and the Lek, is known for its traditional silverware which continues to exist thanks to a few craftsmen. It is linked by a ferry *(veer)* to Lek's south bank.
A picturesque canal crosses the town.
The **Stadhuis** stands on the canal's edge. Dating from the 15C, with a high roof topped by a pinnacle (carillon), it has been modernised.
On Dam, in the centre of the canal, is the **Waag**, an original building of 1617 with a hipped roof. It is now a restaurant.
Near the waag there is a Gold, Silver and Clock Museum, **Nederlands Goud-, Zilver- en Klokkenmuseum** ⊙. It has a fine **collection**★ of wall clocks from Friesland and the Zaan, French dial cases, 18C timepieces as well as a collection of 17 to 20C silverware from several countries, and an important collection of watches.
To the south of the town, the gate, **Veerpoort** which dates from 1601, opens on to the Lek. Some lovely houses can be seen in the town, notably no 37 Lopikerstraat: the 1642 façade is decorated with a double crow-stepped gable and red shutters.

Collectie Nederlands Goud-, Zilver- en Klokkenmuseum

Bracket clock (c1716) by A Witsen

's-GRAVENHAGE See DEN HAAG

GRONINGEN Groningen Ⓟ

Pop 168 702

Michelin map 408 K2
Plan of the conurbation in the current Michelin Red Guide Benelux

Groningen is the provincial capital and the main town in the north of the Netherlands. The town is located at the northern extremity of the Hondsrug *(qv)* with polderlands to the north and peat bogs to the southwest.

HISTORICAL NOTES

A settlement already existed by the year 1000AD. The town was given its first set of city walls in the 12C and by the beginning of the 13C Groningen belonged to the Hanseatic League *(qv)*. A convention concluded in 1251 with the neighbouring cantons made Groningen the only grain market in the region, bringing it six centuries of prosperity. Under the Bishop of Utrecht's authority the town passed into the hands of the Duke of Geldern in 1515. Then, trying to escape from the Habsburg authority, it finally gave in to Charles V in 1536. It joined the Union of Utrecht in 1579 and was taken by the Spanish in 1580 and then by Maurice of Nassau in 1594. An era of prosperity followed with the construction from 1608-16, of a new enclosure (7km - 4 1/2 miles) defended by 17 bastions. In 1614 the university was founded; it very quickly acquired a great reputation and students came from all over Europe. Descartes chose it in 1645 to arbitrate in his conflicts with Dutch theologians.
In 1672 the town resisted against the troops of the Bishop of Munster, ally of Louis XIV. The fortifications were strengthened in 1698 by Coehoorn and rased to the ground in 1874 to allow for the extension of the city. A few remains in Noorderplantsoen (**Y**) have been transformed into a garden.
The town of Groningen is the homeland of the painters **Jozef Israëls** (1827-1911), head of The Hague School *(qv)* and **Hendrik Willem Mesdag** (1831-1915), who was one of its members.

A dynamic town – An important communications junction, Groningen is a stopping place on the way to Scandinavia. Due to its large canals, it is linked to the sea. Its port is installed on the Oosterhaven and the Zuiderhaven.

GRONINGEN

Grote Markt .... Z
Herestraat .... Z
Oosterstraat .... Z
Oude Boteringestr. .... Z 45
Oude Ebbingestr. .... Y 46
Vismarkt .... Z 67

A-Kerkhof .... Z 3
A-Straat .... Z 4
de Brink .... Z 7
Brugstraat .... Z 9
Eeldersingel .... Z 10
Eendrachtskade .... Z 12
Emmaviaduct .... Z 13
Gedempte Zuiderdiep .... Z 18
Lopende Diep .... Y 33
Martinikerkhof .... Z 34
Noorderhaven N.Z. .... Y 37
Noorderhaven Z.Z. .... Z 39
Ossenmarkt .... Y 43
Paterswoldseweg .... Z 49
Rademarkt .... Z 55
Radesingel .... Z 57
Schuitendiep .... Z 58
St. Jansstraat .... Z 60
Spilsluizen .... Y 63
Verlengde Oosterstr. .... Z 66
Westerhaven .... Z 70
Westersingel .... Z 72
Zuiderpark .... Z 76

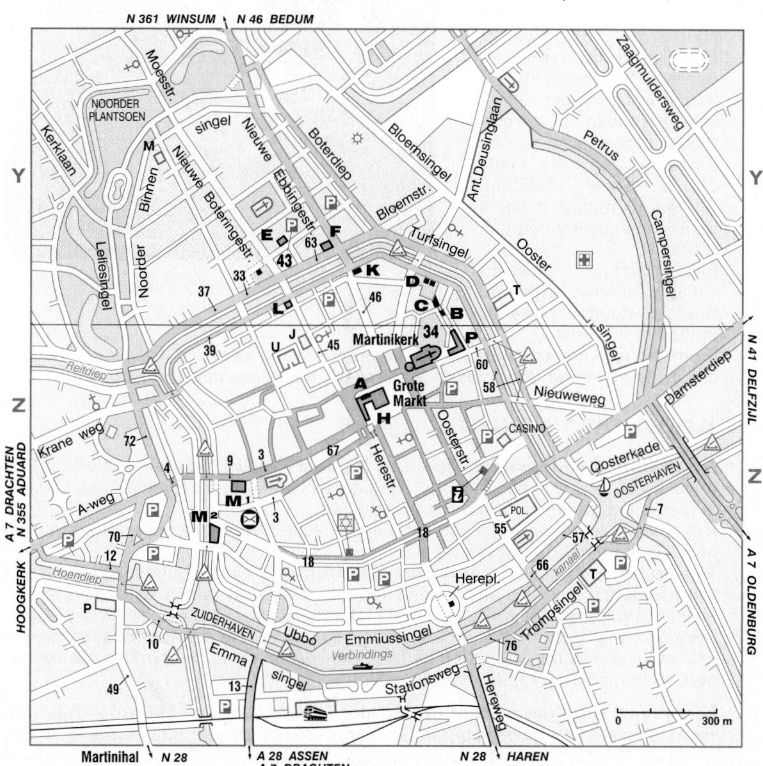

Groningen is a large industrial centre (metallurgy, hi-tech, printing, tobacco manufacture, potato flour factory). The town is the highest ranking in Western Europe for the production of sugar beet. Groningen has built an important congress and exhibition centre, the **Martinihal**, near the racecourse, in the new quarters, which are developing to the south.
The surrounding lakes (Leekstermeer, Paterswoldse Meer, Zuidlaarder Meer) draw watersports enthusiasts. It is also a university town (17 600 students in 1991).

Groningen gas – This town is seen as the capital of the Netherland's power supply. Since 1945 oil has been exploited in the Drenthe near Schoonebeek *(qv)*. In 1959-1960, large deposits of natural gas were discovered in the province of Groningen. The reserves are estimated at more than 2 000 billion m^3, which makes it one of the largest deposits in the world. The region features 29 extraction centres which each have several winding shafts. One of these centres is located in **Slochteren**, east of Groningen. Half the country's production of natural gas is channelled through pipelines towards Belgium, France, Germany and Italy.

Boat trips (Rondvaart) ⊙ – *Departure opposite the station, near the canal* (Z).

AROUND GROTE MARKT *1 1/2 hours*

Grote Markt (Z) – Prolonged by Vismarkt, the fish market, this vast, very busy square where the town's main monuments stand, forms the city centre.
Grote Markt gives onto the different pedestrian precincts; the main shopping street is Herestraat.
A **flea market** ⊙ takes place here.

Stadhuis (Z H) – In neo-classical style (1810), it is linked by a glassed-in foot-bridge to a modern annexe, which by its cubic mass, dwarfs the Goudkantoor.

★ **Goudkantoor** (Z A) – This gracious Renaissance Gold Office built in 1635 has elegant façades with finely worked gables; the windows are topped by shells. Originally the provincial tax collector's office, it was used in the 19C as a place to hallmark precious metal (*goud:* gold, *kantoor:* office).

Martinikerk (Z) ⊙ – Reconstructed in the 15C, the church is known for its tower, **Martinitoren★** ⊙ which is the pride of the people of Groningen. 96m - 315ft high with six storeys, this bell tower is topped by a weathervane in the shape of a horse depicting St Martin's mount. It has a carillon cast by the Hemony brothers.
Inside the church, the chancel is decorated with 16C frescoes depicting scenes in the life of Christ.

B & U International Picture Service Amsterdam/Loek Polders
Martinitoren, Groningen

From the top of Martinitoren there is an interesting **view** over Groningen and its canals, Grote Markt, the roofs of Martinikerk, the Prinsenhof and its garden.

ADDITIONAL SIGHTS

★ **Noordelijk Scheepvaart Museum (Northern Shipping Museum)** (Z M[1]) ⊙ – This museum is housed in two beautiful merchant's houses of the Middle Ages, Canterhuis on the right and Gotisch Huis on the left.
It is devoted to inland water transport and coastal shipping in the northern region of the Netherlands, since the 6C.
The scale models of ships, navigational instruments, charts, paintings and ceramics are particularly well shown and retrace the stages which have marked the history of shipping: the brilliant period of the Hanseatic League to which Groningen belonged, the Dutch East and West India Companies, the activities relative to peat extraction and its transportation by boat, the coastal shipping of bricks and schooners which replaced the traditional galliots.

Niemeyer Tabaksmuseum (Netherlands Tobacco Museum) (Z M[1]) ⊙ – This museum is located at the back of the Gothic House, which also houses the Northern Shipping Museum *(see above)*.

A fine collection of pipes from all over Europe, snuffboxes and jars illustrate the use of tobacco over the centuries.
A 19C tobacco merchant's shop has been reconstituted.

Groninger Museum (**Regional Museum**) (Z **M**[2]) ⊙ – It retraces the town's different historic periods as well as the province's. In the archaeological section one can see the finds excavated from the *terps (qv)*.
A section displays decorative art objects (Chinese and Japanese porcelain, silverware from Groningen).
In the fine arts department there are paintings by Rembrandt, his pupil Carel Fabritius, works of The Hague School *(qv)* and the Expressionist movement, De Ploeg (The Plough), as well as drawings and sculpture from the 16C to the present.
Temporary exhibitions are organised around the works of contemporary artists.

Martinikerkhof (Z **34**) – This lovely square, laid out on the site of a 19C cemetery *(kerkhof)*, is surrounded by renovated houses.
To the northeast is the **Provinciehuis** (Z **P**) rebuilt in 1917 in the 17C style and flanked by an onion-shaped turret.
On its left, the Cardinaal House (Y **B**) has a small Renaissance façade (1559), whose gable is decorated with three heads: Alexander the Great, King David and Charlemagne. This façade is the reconstitution of a Groningen house, which was destroyed. To the north of the square, the **Prinsenhof** (Y **C**), originally built for the Brethren of the Common Life *(see Deventer)* became the Bishop of Groningen's residence in 1568. Preceded by a courtyard and a 17C portal, it is built onto the Gardepoort, a small gateway (1639). Behind the Prinsenhof there is a small 18C garden with two arbours and a rose garden. It opens on to the Turfsingel, a canal where peat *(turf)* was transported, via a gateway called the Zonnewijzerpoort which has an 18C **sundial** (Y **D**) on the garden side.

Ossenmarkt (Y **43**) – It is the former beef market. At no 5 there is a fine 18C **patrician house** (Y **E**); it is a good example of the local architectural style, with its wide façade with rows of rather narrow windows topped by shells.
Not far away, at the corner of Spilsluizen and Nieuwe Ebbingestraat, stand two 17C houses (Y **F**). The one on the left is also characteristic of the Groningen style. On the canal's other side, a lovely sculptured stone depicting a stag (Y **K**) juts out from the wall of a house.
At the corner of Spilsluizen and Oude Boteringestraat is the former guard room, **Kortegaard** (Y **L**) with a portico (1534).

EXCURSIONS

Aduard, Leens and Lauwersoog – *27km – 16 1/2 miles northwest by A-weg* (Z).

Aduard – Of the old Cistercian abbey founded in 1163 only the refectory remains. Built in 1300, it has become a reformed church, **Hervormde Kerk** ⊙. Although the façade is sober, the interior has interesting decorative details: Gothic bays alternating with blind arches with a brick background depicting geometric motifs, bays on the ground floor surrounded by ceramic cable moulding. The 18C furnishings are elegant: pulpit decorated with coats of arms, pews with carved backs, the lords' pews topped by a canopy with heraldic motifs, copper lecterns.

Leens – **Petruskerk** ⊙, built in the 12 and 13C, houses a lovely baroque **organ case**★ (organ concerts) built by Hinsz in 1733.

Lauwersoog – *Local map under Waddeneilanden.* Departure point for ferries to Schiermonnikoog *(qv)*, Lauwersoog is situated near the **Lauwersmeer**, former sea gulf, which has been closed, like the Zuiderzee, by a dike completed in 1969 and around which polders are being reclaimed.
A small museum, **Expozee** ⊙ is housed in a large building. Scale models, photographs, illuminated maps, film and slide projections give interesting documentation on the Lauwersmeer polders and the protection of the Waddenzee.

★ **Rural Churches** – *Round tour of 118km – 73 miles to the northeast. Leave Groningen by Damsterdiep* (Z) *– local map overleaf.*
Every village in the province of Groningen has its brick church which dates from the 12 and 13C and is usually in the transitional Romanesque-Gothic style. Architecturally they are quite simple but they are often adorned with attractive decorative brickwork both inside and outside. These churches in their churchyard setting have a captivating rustic charm as they stand on artificial mounds known as *wierds* locally *(see also terp)*. The saddleback roof of the bell tower often emerges from behind a screen of tall trees. Characteristic features of the interiors are the frescoes, lovely carved furnishings and hatchments. The farmhouses of the region are also quite imposing *(see the Introduction: Farmhouses)*.

Garmerwolde – The 13C **kerk** ⊙ stands in an attractive enclosure near a free-standing bell tower. The flat east end has bays outlined by recessed arches and a gable with blind arcading. The interior still has some 16C frescoes on the vaults and an 18C carved pulpit.

Ten Boer – Pop 6 790. On a mound, a 13C kerk, deconsecrated, topped by a pinnacle, has some lovely decoration, especially on the north side: bays outlined by recessed arches, medallions, multifoil blind arcading and gables both with reticulate brickwork.

Stedum – Built on a mound surrounded by moats, this typical kerk with its tall saddleback roofed bell tower is picturesque. A frieze runs above the modillions sculptured with characters or heads of animals.

Loppersum – This large Gothic **kerk** ⊙ has two transepts with blind arcading on the gables. The interior is interesting for its **frescoes**★, which decorate the upper part of the chancel vaults and the Lady Chapel. In the chapel south of the chancel there are numerous memorial slabs.

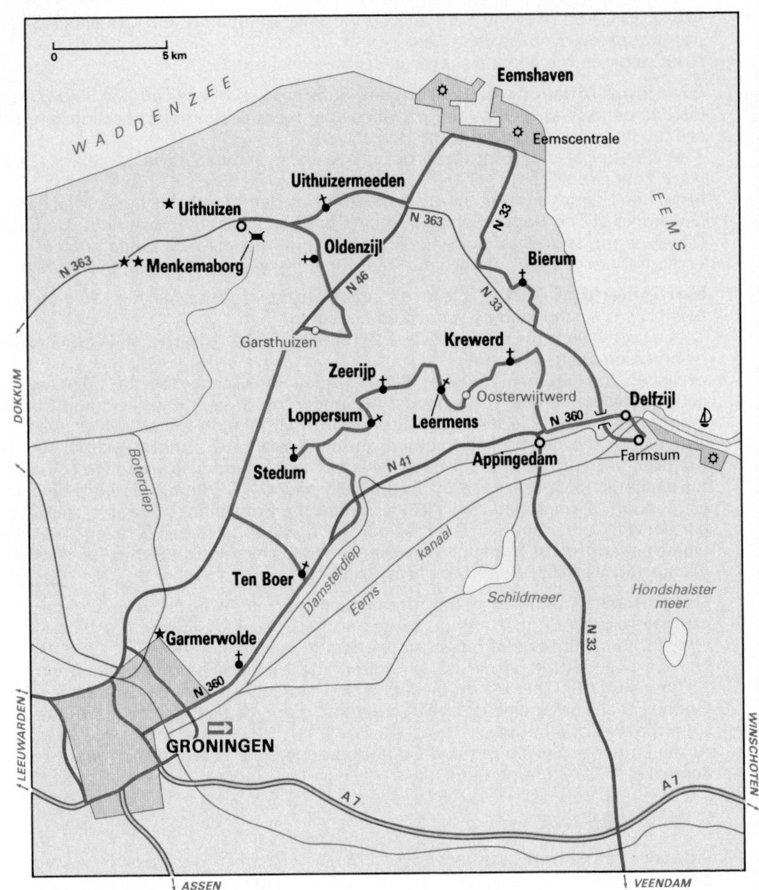

Zeerijp – Next to its free-standing bell tower, the **kerk** ⏲ dating from the 14C has a gable in two parts with blind arcading and brick mosaic.
The interior is remarkable for its **domes★** with brick decoration which varies in each bay: chevrons, interlacing... Blind arcading decorates the end of the nave. The organ, the Renaissance pulpit, and hatchments are also worth seeing.

Leermens – This 13C kerk has a flat east end decorated with blind arcading and a background decorated with brick motifs.

On arriving at Oosterwijtwerd, there is a large farmhouse with four roofs.

Krewerd – This **kerk** ⏲, built on a mound, has vaults decorated with brick motifs. The organ dates from 1531.

Appingedam – Pop 12 508. Renowned for its agricultural markets (April and October), it is a welcoming town with a long pedestrian precinct, Dijkstraat Promenade and crossed by a canal, the Damsterdiep.
From the footbridge (Vrouwenbrug) over the canal there is a fine **view★** of the overhanging kitchens and the town hall's pinnacle. Appingedam's marina is nicely situated in the town centre.
The **old raadhuis**, flanked by a 19C bell tower, dates from 1630. The façade, with bays topped by shells, is decorated with a pelican, a statue of Justice and a voluted pediment.
The 13C **Nicolaikerk** ⏲, has kept lovely frescoes, discovered when it was being restored.

Delfzijl – Pop 31 655. A busy shipping port on Dollard Gulf, linked to Groningen by Eemskanaal, Delfzijl is an industrial city, whose main activities are petrochemicals and the manufacture of soda.
To the south of the town, at **Farmsun**, an aluminium foundry supplied with alumina from Suriname was the first installed in the Netherlands, in 1956. Delfzijl also has a large pleasure boat harbour; **boat trips** ⏲ are organised.
From the dike on the bank of Dollard Gulf, there is a **view** over the harbour and the town, overlooked by a tall wall mill, called **Molen Adam** (1875).
On a square near the station, a monument topped by a swan, **Het Zwaantje**, commemorates the Resistance.
A small **statue of Maigret** on the lawns of the Damsterdiep *(600m - 1/3 mile from the pumping station to the west of Eemskanaal, opposite the RWR warehouses)*, is a reminder that **Georges Simenon** (1903-89) was a visitor in 1929. It is believed that he created his most famous character, police inspector Maigret, while in Delfzijl.

Bierum – On a mound there is a small 13C **kerk** ⏲, whose bell tower was reinforced by a flying buttress. The semicircular east end of the chancel dates from the 14C.

The interior is roofed with geometrically decorated ribbed domes on which a few traces of frescoes remain. The organ dates from 1793, the baptismal font from the early Middle Ages.
Around the church the cemetery has remarkable 19C sculptured memorial slabs depicting symbols of life (trees) and time (hour glasses).

Eemshaven – This new port was built on reclaimed polderland of Emmapolder and Oostpolder. The port started trading in 1973 and has given rise to an important industrial zone. To the east the imposing **Eemscentrale** power station has been powered by natural gas since 1976.

Uithuizermeeden – The **kerk** ⊙ with a 13C nave and a transept (1705) has a white tower rebuilt in 1896-7. The pulpit was sculptured in the 18C.

★ **Uithuizen** – The small **Hervormde Kerk** contains a remarkable organ built in 1700 by Arp Schnitger *(qv)* and a noble's pew from the same period.
To the east is **Menkemaborg**★★ *(qv)* and the **1939-1945 Stichting Museum** ⊙ where the Second World War is evoked by a collection of vehicles and arms.

Oldenzijl Church

Oldenzijl – The small Romanesque church and its churchyard stand on a mound encircled by a moat and a screen of trees. Inside the plainness of the brick walls is broken by several small round windows trimmed with mouldings and the decorative effect of the blind arcading in the chancel.

Return to Groningen by Garsthuizen, St-Annerhuisjes, Ten Boer and the N41.

Campanology
There are three main types of bell installations:

Ringing Peals: up to 12 bells are rung by means of ropes and wheels; each bell swings a full circle to and fro and is struck from the outside, at the end of each swing, by a central clapper or tongue; a ringing peal requires one person per bell; ringing peals or ghange ringing is essentially practised in GB and USA

Carillons: groups of 25 or more bells fixed rigidly and played from a keyboard by one person; the clapper or tongue strikes from inside the bell; operated with the original music cylinders

Chimes of Bells: smaller groups of bells than the carillons but with similar mechanisms; played by one person or mechanically; the range of sound is limited; chimes and carillons are more common on the continent.

★★ DEN HAAG THE HAGUE or 's-GRAVENHAGE Zuid-Holland Ⓟ Pop 444 242

Michelin map 408 D5
Plan of the conurbation in the current Michelin Red Guide Benelux

Seat of the Netherlands' government, of the Parliament, a diplomatic centre, The Hague, whose official name is 's-Gravenhage (generally shortened to Den Haag), is, however, only the provincial capital, the monarch being enthroned in Amsterdam since 1813. Near the sea, it is a pleasant residential town, quiet, airy, with a multitude of squares, parks (more than 700 public gardens) cut across by several lovely canals. Even though The Hague sprawls over a vast area and has a small population density, which has entitled it to being called the "the biggest village in Europe", it is marked by a certain aristocratic charm and is considered as the most worldly and elegant town in the Netherlands.
It is the birthplace of William III (1650-1702), **Christiaen Huygens** *(qv)* the great scientist and the **Jan** (1903-1994) and **Nikolaes Tinbergen** (1907-1988) brothers; one receiving the Nobel Prize for economics (1969) with the Norwegian R. Frisch, the other the Nobel Prize for medicine (1973) with the Austrians K. Lorenz and K. von Frisch.

HISTORICAL NOTES

A meet – Up to the 13C, The Hague was just a hunting lodge set up by Count Floris IV of Holland in the middle of a forest which stretched up to Haarlem *(qv)*. About 1250 his son, William II, who had been proclaimed King of the Romans (1247) by the Pope in his fight against Emperor Frederick II, built a castle on the site of the present Binnenhof. Floris V completed the work of his father by adding the Knight's Hall.
At the end of the 14C, abandoning Haarlem, the Count of Holland, Albert of Bavaria and his suite came to live in The Hague.

C. Sieur/CEDRI

Hofvijver, The Hague

A village... – 's-Gravenhage, the Count's Hedge or Die Haghe, the hedge, rapidly developed without being more than a place of residence and rest. The cloth trade, which started in the 15C was not enough to make it a mercantile town.
In the confederation of cities which was the Low Countries at that time, the other towns would not allow it within their council. However, it was in The Hague that Philip the Good, in 1432 and 1456 held the chapters of the Order of the Golden Fleece.
The absence of fortifications brought destruction upon the city: as from 1528 it was attacked and pillaged by Maarten van Rossum, famous captain of a Gelderland troop of mercenaries. In 1581, the act, declaring Philip II of Spain's disavowal by the States General of the United Provinces, was posted on the door of the Knights' Hall.

...which develops – In the 17C, The Hague found peace and prosperity again. Seat of the States General of the United Provinces, then the government, it became an important centre of diplomatic negotiations. The main coalitions against Louis XIV were sealed here.
From the middle of the 17C to the end of the 18C substantial mansions in Renaissance and baroque style were built round the medieval centre of the Binnenhof.
The French entered The Hague in 1795. Eleven years later the town had to cede its rank of capital to Amsterdam where Louis Bonaparte had installed his government. In 1814 the government and the Court returned to The Hague. But the title of capital remained with Amsterdam, where the king had been enthroned the year before.
The 19C confirmed the residential character of the town which had become the favourite residence of colonials returning from Indonesia. This period marked it so profoundly that it is sometimes considered as the last example of the 19C.

Spinoza – The great philosopher passed the last seven years of his life in The Hague; he died here in 1677. Born in Amsterdam in 1632, this Jew of Portugese origin was a brilliant scholar. In 1656 he had to flee from the Jewish community in Amsterdam. Because he contested the value of the sacred texts, they tried to assassinate him. He took refuge for a time in Ouderkerk aan de Amstel, then went to live in Rijnsburg near Leyden in 1660. For three years he devoted himself to philosophy and polishing lenses to earn his living.
After a few years spent in Voorburg, a suburb of The Hague, in 1670 he moved into a modest residence in Paviljoensgracht (**HJZ**).
It was only after his death that his *Posthumous Works* published in 1677 appeared in Latin; it included the **Ethica**, which became universally famous. His pantheistic doctrine whereby God is a Substance of which only two attributes, extension and thought, are known to us, was violently criticised.

The Hague School – Between 1870 and 1890 a group of painters in The Hague tried to renew painting and notably the art of landscapes in the manner of the Barbizon School in France.
Around their leader, **Jozef Israëls** *(qv)*, painter of fishing scenes and portraits, were grouped: **J.H. Weissenbruch** (1824-1903); **Jacob Maris** (1837-99) painter of dunes and beaches; **H.W. Mesdag** painter of numerous seascapes and the famous *Mesdag Panorama (qv)*; **Anton Mauve** (1838-88) painter of the Gooi heathland *(qv)*; **Albert Neuhuys** (1844-1914) painter of household interiors; **Johannes Bosboom** (1817-91) painter of church interiors; and **Blommers** (1845-1914) painter of the life of fishermen. Neuhuys and Mauve, having worked in Laren, are sometimes attached to the Laren School *(qv)*.
The Hague painters were not looking for brilliance of colour nor the virtuosity of the drawing. In their paintings the prevailing tint was grey or brown, the expression of a certain melancholy.

The diplomatic town – The Hague was chosen several times as a centre for international negotiations: Peace Conferences *(qv)* in particular from 1899 to 1907. Finally the construction of the Peace Palace (1913) established its vocation as a diplomatic town.
It is the seat of the International Court of Justice, an organisation dependant on the UN, the Permanent Court of Arbitration and the Academy of International Law. A number of companies have also made The Hague their headquarters: Royal Dutch (Shell), Aramco, Esso, Chevron.

The modern city – The urban expansion of The Hague has brought it into line with its time. The new district, located mainly to the southwest, is a most pleasing architectural achievement. To the north, the Dutch Convention Centre (Nederlands Congresgebouw) has been open to the public since 1969.
Nestling in an almost rural landscape of copses and meadows, the residential quarters extend up to the dunes that follow the North Sea coast.
The Hague is the seat of the Residentie Orchestra, set up since 1987 in the very modern Anton Philipszaal (seating capacity 1 900) on the Spui. That same year saw the inauguration of the AT & T Danstheater (JZ **T**) (seating capacity 1 000), a venue conceived to house the Nederlands Dans Theater company. Under its Czech-born artistic director, Jiří Kilián, the dance company has acquired a solid reputation for the unorthodoxy of its repertoire and the excellence of its performances.

THE CENTRE *half a day*

Stately mansions line the wide avenues around the Binnenhof, the centre of the country's political life. Nearby, shops are grouped in pedestrian precincts or covered passages: the town has a great many antique dealers and luxury boutiques.

Buitenhof (HY) – It is the "outer courtyard" of the old castle belonging to the Counts of Holland. In its centre stands a statue of King William II.

★ **Binnenhof** (JY) – Enter by the Stadtholder doorway to reach an inner courtyard (binnenhof) in the centre of which stands the Knights' Hall. The buildings all around, dating from different periods in history, act as a symbol of the continuity of the Dutch regime. They now house the Upper Chamber and the Ministry of General Affairs (north wing), part of the State Council (west wing) and the Lower Chamber (south and east wing, as well as the new extensions).
Oldenbarnevelt *(qv)* was executed in this courtyard.

★ **Ridderzaal** (Knights' Hall) ⊙ – An **exhibition** in the cellars of the Knights' Hall (no 8a) explains the origin and workings of the two chambers and the role of the head of state in the monarchy.
The Knight's Hall, destined to be a festival hall for Count William II of Holland, was completed *c*1280 by his son Count Floris V. The building, which looks very much like a church, was located in the prolongation of the old castle. Its façade with a pointed and finely worked gable is flanked by two slender turrets. Inside, the great hall, restored, has recovered its Gothic vault with openwork beams. It is here that since 1904 (3rd Tuesday in September, *see Calendar of Events*) the two chambers of the States General gather for a ceremonial opening session and listen to a speech (on the government's projects to be tackled during the upcoming year) made by the Queen who rides in a ceremonial gold coach.
The back of the building, visible from the Binnenhof's second courtyard consists of the old castle built *c*1250 by Count William II. The main hall became, in 1511, the hall of sessions of the Holland and West Friesland Court, and was called the Roll Court.

Eerste Kamer (Upper Chamber) – Situated in the 17C north wing, in the **Stadtholders' Quarters** (or residence), bordered with a covered gallery, it is the former hall of the Holland and West Friesland States (17C).

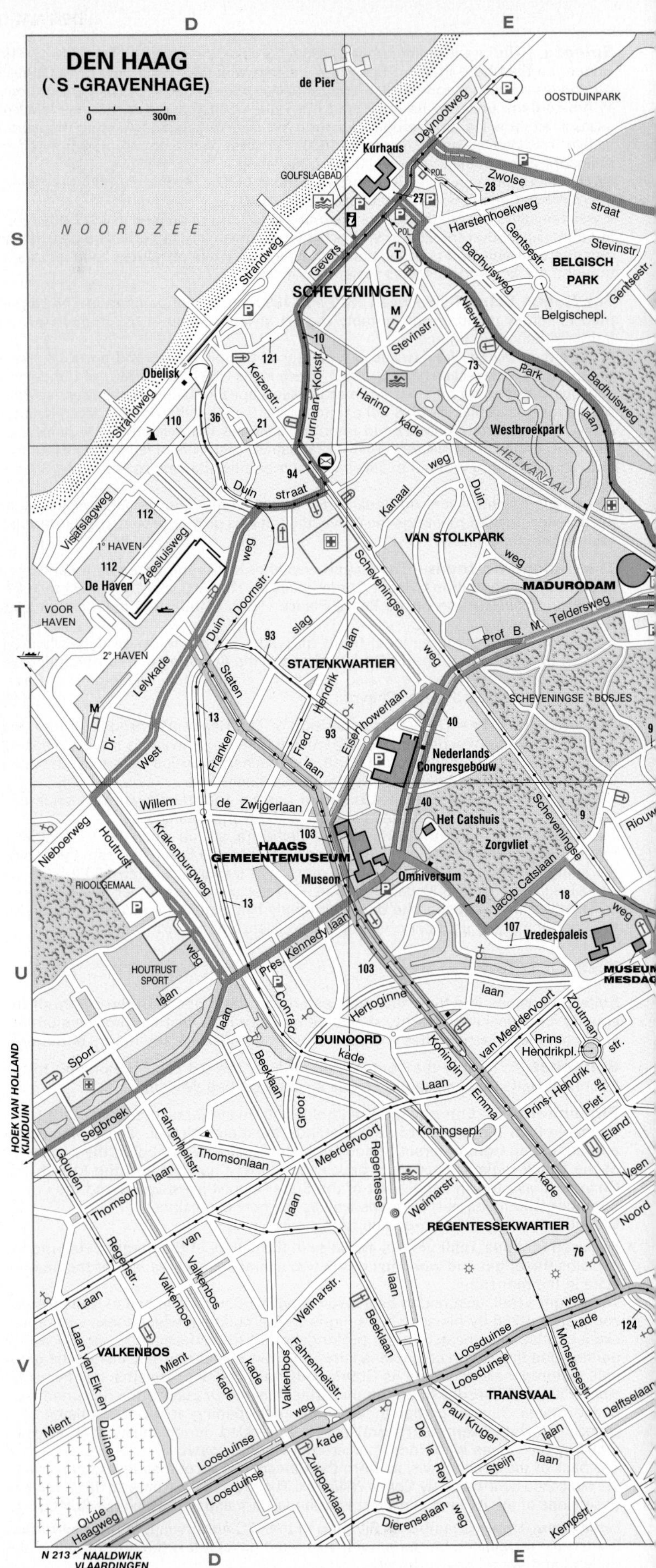
DEN HAAG
('S -GRAVENHAGE)
0 300m
D
E
S
T
U
V
NOORDZEE
de Pier
OOSTDUINPARK
Kurhaus
GOLFSLAGBAD
Deynootweg
Zwolse straat
Harstenhoekweg
Gentsestr.
Badhuisweg
Stevinstr.
BELGISCH PARK
Belgischepl.
SCHEVENINGEN
Strandweg
Gevers
Keizerstr.
Jurriaan Kokstr.
Nieuwe Parklaan
Badhuisweg
Westbroekpark
Haring kade
HET KANAAL
Obelisk
Duinstraat
Kanaal weg
Duin weg
VAN STOLKPARK
Visafslagweg
1° HAVEN
De Haven
Zeesluisweg
MADURODAM
Prof B. M. Teldersweg
VOOR HAVEN
2° HAVEN
Lelykade
Duin weg
Doornstr.
STATENKWARTIER
Scheveningse weg
SCHEVENINGSE BOSJES
Staten
Fred. Hendrik laan
Eisenhowerlaan
Nederlands Congresgebouw
Dr. West
Franken
Willem de Zwijgerlaan
Het Catshuis
Zorgvliet
Scheveningse
Nieboerweg
Houtrust
Krakenburgweg
HAAGS GEMEENTEMUSEUM
Museon
Omniversum
Jacob Catslaan
Vredespaleis
MUSEUM MESDAG
RIOOLGEMAAL
HOUTRUST SPORT
Pres. Kennedy laan
Conrad
Hertoginne laan
Zoutman str.
Prins Hendrikpl.
van Meerdervoort
DUINOORD
kade
Koningin Emma kade
Laan
Prins Hendrik
Piet str.
Eland
Sport laan
Beeklaan
Groot
Segbroek
Fahrenheitstr.
Thomsonlaan
Meerdervoort
Regentesse
Koningspl.
Veen
Noord
Gouden
Thomson laan
Weimarstr.
REGENTESSEKWARTIER
laan
HOEK VAN HOLLAND
KIJKDUIN
Regenstr.
van Valkenbos
Valkenbos
Laan
Weimarstr.
Beeklaan
Loosduinse weg
Loosduinse kade
Monstersestr.
Delftselaan
VALKENBOS
Laan van Eik en Duinen
Mient
Valkenbos kade
Fahrenheitstr.
Paul Kruger laan
TRANSVAAL
Mient
Loosduinse kade
Zuidparklaan
De la Rey weg
Steijn laan
Oude Haagweg
Loosduinse
Dierenselaan
Kempstr.
N 213
NAALDWIJK
VLAARDINGEN

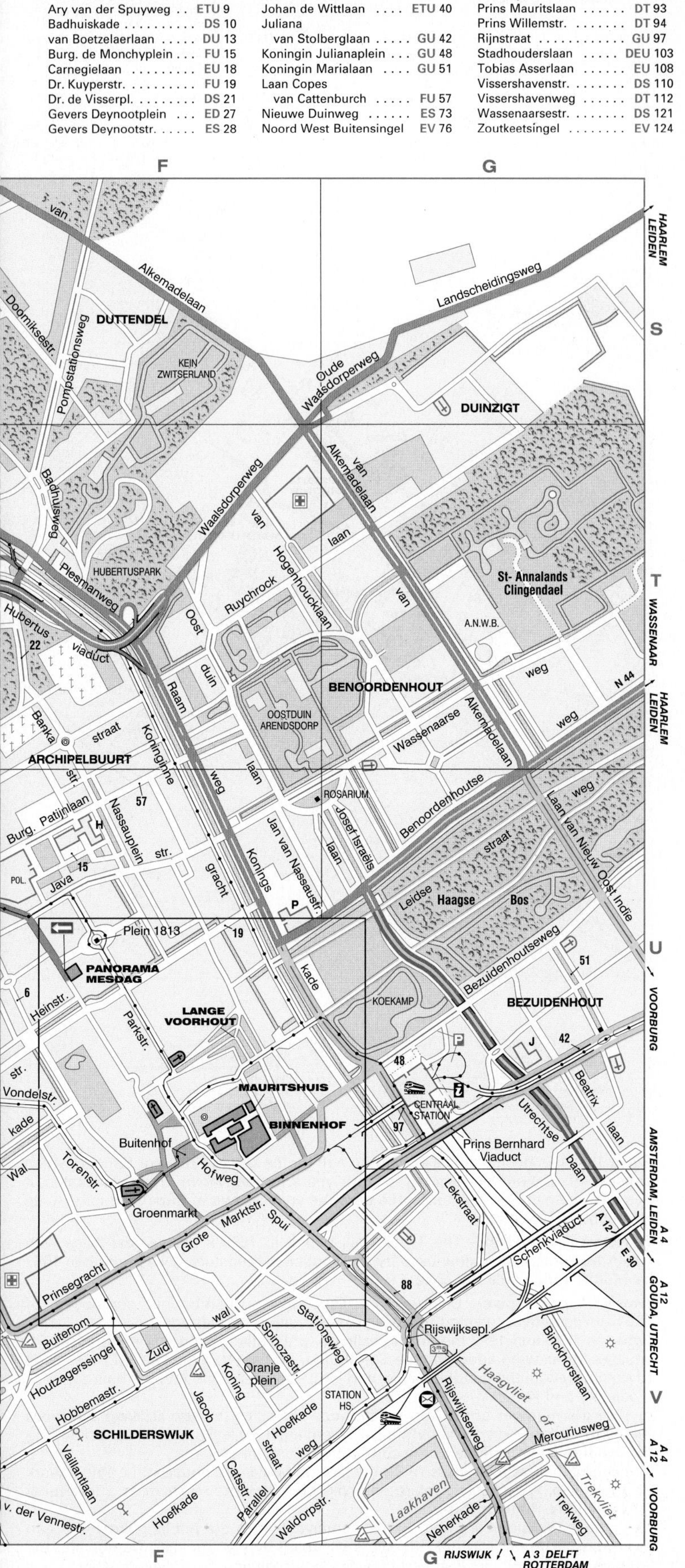
F
G
S
T
U
V
HAARLEM LEIDEN
WASSENAAR
VOORBURG
AMSTERDAM, LEIDEN
A 4
A 12
GOUDA, UTRECHT
RIJSWIJK
A 3 DELFT ROTTERDAM
E 30
N 44
Alkemadelaan
Landscheidingsweg
DUTTENDEL
Doorniksestr.
Pompstationsweg
KEIN ZWITSERLAND
Oude Waalsdorperweg
DUINZIGT
Badhuisweg
Waalsdorperweg
van Alkemadelaan
HUBERTUSPARK
Plesmanweg
Hubertus viaduct
Ruychrock
van Hogenhoucklaan
St- Annalands Clingendael
A.N.W.B.
Oost duin laan
Raam
Koninginne gracht
BENOORDENHOUT
OOSTDUIN ARENDSDORP
Wassenaarse weg
ARCHIPELBUURT
Banka straat
ROSARIUM
Jan van Nassaustr.
Josef Israëls laan
Benoordenhoutse weg
Laan van Nieuw Oost Indië
Burg. Patijnlaan
Nassauplein
Java str.
POL.
Konings kade
Leidse straat
Haagse Bos
Plein 1813
PANORAMA MESDAG
Heinstr.
LANGE VOORHOUT
Parkstr.
KOEKAMP
Bezuidenhoutseweg
BEZUIDENHOUT
Vondelstr.
MAURITSHUIS
BINNENHOF
CENTRAAL STATION
Beatrix laan
Utrechtse baan
Prins Bernhard Viaduct
Buitenhof
Hofweg
Torenstr.
Wal kade
Groenmarkt
Grote Marktstr.
Spui
Lekstraat
Schenkviaduct
Prinsegracht
Buitenom
wal
Stationsweg
Rijswijksepl.
Binckhorstlaan
Zuid
Houtzagerssingel
Spinozastr.
Oranje plein
Koning
Jacob
Hobbemastr.
STATION HS.
Rijswijkseweg
Haagvliet
Mercuriusweg
SCHILDERSWIJK
Hoefkade weg straat
Vaillantlaan
Catsstr.
Parallel
Waldorpstr.
Laakhaven
Neherkade
Trekvliet
Trekweg
v. der Vennestr.
Hoefkade
6
15
19
22
42
48
51
57
88
97

DEN HAAG

Denneweg . . . . JX
Hoogstr. . . . . HY
Korte Poten . . . . JY 54
Lange Poten . . . . JY
Noordeinde . . . . HXY
Paleispromenade . . . . . . HY 81
de Passage . . . . HY 85
Spuistr. . . . . JYZ
Venestr. . . . . HYZ

Vlamingstr. . . . . HZ 114
Wagenstr. . . . . JZ

Amaliastr. . . . . HX 3
Amsterdamse Veerkade . . . . JZ 4
Annastr. . . . . HY 7
Bleijenburg . . . . JY 12
Drie Hoekjes . . . . HY 22
Fluwelen Burgwal . . . . . . JY 24
Groene Wegje . . . . JZ 31
Hooikade . . . . JX 33

Kneuterdijk . . . . HY 45
Korte Molenstr. . . . . HY 52
Korte Vijverberg . . . . JY 55
Lange Vijverberg . . . . . HJY 60
Lutherse Burgwal . . . . . . HZ 64
Molenstr. . . . . HY 70
Paleisstr. . . . . HXY 82
Papestr. . . . . HY 84
Scheveningseveer . . . . . HX 100
Stille Veerkade . . . . JZ 105
Tournooiveld . . . . JXY 108
Vos in Tuinstr. . . . . JX 118

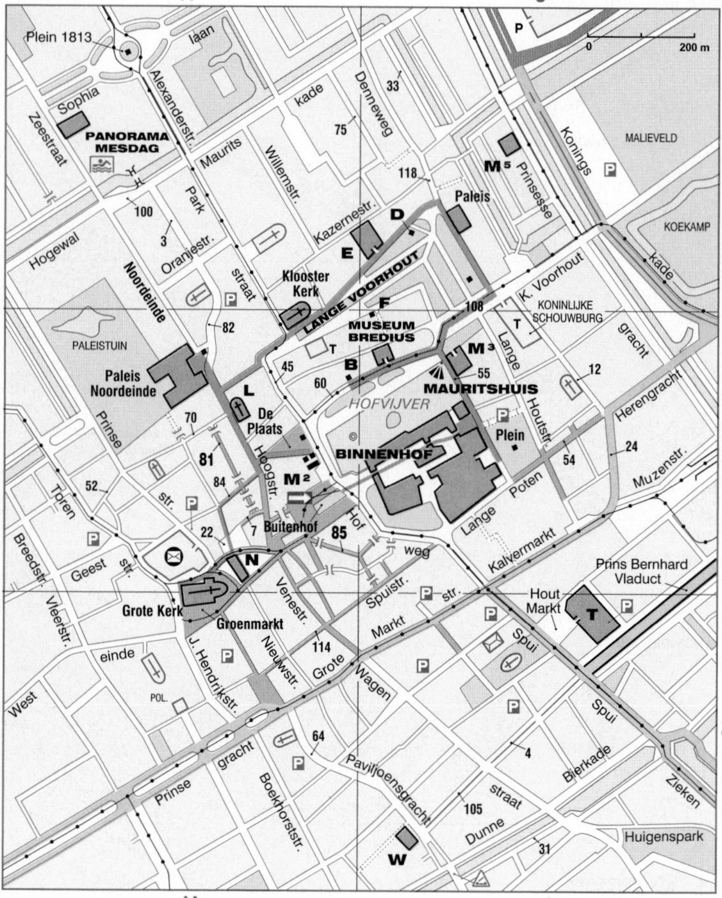

D – de "Flâneur"
F – Pulchri Studio
L – Waals-Hervormde Kerk
M² – Gevangenpoort-Schilderijengalerij Prins Willem V
M³ – Haags Historisch Museum
M⁵ – Rijksmuseum Meermanno-Westreenianum
N – Oude Raadhuis
T – AT & T Danstheater
W – Heilige Geesthofje

Since 1848 has been used as a meeting hall for the Upper House or Senate, which consists of 75 members elected for four years by the twelve Provincial States. It has a wooden ceiling painted in the baroque style by two of Rubens' pupils: A. de Haan and N. Wielingh.

Trêveszaal (Truce Hall) – The Truce Hall, where in 1608 a twelve-year truce with Spain was prepared, is now used by the Council of Ministers. It was rebuilt in 1697 by Marot in the Louis XIV style.

Tweede Kamer (Lower Chamber) – The Lower Chamber is composed of 150 representatives, elected for four years by universal suffrage.

Between 1815 and 1992 the former **ballroom** (presently undergoing restoration ⊙), situated in the wing added by the Stadtholder William V in the late 18C, was used to accommodate the deputies; executed in the style of Louis XIV, the ballroom has a balcony and several boxes.

In 1992 the member of the Lower Chamber moved to the **new buildings** *(Entrance Plein 2A)* ⊙ based on plans by the Dutch architect Pi de Bruijn and set up among the existing constructions to the south of the Binnenhof.

The central hall, whose glass roofing lets in the daylight, houses an original work of art by Lex Wegchelaar, made with marble elements taken from a low relief (1938) by R.N. Roland Holst.

The plenary sessions are held in the hemicycle; from the public gallery one can see, going from left to right, the seats occupied by the Christian Democrats, the Liberals and Labour. Behind the pulpit is a painted panel by R. van de Wint.

Plein (JY) – The Ministry of Defence (Defensie) is situated on this square; in the centre stands the statue of William the Silent (1848). No 23 is a splendid 18C building designed by Daniel Marot. In winter a market selling antique furniture is held on the square.

★★★ **Mauritshuis** (JY) ⊙ – The Royal Picture Gallery is called Mauritshuis, after Prince John Maurice of Nassau (in Dutch: Johan Maurits van Nassau) who had this elegant residence built in the 17C by Pieter Post, from plans by Jacob van Campen. An important restoration, completed in 1987, has adapted the building to the requirements of a modern museum. The exceptional quality of the canvases exhibited makes this museum one of the finest in the world, their relatively small number (about 300), forming a most agreeable collection to visit.

Ground floor – It is devoted to foreign schools and the Flemish School.
The first room of the **Flemish School** *(to the right on entering)* is remarkable with the pathetic *Descent from the Cross* by Rogier van der Weyden, the penetrating *Portrait of a Man* by Memling, *Christ Carrying the Cross* by Quentin Metsys.
There are four lovely portraits by Holbein the Younger (16C), a touching young girl by the German Bartholomeus Bruyn, Holbein's contemporary; two portraits by Antonio Moro, one very vigorous of a silversmith.
Two rooms are reserved for **Rubens** and his contemporaries. *The Adoration of the Shepherds* by Jordaens, canvases by David Teniers are near a rich collection of works by Rubens: *Isabella Brant,* his first wife, *Hélèna Fourment,* his second, *Michel Ophovius,* bishop of 's-Hertogenbosch, and finally the famous *Adam and Eve in Paradise* where the two personages painted by Rubens can be seen against a landscape painted with charming meticulousness by Jan Bruegel (Velvet Bruegel).

1st floor – Amongst the Dutch painters of the Golden Age, **Rembrandt** is the reigning master here *(galleries on the right).*
Between the portrait of the artist when he was 23 (1629), which holds one's attention by its meticulous precision of detail, its taste for scrupulous observation, and the portrait of 1669, one of his last works, with an overwhelming depth, one can see the whole evolution of the painter.
The Anatomy Lesson of Doctor Tulp (1632), his first group portrait painted when he was 26, brought him glory; the research in composition, the contrasts of light give the scene a dramatic intensity already characteristic.
The same emotion appears in the luminous *Susanna* of 1637, one of the rare nudes by Rembrandt, the *Simeon in the Temple* (1631) with its subdued muted light, or in the more fiery works like the pathetic *Saul and David* (1658); *The Two Negroes* (1661).
The museum also has two admirable paintings by **Vermeer**, the *View of Delft* (*c*1658), "the most beautiful in the world" according to Marcel Proust and of which Van Gogh said "It's unbelievable", and the *Young Girl with a Turban* or *With a Pearl* (*c*1658). To these two masterpieces one can compare the *Diana*, one of the first paintings already showing the limpid and serene poetry of the Delft master.
The museum has a number of genre paintings: some Jan Steens, where the verve, malice, and dedicacy bring charming anecdotes *(Merry Company)*, some Van Ostades with scenes of country life *(The Violinist)*, portraits by Frans Hals such as the brilliant *Head of a Child,* some Ter Borchs of great sensitivity, the *Young Mother* by Gerrit Dou...

View of Delft by J. Vermeer

There are also landscape painters; painters of rivers like Van Goyen, Van de Velde, the countryside, like Salomon van Ruysdael and his nephew Jacob van Ruisdael, skaters, like Avercamp, domestic animals, like Paulus Potter *(The Bull Calf)*.
There are also some small gems: the famous *Goldfinch* which Carel Fabritius, Rembrandt's pupil, painted the year of his death aged 32.

Hofvijver (HJY) – From Korte Vijverberg, there is a lovely **view**★ over the court lake in which you can see the Mauritshuis reflected, the octagonal tower of the Prime Minister, the windows of the Truce Hall and the Upper Chamber. In the middle of the lake, which has a fountain, there is an island planted with trees.

Haags Historisch Museum (The Hague Historical Museum) (JY **M**3) ⊙ – The collections of this museum, set up on the former premises of the Archers' Company of St Sebastian (1636), illustrate the history of the town and the life of its inhabitants: archaeological findings, porcelain, work by gold and silversmiths' guilds, views of the city...

Take Lange Vijverberg.

★ **Museum Bredius** (JY) ⊙ – The museum has a privileged setting: a fine hotel built in 1757. The painting collection features many of the works left to the town by Abraham Bredius (1855-1946), an art historian and former director of the Mauritshuis.
In the remarkable section on 17C art, you can admire the famous *Satyr among the Peasants* by Jan Steen, a fine *Christ's Head* by Rembrandt, *Festivities on the Ice* by A. van der Neer, along with canvases by Aelbert Cuyp, Adriaen van Ostade, Willem Pieter Buytewech and J.J. van de Velde.
On the floor above, note the drawings by Rembrandt and Jacob van Ruysdael.
At no 8 (HY **B**) there is a façade by Daniel Marot.

★ **Lange Voorhout** (HJX) – Along the shaded avenues of Lange Voorhout with vast lawns there are some of the most beautiful patrician residences in The Hague. Most of them are occupied by embassies.
Nearby there is a big **antiques market** ⊙. In the spring the lawns are covered with crocuses.

Paleis (JX) ⊙ – The former palace of Queen Emma (1858-1934), wife of William III and mother to Wilhelmina stands at the far end of the main avenue. Its elegant 18C façade is the work of Pieter de Swart. It was the home of a banker when Napoleon stayed in it in 1811.
In front of the Indes Mansion (nos 54-56), there is a lovely statuette of the **"Stroller"** (JX **D**) by the chronicler Elias.

No 34 (HJX **E**) – This edifice was built in 1734-6 by Daniel Marot.
From 1813-4 William I, first king of the Netherlands, lived here. The building now houses the Supreme Court of Appeal.

At no 15, on the left, stands the building bought by Mesdag *(qv)* to house the **Pulchri Studio** company (JXY **F**) of which he was the president from 1889.

Kloosterkerk (HXY) – This former convent chapel built in the 15 and 16C is used for organ concerts and choral services.

Noordeinde (HXY) – This large street with antique shops crosses the square where the **Paleis Noordeinde** (HY) stands. Also called Het Oude Hof, this 16-17C building with two angled wings was occupied by Louise de Coligny, widow of William the Silent, by the Princes Maurice and Frederick Henry, sons of the latter *(p 20)*, and by King William I. Queen Beatrix has installed her offices here.
Opposite there is an equestrian statue of William the Silent.

Return towards the south.

Waals-Hervormde Kerk (HY **L**) ⊙ – The Walloon Reformed Church was built in 1807 by Louis Napoleon to be used by the French-speaking Protestant community of The Hague which formerly met in the castle chapel.
After the mid-16C the Protestant refugees, fleeing persecution in the Southern Netherlands (Belgium), established French-speaking parish communities. These increased in the 17C with Huguenots coming from France.
The cult is still practised today in **Walloon churches** *(qv)* which are dependent upon the Dutch Reformed Church *(qv)*.

De Plaats (HY) – In the Centre of this square is the statue (1887) of Johan de Witt who was lynched here at the same time as his brother Cornelis *(see Dordrecht)*.

Gevangenpoort (HY **M**2) ⊙ – This old curtain wall gate of the ducal castle houses a museum, **Rijksmuseum Gevangenpoort**, which contains a collection of torture instruments. Cornelis de Witt *(see above)* was imprisoned here before being killed on De Plaats.

★ **Schilderijengalerij Prins Willem V** (HY **M**2) ⊙ – In 1773 the Stadtholder of the United Provinces William V converted the second floor of the house adjoining the Prison Gate into a painting gallery. This gallery was open to the public; it may be seen as the very first public museum in the history of the Netherlands. The prince's collection featured mainly 17C landscapes, genre scenes and still lifes. In 1815 King William I donated the collection to the state and it was transferred to the Mauritshuis in 1821.
The gallery has been restored and decorated in the manner of the 18C: the paintings cover almost entirely all the walls, up to the vaulted ceiling embellished with Louis XVI stucco work.

Although it only features a few works belonging to the original collection, the present display of 17C paintings is extremely interesting. It includes landscapes by PH. Wouwerman, *Veere Church* by J. van der Heyde, two works by Steen, *The Bear Hunt* by Paulus Potter, *Portrait of P. Boom* by Thomas de Keyser (son of Hendrick de Keyser), *Head of an Old Man* by Lievens, one of Rembrandt's contemporaries, and a picture by Van de Velde the Younger: *The War Ship at Sunset.*

Groenmarkt (HZ) – It is the central square of The Hague where the town hall and the Grote Kerk stand. Numerous pedestrian precincts start from here, notably **Paleispromenade** (HY **81**) to the north, and **De Passage** (HY **85**), the large covered passage built in 1880, to the south.

Grote- of St.-Jacobskerk (HYZ) ⊙ – Flanked by a tower with a carillon of 51 bells, this great brick hall-type (three naves of equal height) church (*c*1450) is roofed with a wooden vault. In the chancel (*c*1500), there is the tomb of an admiral and the coat of arms of the knights of the Order of the Golden Fleece who held their chapter in this church in 1456. Several stained glass windows are worth seeing in the ambulatory: on one Charles V is shown kneeling at the Virgin's feet. The pulpit of 1550 is beautifully sculptured.

Oude Raadhuis (HY **N**) – The old town hall has a lovely 16C façade with crow-stepped gables. The 18C side façade is elegantly decorated. A modern wing has been added on the east side.

Grand panorama paintings were one of the most popular forms of mass entertainment in the 19C, before the advent of photography and the motion picture. They were usually exhibited in purpose-built rotundas and were often on huge fully cylindrical canvases which entirely surrounded the viewer, who stood on a central viewing platform. The panorama painting technique is related to the exuberant mastery of baroque and the technique of trompe-l'œil and was originally the idea of Robert Barker, an Irishman. By portraying vast panoramas in minute detail the painting enabled the public to glimpse foreign shores with an immediacy never before possible. Panorama paintings were generally executed by teams of artists, often drawing on specialised skills. Their most common subject matter tended to be military, more particularly the glorification of warfare. Preliminary sketches were rescaled onto the enormous canvas using a grid, but this did not entirely eliminate distortions of perspective caused by the curve of the cylindrical canvas. It took about a year to complete a painting, which was then exhibited in its rotunda with the area between it and the viewing platform converted into an elaborate extension of the painting's foreground by the dispersal of relevant objects all over it (known as a faux-terrain) to increase the effect of the illusion. Sadly, the popularity of the grand panorama diminished as that of the cinema grew, and many of the paintings were lost when the rotundas that housed them were demolished or put to other uses. There are now only ten left in western Europe (Austria: Salzburg, Innsbruck; Belgium: Waterloo, Brussels; Germany: Munich, Bad Frankenhausen; Netherlands: The Hague; Switzerland: Einsiedelin, Thun, Lucerne).

OUTSIDE THE CENTRE *half a day – town plan on p 124*

★ **Panorama Mesdag** (HX) ⊙ – Installed in a rotunda on piles, lit by hidden windows, this extraordinary landscape of 120m - 394ft in circumference and 14m - 46ft high shows Scheveningen *(qv)* as it was in 1881. The order for this immense canvas was given in 1880 to the painter **Hendrik Willem Mesdag** *(qv)*. In 1879 from the top of the highest dune in Scheveningen, he had already reproduced the landscape on the glass cylinder shown here.
This work was rapidly carried out: Mesdag painted the sky, the sea, the beach with boats; his wife, Sientje Mesdag van Houten, the village; Théophile de Bock, the dunes; Breitner, the cavalry; Blommers *(qv)*, the woman in costume and her child. Despite the difference in technique it remains a unit; the perspective is marvellous, the sky over the sea of a very soft luminosity, while behind the village the bell towers of The Hague show up.
The spectator 14m - 46ft below this painting appears to be admiring the panorama from the top of a dune where real sand strewn with wreckage joins up with the bottom of the painting. In the absence of a port the flat-bottomed boats *(bommen)* were towed by horses.
In the entrance hall, added in 1910, paintings and watercolours by Mesdag and his wife are exhibited; note the lovely sombre tonalities.

★ **Museum Mesdag** (EU) ⊙ – Mesdag built this residence in 1869 to house his collections. He bequeathed everything to the State in 1903. In this museum an interesting comparison can be made between the Barbizon School (mid-19C) with Millet, Daubigny, Corot, Théodore Rousseau, Courbet, and The Hague School *(qv)* with Bosboom, Mauve, the Maris borthers, Jozef Israëls and obviously Mesdag, the painter of seascapes. In the paintings of the two schools one finds fairly sombre tones, often greyish and the taste for nature and landscapes.

Vredespaleis (EU) ⊙ – The Peace Palace was inaugurated a year before the beginning of the First World War, on 28 August 1913. On the initiative of Czar Nicholas II the first **Peace Conference** took place in The Hague (at Huis Ten Bosch) in 1899.

It was decided at that time to create a Permanent Court of Arbitration which was defined in 1907 during the Second Peace Conference which took place in the Knights' Hall *(p 121)*.
In the meantime the American industrialist and philanthropist, Andrew Carnegie, donated the funds to house this Court and equip it with a library, the Netherlands government donated a park and the French architect Cordonnier was put in charge of the construction.
In 1922 the palace became, in addition, the seat of the Permanent Court of International Justice which in 1946 became the **International Court of Justice** (the United Nation's main judicial organ). It also houses the Academy of International Law of The Hague, founded in 1923. Each nation has contributed to the furnishings and decoration of the palace. The Japanese room, hung with sumptuous tapestries, is where the Administrative Council meets, and where French is the official language; the members sit round an immense table with seats decorated with the various countries' coat of arms. In the marble galleries, on the ground floor, one can see the bust of Grotius *(qv)* and some documents autographed by him.
Walk alongside **Zorgvliet Park** to see the **Het Catshuis** (EU), the Prime Minister's house which belonged to **Jacob Cats** *(qv)*.

Follow President Kennedylaan to reach the Municipal Museum.

★★ **Haags Gemeentemuseum** (DEU) ⏲ – In 1935 Berlage *(qv)* built this municipal museum, consisting of a concrete structure covered by brick facing. A gallery leads to the different exhibition rooms, arranged in a very elaborate manner. The rich and varied collections concern mostly decorative arts, as well as 19 and 20C sculpture and painting. The museum also has a section devoted to musical instruments.

Ground floor – In the decorative arts section, one can admire ceramics from Italy and Spain, Venitian glassware (15 and 16C), blue and polychrome Delftware and glassware manufactured in the Netherlands. The collections of porcelain, ceramics and silverware from The Hague illustrate what this area was able to produce from the 15 to the 19C. Other objects are on display in period interiors dating back to the 17 and 18C. As well as an impressive exhibition of musical instruments from all over the world, the museum presents a remarkable group of European instruments: some of the oldest ones go back as far as the early 16C.
The engravings cabinet is open to visitors by appointment only.

1st floor – The museum houses work by great masters of the 19 and 20C. The French School is well represented. There is a Courbet *(Bridge, House and Waterfall)*, a Sisley *(The Seine at Daybreak)* and three Monets *(The Louvre Quay,* the *Nets* and *Wisteria)*, a Signac *(Cassis, Cape Lombard)*; by Van Gogh, a *Self-Portrait* (1886), the *Poppy Fields* and two other canvases. One can also see: Picasso *(Woman With a Pot of Mustard, Harlequin, Sibyl)*, Braque, Léger, Marquet and two Dutch painters who became Parisians: Van Dongen and Jongkind. The remarkable collection of Expressionists includes works by Kirchner, Jawlensky and Kandinsky.
One can also get an idea of Dutch pictorial production from the 19C to today; the Romantics with W. Nuyen, The Hague School (the Maris brothers, Jozef Israëls, Weissenbruch), the Amsterdam School (Breitner, Verster), modernism with Jan Toorop, a large collection of **Mondrians**, one of the pioneers of abstract art, and artists of the De Stijl movement *(qv)*.
Among the contemporary artists represented are: Karel Appel, Corneille, Constant, Schoonhoven amongst the Dutch, and amongst foreigners, Vasarely, Arp, Max Ernst, Henry Moore and Bacon. The collection of contemporary works has an international flavour and is rapidly expanding. Note the paintings by J. Benys, G. Baselitz, Penck, C. Westerik, Jan Dibbets, Ger Lataster, Marlene Dumas and Per Kirkeby.
The print room displays many of the works by the great engraver **M.C. Escher** (1898-1972), works of The Hague School, those of H. Werkman, and amongst numerous French artists, Daumier, Toulouse-Lautrec, Bresdin and Redon.

Museon (DEU) ⏲ – This modern museum presents, didactically, collections referring to the Earth's origins: geology, biology, ethnology, techniques, physics...

Omniversum (EU) ⏲ – The films and other presentations shown on this huge screen (840m^2 - 9 042sq ft), which also serves as a planetarium, are aimed at familiarising the viewer with the world of science, astronomy and aeronautics. Two projection systems – Omnimax 70mm and the computerised planetary projector Digistar – around forty loud speakers and a great many projectors for special effects make for a wonderful, breathtaking visual experience.

Nederlands Congresgebouw (ET) – The Netherlands Conference Centre was built to plans of the architect J.J.P. Oud by his son between 1964 and 1968. The conference centre is a vast building with walls of sky-blue tiles and yellow bricks, overlooked by a triangular 17-storey tower. The entrance, on the north side, is indicated by a large composition by Karel Appel in red and blue mosaic.
Among the many meeting rooms, the large conference centre (seating capacity 2 000) occupies three floors. It can be used for entertainment: concerts, theatre, ballets. In the basement the festival hall, which can hold 4 000 people, is used for banquets and exhibitions.

Prof. B.M. Teldersweg crosses Scheveningse Bosjes which separates The Hague from Scheveningen.

★ **Madurodam** (ET) ⏲ – *Photograph p 130.* In memory of his son, who died in Dachau in 1945, Maduro built this miniature town for children, which adults will find interesting as well – it is like Gulliver in Lilliput. Madurodam City is a sort of synthesis of the country, gathering together buildings, monuments and characteristic sites. It is a delight to stroll through, recognising the houses of Herengracht in Amsterdam, Kinderdijk's windmills, the port of Rotterdam, Schiphol sairport, fields of flowers, a farmhouse of Zuid-Holland. Trains, cars, buses and boats travel round. At night it is bright with lights.

ADDITIONAL SIGHTS

Haagse Bos (GU) – Crossed by Leidsestraatweg, these woods surround the royal palace, **Huis ten Bosch**, where the first Peace Conference *(qv)* was held in 1899. This edifice was built in the 17C by Pieter Post for Amalia van Solms, widow of the Prince-Stadtholder Frederick-Henry of Orange (3rd son of William the Silent). This is Queen Beatrix' official residence.

Westbroekpark (ES) – This park surrounded by lakes (canoeing) is famous for its **rose garden** *(early July to late September)* where an international exhibition is held annually.

St.-Annalands Clingendael (GT) – This extensive park, with its meadows shaded by majestic trees and strewn with lakes, was once private property; there is a Japanese garden.

Heilige Geesthofje (JZ **W**) – Built in 1616, this almshouse is a charming enclosure with small low houses with crow-stepped dormer windows. Opposite, near the house *(no 74)* where Spinoza ended his days, stands the statue of the illustrious philosopher.

Rijksmuseum Meermanno-Westreenianum (JX **M**^{5}) ⊙ – On Prinsessegracht, lined with 18C rich patrician residences, this museum houses the Baron van Westreenen's collections. The ground floor is usually devoted to exhibitions about books. On the 1st floor, in the library, there are **manuscrits and incunabula** from the medieval period; the oldest dated books printed in the Low Countries were edited in 1473 in Aalst (Belgium) and in Utrecht. The museum also contains Greek, Roman and Egyptian antiquities.

★★ SCHEVENINGEN

Belonging to The Hague administrative district, Scheveningen is an elegant seaside resort with a very large and busy beach. It has often been devastated by storms: the storm of 1570 submerged part of the village: the church, which, in the past, was located in the town centre, is now near the beach. Today Scheveningen is protected by many breakwaters and a high dike.
The **Circustheater** (ES **T**) dating from 1904 was recently refurbished and reopened in 1993 for variety shows and extravaganzas.

The beach – It is a long and wide stretch of fine sand lined for 3km - 2 miles by a boulevard, Strandweg, which is the continuation to the east of a pedestrian path. In summer this is where the holidaymakers can be seen but it is also popular, even in winter, with the townspeople who come to enjoy the invigorating sea breezes or linger with a coffee on one of the café terraces. Some important transformations have recently occurred on this seafront. Overlooking the beach, the **Kurhaus** (ES) an imposing building (1885) contains a casino; events are also held here. The **Pier** (DES) ⊙, a long promenade-jetty leads to four constructions built on piles offering entertainment. An observation tower (45m - 148ft) high offers a panorama of Scheveningen, The Hague, the dunes towards Wassenaar and out to sea.

The port – Beyond the lighthouse, towards the west, the fishing port remains very busy. Two interior docks (binnenhavens), have coasting vessels, pleasure boats and a fleet of trawlers. The **obelisk** (DS) commemorates the place where William I *(qv)* landed in November 1813, from England to take possession of his throne. First situated to the east of the port near the dunes, around Dr. de Visserplein as it is shown on the Panorama Mesdag *(qv)*, the fishing village has grown with new quarters to the south and west of the port: they are vast quadrilateral brick buildings arranged round a courtyard with wide porches.
Old women remain faithful to the traditional costume: black dress and apron with a black cape in winter (on Sundays it is pastel coloured) or a light-coloured shawl in summer.

F. Chazot/EXPLORER

Kurhaus, Scheveningen

The headdress, placed on a metal headband fixed with two hairpins is distinctive: the end of the headband in the shape of an oval buckle of filigree gold stands up on the top of the head. On Sundays the bonnet is of lace *(for more on the female costume see the Introduction).*

Boat trips ⏲ – A day of competitive fishing at sea is organised. *Landing stage: Dr. Lelykade* (**DT**).

EXCURSIONS

Wassenaar – Pop 26 218. *12km - 7 1/2 miles to the north; leave by Benoordenhoutseweg.* Residential suburban town of The Hague, Wassenaar has substantial villas hidden amongst trees.

Voorburg and Zoetermeer – *16km - 10 miles to the east; leave by Brinckhorstlaan.*

Voorburg – Pop 39 813. Situated near Voorburg station, Hofwijck Manor houses the **Huygensmuseum** ⏲. This small manor surrounded by water was conceived by **Constantijn Huygens** (1596-1687) and built by the architect Pieter Post in the years 1641-1643. Part of the symmetrical garden still stands today.

Constantijn Huygens, who acted as first secretary to the stadtholders Frederick Henry, William II and William III, was also a poet and a composer. He decided to have Hofwijck Manor built in order to withdraw from "court life" in The Hague, where he had many social commitments. **Christiaen Huygens** (1629-1695), son of Constantijn, invented the pendulum clock. This great astronomer and physicist enjoyed a worldwide reputation. In 1663 he was made a member of the Royal Society in London, then of the Royal Science Academy *(Académie Royale des Sciences)* in France. After a long and fruitful stay in Paris, Christiaen returned to the Netherlands. He settled into Hofwijck Manor, where he lived until his death. The collections in the museum retrace the history of his family: portraits, original editions of works by Constantijn Huygens and a replica of Christian Huygens' world famous pendulum clock, made in Leyden.

Zoetermeer – Originally the site of this new town was a lake formed by massive peat extraction; it was drained and reclaimed in 1616. The new town was designated to take pressure off The Hague and it was estimated that in its final phase the population would reach 110 000 to 115 000. The new town developments are centred on an existing village with an 18C kerk sporting a Gothic tower and wooden spire (1642). The historic core is now prolonged by a new shopping centre and business complex.

Naaldwijk – Pop 27 987. *16km - 10 miles to the south; leave by Oude Haagweg.* Cross the market-garden region of **Westland**, cut by canals, spread with thousands of greenhouses, orchards and gardens between The Hague, Hoek van Holland and the coastal dunes; flowers are cultivated as well as vegetables (tomatoes, salads, cucumbers). In the heart of Westland, Naaldwijk is a large horticultural centre and has **auctions** ⏲ of cut flowers and potted plants. On Wilhelminaplein, the main square, the old 17C **raadhuis** has a baroque voluted gable. Not far away, behind the Gothic church, the Holy Ghost Almshouse, **Heilige Geesthofje**, groups picturesque, 17C low houses with tall dormer windows arranged round a chapel of the same period.

P. Viard/PIX

Madurodam

★★ HAARLEM Noord-Holland Ⓟ Pop 149 474

Michelin map 408 E4 – Local map see KEUKENHOF
Plan of the conurbation in the current Michelin Red Guide Benelux

Historical capital of the Holland earldom and county town of Noord-Holland province, Haarlem, situated on the Spaarne, is the birthplace of Frans Hals.
It is the centre of a large bulb-growing region.

HISTORICAL NOTES

Haarlem was founded *c*10C on the edge of the offshore bar, near the interior seas, now disappeared, between Haarlem and Wijk (present Wijk aan Zee, *qv*).
Fortified in the 12C, Haarlem was the residence of the Counts of Holland. It obtained its city charter in 1245. In the 13C its inhabitants took part in the Fifth Crusade and the capture of Damietta in 1219. The bells of the Grote Kerk are still called *damiaatjes* in memory of this great deed. In the 14C Haarlem expanded but all that remains of its fortifications is the Amsterdam gateway (late 15C), to the east.

A bloody siege – During the uprising against the Spanish, Haarlem was besieged for seven months (1572-3) by the troops of Dom Frederico of Toledo, son of the Duke of Alba.
During the winter, William the Silent managed to provide the town with supplies by the Beggars, who came on skates over Haarlemmermeer, but despite the heroic defence by the whole population, the town capitulated in June 1573; the inhabitants were massacred. It was only in 1577 that Haarlem sided with the States General.
The 17C marks the peak of Haarlem; the town took advantage of the fall of Flemish cities by developing the linen industry and made a fabric sold all over Europe under the name of holland (a plain weave linen).

HAARLEM

Anegang .... BCY
Barteljorisstr. .... BC 9
Grote Houtstr. .... BYZ
Kruisstr. .... BY
Zijlstr. .... BY

Bakenessergracht .... CY 6
Barrevoetstr. .... BY 7
Botermarkt .... BYZ 13
Damstr. .... CY 18
Donkere Spaarne .... CY 19
Frans Halsstr. .... CX 25
Friese Varkensmarkt .... CXY 27
Gasthuisvest .... BZ 28
Ged. Voldersgracht ...... BY 30
Gierstraat .... BZ 31
Groot Heiligland .... BZ 33
Hagestr. .... CZ 34
Hoogstr. .... CZ 39
Jacobstr. .... BY 40
Keizerstr. .... BY 45
Klokhuispl. .... CY 48
Koningstr. .... BY 49
Nassaustr. .... BY 54
Nieuwe Groenmarkt ..... BY 55
Ostadestr. .... BX 57
Oude Groenmarkt ...... BCY 58
Smedestr. .... BY 66
Spaarndamseweg .... CX 67
Spaarnwouderstr. .... CZ 69
Tuchthuisstr. .... BZ 72
Verwulft .... BYZ 75
Zijlsingel .... BY 79

Haarlemmermeer – Formed by peat exploitation, this great lake of about 18 000ha - 44 460 acres was a threat to Amsterdam and Leyden due to storms. As early as 1641, Leeghwater *(qv)* had suggested draining it by using windmills and making polders. The work was not undertaken until two centuries later when steam powered **pumps** gradually replaced windmills. Three pumping stations were installed (one being the one invented by Cruquius, *qv*) and the work was completed in 1852.
The present territory of Haarlemmermeer, which has become a district borough, is on the average 4m - 13ft below sea level, and Schiphol Airport *(qv)*, which is located there is 4.5m - 15ft below. The silty marine deposits under the peat bogs are very fertile.

The meeting place of artists – Haarlem is the town of **Claus Sluter** (*c*1345-1406), a sculptor who, working for the Dukes of Burgundy in the Charterhouse of Champmol near Dijon *(see Michelin Green Guide Burgundy)* produced works of great realism. In the 15C born in Haarlem were: the painter **Dirck Bouts** who went to live in Louvain (Belgium), **Jan Mostaert** (*c*1475-1555/6) a religious painter influenced by Italian art, while **Geertgen tot Sint Jans** *(qv)* came to live here.
In the 16C **Maarten van Heemskerck** (1498-1574) was the pupil of Jan van Scorel *(qv)* during his stay in Haarlem, from 1527-9. **Cornelis van Haarlem**, Mannerist painter (1562-1638) and **Willem Claesz. Heda** (1594-1680), famous for his still-lifes were born in this town. The engraver **Hendrick Goltzius** (1558-1617), **Pieter Claesz.** (1597-1661), another specialist of still-lifes, and **Pieter Saenredam** (1597-1665) painter of luminous architecture, all ended their days here. **Hercules Seghers** (1589/90-1638) a remarkable landscape painter also lived here.
Born in Haarlem, **Lieven de Key** (*c*1560-1627) was a great Renaissance architect. **Bartholomeus van der Helst** (1613-70), **Philips Wouwerman** (1619-68) painter of horses, imitated by his brother Pieter, **Nicolaes Berchem** (1620-83) who, contrary to his father Pieter Claesz. painted landscapes and herds, were also born in Haarlem.
Salomon van Ruysdael, born in Naarden (*c*1600-70) settled in Haarlem. This serene painter, whose art is very near that of Van Goyen *(qv)* liked wooded shores reflected in calm water, and monochromes.
His nephew and pupil **Jacob van Ruisdael** (1628/9-82) was born in Haarlem. He painted more tormented landscapes, already romantic with dark cliffs, waterfalls, trees menaced by storm, disquieting chiaroscuros. **Meindert Hobbema** (1638-1708) was his pupil.

Frans Hals – This painter was born in Antwerp *c*1582, but his family went to live in Haarlem around 1595. Frans Hals became the portrait painter of the town's bourgeois at a time when the portrait and particularly, group portraits (guilds, brotherhoods) were in fashion.
Frans Hals abandoned the tradition of rigid poses and stilted compositions and he introduced, especially to his commissioned works, a certain vitality and more natural attitudes for his subjects. In some cases he went so far as to catch them unawares, as he did with the arquebusiers during their banquet (painting in the Frans Halsmuseum). His bold and fluent brushwork was considered sloppy at the time.
He enlivened his canvases with bright colours, a riot of colour on scarves and flags. His rapid but expressive brush strokes, which foreshadowed modern art and especially Impressionism, gave his models a life, a mobility which made his portraits real snapshots.
For a long time a frank cheerfulness radiated from his paintings, but after 1640 there was no longer the verve and fantasy in his works. In the famous group of regents and regentesses *(p 110)* the return to black and white, verticality, expressive faces, even disenchanted, left a sinister impression, almost a forewarning of his death two years later (1666).
His style was not captured by his pupils: **Judith Leyster** (1609-60), the Fleming Adriaen Brouwer and **Adriaen van Ostade** (1610-85), painter of village scences. The latter's pupils were his brother Isaack as well as Jan Steen *(qv)*.

Frans Halsmuseum

Banquet of the Officers of the Haarlem Militia Company of St Hadrian by Frans Hals

AROUND GROTE MARKT *1 hour 30 min*

★ **Grote Markt** (BY) – This great square is bordered by the Grote Kerk, the Stadhuis and the former Meat Market.
In the square there is a statue of **Laurens Coster** (1405-84) (his real name is Laurens Janszoon) considered in the Netherlands as the inventor of printing in *c*1430, that is to say about ten years before Gutenberg (who is thought to have completed the printing of the Bible by 1455). Coster is believed to have printed with moveable type; however, no evidence was kept.

★ **Grote of St.-Bavokerk** (BCY) ⊙ – This large 15C church, which should not be confused with the Catholic St Bavo's *(Leidsevaart)*, is topped at the transept crossing by an elegant wooden lantern tower covered with lead, 80m - 262ft high.
Inside admire the short nave and, in the chancel, a lovely cedar-wood ribbed vault. Note, also, a 17C pulpit with a Gothic sounding board, wood choir stalls (1512) carved with amusing subjects, the copper lectern in the shape of a pelican (late 15C) and above all the lovely early 16C **chancel screen**★, backed by finely worked brass.
The **organ**★ ⊙ built by Christiaen Müller in 1738 has been decorated according to the drawings of Daniel Marot. For a long time it was considered as one of the best instruments in the world and it is said that Handel and Mozart (as a child) came to play it. International organ competitions are organised every two years in Haarlem *(see the chapter Practical Information at the end of the guide)*.

Interior of St.-Bavokerk, Haarlem
by P. J. Saenredam, Rijksmuseum, Amsterdam

Rijksmuseum, Amsterdam

★ **Stadhuis** (BY H) ⊙ – Flanked by a turret, it is a 14C Gothic building to which numerous alterations have been made: on the right an advancement over a gallery topped with a voluted gable (15 and 17C), on the left above a flight of steps, a Renaissance loggia.
Inside on the 1st floor, the Counts' Hall, **Gravenzaal**, has kept its former style; the paintings which decorate it are copies of old frescoes from the Carmelite convent and depict the counts of Holland.

★ **Vleeshal** (BY) ⊙ – This elegant building, the former meat hall, in Renaissance style, built in 1603 by Lieven de Key *(qv)* is topped by richly decorated dormer windows. Inside there are exhibits organised by the Frans Hals museum.

Vishal (BCY A) ⊙ – The fish market was built in 1769, up against the northern façade of St-Bavokerk; like the meat market, it is an annex of the Frans Hals museum (temporary exhibitions).

★★ FRANS HALSMUSEUM (BZ) ⊙ *1 hour 30min*

Since 1913, this museum has been set up in a **former almshouse for old men** dating back to 1608; it is said to have been designed by the architect Lieven de Key. The building housed an orphanage from 1810 to 1908.
The façade is characteristic of this type of institution with, on either side of the entrance, a row of low houses topped with a crow-stepped gable with window. The principal façade gives on to the main courtyard around which are the rooms.

Works by Frans Hals – The eight paintings of civic guards (room 21) and regents by Frans Hals constitute a remarkable collection making it possible to follow the evolution of the master's painting. The first painting which marks the already brilliant beginnings of the painter dates only from 1616 when Hals was about 34 years old. It is the **Banquet of the Officers of the Haarlem Militia Company of St George** (no 123). The mobility of the characters and their personality are shown in an extraordinary way. The atmosphere is less restrained in the *Banquet of the Officers of the Haarlem Militia Company of St George* (no 124) and the *Officers of the Haarlem Militia Company of St Hadrian* (no 125), both painted in 1627 and rich in spontaneity and colour.

In the **Officers of the Haarlem Militia Company of St Hadrian** (no 126) of 1662, Frans Hals reached his greatest virtuosity.
The **Officers of the Haarlem Militia Company of St George** (no 127) of 1639, with a self-portrait of the artist (2nd figure on the left, 2nd row) is the last of this genre.
In 1641 a tendency for restraint and solemnity appears in Frans Hals' work and predominates in the *Regents of St Elizabeth's Hospital* (room 25, no 128).
The somber colour of the garments underlines the expression on the faces and the very studied attitude of the hands.
In 1664, Hals was over eighty when he produced *Regents of the Old Men's Home* (room 28, no 129); in this daring, somewhat cynical study of six characters, Hals had the cheek to portray one of them as a drunkard with his hat tilted back. Painted the same year, the painting of the **Regentesses of the Old Men's Home** (room 28, no 130) with furrowed hands, bony faces, unindulgent looks, communicate a sentiment of anguish and discomfort.

Other collections – Apart from Frans Hals, the museum contains rich collections of paintings, furniture and *objets d'art*.
In the series of **old paintings**, first there are the works of Jan van Scorel including the famous *Baptism of Christ,* those of Maerten van Heemskerck and Cornelis van Haarlem *(Baptism of Christ)*.
The main 17C masters notably those of the Haarlem School are represented by landscapes of Esaias van de Velde, Van Goyen, Van Ostade, Salomon van Ruysdael and Jacob van Ruisdael, a scene by Ter Boch, animals by Wouwerman and Cuyp, still lifes by Pieter Claesz., Willem Heda, Floris van Schooten, Abraham van Beyeren. There are also some fine portraits by Verspronck (1597-1662). Note the fine collection of 17 and 18C silverware; a manuscript painted with a tulip by Judith Leyster, pupil of Hals, the reconstitution of an apothecary with Delftware jars and, in a room with Dutch gilded leather, an 18C **dolls house**.
In a modern wing there are **modern and contemporary Dutch paintings**, notably by Isaac Israëls, Jan Sluyters (1881-1957) and the CoBrA Group.
Opposite the museum, the lovely small houses with crow-stepped gables belonged to St Elizabeth's Hospital or **St.-Elisabeths Gasthuis** (BZ **D**), whose regents Frans Hals painted.

ADDITIONAL SIGHTS

Teylers Museum (CY **M**[1]) ⊙ – This museum, the oldest in the Netherlands (1778), is devoted to science and the arts in accordance with the wishes of its founder Pieter Teyler.
Large rooms contain collections of physics and chemistry instruments, fossils and minerals.
However, the main interest of the museum is in a series of 4 000 **drawings**★ from the 16 to 19C, from the Italian, Dutch and French Schools *(exhibited in rotation)*, part of which belonged to Queen Christina of Sweden. Rembrandt and Michelangelo have signed some of these works.
The museum also has a collection of 19C and early 20C paintings.
At the corner of Damstraat stands the **Waag** (CY **E**), built in 1598 in the Renaissance style and attributed to Lieven de Key.

Amsterdamse Poort (CY) – This late 15C gateway, preceded on the town side by two turrets was also a water-gate commanding the Spaarne.

Hofjes (Almshouses) – Among the numerous charitable institutions, which the people of the wealthy town of Haarlem had as from the 15C, there is the **Proveniershuis** (BZ) of 1592 which opens by a large doorway on Grote Houtstraat, the **Brouwershofje** (BZ **L**) (1472) in Tuchthuisstraat and the **Hofje van Loo** (BY **N**) of 1489, visible from Barrevoetestraat.

Kathedrale Basiliek St-Bavo ⊙ – *By Leidsevaart* (BZ). The sacristy of this very large basilica, built between 1895 and 1906 by J.T. Cuypers, son of P.J.H. Cuypers *(qv)* in the style of the time, contains the **treasury**: a large collection of liturgical objects, mainly gold and silverware (15 to 20C). Note the sacerdotal ornaments (early 16C) which come from an old Beguinage in the town.

OUTSKIRTS

Museum De Cruquius ⊙ – *7km - 4 miles to the southeast by Dreef* (BZ). *It is to the northeast of a large bridge on the road to Vijfhuizen. Local map under Keukenhof.*
This museum, on the edge of old Haarlemmermeer *(qv)*, is installed in one of the three pumping stations, which were used to drain it. The station bears the name of the land surveyor **Nicolaes Cruquius** (1678-1754) author of a project (1750) to drain the lake.
The museum presents interesting material on the technical developments in the history of man's fight against water, and on the creation of polders: scale model illustrating the theory of a polder, animated scale model showing the part of the Netherlands which would be flooded by the sea in the absence of dikes and dams. Visitors may also admire the station's original steam engine, fitted with eight beam engines and eight pumps. Built in Cornwall, this unique machine was inaugurated in 1849: its importance was recognised by the American Society of Mechanical Engineers, who awarded it the prestigious title of International Historic Landmark in 1991. This museum also houses the oldest steam machine in Dutch history; it was built in 1826.

Spaarndam – *8km - 5 miles to the northeast by Spaarndamseweg* (CX), *which becomes Vondelweg, then after a bend, take Vergierdeweg on the right.*
The houses of this picturesque village, where one can eat smoked eel, huddle up along both sides of the dike. This is interspersed with several locks making it possible to link the Spaarne and the IJ.

On one of these locks there is a statue of Hans Brinker. According to the legend the young boy plugged a hole he had discovered in a protection dike with his finger for a whole night and thus saved the town from being flooded. The origin of this anecdote: a children's book written in 1873 by the American novelist Mary Mapes Dodge, *Hans Brinker or the Silver Skates.* Beyond this small monument is the pleasure boat harbour; a path makes it possible to walk alongside the marina to reach the Oost- and Westkolk docks; lovely restored houses.

★ **Zandvoort** – Pop 15 649. *11km - 7 miles. Leave by Leidsevaart* (**BZ**). Town plan in the current Michelin Red Guide Benelux.
It is one of the most busy seaside resorts in the Netherlands. A large avenue runs along the dunes which overlook the beach.
Since 1976 Zandvoort has a **casino** installed in Hotel Bouwes, on Badhuisplein.

EXCURSIONS

★★★ **Bulbfields** – *See Keukenhof.*

From Bloemendaal aan Zee to Beverwijk – *35km - 21 1/2 miles to the north by Verspronckweg* (**BX**).

Bloemendaal aan Zee – It is Haarlem's family beach.

Bloemendaal – Pop 17 216. Behind the chain of dunes, this is an elegant residential centre where the villas stretch over wooded hills.
In the open-air theatre or Openluchttheater *(Hoge Duin en Daalseweg 2)* performances are given in summer. Nearby is the highest dune in the country, **Het Kopje** (50m - 164ft). Further to the north are the ruins of the **Kasteel Brederode**, destroyed by the Spanish in 1573.

De Kennemerduinen Nationaal Park ⊙ – *Visitor Centre (Informatiecentrum) at the southeast entry to the park.*
The national park is an estate of 1 250ha - 3 088 acres situated on the long line of dunes edging the North Sea, and criss-crossed by footpaths and cycling tracks. Near the small lakes numerous birds come to breed.

IJmuiden – Famous for its locks, IJmuiden, situated at the far end of the North Sea canal, is also a seaside resort and ranks as Western Europe's first fishing port. About forty trawlers are fitted out here, sometimes, for herring fishing. The fish market auction is very large.
Three **locks**★ (sluizen) make it possible for the biggest ships to sail up to Amsterdam. The north lock, the most recent, begun in 1919, was inaugurated on 29 April 1930. It is 400m - 1 312ft long, 40m - 131ft wide and 15m - 49ft deep.

Beverwijk – Pop 35 165. This small wooded holiday centre has lovely dunes covered with forests which separate it from the seaside resort of **Wijk aan Zee**.

THE HAGUE See DEN HAAG

HARDERWIJK Gelderland — Pop 35 804

Michelin map 408 H4

Harderwijk, a member of the Hanseatic League on the old Zuiderzee, retains a few picturesque lanes, the remains of its brick ramparts and its port, where one can eat excellent smoked eel.
On the edge of **Veluwemeer** *(see under Flevoland)*, Harderwijk which has two pleasure boat harbours and a beach, attracts many tourists. The hinterland, which is part of the Veluwe *(qv)* and where dunes, forests and heathland stretch, is very attractive and includes several nature reserves.
The memory of the famous Swedish botanist **Carolus Linnaeus** (Carl von Linné 1707-78) and pioneer of scientific classification is closely associated with Harderwijk as he attended the university. Founded in 1647, this institution was abolished by Napoleon in 1811.
White ducks are bred in the vicinity.

Boat trips ⊙ – Boat trips are organised along Flevoland.

SIGHTS

★ **Dolfinarium** ⊙ – This vast dolphinarium stands next door to the **Veluwestrand** leisure centre with its beach and not far from the marina. It is the largest marine mammal park in Europe and boasts numerous species: dolphins, sea lions, walruses, seals, black killer whales and friendly skate in a touch-tank.

Old Town – A number of well-restored Renaissance houses and 18C patrician residences with ornamental rococo doorways are the heritage of a more prosperous past. Enter the old town through the charming 14-16C **Vispoort** (near Strandboulevard) which leads to the old fish market. The Kleine Marktstraat on the right leads into the main square, **Markt**, where the **stadhuis** (1837) is recognisable by its portico crowned with a pinnacle.
Donkerstraat is a pedestrian street with numerous grand 18C mansions which rival one another for the elaborateness of their rococo doorways. Looking up Academiestraat on the left one can see the 16C tower, **Linnaeustorentje**, which marks the site of the university's botanical gardens. At the far end of Donkerstraat an 18C mansion at no 4 is now home to the **Veluws Museum** ⊙.

On the ground floor a room is devoted to Veluwe's *(qv)* past. The old gymnasium's rostrum illustrates the importance of education in Harderwijk's past; the part in front was occupied by examination candidates, while the upper seat was reserved for the director. The history of this famous university is evoked on the 1st floor where, notably, there are portraits of professors. Apart from Carolus Linnaeus, Herman Boerhaave *(qv)* and Constantijn Huygens *(qv)* received doctorates in Harderwijk. Coins from the Gelderland Mint, installed in Harderwijk from 1584 to 1806, Veluwe costumes and old Zuiderzee scale models of boats complete the museum's collections.
Taking Smeepoortstraat, a shopping street on the right, pass in front of the **Grote Kerk** ⏲, a tall 14C building.
At the far end of the street, Bruggestraat (lovely 18C portals) returns to Markt.

EXCURSION

Elburg – Pop 20 733 – *20km - 12 miles to the northeast.*
In the 14C Elburg was a busy mainland port looking out on the Zuiderzee and even belonged to the Hanseatic League. Today this small town encircled by its walls and protective canal retains its medieval character but now looks out across the polders of Flevoland. The streets are laid out in a regular grid-iron pattern and often fronted by attractive houses as in the row alongside the Beekstraat Canal. The black and white cobblestones of the narrow pavements make attractive patterns. The only town gate to remain is the one that faced northwards onto the sea, **Vischpoort** ⏲. This 14C tower is flanked by watch turrets. At the other end of the street the **stadhuis** now occupies part of a former convent (Agnietenklooster) dating from 1418. The collections of the Municipal Museum, **Gemeentemuseum**, ⏲) are displayed in the Gothic chapel and other conventual buildings.
The 14C **St.-Nicolaaskerk** ⏲, now Protestant, is dwarfed by its massive square tower. In the neighbouring street, Van Kinsbergenstraat, there is a series of interesting houses, one of which looks like a keep.
Boat trips ⏲ are organised to Veluwemeer and Drontermeer Lakes.

HARLINGEN Friesland — Pop 15 474

Michelin map 408 H2 – Local map see WADDENEILANDEN

Harlingen, Harns in Frisian, which already existed in the 9C under the name of Almenum, received its city charter in 1234. The dike, which protected it, having been submerged, was consolidated by Caspar (or Gaspar) de Robles, governor of the northern regions of the Low Countries in 1573.

The only seaport in Friesland – Harlingen was formerly a great whaling port, with its boats sailing as far as Greenland until *c*1850.
Today, at the mouth of Harinxma Canal, it is a port from where dairy products are shipped to Britain, the departure point for the islands of Terschelling *(see Waddeneilanden)* and Vlieland and a great shrimping centre.
Harlingen now also has two pleasure boat harbours.
Industries have been set up north and east of town; the larger tankers can berth at one of the docks.
Harlingen has a school of fluvial navigation and a educational institute for shipbuilding.
Each year there are Fishing Days *(Visserijdagen) (see Calendar of Events)* and ring tournaments *(ringrijderij – qv)* as well as a naval review.

SIGHTS

The charm of its old streets makes Harlingen an attractive town. It is pleasant to stroll along the main street, Voorstraat and along the quays of the two old ports, the Noorderhaven and the Zuiderhaven. There are some interesting 16 to 18C façades.

★ **Noorderhaven** – This dock, which has become a marina, is lined with picturesque houses and warehouses.
On the north quay, there are some lovely façade stones.
On the south side stands the 18C **stadhuis**, topped by a low relief depicting the archangel St Michael; the rear of the building giving on to Voorstraat is flanked by a tower with a carillon.

Gemeentemuseum "Hannemahuis" ⏲ – *Voorstraat 56.*
Installed in the Hannemahuis, an 18C residence, this museum is devoted to the history of Harlingen and its maritime past.
The regional furniture, the seascapes by Nicolaas Baur, a painter born in Harlingen (1767-1820), engravings, collections of Chinese porcelain, Frisian silverware and scale models of ships, are all beautiful. A room, giving on to the garden, has a lovely collection of earthenware tiles grouped by motif.
At the far end of the street, near the canal, there is the statue of a schoolboy, Anton Wachter, hero of a series of novels by **Simon Vestdijk** (1898-1971), famous writer born in Harlingen; his works tended to describe middle-class provincial life.

De Stenen Man (Stone Man) – At the top of a dike to the south of the port there is a monument crowned with two bronze heads, erected in 1774 in memory of the Governor Caspar de Robles *(see above).*
Behind the dike is Harlingen beach. Fine view over the port.

HAVELTE Drenthe

Pop 5 808

Michelin map 408 J3

This village in the Drenthe, with handsome regional farmhouses covered in thatch, has two *hunebeds (qv)*.

★ **Hunebeds (D 53 and D 54)** – *Take the road to Frederiksoord to the north and opposite a café, there is a road on the right indicating "hunebedden".*
These two megalithic monuments lie in a lovely clearing covered in heather. One is still topped by seven enormous slabs in front of which, on the southeast, is a very conspicuous entrance. The other, smaller one, has a slightly curved shape.

HEERENVEEN Friesland

Pop 38 270

Michelin map 408

Heerenveen was founded in the 16C by Frisian lords, hence its name which means: The Lords' Peat or Fen.
4km - 2 1/2 miles to the south the flowered houses of **Oranjewoud** are hidden among the hundred year old trees of a 17C Nassau Frisian property, crossed by small canals. Two manor houses **Oranjewoud** ⊙ and **Oranjestein** adorn this magnificent landscape *(access by Prins Bernhardlaan)*.
The lovely municipal park, De Overtuin, and paths in the woods make it a pleasant place for walks.

HEERLEN Limburg

Pop 94 344

Michelin map 408 I9 or 212 fold 2 (inset)

This town was the main centre of the Netherlands' coalfields which cross Limburg, continue into Belgium, in the Maaseik region, and the Aachen basin in Germany. Mining started in 1896 and was abandoned in 1975. Nevertheless, a number of industries have established themselves in the region and Heerlen is becoming an important commercial centre.
The city possesses a modern quarter built round a vast pedestrian precinct, **Promenade**, and a theatre (Schouwburg), built in 1961.
The Romanesque St.-Pancratiuskerk has for a tower the old keep of a castle built in 1389 by the Duke of Burgundy, Philip the Bold.

Coriovallum – Heerlen, ancient Coriovallum, was a Roman camp on the great route going from Boulogne-sur-Mer to Cologne and passing by Maastricht. In 1C AD, another route crossed this Roman camp (Xanthus-Trier). Important Roman baths (2 to 4C) were found in Heerlen.

Thermenmuseum ⊙ – There is a slide projection before visiting the Roman baths, the remains of which can be seen from an elevated walkway.
The museum also contains objects found during excavations: coins, bronze statuettes, pottery.

EXCURSION

Kerkrade – Pop 53 282. *10km - 6 miles east of Heerlen.*
This border town has been a centre of mining activity since the Middle Ages. Since mining ceased Kerkrade has diversified its industrial sector.
Every four years *(see Calendar of Events)* an International Music Competiton (Wereld Muziek Concours) is held here; it draws groups of amateur musicians.
To the east is the old abbey, **Abdij Rolduc**★ ⊙. *Go towards Herzogenrath and turn left before the railway.*
The abbey stands high on the valley slope overlooking the Wurm valley, which marks the frontier. The abbey buildings have been transformed to serve as a cultural centre, a gymnasium, a seminary and a museum.
The **abbey church** (abdijkerk) is surrounded by 17 and 18C buildings. Started in the early 12C, it has been restored several times, in particular in the 19C by Cuypers who replaced the Gothic chancel by a Romanesque one. On the west side, it has a façade with a massive porch tower flanked by two square towers.
Inside, on the level of the first and third bays of the nave a sort of transept takes shape in the side aisles. The **capitals**★ in the nave are very varied. Note also the base of certain engaged columns in the side aisles. The heightened apse is trefoil in shape and built above a Romanesque crypt (remarkable capitals).
The mining museum, **Mijnmuseum** ⊙, (inside the abbey) contains interesting documentation on coal mines: geological information (collections of minerals, fossils), evocation of mining activities by machinery, instruments, scale models, photographs.

The Michelin Maps for the Netherlands are shown on the back cover of the guide
The text refers to the maps which, owing to their scale or coverage, are the clearest and most appropriate in each case

DEN HELDER Noord-Holland Pop 61 468

Michelin map 408 F3 – Local map see WADDENEILANDEN

Den Helder owes its importance to the depth of Marsdiep Channel, which separates it from Texel Island.
Originally **Huisduinen**, a simple fishing village, expanded eastwards. In 1500 the new town took the name of Den Helder.
It was the scene of a heroic exploit of Commander Lahure who, crossing the frozen Marsdiep at the head of 400 hussars belonging to Pichegru's army, captured the Dutch fleet blocked in the ice, in January 1795. In 1799 the British Commander, Abercromby landed with 24 000 men joining up with Russian reinforcements, however, he was defeated and went no further than Alkmaar.
In 1811 Napoleon made Den Helder a stronghold. Today it is the Netherlands' chief naval base.

Helders Marinemuseum ⊙ – This museum evokes the Royal Navy since 1813 with a selection of scale models, instruments, photos, uniforms, emblems, maps, paintings and engravings.
Worth noting are a reconstituted ship's bridge and a periscope in working order. Films are shown.

EXCURSION

Callantsoog and Schagen – *27km - 16 1/2 miles to the south.*
The road to Callantsoog runs alongside a dike behind which there are several beaches.

Callantsoog – To the south there is a nature reserve, **Het Zwanewater** (Swan Lake) ⊙. The reserve stretches over 580ha - 1 432 acres amongst coastal dunes and the moors round two lakes which attract many birds. The best time to visit is around mid-May during nesting.
From afar one can see the breeding grounds, generally set in reeds. The spoonbills *(illustration see Waddeneilanden)* arrive from Egypt or Spain at the end of February and leave again in July and August.

Schagen – Pop 16 950. On Thursdays in summer *(see Calendar of Events)* a colourful **market** (Westfriese markt) is held in this town where the costumes of West Friesland are worn.

's-HERTOGENBOSCH (DEN BOSCH) Noord-Brabant Ⓟ Pop 92 057

Michelin map 408 H6 or 212 folds 7 and 8
Plan of the conurbation in the current Michelin Red Guide Benelux

Capital of the Noord-Brabant province, 's-Hertogenbosch is also the seat of a Catholic bishopric. It differs from other towns in the country by its more southern character which can be seen in its tall stone cathedral and its noisy carnival *(see Calendar of Events)*.

HISTORICAL NOTES

Vast forests, which stretched round, were the hunting ground of Duke Godefroy of Brabant, hence the name 's-Hertogen Bosch, the Duke's Wood. Today the town is usually called **Den Bosch**, the Woods. But marshland has replaced the forests.
The castle, built at the end of the 12C, was the centre around which the town grew. 's-Hertogenbosch received its city charter about 1185 from Henry I, Duke of Brabant. The town owes its prosperity to the wool and cloth trades.
In 1561 Philip II of Spain, who reigned over the Low Countries, made 's-Hertogenbosch a bishopric, dependent on the Archbishop of Mechelen.
Taken by the Spanish in 1579, the town only surrendered to the Prince of Orange Frederick-Henry, son of William the Silent, in 1629, after a long siege. Its 17C fortified wall is still clearly marked by a line of bastions and canals in the old moats.
Captured in 1794 by Pichegru after an 18-day siege, Den Bosch became the chief town of the Bouches-du-Rhin *département*.

The modern town – 's-Hertogenbosch, an important road and rail junction, is well situated on the Zuid-Willemsvaart Canal and near the Maas. Numerous commercial and industrial establishments have developed here.
The weekly cattle market, which takes place on Wednesdays in the **Brabanthallen**, is a particularly important one.
The inhabitants have several recreation areas: the **Zuiderplas** (64ha - 158 acres) where one can bathe, go sailing, row, fish, etc; **Oosterplas** (65ha - 160 acres) a large lake (bathing) and the **Prins Hendrik Park** (Y) where there is a stag enclosure and another large lake, **De IJzeren Vrouw** (Y).
A new **Provincial House** (Provinciehuis) was built in 1968-71 to the southeast of the town.

A magician's art – 's-Hertogenbosch is the birthplace of **Hieronymus Bosch** (*c*1450-1516) whose real name was Jeroen van Aeken. The life of this painter is not well known, except that he lived a comfortable life in this town.
Solitary genius, Hieronymus Bosch did not belong to any school. At the most one can see Flemish influence in his landscapes with distant perspectives, and the naturalistic tone given in scenes he paints (precision of plants, study of animals) and in the clear strokes and the somewhat archaic outline drawings of his characters. But with this visionary painter, reality is put to the use of a prodigious imagination.

Objects and animals take strange shapes, men and beasts fill fantastic scenes of a dream-like universe, even nightmarish, where it is impossible to distinguish hell from paradise.
Condemn the bad, denounce the ravages of sin was probably the intention of this mysterious artist who was as passionately interested in alchemy as ethics judging by the presence of numerous symbols in his works. His fantasy-like paintings were enhanced by the harmonious colours applied in fine, successive, slightly transparent coats.
His early works were mostly simple and sober, then later the compositions became more complex and the subjects more and more strange, such as in the most extraordinary of his works, the *Garden of Earthly Delights*, where the painter would have had no cause to envy the Surrealists. This last painting is in the Prado Museum in Madrid *(see Michelin Green Guide Spain)*, but one can see several fascinating works by Hieronymus Bosch in the Museum Boymans-van Beuningen in Rotterdam *(qv)*.
His only successor was Pieter Bruegel the Elder (*c*1529-69), who also showed a certain sense of satire and the unusual in his early works.

★★ ST.-JANSKATHEDRAAL (Z) ⏲ *45 min*

St John's Cathedral is one of the most beautiful religious buildings in the Netherlands. It was assigned to the Protestant faith from 1629-1810, date when Napoleon returned it to the Catholic faith. In 1929 it was given the status of basilica.
Built between 1380 and 1530 in the Brabant Gothic style, it has been much restored since the 19C.
It has a 13C belfry porch whose **carillon**, placed in 1925, has become famous for its concerts.
The cathedral seen from **Parade**, the square to the south, has impressive proportions and a wealth of ornamentation. The fantastic world of grotesque personages astride the flying buttresses may have inspired Hieronymus Bosch. Other amusing figures decorate the side chapels' gable spandrels. The apse is superb with its numerous radiating chapels round the ambulatory. A lantern turret tops the transept crossing.

Interior – The very luminous interior has a grandiose appearance with its five naves, 150 columns which, according to the characteristics of the Late Brabant Gothic, are a cluster of slender columns without capitals.
The last restoration, completed in 1985, has brought to light the vault frescoes, which are very varied. The oldest, in the chancel, dates from the first half of the 15C.
Note the canopy, slightly turned and finely worked, above a statue leaning against a pillar of the transept crossing.
The pulpit with its 16C Renaissance low reliefs, the 15C restored stalls and a 17C Renaissance organ case by Frans Symons of Leyden and Georg Schissler are worth seeing.

Ph. Gajic/MICHELIN

St.-Janskathedraal, 's-Hertogenbosch

's-HERTOGENBOSCH

Hinthamerstr. . . . . Z
Hoge Steenweg . . . . Z 25
Schapenmarkt . . . . Z 54
Visstraat . . . . Z 67
Vughterstr. . . . . Z

Bethaniestr. . . . . Z 4
de Bossche Pad . . . . Z 7
Burg. Loeffpl. . . . . YZ 9
Emmaplein . . . . Y 10
Geert van Woutstr. . . . . Y 12
Graafseweg . . . . Y 16
Havensingel . . . . Y 22
Hinthamereinde . . . . Z 24
Jan Heinsstr. . . . . Y 28
Kerkstraat . . . . Z 30
Koninginnenlaan . . . . Y 31
Maastrichtseweg . . . . Z 34
mMuntelbolwerk . . . . Y 39
van Noremborghstr. . . . . . . Y 40
Oostwal . . . . Z 42
Oranje Nassaulaan . . . . Z 43
Orthenstr. . . . . Y 46
Sint-Jacobstr. . . . . Z 57
Sint-Josephstr. . . . . Z 58
Spinhuiswal . . . . Z 60
Stationsweg . . . . YZ 61
Torenstr. . . . . Z 66
Vlijmenseweg . . . . Z 69
Vughterweg . . . . Z 70
van der Weeghensingel . . . Y 73
Wilhelminaplein . . . . Z 75
Willemsplein . . . . Z 76

The copper baptismal font (1492), in the chapel on the left of the great organ, is the masterpiece of a Maastricht coppersmith. In 1629, when Frederick-Henry, Prince of Orange seized 's-Hertogenbosch, the canons left town for Brussels, taking with them the altarpieces which Hieronymus Bosch had painted for the cathedral.
The rood screen, which from 1610 to 1866, was at the transept crossing was replaced in 1985 by a black stone podium decorated with biblical scenes; the original is now in the Victoria and Albert Museum in London *(see Michelin Green Guide London)*.
Among the stained-glass windows, all made after 1850, note the window in the north arm of the transept made by Marius de Leeuw (1965).
St Anthony's Chapel in the south arm of the transept has a fine **altarpiece★** restored by the Antwerp School (c1500) which came from a local village. The six small scenes of the lower part, in rather naive fashion depict the birth and childhood of Jesus, but the main theme of the altarpiece is the Passion of Christ, with the Calvary in the centre.
The figures carved in wood, notably the Virgin on the right panel (the Lamentation) are particularly remarkable for their expressions.
The Chapel of Our Lady, on the left of the belfry porch, has a miraculous statue of the Virgin (late 13C).
There are numerous memorial slabs on the cathedral floor.

ADDITIONAL SIGHTS

Markt (Z) – This very busy square is in the heart of the city, where one of the main shopping pedestrian precincts starts, **Hinthamerstraat** (Z).
In front of the Stadhuis stands a statue (1929) of Hieronymus Bosch.

Stadhuis (Z **H**) – Dating from the 15C it was given a classical façade in 1670. Part of its **carillon** ⓒ was cast by the Hemony brothers. On the ground floor, the Registrars' Gallery (Trouwkamer) has lovely Cordoba leather hangings. The 16C vaulted cellar (kelder) has been transformed into a café-restaurant.

De Moriaan (Z) – This building, which houses the tourist information centre (VVV), has, to the north of Markt, a brick façade with a 13C crow-stepped gable.

★ **Noordbrabants Museum** (Z M[1]) ⊙ – The North Brabant Museum is set up in the old governor's mansion, built by Pieter de Swart in the years 1768-1769. The ornamental features of the forepart and the pediment serve to counter the severity of the freestone façade.
The museum retraces the history of the North Brabant province, focusing on several themes: the medieval town, the guilds, the Eighty Years' War, cults, popular traditions and archaeology. The highly interesting collection features objects excavated from various sites, including an **amber statue of Bacchus** (*c*200 AD) found in a woman's tomb in Esch. The painting collection presents the admirable *Study of a Brabant Peasant* by Van Gogh and *The Four Seasons* by David Teniers the Younger. One can also see sculptures, costumes and ornamental *objets d'art* (work by gold and silversmiths' guilds, rustic jewellery from the 18 and 19C).
The temporary exhibitions held in the museum concern present-day topics and the Brabant.

Museum Slager (Z M[2]) ⊙ – It houses works by a family of painters, from Petrus Marinus Slager (1841-1912) to Tom Slager, born in 1918.

Museum Het Kruithuis (Y M[3]) ⊙ – This hexagonal brick edifice, dating from 1617-1621, is located in the northern part of town. It is built around a courtyard and was once circled by a moat. Until 1742 it was used as a powder magazine. Today the restored rooms on the ground floor are the setting for exhibitions on design and contemporary art. The first floor presents collections of modern jewellery and ceramics, from 1950 up to the present day.

Boat trips on the Binnendieze ⊙ – A trip along this river, which in places flows under the houses and streets, is a pleasant introduction to the different facets of the city.

EXCURSIONS

Heeswijk-Dinther – Pop 8 581. *14km - 8 1/2 miles to the southeast by Maastrichtseweg.*
Northwest of town stands the 14C **Kasteel Heeswijk** ⊙, set in the woods and surrounded by moats. It contains interesting furnishings and art objects.
At Heeswijk, a farmhouse museum, **De Meierijsche Museumboerderij** ⊙ *(at Meerstraat 20)* retraces the life of Brabant peasants in 1900.

Drunen, Waalwijk and De Efteling★ – *25km - 15 1/2 miles to the west. Leave by Vlijmenseweg.*

Drunen – Pop 18 355. To the south of the locality stretch the **Drunen dunes**.

Waalwijk – Pop 28 821. Main centre of the Netherlands' leather and shoe industry, Waalwijk has a Dutch Leather and Shoe Museum, **Nederlands Leder en Schoenenmuseum**; *Elzenweg 26* ⊙. An important collection of shoes from different countries (Japan, India, North America, Africa); reconstruction of a *c*1930 shoe factory and a 1870 tannery. Other display cases show the evolution of the European shoe.

★ **De Efteling** ⊙ – *South of Kaatsheuvel.*
One of the main attractions of this 72ha - 178 acre theme park is the **Fairy Tale Wood** (Sprookjesbos) (signposted). Here the seven dwarfs weep around Snow White's glass coffin, the animals sing, the giant mushrooms play a harpsichord tune. Further along, in front of an Oriental palace, a fakir zooms through the air on his flying carpet. Droomvlucht (Dream Flight) takes visitors through the magic land of fairy tales. This theme park also features a large haunted castle, a pond with rowing boats, spine-chilling rides, several restaurants and a hotel. A small steam-driven train takes visitors round the park.

Zaltbommel – Pop 9 767. *15km - 9 miles to the north. Leave by Orthenseweg.*
This old stronghold, beside the Waal, received its city charter in 1229.
On Markt, the **stadhuis**, restored, dates from 1763. At no 18 Boschstraat, next to a chemist shop, there is a Renaissance house with caryatids. This, the main street, leads to the 14C water gate, **Waterpoort**.
In Nonnenstraat, to the west of the main street, the **Huis van Maarten van Rossum** *(qv)* has been converted into a regional museum, **Streekmuseum** ⊙.
It has a picturesque façade (1535) with tympana decorated with medallions, corner turrets and crenellations. Inside there is an exhibition of objects from Roman times, discovered during excavations.
At the far end of Nieuwstraat is the 14C **Grote- of St.-Maartenskerk**, restored and abundantly decorated, where the imposing 15C belfry porch, is 63m - 207ft high.
The dikes edging the Waal offer lovely views of the river.

Heusden – Pop 5 858. *19km - 11 1/2 miles to the northwest by Vlijmenseweg.*
On the banks of the Maas, which here becomes the Bergse Maas, Heusden is an old stronghold fortified in 1581. The town has been restored. Inside its ramparts, which have been transformed into an esplanade, it has some fine façades.
Worth seeing is no 4 Hoogstraat (main street), a 17C house with very elaborate scrolls.
The **stadhuis**, rebuilt in 1956, has an automatic **carillon** ⊙ and a Jack-o'the-clock.
The **Vismarkt**, fish market, near the dock, is surrounded by 17C houses. A covered market (Visbank) of 1796 still stands.
Heusden has three post **mills**.

Rosmalen – Pop 27 631. *6km - 3 1/2 miles northeast by N 50.*
The **Autotron Transport Museum** ⏲ is part of an amusement park (stream train, airplanes and other attractions). The **collection of vehicles★** is displayed in the outbuildings of a Brabant farm. Each period in the development of the motor car is well represented: replica of the petrol powered car invented by Benz in Germany, several De Dion Boutons and Panhard-Levassors, a Ford Model T (1909), Mercedes (1933) belonging to the ex-Kaiser of Germany Wilhelm II *(qv)*, American-built limousines (1940s), a Tatra 600 (1947) and a 1958 Daf. The racing cars include the 1978 Jameson Concorde, which was the most powerful car in the world with a top speed of 350km/h - 217mph. In the lakeside pavilion admire the magnificent models of the Dutch manufacturer Spijker (1899-1925); the prestige and refinement of the Spijker C4 was such that it was nicknamed the continental Rolls-Royce.
On the far side of the lake is the House of the Future, **Huis van de Toekomst**⏲, a glass and steel structure (1988-89) with a dramatic form. The futuristic vision of a home demonstrates how today's technology will change the home environment and the quality of life in the early 21C. Here the architectural reality addresses the problems of environment, energy-saving, safety and longer life expectancy to produce a design which shapes up to the 21C.
It is as one would expect an intelligently designed and largely automatic home: magnetic cards replace door knobs and keys; taps, lights and curtains are all operated by infra-rouge; the entrance gates and the conical bathroom roof are opened by voice command. Computers are everywhere: in the kitchen where they record the food stocks, in the sitting room where they provide direct links with the bank, stock market and the shops. In the bedroom the glass wall can be transparent or opaque; in the toilets a jet of water replaces the toilet paper and solar energy is a must. New technologies will be incorporated as they develop.

The Cartographers of 17C Europe

The daring and enterprise of Dutch merchant-seamen and navigators lead to the rise of the United Netherlands as a maritime power. Amsterdam became not only the centre of international commerce but also of commercial cartography. The map-makers of the period were often indifferently engravers, publishers or cartographers.
Great names of Dutch cartography included Petrus Plancius; Mercator (of the projection and Atlas 1606); Hondius who revised Mercator's Atlas and mapped Sir Francis Drake's round the world voyage; Blaeu (Willem Jansz) publisher of the poet and dramatist Vondel and cartographer to the East India Company from 1634; his arch rival Johannes Jansonius, son-in-law to Hondius and successor to the family firm; and Van Keulen founder of a publishing house famous for its nautical charts.

★★★ HET LOO Gelderland

Michelin map 408 15

William and Mary chose the great stretch of heath and forest the Hoge Veluwe *(qv)* as the site of their new palace. These enthusiastic improvers of royal residences (both in the Netherlands and England) created a small but elegant palace and Het Loo more than anywhere else retains their imprint. The palace's unique gardens are a baroque masterpiece and were laid out in typically Dutch formal style by William for his English Queen, Mary.
Het Loo Royal Palace and its gardens were opened to the public in 1984 following an extensive restoration programme. A 650ha - 1 626 acre **park** ⏲ is the immediate setting for the palace.

HISTORICAL NOTES

When **William III** (1650-1702), Prince of Orange and Stadtholder of the United Provinces bought the 14-15C Het Oude Loo Castle in 1684, this ardent huntsman was fulfilling a lifetime's dream. In 1685 the first stone of Het Loo Palace was laid, about 300yds from the site of the old castle, by William's wife Princess **Mary**, daughter to James II.
The palace was intended for the princely couple with their court and guests, as well as their large hunt. The presence of spring water made it possible to provide water for horses and dogs and decorate the gardens with fountains. Situated in the heart of the Veluwe and abounding in game, it had a privileged location.
The Royal Academy of Architecture in Paris supplied the plans for the palace while **Jacob Roman** (1640-1716) pupil of Pieter Post *(qv)* can be considered as the main architect. The interior decoration and the design of the gardens were commissioned from **Daniel Marot** (1661-1752), a Parisian Huguenot, who probably arrived in Holland shortly after the Revocation of the Edict of Nantes (1685).
In 1689 William III was proclaimed King of England after his father-in-law and uncle, James II, had fled the country. Het Loo Palace was to become a royal palace, and had to be enlarged: the colonnades which linked the main part of the building to the wings were replaced by four pavilions and the gardens were further embellished.

1684 **William III**, Prince of Orange and Stadtholder of the United Provinces, buys Het Oude Loo.
1685 Building starts at Het Loo. Revocation of the Edict of Nantes.
1688-97 War of the League of Augsburg.
1689 William and Princess Mary crowned King and Queen of England.
1692 An extension is made to the palace.
1694 Queen Mary dies in England.
1702 The Stadtholder-King William III dies without a successor.
1747-51 **William IV**, son of John William Friso, hereditary Stadtholder of the United Provinces.
1751-95 **William V**, son of the precedent stadtholder.
1795 Conquest of the country by the French army; William V flees to England. Het Loo seized by the French suffers from the destructive rage of the soldiers.
1795-1806 The Batavian Republic.
1806-10 Louis Bonaparte, King of Holland, puts rough-cast on the palace façade and commissions an English style park.
1810 The Kingdom of Holland is attached to the French Empire.
Oct. 1811 Emperor Napoleon stays briefly in Het Loo Palace.
1815 Het Loo, now State property, is offered to **King William I** as a summer residence.
1840 In Het Loo Palace, William I abdicates in favour of his son **William II**.
1849-90 Reign of William III.
1890-8 Regency of **Queen Emma**.
1898 **Wilhelmina**, only daughter of William III and Emma, accedes to the throne.
1901 Marriage of Queen Wilhelmina to Duke Henry of Mecklenburg-Schwerin.
1904-14 The State decides to extend and refurbish the palace.
1948 Abdication of Queen Wilhelmina, who retires to Het Loo Palace.
1962 Death of Queen Wilhelmina.
1967-75 Princess Margriet, daughter of Queen Juliana, and her family were the last members of the royal family to live in Het Loo.
1969 Queen Juliana gives up the use of the palace by the royal family and the creation of a museum is decided.
1977-84 Restoration of the palace and gardens.
June 1984 Opening of the **National Museum**.

PALACE AND NATIONAL MUSEUM ⏲ *about 3 hours*

It is advisable to choose a sunny day to visit the palace in order to appreciate certain poorly lit rooms.
After having walked alongside the **royal stables** (fine series of cars and sleighs, late 19 - early 20C) one reaches a wide avenue, where the beech trees form a magnificent vault; then one reaches the vast brick building flanked with long wings which surrounds the main courtyard.
A grille, painted blue and gold, closes the main courtyard, where a fountain decorated with dolphins was used to water the horses.
The finely proportioned building, built on a north-south axis, is impressive for its severe sobriety, characteristic of the Dutch baroque style. The only decorative elements are the tympana in sandstone of hunting scenes, and the window sills. The east pavilions were intended for Queen Mary while those situated to the west included those of the King Stadtholder William III. The sash windows of the main part of the building and the pavilions were a novelty often believed to be a Dutch invention and characteristic of English Georgian style.

East Wing – It contains a collection of historic documents, ceramics, paintings and prints as well as *objets d'art* regarding the most illustrious members of the House of Orange. Many of the documents were written in French, the language used by the Dutch court until the regency of Queen Emma (1890).

West Wing – On the ground floor there is a **video film show** on the history of the palace and its restoration.
On the 1st floor the **Museum of the Chancery of the Netherlands Orders of Knighthood** (Museum van de Kanselarij der Nederlandse Orden) exhibits insignia, uniforms, Dutch and foreign Orders.

★★★ **Apartments** *Access by a staircase on the side of the steps leading to the main building.*

From the vaulted cellars a staircase leads up to the **great hall** (**1**) where two 17C garden vases, after drawings by Daniel Marot, are exhibited.
The **old dining room** (**2**) is hung with 17C Antwerp tapestries. Note the cabinet (Antwerp, 1630), with biblical scenes painted by Frans Francken the Younger.
The remarkable **new dining room**★★★ (**3**) (*c*1692) is a very good example of Marot's contribution to the palace's interior decoration. The white columns and pilasters, decorated with gold bands and the coffered ceiling give this room, hardly bigger than the old dining room, a majestic character. On the walls, the Brussels' tapestries (*c*1690) depict the armorial bearings and monograms of William III and his Queen, as well as a mirror (1689), in finely carved gilded wood, which came from Honselersdijk Kasteel (south of The Hague; the castle has since been demolished).
Here, as in other rooms, there are some admirable Dutch chairs (late 17C) with their high backs of finely worked wood.

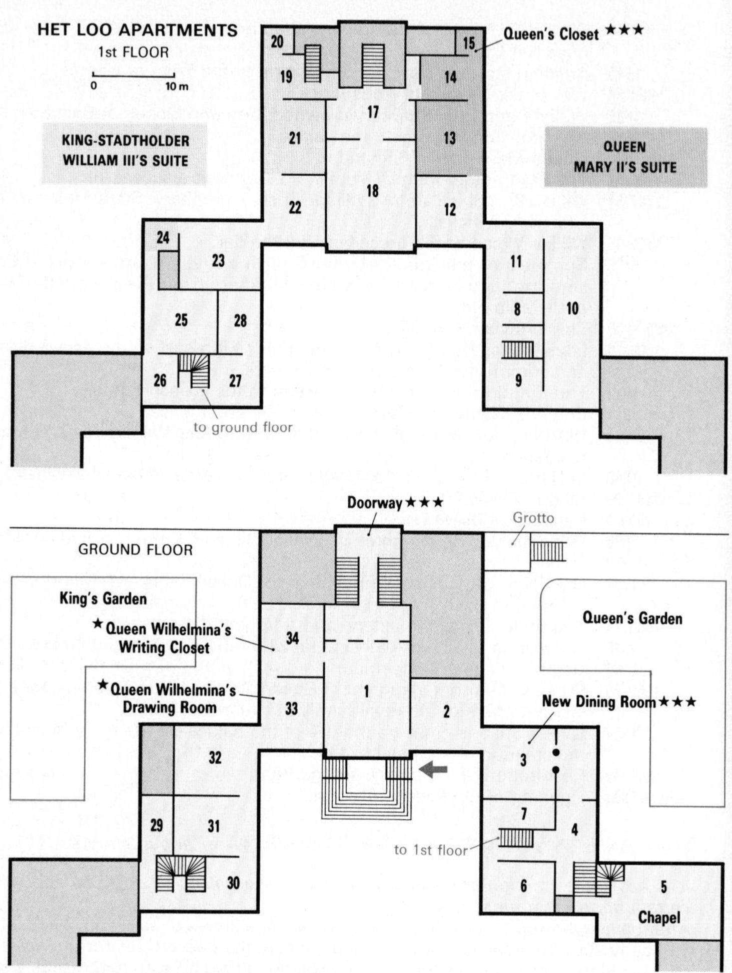

At the end of the **white hall (4)** which has portraits of members of the Nassau family, who lived in Friesland *(qv)*, a staircase leads up to the **chapel (5)** where **organ concerts** are held. The coffered stucco ceiling is by Marot. The Bible exhibited is a gift from the Dutch people to their King, William III, who had shown generosity during the 1861 floods. It was in this chapel where many Dutch filed past to bid farewell to Queen Wilhelmina (her funeral took place in Delft - *qv*).

Go back down the stairs and take the left corridor.

At the end of the corridor and on the left **Prince William IV's Chamber (6)**, a luminous room due to the yellow silk damask, has, apart from portraits of the stadtholder and his wife Anne of Hanover, Princess of England, daughter of George II, a crystal chandelier (*c*1747) decorated with the coat of arms of the United Provinces and those of William and Anne.

The walls of the **Frisian Cabinet (7)**, opposite, are covered with gilded leather (18C); portraits of the Frisian Nassaus.

On the 1st floor one passes through the **library (9)**, laid out after Marot's drawings and decorated with a stucco ceiling inlaid with mirrors, to reach the **gallery (10)**. In its lovely decor of panelling and green damask, this gallery, with magnificent chandeliers, contains a lovely collection of paintings. Next to the window giving on to the main courtyard, there are portraits of René de Chalon *(qv)* and his wife Anne of Lotharingia (1542); William the Silent (two first portraits on the left) inherited the Principality of Orange from René de Chalon. Adriaen van de Venne (1589-1662) has depicted the sons and nephews of William the Silent on horseback. On either side of the chimney there are William III and Mary II, King and Queen of England, Ireland and Scotland, by G. Kneller. The portrait above the chimney showing the king-stadtholder on horseback, is a study for a large painting exhibited in Hampton Court in London.

After having crossed the **drawing room** of the **Stadtholder William V (11)** where a porcelain chandelier from Berlin hangs from the stucco ceiling, and portraits (1795) of William V and his wife, Princess Wilhelmina by John Hoppner, one enters the drawing room of the first Dutch King, **William I (12)**. The Empire chairs, covered in blue and gold cloth, were made in the Dutch workshop of A. Eeltjes (1751-1836) for Het Loo Palace at the request of Louis Napoleon. On the walls there are portraits of the king and his daughter Marianne.

One then visits the apartments of Queen Mary and the King-Stadtholder William III, reconstructed in their 17C layout.

In **Mary Stuart's Bedroom (13)** the sumptuous canopied four-poster bed (*c*1685) is covered in Genova velvet; it comes from Kensington Palace in London. The table, the two pedestal tables and the mirrors in silver and gilt silver (*c*1700) are the work of an Augsburg gold and silversmith, J. Bartermann. The decoration on the ceiling, where the four elements and the four cardinal virtues are depicted, is by the painter Gerard de Lairesse (1641-1721).

Mary Stuart's Dressing Room (14), where the walls are covered with 17C Dutch tapestries, adjoins the **Queen's Antechamber★★★ (15)**, which is decorated mainly in red and green. This lovely little room, where Mary had a splendid view over the gardens, has a lacquer cabinet (1690) made in England as well as Delft and Chinese porcelain.

The **great staircase (17)**, designed by Marot, has been reconstructed by W. Fabri at the request of Queen Wilhelmina. The landscapes on the walls of the **great hall (18)** were painted by J. Glauber (1646-1726); this room with lovely grisailles on a golden background is where King William I abdicated in 1840.

A passage with gilded leather hangings **(19)** leads to the **King-Stadtholder William III's Closet (20)**. There is a fine Dutch writing-desk (late 17C). In **William III's Bedroom (21)** the colours of the wall hangings are again blue and gold, the colours of the House of Orange-Nassau. The next room **(22)** was laid out according to the taste of **King William II**, with neo-Gothic rosewood furniture (*c*1845). On the right of the king's portrait, there is a portrait of his wife, Princess Anna Pavlovna by J.B. van der Hulst.

When reconstituting **Sophia's Drawing Room (23)**, Princess of Würtemberg and first wife of William III (1817-90), the watercolours painted at the queen's request, which depict the rooms she occupied, were an excellent reference. The 19C German artist Franz Xaver Winterhalter painted the portrait of Queen Sophia in a black dress.

The small room **(24)** which gives on to the King's Garden was the **King-Stadtholder William III's Closet**. At the request of the sovereign, Melchior d'Hondecoeter (1639-*c*95) painter of still lifes and animals, decorated the mantelpiece. The furnishings in **King William III's Bedroom** (1817-90) **(25)** are in walnut and ebony, inlaid with ivory, brass, mother-of-pearl and semi-precious stones.

The following three small rooms contain, respectively, objects relating to **Prince Henry** (1820-79) **(26)**, brother of William III, a **collection of watercolours (27)** (note the painting on the left showing the palace's rear façade with the English garden) and toys and furniture which had belonged to **Queen Wilhelmina** as a child **(28)**.

On the ground floor **Queen Sophia's Closet (29)** has been fitted out in Moorish style. There is also the **trophy room (30)** of Prince Henry, husband of Queen Wilhelmina. On the left of the windows there is the prince in hunting costume (1917) by J. Kleintjes.

Queen Emma's Drawing Room (31), second wife of William III, and that of **Prince Henry (32)** are furnished according to the tastes of the time. The palace visit ends with **Queen Wilhelmina's Drawing Room and Office★ (33** and **34)** arranged as they were when she was alive. The statuette on the chimney in the second room is of Gaspard de Coligny (father to William the Silent's fourth wife, Louise) who led the Huguenots in the 16C.

Go down to the vaulted cellars, then pass between the two staircases and turn right, then left to reach the gardens (tuinen).

On your way, do not miss seeing the small **kitchen** covered in Delft tiles. Queen Mary used this room, when she prepared jam with fruit from her garden. The small **grotto**, restored, has shells, fine stones and marble decoration.

★★ Gardens – *Go up to the terrace.*

The superb **garden gate★★★** in gilded wrought iron used to provide access to the terrace. It took one year for a Dutch craftsman to recreate this masterpiece designed by D. Marot by resorting to the techniques used in those days. Under the crown can be seen the initials of William and Mary (W and M), and in the lower part, orange trees and acanthus leaves.

The terrace, flanked by two statues in sandstone, symbolising the rivers which edge the Veluwe, affords a fine view over the gardens (6.5ha - 16 acres). Documents of the time as well as traces discovered under the layers of sand in the 19C English garden have made it possible to reconstitute the 17C gardens. In addition the choice of plants decorating the flower beds has been limited to species known at the time.

Ph. Gajic/MICHELIN

Garden Gate, Het Loo

There are four gardens:

The **lower garden**, surrounded on three sides by terraces, consists of four *parterres de broderie* (embroidery-like pattern) and four English-style parterres decorated with statues representing Flora and Baccus *(east side)*, Apollo and Venus receiving a golden apple from Paris *(west side)*. The Venus adorning the central fountain is the replica of a statue by Gaspar Marsy (1625-81) which is in Versailles. Note the terrestrial and celestial globes; the first reflects the world as it was known in Europe at the end of the 17C, whereas the positioning of the second corresponds to that of the sky above Het Loo at the birth of Princess Mary Stuart. The waterfall in the middle of the east slope is decorated with a very graceful statue of Narcissus gazing at himself in the water, the copy of a work by the Belgian sculptor Gabriel de Grupello (1644-1730).

Beyond the path lined with a double row of oak trees which led to Het Oude Loo (a few turrets can be seen) extends the **upper garden**. This is delimited by colonnades – go up the staircase to see the view – and amongst the large trees in the English-style garden, there is a tulip tree, recognisable by its leaves ending not in a point but in a V-shaped notch. The king's fountain symbolises the power of the sovereign William III who wished it to shoot water higher into the air than those of his rival Louis XIV.

Distinguished people have witnessed to the qualities of the water: contrary to the water of Versailles, that of Het Loo was limpid and odourless.

The **King's Garden** *(to the west of the palace)* where blue and orange are the dominant colours, has a lawn, once a bowling-green. The lovely Canadian maple tree in the corner of the lawn was a present from Queen Juliana to her mother Wilhelmina.

For the **Queen's Garden** *(to the east of the palace)* of more intimate character with its arbour of greenery, flowers in pastel shades have been chosen, as well as fruit trees (orange, apricot, cherry-plum, morello cherry trees).

Consult the Index to find an individual town or sight

HILVERSUM Noord-Holland

Pop 84 606

Michelin map 408 G5 – Town plan in the current Michelin Red Guide Benelux

Hilversum in the picturesque moors and woods of the Gooi is, in a way, a large residential suburb of Amsterdam: it is an extensive residential area with villas scattered amongst the trees.

In Hilversum and its surroundings to the north, towards Bussum, there are broadcasting stations and the seat of the Netherlands television installations and studios.

★ **Raadhuis** – *To the north of town, Hoge Naarderweg.* Built between 1928 and 1932, it is the work of **Dudok** (1884-1974). For the most part it is a harmonious juxtaposition of cubic masses where the different volumes fall nicely into place offering a play of horizontal and vertical lines overlooked by a tall clock tower. On the south side the clock tower is reflected in a lake. The bare walls are of a fairly discreet yellow tinted brick. Inside all is functional and rational.

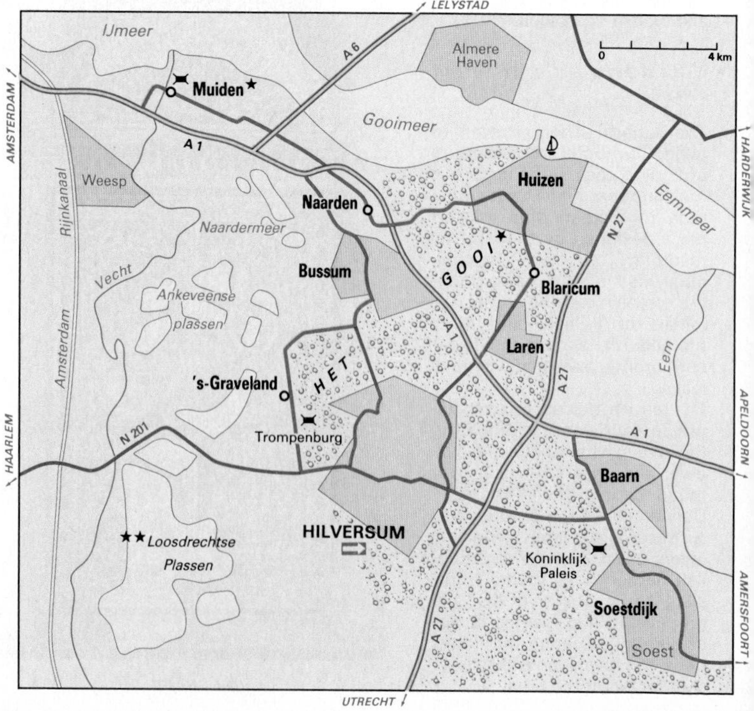

★ GOOI

Round tour of 62km - 38 1/2 miles – allow a day – local map opposite

Leave Hilversum to the southeast.

Soestdijk – To the north of town is the Royal Palace, **Koninklijk Paleis**, residence of the Queen Mother (Princess Juliana). This former hunting lodge was used in the summer by the Dutch sovereigns until the marriage of Princess Juliana to Prince Bernhard of Lippe-Biesterfeld, when it became their residence.

Baarn – Pop 24 847. Pleasant holiday resort near coniferous forests.
Near Laren one enters **Gooi**. This densely wooded region of Noord-Holland is in fact an immense residential suburb with many substantial houses tucked away in lovely parks where Amsterdamers have chosen to live. There are still several tracts of heathland in the vicinity.

Laren – Pop 11 377. A residential town in a very pleasant site, Laren is a painter's haven. At the end of the 19C the **Laren School** gathered together several painters under the guidance of Neuhuys and Anton Mauve; several of the artists were also members of The Hague School.
In the town's centre, around the villa (1911) of the American painter William Henry Singer (1868-1943), a cultural centre (Singer-museum en Concertzaal) was built in 1956 by the painter's widow. It includes a theatre and a museum.
The interesting collections of the **Singermuseum** ⊙ are shown by rotation: works by Singer with Impressionist tendencies; 19C and 20C French paintings (Le Sidaner); the Laren (Hart Nibbrig), Amsterdam and Hague Schools (Maris, Bosboom and Isaac Israëls). Sculpture is dispersed throughout the museum and garden.

Blaricum – Pop 10 511. Lovely residential town in the heart of Gooi.

Huizen – Pop 42 001. Since the closing of the Zuiderzee *(qv)*, this town has become industrialised and has a large marina.

Naarden – *See Naarden.*

P. van Riel/EXPLORER

Muiderslot

★ **Muiden** – Pop 6 745. Near this small harbour used frequently by pleasure boats is **Muiderslot**★ ⊙ standing on the banks of the IJmeer and at the mouth of the Vecht. It is an old brick fortress with stout corner towers, surrounded by a moat; its massive silhouette is visible from afar.
Built *c*1204 to defend the mouth of the Vecht, it was rebuilt by Floris V, Count of Holland. He was assassinated here in 1296 by the nobles, who felt he granted too many privileges to the common people.
As of 1621 the castle became the meeting place for the **Muiderkring** (Muiden Circle), an intellectual and literary circle which gathered around the then owner of the premises, the historian and poet **Pieter C. Hooft** (1581-1647). The distinguished participants included the jurist Hugo Grotius, the poets Joost van den Vondel and Constantijn Huygens and the writer Maria Tesselschede.
Whan Hooft died the castle fell into neglect but today the rooms have been resfurbished and display their former 17C glory.

Bussum – Pop 31 572. An important residential town on the edge of Gooimeer.

On leaving Bussum, turn right towards 's-Graveland.

's-Graveland – Pop 9 129. In the vicinity of this town, there are a number of fine manorhouses. **Trompenburg** is the most elegant with its gracious silhouette reflected in the waters of the lake. Built by Admiral Cornelis Tromp, son of the famous Admiral *(qv)*, it is a rectangular building linked to a domed pavilion.

Return to Hilversum.

HINDELOOPEN Friesland

Michelin map 408 H3 – Local map see SNEEK

This small town (Hynljippen), on the banks of IJsselmeer, is one of the eleven cities of Friesland. Member of the Hanseatic League, it was formerly very prosperous due to its trade with Norway.
Away from the road, with its lanes winding between houses and gardens, its footbridges spanning small canals, the tranquility of Hindeloopen is roused in the summer by the presence of many pleasure boats.

Furniture and costumes – Since the 18C Hindeloopen has specialised in hand painted furniture, where red and a dull green prevail. The colours as well as the motifs and shapes are inspired by Scandinavian styles seen by sailors during their long journeys. Hindeloopen is a close knit community and each drawing had a ritual meaning.
The costumes also owed much to the Far East: made of cotton with large foliage in reds, greens or blues on a white background *(sits, see Traditions and Folklore in the Introduction)*.

★ **Hidde Nijland Stichting** ⊙ – Located near the church, this museum captivates by its reconstituted interiors, collections of fine traditional costumes, a series of tiles or earthenware pictures and its images of the great sailing ships of the past.

The Elfstedentocht – Eleven Towns Race – links 11 Frisian towns in a 210km - 131 mile skating race held only when it is cold enough for the waterways that link them to be rock solid. 400 qualify as competitors but hundreds of other skaters are allowed to follow the competitors as touring skaters. The race begins at 0500 and the course may take 7 punishing hours to complete.

★★★ DE HOGE VELUWE Gelderland

Michelin map 408 I5

The De Hoge Veluwe National Park, which covers 5 400ha - 13 338 acres, is a beautiful park with a famous museum.

★★★ PARK ⊙ *2 hours*

A desolate landscape of heathlands, sand dunes and lakes is interspersed with clusters of tall oak and beech trees, pine and birch woods.
The park has a rich wildlife ranging from red deer, moufflons, wild boar, roe deer and a wide variety of birdlife. The birdlife is best seen from the observation hide (Wildkansel) or the place called Vogelvijvers. The best time to observe the animals is in the late afternoon in winter and spring (ie till the end of May).
The park has a good road network as well as a choice of cycling paths and trails.

★★★ RIJKSMUSEUM KRÖLLER-MÜLLER ⊙ *3 hours*

The Kröller-Müller Museum was built to the designs of Henry van de Velde and owes its name to its founders Willem Kröller and his wife Hélène, born Müller. The museum was inaugurated in 1938 and then in 1960 a Sculpture Garden was created. 17 years later W Quist was commissioned to build a new wing. The museum houses an important collection of paintings, sculptures and drawings, including works by Van Gogh.
To the right of the main entrance is the **sculpture room** (Beeldenzaal): *The Rider and Horse* by Marini (1952) is near works by Zadkine. Early 20C paintings are hung in the series of rooms that follow. There are a number of canvases by **Mondrian** *(qv)* showing his diversity of style. The paintings by Van der Leck are followed by works of the **Constructivists** (Strzeminsky) and **Futurists** (Ballà and Severini). **Cubism** is represented by Picasso, Braque, Juan de Gris and Fernand Léger (*Soldiers Playing Cards,* 1917).
Further along, there are works by James Ensor and a few Pointillist canvases by Seurat *(Ile Chahut)* and Signac.
A particularly good selection of works by **Van Gogh** is grouped around a patio: *The Olive Grove, Old Man in Sorrow, The Good Samaritain,* after a painting by Delacroix, *Cypress with a Star, Café Terrace at Night, The Bridge at Arles, Willows at Sunset, The Postman Roulin,* and *L'Arlésienne,* copied from a drawing by his friend Gauguin. There are also works of 1887 like the *Sunflowers,* which was Mrs Kröller's first acquisition and a *Bouquet of Flowers in a Blue Vase.* Other paintings – *Potato Eaters* and *Weaver's Workshop* – are typical of his earliest more sombre style.
In another room, next to the **French Impressionists** (Cézanne, Renoir and Monet), there is a landscape by Jongkind. Strange Symbolist works are signed by the Dutch artist Jan Toorop.
Then come the Dutch painters of the Golden Age (Avercamp, Van Goyen and Van de Velde the Younger) and masters of the 16C such as Bruyn the Elder *(Portrait of a Woman with a Carnation,* with a vanitas on the reverse side) and a *Venus and Cupid* (1525) by Hans Baldung Grien which compares favourably with Cranach's version.
The museum also has on display Greek ceramics, Chinese and Japanese porcelain and 19C ceramics (Mendes da Costa).
The **new wing** is used alternately for displaying contemporary sculpture (Minimal Art, Zero Group and Arte povere) or temporary exhibitions of recent sculpture and architecture.

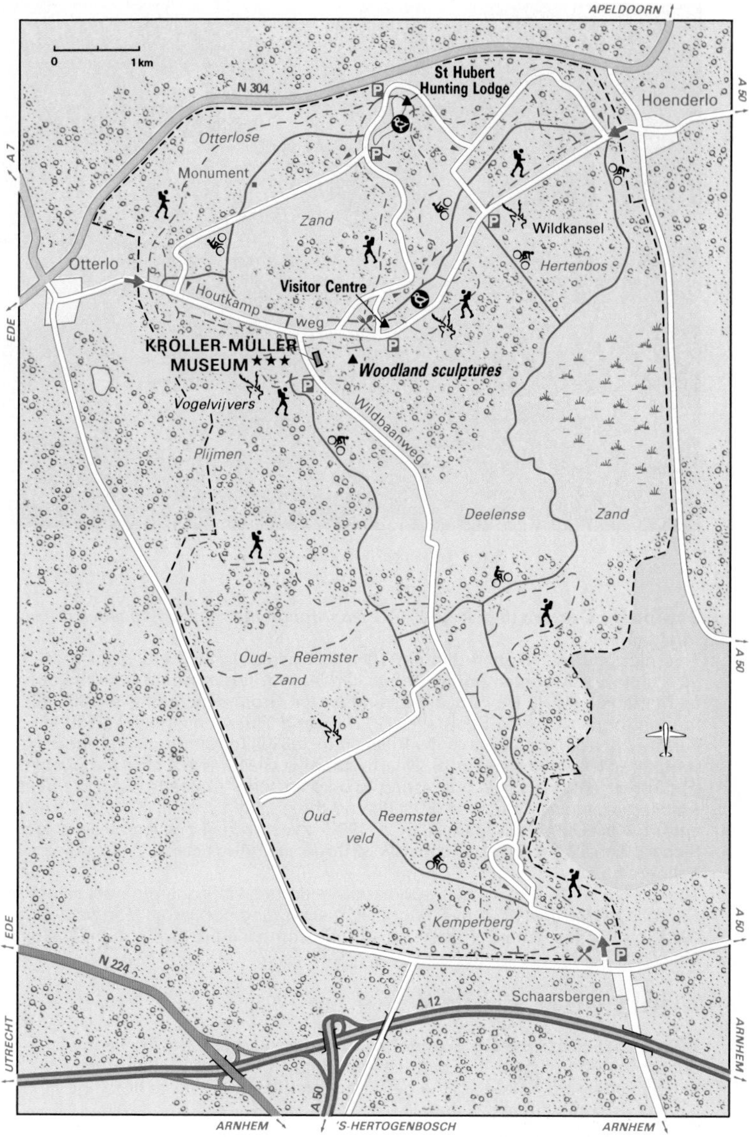

APELDOORN
0
1 km
N 304
St Hubert
Hunting Lodge
Hoenderlo
A 50
A 7
Otterlose
Monument
Zand
Wildkansel
Hertenbos
Otterlo
Visitor Centre
Houtkamp
weg
EDE
KRÖLLER-MÜLLER
MUSEUM ★★★
Woodland sculptures
Vogelvijvers
Wildbaanweg
Plijmen
Deelense
Zand
Oud-
Reemster
Zand
A 50
Oud-
Reemster
veld
Kemperberg
EDE
A 50
N 224
Schaarsbergen
A 12
UTRECHT
ARNHEM
A 50
ARNHEM
'S-HERTOGENBOSCH
ARNHEM

DE HOGE VELUWE
NATIONAL PARK
Birds
Game observation hide
Cycling path
Waymarked trail
Restaurant
Car park
One-way
Houtkamp
weg
★★★ KRÖLLER-MÜLLER
MUSEUM
Rietveld Pavilion
F
G
B
E
Sculpture
C
D
Garden ★
Wildbaanweg
Enamel
Garden
H
0
100 m
Woodland sculptures

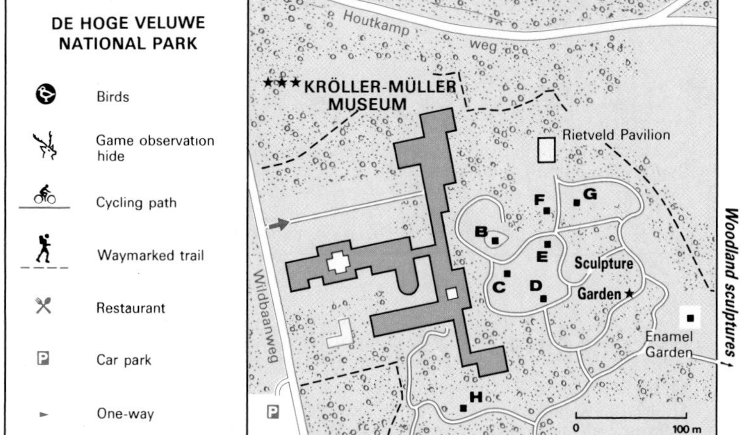

For a quiet place to stay

Consult the annual Michelin Red Guide Benelux which offers a selection of pleasant and quiet hotels in a convenient location

Ph. Gajic/MICHELIN

Sculpture Garden, Rijksmuseum Kröller-Müller

★ **Sculpture Garden (Beeldenpark)** ⏲ – *Go through the museum to reach the sculpture garden.*

This pleasant tree-shaded garden (10ha - 25 acres) is the setting for more than 90 sculptures by contemporary artists. On leaving the museum note the polyster by Marta Pan (1961) **(B)**, *Niobe Weeping on the Ground* by Permeke (1951) **(C)**, the thoughtful *Penelope* by Bourdelle (1912) **(D)** and *The Air* by Maillol (1939) **(E)**.

Further on, a **pavilion** designed by Rietveld in 1953 is for the smaller or more fragile sculptures (Barbara Hepworth). Nearby there is Giacometti's *Walking Man* (1960) **(F)**. Some of the more interesting works include *Concette Spaziale Nature, 5 Spheres* by Lucio Fontana (1965) **(G)** and the gigantic *Trowl* (1971) by Claes Oldenburg. Visit Dubuffet's **Enamel Garden** (1975) a vast white-honeycomb construction. Richard Serra's *Spin Out* **(H)** consists of three steel discs carefully arranged in the hollow of a sand dune.

The garden leads onto a small woodland site dotted with contemporary sculptures: *Herbaceous Border* (1987) by F. Morellet, the amazing beech tree (*Faggio di Otterlo*, 1988) by Penone, André Volten's quadruple composition *1 : 4 = 1 × 4* (1986) and *One* (1988), a bronze by Serra.

ADDITIONAL SIGHTS

Bezoekerscentrum De Aanschouw (Visitor Centre) ⏲ – The centre provides documentation on both the national park and the Kröller-Müller Museum. Other exhibits cover the history of the park, its varied landscapes, its flora and fauna as well as its recreational facilities.

Jachtslot St-Hubertus (St Hubert Hunting Lodge) ⏲ – The pavilion was built to the designs of Berlage and it was here that both Mrs and Mr Kröller died in 1939 and 1941 respectively.

Naar foto Tegelmuseum

17C and 18C ceramic tiles, Nederlands Tegelmuseum, Otterlo

EXCURSIONS

Otterlo – *1km - 1/2 mile from the west entrance to De Hoge Veluwe National Park.*

Otterloo has a Museum of Ceramic Tiles, **Nederlands Tegelmuseum**⏲, which presents a large collection of Dutch earthenware tiles dating from the 14C to the present day: polychrome from *c*1600, blue from around 1620, blue and purple in the 18C and 19C. The influence of Italian earthenware and then Chinese porcelain are evident in the 16C pieces while in the following century typical Dutch themes come into their own.

Landscapes and pastoral scenes were popular in the 18C. Note the late 18C biblical scenes on the mantelpiece from Zaanstreek *(qv)*. Admire also the colourful pictures or panels made from the 18C on with blue, purple or polychrome tiles as well as the collection of foreign tiles.

★ HOORN Noord-Holland

Pop 58 225

Michelin map 408 G4 – Plan of the conurbation in the current Michelin Red Guide Benelux

Hoorn is one of the most typical of the old Zuiderzee ports. With the creation of the freshwater lake, IJsselmeer, it now enjoys the status of lakeside town and sailing centre. Despite the loss of its maritime activities Hoorn has remained a busy commercial centre.

The town looks over what was to have been the fifth polder the Markerwaard *(see IJsselmeer).*

A **tourist train** (Stoomtram Hoorn-Medemblik) ⊙ runs from Hoorn to Medemblik where the journey can be continued by boat to Enkhuizen *(qv)*. The original steam locomotives and carriages take travellers back in time to the glorious days of steam.

HISTORICAL NOTES

A town was founded *c*1300 on the shores of the natural haven and it grew rapidly to become the main settlement of Western Friesland. Overseas trade and fishing brought great prosperity to Hoorn.

It was in Hoorn that the first large fishing net was made in 1416, marking the beginning of what was to become a flourishing industry.

To the north of the town centre, gardens mark the coursel of the moats of the early 16C fortifications.

In October 1573 the famous naval engagement the Battle of the Zuiderzee took place just outside the harbour; the combined fleets of the towns of Hoorn, Enkhuizen, Edam and Monikendam – all towns already in the hands of the Sea Beggars – defeated the Spanish under Admiral Bossu. However Hoorn's hour of glory came in the 17C when it served as the administrative and commercial centre of all Holland north of Amsterdam.

The town had one of the six "chambers" *(kamer)* which comprised the federal organisation of the Dutch East India Company *(see Introduction: Overseas Expansion)*.

In 1616 **Willem Schouten** (1580-1625) was the first to round the southernmost tip of South America, 96 years after Magellan had discovered the Magellan Strait. Schouten named the ultimate rocky headland of Tierra del Fuego, Cape Horn, after his native town.

Jan Pieterszoon Coen (1587-1629), also a native of Hoorn, was the enterprising Governor General of the Dutch East Indies from 1617 to 1623 and again from 1627 to his death in 1629. He founded Batavia, today Jakarta, and is generally considered to be the founder of the Dutch commercial empire in the Dutch East Indies (Indonesia).

Like the rest of the country Hoorn declined in the 18C and it was two centuries later before it was to see a recovery.

HOORN

Street	Ref	Street	Ref	Street	Ref
		Breestraat	Y 6	Noorderstraat	Y 35
		Hoge Vest	Y 10	Noorderveemarkt	Y 36
		Joh. Messchaertstr.	Y 12	Onder de Boompjes	Y 38
Breed	Y	Keern	Y 15	Oude Doelenkade	Z 39
Gedempte Turfhaven	Y 9	Kerkplein	Z 17	Scharloo	Y 41
Gouw	Y	Kerstraat	Z 18	Slapershaven	Z 42
Grote Noord	YZ	Koepoortsplein	Y 20	Spoorsingel	Y 44
Lange Kerkstraat	Z 26	Korenmarkt	Z 23	Stationsplein	Y 45
Nieuwsteeg	Y 32	Korte Achterstr.	Y 24	Veemanskade	Z 47
		Muntstraat	Y 29	Westerdijk	Z 48
Achterstraat	Y 2	Nieuwendam	Z 30	Wijdebrugsteen	Z 50
Bierkade	Z 5	Nieuwstraat	YZ 33	Zon	Z 51

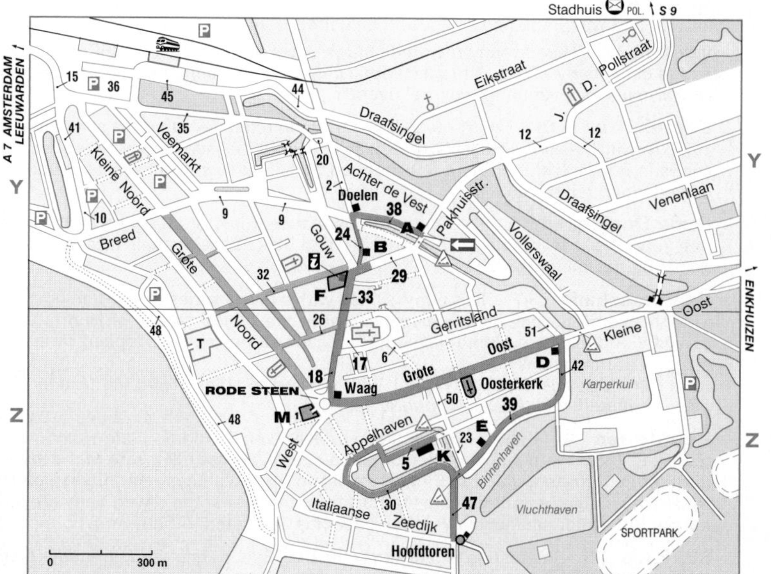

★ OLD TOWN *3 hours*

This was the original site of Hoorn and today a succession of old façades, many with lovely sculptured stones with a sea-faring theme, can still be seen.

Onder de Boompjes (Y 38) – At the east end of the quay an old storehouse (Y A) of 1606 is decorated with a sculptured facade stone depicting two sailing ships of the Dutch East India Company. At the other end the **Dolen** (Y) was the local archers' guild hall. Above the fine porch of the central facade, dated 1615, is a bas relief showing the martyrdom of St Sebastan the patron saint of archers.

Korte Achterstraat (Y 24) – At no 4 in this street is the old orphanage, **Weeshuis** (Y B). A commemorative plaque recalls that Admiral Bossu was imprisoned in Hoorn after his naval defeat *(see above)*.
Not far away at no 4 Munststraat, the house with the voluted gable adorned with the letters VOC (Verenigde Oostindische Compagnie) once belonged to the East India Company.

Nieuwstraat (YZ 33) – In this shopping street stands the old **stadhuis** (Y F) with its double crow-stepped gabled façade (1613), housing the tourist information centre. The house, at no 17, presents a façade with Poseidon and Aphrodite accompanied by dolphins.

Kerkplein (Z 17) – At no 39 opposite a church (secularized), the **De Boterhal** or butter market, formerly St John's almshouse (St-Jans Gasthuis), is a fine 1563 residence with a gable decorated with sculptures.

Kerkstraat (Z 18) – At no 1 there is an attractive 1660 façade.

★ **Rode Steen** (Z) – This picturesque square is overlooked by the Westfries Museum and by the waag. In the centre stands a 19C statue of Jan Pieterszoon Coen *(see above)*.
The house at no 2 has a façade stone depicting a blacksmith, hence its name: *In Dyser Man* (to the Iron Man).

Westfries Museum (Z M[1]) ⊙ – Built in 1632 the West Friesland Museum is an elegant edifice in the baroque style. Its tall **façade★** is imposing with its large windows, very colourful coats of arms (House of Orange and West Friesland) and cornices topped by lion supporters bearing the coats of arms of seven local towns. It was the seat of the States' College: consisting of delegates from seven important towns, it governed West Friesland and the Noorderkwartier (Northern Quarter).
In the entrance note a lovely gate (1729).
In the basement there is an exhibition of finds from local excavation sites (Bronze Age tombs...).
On the ground floor there is a fine hall (Grote Voorzaal) decorated with a lovely chimney and guild paintings; the beams are supported by corbels sculptured with coats of arms of the region's towns. On the 1st floor, the rooms decorated with lovely furniture and *objets d'art* reproduce the refined interiors of the 17 and 18C including a great number of items brought back from the Far East by the Dutch East India Company.
The 2nd floor is dedicated to Hoorn's maritime activities. There is a **portrait of Admiral De Ruyter** by Ferdinand Bol (1667). Amongst the scale-models of ships, there is a *flute* (a fly-boat) built in Hoorn in 1595. A small collection of regional, naive paintings by contemporary artists is displayed in a room giving on to the garden.
In the attic there are shop signs, scale-models of mills and ships, pottery.

Waag (Z) – Probably the work of Hendrick de Keyser, it is a fine 1609 building in blue stone, which today houses a restaurant. In a niche, a unicorn holds a shield depicting a cornucopia.

Grote Oost (Z) – In this street the houses near the square are very steeply inclined and topped with imposing sculptured balustrades in the rococo style.

Oosterkerk (Z) – This recently restored church dates from the 15 and 16C; a façade, added in the early 17C, was topped with a charming wooden pinnacle. The church is now used as a venue for cultural events.

Bossuhuizen (Z D) – The frontage has a frieze in relief depicting the sea battle of 1573, in which Admiral Bossu was defeated. The left façade is very typical of old shops in Hoorn, with a ground floor topped by tall narrow windows separated by carved wood pilasters.

Oude Doelenkade (Z 39) – On the Binnenhaven quay, or inside harbour, there is a row of old warehouses, note nos 21 and 19 (Z E) with their façade stones depicting navigational scenes.

★ **Veermanskade** (Z 47) – This quay is lined with a lovely series of restored houses. Most of them old merchants' residences have the typical façade of Hoorn, with carved wood pilasters. Some have lovely façade stones and are topped by crow-stepped or bell gables.
Note the birthplace of the navigator **Willem Bontekoe** (1587-1630); the façade displays a spotted cow (*koe:* cow; *bonte:* spotted).

Hoofdtoren (Z) – Built in 1532 to keep watch over the port's main *(hoofd)* entrance; in 1651 it was topped by a wooden pinnacle. On the other side of the tower a sculpture depicts a unicorn. Since 1968 a trio of ship's boys – bronze sculpture by Jan van Druten – contemplate the port from the foot of the tower. They are the heroes of a children's novel by Johan Fabricius dedicated to Bontekoe.

Bierkade (Z 5) – Interesting façades (nos 10 and 13) (Z K) line this beer quay (*bier:* beer).

HULST Zeeland — Pop 18 540

Michelin map 408 B D8 or 212 fold 14

At the frontier with Belgium, Hulst is a small town with cheerful, colourful houses and streets paved with pink brick. It is an old fortified town which was located on an important defence line made up of 13 bastions.
In the past it was the capital of the said Vier Ambachten region (*mestiers* meaning administrative district) comprising Axel, Assenede and Boechout (these last two cities became Belgian in 1830). Hulst's 17C ramparts and numerous bastions, still encircled by moats, have been transformed into a grassy esplanade shaded by fine trees.

Reynart's city – The surroundings of Hulst are evoked in the Dutch tale written in the mid-13C and inspired by the medieval epic *Reynart the Fox*.
Near Gentsepoort is a monument (Reinaertmonument) in honour of Reynart.

SIGHTS

Grote Markt – The **stadhuis** with a perron flanked by a square tower, dates from the 16C.
The **St-Willibrordusbasiliek** is a fine Gothic edifice. Its tower (restored) has an excellent carillon. For more than a century (1807-1931), the church was used by both Catholics and Protestants: the chancel and ambulatory being reserved for the first, the nave for the second.

Dubbele Poort – Near one of the town's gateways, important excavations have uncovered the remains of this early 16C gateway. A water gate as well, it stood over a navigable tunnel giving access to a military port.
From the top of the nearby ramparts, one can see the crow-stepped gable and octagonal turret of the **hostel** which belonged to Dunes Abbey, near Koksijde in Belgium. This hostel houses a **Streekmuseum** ⊙ of local and regional history.

Stadsmolen – This windmill on the ramparts was built by the garrison in 1792.

EXCURSION

Terneuzen – Pop 35 065. *24km - 15 miles to the northwest.* This port at the mouth of the Scheldt commands the entrance to Ghent Canal in Terneuzen.
Accommodating ships of up to 70 000 metric tons, it has three **locks**, the most important being 290m - 951ft long and 40m - 131ft wide.
In this complex of locks one can examine their workings closely.

★ HUNEBEDDEN Drenthe and Groningen

Michelin map 408 K2, 3, L2, 3

A prehistoric funerary monument, a *hunebed* is a kind of covered passage formed more or less by an alignment of several dolmens. It has a side entrance usually orientated to the south. Megaliths of this type, which exist in the Netherlands, are grouped in the Drenthe where 53 have been registered and numbered (D1, D2...). Only one is not included, that of Noordlaren *(qv)* which is in the province of Groningen (G1).

Ph. Gajic/MICHELIN

Emmerdennen hunebed

Imposing dimensions – The smallest *hunebeds* are not less than 7m - 23ft long whereas a length of 25m - 82ft is usual. The biggest covered alleyway is near Borger: the slabs which form it weigh more than 20 metric tons. The megaliths used to build *hunebeds* are erratic boulders from the *Hondsrug* (Dog's back), an end moraine deposited by a Scandinavian glacier, which extended from Groningen to Emmen. At present *hunebeds* have lost their original aspect. In early days, in fact, the *hunebed* was hidden under a small burial mound, the earth being held up by a ring of upright stones; the space between these uprights was filled in by small rocks. In Emmen *(qv)* and especially south of Schoonoord *(qv)* one can see reconstructed *hunebeds.*

A funerary monument – Hunebeds prove that prehistoric man lived in the Drenthe from 3 000 or 2 000 BC. They were used as collective burial chambers. Dishes, plates, tools and even jewellery were placed next to the bodies. Consequently the excavations made under the *hunebeds* have been very fruitful. The objects discovered, notably pottery, have made it possible to connect *hunebeds* with the civilisation known as the Bell-Beaker folk.

★ HUNEBED TRAIL

From Emmen to Noordlaren

52km - 32 miles – allow 1 day – local map right

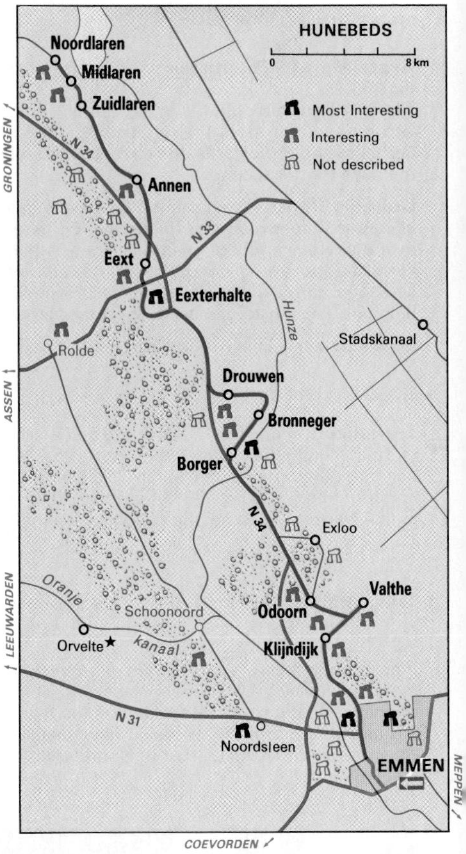

Emmen – *See Emmen.*

Klijndijk – *Go towards Valthe on the right.* On leaving the village turn right on to a sandy path, then left. Skirting the woods one reaches a long *hunebed* where two capstones remain.

Valthe – On leaving the village towards the north-east, on the right before a petrol station, a lane marked *hunebed (about 400m - 1/4 mile)* leads to *hunebed* D 37, surrounded by oaks. It is in fact two covered alleyways, one of which has been knocked down by three large oaks.

Going towards Odoorn, on the left after a wood, there is a small lane marked hunebed *which leads to* hunebed *D 34.*

Set among heather, it is a small covered alleyway with two leaning slabs.

Odoorn – Pop 12 314. At Odoorn, centre of a sheep rearing region, a very important sheep market is held annually.

At **Exloo** *(4km - 2 1/2 miles north of Odoorn)* the sheperds' feast (Schaapscheerdersfeest) and an ancient handicraft festival are held each year *(for these two events see Calendar of Events).*

On leaving Odoorn, *hunebed* D 32 reached by a small path marked *hunebed,* is hidden behind a curtain of trees. It is topped by four capstones.

Borger – Pop 12 498. *In the main street, take the road to Bronneger.* At the fork there is the **Nationaal Hunebedden Informatiecentrum** ⊙ (Visitor Centre) devoted to *hunebeds* and life during prehistoric times.

A little further on, surrounded by trees, is the Borger **hunebed**★ (D 27), the biggest of all. It is still stopped by nine enormous capstones. Its entry on the south side is clearly visible.

Bronneger – *In this hamlet, a path marked hunebed leads to an oak wood.* There are five small *hunebeds* (D 23/25 and D 21/22).

Drouwen – The *hunebeds* (D 19/20) are on a rather bare mound, near the main road (they are visible from the road). One is surrounded by a circle of stones.

6km - 3 1/2 miles to the north of Drouwen, go left towards Assen, then turn right towards Eext.

Eexterhalte – Shortly after the fork, on the right there is a **hunebed**★ (D 14) topped by six capstones. One can still see some of the stones encircling it.

Eext – In this village, in line with a bend, a path on the left leads to a *hunebed* (D 13), which has kept its original appearance; set in a cavity at the top of a mound, it consists of a square of uprights pressed closely together, and still has one of the capstones which served as the roof. Two stones set further apart mark the entrance, located, exceptionally, on the east side.

Annen – Small *hunebed* (D 9) on the left of the road.

Zuidlaren – Pop 10 945. Important tourist centre.

Midlaren – The village has two *hunebeds. Turn left, between two houses, on to a dirt track called* Hunebedpad.
200m - 656ft away, after having crossed a road, and behind two houses shaded by large trees there are two covered alleyways (D 3/D 4) each one made of several enormous slabs.

Noordlaren – *Before reaching the mill, take a lane on the left marked* hunebed *which leads to a grove.*
This *hunebed* (G 1), where there still remain two capstones resting on five uprights, is the only one in the Groningen province.

IJSSELMEER Flevoland-Friesland-Gelderland-Noord-Holland-Overijssel

Michelin map 408 G2, 3, 4, 5, H2, 3, 4, 5 – Local map see below

IJsselmeer is the name that has been given to the Zuiderzee since it was cut off from the sea by the construction of a Barrier Dam in 1932.

HISTORICAL AND GEOGRAPHICAL NOTES

The old Zuiderzee – The IJssel river formerly flowed into a series of small lakes. Enlarged progressively they developed into a large lake called **Lake Flevo** by the Romans and in the Middle Ages, known as **Almere** or Almari. In 1287 a tidal wave destroyed part of the north coast, enlarged the mouth of the Vlie, the lake's outlet and invaded the low-lying regions which surrounded it, turning it into a large gulf open to the North Sea.
It owes its name of Zuiderzee or South Sea to the Danes.
From the 13 to 16C commercial ports developed such as Staveren, Kampen, Harderwijk, affiliated to the **Hanseatic League**, an association of towns in Northern Europe which had the monopoly of traffic in the Scandinavian countries. In the 17 and 18C, trade turned towards the Far East and brought prosperity to such towns as Amsterdam, Hoorn, Medemblik, Enkhuizen, etc.
The Zuiderzeemuseum in Enkhuizen *(qv)* provides an interesting insight into the daily lives of those who lived in the old fishing villages of the Zuiderzee region.

Creation of IJsselmeer – The idea of closing the Zuiderzee by a dike goes back to 1667 when **Hendrick Stevin** published a work in which he proposed this means of fighting against the devastation created by the North Sea. In 1825 a violent storm ravaged the coasts of the Zuiderzee. In 1891 a project was presented by the engineer **Dr. C. Lely** (1854-1929). It was only adopted by Parliament in 1918, following the terrible floods of 1916 and when Lely had become Minister of Public Works for the third time.
The aim envisaged was triple: by the construction of a dike to put an end to the floods which menaced the banks of the Zuiderzee, make a reserve of fresh water to stop the increasing salinity of the soil, and with the creation of polderland to gain 225 000ha - 555 750 acres of fertile land.
The work on IJsselmeer started in 1919; in 1924 the small Amsteldiep dike linking **Wieringen Island** to the continent was completed.

Wieringermeer Polder – From 1927 to 1930 this polder was reclaimed. It stretches over 20 000ha - 49 400 acres in a former gulf of the Zuiderzee between Medemblik and the former Wieringen Island. Immediately after the drainage, the polder presented a surface of muddy clay, so in order to continue the work it was necessary, even before the end of pumping (700 million m³ - 24 720 million ft³ of water) to drain the future collection ditches.
In 1945, two weeks before their surrender, the Germans blew up the Wieringermeer Polder dike and flooding ensued. The surging water created two gaps of more than 30m - 98ft deep, engulfing a farm. These gaps could not be repaired and the dike had to be rerouted: it is the place called **De Gaper** (the Yawner). Again drained and returned to its former state, the polder is now a flourishing agricultural region.

Construction of the dike – The barrier dam, Afsluitdijk *(see below)*, was undertaken in 1927 between the Frisian coast and the former Wieringen Island by means of an artificial island (Breezand) built between the two points.
With clay dredged from the bottom of the Zuiderzee, a dike was built, against which sand was deposited; the sand doubled by a layer of clay was collected on the spot by pumping. As the work advanced the current grew stronger and the remaining channel was sealed off with great difficulty.
The barrier dam was completed on 28 May 1932. 30km - 19 miles long and 90m - 295ft wide at sea level, it overlooks the sea by more than 7m - 23ft and forms a new lake, IJsselmeer.

Three large polders – Once the barrier dam was completed, the creation of the second IJsselmeer polder was undertaken, the **Noordoostpolder** *(qv)* and then the two **Flevoland**★ polders *(qv)*.
The project concerning the development of the very last IJsselmeer polder (Markerwaard) has been abandoned. Only the northern part of the surrounding dike has been completed: it links Enkhuizen to Lelystad.

G. Sioen/CEDRI

Afsluitdijk - Barrier Dam

★★ AFSLUITDIJK (BARRIER DAM) *30km - 10 1/2 miles*

On the **Den Oever** side, at the dam's entrance, stands a **statue** of the engineer Lely on the left. On the seaward side the barrier dam has a breakwater which protects a bicycle path and a dual carriageway. Below the barrier dam on the IJsselmeer side, fishermen come to place their nets on the bottom of the lake, mainly to catch eels.
The **Stevin Lock** which bears the name of the engineer Stevin *(see above)*, forms the first group of locks for ships to pass through. They are also used to evacuate water.
At the point where the two sections of the barrier dam joined in 1932, there is now a **tower** with the inscription "A living nation builds for its future". From the top of this monument there is a **panorama** over Waddenzee and IJsselmeer. Near this edifice a footbridge spans the road.
Further on, a viaduct built in 1970 makes cross traffic possible between the two ports of **Breezanddijk** and gives drivers the possibility of turning back.
Beyond **Lorentz Lock**, the second group of locks crossed by a viaduct, the barrier dam rejoins the eastern side of IJsselmeer.

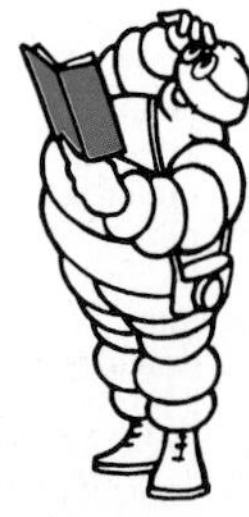

★ KAMPEN Overijssel Pop 32 679

Michelin map 408 I4 – Town plan in the current Michelin Red Guide Benelux

Kampen extends along the IJssel's west bank, near the mouth of the river. In the Middle Ages it was a very prosperous port due to the herring trade. It was a Hanseatic League city *(qv)* with commercial ties extending over the whole Baltic basin.
In the 16C there was a very rapid decline in the town brought about by the wars, which ruined the hinterland, and by the silting up of the IJssel. In the 19C a channel was made leading to the Zuiderzee but the closing of this sea reduced Kampen to the state of a river harbour.

Hendrick Avercamp (1585-1634) – This artist called the Mute of Kampen (due to his disability) came to work in the town in the early 17C. From his Flemish master Gilles van Coninxloo, he learnt Bruegel's style. But by the delicacy of the tones used, the presence of innumerable people and the serene atmosphere, his winter scenes have a surprising originality.
His nephew **Barent Avercamp** (1612-79) was his pupil and faithful imitator.

Foto © Mauritshuis

Winter scene (detail) by Hendrick Avercamp, Mauritshuis, The Hague

★ **Viewpoint** – From the east bank of the IJssel, there is an overall view of the town, which is particularly beautiful at sunset. In the centre, the onion-shaped turret of the Oude Raadhuis and the Nieuwe Toren stand out, to the right the 14C Buitenkerk (1), to the left St.-Nicolaas and the large towers of the Corn Market Gateway.

Boat trips ⏲ – *Boat trips are organised to Urk and Enkhuizen as well as cruises on the IJssel.*

SIGHTS

Oude Raadhuis (2) ⏲ – A little dwarfed by the new 18C town hall, it is a small edifice of 1543 crowned with galleries and flanked at the back by a slightly leaning octagonal tower with an openwork onion-shaped dome. Its pinnacle gable is surrounded by bartizans. On the façade the statues were replaced at the beginning of the century.
The **Magistrates' Hall★** (Schepenzaal), with somber 16C oak wainscotting forming the seats, has an oak **bench** richly decorated with Renaissance style reliefs, next to a monumental **chimneypiece★** by Colijn de Nole (1545). Dominated by the head and coat of arms of Charles V, the chimneypiece has a gracious statue of Charity in its centre.

Oude Vleeshuys – *Oudestraat 119.* On the stone façade (1596) of the old butcher's shop the town's coat of arms is engraved: two lions framing a fortified gateway.

Nieuwe Toren ⏲ – It is a tall square tower, erected in the 17C, topped by an octagonal bell tower with a carillon cast by the famous Hemony brothers.

Gotische huis – *On the right of the Nieuwe Toren.* This elegant residence with a very tall façade, crowned with pinnacles and pierced with numerous windows, contains the municipal museum, **Stedelijk Museum** ⏲.
There is, notably, a collection of silverware of the boatmen's guild with a fine 1369 **goblet★** of horn and silver and costumes of the region (Kampereiland) which included former Schokland Island.

Pass under the Nieuwe Toren and follow Nieuwe Markt to Burgwal, a quay running alongside Burgel Canal, which crosses the town; turn left.

Broederkerk (3) – This is the former church of the Minorites (Franciscans).

Broederweg – On the right side of this street, there is a Gothic chapel, a former Walloon church *(qv)* which in 1823 became a **Mennonite church** (4).

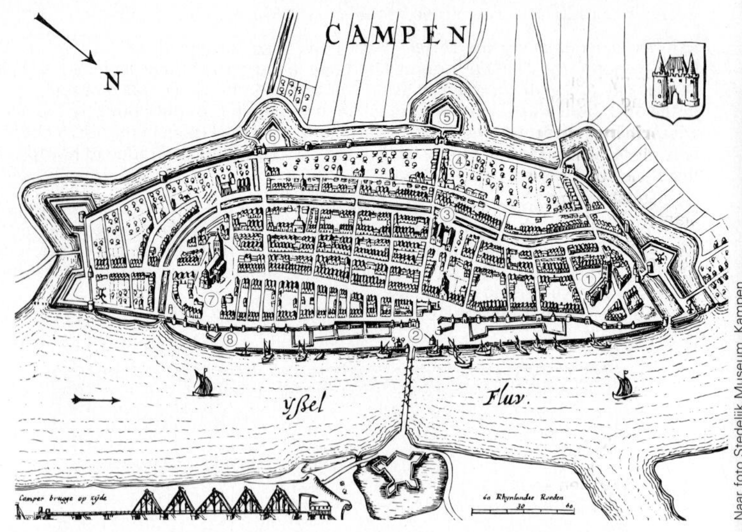

Naar foto Stedelijk Museum, Kampen

Broederpoort (5) – It is a lovely gateway with a voluted gable (1465) flanked by graceful turrets.

After the gateway, turn left.

Plantsoen – This is the name of the pleasant park which follows the old ramparts: the moats form the Singelgracht.

Cellebroederspoort (6) – An elegant building flanked by steeply pitched roofed towers, this gateway, which was part of the 15C walls, was altered in the 17C in the Renaissance style.

Go through the gateway and follow Cellebroedersweg then Geerstraat. By Boven Nieuwstraat, on the right, one reaches Muntplein.

St.-Nicolaas or Bovenkerk (7) ⏲ – It is a vast Gothic edifice of the mid-14C, overlooked by a tower 70m - 230ft high.
The interior is vast: nave and four aisles, a wide transept and a large ambulatory with radiating chapels. Note the 16C chancel screen and a Late Gothic pulpit.
The **organ** ⏲ dating from 1676, was altered in 1741 by Hinsz.

Koornmarktspoort (8) – It is the oldest gateway to the town. Dating from the 14C and situated on the old corn market, Koornmarkt, near St-Nicolaas, the gateway has kept its defensive character with a massive central keep flanked, since the 15C, by two squat towers.
The municipal museum holds exhibitons inside.

Campanology
There are three main types of bell installations:

Ringing Peals: up to 12 bells are rung by means of ropes and wheels; each bell swings a full circle to and fro and is struck from the outside, at the end of each swing, by a central clapper or tongue; a ringing peal requires one person per bell; ringing peals or ghange ringing is essentially practised in GB and USA
Carillons: groups of 25 or more bells fixed rigidly and played from a keyboard by one person; the clapper or tongue strikes from inside the bell; operated with the original music cylinders
Chimes of Bells: smaller groups of bells than the carillons but with similar mechanisms; played by one person or mechanically; the range of sound is limited; chimes and carillons are more common on the continent.

★★★ KEUKENHOF Zuid-Holland

Michelin map 408 E5

The springtime floral displays of Keukenhof, in the heart of the bulbfields, attract visitors by their hundreds of thousands. The journey to the park through the surrounding bulbfields gives the visitor a foretaste of the extravaganza to come.

An original speculation – The tulip is said to have been brought from Turkey by Ogier Ghislain de Busbecq (1522-92) the Austrian ambassador, who gave bulbs to Charles de l'Ecluse (1526-1609), better known under the name of **Carolus Clusius**, a scientist, who at the time was in charge of the Emperor's garden of medicinal plants in Vienna. Professor at the University of Leyden in 1593, Clusius started to cultivate tulips on the sandy and humid soil which stretched along the North Sea between Leyden and Haarlem. This experiment was a great success.
Meanwhile other flowers such as hyacinths and gladioli had been introduced but it was the tulip which attained the highest bids. Between 1634 and 1636 speculation was rife and "tulipmania" reached insane proportions. A rare tulip bulb was sold for 6 000 florins. Buyers even went so far as to exchange one bulb for a coach and two horses, for acres of land or for a house. The Dutch States put an end to this speculation in 1636 and the flower industry was regulated. At the end of the 17C the tulip craze was taken over by that of the hyacinth.

A few figures – Today bulbs cover an area of 16 500ha - 41 230 acres in the country. The main production areas are in the south of Haarlem and to the north of the line formed between Alkmaar and Hoorn. The bulbs are exported in both hemispheres and the total of these exports represents about one milliard florins per annum.

Bulb growing – The most widespread species in the Netherlands are the tulip, gladiolus, narcissus, lily and hyacinth but numerous other flowers are cultivated such as the iris, dahlia, crocus, anemone and freesia. Towards mid-March the bulbfields take on their first colour with the blossoming of orange and violet **crocuses**, which are followed by white and yellow **narcissi** (end March). Mid-April the **hyacinths** flower as well as the early **tulips**. A few days later the most beautiful tulips open out. It is, therefore, at the end of April that the plain is usually at its most beautiful. Divided into multicoloured strips separated by small irrigation canals, it looks like an immense patchwork. It is the time of the floral floats on the road from Haarlem to Noordwijk *(see Calendar of Events)*. The fields are then covered by irises, then **gladioli** (August). Another floral float procession takes place in September *(see Calendar of Events)* between Aalsmeer and Amsterdam.
Shortly after blossoming the stems are cut off by mechanical means, in order to strengthen the bulb. Once harvested, the large bulbs are sold. The bulbules are replanted in autumn.
Crossing the bulbfields by railway offers lovely views; flying over them in an **airplane** ⊙ is even better.

★★★ VISIT TO THE PARK ⊙ *allow 2 hours 30min*

The site was originally Jacoba's kitchen garden (*keuken:* kitchen and *hof:* garden); the countess used the castle, which still stands nearby, as her hunting seat. Over 150 years ago the castle grounds were landscaped in the English style by J D Zocher the Younger.
When a group of bulb growers was looking for an exhibition site, Keukenhof was chosen as the ideal location and has ever since served as the showcase for Dutch bulb growers. Each year the garden attracts over 900 000 visitors to admire the dazzling display of six million bulbs in flower in an attractive parkland setting. The layout is changed each year and planting starts in September and must be completed before the first frosts in December. The bulbs are planted in layers to ensure continuity of flowering from the end of March to late May. The tulips are in bloom throughout the entire period while the daffodils are out in April and the hyacinths are best during the last fortnight of April. In addition to the outside displays there are a number of thematic gardens and glasshouses where over 450 tulip varieties and more fragile species are on show. There is a splendid **view★★** of the surrounding bulbfields *(see overleaf)* from the windmill.

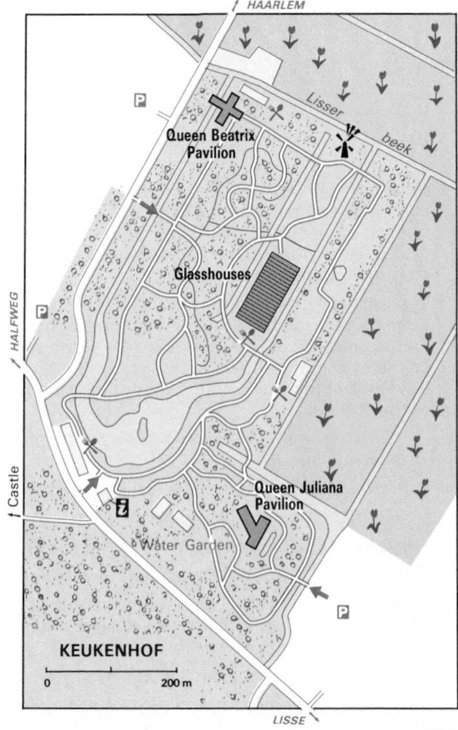

★★★ BULBFIELDS (BOLLENVELDEN)

From Haarlem to Leyden *46km - 29 miles - half a day*

★★ **Haarlem** – *Sightseeing: 3 hours. See Haarlem.*

Leave Haarlem to the south by V. Eedenstraat.

Going through the outskirts of Haarlem there is a succession of fine houses in spacious grounds before the first bulbfields appear. On the right is the 17-18C mansion, Huis de Manpad.

Take the first road on the right in the direction of Tulipshow and once over the level-crossing turn right.

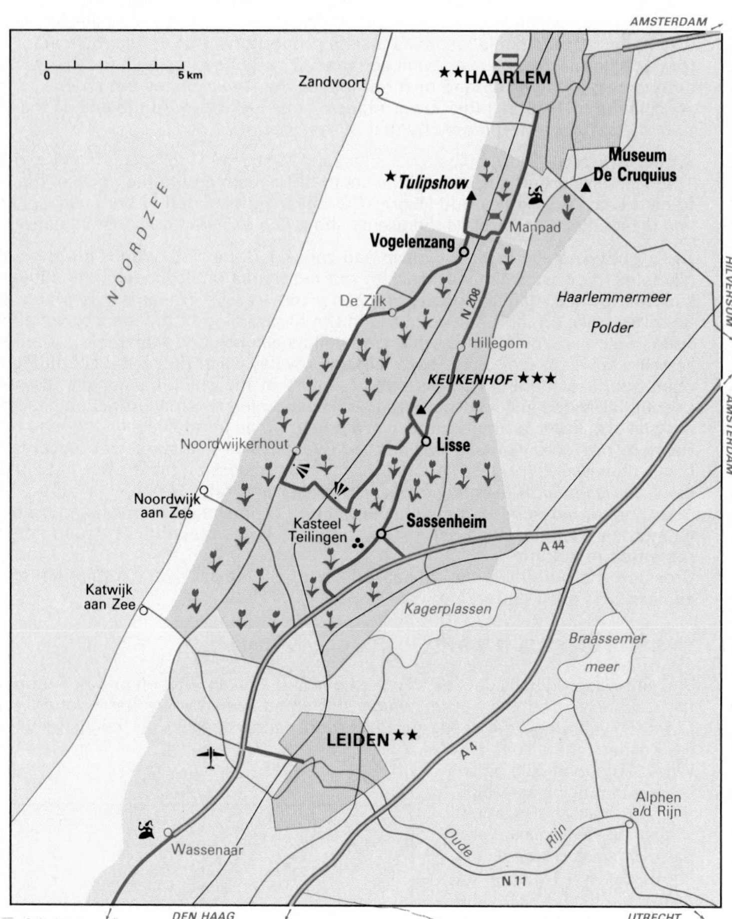

★ **Tulipshow** ⊙ – *1.5km - 3/4 mile to the north of Vogelenzang.* This garden centre cum nursery dates from 1789. In addition to its exhibition garden, there are glass-houses and the bulbfields, all of which are open to the public. A clog-maker also has his workshop on the premises and gives demonstrations of traditional clog-making methods.

Vogelenzang – The village is pleasantly set amidst woods not far from the coastal dunes. Once again there are some prestigious villas in well-tended grounds.
To the south of De Zilk the pale tints of the sand dunes contrast with the brightly coloured carpet of flowers.
Beyond Noordwijkerhout the road starts climbing and soon offers splendid **views★** of the bulbfields.

Turn left in the direction of Sassenheim and then left again after crossing the railway line.

From the railway bridge there are lovely **views★** of the bulbfields.

Turn left towards Keukenhof.

★★★ **Keukenhof** – *See Keukenhof.*

Lisse – Pop 21 312. One of the main towns in the bulb-growing area.

Sassenheim – Pop 14 422. An important bulb-growing centre.
Nearby are the ruins of **Kasteel Teilingen**, where Jacoba or Jacqueline of Hainaut spent the last years of her life.

Take the motorway back to Leyden.

Leyden – *Sightseeing: 5 hours. See Leiden.*

★ LEEUWARDEN Friesland P — Pop 85 693

Michelin map 408 I2 – Local map below
Plan of the conurbation in the current Michelin Red Guide Benelux

Leeuwarden – Ljouwert for the Frisians – crisscrossed by canals, is an attractive, busy town and the Frisians' cultural centre.
The town is the centre of a thriving dairy farming industry and herds of the famous black and white cattle are a regular feature of the surrounding countryside. The famous Frisian cow has been immortalised by a larger than life bronze statue on the Harlingersingel-Harlingerstraatweg roundabout. The locals affectionately refers to it as **Us Mem** (BY), Our Mother. The Friday cattle markets and Frisian bull sales held in the large, modern Frieslandhal at the western end of Tesselschadestraat (BZ **42**) are some of the most important in the country *(see Calendar of Events)*.

HISTORICAL NOTES

Founded from the linking of three mounds located on the edge of the old **Middelzee**, a sort of gulf, drained between the 14 and 18C, Leeuwarden gained some importance in the 12C when it was fortified.

Capital of Friesland – Friesland was a bone of contention between the Counts of Holland and the Dukes of Saxony whose feudal lord was the German emperor. In 1499 the Emperor Maxilian gave the fief to **Duke Albert of Saxony** who elected to reside in Leeuwarden which had become the provincial capital. In 1516 the Emperor Charles V gave the town a new set of fortifications.
After the independence of the United Provinces, Leeuwarden became the residence of the **stadtholders** of Friesland and Groningen in 1584. The first was **William Louis** of Nassau (1560-1620) son of John of Nassau (brother of William the Silent). In 1675, under Henry Casimir II (1657-96), the Frisian stadtholdership became hereditary.
John William Friso (1648-1711) received the title of Prince of Orange as a legacy from the Holland stadtholder (and king of England) William III. Friso's son **William IV** (1711-51) stadtholder of Friesland was chosen the first hereditary stadtholder of the whole country in 1747.
The present dynasty in the Netherlands stems from him, the first king being his grandson William I *(see family tree in the Introduction)*.
In 1580 Leeuwarden received its new curtain wall and, in the beginning of the 17C, a few bastions to the north and west, which were razed in the 18C and today have been converted into an esplanade bordered by the Stadsgracht.

LEEUWARDEN

Naauw	CZ 24	de Brol	CZ 6	Schoenmakersperk	BY 34
Nieuwestad	BZ	Druifstreek	CZ 9	St. Jacobsstr.	CY 36
Over de Kelders	CYZ 27	Groningerstraatweg	CZ 13	Sophialaan	BZ 37
Peperstr.	CZ 28	Harlingersingel	BY 15	Speelmansstr.	CY 39
Voorstreek	CY	Harlingerstraatweg	BY 16	Tesselschadestr.	BZ 42
Wirdumerdijk	CZ 51	Hoeksterend	CY 18	Torenstr.	BY 43
Bagijnestr.	BYZ 3	Kleine Kerkstr.	BY 21	Turfmarkt	BY 45
Blokhuispl.	CZ 4	Monnikemuurstr.	CY 22	Tweebaksmarkt	CZ 46
		Nieuwe Kade	CY 25	Waagplein	CZ 48
		Prins Hendrikstr.	BZ 31	Westerplantage	BYZ 49

In 1876 Margarethe Geertruida Zelle was born here. Having learnt to dance in the Dutch Indies (Indonesia), she went to Paris in 1903 and became famous as a dancer under the name of **Mata Hari** (In Malayan: Eye of the Day). She was shot in 1917 for spying for the Germans.
Since 1909, Leeuwarden is the departure point of the famous **Eleven Towns Race** (Elfstedentocht) a race where, when the Frisian canals are frozen, skaters compete over a distance of about 210km - 131 miles. The race may last 7 punishing hours and the last one took place in 1986.

SIGHTS

Kanselarij (Chancellery) (CY **K**) – These former law courts in the Renaissance style (1566) reveal, on Turfmarkt (peat market), a wide, heavily decorated façade, and topped by a slender dormer window with a statue of Charles V. The perron is flanked by heraldic lions. It is reminiscent of the town halls of Bolsward and Franeker.

★★ **Fries Museum** (CY **M**) ⏲ – Installed in a late 18C mansion, enlarged in the 19 and 20C, this museum gives an excellent idea of Frisian civilisation.
On the ground floor the **gold and silversmith** section is remarkable, with 16C Leeuwarden plate, a nautilus made into a goblet in the 17C, rare in Friesland, brandy bowls *(see photograph in the Introduction)*, the Popta treasure which shows 17C elegance and 18C rococo silverware.
The **archaeological** section concerns the *hunebed* period *(qv)*, the urnfield culture and the *terp* culture *(qv)*.
On the ground floor, interiors have been rebuilt. In the painting gallery (Schilderijenzaal) on the 1st floor there is a canvas from Rembrandt's studio; it is the portrait of Saskia van Uilenburg, daughter of the burgomaster of Leeuwarden and the painter's fiancée (married in 1634).
Several rooms are devoted to the 19C painter C. Bisschop, another room to Chinese porcelain and Frisian handicrafts.
The **furniture** of Hindeloopen and Ameland are painted in bright colours.
On the 2nd floor: reconstitutions of old shops (apothecary, grocer, tobacconist) and an interior from Workum with walls covered with tiles in the Louis XVI style, 18 and 19C **costumes** some of which are from Hindeloopen *(qv)*, a gold and silversmith's workshop, and 17 to 19C Frisian pottery.
In the cellars, medieval sculptures and a Frisian kitchen of the 18 and 19C.
A new wing is devoted to temporary exhibitions.

Over de Kelders (CYZ **27**) – One of the quays on this canal is dug out of cellars *(kelders)*. From the bridge to the north there is a fine view over the quays of Voorstreek and the bell tower of St Boniface.
The small **statue of Mata Hari** (CY **D**) was erected in 1976 for the anniversary of her birth.

Waag (CZ **E**) – On Waagplein, in the centre of the town, this is a 1598 building of red brick, the 1st floor cantoned with heraldic lions. Above them is a frieze sculptured with alternating motifs (flowers, animals, cherubs). The weighing of butter and cheese took place here up to 1884.

Weerd (BYZ) – This narrow street which plunges into Leeuwarden's old quarter is lined with lovely shops.

Hofplein (BCY) – The **stadhuis** (**H**) is on this square, a sober, classical building (1715) topped by a 17C carillon. At no 34 note a fine façade stone (1666) depicting Fortune. In the stadhuis annexe, added in 1760, the Council Room (Raadzaal) has a façade with rococo decoration topped by the lion which appears on the town's coat of arms.
Opposite this is the **Hof** (BY) or former residence of the Frisian stadtholders.
In the centre of the square there is a statue of William Louis, first hereditary stadtholder, called by the Frisians "Us heit" (Our Father).
At no 35 a façade stone depicts a stork.

Eewal (BCY) – This wide main road is lined with elegant 18C residences. Some still have lovely façade stones (no 52: sailing ship, no 58: St James as a pilgrim).

Grote- of Jacobijnerkerk (CY) ⏲ – Dating from the 13C, the Jacobin Church was reconstructed in the 15 and 16C. Devastated by the revolutionaries in 1795, it was restored, notably in 1976.
Since 1588 it has been the Nassau Frisian mausoleum.
Concerts ⏲ are given on the organ built in 1724-7 by Christiaen Müller *(qv)*.

Grote Kerkstraat (BCY) – The tall house where Mata Hari probably lived has been converted into a museum, **Fries Letterkundig Museum**. (BY **M**[1]).
Further on at no 43 there is a fine façade stone depicting a lion and a fortified castle, then near the corner of Doelestraat, at no 17, a lovely baroque portal is decorated with garlands in the Frisian style.

★★ **Museum het Princessehof, Nederlands Keramiek Museum** (BY) ⏲ – During the 18C, this 17C palace (hof) decorated with garlands and cherubs' heads was the official residence of Princess Marie-Louise of Hesse-Kassel, widow of the Frisian stadtholder John William Friso, Prince of Orange. Her dining-room (eetkamer van Marijke Meu) on the ground floor is richly decorated: stucco ceiling, gold curtains, portraits and Chinese porcelain.
This palace has been turned into a ceramics museum. Thirty rooms contain stunning collections of porcelain, pottery and stoneware pieces from many different countries.

Museum het Princessehof

Famille rose (1730-50), Chinese porcelain, Collectie Museum het Princessehof

The exhibits from **Asia** are displayed in chronological order (7 rooms). Some samples of the **Japanese production** are on show but the most splendid of all are the **Chinese ceramics**. They illustrate the development of the industry from the terracotta pieces made in the 3rd millenium BC up to the objects manufactured under the Ching dynasty (1644-1912), renowned for its *famille verte, noire* and *rose,* much sought-after by European collectors.
European ceramics (3 rooms) are the subject of a beautiful display: majolica from Italy, Delftware, Wedgwood, porcelain and *Art-Nouveau* ceramics.
The museum also presents an extensive collection of **earthenware tiles** from Spain, France, Portugal and the Netherlands. Two rooms are devoted to **contemporary ceramics** from several European countries, in particular from the Netherlands.

Oldehove (BY) ⊙ – This massive Gothic tower in brick was never completed due to the instability of the ground, which explains why it leans sharply.
The plan of the adjacent church, which was destroyed in 1595, is indicated on the square by coloured paving. From the top of the tower, there is an overall **view** of the town and its main monuments. Nearby, the old wooded ramparts make a pleasant walk along **Stadsgracht** (BY), a wide canal which follows the outline of the fortifications.

EXCURSIONS

Marssum – *5km - 3 miles to the west by Harlingerstraatweg* (BY).
Poptaslot ⊙ or Heringastate, preceeded by a 17C gatehouse with voluted gables, houses 17 and 18C furnishings.
Nearby the old almshouse, **Popta-Gasthuis**, founded in 1711 is a picturesque group of low buildings with a monumental portal.

Drachten – *27km - 16 1/2 miles to the southeast by Oostergoweg* (CZ).
In the Frisian countryside with rich meadows bordered by poplar trees, Drachten spreads with its great apartment complexes and brick houses. This town is a commercial and industrial centre with busy streets and pedestrian precincts, adorned with statues. It has numerous schools.

Terpenland (Terp Region) – *Round tour of 118km - 73 miles – local map overleaf. Leave by Groningerstraatweg* (CY). *Turn left after 9km - 5 1/2 miles.*
From the beginning of 5C BC and up to 12C AD in the low regions liable to sea or river flooding, the Frisians established their farmhouses and later their churches on manmade mounds called **terps**. There are still about a thousand of which two thirds are in the province of Friesland, and the rest in the province of Groningen where they are called *wierden*. Their average height is between 2 and 6m - 6 1/2 and 19 1/2ft, and their area between 1 and 12ha - 2 1/2 to 29 1/2 acres. The excavations have been very successful.
The tour covers a region where most of the villages have a *terp* with a church of tufa and brick with rustic charm, and a tower with a saddleback roof rising from a curtain of trees indicating its presence. The typical Frisian countryside is scattered with lovely farmhouses with gables decorated with a *uilebord (qv)* and a few windmills.

Oenkerk – This lovely forest-like castle park, **Stania State**, is open to the public.

Oudkerk – This village, known as Aldtsjerk in Frisian language, has a castle and a church on a *terp*.

Rinsumageest – The **kerk** ⊙, built on a *terp*, has a Romanesque crypt with two elegantly sculptured capitals. The interior is typical of Frisian churches.

Dokkum – *See Dokkum.*

Follow the canal to the southeast.

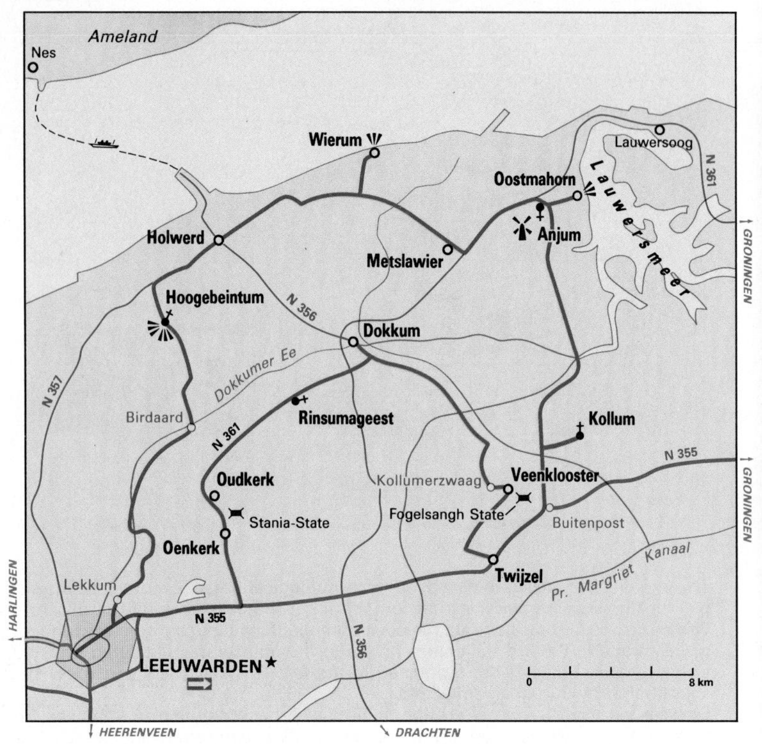

The route soon rises, the tree-lined canal becomes more pleasant.

Turn right towards Kollumerzwaag.

Veenklooster – Charming village with thatched cottages round a *brink (qv)*. A fine alley leads to **Fogelsangh State** ⏲ built in 1725; museum on the site of an abbey and surrounded by a park.

Twijzel – All along the main road, which crosses this town for a couple of miles, stand a row of magnificent **farmhouses★**. Behind the pleasant façade, more urban than rural, an enormous barn, often covered with a thatched roof, is hidden *(p 33)*.

At Buitenpost, turn left.

Kollum – This town has a 15C Gothic **kerk** ⏲ preceeded by a 13C tower. The nave is separated from the side aisles by stocky columns. The vaults with painted ribs are decorated with naive frescoes, as is the north wall where one can see a St Christopher.

Oostmahorn – From the top of the dike, there is an overall view of **Lauwersmeer** *(qv)*. Like the Zuiderzee, this low-lying region was flooded by the sea in the 13C. To avoid floods and create new polders a barrier dam has been built. The lake is now a popular centre for watersports.

Anjum – This village has kept an 1889 windmill. On a small *terp* there is a Romanesque church, enlarged in the Gothic style.

Take the road to Dokkum, then turn right towards Metslawier.

Metslawier – Grouped round the old Gothic church, the old, remarkably restored, houses form a harmonious whole.

Wierum – This is a small harbour with modest homes; its church is built on an oval *terp* and surrounded by a cemetery.
A staircase leads to the top of the dike: **view** over the Waddenzee *(qv)*, which at low tide appears, here, like an immense beach. The islands of Ameland and Schiermonnikoog are visible on the horizon.

Holwerd – It is the departure point for boats going to Ameland Island *(qv)*.

After Blija, turn left to Hoogebeintum.

Hoogebeintum – This village on the highest *terp* in Friesland (nearly 9m - 30ft above sea level) has a **kerk** ⏲ typical of the northern Netherlands with a bell tower with a saddleback roof and surrounded by a cemetery. It offers a fine view over the neighbouring countryside. The interior is interesting for the series of 16 **hatchments★** (from the 17 to the early 20C) which decorate the walls. On each carved wood panel, there is a coat of arms adorned with baroque motifs, symbols of death (scythe, hour glass, skulls and bones) and heads of cherubs in naive and rustic style. There are also some lovely seignorial pews in wood, and on the ground numerous memorial slabs.

Reach Birdaard to the south and follow the Dokkumer Ee Canal towards the south. Via the village of Lekkum, Prof. Mr. P.S. Gerbrandyweg and Groningerstraatweg, one returns to Leeuwarden.

★★ LEIDEN (LEYDEN) Zuid-Holland Pop 111 949

Michelin map 408 E 5 – Local map see KEUKENHOF
Plan of the conurbation in the current Michelin Red Guide Benelux

Built on the Oude Rijn, Leyden is an agreeable town crisscrossed by canals. It is famous for its university, the oldest in the country, and has numerous museums. It is also a prosperous town where graphic arts and the manufacture of building materials are important.
To the south east of the town stretches the Vlietland, a large recreational area.

Boat trips ⏲ – Boat trips are organised on the Oude Rijn, departure point: Oude Singel (EY) as far as Avifauna *(qv)* and on the city's canals, departure point: Beestenmarkt (CY).

HISTORICAL NOTES

In Roman times Leyden was called Lugdunum Batavorum. The medieval town grew at the foot of a fortified castle, the Burcht, erected in the 9C on an artificial mound. It owed its prosperity to its location on the Oude Rijn, which was then the main branch of the river, but the displacement of the mouth towards Rotterdam reduced the town's role to that of an inland market.
In the 14C Leyden regained a certain prosperity with the linen industry introduced by weavers from Ypres (Belgium) taking refuge from the Black Death.
John of Leiden was born here in 1509. He was the leader of the Anabaptists, members of a religious sect, who took refuge in Münster, Germany in 1534, where they formed a theocratic community. Beseiged, the Anabaptists had to surrender in 1535 and John of Leiden died the following year.

A heroic siege – In the 16C the town was besieged twice by the Spanish. The first siege (end 1573 - March 1574) failed. The second, started a month later was terrible.
The population reduced to half due to plague and starvation revolted against the burgomaster Van der Werff, who offered his body to the famished. Revived by the courage of their leader, the inhabitants continued their resistance.
Finally, William the Silent had the idea of breaking the dikes to flood the surrounding country.
On 3 October, the Spanish were attacked by the Sea Beggars, who had sailed in over the flooded land on flat-bottomed boats; the Spaniards raised the siege, abandoning, at the foot of the ramparts, a big pot of beef stew *(Hutspot)*.
The inhabitants of Leyden were then supplied with bread and herring.
From then on a commemorative feast, **Leidens Ontzet**, takes place annually *(see Calendar of Events)* with a historical procession, distribution of herring and white bread and eating of beef stew *(hutspot, qv)* in memory of the pot left by the Spanish.
To reward the town, William the Silent founded a university here.

Leyden University (1575) – It was the first in the Low Countries liberated from Spain and for a long time rivalled that of Louvain, which had remained Catholic; it very quickly acquired an European reputation due to its relatively tolerant spirit and the great minds it drew there: the Flemish humanist Justus Lipsius (1547-1606); the philologist Daniël Heinsius (1580-1655); the famous theologians **Gomarus**, Arminius and Episcopius *(qv)*; the Frenchmen Saumaise (1588-1653), philologist, and Joseph Scaliger (1540-1609) philosopher; the physician and botanist **Boerhaave**, master of clinical education (1668-1738); and **Van Musschenbroek** (1692-1761), inventor in 1746 of the Leyden jar, the first electrical condenser.
In 1637 **René Descartes** (1596-1650), published anonymously in Leyden, his *Discourse on Method* written in Utrecht, where he had formerly lived.
The influence of the university was increased by the fact that Leyden had become a great centre of printing in the 17C due to the illustrious **Elzevier** family; the family's first member, Louis who came from Louvain (Belgium) settled in Leyden in 1580.

The Protestant refuge – In the 16 and 17C Leyden welcomed numerous Flemish and French Protestants (who fled in 1685 because of the Revocation of the Edict of Nantes) as well as English.
In 1609 a hundred or so English Puritans arrived via Amsterdam, led by their spiritual leader **John Robinson** (*c*1575-1625), who had left their country under the threat of persecution. Former farmers from Scrooby, Nottinghamshire they had to adapt themselves to their new urban condition and applied themselves to various handicraft trades. A printing press published religious works exported to England and Scotland.
Their stay became difficult and the Puritans decided to leave Leyden and go to America. Sailing from Delfshaven *(qv)* on the *Speedwell* they reached England and embarked on the *Mayflower* in Plymouth.
The 102 emigrants amongst which there were 41 Puritans or **Pilgrim Fathers** landed in December 1620 on the southeast coast of Boston and founded Plymouth Colony, the first permanent settlement established in New England *(see Michelin Green Guide New England)*. Robinson intended to join them later but died before.

Botanical gardens and the early medical schools
When Leyden's Hortus Botanicus was founded in 1587 it was one of only five in Europe. These "physic gardens" were used by professors of medicine – often botanists – to teach their students and as a source of herbal remedies. Carolus Clusius, of tulip fame, came to Leyden as an honorary professor of botany from Vienna where he was Director of the Emperor's garden.

LEYDEN PAINTERS

Leyden School – From the 15 to the 17C a great number of painters were born in Leyden.

Geertgen tot Sint Jans (*c*1465-*c*95), who died in Haarlem, is the most gifted painter of the late 15C. Still turned towards the Middle Ages, he showed, however, virtuosity in the treatment of folds and gave great importance to landscape.

Cornelis Engebrechtsz. (1468-1533) remained Gothic as well, with crowded compositions and rather tormented linear painting (Stedelijk Museum De Lakenhal).
His pupil **Lucas van Leyden** (1489 or 1494-1533) is the great Renaissance painter. Influenced by Italian art, his *Last Judgment*, which can be seen in the Stedelijk Museum De Lakenhal Museum is a very fine work, for the balance of composition, sense of depth, elegant draughtsmanship and fine colours. Lucas van Leyden also originated the genre scene, using it for numerous engravings. In the beginning of the 17C a few painters of the Leyden School painted *vanitas*, still lifes where certain specific objects: representing the arts and sciences (books, maps...), wealth (jewellery...), earthly pleasures (goblets, playing cards), death (skulls)... are depicted with great precision often with a moralistic message. These subjects were appreciated by Jan Davidsz. de Heem *(qv)* when he stayed here before going to Antwerp.

Jan van Goyen, born in Leyden in 1596 went to live in Haarlem in 1631 where he died (1656). He was a great painter of pale, monochromatic landscapes: immense skies covered with clouds, shimmering water and skiful use of light and shadow.
Son of **Willem van de Velde the Elder** (*c*1611-93), **Willem van de Velde the Younger** (1633-1707), specialised, like his father, in sea battles: the sun piercing through the clouds flooding light onto the sails and golden sterns of large warships and shimmering on a calm sea. The Van de Veldes ended their lives in London where they were called to be court painters to Charles II. Oddly enough, the Van de Veldes were artists of sea battles who changed from the Dutch side to the English side in the middle of the Dutch Wars.

Gerrit Dou (1613-75) is perhaps the most conscientious of all the intimist masters of Leyden. He took to chiaroscuro when in touch with his master, Rembrandt, but he mainly tried to render with the patience of a miniaturist and a stylistic touch, recalling his first trade as a glazier, scenes of bourgeois life *(Young Woman Dressing*, Museum Boymans-van Beuningen in Rotterdam).
His pupil **Frans van Mieris the Elder** (1635-81) depicted smiling people in refined interiors. **Gabriel Metsu** (1629-67) genre painter, master in his manner of treating fabrics and the substance of objects, treated with great sensitivity slightly sentimental subjects (*The Sick Child*, Rijksmuseum, Amsterdam).

Contrary to his contemporaries, **Jan Steen** (1626-79) depicts very busy scenes with humour. His paintings are the theatre of the whole human comedy where somewhat dishevelled people indulge in various pleasures; they play music, drink, eat and play in a very unruly atmosphere (*Merry Company*, Mauritshuis in The Hague).

Rembrandt – Rembrandt Harmensz. van Rijn was born in Leyden in 1606. Son of a miller he lived near the Rhine, hence his name Van Rijn. His childhood remains mysterious. In 1620 he enrolled at Leyden University, but attracted by painting, he soon became an apprentice to Jacob van Swanenburgh, then, in 1623 in Amsterdam, to **Pieter Lastman** (1583-1633), a great admirer of Italy and Caravaggio.
Although he painted numerous portraits and even self-portraits, Rembrandt right from the start showed a leaning towards biblical history, which he first painted with minute detail typical of the Leyden School.
The artist, who never studied in Italy, contrary to the great painters of his time, adopted a very personal style. His chiaroscuro was not that of Caravaggio, where strong contrasts between light and shade existed, but an imperceptible change from shadow to people suffused with a warm light who occupied the centre of the painting. His works are steeped in a mysterious atmosphere from which an intense emotion and profound spirituality emanate.
Beginning in 1628 he took up etching and drawing, sometimes seeking inspiration from ordinary people

Rembrandt, Self portrait aged 23, Mauritshuis, The Hague

(beggars, etc.). At the end of 1631, he settled in Amsterdam; it was then that he painted the famous **The Anatomy Lesson of Doctor Tulp** (1632). This group portrait brought glory to the young painter of 26. Orders started flowing in.
Rembrandt met Saskia *(qv)* whom he married in 1634. Several children were born (all died soon after birth), one of whom Titus, was born in 1641.
In 1639 he moved to a house in the Jewish quarter, the present Rembrandt Huis.
In 1642 he painted his greatest work, the **Night Watch**, group portrait of members of the civic guard. This genre, which had already been revived by Frans Hals, is treated by Rembrandt with daring and complexity of technique up to then unequalled. However, not much interest was shown in this painting at the time, which became his most famous.
In addition, 1642 marked the beginning of the painter's misfortune: he lost his wife Saskia; he had already seen his parents die in 1630 and 1640.
He painted numerous portraits including that of the young Titus (1655), a solemn *Self-Portrait* (1652) but the wealthy art patrons began to abandon him with the exception of the burgomaster Jan Six. In 1657 and 1658 he was unable to pay his debts and had to sell his house and goods.
In 1661 his *Conspiracy of Julius Civilis*, ordered for the town hall was refused (National Museum of Stockholm). In 1662 he lost his mistress Hendrickje Stoffels. **The Sampling Officials of the Drapers Guild** (1662) was his last group painting, but he still did some marvellous paintings like the *Jewish Bride* before passing away, forgotten, a year after his son Titus, in 1669. He had just completed his last self-portrait.
The Rijksmuseum *(qv)* in Amsterdam has an exceptional collection of the master's works.
Among Rembrandt's numerous pupils in Amsterdam, there was the landscape painter **Philips Koninck** (1619-88) and several painters originating from Dordrecht *(qv)* or Leyden like Gerrit Dou.

★★ THE OLD TOWN AND ITS MUSEUMS *5 hours*

★★ **Rijksmuseum voor Volkenkunde** (CY M[1]) ⊙ – This ethnology museum, famous for its collections of non-Western civilisations, is presently undergoing restoration work. Until its official reopening, it will be used as a venue for temporary exhibitions, film presentations and conferences.

Molen De Valk (CY) ⊙ – This wall mill, the last in Leyden, built in 1743, bears the name of a bird of prey (*valk*: falcon). It has seven floors and the first ones were the living quarters where ten generations of millers succeeded each other until 1964. Restored, it has become a museum.
The tour includes the repair workshop, the forge, the drawing room (zondagkamer) and a retrospective of Dutch windmills. In season its sails turn, but it no longer mills grain *(for more information on windmills see Introduction).*

★★ **Stedelijk Museum De Lakenhal** (DY M[2]) ⊙ – Installed in the old cloth merchants' hall (lakenhal), this is a museum of decorative arts (furniture, silverware, pewterware), which also contains a fine section of paintings. The whole history of the town unravels within these rooms.
On the 1st floor the **guild rooms** (gildekamers) have been reconstituted: the surgeons', civic guards', tailors', brewers' and clothmakers' rooms.
On the 2nd floor the town's religious history is evoked with an Old Catholic church *(qv)*, and the execution of the Remonstrants *(qv)* in 1623.
On the ground floor there is a fine collection of glassware, furnished rooms (stijlkamers) in the Louis XV, Louis XVI and Renaissance styles.
In the **painting section**, numerous Leyden masters are shown.
By Cornelis Engebrechtsz. (room 17) there are two admirably detailed triptyches: *Crucifixion* and *Descent from the Cross*, as well as a small *Carrying of the Cross.*
But the works of **Lucas van Leyden** dominate. In his luminous triptych of the **Last Judgment** painted with assurance of draughtsmanship, the painter knew how to free the figures from constraint and rigidity. The central panel shows the Son of Man enthroned in thick clouds for the Supreme Judgment. On the panels heaven and hell are painted; on the back, St Peter and St Paul.
Among the 17C Leyden painters exhibited are Gerrit Dou, Jan Steen (animated scenes) and refined works by Mieris the Elder.
The museum also possesses some fine 17C paintings: a still life by J. Davidsz. de Heem, *Horse Market* by Salomon van Ruysdael, *View of Leyden* by Van Goyen and an early work by Rembrandt.
To the south of **Turfmarkt** (CY **57**) there is a lovely **view** over the harbour and the mill. Further on, from **Prinsessekade** (CY **51**) there is an old warehouse (CY **A**), restored, giving on to Galgewater harbour.

★ **Rapenburg** (CZ) – It is the most beautiful canal in Leyden, spanned by triple-arched bridges and lined with trees. On the west side there are some fine houses: nos 19, 21, 25, 29, 31, 61 and 65.

★★ **Rijksmuseum van Oudheden** (CZ M[3]) ⊙ – Apart from the particularly rich Egyptian and Classical sections, this antiquities museum has prehistoric and oriental collections.

Ground floor – In the hall the Temple of Taffeh (Nubia) has been reconstructed, a gift to the Netherlands by the Egyptian State; it dates from the Augustan Age. Also exhibited are Greek and Roman sculptures, notably the sarcophagus of Simpelveld (Limburg), a remarkable collection of Egyptian sculpture with the reconstruction of two tombs of the 5th and 19th dynasties, low reliefs from the tomb of Horemheb (*c*1330BC) and the famous statues of Maya and Merit (*c*1300BC).

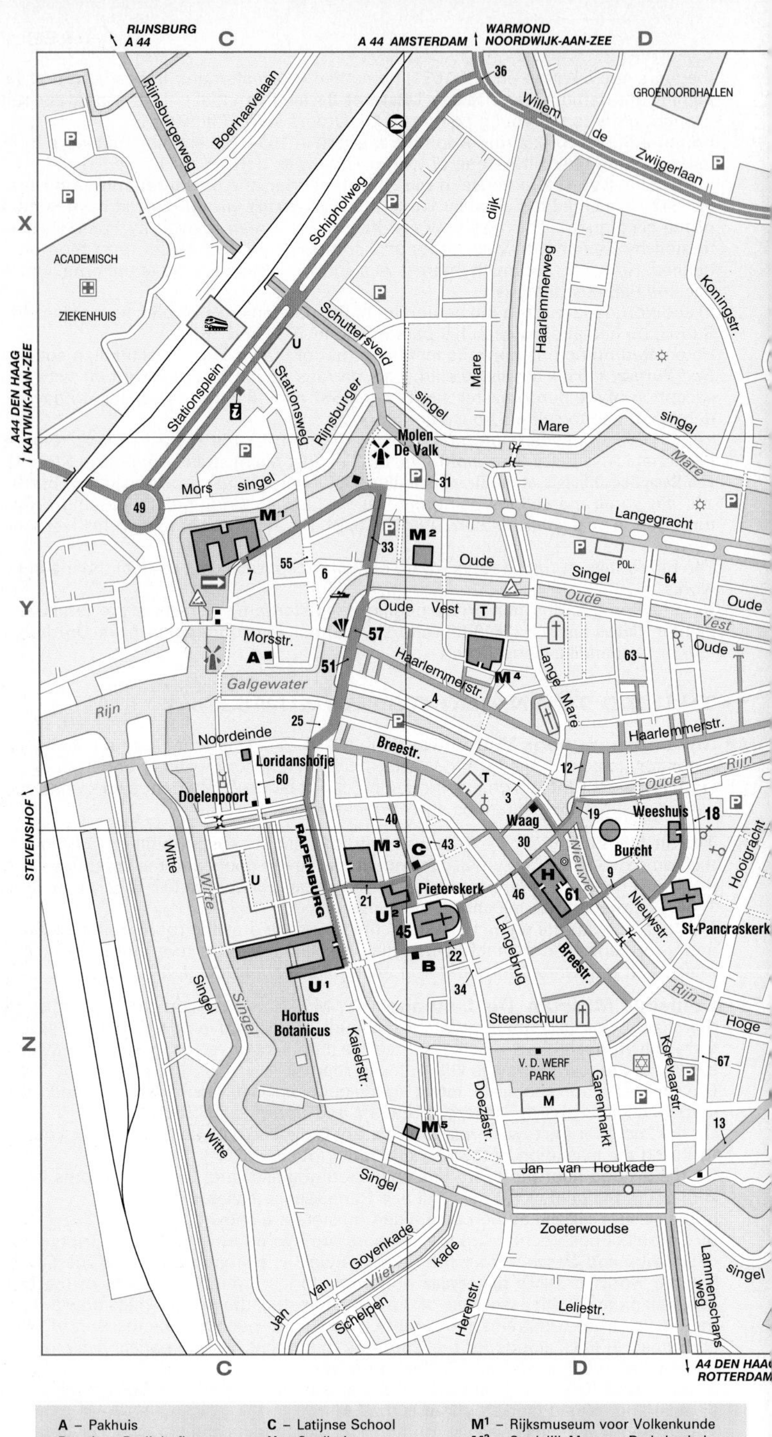

A – Pakhuis
B – Jean Pesijnhofje
C – Latijnse School
H – Stadhuis
M[1] – Rijksmuseum voor Volkenkunde
M[2] – Stedelijk Museum De Lakenhal

400 years ago

In 1594 the Dutch botanist Carolous Clusius introduced the tulip from Constantinople. The first plant caused such a stir when it flowered that tulipmania ensued and some were even prepared to pay the price of a canal house in Amsterdam to purchase some bulbs. Ever since the Netherlands has been associated with this flower which has become a sort of national emblem.

Tulips were portrayed in paintings (Judith Leyster), engravings, carvings and on porcelain.

Even today thousands of visitors flock to see the dazzling bulb displays at the Keukenhof, where 6 million bulbs are planted annually, and in the fields of the bulb-growing areas..

LEIDEN

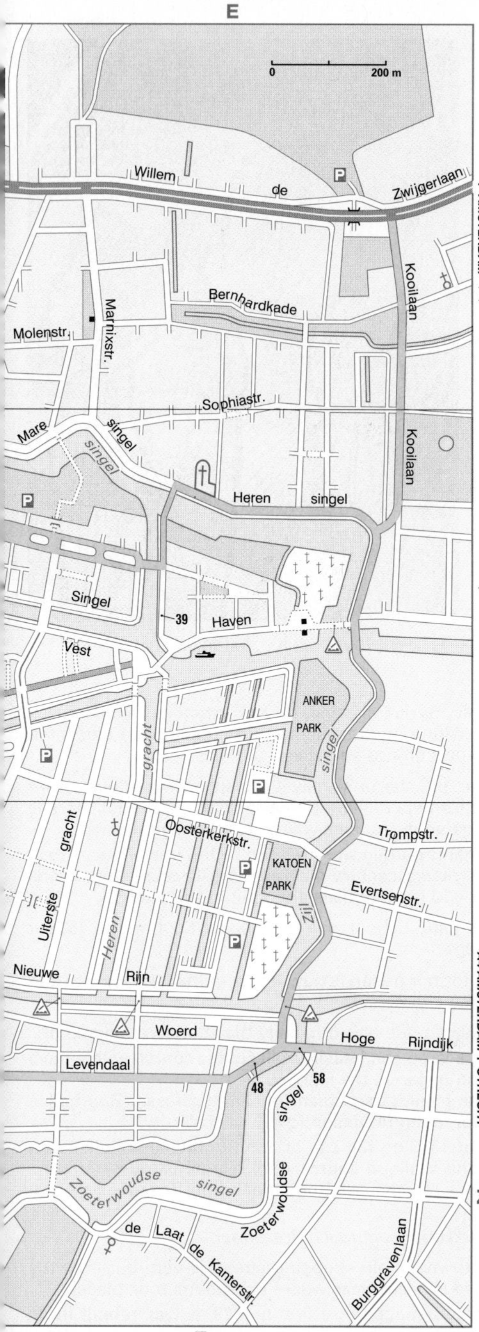

Breestraat . . . . DYZ 12
Donkersteeg . . . . DY
Haarlemmerstr. . . . . DEY
Aalmarkt 3
Apothekersdijk . . . . DY 4
Beestenmarkt . . . . DY 6
Bernhardkade . . . . CY
Binnenvestgracht . . . . EX 7
Boerhaavelaan . . . . CY
Burggravenlaan CX
Burgsteeg . . . . EZ 9
Doezastr. . . . . DZ
Evertsenstr. . . . . DZ
Garenmarkt . . . . EZ
Geregracht . . . . DZ 13
Haarlemmerweg . . . . DZ
Haven . . . . DX
Herensingel . . . . EY 88
Herenstr. . . . . EY
Hogerijndijk . . . . DZ
Hogewoerd . . . . EZ
Hooglandse Kerkgracht . . . . DEZ 18
Hoogstraat . . . . .DYZ 19
Hooigracht . . . . DY
Houtstraat . . . . DZ 21
Jan van Goyenkade . . . . . CZ
Jan van Houtkade . . . . CZ
Kaiserstr. . . . . DZ
Kloksteeg . . . . CZ 22
Koningstr. . . . . DZ
Kooilaan . . . . DX
Korevaarstr. . . . . .EXY
Kort Rapenburg . . . . DZ 25
de Laat de Kanterstr. . . . . CY
Lammenschansweg . . . . . EZ
Langebrug . . . . DZ
Langegracht . . . . DZ
Langemare . . . . DY
Leliestr. . . . . DY
Levendaal . . . . DZ
Maarsmansteeg . . . . EZ 30
Maredijk . . . . .CYZ
Maresingel . . . . DX
Marnixstr. . . . . .DEX
Molenstr. . . . . EX
Molenwerf . . . . EX 31
Morssingel . . . . .CDY
Morsstr. . . . . CY
Nieuwe Beestenmarkt . . . . CY 33
Nieuwerijn . . . . CY
Nieuwsteeg . . . . EZ 34
Nieuwstr. . . . . DZ
Noordeinde . . . . DZ
Oegstgeesterweg . . . . CY 36
Oosterkerkstr. . . . . DX
Oude Herengracht . . . . . . EZ 39
Oudesingel . . . . EY
Oudevest . . . . DEY
Papengracht . . . . DEY 40
Pieterskerkgracht . . . . . . CYZ 43
Pieterskerkhof . . . . DYZ 45
Pieterskerkkoorsteeg . . . . .CDZ 46
Plantagelaan . . . . DZ 48
Plesmanlaan . . . . EZ 49
Prinsessekade . . . . CY 51
Rapenburg . . . . CY
Rijnsburgersingel . . . . . . CZ
Rijnsburgerweg . . . . .CDX
Schelpenkade . . . . CS
Schipholweg . . . . CZ
Schuttersveld CX
Sophiastr. CX
Stationsplein . . . . EX
Stationsweg CX
Steenschuur CX
Steenstr. . . . . DZ 55
Trompstr. . . . . CY
Turfmarkt . . . . EZ 57
Uiterstegracht . . . . CY
Utrechtsebrug . . . . EZ 58
Varkenmarkt . . . . EZ 60
Vismarkt . . . . CY 61
Vollersgracht . . . . DZ 63
Volmolengracht . . . . DY 64
Watersteeg . . . . DY 67
Willem de DZ
Zwijgerlaan . . . .
Wittesingel . . . . .DEX
Zoeterwoudesingel . . . . . CZ
DEZ

M^3 – Rijksmuseum van Oudheden
M^4 – Museum Boerhaave
M^5 – Pilgrim Fathers Documentatie Centrum
U^1 – Universiteit
U^2 – Gravensteen

Selection of words appearing in the text

abdij	***abbey***	***kerk***	***church***
basiliek	***basilica***	***markt***	***market square***
beurs	***stock exchange***	***molen***	***windmill***
brink	***village green***	***poort***	***gate in city wall***
brug	***bridge***	***singel***	***ring canal***
gracht	***canal***	***slot***	***castle***
haven	***harbour, port***	***stadhuis***	***town hall***
hofje	***almshouse***	***toren***	***tower***
huis	***house***	***waag***	***weigh house***
kasteel	***castle***	***weeshuis***	***orphanage***

In the stele section note the expressive features so carefully carved in the sandstone of the stele (1300BC) from Hoey.
A separate room offers a brief presentation of Dutch archaeology until this department is officially reopened.

1st floor – Here there are collections of glassware (Egyptian, Roman, Syrian and Persian) and ceramics (Greece and Southern Italy) where the vases painted with mythological scenes of the classical period are at their apogee. The cult of the dead in Egypt is evoked by a great number of painted sarcophagi, mummies of men and animals, furniture and funerary urns.
Bronze statuettes, jewellery, amulets, pottery give a fairly good overall view of decorative arts in Ancient Egypt. Egyptian art of Roman times and Coptic art are also evoked.

Rijksmuseum van Oudheden

Stele (detail), ± 1300 BC from Hoey

The Middle East section presents archaeological finds excavated in Mesopotamia, Syria-Palestine, Turkey (Anatolia) and Iran. As well as samples of cuneiform writing, the museum houses decorative and functional objects made of stone, ivory, bronze and silver.

Academie (CZ U^1) – Since the 16C the university's administrative offices have been housed in the chapel of a former convent. Upstairs on the first floor there is a "sweating room" where the nervous students waited to take their exams.

Hortus Botanicus (CZ) ⊙ – The botanic garden was founded by the university in 1587 in a lovely riverside setting. Rare plants, century-old trees and attractive flowerbeds add to its charm. The orangery and greenhouses are open to the public.

Latijnse School (DZ C) – The Latin School was founded in 1324 and in 1599 it was given a Renaissance frontage.

Gravensteen (CDZ U^2) – This former prison is now home to the Law Faculty and has a lovely classical front on the church side.

Pieterskerkhof (CDZ 45) – This square was originally the churchyard (kerkhof).

Pieterskerk (DZ) ⊙ – St Peter's is a large and heavily built Gothic church with a nave and 4 aisles, whose construction began in the late 14C.
There are memorial slabs to the painter Jan Steen *(qv)* and Professor Boerhaave *(qv)* as well as the Puritan leader, John Robinson *(qv)*.

Jean Pesijnshofje (DZ B) – Built in 1683 on the site of John Robinson's house and intended for the members of the Walloon church *(qv)*, this almshouse took the name of its founder, Jean Pesijn, a merchant of Huguenot origin. There is a memorial slab to John Robinson.

By a narrow lane, Pieterskerkkoorsteeg, reach Breestraat.

Breestraat (CDY) – This, the town's main shopping street, is very busy. At the point where one crosses it, there is a **blue stone** where executions took place.

Stadhuis (DZ H) – Built *c*1600 and damaged in a fire in 1929, it was rebuilt in its original style. Preceded by a perron, it is topped with a highly decorated gable.

Vismarkt (DZ 61) – It is the old fish market.
At the beginning of Nieuwstraat one can see the 17C entrance doorway of the **Burcht** topped by a lion with the town's coat of arms (two keys). This fortress was built on an artificial mound at the confluence of the Oude Rijn and the Nieuwe Rijn. There remains a stout curtain wall with crenellations and loopholes. Its watch-path offers a panorama over the town.

St.-Pancraskerk or Hooglandsekerk (DZ) – On the outside of the transepts' arms, this 15C church has interesting Flamboyant style sculptured portals.

Hooglandse Kerkgracht (DYZ 18) – Alongside this filled-in canal is the old orphanage, **Weeshuis**, with a decorative panel above the doorway depicting foundlings.

Waag (DY) – The weigh house was built in 1657-9 by Pieter Post.

ADDITIONAL SIGHTS

★ **Museum Boerhaave** (DY M^4) ⊙ – The museum is named after the famous physician and botanist Herman Boerhaave *(qv)* and contains scientific instruments and documents concerning the evolution of scientific and medical studies from the 17C onwards. The exhibits include Christiaen Huygens collection of astronomical and surgical instruments as well as microscopes. Of particular interest is the microscope of the naturalist, Antonie van Leeuwenhoek.

Pilgrim Fathers Documentatiecentrum (CDZ M[5]) ⊙ – In a small house behind the municipal archives is a collection of objects and documents associated with the Pilgrim Fathers *(qv)*. The varied collection comprises a printing press, theological books and a model of the *Mayflower*.

Loridanshofje (CY) – The 1656 **almshouse** at no 1 Varkensmarkt (pig market) has an unusually plain inner courtyard.
Further along the street is the 1645 gateway, **Doelenpoort** (CY), crowned with an equestrian statue of St George, the patron saint of archers guild *(doelen)*.

EXCURSIONS

★★★ **Bulbfields** – *See Keukenhof.*

Alphen aan den Rijn – Pop 62 401. *17km – 11 miles to the east by Hoge Rijndijk.* This small industrial town on the banks of the Oude Rijn has a large bird garden, **Avifauna** ⊙, with numerous exotic species. Ducks and pink flamingos monopolise the pools and ponds while the more exotic birds are confined to the aviaries. **Boat trips** ⊙ leave from the garden to Braassemeer to the north of the town.

Katwijk aan Zee and Noordwijk aan Zee – *18km – 11 miles to the northwest; leave Leyden by Oegstgeesterweg. Local map see Keukenhof.*

Katwijk aan Zee – This is a popular resort not far from the bulbfields. The long sandy beach is backed by lines of dunes.

Noordwijk aan Zee – This fashionable seaside resort has excellent amenities for the visitor. Again a wide sandy beach stretches seawards from the chain of high dunes. The annual flower parade *(see Calendar of Events)* leaves Leyden in the morning and arrives at Noordwijk in the evening.

★★ MAASTRICHT Limburg Ⓟ — Pop 117 417

Michelin map 408 or 212 fold 1
Plan of the conurbation in the current Michelin Red Guide Benelux

Once prized for its strategic location at the confines of Belgium and Germany, Maastricht is now the bustling cosmopolitan provincial capital of Limburg. The city has developed on the banks of the great Maas river from which it takes its name. The town is quite distinct from the rest of the country with its bustling pedestrian precincts, its squares with sprawling café terraces and an almost Mediterranean atmosphere, its Mosan-type stone houses and its undulating hinterland.
A university town since 1976, Maastricht has five faculties, attended by a student population of around 7 000 (in 1991).

HISTORICAL NOTES

The original settlement grew around a fortified bridge built by the Romans on the Roman road from Bavay (in northern France) to Cologne, hence its name which means the Maas crossing (Mosae Trajectum).
St Servatius finding it safer than Tongeren (Belgium) transferred his bishopric here in 382. In 722 St Hubert moved it to Liège. The town already belonged to the Frank kings. In 1204 it passed into the trusteeship of the Duke of Brabant who, in 1283, shared his power with the Prince-Bishop of Liège.
It was given its first defensive walls in 1229.

The sieges of Maastricht – Maastricht having rallied to the Revolt of the Netherlands, the Spanish led by the Duke of Parma, besieged the town in 1579, took it by surprise, devastated it and left only 4000 people alive.
The United Provinces annexed the town in 1632.
In 1673, 40 000 French, commanded by Louis XVI appeared in front of Maastricht. The siege was terrible, the Dutch defense fierce. England contributed some 6 000 troops under the command of the Duke of Monmouth. But Vauban, who was directing the operations, won the victory for the French who left 8 000 men on the battlefield, amongst them **D'Artagnan** *(qv)*, officer of the musketeers.
The French captured Maastricht again in 1748, due to a clever move by Maurice de Saxe, Marshal of Saxony.
Taken by Kleber in 1794, Maastricht was annexed to France, as was Breda.
In 1814 the town became part of the Netherlands kingdom.
In 1830 the garrison resisted against the Belgians, thus obtaining the right to remain part of the Netherlands, but this was only confirmed by the Treaty of London in 1839. The fortifications were partly demolished in 1867.

During the occupation, Maastricht was the German communications centre in the west. One of the first towns liberated, in September 1944, only its bridges were damaged.

The Maastricht Treaty – The town of Maastricht shot to fame during a European summit held in December 1991, when the various heads of state and government leaders of the twelve EC members signed a treaty advocating commercial, monetary and political unity.

Maastricht today – Continuing its tradition of a busy medieval centre on an important trading route, Maastricht is an active industrial centre specialising in ceramics, paper making and cement. The presence of the Albert Canal, which provides a direct link with Antwerp and the North Sea, has served as a stimulus to the industrial sector. However Maastricht is gaining a growing reputation as a business and conference centre. Every year the **European Fine Art Fair** is held in the Maastricht Exhibition and Congress Centre (Maastrichts Expositie en Congress Centrum) which lies to the south-east of the town centre *(see Calendar of Events)*.
The annual **carnival★** *(see Calendar of Events)* is a highly popular event which draws large crowds of townspeople and visitors to the general merry-making. In this pre-Lenten carnival the decorated floats and bands are led by His Cheerfulness the Carnival Prince. The town is also known for its, great male choir the **Maastreechter Staar** ⏲.

Boat trips ⏲ – Boat trips are organised down the Maas to the Belgian frontier.

★ OLD TOWN *1/2 day*

Vrijthof (AY) – This square is the heart of the town, a vast esplanade surrounded by cafés and restaurants and overlooked by two churches, St.-Servaasbasiliek and St.-Janskerk.
To the south there is the Gothic façade of the Spanish Government House **Spaans Gouvernement**, (AY A) where William the Silent *(qv)* was declared an outlaw by Philip II of Spain.
Numerous shopping pedestrian precincts start from this square.

★★ **St.-Servaasbasiliek** (AY) ⏲ – This imposing monument, one of the oldest in the Netherlands, although often altered, was begun *c*1000 on the site of a 6C sanctuary. It then had one nave and side aisles, a transept and a flat east end. In the 12C it was enlarged on the one hand by the present chancel, flanked by two square towers and an apse, and, on the other hand, by a monumental **westwork**. The westwork is characteristic of the Rhenish-Mosan style; the basilica is one of the first examples of this style. Topped by two towers, it is decorated with Lombard arcading between which are twin arches. Its **carillon** ⏲ is excellent.

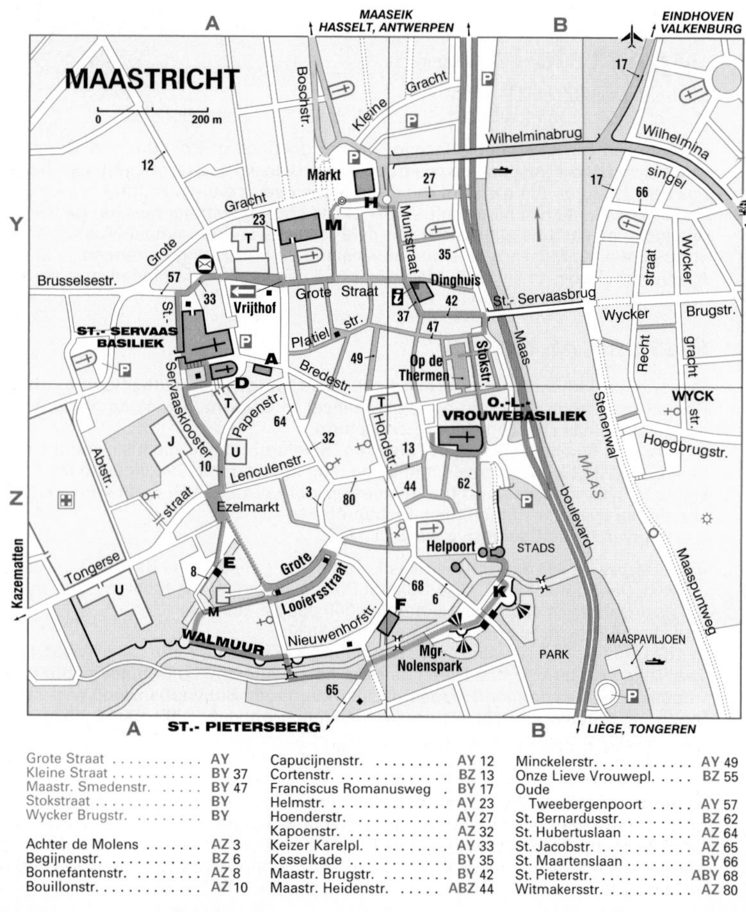

In the 13C the lovely south portal or **royal portal★** (Bergportaal) was built and is now painted with vivid colours; the tympanum illustrates the death, ascension and crowning of the Virgin. In the 15C the side chapels and the north portal were added. The north portal gives on to cloisters also built in the 15C.
The whole building underwent extensive restoration on two occasions; in the late 19C and in the years 1981-1991.

Interior – On the basilica's entrance portal there is a 15C statue of St Peter.
The **chancel★** vaults (restored) have recovered their 16C paintings. It is harmonious with its tall pillars and the gallery above the ambulatory.
Inside the westwork, on the 1st floor, is the Emperor's Room (Keizerszaal), topped by a dome. The **capitals★** of the westwork are interesting for their rich decoration.
The last chapel on the north aisle, towards the transept, has a Sedes Sapientiae (Seat of Wisdom) and a seated Virgin and Child, of 13C Mosan type. Nearby is a doorway, formerly the main access to the church, opening onto cloisters. Outside it is topped by a lovely tympanum depicting Christ in Majesty.
The **crypt**, which is under the nave, contains the tomb of St Servatius, behind the grille is the sarcophagus of Charles of Lorraine son of the Carolingian King, Louis IV d'Outremer, and on the old altar of St Peter, the sarcophagus of the Bishops Monulfus and Gondulfus, founders of the primitive church in the 6C, as well as two other bishops, Candidus and Valentinus.
The neighbouring crypt with square pillars, under the chancel, belonged to the 6C primitive church.

★★ **Treasury** (Kerkschat) ⊙ – The collegiate chapel (12C) house the treasury: a rich collection of liturgical objects, mainly gold and silversmiths' work, ivory, sacerdotal ornaments, paintings, altarpieces, statues.
There is notably a bust of St Servatius, a symbolic silver key decorated with foliated scrolls which would have been given to him by St Peter, the pectoral cross said to have belonged to St Servatius (late 10C), pieces of oriental cloth (*c*600AD), as well as a great number of reliquaries and shrines of the late 12C.

St Servatius's shrine

Stichting Schatkamer St.-Servaas

The most remarkable object is **St Servatius's shrine** called Noodkist *(illustration above)*. In oak, covered with gilded copper, enamelled, chased and decorated with precious stones, it is an important work of the Mosan School (*c*1160); at each end Christ and St Servatius are depicted, on the sides, the apostles.

St.-Janskerk (AY **D**) – This Gothic church, Protestant since 1632, was built by the canons of St Servatius to be used as a parish church. Dating from the 12C, it was enlarged in the 15C with a chancel and a tower 70m - 230ft high, decorated in the Utrecht style.

Take a few steps along Bonnefantenstraat.

From this street there is a fine viewpoint over a 17C house with crow-stepped gables (AZ **E**) and the botanical garden of the Natural History Museum, located on the other side of the canal.

Turn back and take Looiersgracht.

Grote Looiersstraat (AZ) – On this charming shaded square surrounded by old houses, a sculptured group depicts children listening to the popular Maastricht storyteller, Fons Olterdissen.

★ **Walmuur** (ABZ) – The defensive walls still preserved to the south of town and dominated by numerous towers, shaded by beautiful trees and surrounded by pleasant gardens, are one of Maastricht's charms. On the two sections which exist one can go round the watchpath from where there are fine views.

Follow the watchpath, then leave it to take a footbridge crossing the ring canal.

Monseigneur Nolenspark (BZ) – A lovely park laid out at the foot of the ramparts. Animals (deer, etc) are kept in enclosures.

Take the watchpath again.

From the top of the first tower one overlooks the lakes where swans and ducks swim. On the north side of the ramparts one can see the **Bejaardencentrum Molenhof** (BZ **F**) building. Beside it, near the Jeker, hides an old watermill.
Continuing, one reaches the tower, **De Vijf Koppen** (BZ **K**) where one overlooks a vast lake.

Helpoort (BZ) – This gate, flanked by two round towers, belonged to the 13C curtain wall.

★ **Onze Lieve Vrouwebasiliek** (BZ) ⊙ – This is the oldest monument in town. It is thought that it is on the site of an old Roman temple where a cathedral was built at the time when Maastricht was the episcopal see.
The edifice already existed in the year 1000. The very tall **westwork** which precedes the church, as it does at St.-Servaasbasiliek, dates from this period. It is flanked by two round turrets; its upper part, added *c*1200 is decorated with Romanesque blind arcading. The nave and the beautiful apse date from the 12C.
Among interesting sculptures grouped under the left porch of the westwork, note the effigy of a bishop (*c*1200).
Inside, the **chancel**★★ with an ambulatory topped by a gallery, thus forming two rows of superimposed columns, like the one at St.-Servaasbasiliek, is remarkable. Furthermore, the richly decorated capitals are very varied.
The nave, like that of Kerkrade *(qv)* has alternating thick and thin pillars supporting the vault, redone in the 18C. The transept was given pointed vaulting in the 15C. The organ case dates from 1652.
The church has two Romanesque crypts, one under the transept crossing (1018), the other under the westwork, and 16C cloisters.

Ph. Gajic/MICHELIN
Westwork of Onze Lieve Vrouwebasiliek, Maastricht

Treasury (Kerkschat) ⊙ – The treasury has precious reliquaries and shrines, ivory, liturgical ornaments including Bishop Lambert's early 8C dalmatic.

Stokstraat (BYZ) – It is a pleasant pedestrian precinct where the lovely 17 and 18C restored houses, decorated with pediments, façade stones and signs, are now art, antique and print shops.
At no 28 there is a façade decorated with sculptured friezes.
To the west, on a small square called **Op de Thermen** (BY), paving stones indicate the site of old Roman baths discovered here in 1840.

Dinghuis (BY) – This former 16C law court is narrow and picturesque.

Markt (AY) – On this busy main square a market takes place.
The **Stadhuis** (AY H), built 1659-65 by **Pieter Post**, who designed Huis ten Bosch in The Hague, is an imposing quadrilateral building preceded by a large perron and topped by a bell tower with a **carillon**. ⊙

Return to Vrijthof by the pedestrian precinct crossing the shopping quarter.

ADDITIONAL SIGHTS

★ **Bonnefantenmuseum** (AY M) ⊙ – *See Admission Times and Charges for new address.* This museum devoted to art, archaeology and history will shortly move premises. Meanwhile, part of the exhibitions are displayed to the public.

Kazematten ⊙ – *By Tongerestraat* (AZ). The casemates are to be found in Waldeckpark. They belonged to a system of fortifications which was built between 1575 and 1825. Most of the fortifications above ground were razed in 1867 but the network *(10 km - 6 miles)* of underground galleries remains. Some of these galleries are open to the public and visitors who are able to tackle the labyrinth of corridors and stairs can visit the **Waldeck Bastion** with its domed vaults, gunpowder stores and lookout posts.
Not for away, near the fortified walls there is a bronze statue of D'Artagnan *(qv)*.

OUTSKIRTS

★ **St.-Pietersberg** – *2km - 1 mile to the south by Sint Hubertuslaan and Luikerweg* (ABZ).
Between the valley of the Maas and the Jeker, St Peter's Mount rises to more than 100m - 328ft high. It is above all famous for its **caves**, old quarries which have been worked since Roman times. The stone, a sort of marl that hardens on exposure to the air, had been used for building numerous edifices in Maastricht. Today the

galleries extend for more than 200km - 124 miles and are 12m - 39ft high. They were excavated by lowering the floor level so that now the oldest charcoal drawings covering the walls are near the roof. The rock sedimentary in origin, contains a large number of fossils. In 1780 the head of a Prehistoric animal was found; it was called Mosasaurus (*Mosa*: the Maas).
During all the troubled periods the caves have been used to shelter the people of Maastricht; they have kept traces of these periods of refuge.
The temperature is about 10°C-50°F and it is very humid.

Fort St.-Pieter ⏲ – From the fort's (1701) terrace, there is an overall view of the town.

Mergelgrotten - Noorderlijk Gangenstelsel ⏲ – During the Second World War these caves sheltered Rembrandt's painting *The Night Watch*. There are graffiti here and amusing low reliefs like that of the Mosasaurus.

Continuing along the road then taking the second on the left, one reaches other caves.

Gangenstelsel Zonneberg ⏲ – These caves are very similar to the preceding ones, steeped in history and a maze of corridors covered with graffiti.

EXCURSIONS

Cadier en Keer – *5km - 3 miles to the east by ④ on the town plan.*
The **Afrika-Centrum** ⏲ exhibits interesting artistic and ethnographic collections concerning western Africa.

From Meerssen to Susteren – *35km - 21 1/2 miles. Leave by ① on the town plan.*

Meerssen – Pop 20 556. Former resisdence of the Frankish kings. In 870 a treaty was signed sharing Lotharingia, the domain of King Lothair II (855-869) between the two brothers Louis the German and Charles the Bald, the King of France (in 879 the whole of Lotharingia came into the hands of the German Emperor).
In the 13C Meerssen attracted the monks from the Abbey of St Remy in Rheims. They built the fine **basilica** of the Blessed Sacrament (13-14C). The chancel has a stone tabernacle in the Flamboyant Gothic style (early 16C), richly decorated, but unfortunately, greatly restored.

Stein – Pop 26 687. Stein is the home of a small archaeological museum, **Archeologisch reservaat** ⏲ *(Hoppenkampstraat 14a)*. Built to house a megalithic tomb (*c*2800BC), the museum also has collections associated with Prehistoric, Roman and Merovingian sites in the region.

Sittard – Pop 45 883. Sittard which obtained its city charter in 1243, was a very disputed stronghold. A large part of the city is still surrounded by ramparts. It is a busy commerdial and industrial city (chemistry, electrical engineering, Volvo automobile factory). It has pedestrian precincts and a theatre (Stadsschouwburg) which seats 800 *(Wilhelminastraat, near the station)*.
Amongst the numerous festivities in the town, note in particular the carnival *(see Calendar of Events)*.
On the **Markt**, the main square, there stands St.-Michielskerk, in the 17C baroque style, and a picturesque half-timbered house with a corbelled gable built *c*1500. In Rosmolenstraat, **Kritzraedthuis** is a lovely bourgeois house of 1620 where temporary exhibitions are held.
The 14C **Grote- of St.-Petruskerk** ⏲ has carved wood Gothic stalls, which are probably the oldest in the country.

Susteren – Pop 13 089. **St.-Amelbergakerk,** ⏲ an old abbey church, was built in the Romanesque style probably during the first half of the 11C.
The nave, very simple, covered with a flat ceiling, leans on square pillars alternating with squat columns. The crypt, outside the apse was probably inspired by that of Essen Cathedral in Germany. It contains an 8C sarcophagus and a 13C calvary.

The length of time given in this guide
– for touring allows time to enjoy the views and the scenery
– for sightseeing is the average time required for a visit

★ MARKEN Noord-Holland

Michelin map 408 G 4

Separated from the continent in the 13C during the formation of the Zuiderzee, Marken was an island 2 1/2km - 1 1/2 miles from the shore until 1957. Now connected to the mainland, it is on the edge of the Gouwzee, a sort of inland sea.
Marken, whose population is Protestant, has from the beginning, formed a close community. It has kept its atmosphere of days past with its wooden houses and inhabitants who, in season, wear the traditional costume.
Before the IJsselmeer was created, the population earned its living from fishing; today it lives partly from tourism.

★ **The village** – The village includes two quarters: Havenbuurt, near the port and Kerkbuurt, around the church. For protection against high tides, the houses are grouped on small mounds and built on piles which, before the closing of the Zuiderzee were left open for the passage of waves. Most of the houses are painted a sombre green, with slightly corbelled side gables. The **interiors,** ⏲ painted and polished, are richly decorated with crockery and bibelots. Beds are fitted in alcoves where there is also a small drawer, which was used as a cradle.

★ **Costumes** – The women wear a wide skirt and a black apron over a striped petticoat.
The striped blouse, worn in summer, is covered with a corselet and a printed front.
The headdress is just a gaily coloured lace and cotton skullcap from which a fringe of starched hair sometimes sticks out like a peak.
The men wear a short vest, baggy trousers tightened at the knees and black socks.
The children more rarely wear a costume; boys and girls wear a skirt and bonnet, only the shapes and colours differ.
The costume worn on feast days, and particularly at Whitsun, is more elaborate.

G. Sioen/CEDRI

Traditional costumes of Marken

MEDEMBLIK Noord-Holland Pop 7 011

Michelin map 408 G 3

Medemblik received its city charter in 1289, when it became the capital of West Friesland. It was then part of the Hanseatic League. Today it is one of the "ghost towns" of the former Zuiderzee region.
The dike that limits the Wieringermeer Polder *(qv)* to the east starts at Medemblik. To the north of the town, the Lely pumping station is the most important one used to dry out the polder.
A tourist railway links the town to Hoorn *(qv)* and a boat service runs between Medemblik and Enkhuizen.

SIGHTS

Nieuwstraat – One of the most charming features of Medemblik is its main street, Nieuwstraat, which still has several old houses with pretty stone façades. At no 26 stands an unusual house: its 1613 façade presents a lintel decorated with four coats of arms.
The **Waag** at the end of the street boasts a façade with crow-stepped gables, embellished with a carved façade stone depicting a pair of scales.

Westerhaven – This quay, stretching along one of the port's two main basins – Westerhaven means western basin – retains several fine houses: nos 9 to 14, with crow-stepped gables, and nos 16 to 20.
In Torenstraat, which begins at Westerhaven, the old orphanage, **Weeshuis**, has a gateway surmounted by a naive low relief depicting four orphans (18C).

★ **Oosterhaven** – Along the quay skirting this basin – Oosterhaven means eastern basin – stand a great many old façades: nos 22, 43 and 44 have carved stones. The far end of the quay affords a pleasant view of IJsselmeer.

Kasteel Radboud ⊙ – The castle stands on the opposite side of Oosterhaven. It was built in the 8C by Radboud, King of Frisia. Around 1288 the Count of Holland Floris V fortified and altered the castle. Only one restored part exists today, surrounded by moats, the rest having been destroyed in the 17 and 18C.
The castle houses a small museum: coins, pitchers, etc... from excavation sites.

★★ MENKEMABORG Groningen

Michelin map 408 L 1

The castle stands to the east of Uithuizen *(qv)* and is screened by tall trees with a heronry, where herons nest from February to June. There are over a hundred nests. **Menkemaborg** ⊙ is surrounded by a moat and a typically Dutch garden laid out in Renaissance and Baroque tradition; the grounds also feature a maze, an orchard and a vegetable garden.
The oldest part (14C) of the building, with only a few small windows, was extended by the addition of two wings in the 17C and 18C.
The interior is pleasantly furnished and decorated and gives some idea of how the local nobility lived during the 17C and 18C. The kitchen in the basement occupies the oldest part of the castle. In the other rooms note the 1700 oak chimneypieces sumptuously carved with acanthus leaves, cherubs and female figures, portraits of past owners, a four-poster bed by Daniel Marot and lovely pieces of 17C Chinese porcelain.

★ MIDDELBURG Zeeland Ⓟ Pop 39 617

Michelin map 408 B7 or 212 fold 12 – Local map see DELTA

Middelburg used to be the pearl of the Walcheren district. A very busy tourist centre, this old town is surrounded by canals and moats marking the limits of its fortified walls. Two 18C wall mills (AZ) still stand.

HISTORICAL NOTES

Formerly Middelburg was a prosperous commercial city, with its cloth trade and its importing of French wine from Argenteuil and Suresnes, shipped from the port of Rouen to Rouaansekaai.

The Sea Beggars captured it in 1574. In 1595 and 1692 the town was given its first line of fortifications with bastions. These have remained more or less intact up to the present, but the only old gate which remains is **Koepoort** (BY) to the north.

It is said that a spectacle manufacturer of Middelburg, Zacharias Jansen invented the microscope in 1590 and the telescope in 1604. However, some people prefer to attribute the invention of the microscope to Van Leeuwenhoek.

Middelburg continued to prosper in the 17 and 18C due to the Dutch India Company which had a trading post here.

In 1940 a violent German bombardment destroyed the historic centre of the town. Its monuments have been rebuilt and it remains the great Walcheren market.

In July and August, on the Molenwater, one can watch a **ringrijderij**, a sort of tournament where the stake consists in unhooking a ring. On Vismarkt, in summer *(Thursdays)*, there is an antiques market and the first Saturday of each month, a flea market.

THE HEART OF TOWN

★ **Stadhuis** (AZ **H**) ⊙ – Overlooking **Markt** (AZ) or main square, where the market takes place *(Thursdays)*, this imposing building, begun in 1452 by two architects of the Keldermans family from Mechelen (Belgium), is inspired by the Brussels town hall. Partly destroyed in May 1940, it has been rebuilt. The main façade is remarkable with its ten, first floor, Gothic windows with finely worked tympana. Between each window double niches have statues, remade in the 19C, depicting the Counts and Countesses of Zeeland back to back. The roof is decorated with three tiers of dormer windows and, on the left, an elaborately pinnacled gable. The central perron was added in the 18C.

An octagonal turret, finely decorated and flanked by an openwork balustrade in the 17C, stands on the right.

A highly distinctive belfry 55m - 180ft high, is quartered by four pinnacles and dominates the whole.

The interior contains antique furnishings, in particular the immense **Burgerzaal**, the former cloth hall.

Behind the town hall there is a lovely restored chapel called the English Church **Engelse Kerk** (AZ). At one point the building became a tapestry workshop *(see the Zeeuws Museum overleaf)*.

B & U International Picture Service Amsterdam/Herman Scholten, Huizen

Stadhuis, Middelburg

MIDDELBURG

Lange Delft .... ABZ
Langeviele .... AZ
Markt .... AZ
Nieuwe Burg .... AZ 24
Plein 1940 .... AZ 30

Achter de Houttuinen .... AZ 3
Bierkaai .... BZ 4
Damplein .... BY 6
Groenmarkt .... AYZ 7
Hoogstr. .... AZ 9
Houtkaai .... BZ 10
Koepoortstr. .... BY 12
Koestr. .... AZ 13
Koorkerkstr. .... BZ 15
Korte Burg .... AY 16
Korte Delft .... BYZ 18
Korte Noordstr. .... AY 19
Lange Noordstr. .... AY 21
Londensekaai .... BZ 22
Nieuwe Haven .... AZ 25
Nieuwe Vlissingseweg .... AZ 27
Nieuwstr. .... BZ 28
Rotterdamsekaai .... BY 31
Segeersstr. .... BZ 33
Sint Pieterstr. .... BY 34
Stadhuisstr. .... AY 36
Vismarkt .... ABZ 37
Vlissingsestr. .... AZ 39
Volderijlaagte .... AY 40
Wagenaarstr. .... AY 42
Walensingel .... AYZ 43

★ **Abdij** (ABY) – Today the seat of the provincial government of Zeeland, this vast monastic building was, in the 12C a Premonstrant abbey (order founded by St Norbert in 1120), a dependance of St Michael in Antwerp. It was secularised after the capture of the town by the Sea Beggars.
To the east, the defensive gate, the **Gistpoort** (BY) on Damplein, has a lovely 16C façade still marked by the Gothic style.

Abdijkerken (ABY A) ⏲ – To the south of the abbey standing side by side are two churches. The **Koorkerk** with a 14C nave and apse has a 15C organ, whose case was renovated in the 16C. The 16C **Nieuwe Kerk** holds organ concerts in summer. Against the former leans the **Lange Jan Tower** ⏲. This 14C octagonal construction in stone, crowned with a small 18C onion-shaped dome, rises 85m - 279ft. From the top there is a fine view over the abbey, the town and its canals.

★ **Zeeuws Museum** (AY M[1]) ⏲ – The Zeeland Museum has been laid out in the old hostelry which is flanked by fine turrets. It has very varied regional collections.
In the archaeological section a room is devoted to the Celtic goddess **Mehallenia**; several votive steles dating from Roman times were found in 1647 in Domburg *(qv)* and in 1970 at Colijnsplaat (island of Noord-Beveland). The goddess is often shown sitting, wearing a long dress and a wide-brimmed hat, accompanied by a dog and carrying a basket of fruit. On the ground floor there is a collection of animal bones (stag, mammoth) discovered at the mouth of the Scheldt, and a roomful of rarities where notably a planetarium can be seen.
On the 1st floor, in a large room, there is a fine series of local late 16 and early 17C **tapestries**, several illustrate Zeeland naval victories over the Spanish.
After having crossed the 17 and 18C decorative art rooms where Zeeland furniture and silverware, Chinese porcelain and Delftware can be admired, one reaches the attic which contains a remarkable collection of Zeeland **costumes** and headdresses; in a revolving show-case interior scenes are reconstituted.

ADDITIONAL SIGHTS

Kloveniersdoelen (AZ B) – It is the former arquebusiers' mansion, built in 1607 and 1611 in the Flemish Renaissance style. As of 1795 it was used as a military hospital. It has a very wide façade in brick streaked with white stone and brightened by painted shutters. The central voluted gable bears a sculptured low relief of arquebuses, cannon balls and topped by an eagle. The tall slate roof is pierced by dormer windows with painted shutters. Behind is an octagonal turret with an onion-shaped dome.

★ **Miniatuur Walcheren** (ABY) ⊙ – It is an open-air scale model of Walcheren Peninsula with its roads, dikes, ports and main buildings, made to a scale of 1:20. Opposite stands the austere Koepoort (1735).

The quays (BYZ) – The **Rotterdamsekaai, Rouaansekaai** and **Londensekaai** are lined with fine rows of 18C houses, witness to the prosperity of that time.

Oostkerk (BY) – This octagonal church with an onion-shaped dome is of a fairly usual type amongst 17C Protestant buildings. **Pieter Post** was one of the architects who built it between 1646-67.

St.-Jorisdoelen (ABY **D**) – These old premises of the civic guard dating from 1582 were rebuilt in the original style in 1970. Similar to the old military hospital (Kloveniersdoelen), its central voluted gable is topped by a statue of St George (Sint Joris).

EXCURSION

Round tour of the Walcheren Peninsula – *49km - 30 miles – allow 2 hours – local map see Delta.*

Leave by ③ on the town plan.

Domburg – Pop 4 021. This seaside resort with a large beach situated at the foot of high dunes is very popular. To the west, the top of the highest dune offers an interesting **view** over Domburg and the coast.

The route follows the dunes which isolate Walcheren Peninsula from the sea. A few farmhouses surrounded by a curtain of trees line the route.

Westkapelle – Pop 2 705. This town is on the western point of Walcheren Island, where the dunes are not strong enough to hold out against currents and are reinforced by **dikes**. These extend over 4km - 2 1/2 miles and their highest crest is 7m - 23ft above sea level. In 1944 they were bombarded by the Allies, which caused flooding of the island and made it possible to evict the Germans. In 1945 the gaps were filled in. Westkapelle, a family seaside resort, has a beach facing south. The **lighthouse** is on the top of the bell tower of an old Gothic church destroyed by fire.

Zoutelande – Small seaside resort.

Flushing (Vlissingen) – *See Vlissingen.*

Return to Middelburg by ② on the town plan.

The Michelin Map 408 (scale 1:400 000), which is revised regularly, indicates:

– difficult or dangerous roads, steep gradients

– roads and bridges with tolls

– car and passenger ferries

Keep the current Michelin Map in the car at all times

NAARDEN Noord-Holland — Pop 16 255

Michelin map 408 G 5 – Local map see HILVERSUM

Naarden used to be the capital of Gooi *(qv)*. Washed by the Zuiderzee, the town was engulfed in the 12C.

Rebuilt further inland in the 14C, Naarden became an important stronghold, taken by the Spanish in 1572, then by the French in 1673.

Today it is a peaceful city, still circled by its extensive 17C **fortifications**, shaped as a twelve-pointed star with six bastions surrounded by marshes.

The memory of **John Amos Comenius** (1592-1670), the educational reformer, is perpetuated in Naarden. Born in Moravia, this Czech humanist became bishop of the Bohemian Brothers or Moravian Brothers in 1648 *(qv)*. Persecuted, he fled to Poland, then in 1656 went to Amsterdam, where he died. He devoted himself primarily to educational research.

Founder of the pedagogic methods concerning the development of a child's individual observation, a strong advocate of more stimulating teaching methods, he was one of the first to advocate education for all.

SIGHTS

Stadhuis ⊙ – This fine Renaissance building with crow-stepped gables dates from 1601. The interior is embellished with old furniture; it contains 17C paintings and a scale model of the 17C fortifications.

Comenius museum ⊙ – *Kloosterstraat 29.*
The collections displayed here illustrate the life and work of the Dutch humanist. His tomb lies nearby, in the old Waalse Kerk, **Comenius Mausoleum** ⊙

Het Spaanse Huis – *Turfpoortstraat.*
The façade stone of this building depicts the massacre of the townspeople by the Spanish in 1572, hence its name Spanish House.

Vestingmuseum (Fortress Museum) ⊙ – *Westwalstraat.*
The pillboxes of one of the bastions *(turfpoort)* have been made into a museum; cannon and other weapons, written documents and photographs retrace the eventful history of Naarden.

★ NIJMEGEN Gelderland — Pop 145 782

Michelin map 408 I 6
Plan of the conurbation in the current Michelin Red Guide Benelux

The only town in the Netherlands built on several hills, Nijmegen is the gateway to the river region, due to its location on the Waal, main branch of the Rhine, and near the canal, the Maas-Waalkanaal.

HISTORICAL NOTES

An old Batavian oppidum, Nijmegen was conquered by the Romans under Emperor Augustus then burnt down in 70AD by the Roman, Cerialis, General of Emperor Vespasian who was trying to quell the **Batavian revolt** stirred up the year before by **Gaius Julius Civilis**. It subsequently became a prosperous Roman city called Ulpia Noviomagus. Charlemagne who considered the town one of his favourite places to stay, built himself a castle on the present Valkhof. In the Middles Ages the town expanded west of this castle.
In the 14C it became a member of the Hanseatic League. In 1585 it was taken by Alessandro Farnese, Duke of Parma, but recaptured in 1591 by Maurice of Nassau.

The peace of Nijmegen – After the French, under the leadership of Turenne, captured it without difficulty in 1672, Nijmegen gave its name to three treaties which were signed there between France, the United Provinces, Spain (1678) and the German Empire (1679). They mark the peak of Louis XIV's reign who, at the outcome of the war against the United Provinces, which had started in June 1672, annexed to France the Franche-Comté and a part of Flanders. The United Provinces remained intact. It was during the preliminary conferences for these treaties that the French language began to impose itself as the diplomatic language (despite this the treaties were written in latin as was customary). The first treaty written in French was that of Rastatt in 1714.
In February 1944 the town was bombarded by the Americans. At the time of the Battle of Arnhem *(qv)* in September, Nijmegen was in the midst of heavy fighting. The bridge over the Waal, Waalbrug, built in 1936, which the Germans were threatening to destroy, was saved by a young inhabitant of the town, Jan van Hoof. A tablet to his memory has been put up in the centre of the bridge, on the east side. A monument (**C A**) at the southern end of the bridge commemorates the liberation of the town.
The Netherlands Catholic University founded in 1923 has been, since 1949, installed in a campus to the south of the town on the road to Venlo.
Nijmegen is the birthplace of **St Peter Canisius** (1521-97); he was named doctor of the church, when he was canonised in 1925.

Boat trips (C) ⏲ – Boat trips are organised on the Waal.

NIJMEGEN

Street	Ref	Street	Ref	Street	Ref
		Barbarossastr.	C 6	Mr. Frankenstr.	C 34
		van Berchenstr.	B 7	Nassausingel	B 37
		in de Betouwstr.	B 9	Nonnenstr.	B 40
		Bisschop Hamerstr.	B 10	van Oldenbarneveltstr.	B 42
		van Broeckhuysenstraat	C 12	Prins Bernhardstr.	C 46
Augustijnenstr.	B 4	van Diemerbroeckstraat	B 13	Prins Hendrikstr.	C 48
Bloemenstr.	B	Gerard Noordstr.	C 15	Regulierstr.	B 49
Broerstr.	BC	Graadt Roggenstr.	C 16	van Schevichavenstraat	C 51
Burchtstr.	B	Groesbeekseweg	B 18	Stationspl.	B 55
Lange Hezelstr.	B	Grote Markt	B 19	Stikke Hezelstr.	B 57
Molenstr.	B	Grotestr.	C 21	van Trieststr.	B 58
Passage Molenpoort	B 45	Julianapl.	C 28	Tunnelweg	B 60
Plein 1944	B	Keizer Traianuspl.	C 30	Tweede Walstr.	B 61
Ziekerstr.	BC	Kelfkensbos	C 31	Wilhelminasingel	B 64

SIGHTS

Grote Markt (B 19) – In the centre of the square the **Waag★**, built in 1612 in the Renaissance style, has a lovely façade with a perron where the red and black colouring of the shutters and the somber red brick merge harmoniously. The ground floor is now a restaurant.

There is also a bronze statue of **Mariken van Nieumeghen** (B **D**), heroine of a late 15C religious drama in which, seduced by the devil, she followed him seven years before repenting. The hands of the statue have three iron rings with which the Pope had ordered Mariken to chain her neck and arms. They loosened themselves, when she had atoned for her sin.

Near the weigh house there is a group of four 17C houses (B **E**). One, the **Kerkboog** is identifiable by its decorated gable (1605) above a vaulted passage; the passage leads to St.-Stevenskerk.

Near the chevet of the church, the old **Latijnse School** (B **F**) is a fine building of 1554.

St.-Stevenskerk (B) ⏲ – This large 13C Gothic church, enlarged in the 15C, is flanked by a massive square tower with an octagonal onion-shape domed pinnacle (1604) which has an 18C **carillon** ⏲.

The interior contains some lovely **furnishings**: the back of the door of the south arm of the transept (1632), the local gentry's pews in the Renaissance style by Cornelis Hermansz Schaeff of Nijmegen and the Renaissance pulpit by Joost Jacobs.

Note also the 18C princes' pew decorated with the armorial bearings of the town (eagles) and the province (lions), the **organ** ⏲ built in the 18C by König and the copper chandeliers.

Toren ⏲ *Access by the west façade.*

From the top (183 steps) there is a panorama over the town and the Waal. Note an old 15C curtain wall tower in Kronenburger Park (B **L**).

The church's precinct has been restored; a flea market takes place here on Monday mornings.

To the north there are some lovely houses with gables, **Kannunikenhuizen** (B) or the canons' houses.

Nijmeegs Museum "Commanderie van St.-Jan" (BC **M**[1]) ⏲ – This 15 and 16C brick building (restored) overlooking the Waal, is an old hospital. Founded is the 12C to shelter pilgrims going to the Holy Land, in the 13C, it came into the possession of the Order of the Hospital of St John of Jerusalem.

The town's history is unveiled in this museum where engravings, objects, scale models and paintings are pleasantly exhibited. The anonymous triptych depicting a *Calvary* (1526) with St Peter Canisius' family, a *View of the Waal with the Valkhof* by Van Goyen, the *Peace of Nijmegen* painted for Louis XIV in 1678, and the collections which belonged to corporations and guilds (silver chains, pewter pots) are particularly remarkable.

The museum also organises temporary exhibitions of ancient and modern art.

Naar foto Nijmeegs Museum "Commanderie van St.-Jan"

Chain of Office, Nijmeegs Museum

Stadhuis (C **H**) ⏲ – This fine 16 and 17C building, partly destroyed by the bombardments, was restored in 1953. It is flanked by an onion-shaped turret. The outside is decorated with statues carved by Albert Termote depicting the emperors who were Nijmegen's benefactors or who had played a part in its history. On the corner is a statue of the Virgin.

Inside there are lovely rooms decorated in the old style, the Aldermen's Room (Schepenhal), the Registrar's Office (Trouwzaal). In the Truce Hall, **Trêveszaal**, where the walls are covered with verdure tapestries, the treaties of 1678 and 1679 were signed. In the Council Room (Raadzaal) and the Great Hall (Burgerzaal) hang other tapestries.

Valkhof (C) – This park has been laid out on the site of a castle built by Charlemagne. It took the name of "falcon's tower" because Louis the Pious, son of Charlemagne and heir to his father's empire, bred falcons here for hunting. The castle rebuilt by Frederick Barbarossa in the 12C was destroyed in the 18C.

St.-Maartenskapel (C **Q**) – In the centre of the park are the remains of the Romanesque chapel of Frederick Barbarossa's castle. There remains a finely decorated oven-vaulted apse at the chancel's entrance, two columns with foliated capitals, and blind arcades outside.

★ **St.-Nicolaaskapel** (C **R**) – Near a terrace from where there is an interesting **view** over the Waal, this old chapel of the Carolingian castle stands hidden behind trees. It was probably modified in the 11C.

It has 16 sides and is topped by an octagonal turret. Inside one can see the pillars which encircle a central octagonal-shaped space. Upstairs there is a gallery with twin bays.

Belvedere (C) – It is the name of an old watch tower (1640) of the old curtain wall, now converted into a restaurant, the terrace offers a fine **view** over the Waal.

Provinciaal Museum G.M. DAM (C M^2) ⊙ – It contains a collection of antiquities (objets dating from Prehistoric times, the Roman era and the early Middle Ages) found mainly during excavations in Nijmegen and its surroundings.
The ground floor evokes Roman Nijmegen (from the birth of Christ to 400AD): the town, the necropolis and the military camps. Note the pottery pieces and the trappings of a Roman centurion.
The exhibits in the hall focus on different themes: tombs from the Iron Age in which chariots were found, sanctuaries and small cities in Roman times, tomb of a warrior belonging to a Frankish tribe. The display also presents a bronze portrait of the Emperor Trajan, silverware, jewellery and coins. The first floor boasts superb collections of Roman glassware, bronze crockery and household items.

EXCURSIONS

Heilig Land Stichting ⊙ – *4km - 2 1/2 miles to the southeast by Groesbeekseweg* (B); *the museum is just north of the town of Groesbeek.*
This **Open-air Bible Museum** takes you back to the Palestine of biblical times with displays illustrating a variety of aspects – religious, cultural, historical and archaeological – of life at the time.
The history of the different peoples of the Bible is recounted in the main building while the open-air section (49ha - 120 acres) evokes the country during Jesus's lifetime through a series of reconstitutions: the Palestinian village with its synagogue, an inn, a fishing village and the Via Orientalis, a depiction of Jerusalem with its Jewish, Roman, Greek and Egyptian houses.

Berg en Dal – *6km - 3 1/2 miles to the east by Berg en Dalseweg* (C).
This locality is located in a region appreciated for its wooded and undulating countryside.
The **Afrika Museum** ⊙ is installed to the south. *Postweg 6.* It contains a collection of sculpture including masks and objects used daily, laid out in a modern building, and reconstitutions in the open-air (Ghana and Mali dwellings, houses on piles).
The **Duivelsberg**, a wooded hill 76m - 249ft high, is crisscrossed with paths. By following the signs "Pannekoeken" (restaurant) one reaches a car park. From there a signposted path leads to a belvedere: **view** over the German plain and Wijlermeer.

Doornenburg – *18km - 11 miles to the northeast. Leave by Waalbrug* (C) *and turn towards Bemmel and Gendt.*
This village has a 14C **Kasteel** ⊙ which was rebuilt after the Second World War. It is a tall square fortress surrounded by water, topped by turrets and linked by a footbridge to a fortified courtyard where there is a chapel and a farmhouse.

NOORDOOSTPOLDER Flevoland — Pop 38 278

Michelin map 408 H 3, 4, I 3, 4 – Local map see IJSSELMEER

The Noordoostpolder was the second area to be reclaimed in the process of draining the Zuiderzee *(qv)*, but only once the sea had become a freshwater lake.

Drainage – The polder covers more than 48 000 ha - 118 560 acres. The 55km - 34 miles long enclosing dike was built between 1937 and 1940. As of 1941 three pumping stations at Vollenhove, Urk and Lemmer evacuated 1.5 billion m^3 - 52 971 billion ft^3 of water. Collection and drainage ditches completed the draining process.
The polder includes the former island of Urk (alt: 9m - 30ft) and Schokland (alt: 3.5m - 11ft). Urk is the highest point while the lowest is 5m - 16ft below the Amsterdam Reference Level *(qv)*.

Development – Once the land had been drained 500km - 310 miles of roads were built and the future capital **Emmelord** was built in the middle of the polder.
After years (1942-62) of improving and fertilising the soil the Noordoostpolder is now mainly devoted to agriculture and over 1 650 farmhouses were built. The smaller units were clustered round the villages while the larger farms were dispersed in the outlying areas. The main crops are wheat, potatoes and sugarbeet with an occasional field of flowers; cattle and sheep graze the meadows.

SIGHTS

Emmeloord – Pop 38 585. The capital of the polder was laid out according to town planning concepts of the time. Right in the centre of the town the **watertoren** ⊙ built in 1957 provides water for the whole polder and true to Dutch traditions has a carillon of 48 bells.
The **view** from the summit stretches north to the Frisian Coast, southwest to Urk and the power station on the Oostelijk Flevoland Polder.

Schokland – *Between Ens and Nagele.* This former island in the Zuiderzee was low-lying and difficult to defend against the sea. Its three villages were abandoned in 1859. The former church and a modern building have been converted into the **Museum Schokland** ⊙ which relates the island's past: geology, prehistory and more recent times. Items on display include archaeological finds made during reclamation work on the polder.
Behind the presbytery there are remains of the stockade which protected the island from the onslaught of the sea. Stelae set into the walls of the church and the presbytery indicate the levels of past floods.
Visitors may follow a path around the former island.

G. Biollay/DIAF

Fishing port of Urk

★ **Urk** – Pop 13 346. The Zuiderzee's other island was joined to the polder and today its small port is popular with holidaymakers. A **boat service** ⏲ links Urk to Enkhuizen in Noord-Holland. The fishermen of Urk fish both the North Sea and IJsselmeer and the town has the biggest fish market in the country. Urk once specialised in eel fishing. The busy **harbour** makes an attractive picture with the gaily painted eel fishing boats. Urk has retained some of its insular traditions. The older people still wear the traditional costume: for the men a black suit with a striped shirt; for the women a black skirt with a floral or embroidered panel on the front of the blouse, a lace headdress worn over a metal hairband ending in animal head motifs.
From beside the church on its mound there is a **view** of the enclosing dike and IJsselmeer beyond.

NUENEN Noord-Brabant — Pop 21 110

Michelin map 408 H 7 – or 212 north of fold 18 (8km – 5 miles to the northeast of Eindhoven)

This town preserves the memory of **Vincent van Gogh** *(qv)* who, after having spent several months in the Drenthe, came to live, in the presbytery where his parents lived from December 1883 to November 1885. It was then that he really started to experiment with oils before leaving for Antwerp. He painted several portraits of country people, which he used as studies for his great canvas *The Potato Eaters* in the Rijksmuseum Kröller-Müller.

SIGHTS

Monument to Van Gogh – *On a small triangular square at the junction of the road to Mierlo, near a large lime tree surrounded by lime shoots.* This work by Hildo Krop in 1932 is a sober black stone stela, engraved with a sun and lying on a round pedestal with an inscription concerning Van Gogh's stay here.

Het domineeshuis – Just south of the monument, on the main street, at no 26 Berg is the presbytery where Vincent van Gogh's father died in March 1885. It looks exactly as the artist painted it.

Van Gogh Documentatiecentrum ⏲ – A custom-built building beside the new town hall (Gemeentehuis) houses an exhibition of photos and documents concerning the painter's stay in Nuenen.

Molen – *To the north, take a right off the main road towards 't Weefhuis (weaver's house).* Near a pond there is a mill perched on a mound.

ROERMOND Limburg — Pop 42 556

Michelin map 408 J 8 – or 212 fold 20
Town plan in the current Michelin Red Guide Benelux

At the confluence of the Maas and the Roer, near the German and Dutch frontier, Roermond, the most important city of central Limburg, is an industrial town (Philips, insulators, paper, chemicals, dairy products). Due to its bisphoric founded in 1559 it is also the religious capital of this very Catholic province. Roermond was formerly the county town of Upper Gelderland.
It was granted its city rights in 1232 and was soon given a fortified wall of which the 14C **Rattentoren** on the Buitenop, remains.
Roermond was one of the first towns caputred in 1572 by William the Silent coming from Dillenburg, but is was recapturerd by the Spanish in October.

Roermond then passed to Austria, France, and was only returned to the Netherlands Kingdom in 1815.
The town which suffered greatly in the last war has been partly rebuilt. It includes two marinas and vast stretches of water between the Maas and a side canal.

SIGHTS

O. L. Vrouwekerk or Munsterkerk ⊙ – *Munsterplein, in the town centre.* It is the old church of a Cistercian abbey. In Rhenish style, it was started in 1218 in the transitional Romanesque-Gothic style and restored at the end of the 19C by Cuypers (who was born here in 1827). On the west it is flanked by a massive porch framed by two towers with spires and topped by a dome flanked by two turrets at the transept crossing. The trefoil plan of the western part, with the transept arms ending in semicircles, the apse's outside gallery, the roofs of the towers and turrets in the shape of bishops' mitres, and the decoration of Lombard arcading are characteristics typical of Rhenish edifices.
The church has a Brabant altarpiece (*c*1530) in carved and painted wood and at the transept crossing there is the tomb of the abbey's founders, the Count of Gelderland Gerald IV and his wife Margaret of Brabant.
Near the church, at the corner of Pollartstraat, the **Prinsenhof**, built between 1660-70 is the old palace of the stadtholders of Upper Gelderland, during Spanish rule.

Take Steenweg, the main shopping street and a pedestrian precinct.

Kathedrale Kerk ⊙ – Dedicated to St Christopher, it stands near Markt. Built in 1410 in regional Gothic style, it was damaged during the last war, but since restored.
Opposite the cathedral there is a small 1764 **baroque house** (converted into a restaurant).

EXCURSION

★ **Thorn** – Pop 2 660. *14km - 8 1/2 miles southwest of Roermond. Leave by ⑤ on the town plan.* Not far from the Belgian frontier, this large village built of pink brick, often painted white, has charm. Near Plein de Wijngaard, its paving decorated with geometric motifs, stands the **abdijkerk** ⊙ preceded by a high brick tower striped with white stone. This is the old church of a women's abbey founded at the end of the 10C by Ansfried (who became Bishop of Utrecht in 995) and his wife Hilsondis. Rebuilt at the end of the 13C in the Gothic style, it has preserved from Romanesque times two staircase turrets and a crypt on the west side. It was enlarged in the 15C, and remodelled in the baroque style at the end of the 18C. It was restored by Cuypers at the end of the 19C. The interior is surprisingly white. The eastern chancel, raised and decorated by a baroque altarpiece overlooks a Gothic crypt. The chapels in the aisles have interesting low reliefs. In the south aisle there are charming 17 and 18C statues of saints in the folk art tradition. At the end of the nave, a double flight of stairs leads to the canonesses's chancel. From here one reaches a small **museum** installed in the old chapterhouse and the archives both of the 14 and 15C: treasury (reliquaries, crowns), engravings, documents. In the western crypt, which is Romanesque, there is a sculptured stone baptismal font (15C).

Take the main street (Akkerwal, Akker, Boekenderweg). At the second oratory (St.-Antoniuskapel) turn left.

On a small shady square, the 1673 Chapel Under the Lime Trees, **Kapel onder de Linden**, was enlarged in 1811. Inside, the oldest part on the east side has fine baroque decoration (stucco work, paintings) while the 19C part was decorated in the Empire style.

G. Biollay/DIAF

Thorn

★★ ROTTERDAM Zuid Holland

Pop 582 266

Michelin map 408 E 6, folds 25 and 26 (inset) – Local maps see DELTA and ROTTERDAM
Plan of the conurbation in the current Michelin Red Guide Benelux

The second most populated city in the kingdom, Rotterdam, the world's largest port, is located on the **Nieuwe Maas**, with 2 150ha - 5 313 acres of water and 30km - 19 miles from the North Sea. Rotterdam, at the mouth of two important waterways – Rhine, Maas and their tributaries – leading into the industrial heartland, is the meeting point of maritime and fluvial traffic. The city of Rotterdam sprawls over both banks of the river and is linked by tunnels, bridges and the underground. It is part of the **Rijnmond** a group of 23 municipalities part of **Randstad Holland** *(qv)*.
The university, named after Erasmus, was founded in 1973 by amalgamating the School of Advanced Economic Studies and Social Sciences with the Faculty of Medicine.
Destroyed during the last war, Rotterdam has been entirely rebuilt.

Boat trips ⊙ – Besides a visit to the port *(see below)*, excursions are also organised in the Delta, landing stage Leuvehoofd *(KZ on town plan p 192)*.
In addition Rotterdam is the departure point for cruises on the Rhine.

HISTORICAL NOTES

Rotterdam was originally a small village built on the dike (dam) on the small river Rotte. The town was still of little importance when Erasmus was born there.

Erasmus Roterodamus – This was the way the great humanist Geert Geertsz signed his name throughout his life. He was born here in 1469 but spent little time. As a child, Erasmus lived in Gouda, studied in Utrecht, then in the school of the Brethren of Common Life at Deventer and later at 's-Hertogenbosch.
An orphan with nowhere to turn, Erasmus became a monk in 1488 at the convent of Steyn, near Gouda, and studied the Antique world.
In 1493 having left the convent, he became secretary to the Bishop of Cambrai, whom he accompanied on his travels. He was, however, attracted by learning, and succeeded in getting a scholarship to study theology at the Sorbonne, while continuing to write many works.
During a stay in England, in 1499, he met Thomas More, the author of *Utopia*, who was to become his best friend. In 1502, fleeing the plague, which had spread through France, he arrived at the University of Louvain and soon became a professor there.
A tireless traveller, Erasmus was in Italy in 1506, where he published his **Adagia**, a commentary on quotations and proverbs from Antiquity; then in London in 1509 where he wrote and published two years later his *In Praise of Folly*. In Basle in 1514, Erasmus met Holbein who in 1515 illustrated an edition of *In Praise of Folly* and made several portraits of the humanist.
When, in 1517, Luther put up the ninety-five theses which triggered the Reformation, Erasmus was in Louvain. He at first refused to take part in religious quarrels but, when the Faculty of Theology condemned Luther's Theses, his neutrality brought him problems. After spending some months at Anderlecht, near Brussels in 1521, he left for Switzerland where he calmly continued with his literary endeavours and published, in 1526, an enlarged edition of his **Colloquia Familaria**, satyric dialogues, which was very successful.
The Prince of Humanists died in Basle in 1536.

Expansion – In 1572 the Spaniards pursued by the Sea Beggars, who had just captured Brielle, pleaded with the inhabitants of Rotterdam to be allowed entry. Once inside, Admiral Bossu allowed his troops to pillage the town. After this betrayal, Rotterdam joined the revolt. From 1576 to 1602 ports were constructed which were used by the Sea Beggars' fleet; the town rapidly surpassed its rival, Dordrecht, and became the second largest in Holland. Nevertheless, when Rotterdam was captured by the French in 1794, its trade severely suffered.

Major dock work – It was only after Belgium and the Netherlands separated in 1830 that Rotterdam once again became a transit port for the Rhine. As the depth of the river in the estuary (Brielse Maas) had become inadequate for the increasingly large ships, an access canal had to be built across the island of Voorne in 1830, the Voornsekanaal.
The Voornsekanaal, also, became insufficient and in 1863 the Minister Jan R. Thorbecke approved the plans drawn up by the young hydraulic engineer **Pieter Caland** (1826-1902) for the construction of a waterway crossing the sandy plains separating Rotterdam from the North Sea. The **Nieuwe Waterweg**, a waterway 18km - 11 miles long and 11m - 36ft deep at low tide, was dug between 1866 and 1872, and is comparable to Amsterdam's Noordzeekanaal, without locks. The port of **Hoek van Holland** was built at the sea-end for passenger travel.
New docks started to be built on the south bank of the river towards 1870 (Binnen Dock, Entrepot Dock, Spoorweg Dock) which were bigger than the old ones and linked to the railway.
Between 1876 and 1878 two bridges were built across the Maas (Willemsbrug and Koninginnebrug) as well as a railway viaduct 1 400 m - 4 598ft wide spaning the river.
Three man-made harbours were built, the Rijn Dock (1887-94), the Maas Dock (1988-1909) and the Waal Dock (1907-31), which became the largest artificial harbour in the world. Subsequently the port was extended along the north bank of the Maas, to the west (Merwe Dock, 1923-1932).
By 1886 Rotterdam had engulfed **Delfshaven** *(qv)*.

A martyred city – On 14 May, 1940 Rotterdam suffered German bombings that destroyed almost all of the old town. Only the town hall, the central post office, the stock exchange and Erasmus' statue were spared.
In March 1943, Allied bombing completed the destruction. 280ha - 692 acres were razed, 30 000 houses and buildings set on fire.
The port was also very badly bombed during the last war and, moreover, was sabotaged in 1944 by the Germans who destroyed 7km - 4 miles of docks and 20% of the warehouses.

A NEW CITY

Reconstruction of the city – Immediately after the war Rotterdam began rebuilding. Rational urban planning was adopted, which allowed for more open spaces and a cultural and commercial city centre.
The population emigrated outside the city which led to the spectacular development of the built-up area. Many communities were set up almost overnight, such as **Hoogvliet** in the south and **Alexanderpolder** in the east, and Prins Alexanderpolder (1871).
The quarter south of the Maas was given a shopping centre, the **Zuidplein** (GX), a theatre and an enormous sports complex, the **Ahoy** (concerts, exhibitions).
To facilitate the inhabitants' of this considerable urban area's leisure activities, large recreational facilities were set up nearby, in particular on a peninsula of the Maas near Brielle, to the west and to the northeast along the Rotte.

The new port – *See also p 193 and the inset on map 408.*
In 1945 the reconstruction of the port began. It was decided that national industry should be developed. A new port, Botlek, was built in 1954 on the island of Rozenburg, where refineries and petro-chemical plants were subsequently set up. When these facilities became inadequate, the new **Europoort** was added.
Finally, to accommodate the giant tankers, open-sea docks were built to the south of the Nieuwe Waterweg, in the Maasvlakte region, where an industrial zone was created around the port and its installations.

M. Koner/RAPHO

Port of Rotterdam

Port activity – With a total goods traffic of 292 million metric tons for 1991, Rotterdam is the world's largest port (the same year the overall goods traffic for all French ports was estimated at 304 million metric tons). This gigantic concern employs altogether 300 000 people.
Petroleum and its by-products account for 117 million metric tons, or around 40% of the total activity.
Four important refineries (Shell, Esso, Kuwait Petroleum and Nerefco) have been set up between Rotterdam and the sea. They have led to the creation of a powerful chemical industry (ICI, AZCO, DSM, ARCO, Shell, etc.).
The port of Rotterdam enjoys a privileged situation at the mouth of two big European rivers and within easy reach of major road and railway networks. Not to mention the presence of two nearby airports: Schipol and Zestienhoven (a mile or so north of the town).

More than 80% of goods arriving in Rotterdam are in transit; 60% of them are headed for foreign countries. Both a home port and a port of transit, Rotterdam counts over 300 regular international shipping lines; in 1990 it received around 32 150 deep-sea ships.
The port facilities have had to adapt to the remarkable increase in **container traffic** (2 400 475 container ships in 1990, as against only 242 325 in 1970). Transhipment centres *(distriparken)* have been set up, offering storage, distribution and reassembling services; they are located near the huge shipping terminals designed to receive the container vessels.

Transportation – There are 4 main urban road links between the north and south banks:

Maastunnel (FX) – Opened in 1942, the Maas Tunnel is 1 070 m - 3 510ft long of which 550m - 1 804ft are under the river. Covered with yellow tiles, it has four separate galleries: two one-way roads for cars (6 000 an hour) placed side by side, and two upper levels for cyclists (8 000 an hour) and pedestrians (40 000 an hour) with eight escalators.

Beneluxtunnel – This was built in 1967 to relieve some of the traffic from the Maastunnel, which had become inadequate, and to allow a crossing between the two banks while avoiding the city centre. It is 1 300m - 4 265ft long and the river bed was dredged 22.5m - 74ft deep.

Willemsbrug (HV) – This bridge was opened in 1982.

Van Brienenoordbrug – This bridge to the east was inaugurated in 1965. It has a single span 297m - 974ft long, rising 25m - 82 ft above the water. It ends in a bascule bridge on the north side. Since 1992 the twelve-lane Tweede Brienenoordbrug (Second Bridge) has regulated traffic flow in the area.
Moreover, the city has acquired an extensive quadrilateral ring road which enables drivers to avoid the city centre.
A major railway junction, Rotterdam is presently undertaking the construction of a 3km - 2 mile tunnel which will replace the railway viaduct and the railway bridges spanning the Maas in 1995.
The Rotterdam underground, the first in the country, opened in 1968.

THE CENTRE

From the railway station – to the Museum Boymans-van Beuningen *about 5 hours*

The 1985 Inner City Plan set out to create in the heart of Rotterdam an attractive mix of commercial and cultural facilities, residential districts, public buildings and green spaces with the renewal of the decaying harbour area as a recreational attraction point. The decorative detailing has been provided by a variety of statues and sculptures.

Stationsplein (JY) – With one's back to the **Centraal Station**, built in 1957, the Wholesale Trade Centre **(Groothandelsgebouw)** (JY) can be seen on the right. Built in 1952, the massive building covering 2ha - 5 acres, houses 200 firms and employs 5 000 people.
On the left stands the building housing the **Nationale Nederlanden** insurance company (JY **N**), easily recognisable by the huge tower soaring above them.

Kruisplein (JY **52**) – To the right is the **Bouwcentrum** or **Building Centre** (JY) whose façade has an enormous reproduction of Picasso's **Sylvette**. Inside the building there are architectural exhibitions. On the side façade overlooking the Weena, note Henry Moore's brick **Relief** (1955).

De Doelen (JY) – It is an immense concert hall and congress centre built in 1966; the main auditorium seats 2 222 people.
To the north of Westersingel stands a statue symbolising the Rotterdam Resistance.

Schouwburgplein (JY **88**) – Built over an underground car park, this square is a vast esplanade with many benches where visitors can sit and relax. The new theatre (**T**), inaugurated in 1988, features two rehearsal rooms where dance companies and theatre troupes can make use of state-of-the-art facilities.

★ **Lijnbaan** (JKY) – This is the shopping quarter's main street, built by Jacob B. Bakema from 1952-4, with pedestrian precincts and flower beds. One can stroll by pretty shops or relax in outdoor cafés.

Cross Lijnbaan to reach the town hall.

Note the charming little sculpture by Anne Grimdalen, **The Bear Cubs** (*De Beertjes*, 1956). Opposite the town hall is the **War Memorial**. It was made by Mari Andriessen in 1957 and three generations are depicted.

Coolsingel (KY) – This is the city's main thoroughfare and the town hall, the post office and the stock exchange are situated here. There are many modern compositions on the sidewalks and building façades, as well as several statues. Shaded lawns make it a pleasant place to walk.

Naar foto VVV Rotterdam

The Bear Cubs by Anne Grimdalen

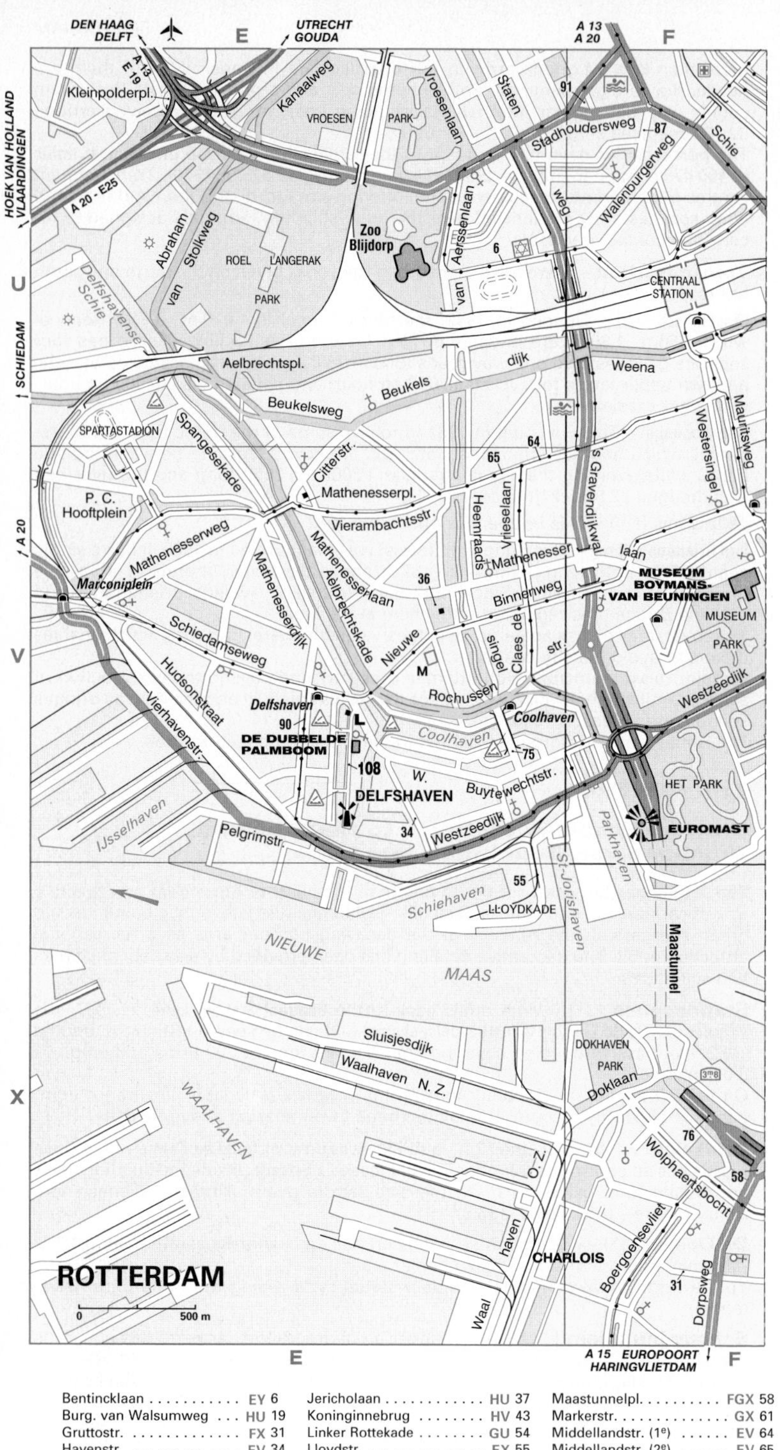

Bentincklaan .... EY 6	Jericholaan .... HU 37	Maastunnelpl. .... FGX 58
Burg. van Walsumweg ... HU 19	Koninginnebrug .... HV 43	Markerstr. .... GX 61
Gruttostr. .... FX 31	Linker Rottekade .... GU 54	Middellandstr. (1e) ...... EV 64
Havenstr. .... EV 34	Lloydstr. .... EX 55	Middellandstr. (2e) ...... EV 65
Heemraadspl. .... EV 36	Maashaven O.Z. .... HX 57	Mijnsheerenlaan .... GHX 67

Stadhuis (KY **H**) ⊙ – Built between 1914-20, a good example of period architecture, it is one of the few edifices which was spared. It has an excellent **carillon** ⊙. Among other statues, in front of the building, is one of the great jurist, Grotius, by Hettema (1970). On the façade of the building opposite there is a mosaic (1954) (KY **C**) by Van Roode depicting Erasmus on his way to Basle.

The **post office**, dating from the same period as the Town Hall, features, in its interior, a remarkable concrete framework. Facing the Stock Exchange, in front of the department store De Bijenkorf (The Beehive), stands a gigantic metal **"Construction"** (KY **E**); it is the work of Naum Gabo (1957) and illustrates the reconstruction of the town. The Stock Exchange, **Beurs** (KY), built in 1936-1940, is surmonted by a bell tower. The **World Trade Center** (1983-1986) a 23-storey block erected above the Stock Exchange hall, is a distinctive landmark: it has the shape of a flattened ellipse and presents glass façades of green.

Go between the post office and Beurs to cross Rotte Canal.

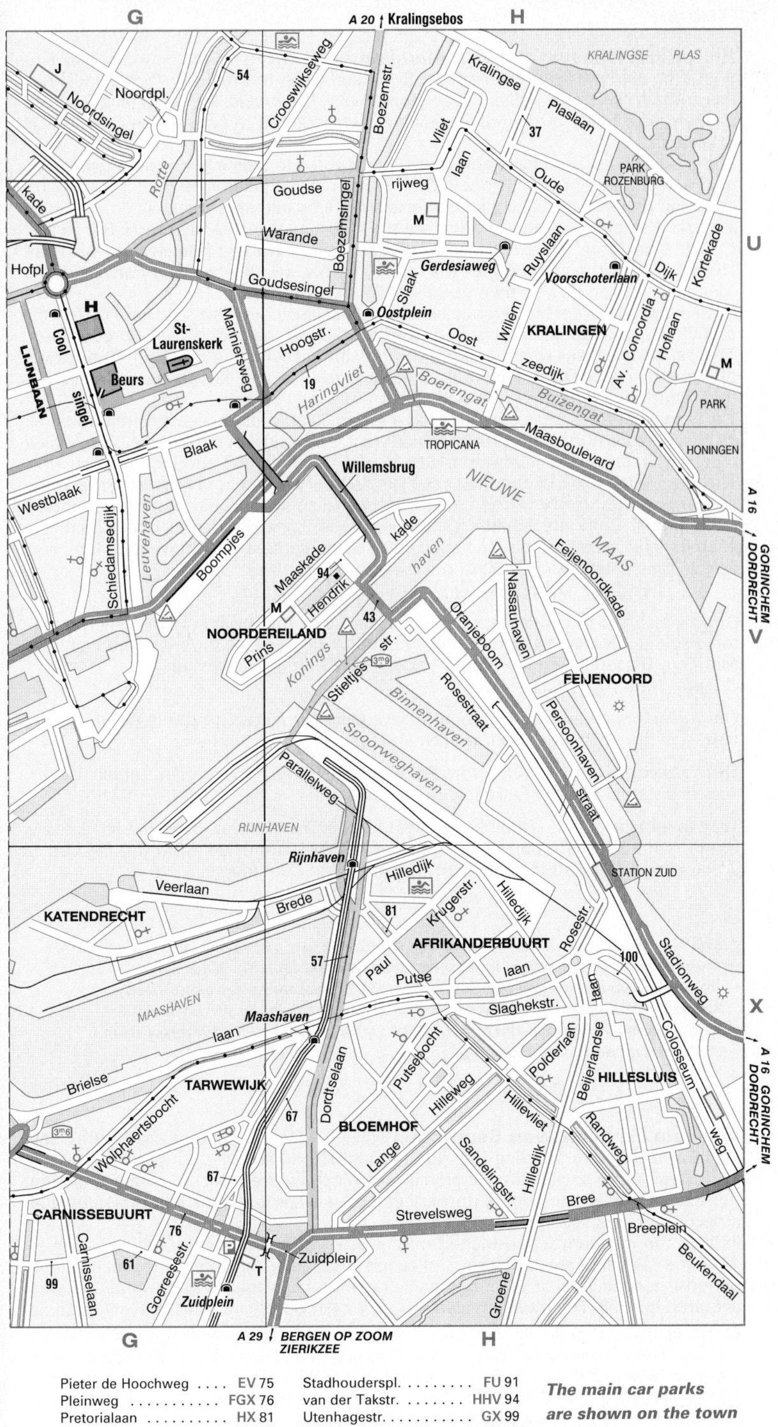

Pieter de Hoochweg	EV 75	Stadhouderspl.	FU 91
Pleinweg	FGX 76	van der Takstr.	HHV 94
Pretorialaan	HX 81	Utenhagestr.	GX 99
Schepenstr.	FU 87	Varkenoordsebocht	HX 100
Spanjaardstr.	EV 90	Voorhaven	EV 108

The main car parks are shown on the town plans in this guide

The Statue of Erasmus on the parvis of St.-Laurenskerk is the work of Hendrick de Keyser and was finished in 1622, after his death (1536).

Grote- of St.-Laurenskerk (KY) – Completed in 1646, with its truncated tower built into the transept, this Gothic church was destroyed in 1940, then restored. It now has, once more, a fine façade with a new bronze portal (1968) by Giacomo Manzù *(War and Peace)* and a chevet with Gothic tracery.

The **interior★** is spaciously conceived in the Gothic Brabant style, the severity of which is attenuated by the warm colours of the panelled vaults, the copper chandeliers, the great red and gold organ (1973), and the 18C gilded ironwork of the sanctuary. The slightly protruding transept contains 17C admirals' tombs and a fine 16C organ case. The organ case in the chancel dates from 1725. The bronze baptismal font (1959) is by Han Petri.

Cross the pedestrian bridge spanning the Rotte. When you reach the back of the Stock Exchange (Beurs), turn left into Korte Hoogstraat.

★ **Historisch Museum Het Schielandshuis** (KY M4) ⊘ – Built between 1662-5 to house the administrative centre of the Schieland dikes, this mansion (Schielandshuis) has a main façade in white ashlar stone, richly decorated and brightened by red shutters. The finely proportioned building was restored to hold the city's historical collection.

The ground floor and basement rooms are devoted to artistic production (paintings, gold and silversmith work, clockwork...). Three reconstructed interiors (Louis XVI, rococo and Regency styles) contain objects sought by 18C art collectors.

Among the paintings worth noting are the interior scenes painted by H. Sorgh and C. Saftleven (both 17C artists) and, especially, the works of **Adriaen van der Werff** (1659-1722); his technique and the quality of his works – see *Self-Portrait in the Medallion* – brought this painter international recognition.

Note in the basement the ceramic tile scene *In Duijsent Vreesen (To Live 1 000 Fears, c*1600) where the green tone is evident and typical of the period's local production.

The 1st floor evokes institutions and municipal activities: more than 40 portraits of directors of the Dutch East India Company *(qv)*, 18 and 19C canvases (reflecting the importance of commercial activities.

The remains of the city's churches have a particular importance: Rotterdam lost all its old churches during the 1940 bombardment. The model of the wooden spire which crowned St.-Laurenskerk between 1619-45 was designed by Hendrick de Keyser *(qv)*.

The mezzanine exhibits the **Atlas van Stolk Collection** with engravings and drawings concerning the history of the Low Countries (displayed in part during temporary exhibitions). Daily life (children's kitchen – 1853; reconstitution of a grocer's – 1910-68, etc) occupies the attic space; it also presents a collection of clothes and accessories dating from 1760 to the present day.

Cross Blaak to reach Plein 1940.

At the north end of Leuvehaven, stands a statue by the Russian-born French sculptor, Zadkine, **Destroyed City** (1953) (KY **F**), which symbolises the martyred city. The Maritiem Museum "Prins Hendrik" *(qv)* is located on Leuvehaven.

Return to Coolsingel

On Coolsingel an amusing statue portrays **Monsieur Jacques** (KY **K**) (1959), a typical citizen of Rotterdam by Wenckebach (1959).

Binnenwegplein (KY **10**) – Note **Het Ding** (the Thing; 1969) a giant mobile by the American artist George Rickey.

Westersingel (JYZ) – Rodin's headless statue, **The Man who Walks** (JZ **N**), is to be found in the southern part of the gardens laid out alongside a former ring canal. Westersingel leads to the Museum Boymans-van Beuningen.

The Het Museumpark has become the cultural heart of the city and the venue for a wide range of activities. Museums close at hand include: Museum Boymans-van Beuningen (qv); Kunsthal (1992) for temporary exhibitions; Natuurmuseum; Chabot Museum to the artist of the same name; and the Nederlands Architectuurinstituut (1988-1993) covering interior decoration, architecture and town planning.

★★★ **Museum Boymans-van Beuningen** (⊘) JZ – On the edge of a park, this fine art museum is in a building inaugurated in 1935, to which a wing was added in 1972. Besides an excellent collection of Old Masters, the museum contains a large number of modern and contemporary works of art, engravings and drawings and a decorative arts section.

In 1958 the museum was enriched by the D.G. Van Beuningen donation, while in 1972 the Willem Van der Vorm Collection was given on loan. The Vitale Bloch bequest, a collection of paintings and drawings from the 15 to the mid-20C was acquired in 1978. The museum also organises temporary international exhibitions.

Old Masters – *Old building, 1st floor.* There is a remarkable collection of primitive art. *The Three Marys at the Open Sepulchre* is a major work by the **Van Eycks**. There are admirable paintings by **Hieronymus Bosch**, *The Marriage at Cana, St Christopher*, and in particular *The Prodigal Son* where one can appreciate the painter's poetic humour, his flights of imagination, and his mastery of colour. Note a Virgin and Child surrounded by angel musicians, *The Glorification of the Virgin*, a masterpiece by **Geerten tot Sint Jans**. The Prophet Isaiah is shown on the left panel of the famous altarpiece by the **Master of the Annunciation of Aix** (Aix-en-Provence).

The Tower of Babel by **Bruegel the Elder**, the delightful *Portrait of a Young Scholar* in a red beret (1531) by **Jan Van Scorel**, and works by **Pieter Aertsen** etc represent the 16C.

17C painting is particularly interesting. There are two portraits by **Frans Hals**; church interiors with masterful use of light by **Pieter Saenredam** and **Emanuel de Witte**; a portrait by **Rembrandt** of his young son Titus; the distant horizons of **Hercules Seghers** and **Van Goyen**; and nature's atmosphere rendered by **Hobbema** and **Jacob van Ruisdael**. There are also interior scenes by **Jan Steen** and **Gerrit Dou**.

The **Rubens** collection has, among other sketches, a remarkable series on the theme of Achilles' life.

In the fine group of Italian paintings from the 15 to 17C, there are works by the Venetians: Titian, Tintoretto and Veronese.

Willem Van der Vorm Collection (Verzameling) – It includes, notably, an interesting series of 17C paintings with Rubens, Van Dyck, Rembrandt *(Tobias and his Wife)* and many Dutch masters such as Gerrit Dou, Ter Borch *(Woman Spinning)* and Van de Velde with two seascapes.

Woman Spinning by G. Ter Borch

19C French painting is represented by the Barbizon School. There are works by Daubigny, Théodore Rousseau and Corot *(Ville d'Avray)*. For the 18C, Hubert Robert, Chardin and Watteau should be mentioned for France, and the Venetian Francesco Guardi, for Italy.

Prints and Drawings – *New Wing Cabinet.*
This important collection, a part of which is exhibited during temporary exhibitions, covers the 15C to the present day. It includes works by Albrecht Dürer, Leonardo da Vinci, Rembrandt, Watteau, Cézanne and Picasso.

Modern and Contemporary Art – *Old building, 1st floor and new wing.*
It covers the period from 1850 to the present. The Impressionist artists Monet, Sisley and Pissaro are represented as well as Signac, Van Gogh, Mondrian and Kandinsky *(Lyrisches)*. Note the small 14-year old ballet dancer, a graceful statuette by Degas. Among the Surrealist works there are paintings by Salvador Dali *(Sundial, Impressions of Africa)* and René Magritte *(The Red Model, Reproduction Forbidden)*.
The contemporary art collection is exhibited by rotation; it includes sculptures by Richard Serra, Oldenburg, Joseph Beuys, Bruce Nauman and Walter De Maria, and Donald Judd and paintings by the Germans Kiefer and Penck, the Italians Cucchi, Clemente and Chia. Dutch contemporary art is represented by Van Elk, Carel Visser, Rob van Koningsbruggen and René Daniels.
Among the contemporary trends are works by Milan Kunc and Salvo as well as sculptures by Thomas Schütte, Bazilebustamente and Niek Kamp.

Decorative Arts – *Old building, ground floor.* The museum also has a very rich collection of objets d'art; glassware (17C), silverware, majolica and Persian, Turkish (13C), Spanish, Dutch, Italian (15-16C) and Delft earthenware.

DELFSHAVEN

From Delfshaven, Delft's *(qv)* old port, the Pilgrim Fathers *(qv)* embarked in 1620 for England from where they sailed for the New World.

Piet Hein was born here in 1577, the Admiral who distinguished himself in Mexico, in 1628, against the Spanish. The painter **Kees Van Dongen** was born here in 1877 (d1968). He portrayed violently coloured female figures.

Voorhaven (EV **108**) – It is a picturesque quay and has a chapel with a pinnacle known as the Pilgrim Fathers' Church, and a charming lever bridge.

★ **Museum De Dubbele Palmboom** (EV) ⏲ – This museum has been remarkably installed in converted warehouses.
Photographs, scale models and a great variety of *objets d'art* and arts and crafts are shown throughout the five storeys of the building to illustrate the history of Rotterdam. From the top storey, the city can be seen towards the east (orientation table); note below, opposite Coolhaven, the statue of Piet Hein (1870).

ROTTERDAM

Street	Grid
Beursplein	KY 9
Binnenweg	JY
Botersloot	KY 13
Coolsingel	KY
Hoogstr.	KY
Karel Doormanstr.	JY
Korte Hoogstr.	KY 46
Korte Lijnbaan	JY 48
Lijnbaan	JKY
Stadhuispl.	KY 93
Aert van Nesst.	JKY 4
Binnenwegpl.	KY 10
Delftsepl.	JY 21
Delftsestr.	JY 22
G. J. de Jonghweg	JZ 24
Grotekerkpl.	KY 30
Haagseveer	KY 33
Jonker Fransstr.	KY 39
Keizerstr.	KY 40
Kruiskade	JKY 51
Kruisplein	JY 52
Nieuwestr.	KY 70
van Oldenbarnevelt-straat	JKY 72
Pompenburg	KY 78
Posthoornstr.	KY 79
Scheepstimmermanslaan	KZ 85
Schouwburgplein	JY 88
Veerhaven	KZ 102
Veerkade	KZ 103
van Vollenhovestr.	KZ 107
Westewagenstr.	KY 110
Witte de Withstr.	KZ 112

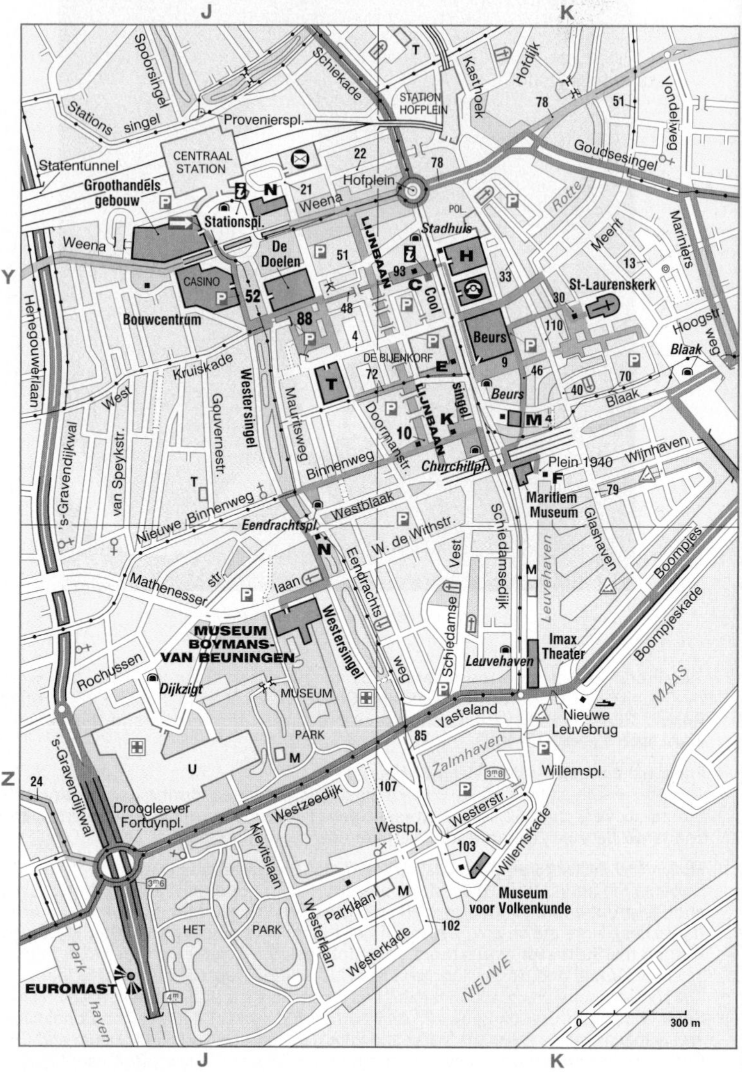

C – Mozaiek van Van Roode
E – Constructie van Naum Gabo
F – Monument van Zadkine
H – Stadhuis
K – Monsieur Jacques, an Wenckebach
M4 – Historisch Museum Het Schielandshuis
N – Toren Nationale Nederlanden

Zakkendragershuisje (EV L) ⊙ – To the north of Voorhaven, this old porters' house has been renovated and contains a tin smelting works where traditional methods are still used.

Nos 34 and 36 have interesting façade stones with sculptured animals.

ADDITIONAL SIGHTS

★ **Euromast** (JZ) ⊙ – This boldly designed tower was built in 1960 to celebrate the opening of Floriade, the World Horticultural Show; it is situated in Rotterdam Park, close to Parkhaven.

From the terrace, which is 100m - 328ft high, there is a remarkable **view★** of the city and the port.

The **Space Tower** ⊙, added in 1970, rises 185m - 607ft on an axis. The spectacular glass lift revolving around it holds 32 people who may admire a **panorama★★** stretching 30km - 19 miles in all directions, including the immense Delta formed by the Maas and the Rhine, hemming in the Europoort. At night the sight is truly breathtaking.

Maritiem Museum "Prins Hendrik" (KY) ⏲ – Located on Leuvehaven, Rotterdam's first harbour basin onto the sea, this museum is devoted to European seafaring in the past and present with special emphasis on the Netherlands. The main building houses not only the temporary exhibitions but scale models, paintings, maps, globes and navigational instruments as well.
In Leuvehaven note the **Buffel** (1868), the Royal Navy's old ship. Cabins belonging to the different crew members are on view as well as the prison cells and the well-appointed captain's cabin.

IMAX (KZ) ⏲ – *Enter from the quayside.* From the comfort of your seat enjoy the images projected by the IMAX system from a 70mm film – double that of a conventional one – onto a slightly curved screen (23m - 75ft high and 17m - 56ft across).
Stereo sound from 6 loudspeakers intensifies the whole experience. The difference with the Omniversum auditorium in The Hague is that it has a screen shaped like a dome which completely surrounds you.

Museum voor Volkenkunde (KZ) ⏲ – On the quays of the Nieuwe Maas, this Ethnography Museum which is in the old Royal Yacht Club building, is devoted to the cultures of non-Western peoples.

Diergaarde (EU) ⏲ – In a floral park, this zoo contains an interesting collection of over 2 000 animals, including some rare species (okapies, etc). The Riviera-Hal includes aquariums, a vivarium (reptiles), a tropical hothouse and aviaries.

Kralingsebos (HU) – This wood surrounds a big lake (Kralingseplas) and has two **windmills** on the north side.
In one of them, **Molen De Ster** ⏲, an old spice mill dating from 1740, rebuilt in 1969, snuff manufacture can be seen.

★★ THE PORT

See p 186 and the inset on map **408**

Nieuwe Maas

Short boat trip to Eemhaven ⏲ – The boat sails down the Maas to Eem Dock. Landing stage: *Leuvenhoofd (town plan see above,* KZ*).*
The boat heads west, following the north bank. It passes on the right the park (Het Park) with Euromast. The air vents of Maastunnel can be seen.

Lloyd Kade – This is the dock for ships trading with Indonesia.

Delfshaven – This is Delft's old port *(qv)*.

Merwehaven – This is the biggest dock for miscellaneous goods, on the north bank.

Schiedam – *See Schiedam.*

Wilhelminahaven – Naval repairs on a floating dock.

To the west the gulf, then **Wiltonhaven** can be seen; it is used for naval construction and repair workshops.

Here the boat turns round and crosses the river to sail back up the opposite bank towards Rotterdam.

Pernis – Chemical industries, including petrochemicals and artificial fertilisers.

Eemhaven – The boat enters this vast series of docks specialised in container traffic and transhipment of goods.

Waalhaven – Originally built for iron and copper ore tankers, at present this dock also handles containers and miscellaneous goods.

Maashaven – Beyond Maastunnel, this grain dock, now supplanted by Botlek and Benelux Dock, also handles miscellaneous goods.

Rijnhaven – This dock is lined by quays, where in the past, the great transatlantic liners of the Holland-America Line moored.
Note the fine rectilinear constructions.

Long boat trip ⏲ – This tour goes all the way to Botlek. *Description of Vlaardingen and Botlek on next page.*

Europoort and Maasvlakte

The vast installations of Europoort, built between 1958 and 1975, cover 3 600ha - 8 892 acres on the south bank of Nieuwe Waterweg. Europoort continues to the west by Maasvlakte whose development dates from 1965-71. Some docks can take cargo boats drawing 21.95 m - 72 ft of water.

Car tour – *79km - 49 miles to Maasvlakte. Leave by the A20 motorway and take the Beneluxtunnel on the left.*
At the south exit there is a fine view of **Pernis** oil terminal.

Take the motorway on the right, running alongside a railway line.

Botlektunnel – Opened in 1980 under the Oude Maas which comes from Dordrecht *(qv)*, this tunnel has a single carriageway 500m - 1 640ft long and 21m - 69ft below sea level. It supplements an old bridge.

Botlek – It is a grain port and oil terminal. Moreover, it has installations for chemical products, bulk transport and naval repairs.

Leave the Europoort road opposite, and continue right to rejoin the river.

Rozenburg – On the **Het Scheur**, the river's opposite bank, is the Maassluis *(see below)* industrial sector. Near the Rozenburg church there is a **windmill**.

Shortly afterwards leave the Europoort road on the left to take Noordzeeweg which runs between the Nieuwe Waterweg and the Caland Canal.

On the left unloading facilities for oil tankers of different companies can be seen. The end of the road goes around an old radar station: there is a **view** of the Hoek van Holland, Europoort and the estuary which is divided by a dike; towards the north, there is the entrance to the Nieuwe Waterweg leading to Rotterdam, and to the south, the entrance to Europoort – 30 000 ships pass through the estuary every year.

Return by the same route and take the bridge over the canal or Calandbrug, then go under Brielsebrug to reach Europoort.

To the right one goes alongside the oil terminals which have already been seen, and to the left **Hartel Canal**, which has recreational areas on either side of it; and on the edge of **Brielse Meer** an artificial lake for pleasure boats and once a branch of the Maas, the Brielse Maas.

Dintelhavenbrug – A bridge over an access canal to Dintelhaven, the mineral port. From this bridge one can occasionally see a ferry in **Beneluxhaven**, which like Hoek van Holland, is a port for ferries between England (Kingston-upon-Hull) and the Netherlands.

Once over the Suurhoffbrug, turn right towards Maasvlakte.

Oostvoornse Meer – This lake was created by the closing of the Brielse Gat in 1965; it has been adapted for swimming and sailing.

Maasvlakte (Mass Plain) – A stretch of sandy land reclaimed from the North Sea to accommodate the inevitable extension (around 1 200ha - 3 000 acres) of Rotterdam's port. At present, the **8th Petroleumhaven** houses an oil terminal (Maasvlakte Olie Terminal). A container terminal (Europe Container Terminus B.V.), an electric power station (E.Z.F.) and a security firm have been set up on **Europahaven**. A company specialised in the handling of goods lies near **Amazonehaven**. Facilities for the storage and transhipment of minerals (E.M.O.), along with a branch of Holland's national gas board (Nederlandse Gasunie) are in the **Mississippihaven**.
A new lighthouse has replaced that of Hoek van Holland as the Maasvlakte development had left it stranded inland. To the west stretches a beach *(strand)*.

Boat trip ⏲ – The tour allows one to grasp the extent of the port installations. The boats leave from Leuvehoofd *(plan p 192,* **KZ**).

EXCURSIONS

From Schiedam to Hoek van Holland – *31km - 19 miles by the AZO motorway going west.*

Schiedam – *See Schiedam.*

Vlaardingen – Pop 73 719. This major river and sea port used to specialise in herring fishing.
Today it is also an important industrial and commercial centre. From the banks of the Nieuwe Maas one can look at the unending traffic of ocean-going ships toing and froing from Rotterdam. Downstream along the south bank is the Botlek oil terminal.

Maassluis – Pop 33 272. This port is on Het Scheur, between the Nieuwe Maas and the Nieuwe Waterweg. A new dam designed to withstand stormy weather on the Nieuwe Waterweg is presently being built between Maassluis and Hoek van Holland.

Hoek van Holland – At the mouth of the Nieuwe Waterweg, this is the passenger port for Rotterdam and for ferries going to England (Harwich). It is an impressive sight to see the ships heading for Rotterdam or the North Sea. Opposite are the Europoort installations.
An artificial beach was created north of Hoek van Holland in 1971.

Brielle and Oostvoorne – *41km - 25 1/2 miles to the southwest. Leave Rotterdam by Dorpsweg* (**FX**).

Brielle – *See Brielle.*

Oostvoorne – This is a seaside resort situated near a chain of dunes.
A 311ha - 768 acre nature reserve, the **Duinen van Voorne**, has been laid out in the dunes; the reserve is crisscrossed by paths. A visitor centre (Bezoekerscentrum) provides information about the reserve's plants and animals.

Windmills and polders – *Round tour of 81km - 50 miles – about 3 hours – local map see above. Leave Rotterdam by Maasboulevard* (**HV**) *and go towards Gorinchem and turn off towards Alblasserdam.*
The narrow dike road follows the Noord, a stretch of water frequently used. Between the Noord and the Lek lies the **Alblasserwaard**. This old **waard** (low land surrounded by rivers) has a ring of dikes around it and has been made into a polder.

Alblasserdam – Pop 17 468. This town has shipyards for naval construction.

Kinderdijk – Kinderdijk means children's dike for it is said that during the great floods which occured on St Elisabeth's feast day in 1421, the sea washed up on the dike a crib with a crying baby and a cat.

Towards the end of the village an opening between houses on the right gives a pretty **view** of the windmills which dot the plain.

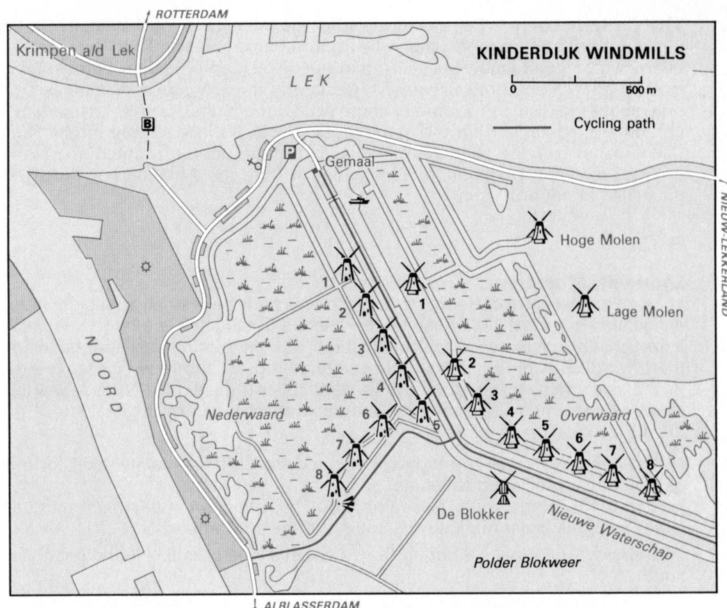

★★ **Kinderdijk Windmills** (Molens van Kinderdijk) ⊙ – *For details and illustrations of the different kinds of windmills, see the Introduction: Windmills.*

Near the Nederwaard pumping station *(gemaal)*, along the canals, amidst meadows and reeds stand 19 windmills. Their exceptional number, their size and the beauty of the marshy plain have made them famous. Up to 1950 they helped drain the Alblasserwaard.

Today their sails turn for tourists only on Windmill Days *(see Calendar of Events)*. One can walk along the dikes or take a **boat trip** ⊙.

The eight tall polder mills *(bovenkruier)* lined up towards the west are truncated-shaped brick drainage mills with rotating caps dating from 1738 (1 to 8).

The second **windmill** ⊙ can be visited.

A little further on there is a smaller hollow post mill, the *wipmolen* type, called De Blokker.

There are also eight windmills with rotating caps along the other canal, but octagonal in shape and thatched (**1** to **8**) dating from 1740. Hidden behind them are two other windmills built in 1740 and 1761.

Continue by car along the dike road which follows the Lek.

From Nieuw-Lekkerland on, just down to the right of the dike, large T-shaped farmhouses can be seen; they are thatched and have haystacks beside them protected by a little roof *(illustration p 33)*. Orchards surround these farmhouses. Other windmills can soon be seen.

At Groot-Ammers take the Molenaarsgraaf road.

Soon four windmills appear in single file along the canal. Three are hollow post mills, the fourth is an octagonal polder mill.

Further on rejoin the large canal which crosses the Alblasserward and follow the south bank until you come to Alblasserdam.

The **road**★ which is almost at water-level is picturesque. There are large hall-farmhouses *(see Introduction: Farmhouses)* and windmills along the way in a very lush countryside. Some of these farmhouses have a safety exit a little above ground level, which led into the living room and which was used during floods.

Return to Rotterdam by Maasboulevard.

SCHIEDAM Zuid-Holland — Pop 70 207

Michelin map 408 E 6, fold 24 (inset) – Local map see ROTTERDAM

Schiedam (pronounced sridam) is a typical small town whose centre is surrounded by canals, lined with several windmills.

Shipbuilding yards and numerous industries make it an animated town. But it is mainly juniper which brought it fame.

HISTORICAL NOTES

About 1260 a castle was built in Schiedam and one of its towers still stands near the new town hall. It received its city rights in 1275. In 1574 the castle was destroyed by the inhabitants so that it would not fall into the hands of the Spanish.

Schiedam is the homeland of **St Lydwine** (1380-1433), a mystic whose life was retraced by J.K. Huysmans *(St Lydwine of Schiedam, 1901)*.

The town has a large park, **Beatrix Park** to the north with lakes, and nearby the **Groenoord** open-air swimming-pool.

The juniper town – Beginning in *c*1600 the inhabitants of Schiedam started to make alcohol from second-class wine imported from France. Then they made spirits from grain, and finally specialised in the distillation of juniper berries *(jenever)* making gin. At one time Schiedam had nearly three hundred distilleries. Today, only about ten distilleries remain, some use young juniper berries *(jonge genever)* and others old juniper berries *(oude jenever)* which make a more full-bodied gin. Called Jenever in the Netherlands, this kind of gin often presented in a stone jar or crock is called Hollands, distinguishing it from the American or British-made gin called London Dry gin.

SIGHTS

Stedelijk Museum ⏲ – *Hoogstraat 112.*
Located in the centre of Hoogstraat, the town's main pedestrian street, the museum is installed in an old 1787 hospital, St.-Jacobs Gasthuis; it is a large building with a portico. Its collections concern archaeology, contemporary art and the history of the town (CoBrA group, systematic painting, Pop Art and New Figurative Art).
In the basement, there is the National Distillery Museum, **Nationaal Gedistilleerd Museum.** Instruments, documents and scale models evoke the making of gin in the 19C; collection of miniature bottles.

Mills – The town was formerly surrounded by 18 mills, mainly used for milling grain intended for the distilleries.
Four tall 18C stage mills *(see illustration Introduction: Windmills)* exist along Noordvest, the canal marking the course of the old ramparts.

De Walvisch (The Whale) – Dating from 1794 this type of mill is found mostly in the south.

Continuing along the quay towards the north, one can see the three other mills.

De Drie Koornbloemen (The Three Corn Flowers) – This mill of 1770 was used to grind cattle food.

De Vrijheid (Freedom) – Started in 1785, it still mills grain.

De Noord (The North) – This mill of 1803 is thought to be the tallest in Europe (33.33m - 109ft including the cap, maximum height of sails 44.56m - 146ft). Its premises are used for tasting by an important distillery, whose buildings are opposite.

Zakkendragerhuis (Porters' House) – *Take the road opposite the Stedelijk Museum and cross the Lange Haven, the town's central canal.* Fine view over the picturesque quays. Then follow the quay Oude Sluis, on the right. Behind the old Grain Exchange or **Korenbeurs,** there is a gracious 1725 building with a curving gable topped by a turret.

Maasboulevard – From this boulevard near the pleasure boat harbour, there is an interesting **view** over the heavy maritime traffic between Rotterdam and the sea.
The port of Pernis, on the opposite bank, is linked to Schiedam by the Beneluxtunnel.

SLUIS Zeeland — Pop 2 876

Michelin map 408 B 8 or 212 fold 12

This small touristic town, pleasant and busy, is situated near the Belgian frontier. With Damme it was an outer harbour of Bruges in the 14C when it was at the mouth of the Zwin, today silted up. Its old French name, **l'Écluse** (the Lock) evokes the naval battle which took place here in 1340 at the beginning of the Hundred Years War. Edward III's English fleet repelled 190 French ships, winning the first naval battle of that war.
The grassy mounds which one sees on entering the town are remains of the old ramparts, turned into an esplanade.

SIGHTS

Stadhuis ⏲ – It is overlooked by a tall 14C **belfry,** the only one existing in the Netherlands. It is decorated with four turrets and a Jack-of the clock. From the top of the bell tower there is a fine **view** stretching over the plain. Sluis memorabilia can be seen in the staircase. The Council Room has a lovely 18C grille.

Molen De Brak ⏲ – This wall mill, destroyed in 1944, was rebuilt in 1951. Its three floors reached by steep ladders make it possible to understand how it works. From the handrail the **view** extends over the surrounding countryside and the Zwin.

EXCURSIONS

St.-Anna ter Muiden – *2km - 1 mile to the northwest, near the frontier.* At the foot of the church's imposing 14C brick tower, the small triangular **square,** the rustic houses and the water pump form a charming picture. Note a thatched wooden barn at the far end of the square.

Aardenburg – Pop 3 710. *8km - 5 miles to the southeast.* Its fine Gothic church, **St.-Bavokerk,** ⏲ with characteristics of the Scheldt Gothic style (which developed in Belgium), contains 14 and 15C sarcophagi, with interesting paintings on their inside panels.

IJzendijke – *22km - 14 miles to the east.* This old stronghold only has a small halfmoon shaped bastion or ravelin remaining from its ramparts, covered with earth and surrounded by water. Nearby, there is a lovely windmill.
The spire topped with a golden cock, which one sees in the middle of this small town, belongs to the oldest Protestant church (1612) in Zeeland.
At no 28 Grote Markt is the Regional Museum **Streekmuseum West Zeeuws Vlaanderen** ⊙. Apart from a rustic interior of 1850 from Cadzand with its fine stove, there are instruments used in the cultivation of flax and madder and a section devoted to the Zeeland plough horses.

Breskens – *29km - 18 miles to the north.* A fishing port at the mouth of the Westerschelde, Breskens is the departure point for the **Vlissingen** *(qv)* **ferry** ⊙. It also has a pleasure boat harbour.
From the pedestrian Promenade laid out on top of the dune, between the fishing port and the ferry terminal to the west, there are fine **views** over the beaches and the Scheldt.

SNEEK Friesland — Pop 29 282

Michelin map 408 I Z – Local map overleaf
Town plan in the current Michelin Red Guide Benelux

Sneek (Snits for Frisians) is a small, active and very popular tourist centre. In the Middle Ages it was a port on the Middelzee, an inland sea, since disappeared.

Gateway to the Frisian Lakes – Sneek is situated in the centre of a region much appreciated for its lakes, in particular Sneekermeer which is used for different water sports.
Sneek has a marina and several sailing schools. One can hire motorboats, sail boats, or participate in boating excursions in season *(apply to the VVV).*
Every year regattas are organised during the great **Sneekweek**. In addition, every summer for a fortnight, the **skûtsjesilen**, regattas with *skûtsjes* are held on the Frisian Lakes and IJsselmeer. Several Frisian towns have one of these old trading boats *(skûtsjes)* with dark brown sails and a wide and flat hull flanked by two leeboards. *See Calendar of Events.*

D'après photo Ch. Cuzol, MICHELIN

Waterpoort

SIGHTS

★ **Waterpoort** – This elegant 1613 gateway in brick decorated with sandstone protected the entrance to the port. Its central part pierced with arcades and forming a bridge over the Geeuw is flanked by two turrets.

Stadhuis ⊙ – Dating from the 16C, modified in the 18C, the Stadhuis has a lovely rococo façade, with tall windows and green shutters, and a richly carved perron guarded by heraldic lions.

Fries Scheepvaart Museum en Sneker Oudheidkamer ⊙ – *Kleinzand no 14.*
This museum is devoted to Frisian navigation, both fluvial and maritime, with a large collection of boat models used in the 18 and 19C, reconstituted pleasure boat interiors, 17, 18 and 19C paintings, sail and mast workshops, navigational instruments...
In the house, beside the canal, admire the lovely collection of Frisian silverware, especially from Sneek. Several interiors have been recreated including the delightful room, from a neighbouring farm, decorated with naive 18C Frisian landscape paintings.

★ FRIESE MEREN (FRISIAN LAKES)

Round tour of 134km - 83 miles – about 1 day – local map see overleaf

Leave Sneek in the direction of Bolsward.

Here and there one can catch a glimpse of a church on an artificial mound, called *terp (qv)* hidden behind a screen of trees.

★ **Bolsward** – *See Bolsward.*

Near the Workum crossroads, take a minor road towards Exmorra.

Exmorra is situated on the tourist route known under the name of Aldfaers Erf.

Exmorra – In the small **museum** ⊙ a country grocer's shop, a rural house and a classroom of 1885 have been reconstituted.
Further on, the charming 13C church on a *terp*, surrounded by a cemetery, has been restored.

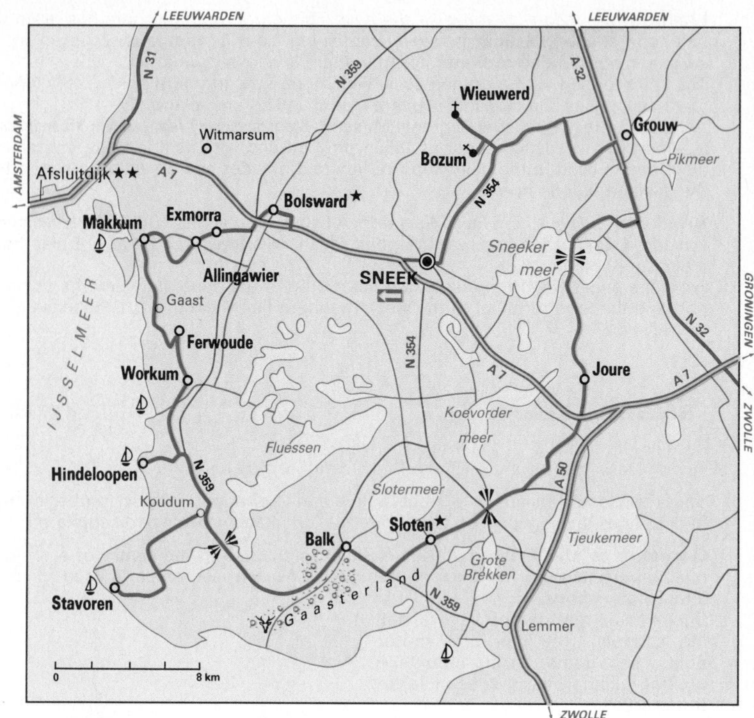

Allingawier – Near the church with a saddleback roofed bell tower one can visit a typical old Friesland **farmhouse** ⊙ named Yzeren Kou: a large building contains the huge barn and the stable; the annexe, the living quarters, are raised higher to leave room underneath for the dairy.

Makkum – It is a picturesque fishing port on the edge of IJsselmeer and crossed by a canal. It has naval shipyards.
Since the 17C tin-glazed earthenware is made here and above all tiles similar in style to those of Delft, but more rustic. On the main square, the **Waag** is a fine construction of 1698. It houses the tourist information centre (VVV) on the ground floor and the Museum of Frisian Ceramics, **Fries Aardewerkmuseum De Waag** ⊙, in the two attics and in the adjacent house. The museum displays objects used daily or for decorative purposes (plates, platters, hot plates) from 1600-1880. Note especially the objects (blue paintings on white backgrounds) from Makkum and Harlingen *(qv)* dating from the 18C, the period when Frisian earthenware was at its peak. Among the painted tile scenes note the one on the chimneypiece from a wealthy Makkum farmhouse and the scene depicting a Frisian earthenware factory in 1737 (a copy; the original is in the Rijksmuseum in Amsterdam).
In Tichelaar's Royal Pottery and Tile Factory, **Tichelaars Aardewerk- en Tegelfabriek** ⊙, founded in 1594, one can see an exhibition of earthenware and visit the workshops to see the different stages in pottery making.

Take the narrow road in the direction of Workum. The road runs parallel to the dike on one side and the canal on the other. Keep your eyes open for herons.

In Gaast, turn left to reach Ferwoude.

Ferwoude – In this locality an old **farmhouse** ⊙ and its carpentry workshop (1845) is open to the public. Opposite, the village church, topped by a pointed spire, has been attractively repainted.

Workum – *See Workum.*

Hindeloopen – *See Hindeloopen.*

Stavoren – *8.5km - 5 1/4 miles leaving from Koudum.* A fishing village, Stavoren (Starum in Frisian) has two pleasure boat harbours. It is linked to Enkhuizen by a boat service. In the past Stavoren was the capital of the Frisian kings, then a member of the Hanseatic League. Evangelised in the 9C by St Odulphus, it flourished in the 11C. Its port was excellent in the 14C. Then it silted up, as legend has it, because of a rich widow of Stavoren who ordered one of her ships' captains to bring her a precious cargo. The latter returned to Stavoren with wheat: furious the widow had all the wheat thrown into the port.
After Koudum there is a fine **view**, from the lever bridge, over the two lakes on either side of the road.
One soon crosses the wooded region of **Gaasterland**, which stretches southwest of Balk.

Balk – Near Slotermeer, this locality is crossed by a canal bordered with several lovely 18C houses, witness to a former prosperity due to its butter trade, for which Balk was the centre.

★ **Sloten** – Near Slotermeer and on the fringe of the wooded Gaasterland region, Sloten (Sleat for the Frisians) an old fortified city, seems as though it was built on a reduced scale, which accentuates its charm; narrow streets, tiny 17 and 18C houses run alongside the small canal lined with lime trees.
Following the quays, where ducks waddle, one reaches **Lemsterpoort**, an old water-gate and its **mill** of 1755; lovely view over the canal and the lakes where yachts sail in season.

From the lever bridge near Spannenburg, there are lovely **views** over a wide canal which links the two lakes.

Joure – Since the 17C this town has specialised in clock-making. It also has a large firm dealing in tobacco, tea and coffee.

A few miles north of Joure, the road runs along a narrow strip of land between two lakes; there are some fine **views**. On the left **Sneekermeer** is one of the most frequented Frisian lakes.

Grouw – Near a lake, it is a very popular water sports centre.

Wiewerd – The village **kerk** ⊘ has a crypt with strange powers. Built in the 14C on a small *terp* surrounded by a cemetery, this small church, altered in the 19C was used as a tomb in the 17 and 18C for eleven people. The corpses were protected from decomposition by an antimonious gas which rose from the ground: four of the mummies are exhibited under a sheet of glass. To illustrate this phenomenon several birds, one of which in 1879 was a parrot, were suspended from the vault.

Bozum – This charming village has a 12 and 13C **Romanesque kerk** ⊘, restored, built of tufa and brick in front of a tower with a saddleback roof, and lined on the west by a semicircle of lovely low houses. The inside is rustic and the paintings in the chancel (*c*1300) are very faded.
In the pond nearby there are often a multitude of mallards dabbling about.

Return to Sneek by ① on the town plan.

STADSKANAAL Groningen — Pop 32 936

Michelin map 408 L 3

In this former fenland area, which has been reclaimed as agricultural land, the villages are linear settlements strung out along the main canals and they give the impression of being one long village. Stadskanaal (canal town) is one of them and well merits its name.

EXCURSIONS

Ter Apel – *20km - 12 miles to the southeast.*
Ter Apel's former convent **Museum-Kloster** ⊘ is pleasantly situated in a park which boasts some splendid oak trees. The church and two ranges of the cloisters are all that remain and the visitor can visit the cloisters, the refectory and the cellar, where the sarcophagi that were found during excavations in the cloister garth are now on show. The **church** has a Gothic rood screen of carved wood (1501) and stalls of the same period which are quite plain but have misericords carved with quaint figures. Note the attractive gallery in the chancel.

Nieuweschans – *35km - 22 miles to the northeast.*
This small quiet village lies in the eastern part of the province of Groningen quite near to the German border. The low houses have been tastefully restored.

Frisian place names
In Friesland signposts are either in Frisian or Dutch or they are bilingual. Given below are some of the places described in the guide.

Dutch	Frisian	Dutch	Frisian
Grouw	*Grou*	*Sloten*	*Sleat*
Hoorn	*Hoarne*	*Twijzel*	*Twizel*
Oudkerk	*Aldtsjerk*	*West-Terschelling*	*West-Skylge*
Rinsumageest	*Rinsumageast*	*Workum*	*Warkum*

★ STAPHORST Overijssel

Pop 13 837

Michelin map 408 J 4

The neighbouring towns of Staphorst and **Rouveen** form a world of their own. The townspeople belong to a strict form of Protestantism, a bastion against the innovations of modern life: thus in 1971 vaccinations were forbidden and even now cars are not allowed to run during Sunday services. Women, young and old alike, wear the traditional costume but refuse to be photographed.

★ **Farmhouses** – The two villages stretch out along the road for over 8km - 5 miles. The thatched hall-type farmhouses are all identical with trimly painted green doors and blue window frames.
Another characteristic of these farmhouses is the line of doors along one of the side walls. On the right side of the farm house the blue shelf for the empty milk cans is often finely carved.

Costume from Staphorst

★ **Costumes** – The very graceful woman's costume is worn quite often. Although rather dark (black shoes, stockings and pleated skirt with a blue or black apron) it is brightened up by a floral bodice-front *(kraplap)* and with a matching bonnet.
A red (blue if in mourning) tartan fichu is sometimes worn over the shoulders. In winter a blue cardigan is worn over the costume.
The older women still wear the head band with spiral antennae *(see Introduction: Colourful Costumes)*. The bonnet is reserved for small girls. When the children come out of school (around noon and 1600) one can see young girls prettily attired in their local costumes pedalling past on their bicycles.

The key on p 2 explains the abbreviations and symbols used in the text or on the maps

TIEL Gelderland

Pop 32 395

Michelin map 408 H 6

Tiel is nicely situated on the banks of the Waal in the centre of a fruit growing region the **Betuwe**; the orchards make a magnificent sight when the trees are in blossom.
Tiel was another of the Dutch towns which belonged to the Hanseatic League.
A harvest thanksgiving procession celebrates the end of the fruit picking *(see Calendar of Events)*.

EXCURSION

Buren and Culemborg – *19km - 12 miles to the northwest.*

Buren – 9 910. This small town hemmed in by its walls has been the object of some quite extensive restoration work. In 1492 it became the seat of a countship which passed to the House of Orange when Anne of Buren married William the Silent.
The old **orphanage** dating from 1613 is a fine building with green and red shutters and a porch with heavy ornamentation. It contains the **Museum der Koninklijke Marechaussee** ⏲ retracing the history of the gendarmerie and police force in the Netherlands. Not far away, part of the curtain wall bordering the river has been turned into a promenade and affords lovely **views** over the river and the Betuwe orchards.
In the main street, Voorstraat, is a **church** with a 15C bell tower crowned by an octagonal Renaissance upper part itself topped out with a pinnacle turret. The **stadhuis**, recognisable by its rococo doorway, was rebuilt in the 18C. Nearby, in a building against the wall, is a small cart museum, **Boerenwagenmuseum** ⏲ *(Achter Boonenburg 1)*.
At the far end of Voorstraat is a brick town **gateway** and a 1716 **wall mill** named after the Prince of Orange.

Culemborg – Pop 22 052. This historic city received its charter in 1318 and became the seat of an earldom in 1555. Some sections of its old city walls still stand. It was the birthplace of **Jan van Riebeeck** (1619-77), who in 1652 founded the Cape Colony (now Cape Town) for the Dutch East India Company as a stopping place on the way to the East Indies. In **Marktplein** the Flamboyant Gothic stadhuis sports heraldic lions above the perron. The **Binnenpoort** is the only gateway to remain.

TILBURG Noord-Brabant Pop 158 846

Michelin map 408 G 7 and 212 fold 7 – Town plan in the current Michelin Red Guide Benelux

The industrial town of Tilburg stands on the banks of the Wilheminakanaal and is a great textile centre and one of the country's largest towns. The Catholic university has Economics, Social Science, Theology and Law faculties.
King William II liked to live in this town and it was here that he died in 1849 thus ending his 9-year reign.

SIGHTS

Stadhuisplein – There are quite a number of recent buildings in Tilburg's main square. The shopping streets leading off to the north are now pedestrian zones.

Stadsschouwburg – The 1961 municipal theatre was the work of the architects Bejvoet and Holt. Glass curtain walls adjoin incurved surfaces of bare brick.

Stadhuis – The sober lines of the black granite-clad town hall were the work of Kraayvanger. This extension was added in 1971 to the old town hall, which was a crenellated building dating from 1849 and was originally built as a residence for King William II.

Nederlands Textielmuseum ⊙ – *Goirkestraat 96, to the north of the railway station.*
This museum gives an interesting presentation of the local textile industry; machines and looms for spinning and weaving, precious and exotic fabrics, materials, lace and tapestries as well as tools used in the cottage industries of the 18C and 19C.

EXCURSIONS

★ **Beekse Bergen** – *4km - 3 miles to the southeast.*
This country park lies to the north of Hilvarenbeek and covers a total area of 425ha - 1 050 acres. It incorporates a small zoo, a safari park and an amusement park.

Safari park ⊙ – This spacious park (100ha - 247 acres) is now home to over 800 animals free to roam at liberty within their enclosures. Lions, rhinoceroses, hyenas, cheetahs, antilopes, zebras and baboons are only some of the residents of the drive-through area. The section with the penguins, flamingos, squirrel monkeys and other rare species can be visited on foot. For the children there is a small **zoo** with a collection of young animals.

Strandpark ⊙ – This amusement park (70ha - 173 acres) centres on a lake where there are various types of craft for hire (pedalos and canoes) and organised boat trips (rondvaartboot); bathing is also permitted. A cable-car (kabelbaan) gives visitors a bird's eye view of the whole park. The trampolines and mini-golf are added attractions.

★ **Oisterwijk** – Pop 18 619. *10km - 6 miles to the east.* This pleasant holiday centre offers a choice of excursions in its immediate vicinity, where wooded dunes, heather clad moors and numerous lakes are to be found. In the town itself the **house** at nos 88-90 Kerkstraat dating from 1633 has an elegant gable. The charming square, **De Lind**, in front of the stadhuis is planted with lime tree to form a marriage way traditionally followed by wedding processions.
Take the Oirschot road to the southeastern outskirts of town and the open-air theatre where there is a bird park, **Vogelpark** ⊙ with numerous exotic birds in a pinewood setting.

★★ UTRECHT Utrecht Ⓟ Pop 231 231

Michelin map 408 G 5 – Local map see UTRECHT: Excursions
Plan of the conurbation (showing motorway network with access roads) in the current Michelin Red Guide Benelux

Utrecht is a religious metropolis – the Catholic primate of the Netherlands lives here – is intellectual due to its university and commercial due to its well-known international trade fair, founded in 1916. Furthermore, it is an important communication network junction.
Every year a Festival of Ancient Music is held here. The Dutch Film Week, held in September, organises screenings of all the films made in Holland during the previous year *(see Calendar of Events)*.

HISTORICAL NOTES

Utrecht was founded at the beginning of our era on the Rhine (now called Oude Rijn), which passed through the town at that time. Under the Roman Empire the town was called Trajectum (ford) from which it gets its present name.
In the 7C it was chosen as the seat of Friesland missions. **St Willibrord** (658-739), a Northumbrian, was made Bishop of the Frisians in 695, settled in Utrecht, Friesland then being considered a dangerous place. He died in Echternach in Luxembourg.
At the time of Charlemagne, who extended his empire northwards, the area became part of the Carolingian Empire. After the Treaty of Meerssen *(p 175)*, Utrecht became a fief of the German emperors. Under their domination, Bishop Balderik (918-976) succeeded in enlarging the bishopric's jurisdiction. Having become very powerful, the bishops extended their sovereignty over the present-day provinces of Utrecht, Overijssel, Drenthe and Groningen: their territory was called the **Sticht**. The town received its charter in 1122 and was surrounded by ramparts (rebuilt 14C).
Born in Utrecht in 1459, **Adrian VI**, tutor to Charles V and then a professor in Louvain (Belgium), was the only Dutch pope (1522-3).
Charles V took possession of the Sticht in 1528. Made an archbishopric by Philip II of Spain in 1559, the bishopric of Utrecht, from that time, covered all the main towns of the area, except 's-Hertogenbosch. However, the town's prosperity was coming to an end as the commercial centre had moved towards the coast.
In 1577 the inhabitants expelled the Spanish garrison.
In 1585, Elizabeth I, after signing the Treaty of Nonsuch, sent Robert Dudley, Earl of Leicester (*c*1532-88), to the Low Countries, to help the United Provinces against Spain. He was appointed Governor and chose to reside in Utrecht.

The Union of Utrecht – In January 1579 the representatives of the states of Holland and Zeeland, and the territories of Groningen and Utrecht, and the stadtholder of Gelderland united to sign the Union of Utrecht; they decided that no separate agreement would be made with Philip II and that the Protestant religion would be the only one authorised in Holland and Zeeland; in the other regions, practice of the Catholic religion would not lead to prosecution. In the same year signatures were added by representatives from Overijssel, Friesland and Drenthe and some southern towns such as Antwerp.
This treaty, following the Union of Arras by which the Duke of Parma had forced the southern states to submit to Spain, was the cause of the split between South and North Low Countries (which later became the United Provinces).

Intellectual Utrecht – In 1635, Descartes stayed in Utrecht *(Maliebaan 36 - 38)* and wrote the *Discourse on Method* which was published in Leyden.
The year 1636 was marked by the founding of Utrecht University, the second in the country after the one in Leyden. James Boswell studied civil law here in 1763-4, following in his father's footsteps.

The schism of the Old Catholics – In the 15C a first schism shook the bishopric of Utrecht, where the chapter had retained the privilege of electing its bishops. In 1423, opposition to a pontifical candidate caused a bitter conflict between the partisans of the two opposing bishops.
In 1702 the Archbishop of Utrecht, Petrus Codde, accused of Jansenism, was dismissed from his duties by the pope. In 1723 the Chapter of Utrecht elected a successor, Cornelis Steenoven, without pontifical agreement. Thus, in 1724, the Old Catholics Church was formed in Utrecht. A large number of French Jansenists, fleeing to the Netherlands after the condemnation of their religion by the papal bull *Unigenitus* in 1717, became members of this independent church with Jansenist tendencies.
In 1870 a group of Germans, refusing the dogma of pontifical infallibility, joined the Church of Old Catholics in Utrecht. In 1889 a great meeting of members of this Church, coming from several countries, took place in Utrecht. This religion is still practised in the Netherlands where it has about 10 000 followers (as well as in the U.S., Switzerland, Germany, Austria...)

The Utrecht School of painting – In the 16C a school of painting with a strong Italian influence developed in Utrecht.

Jan van Scorel (1495-1562) born near Alkmaar, lived in Utrecht, apart from a visit to Italy and a stay in Haarlem *(qv)*. He helped spread the Italian influence in his country; *The Baptism of Christ* (in the Frans Halsmuseum in Haarlem) is one of his best works.

Maarten van Heemskerck *(qv)* his pupil, was also a Romanist painter (16C Northern European artists who were greatly influenced by the Italian Renaissance). Excellent portrait painter *(Portrait of a Young Scholar* in the Museum Boymans-van Beuningen in Rotterdam), Jan van Scorel also had as a pupil **Antoon Mor** (1517-76) who made his career particularly in Spain, under the name of **Antonio Moro**, where he painted with talent the court of Philip II.

In the beginning of the 17C, **Abraham Bloemaert** (1564-1651), born in Gorinchem, passed on his taste for Italian painting to many of his pupils: Hendrick Ter Brugghen or **Terbrugghen** (1588-1629) who, born in Deventer, worked mostly in Utrecht; on his return from Italy he was one of the first to take his inspiration from Caravaggism (those artists greatly influenced by Caravaggio's chiaroscuro), **Gerard van Honthorst** (1590-1656) born in Utrecht, also became, after a visit to Italy, a faithful imitator of Caravaggio; **Cornelis van Poelenburgh** (*c*1586-1667), who painted with precision luminous landscapes scattered with Roman ruins.

One who remained uninfluenced by the problems of chiaroscuro was **Jan Davidsz. de Heem** (1606-1683-4). He was born in Utrecht and lived in Leyden and then in Antwerp, and specialised in the *vanitas* still lifes, especially paintings depicting a table loaded with plates, glasses and dishes of food. His son, Cornelis de Heem, imitated his subjects as well as his sophisticated style.

From the 17C to the present – In the 17C Utrecht was a very important fortified town: a ring of canals, today, marks the course of the fortifications. The town was occupied by the armies of Louis XIV from 1672-4 and in 1712. Prepared in Utrecht's town hall in January 1712, the **Peace of Utrecht** was signed in 1713 in Het Slot van Zeist *(see Excursions)* and brought an end to the Spanish War of Succession which, caused by the accession to the throne of Philip V, Louis XIV's grandson, had broken out in 1701.

In 1806 the King of Holland, Louis Bonaparte, stayed with his court in a private mansion in Utrecht (*at no 31 Drift* – BX).

The famous **Utrecht velvet** with its long strand and embossed ornamentation, used for covering walls, is no longer made in the area. It was a velvet woven with linen, goats' hair (which replaced silk) and cotton.

Utrecht has been expanding since the middle of the century and has many new quarters and buildings. Amongst many achievements there is a very large shopping centre, the Hoog Catharijne, a municipal theatre (1941) by Dudok, the Rietveld Schröderhuis by Rietveld *(qv)* and the Kanaleneiland (or island of canals) quarter to the west near the Amsterdam-Rijnkanaal and the music centre.

There are many statues in the town. Amongst them the *Fountain of the Muses'-Feast* (1959) by J.C. Hekman in front of the theatre, and *Queen Wilhelmina* by Mari Andriessen in Wilhelmina Park (1968). Others are cited in the text on the tour of the town.

The university of Utrecht, which enjoys a vast campus to the east (De Uithof), with approximately 24 000 students, is the largest university in the Netherlands.

One of the better known specialities of Utrecht is the *spritsen*, a type of shortbread biscuit.

Boat trips ⊙ – Boat trips are organised on the city's canals, on the Vecht, Kromme Rijn and the Loosdrecht Lakes. Boats leave from Oudegracht (ABX) and Weerdsluis (AX).

★★ OLD TOWN *half a day*

The very shaded **canals** (Oudegracht and Nieuwe Gracht) of Utrecht's centre are edged by quays which are much lower than the road level, on to which open vaulted cellars.

Vredenburg (AY) – Most of Utrecht's animation is concentrated on this large square which links the old town with the new quarters. The old fortress of Charles V stood here, the foundations having been found during the laying out of the square. A Music Centre (Muziekcentrum) (AY **A**) with an original design by the architect Herzberger has stood here since 1978.

A market takes place on Wednesdays and Saturdays.

To the west, the new **Hoog Catharijne** (AY) shopping centre extends to the station. This vast urban complex includes shopping galleries with air-conditioning in the basement, a large hotel and the **Beatrixgebouw**, the main building of the Exhibition Palace (Jaarbeurs) where there are international fairs and a permanent commercial exhibition.

From Oudegracht bridge, there is a fine **view** over the canal.

★ **Oudegracht** (ABXY) – Narrow, spanned by numerous bridges, this old canal which crosses the town from one end to the other, originally linked the Rhine to the Vecht. It is one of the city's animated centres, both on the upper quays and the lower quays, which are lined with shops and restaurants.

At the point where it forms a bend one can see the **Drakenborch** (BXY **B**), a house rebuilt in 1968 in the old style.

Opposite at no 99, the 14C **Het Oudaen** house (ABY **T**) has a tall façade topped by crenellations.

Cross the first bridge (Jansbrug).

The quay on the opposite side is reserved for pedestrians. One soon has a lovely **view★** of the cathedral's tall Domtoren.

Return to the other quay.

On the bridge, Bakkerbrug, a statue has been raised in honour of Katrijn van Leemput, a heroic Utrecht woman, who distinguished herself fighting against the Spanish in 1577. On this bridge and along Oudegracht there is a flower market on Saturdays.

Pass in front of the stadhuis with its neo-classical façade (1826) which conceals ruins dating from the Middle Ages.

Vismarkt (BY **133**) – This is the old fish market. Several houses have façade stones: a golden falcon, three swords (at no 9), a boat (at no 10).

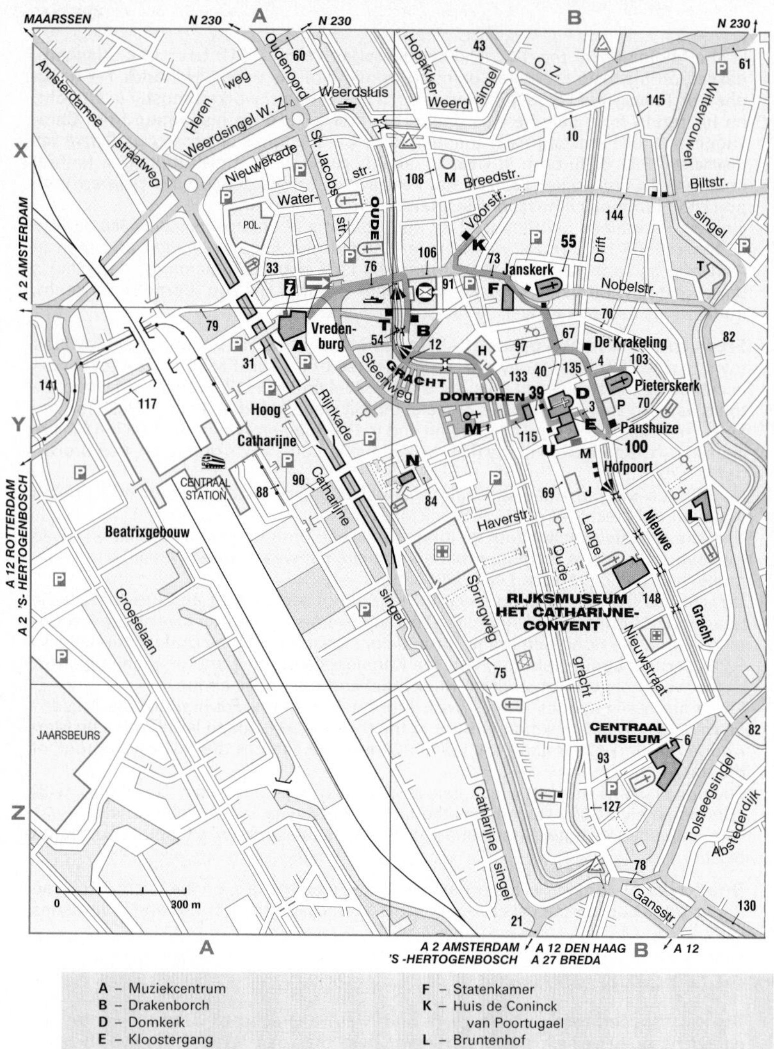

★ **Nationaal Museum van Speelklok tot Pierement** (BY M[1]) ⊙ – Located in the old hall-church, Buurkerk, this Mechanical Musical Instruments Museum (the guide operates several instruments during the tour) presents a magnificent collection of 18 to 20C mechanical musical instruments.

Exhibited are old clocks and music boxes, player pianos and a type of organ which imitates orchestral instruments, similar to the Hupfeld automatic violin (1910). The museum also houses a superb collection of barrel organs *(qv)*, small street organs and enormous fair or dance organs.

★★ **Domtoren** (BY) ⊙ – This bell tower was formerly linked by an arch to the nave of the cathedral, which was destroyed shortly after a church service in 1674, by a hurricane, which also devastated the town. Built between 1321-82 in the Gothic style, restored at the beginning of this century, it influenced many other bell towers in the country, of which it is the highest. Its three recessed floors, the first two are square and of brick, the last, octagonal and of stone, soar up to 112m - 367ft in height. It has a fine carillon, most of the bells having been cast by the Hemony brothers.

From the topmost gallery (465 steps), there is an immense and magnificent **panorama**★★ over the town and the province.

Domplein (BY 39) – This square extends between the Domtoren, and the cathedral remains. A line of paving stones indicate the nave's old layout. In the centre of the square, there is a statue (1887) of Count **John of Nassau**, brother of William the Silent, who presided over the Union of Utrecht.

★ **Domkerk** (BY D) ⊙ – The tall silhouette of its transept stands miraculously preserved, hidden behind it is the chancel. Both are Gothic, built between 1254 and 1517 on the site of St.-Maartenskathedraal, destroyed by fire. The chancel with five chapels radiating round the ambulatory was inspired by that of Tournai Cathedral. Inside there are **funerary monuments**, in particular, in the second chapel, south side of the ambulatory, the black marble tomb of Bishop Guy of Avesnes, who died in 1379.

The organ, built in 1831, is used for concerts.

The title of cathedral is now held by the church, Catharijnekerk (BY).

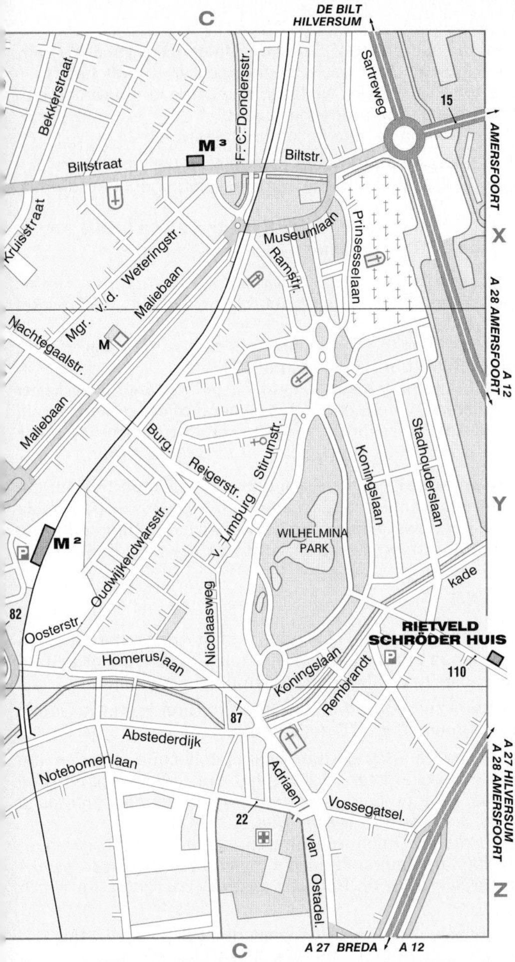

UTRECHT

Lange Viestr. .... AX 76
Nachtegaalstr. .... CY
Oudegracht .... BXYZ
Steenweg .... ABY
Voorstr. .... BX
Vredenburg .... AY

Achter de Dom .... BY 3
Achter St Pieter .... BY 4
Agnietenstr. .... BZ 6
van Asch
van Wijckskade ...... BX 10
Bakkerbrug .... BY 12
Biltsestraatweg .... CX 15
Bleekstr. .... BZ 21
Bosboomstr. .... CZ 22
Catharijnebaan .... AY 3
Catharijnekade .... AX 33
Domplein .... BY 39
Domstr. .... BY 40
Duifstr. .... BX 43
Jansbrug .... ABY 54
Janskerkhof .... BX 55
Kaatstr. .... AX 60
Kleinesingel .... BX 61
Korte Jansstr. .... BY 67
Korte Nieuwstr. .... BY 69
Kromme
Nieuwegracht .... BY 70
Lange Jansstr. .... BX 73
Lange Smeestr. .... BY 75
Ledig Erf .... BZ 78
Leidseveer .... AXY 79
Maliesingel .... BCYZ 82
Mariaplaats .... BY 84
Mecklenburglaan ..... CYZ 87
Moreelselaan .... AY 88
Moreelsepark .... AY 90
Neude .... BXY 91
Nicolaasstr. .... BZ 93
Oudkerkhof .... BY 97
Pausdam .... BY 100
Pieterskerkhof .... BY 103
Pottestr. .... BX 106
Predikherenkerkhof ..... BX 108
Prins Hendriklaan ...... CY 110
Servetstr. .... BY 115
van Sijpesteijnkade ..... AY 117
Twijnstr. .... BZ 127
Venuslaan .... BCZ 130
Vismarkt .... BY 133
Voetiusstr. .... BY 135
Westplein .... AY 141
Wittevrouwenstr. ...... BX 144
Wolvenplein .... BX 145
Zuilenstr. .... BY 148

M1 – Nationaal Museum van Speelklok tot Pierement
M2 – Nederlands Spoorwegmuseum
M3 – Universiteitsmuseum
N – Kloostergang van St-Marie
T – Het Oudaen
U – Rijksuniversiteit

Rijksuniversiteit (BY U) ⊙ – Built at the end of the 19C in the neo-Renaissance style, it incorporates the cathedral's old **chapterhouse** (1409), the present great lecture hall or **Aula**. The Union of Utrecht was signed here. The seven coats of arms on the stained glass windows evoke the provinces and the signatory regions. On the wall seven tapestries woven in 1936 bear the emblems of the various faculties.

Kloostergang (BY E) – A replica of a 10C runic stone from Jelling (Denmark), evoking the conversion of the Danes to christianity, stands at the entrance to the cathedral cloisters. Around the cloisters, the gables over the Flamboyant tracery have low reliefs illustrating the life of St Martin, patron saint of the old cathedral. The **view** of the transept and the apse of the cathedral is very pretty.
To the south of the cloisters there is the old chapterhouse where the Union of Utrecht was signed.

Pausdam (BY 100) – At the junction of two canals, this is a peaceful square where the **Paushuize** (BY) stands. This house, intended for Pope *(paus)* Adrian VI was only completed in 1523, the year of his death. On the left side there is a statue of Christ.

Nieuwe Gracht (BY) – Similar to the Oudegracht, the new canal is also lined by elegant residences. One can see Hofpoort (BY), a 17C baroque doorway of the Law Courts, and at nos 35 and 37, lovely old houses.
Further on, at no 63, is the Het Catharijneconvent.
From the bridge, a fine **view** over the canal and Domtoren can be had.

Pieterskerk (BY) ⊙ – Assigned since 1656 to the Walloon Protestant cult, this interesting Romanesque church was built in 1048. Pieterskerk is one of the four churches in the shape of a cross which Bishop **Bernulphus** wished to build round the cathedral. Two of these churches have disappeared: abbey church of St.-Paulusabdij and St.-Mariakerk, where only the cloisters remain. The two others, Pieterskerk and Janskerk are all that remain of the famous **Bernulphus's Cross.**
The vaults in the transept are Gothic, but the nave in pure Romanesque style is roofed by a wooden barrel vault held up by ten red sandstone columns with plain capitals. Some of the columns have been moved to the end of the church and replaced by copies. The raised chancel is built over the crypt. Four **low reliefs**★ (*c*1170), found during the church's restoration, are embedded in the wall in front

of the chancel. They concern the Judgment of Christ by Pilate, his death and resurrection. The Romanesque baptismal font has corners decorated with heads. In the chapel towards the left, which has oven vaulting, one can see the remains of Romanesque frescoes: the Virgin on the moon's crescent.
Concerts ⏲ are given on the new organ at the far end of the church.

★ **Crypt** – The groined vaulting leans on stout fluted columns. In the apse there is a red sandstone sarcophagus which contains the remains of Bishop Bernulphus, founder of the church.
At no 8, on the corner of Achter St.-Pieter and Keistraat, there is a lovely house, **De Krakeling** (BY), with a façade (17C) of garlands.

Janskerkhof (BX 55) – On this square stands **Janskerk** (BX) a restored Gothic church, and several elegant 17 and 18C houses, notably no 13. A flower market takes place here on Saturdays.
A small emblazoned building adjoins the church. In front of it is the **statue of Anne Frank** *(qv)* by Pieter d'Hont, sculptor born in Utrecht in 1917.
To the south of the square the Anatomy Institute is in the old restored **Statenkamer** (BX F) (former Franciscan cloisters), where the States General of the province met. In front one can see the statue of Professor Donders *(qv)* and further on the **statue of St Willibrord** by A. Termote (1887-1978), Dutch sculptor of Belgian origin.

Huis De Coninck van Poortugael (BX K) – Dating from 1619, the House of the King of Portugal has a charming Renaissance façade with a crow-stepped gable and above the ground floor, windows display the coat of arms of Nijmegen *(qv)* and Portugal around a man brandishing a sceptre, probably the King of Portugal.

ADDITIONAL SIGHTS

★★ **Centraal Museum** (BZ) ⏲ – Housed in the old convent of St Agnes, the museum houses a rich section of paintings and decorative arts relating to Utrecht and its surroundings. The museum hosts several important temporary exhibitions.

Ground floor – Visitors can admire six rooms with ancient furniture, from the Gothic to the Louis XVI style, and an interesting 17C dolls house.

Mezzanine and former stables – The Van Baaren (mezzanine) collection includes late 19 to early 20C Dutch and French artists. To be noted are: J.B. Jongkind *(Full Moon)*, Van Gogh *(Underbrush)*, Fantin-Latour (portrait), Daubigny *(Iles Vierges at Bezons)*, J. Maris *(Five Mills)*, and I. Israëls *(At the Beach, c*1915).
Modern art (former stables) – mainly Dutch – encompasses the De Stijl *(qv)* movement to the present. Rietveld's armchairs, P. Koch's mysterious canvases, works by members of CoBrA and a few of Bram Bogart's abstract paintings are worth admiring.

1st floor – Devoted mainly to ancient art, this floor includes Primitives to the 18C with painters from the Utrecht School (Jan van Scorel, Abraham Bloemaert) and Caravaggists (Terbrugghen – *The Calling of St Matthew* – Gerard van Honthorst). Several rooms are reserved for prints, drawings and silverware.
The costume gallery offers a brief presentation of fashion, from the mid-18C to the present day.

2nd floor – The attic has an archaeological section with objects found in excavations dating from Roman and Carolingian times, and a historical part relating to Utrecht's medieval past (churches, walls) or the Golden Age (ceremonial entry of Maurice of Nassau in 1635).
The Muntenkabinet exhibits a rich collection of coins and medals.
In the basement, the **Utrecht boat** (c1100) is worth seeing, a small craft of about 13 metric tons discovered in 1930.
Part of the museum, the **Van Renswoude Foundation**, built in 1756 as a school for orphans, has an imposing baroque façade on Agnietenstraat.
Opposite, there is a fine group of low brick houses belonging to an almshouse, **Hofje van Pallaes** (1561). Next to it is another almshouse, **Beyerskameren**, founded at the end of the 16C.

Centraal Museum, Utrecht

Christ's Entry into Jerusalem (central section from the Lochorst Triptych)
by Jan van Scorel, Collectie Centraal Museum, Utrecht

★★ **Rijksmuseum Het Catharijneconvent** (BY) ⏲ – The old convent of St J of Malta contains collections of sacred art from Utrecht's Archiepiscopal Museu Haarlem's Episcopal Museum and the Old Catholics Museum. The collections evoke Christianity in the Netherlands from its beginnings to the present. The **medieval art** section is the most important in the Netherlands.

The stages marking the evolution of Catholic and Protestant churches are shown in their historical context. Various themes are evoked: the churches (construction, style, decorative elements), the religious universe and the works of art it inspired, the different ceremonies, the role taken by faith in daily life, the relationship between the Church and the State.

Amongst the collections there are: altarpieces, gold and silversmiths' work, liturgical garments (15C cope of David of Burgundy), sculptures (*Christ in bonds*, of 1500, is particularly expressive), manuscripts and minatures (the gospel-book of St Lebuinus incrusted with ivory and semi-precious stones), paintings (*Christ as Man of Sorrows* by Geertgen tot Sint Jans, the triptych of Jan van Scorel, the *Portrait of Stenius* by Frans Hals).

Nederlands Spoorwegmuseum (CY M2) ⏲ – The former Maliebaan Station is the setting for the Dutch Railway Museum.

Inside, paintings, documents and scale models reconstitute the history of the Dutch railways. Scale models and a film give an idea of present railway traffic. Outside on the tracks, no longer used, there are, in particular, shining steam engines and trams. One can see the reproduction of the engine *De Arend* (the eagle) which in 1839 with another engine *(De Snelheid)* drew the first train to run in the Netherlands, between Amsterdam and Haarlem.

Universiteitsmuseum (CX M3) ⏲ – *Biltstraat 166.*

The University Museum assembles an interesting collection of **old instruments** formerly used by members of the university: astrolabes and sundials, air pumps, surgical instruments...

Through documents it also evokes distinguished members of the university like the physician **Frans Cornelis Donders** (1818-89), who researched and diagnosed the problems of the eye – short-sightedness, long-sightedness and astigmatism; the quarrel between Descartes and **Voetius** (1589-1676) a Protestant theologian who was professor at the university, and the meteorologist Buys Ballot (1817-90).

Bruntenhof (BY L) – This picturesque line of low houses forms part of a 1621 **almshouse**. The main entrance has a baroque portal.

Kloostergang van St.-Marie (ABY N) – Only the Romanesque cloisters in brick remain of this church built in the 11C, one of the four churches of Bernulphus's Cross *(see Pieterskerk)* which was destroyed in the 19C.

Ph. Gajic/MICHELIN

Rietveld Schröderhuis, Utrecht

★★ **Rietveld Schröderhuis** (CY) ⏲ – Restored after the owner's death (Mrs Schröder, in 1985), this house, built in 1924, illustrates perfectly the architectural theories of the De Stijl movement to which Gerrit Rietveld (1888-1964) belonged.

In response to Mrs Schröder's demands, she attached a great deal of importance to communicating with nature (every room has a door to the outside), Rietveld created an open plan where the different elements placed at right angles determined the space. Breaking away from the traditional house, Rietveld limited himself to neutral tones – white and grey – for the large surfaces and primary colours for the linear details.

Visiting the interior enables one to appreciate the originality of the layout both simple and clever. On the ground floor the rooms are clearly divided while, the 1st floor is a vast open space with sliding partitions to close off the living room and bedrooms.

SIONS

; 59 357. *10km - 6 miles. Leave Utrecht by Biltsestraatweg* (**CX 15**).
…harming and elegant holiday resort nestling among lush woods. In the … the town, a path leads to **Het Slot van Zeist**, built in 1677 and used as a venue for temporary exhibitions. On either side of the path stand the buildings which house the **Moravian Brotherhood** community.

The sect was reinstated in the early 18C by the Count of Zinzerdorf. On his land in Germany he had sheltered the Moravian Brotherhood (or Bohemian Brotherhood) refugees from Moravia and Bohemia and disciples of Jean Hus, burned at the stake in 1415. The members of this sect are dedicated to the mystical adoration of God and Christ, preach fraternity among all men and live in a community. There exist around 430 000 representatives of this sect throughout the world.

★★ **Loosdrechtse Plassen** – *Round tour of 70km - 43 1/2 miles – allow 1 day – local map below. Leave Utrecht by Sartreweg* (**CX**).

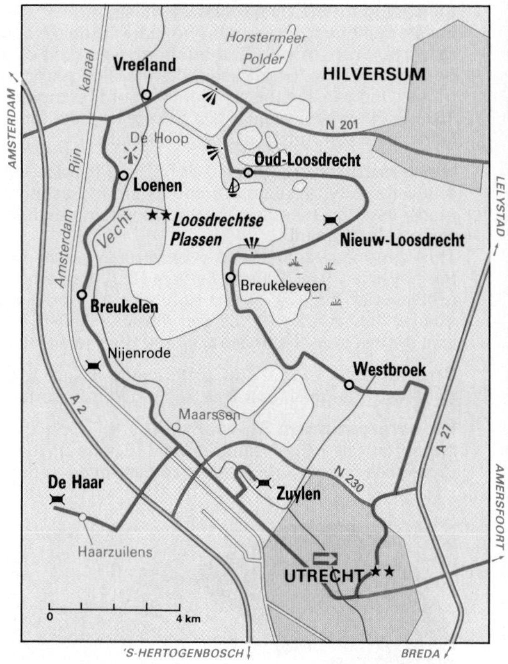

Westbroek – The picturesque route is edged by canals spanned by small bridges, each one leading to a house surrounded by a charming garden.

Set between verdant strips of land bathed in soft sunlight, the **Loosdrechtse Plassen★★** cover more than 2 500ha - 6 175 acres producing a rather silent end desolate landscape.

These lakes are flooded peat workings. Particularly favourable for water sports, they are served by numerous pleasure boat harbours.

The road is lined with villas.

After **Breukeleveen** one goes along the lake's edge; there is a fine **view**.

Nieuw-Loosdrecht - Kasteel Sypesteyn ⊙ rebuilt from 1912 to 1927 on the original plans, has been converted into a museum. Displayed inside are furniture, family portraits painted by N. Maes and C. Troost, old *objets d'art* and, in particular, Loosdrecht porcelain.

The castle is surrounded by a charming park (rose garden, orchard, maze).

Oud-Loosdrecht – This is the main tourist centre in the region. It has a large pleasure boat harbour.

Turn right then left towards Vreeland.

The road soon returns to the water; it has lovely **views**.

Vreeland – An attractive **lever bridge** makes it possible to cross the Vecht, which one subsequently rejoins at Loenen aan de Vecht. The **Vecht**, formerly a great navigation way, since 1952, is doubled by the canal (Amsterdam-Rijnkanaal) from the Rhine to Amsterdam.

The road runs along this peaceful and winding river, on whose banks are charming villas and small manor houses surrounded by magnificent parks.

Loenen – Pop 8 270. This small town with trim and flowered houses has a tall stage mill, with a handrail, called De Hoop (hope).

Breukelen – Pop 13 822. In the 17C this locality gave its name to a quarter in New York founded by Dutch settlers: Breukelen, pronounced in English as Brooklyn.

To the south of Breukelen, there is a pleasant **route★** which offers views of lovely estates along the Vecht.

To the right of the road the 17C **Kasteel Nijenrode** was restored at the beginning of the 20C. The castle and its estate are now the seat of Nijenrode University, the Netherlands Business School.

Kasteel De Haar ⊙ – It stands to the west of **Haarzuilens** in the middle of a large park. This castle is an enormous 14 and 15C brick construction. It was burnt by Louis XIV's troops in 1672-3, then rebuilt by Cuypers, as from 1892 in the original style. The main building, with pepperpot roof towers, is surrounded by wide moats and linked to a large entrance fort by a covered bridge.

The interior, which is still inhabited in summer, contains the exceptional **collections★** of Baron van Zuylen van Nyevelt, notably lovely old furnishings, 16 and 17C tapestries, Persian carpets, paintings and ceramics.

In the main hall there is a 14C *Virgin and Child*.

Return to Haarzuilens, cross over the motorway and the canal, then turn right, then left to reach Oud-Zuilen.

Slot Zuylen ⏲ – Situated near the Vecht at **Oud-Zuilen**, this **castle** is a solid medieval construction flanked by four octagonal towers. In the 18C it was enlarged with two wings. Belle van Zuylen was born here in 1740, better known under the name of **Belle de Charrière**. This famous woman of letters, who wrote in French, a friend of Madame de Stael, Benjamin Constant and the diarist and biographer James Boswell *(Life of Johnson)*, spent her childhood in the castle. After her marriage in 1766 she lived near Neuchâtel in Switzerland where she died in 1805. The castle houses ancient objects illustrating the daily life of the past, lovely furniture and a Chinese porcelain collection.

One room is decorated with a large tapestry (1643) woven in Delft and depicting a landscape with a multitude of birds.

In the rooms where Belle de Charrière lived, a portrait of her by a Danish artist, a few books and engravings evoke the life of the writer.

Return to Utrecht by Amsterdamsestraatweg (AX).

To plan a special itinerary:

– consult the **Map of Touring Programmes** ***which indicates the tourist regions, the recommended routes, the principal towns and main sights***

– read the descriptions in the **Sights** ***section which include Excursions from the main tourist centres***

Michelin Maps nos 408 and 212 indicate scenic routes, places of interest, viewpoints, rivers, forests ...

★ VALKENBURG Limburg — Pop 18 116

Michelin map 408 I 9 or 212 fold 1 – Local map see below

VALKENBURG

Street	Grid
Berkelstr.	Z 3
Grendelpl.	Z 7
Grotestr.	Z 9
Louis van der Maessenstr.	Y 18
Muntstr.	Z 19
Plenkertstr.	YZ
Theodoor Dorrenpl.	Y 28
Wilhelminalaan	YZ
Dr. Erensstr.	Y 4
Emmalaan	Y 6
Halderstr.	Z 10
Hekerbeekstr.	Y 12
Jan Dekkerstr.	Y 13
Kerkstr.	Z 15
Kloosterweg	Y 16
Oranjelaan	Y 21
Palankastr.	Z 22
Poststr.	Y 24
Prinses Margrietlaan	Y 25
Sittarderweg	Y 27
Walrampl.	Z 30
Walravenstr.	Z 31

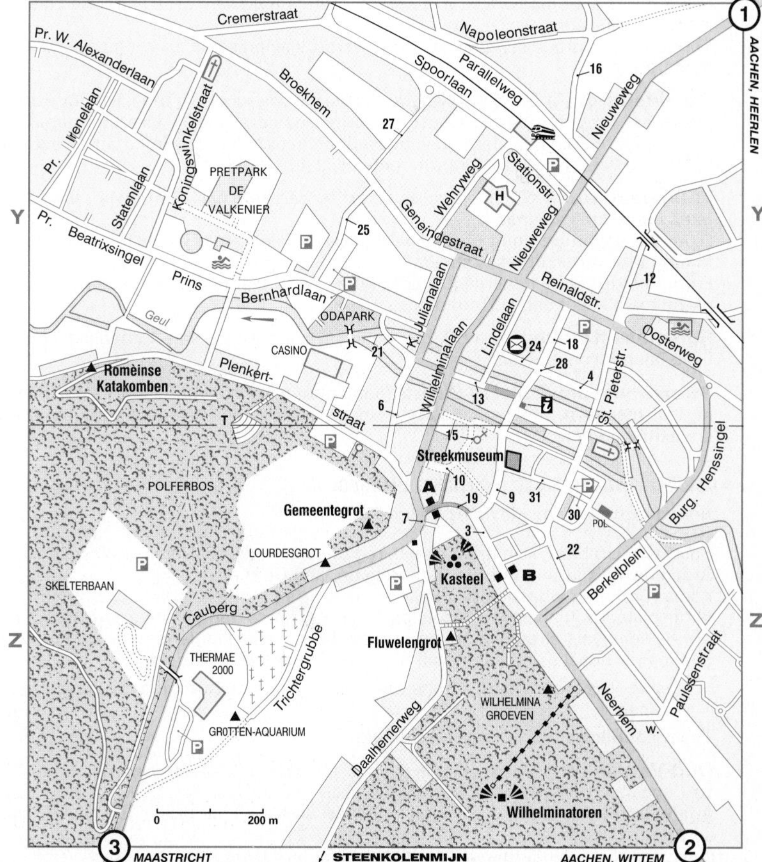

Valkenburg is situated in the charming Geul Valley, between two branches of the river, a very old, little town, it belongs to the district borough of Valkenburg-Houthem.
It is much frequented in the summer by holidaymakers attracted by the gentle hills surrounding its fine parks and its other attractions.
The town has preserved two fortified gateways: 14C **Grendelpoort** (Z **A**) and 15C **Berkelpoort** (Z **B**) with its footbridge.

The caves – Marl stone, a sort of limestone, predominates in the surrounding hilly countryside as at St.-Pietersberg not far from Maastricht. Marl stone has been quarried locally for centuries for its qualities as a building stone. A certain number of these caves and galleries *(70 km - 44 miles)* can now be visited and quite a number have been transformed into museums or other tourist attractions.

SIGHTS

Kasteel-Ruïne (Z) ⊙ – The ruins of the castle of the Lords of Valkenburg dominate the city. Only parts of walls and broken arches still remain of this fortress. It was built in *c*1087 and was altered in the Gothic period. It was subjected to a great number of sieges; notably by the Count of Louvain (1122).
Louis XIV captured it in May 1672. It was taken back in December and razed to the ground the following year by order of the King-Statdholder William III.
Many legends are attached to the ruins, such as that of Walram and Reginald of Valkenburg, who were in love with Alix, the daughter of the Count of Juliers. Walram married Alix but the young couple was assassinated by Reginald.
From the top of the ruins there is a view over the town and the Geul Valley.

★ **Steenkolenmijn Valkenburg** ⊙ – *Access from Daalhemerweg* (Z).
A coal mine has been reconstituted in the galleries of an old quarry. The visit provides information on the methods of coal extraction as practised in Limburg before the last workings were closed.
A film provides a realistic picture of a coal mine. Then walk along the galleries to see: the trains for the transportation of miners or coal, the water pumps, the tunnel with the working coal face, with portable shaft supports, the evacuation of the coal and the different security systems.

Gemeentegrot (Z) ⊙ – These are ancient marl quarries which were already known to the Romans. They were used by non-juring priests during the French Revolution and sheltered the population in time of war, notably in September 1944 on the town's liberation.
The sedimentary marl stone contains many fossils. The caves remain at a constant temperature of 14°C-57°F. The walls are covered with charcoal drawings and low reliefs, some representing the animals whose fossils have been found, such as the Mosasaurus *(see Maastricht: Excursions)*; others represent artistic (Mona Lisa) or religious subjects.
The stone was gradually quarried downwards, leaving some drawings placed very high up.

Fluwelengrot (Z) ⊙ – This system of caves is connected to the castle by secret passages. They are named after their former owner, Fluwijn. Like the municipal caves, they are old quarries which housed refugees, who have left many drawings and low reliefs. Their temperature remains at 10°C-50°F.

Wilhelminatoren (Z) ⊙ – *Access either by car from Daalhemerweg, then turn left by chairlift* (kabelbaan).
From the departure point of the chairlift, **caves** (Panorama-Grot) can be visited. A film on Prehistoric times is shown.
From the top of the tower (160 steps), 30m - 98 1/2 feet high, there is a good view of the town's wooded surroundings.

Romeinse Katakomben (Y) ⊙ – In the old quarries a dozen Roman catacombs have been reconstructed.

Streekmuseum (Z **M**) ⊙ – Objects found during excavations of the castle, paintings of the town, reconstructed workshops, mementoes of shooting companies are exhibited here.

★ ZUID-LIMBURG (SOUTHERN LIMBURG)

Round tour of 58km - 36 miles – about 1/2 day

Southern Limburg is a transitional region between the Dutch plains and the Ardennes hills jutting out between Belgium and Germany.
It is a rural area whose appearance is not marred by the region's coal mines. Its fertile plateaux, lush valleys, its fields shaded by apple trees, its hilltops from which can be seen vast stretches of countryside, form a pleasant landscape dotted with fine manor houses and white half-timbered farms *(see Introduction)*.

Leave Valkenburg by ② on the town plan, going eastwards in the direction of Gulpen.

The road follows the verdant Geul Valley.

Oud-Valkenburg – On the left is the fine 17C **Kasteel Schaloen**, restored in the 19C by Cuypers. The park is watered by a branch of the Geul.
A little farther on, behind a chapel, is **Kasteel Genhoes**, built in the 16 and 18C and surrounded by moats.
After Wijlre, notice on the left **Cartils Kasteel**, in the middle of a fine park.

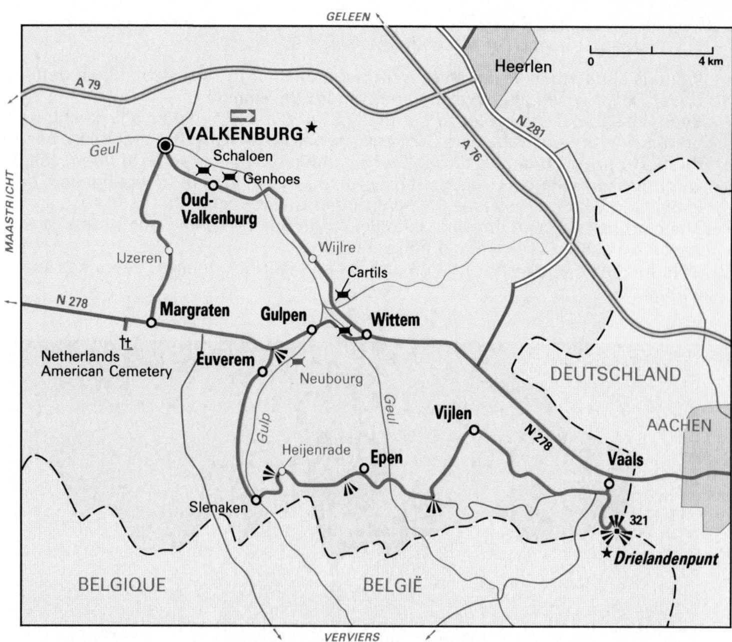

Wittem – Pop 7 769. On the right, the **Kasteel Wittem** is a 15C building, restored in the 19C in the neo-Gothic style. It is now a hotel-restaurant.

A road over the plateau leads to Vaals.

Vaals – Pop 10 781. A resort which owes its animation to the proximity of the German frontier and Drielandenpunt.

A winding road climbs through the woods to Drielandenpunt. 500m - 1/2 mile before the end of the road, on the left, there is a fine **panorama★** of Aachen (Aix-la-Chapelle).

★ **Drielandenpunt** – It is the meeting point *(punt)* of three *(drie)* countries' *(landen)* frontiers: Germany, Belgium and the Netherlands. It is also the highest point in the Netherlands being at 321m - 1 053ft.

From the top of **Boudewijntoren** (a metal building) ⏲ there is a **panorama★** over the region, Aachen close by, Germany's Eifel Forests, and in the distance, towards the west, Maastricht.

Return towards Vaals and go to Vijlen.

Vijlen – This village still has many half-timbered houses.

By a road through the woods one reaches the road from Vaals to Epen: pretty **view** over the hills to the south.

Epen – Resort where several houses still have half-timbered walls.

Before reaching the church, turn left.

A fine half-timbered farmhouse can be seen on leaving the village.

The climb gives fine **views★** over the frontier hills to the south.

After Heijenrade there is a fine **view** on the right over Gulp Valley which one crosses at **Slenaken**, a small frontier village.

Then follow the river towards Gulpen. This is a pleasant drive through a landscape of lush fields.

Euverem – In pools near the Gulp nearly 500 000 trout are raised every year. Some of them are sent to neighbouring fish ponds.

At the junction of the road from Gulpen to Maastricht, there is a **view** on the right of Kasteel Neubourg. It lies at the bottom of a valley and is a vast building flanked by a square tower with an onion-shaped dome; it is now a hotel.

Gulpen – Pop 7 334. A resort at the confluence of the Gulp and the Geul.

Margraten – Pop 13 463. At the west of town lies the **Netherlands American Military Cemetery**, which was laid out in 1944 by the American Army. On the left of the entrance a small museum retraces the episodes of the war. On the walls the names of the 1 722 missing are engraved.

In the cemetery, dominated by a tall tower (chapel inside) lie the graves of 8 301 soldiers marked out by crosses placed in a semi-circle; these soldiers fell during the breakthrough of the Siegfried Line.

Return to Valkenburg through IJzeren and Sibbe over the plain, entering by Daalhemerweg.

The main through routes are clearly indicated on all town plans

★ VEERE Zeeland Pop 4 910

Michelin map 408 B 7 or 212 south of fold 2 – Local map see DELTA
Town plan in the current Michelin Red Guide Benelux

Veere is situated on **Veerse Meer**, a former branch of the sea closed by a dam *(see under Delta)* which links Walcheren to Noord-Beveland.

Veere was under the protection of the Lord of Borsele and was a flourishing port because of its wool trade with Scotland – it was in the early 16C that Veere became the port on the continent through which staple goods (exports of linen, salt and wool) passed. The port was gradually ruined by the War of Independence. Veere is twinned with Culross *(see Michelin Green Guide Scotland)*.

The dam has stopped any access to the North Sea by fishing boats, so Veere has become a sailing centre and a holiday resort.

With its paved alleyways, its monuments and its brick houses, Veere has kept its character.

Veere

Van der Leeden/RENFLUX PRESS B.V.

Campveerse Toren – This 15C tower is part of the town's old fortifications. It is built of brick and decorated with bands of white stone and has a crow-stepped gable. It is now a restaurant.

★ **Schotse Huizen** ⊙ – *Nos 25 and 27 on the quay (Kade).* Built in the 16C in the Gothic Flamboyant style, these two buildings were used as offices and warehouses by the Scottish wool merchants who lived in Veere. The tympana of the windows and doors are richly decorated. At no 25 the façade stone represents a lamb, symbol of the wool trade; at no 27 it shows an ostrich.

Inside there are Zeeland costumes, porcelain and furniture, including a *sterrekabinet* encrusted with designs of stars *(p 31)*. In a fine Gothic room there are the original statues of the lords and ladies of Veere, which once decorated the stadhuis.

★ **Oude Stadhuis** ⊙ – This is a charming little two storey Gothic building made of sandstone. It was started in 1474. The openings on the 1st floor are separated by recesses surmounted by canopies, under which are statues, remade in 1934, of four lords and three ladies of Veere.

The roof is flanked with octagonal turrets and dominated by a 1591 onion-shaped belfry, crowned with a balustrade with pinnacles and small columns. Inside there is a **carillon** ⊙ of 48 bells.

In the audience chamber "Rechtszaal" on the ground floor, one of the oldest in the Netherlands, there is the silver gilt goblet which Emperor Charles V gave to Count Maximilian of Buren in 1546. The portraits displayed in the Council Chamber depict marquis and marchionesses from Veere, members of the house of Orange-Nassau.

Grote- of O.L.Vrouwekerk ⊙ – A massive 14C structure, in front of which stands a large tower-porch, which was never completed.

Next to the church is the **municipal fountain**, a lovely Gothic monument of 1551, composed of an octagonal rotunda with diagonal arches and small columns.

The length of time given in this guide

– for touring allows time to enjoy the views and the scenery

– for sightseeing is the average time required for a visit

VENLO Limburg — Pop 64 392

Michelin map 408 J 7 or 212 fold 20
Plan of the conurbation in the current Michelin Red Guide Benelux

In the northern part of the province of Limburg, near the German-Dutch frontier, Venlo is a small industrial town on the banks of the Maas.

HISTORICAL NOTES

A legend of the Middle Ages gives 90AD as the date of Venlo's foundation by Valuas, chief of a Germanic tribe, the Bructeri. The name of the town's founder is commemorated at all the celebrations, parades and processions; the effigies of two giants representing Valuas and his wife are carried through the town.
Venlo was prosperous in the Middle Ages and was given city rights in 1343. In 1364 it became a member of the Hanseatic League.
Today it is the centre of a large market gardening area (asparagus, mushrooms, flowers, tomatoes, gherkins), which stretches north to the outskirts of Grubbenvorst. The town's immediate surroundings are covered with hothouses.
The carnival *(see Calendar of Events)* is a very lively one.

Boat trips ⏲ – Boat trips are organised on the Maas. Landing stage: Maaskade (Y).

SIGHTS

Stadhuis (Y H) – In the middle of Markt, the town hall is a fine quadrilateral Renaissance building (*c*1600).

St.-Martinuskerk (Y) ⏲ – Dating from the beginning of the 15C, it was damaged during the last war but has been restored and its tower, which has a carillon of 48 bells, rebuilt. The interior has interesting **furnishings★** and *objets d'art.*
The 15C Gothic **stalls** are carved to represent about twenty scenes of the Old and New Testaments; the misericords are decorated with various subjects (heads, evangelist symbols, foliage, proverbs, fables, etc. On the left of the triumphal arch note a 16C *Virgin and Child;* on the right a 17C Christ; in the chancel of Sacraments, north of the high altar, a carved 16C oak bench; in the chancel of Our Lady on the right of the high altar, a 15C limestone *Pietà* and an *Ecce Homo* painted by Jan van Cleef, a painter born in Venlo (1646-1716). The pulpit is baroque. A beautiful brass **baptismal font**, dating from 1621, stands at the back of the south side aisle.

In the same street (Grote Kerkstraat), at nos 19-21, there is the interesting façade of the **Schreurs House** (Y A) built in the Renaissance style (1588), topped by a voluted gable; on the 1st floor, blind arcades lean on two corbels carved with the head of a lion; note also the carved coat of arms and the medallions.

Goltziusmuseum (Y M^1) ⏲ – This regional museum deals with archaeology, history and art.
The ground floor is devoted to Prehistory, the Roman occupation and the town's history.
The 1st floor exhibits decorative arts. These are also collections of silverware, pewter, coins and weapons. The museum also organises temporary exhibitions.

Museum van Bommel-van Dam (Z M^2) ⏲ – On the edge of Juliana Park, it is a pleasant modern and contemporary Dutch art museum which mainly holds temporary exhibitions.

Romerhuis (Z B) – A 16C house with crow-stepped gable and pinnacles.

VENLO

Street	Grid
Gasthuisstr.	Y 12
Grote Kerkstr.	Y 16
Klaasstr.	Z 24
Koninginnesingel	Z 27
Lomstr.	Y 31
Parade	Z
Sint-Jorisstr.	Y 51
Vleesstr.	Z
Eindhovenstr.	Z 9
Goltziusstr.	Y 13
Grote Beekstr.	Z 15
Havenkade	Z 18
Koninginnepl.	Z 25
Nassaustr.	Z 36
Peperstr.	Y 39
Prinsessesingel	Z 42
Prof. Gelissensingel	Z 43
Puteanusstr.	Y 45
Roermondsepoort	Z 46
Roermondsestr.	Z 48

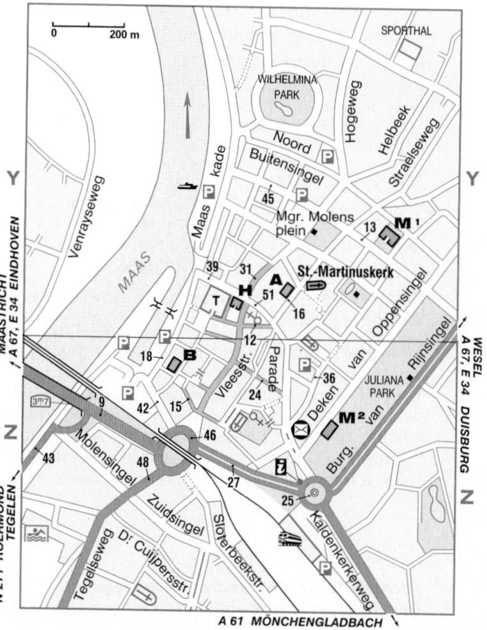

EXCURSION

Tegelen – Pop 19 101. *4km - 2 1/2 miles to the southwest by Prof. Gelissensingel* (Z **43**). This is a small industrial town well-known for its **Passion Plays** (Passiespelen) enacted every five years with all the population taking part *(see Calendar of Events.* Tegelen has the **Museum Steyl** ⏲, *St Michaëlstraat 7.* Housed in the buildings of a missionary community, it contains artefacts from Indonesia, New Guinea, the Far East, Africa, Chinese *objets d'art,* butterflies and stuffed animals from all over the world.
Not far from the museum *(Maashoek 2 b, Steijl),* there is a botanical garden, **Jochum-Hof** ⏲. It is an open-air garden with plants from the north of Limburg and a tropical hothouse (cacti, orchids, banana trees).

VENRAY Limburg

Pop 34 414

Michelin map 408 I 7 or 212 south of fold 10

On Grote Markt, **St.-Petrus Bandenkerk** ⏲, a large Gothic church, contains some interesting furnishings. Apart from the baroque pulpit note a fine late 15C brass lectern and a remarkable series of wooden **statues** and the one in stone of St Paul; the oldest is of St James (15C). The Apostles, with their attributes, stand against the pillars of the nave. In the aisles there is a series of saints (a beautiful St Lucy) which come from old altars no longer in existence. At the entrance there is a baroque statue of St Peter, shown as pope.

EXCURSION

Overloon – *7km - 4 miles to the north.* For three weeks in the autumn of 1944 the British and Americans fought a battle round this village to support the Operation Market Garden *(qv),* one of the biggest tank battles of the war, often compared to the one at Caen because of the terrible artillery bombardment and the number of tanks involved.
The National War and Resistance Museum, **Nederlands Nationaal Oorlogs- en Verzetsmuseum** is to the east of Overloon in the woods where the fighting occured.
A signposted route is marked out in this 14ha - 34 1/2 acre enclosure to display the large collection (70 items) of German and Allied material which remains from the battle: tanks, planes, one-man submarine, a complete V1, a pocket submarine, guns, landmines, bombs, torpedoes, etc.
One then reaches a building with a gallery of hand guns and a large amount of graphic documentation about the Netherlands during the war.
In a building devoted to concentration camps (Kampengebouw), a standing exhibition illustrates the tragic plight of the victims through photographs, films, documents and various other objects.

VLISSINGEN (FLUSHING) Zeeland

Pop 44 179

Michelin map 408 B 7 and 212 fold 12 – Local map see DELTA

The only large maritime port at the mouth of the Scheldt, Flushing became important in the 14C on account of its commercial activities and herring fishing industry. Philip II embarked here in 1559 when he finally left the Low Countries for Spain. From 1585 to 1616 the town was pledged to the English as a guarantee of the costs incurred by the Earl of Leicester's army to uphold the United Provinces after the assassination of William the Silent.

Admiral de Ruyter (1607-1674), born in Flushing, distinguished himself during the third war against England (1672-4) and was fatally wounded during a battle near Syracuse. The French draughtsman **Constantin Guys** (1802-1892), nicknamed "the painter of modern life" by the poet Charles Baudelaire, was also a native of Flushing.

The town today – Flushing, which commands the entry to the Walcheren canal, is both a fishing port and an industrial centre with large naval shipyards. Warships are moored here. A maritime terminal runs a car ferry service towards England (Sheerness) and Flemish Zeeland (Breskens).
Flushing also has a Naval College.

Boat trips ⏲ – Flushing is the starting-point for boat trips along the coast of Walcheren Peninsula.

The Boulevard – The town's sea front is a long avenue flanked by an esplanade known as the Boulevard.
The 15C **Gevangentoren** or Prison Tower stands here. Down below stretches a wide beach sheltered from northern winds. At the far end of the boulevard, on an old bastion built by Charles V, note the little lighthouse and the statue of Admiral de Ruyter. From there one has a nice **view** of the port below and the **Old Exchange** of 1635, a fine building with green shutters surmounted by a pinnacle.

★ VOLENDAM Noord-Holland Pop 24 839 (with Edam)

Michelin map 408 G4

Volendam stands on a small land-locked sea, Gouwzee. It is equipped for eel fishing and is one of the best known ports of the old Zuiderzee. Its inhabitants wear the traditional costume in summer which has become Netherlands' symbol abroad. Tourism is, also, an important activity of Volendam.

Village – The long street, which runs along the top of the high dike, is just a line of shops, but behind and below the dike there are picturesque narrow alleyways winding between small brick houses with wooden gables.

★ **Traditional costume** – The men wear black trousers with silver buttons, short jackets over striped shirts, and round caps. The women's costume consists of a black skirt with a striped apron or a striped skirt with a black apron, a shirt with a flowered front under a black short sleeved overblouse, a necklace of large coral beads with a gold clasp, hidden in winter by a blue and white shawl. When they are not wearing a pointed black bonnet they wear a lace cap for feast days, very tall with turned up wings, whose shape is famous. Men and women wear clogs or buckled shoes. Visitors should watch the congregation leaving after morning or evening service on Sundays or feast days when the couples cross the little wooden bridge in front of the Catholic church.

★★ WADDENEILANDEN (WADDEN ISLANDS)

Michelin map 408 F2, 3, G2, H1, I1, J1 – Local map see overleaf

In the north of the country between the North Sea and the Waddenzee lie the Wadden Islands: **Texel** (province of Noord-Holland), the **Frisian Islands** of which the main ones are Vlieland, Terschelling, Ameland and Schiermonnikoog; and two smaller islands belonging to the province of Groningen; Rottumeroog and Rottumerplaat, which before 1950 were sometimes under water.

The formation of the islands and the Waddenzee – The islands, formed during the Tertiary Era and were subsequently modified, especially on Texel, by the movement of large Scandinavian glaciers which covered the north of Europe in the Quaternary Era. But the Wadden Islands are, above all, along with the German and Danish islands which are an extension of them, the remains of an ancient chain of dunes, wind blown, which stretched as far as Jutland in Denmark.
As far back as the Roman epoch the sea had broken up the chain of dunes and invaded the flat hinterland forming the **Waddenzee**. In the 13C this connected to a vast gulf which had just been formed, the Zuiderzee *(qv)*.

Tides and current – The islands are still subject to the strong action of sea currents and the North Sea continues its insidious undermining process to the west of the islands. Numbered posts are planted in lines on the beaches making it possible to estimate the sand's movement, which breakwaters, built out perpendiculary from the coast, attempt to reduce.
The wind then accumulates the sand behind the dunes as well as to the southwesterly point of the islands, where it forms immense desert stretches.
To the east, the currents contribute to the filling up of the Waddenzee. At low tide, the sea leaves huge stretches of mudflats or sand, called *wadden*, which are much appreciated by birds, but force ships to make large detours to avoid them and take marked channels.
The Waddenzee can be crossed over by **fording** it (called *wadlopen*) ⏲ with a guide, weather permitting.

Hug/EXPLORER

Texel

Storms – These have always been a threat to the Waddenzee and its low-lying islands, which are only protected from the sea by a chain of dunes on the west and a dike on the east.
The small island of **Griend,** between Vlieland and Harlingen, was a prosperous island in the 13C; little by little it was eroded by the high tides, and had to be abandoned in the 18C. In 1851 part of Texel was lost to the sea.

Landscape – The north of the islands have wonderful **beaches** of very white sand bordered by **dunes** on which abundant vegetation grows. They are particularly high and wide on Texel. To the south the very flat coast is protected by a dike. Inland the villages and **farms** are protected from the wind by thick curtains of trees. The farmhouses on the Frisian Islands have the same features as those of Friesland, whereas those of Texel are similar to the pyramid-shaped farmhouses of Noord-Holland. The countryside is generally subdivided into several **polders** separated by small dikes, where numerous herds of cows and a few horses graze. Texel specialises mainly in sheep raising.
There are also several small **ports** on the Waddenzee. They were once the departure point for fishing and whaling, formerly the chief activity of Ameland.

Fauna and flora – All these islands make up a kind of nature reserve for seabirds. Some come to lay their eggs: different types of gulls, spoonbills, pintail ducks.
In the autumn a great number of **migratory birds** from northern Europe (Scandinavia, Iceland) and from Siberia stop for a time on the Waddenzee, which is rich in food of all kinds (fish and shellfish), then continue on their way to warmer climates (France, Spain, North Africa). This is so with the avocet. Others spend the winter on the Waddenzee: they include among the waders a large number of different types of dunlins and oyster catchers.
Nature reserves have been laid out on each island; some of them are forbidden to visitors unaccompanied by a guide. The largest belong to the Forestry Commission (Staatsbosbeheer).
Seals, which used to come in great numbers to the sand banks on the north side of the islands, are unfortunately decreasing.
On the dunes, among which a number of small ponds nestle, the **vegetation** is rich and exceptional. Among the most common species to be found are shrubs such as the sea buckthorn with its edible orange berries, the Burnet rose, and grasses such as scurvy grass, Parnassus grass with white flowers and succulent plants such as milkwort.

Tourism on the islands – Even if not interested in ornithology or botany, many tourists enjoy the natural beauty of the islands, hardly polluted (clear seas, wild dunes and a healthy climate), the calm (on two of the islands only public commercial vehicles are allowed), the signposted paths (for walking, bicycling, horseriding) in the woods or on the dunes, and the possibilities for other activities such as fishing, sailing, etc.

The drawbacks – The Wadden Islands are coveted: the army, for instance, has built several military bases (Texel, Terschelling, Vlieland) which have scared away some bird species.
In addition very rich resources of natural gas have been found under the Waddenzee: a drilling platform has already been built between Den Helder and Texel.

Some practical advice – The best way to get about on the islands, which are forbidden to cars, or across the nature reserves or dunes which have cycling paths (Boschplaat to Terschelling for example), is by bicycle. They can be hired on each island and in most villages. However, in season they are not always available, therefore, it is highly advisable to embark from the mainland with your own bicycle, which is accepted on all ships.
In season, it is recommended to reserve rooms through the island's tourist information centre. There are few hotels but private houses take lodgers.

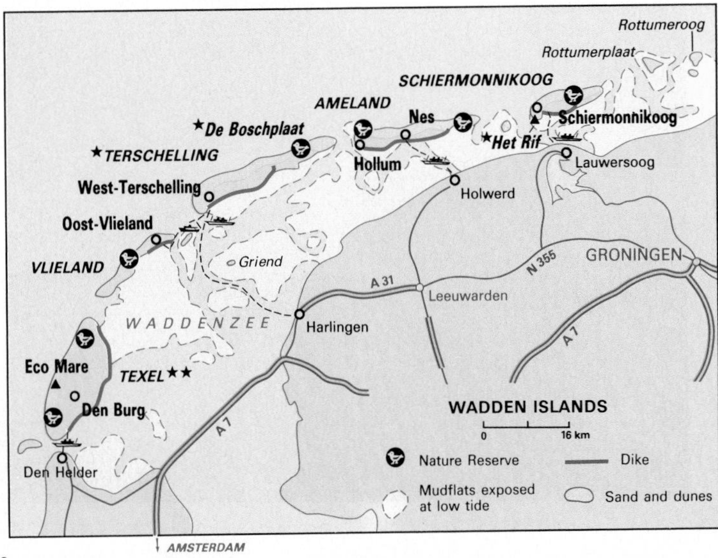

AMELAND Friesland — Pop 3 227

Access ⊙ – *From Holwerd.* This long island covering about 5 800ha - 14 326 acres with its large stretches of dunes, fine sandy beaches on the North Sea, and woods, is very popular with tourists, including a large number of Germans who come here in the summer. Several bicycle tracks *(90 km - 56 miles)* cross the island passing through woods and over dunes.
Like the other Wadden Islands, Ameland has its **nature reserves** for birds.
The inhabitants of Ameland formerly specialised in **whaling.** This activity was discontinued in the mid-19C but the captains' *(commandeurs)* houses can still be seen here and there on the island, and in some places whale bones are still used as fences.
The farmhouses in Ameland are of the same type as the Frisian farmhouses *(see Introduction: Farmhouses).*

Nes – This is the island's chief locality, overlooked by an isolated **bell tower** with a saddleback roof, dating from 1732. In Rixt van Doniastraat, there are several old captains' houses, **Commandeurshuizen,** one-storey houses with a small lean-to on the side, and where the entrance door is slightly off-centre. A cordon of bricks or a geometric frieze outlines each floor. The façade anchors often show an old date.
To the east, on the road to Buren, past the new Catholic cemetery, the old **cemetery** is accessible by a small road on the left. It still has ancient steles, some decorated with a weeping willow, others are very narrow and nearly 2m - 6 1/2ft high. Several graves of British airmen are grouped in this cemetery.

Ballum – The **tower** of an old church stands in the village centre. Take Smitteweg to the southeast to reach the **cemetery** where some of the old tombstones depict sailing ships or weeping willows.

Hollum – To the south of the town stands a typical but attractive church with a saddleback roofed bell-tower. In the surrounding **cemetery** there are more 18C tombstones showing sailing ships.
Hollum was home to many of the captains of the whaling ships which operated out of Ameland and one of these houses has been converted into a museum, **Sorgdragermuseum** ⊙. Pieces of local furniture and tiled walls grace the interiors which make an ideal setting for the collections of earthenware, pottery, costumes and other objects related to whaling.

M. et G. Morand-Grahame/CEDRI

Churchyard in Hollum

The great hangar-like building in Oranjeweg is now a lifeboat museum **Reddingsmuseum Abraham Fock** ⊙.
This was the home of the famous **lifeboat** (*Redding-boot*) drawn down to the water by a team of horses.

SCHIERMONNIKOOG Friesland — Pop 933

Access ⊙ – *From Lauwersoog.* It is the smallest of Wadden Sea's inhabited islands: an area of 4 000ha - 9 880 acres, it is 16km - 10 miles long and 4km - 2 1/2 miles wide and has recently become a national park.
The only town, Schiermonnikoog, has two large beaches and a small lake (pleasure boats), the Westerplas.
To the east, there is a nature reserve of 2 400ha - 5 928 acres: **De Oosterkwelder.**
With its wild scenery, its dunes, woods, beaches and its tranquillity, Schiermonnikoog is one of the most pleasant islands in the group. In 1989 it was made a National Park.
The island became Frisian in 1580 before passing into the hands of several land-owning families from 1639 to 1858 and finally becoming state property in 1945.

Schiermonnikoog – The houses of this small town are built among the trees. The town developed after Cistercian monks from Friesland settled here *c*1400. The name of the island derives from *schier* meaning grey, *monnik* monk and *oog* island. A statue of a monk on the green in the town centre is a reminder of its past.

Nearby, an arch made of two huge whale bones recalls the whale hunting of earlier times. The museum, **Bezoekerscentrum en Natuurhistorische Museum,** ⊙ is housed in an old power station and contains documents concerning the island.
In Middenstreek, which runs towards the west, and in the parallel Langestreek, there are interesting **old houses** with asymmetrical roofs.

★ **Het Rif** – Past the Westerplas, at the southwestern point of the island, lies a vast stretch of immaculate white sand and reaching 1,5km - 1 mile in width. From it, there is a **view★** of the whole of Westerburenweg, a path which ends in the dunes.

★ TERSCHELLING Friesland — Pop 4 552

Access ⊙ – *From Harlingen.* This very long island (28km - 17 1/2 miles) covers 11 000ha - 27 180 acres and is the second largest of the Wadden Islands, after Texel.
It welcomes many holidaymakers in summer, who enjoy its huge sandy beaches. Terschelling (pronounced Ter-srelling) has kept in some places its wild aspect. It is covered with vast areas of dunes where an abundant vegetation of various grasses, flowers and moss grow. It also has several **nature reserves,** of which the largest is De Boschplaat.
Many bicycle paths cover the island, which makes it possible to discover the most unusual scenery.
The **farmhouses** of Frisian type *(see Introduction: Farmhouses)* have the distinctive feature of barns pierced by a high portal where the carts enter, and which forms a kind of transept.
Cranberry wine *(cranberrywijn)* has been a speciality of Terschelling ever since a sailor found a barrel of cranberries washed up on the dunes.
Terschelling is the homeland of **Willem Barents** or Barentsz (*c*1555-97), the navigator who, while trying to seek a northeast passage to India, discovered Novaya Zemlya in 1594 and Spitsbergen in 1596. The portion of the Arctic Ocean, which lies between these two archipelagos bears his name, the Barents Sea. On his third expedition (1596-7), his boat was caught in the ice. He spent the winter in Novaya Zemlya in a hut made from boat planks, and died in the attempt to reach inhabited land. In 1871 the ship's log was found.

West-Terschelling – The capital of the island is a small port well situated in a large bay. It is overlooked by a square tower 54m - 174ft high, the **Brandaris,** a lighthouse built in 1594 to replace the bell tower (used as a lighthouse) of St Brandarius Chapel which, located on the island's southwest side, had been engulfed by waves.
At the foot of the tower lies a large **cemetery.** The 19 and early 20C steles, engraved with naively depicted boats, recall the maritime past of its inhabitants. One of the steles, in the middle of the cemetery, recalls the episode during which on 3 January 1880, five of the island's life savers tried to pick up the survivors from the wreck of the *Queen of Mistley.*

Gemeentemuseum 't Behouden Huys ⊙ – *Commandeurstraat no 30.* This pleasant regional museum is housed in two dwellings belonging to captains (commandeurs-huizen)(1668) with charming crow-stepped gables. It bears the name of the hut in which Willem Barents spent the winter. At the entrance and at no 14 of the same street, note the fine sculptured paving stones.
The reconstructed interior with its furniture, household items, costumed figures, gives a picture of local life. One section of the museum exhibits objects pertaining to the navy and whaling.

Formerum – A small windmill, **De Koffiemolen** (the coffee mill) is worth seeing. It has a thatched roof and dates from 1876; and is now used to mill grain.

Hoorn – This 13C church built of brick in the Frisian style is surrounded by gravestones. The oldest date from the 19C and are topped by a low relief depicting a ship.

★ **De Boschplaat** ⊙ – *Access forbidden to cars but bicycles allowed (bicycle paths in the western part).*
This nature reserve covers 4 440ha - 10 868 acres of the island's eastern point, which is uninhabited; it is the only European nature reserve to be found in the Netherlands. On the dunes and near the estuaries, large numbers of birds come to nest. The vegetation is most remarkable, as unique types of halophyte plants can be found (those growing on salty soil).

★★ TEXEL Noord-Holland — Pop 12 726

Access ⊙ – *From Den Helder.*
Texel (pronounced Tessel) is 24km - 15 miles long and 9km - 5 1/2 miles wide and is the largest of the Wadden Islands.
The capital, **Den Burg,** is in the centre. **De Koog,** to the west, gives access to the main beach. **Oudeschild** is a small fishing and pleasure port. **De Cocksdorp** is the most northern locality.
After agriculture and tourism the island's main activity is sheep breeding (about 20 000 head).

Bird Island – Birds are one of the most interesting features of Texel. The most varied species live here, lay their eggs and hatch them on the dunes or on the freshwater lakes here. Texel has several **nature reserves★** ⊙ belonging to the State.
The waymarked nature trails are for walkers only.

De Eijerlandse duinen – These dunes belonged to an island, Eyerlandt, which has been joined to Texel since 1629 by a sand bar. Numerous birds nest here from the end of March to the end of July, especially eiders which provide the down to make eiderdowns.

De Slufter – This is a large area surrounded by dunes, linked to the sea by a gap. The vegetation growing here is impregnated with salt. About forty different species of birds nest here.
From the top of the dunes, at the end of the Slufterweg, which can be reached by a stairway, there is a **view★** over this amazing wild landscape which in July and August is covered with a mauve flower called sea lavender.

De Muy – This is a partly marshy area in the hollow of the dunes, where nearly fifty species of birds nest, especially white spoonbills with their characteristic beak, and the grey heron. There are interesting plants (orchids, pyrola, and Parnassus grass).

De Westerduinen – On these dunes, near the beach, herring gulls nest.

De Geul – This lake was formed in the dunes at the end of the last century. Several other small lakes have formed since. In the reeds one can see the spoonbill, the grey heron and the pintail duck.
Nearby interesting plants grow on the dunes and marshes.
A fine viewpoint can be had over the reserve from the belvedere built on the **Mokweg.**

F. Roux/JACANA

Spoonbill

Eco Mare ⊙ – *Ruyslaan 92. Access by De Koog road and the road numbered 13.*
In these dunes northwest of Den Burg a building houses this centre devoted to the Wadden Islands and the North Sea, as well as a small Natural History Museum, **Natuurhistorisch Museum** with collections on Texel.
The first section is about the island's evolution, from its geological formation during the Ice Age, up to its transformation into polders, and from its prehistoric inhabitants until the present tourist invasion.
In another section, the nature reserves' flora and fauna can be studied with the help of dioramas, show cases with stuffed birds and photographs of plants. Aquariums, shell collections, reproductions of the sea bed evoke the maritime environment of the island.
The seals, which were once very common in the Waddenzee, cavort in the salt water ponds outside; **feeding times** ⊙ are lively occasions.

Oudheidkamer ⊙ – *In Den Burg, in Kogerstraat, on a small shady square called Stenenplaats.* This house, buit in 1959, with a pinnacled gable contains a museum of paintings and costumes recalling local life.

Agrarisch en Wagenmuseum ⊙ – *At De Waal, north of Den Burg.*
The agricultural collection includes a collection of wagons and carriages which were formerly used on the island. Some of the Frisian sledges are especially elegant.

VLIELAND Friesland — Pop 1 0642

Access ⊙ – *From Harlingen or from Terschelling.*
This island, composed of dunes and woods, covering 5 100ha - 12 597 acres is 20km - 12 1/2 miles long with a maximum width of 2.5km - 1 1/2 miles. There is only one small town, Oost-Vlieland. A single main road crosses it from east to west. Only the army at the western end and tourists in season come and spoil the peace of this wild countryside.

Oost-Vlieland – In Dorpsstraat, the main street, there are a few old houses. On the south side of the street a house called **Tromps' Huys** ⊙ has been made into a museum.
This is a typical island home, with panelled rooms, some painted blue, with fine furniture and porcelain and earthenware collections.
A small visitor centre, **Bezoekerscentrum** ⊙, has been fitted out near the church. Photographs provide documentation on the island's flora and fauna and especially about the main species of birds which live on the shores.
The **kerk** ⊙ contains whale bones.
The **cemetery** beside the church contains some interesting carved funerary steles, as well as graves of Commonwealth soldiers killed during the Second World War. From the hill on which the lighthouse (vuurtoren) stands, west of town, there is a **view★** over the island, Oost-Vlieland, the dark green woods forming a contrast to the pale colour of the dunes, and Waddenzee, where at each low tide vast stretches of mud flats appear, covered with flocks of birds.

WORKUM Friesland

Michelin map 408 H3 – Local map see SNEEK

This small town (Warkum in Frisian) was once a prosperous seaport where the eel trade flourished. Now it is a large holiday and water sports centre.
It is well-known for its glazed pottery which is brown in colour and often decorated with a frieze of white scrolls.
Workum still has several interesting houses with crow-stepped or bell-shaped gables *(kolkgevel)*.

Merk – It has a picturesque collection of old buildings.

Stadhuis – This has a tall 18C façade.
On the left is the old town hall, a small Renaissance building decorated with a carved stone.

St.-Gertrudiskerk ⏲ – This large Gothic church was built in the 16 and 17C and has an imposing separate **bell tower** crowned with a tiny onion-shaped dome.
Inside the church there is a fine 18C pulpit and nine painted **biers** (gildebaren) illustrating the activities of the guilds. They were used during funerals to carry the corpses of guild members to the cemetery. The organ dates from 1697.

Waag – A fine 17C building with stepped dormer windows. Inside is a small **Museum Warkums Erfskip** ⏲.

Use Michelin Maps with Michelin Guides

★ ZAANSTREEK Noord Holland

Michelin map 408 F4 and fold 27 (inset) – Local map see opposite

The Zaanstreek or Zaan Region is an area bordering the River Zaan to the north of Amsterdam.
The succession of riverside towns were regrouped in 1974 to form the district of **Zaanstad** (pop 130 705).
Originally the inhabitants gained a living from fishing. Then in 1592 Cornelius Corneliszoon built the first wind-powered saw mill. Many other windmills were built for industrial purposes and there were soon more than 500 locally. The timber in particular was used to build the warships for the navy and the great sailing vessels for Dutch merchants. The shipyards reputation was such that in 1697 the **Czar Peter the Great** paid a visit incognito to undergo a period of training with a local shipbuilder.
Many of the windmills still exist. These industrial mills are usually very tall as they were built over the workshop; their sails were driven from a platform *(see Introduction: Windmills)*.
The local houses also had a very characteristic style and quite a number have been reassembled in the Zaan Quarter.

PICTOR International

Typical houses from Zaanstreek

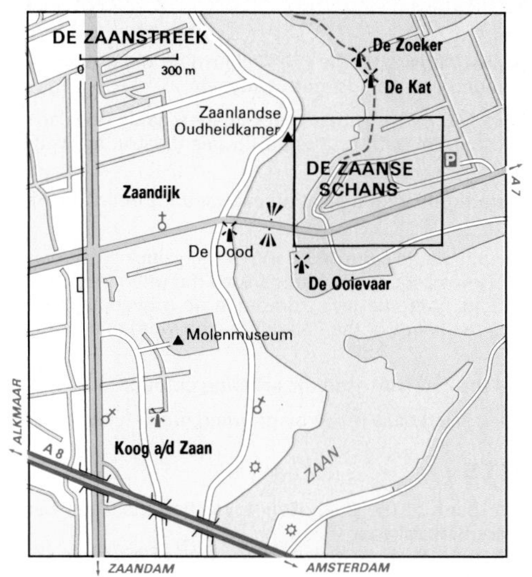

Industrial mill,
Zaanstreek

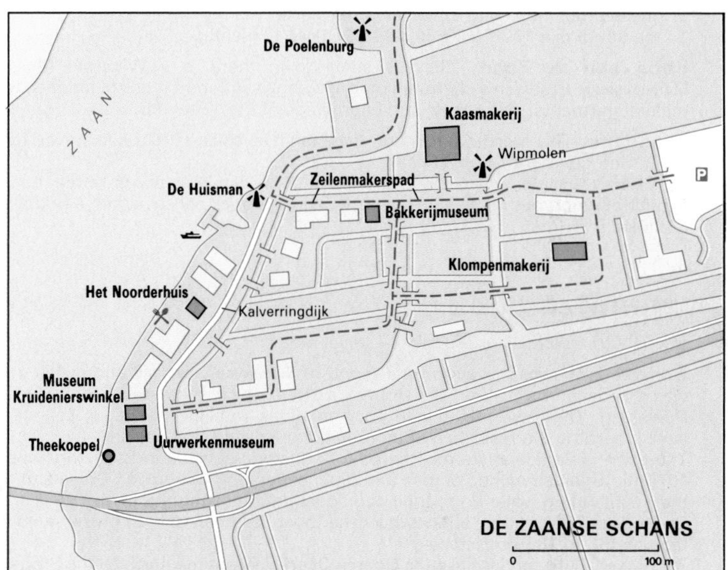

★ DE ZAANSE SCHANS (ZAAN QUARTER)

This quarter has taken its name, De Zaanse Schans, from a redoubt built at the end of the 16C as a protection against Spanish troops and which no longer exists.
Since 1950 a village has been laid out here consisting of 17 and 18C houses and public buildings brought in from different localities, especially from Zaandaam. They have been reconstituted and restored to form a kind of open-air museum.
The village is inhabited and its windmills are still active. It is built along a dike, **Kalverringdijk**, beside which runs a ditch crossed by little humpbacked bridges. Some of the houses border secondary canals, along which run paths such as Zeilenmakerspad.
Most of the houses are of wood with gables of different shapes. These are painted green or tarred black and their doors, windows and gables are outlined in white. On top of each gable is a small wooden ornament, the *makelaar.*
Several of the houses, shops and windmills can be visited.
South of the village and bridge there is an oil mill, called **De Ooievaar** (the stork).

Boat trips ⏲ – Boat trips are organised along the Zaan. *Landing stage on the local map above.*

Klompenmakerij ⏲ – There are demonstrations of traditional clog-making.

Zeilenmakerspad – On this path there is a tiny hollow post mill or **wipmolen**.
At no 4, a 17C house called In de Gecroonde Duijvekater (the crowned bread-roll), there is a Bakery Museum, **Bakkerijmuseum** ⏲.

Kaasmakerij ⏲ – Gouda and Edam are made in the dairy in the traditional manner.

Theekoepel – It is a pavilion in the form of a rotunda at the bottom of a garden; once a tea house (theekoepel), it now houses a pewter foundry, **Tinnegieterij** ⏲.

Uurwerkenmusem ⏲ – A collection of all different types of clocks made in the country.

Museum Kruidenierswinkel Albert Heijn ⊙ – A charming old grocery shop in a 19C house selling out-moded products (sugar candy, etc).

Het Noorderhuis ⊙ – In this 18C house with its neck-shaped gable one can visit the grand drawing room and a room with costumed figures illustrating wedding preparations.

De Huisman – An 18C mustard mill with a rotating cap *(see Introduction: Windmills)*.

De Poelenburg – This saw mill dates from 1869 and is the **paltrok**-type *(paltrokmolen):* it is built above the big workshop which turns with the mill when the sails are oriented to face the wind. Its name derives from its large moveable base like the *Pfalzrock,* a dress worn by the ladies of the Palatinate who were once refugees in the Netherlands.

De Kat ⊙ – This mill, called the cat, was used for grinding colours.

De Zoeker ⊙ – In this oil mill, salad oil is made by grinding many types of seeds.

ADDITIONAL SIGHTS

Zaandijk – On the opposite bank of the Zaan, this town has the Zaan Region Antiquities Museum **Zaanlandse Oudheidkamer** ⊙.
It is the brick built house of a rich 18C merchant and consists of a drawing room with 19C furniture and a "good year room", a room added to the house when business prospered, with a tiled chimneypiece.
To the south is a 17C flour mill called **De Dood** ⊙ (death).

Koog aan de Zaan – In this small town there is a Windmill Museum, **Molenmuseum** ⊙. It is in a charming park and shows different types of ladders, tools, millers' garments, documents and engravings of the 17 to 19C.

Zaandam – This industrial town on the Zaan has, since 1876, been served by the North Sea Canal (Noordzeekanaal).
Het Czaar-Peterhuisje, where the Czar lived in 1697, can be seen on Krimp, no 23. It is built of wood but in 1895 it was enclosed by a brick construction, a gift of Czar Nicholas II.

★ ZIERIKZEE Zeeland — Pop 9 813

Michelin map 408 C7 or 212 fold 3 – Local map see DELTA

Zierikzee is the main town on the island of **Schouwen-Duiveland** and in the past it was a prosperous port on the Gouwe, a strait which separated Schouwen from Duiveland. The town maintained good relations with the Hanseatic League and later it became the residence of the Counts of Holland and Zeeland.
The town is particularly remembered for a historic episode in its history when in 1576 the Spanish waded across the Zijpe, separating Schouwen-Duiveland from the mainland, in water up to their shoulders before taking the town.
Decline set in from the 16C; however the town has been able to preserve its heritage of 16C to 18C houses.
Schouwen-Duiveland is linked to Goeree Overflakkee in the north by the Brouwersdam and the Grevelingendam and to Noord-Beveland in the south by the Oosterschelde storm barrier and the Zeelandbrug *(see Delta map)*.

Boat trips ⊙ – *Boats leave from the haven* (Z). Zierikzee is the departure point for boat trips on the Oosterschelde.

SIGHTS

★ **Noordhavenpoort** (Z **B**) – This double gateway presents two 16C Renaissance gables on the town side and an older crow-stepped gable on the outside.
The **Zuidhavenpoort** (Z **E**) takes the form of a square tower quartered by four 14C corner turrets and is linked to the previous gateway by a lever bridge.

Oude haven (Z **32**) – Rows of elegant 17C and 18C houses line the quaysides of the old harbour.

Havenpark (Z) – On the north side of this square the house, **De Witte Swaen** (Z **N**) dating from 1658 has a lovely baroque gable. The house itself was rebuilt after the 1953 floods.
Adjoining the Gasthuiskerk is a former **market** (Z **L**) consisting of a Renaissance arcaded gallery with Tuscan columns at street level.

's-Gravensteen (Z **M1**) – This onetime prison has a 1524 crow-stepped gable with ornamental wrought-iron grilles on the first floor windows. It is now home to the **maritiem museum** ⊙ with its maritime collection.

Stadhuis (Z **H**) ⊙ – This was a covered market. The outstanding feature of the building which has been altered several times is the usual wooden **tower** topped with an ornamental onion-shaped dome (1550) surmounted by a statue of Neptune. The tower has a **carillon** ⊙. Two decorative gables provide further ornamentation to the façade. The decorative pieces of wrought iron were for holding lighted torches. The **stadhuismuseum** ⊙ inside is a local history museum. Most of the exhibits are displayed in the Harquebusiers' Hall with its fine timber ceiling.
Across from the stadhuis the 14C Huis De Haene, often called the **Tempeliershuis** (Z **S**) is the oldest in town. The influence of Bruges (Belgium) architecture can be seen in the ogee-shaped mouldings of the windows.

ZIERIKZEE

Appelmarkt .... Y 2
Dam .... Z 5
Meelstr. .... Z
Melkmarkt .... Z 28
Poststr. .... Z

Basterstr. .... Z 3
Fonteine .... Z 7
Hoofdpoortstr. .... Z 12
Julianastr. .... Z 14
Karsteil .... Z 16
Kerkhof N.Z. .... Z 17
Kerkhof Z.Z. .... Z 18
Klokstr. .... Z 20
Korte Nobelstr. .... Y 22
Lange Nobelstr. ..... Y 25
Lange St Janstr. ..... Z 26
Minderbroederstr. .... Z 30
Oude Haven .... Z 32
P.D. de Vosstr. ...... Y 34
Ravestr. .... Z 36
Schuithaven .... Z 38
Schuurbeque Boeyestr. Y 39
Verrenieuwstr. ...... Y 42
Watermolen .... Y 44
Wevershoek .... Z 45
Zevengetijstr. .... Y 48
Zuidwellerstr. .... Y 50

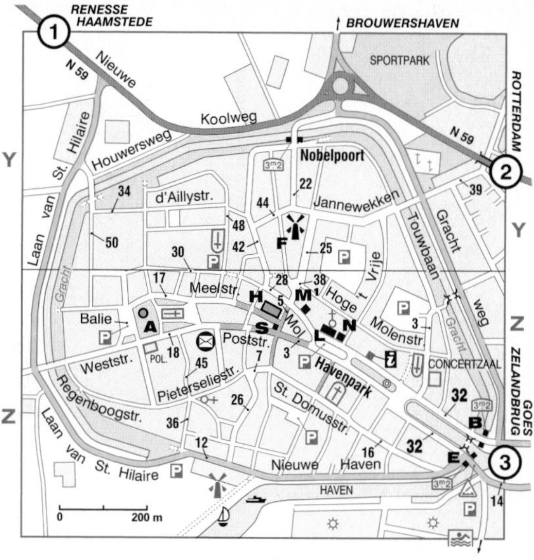

St.-Lievensmonstertoren (Z A) ⊙ – It is the bell tower of the old Gothic cathedral, which was destroyed by fire in 1832. Building work on the tower started in 1454 and was supervised by a member of the Keldermans family, who were also responsible for the Middelburg stadhuis *(see photograph under Middelburg)*. The tower rises to a height of 56m - 184ft but it remains unfinished.
Next door is a great neo-classical church (1848) preceded by a portico.

Nobelpoort (Y) – In the northern part of the town this late 14C square was one of the town gateways. The outer side of the gate is flanked by two tall towers, both later additions, topped by tall tapering pepperpot roofs.
Back towards the centre of town there is a tall 19C **windmill** (Y **F**) with a hand-rail called hope (De Hoop).

When driving north from the Channel Tunnel take the ***Michelin Green Guide Belgium and the Grand Duchy of Luxembourg*** *to discover these countries of contrast.*

★ ZUTPHEN Gelderland — Pop 31 127

Michelin map 408 fold 12

Zutphen lies at the confluence of the IJssel, Berkel and Twentekanaal not far from the heathlands of Veluwe *(qv)*.
This pleasant historic city is the capital of the beautiful wooded region **Achterhoek** *(qv)*. It is an important commercial centre and its pedestrian precincts come alive on market days.

HISTORICAL NOTES

The county town of Zutphen became part of Geldern in 1127. In 1190 the town received its burgh charter but 10 years later (1200) it was transferred to the see of Utrecht. In the 14C the town belonged to the Hanseatic League and built an enclosing wall which was extended the following century.
Zutphen was then recognised as an important strategic point due to its easily defendable position in the surrounding marshland (the name Zutphen, sometimes spelt Zutfen, comes from Zuidveen, the southern peat bog). Zutphen became one of the richest towns in Gelderland and in the 16C it was given a second town wall of which several sections still remain. The town was captured by the Spanish in 1572 and only retaken by Maurice of Nassau in 1591. In 1586 the English poet Sir Philip Sidney died of wounds received in an action to prevent the Spaniards from sending supplies into the town. The French occupied Zutphen from 1672 to 1674 and recaptured it again in 1795.

★ OLD TOWN *3 hours*

's-Gravenhof – Both the St.-Walburgskerk and the stadhuis are to be found in this square. During excavations on the site in 1946 remains of the Counts of Zutphen's castle were uncovered and today the outline of the castle can be traced on the pavement.

St.-Walburgskerk ⊙ – This early 13C Romanesque church dedicated to St Walburga, was given successive extensions in Gothic style up to the 16C. The church was damaged in 1945 and lost the upper storey of its tower three years later. The original tufa facing of the tower has been repaired with limestone.

ZUTPHEN

Beukerstr. .... Y
Frankensteeg .... Y 4
Houtmarkt .... Y
Korte Beukerstr. ..... Y 9
Korte Hofstr. .... Y 10
Sprongstr. .... Z 21
Turfstr. .... Y 22
Vaalstr. .... Z 24
Zaadmarkt .... Z

Berkelsingel .... Y 32
Brugstr. .... Y
's Gravenhof .... Z
Groenmarkt .... Y 6
Hagepoortpl. .... Y 7
Houtwal .... Z
IJsselkade .... YZ
Isendoornstr. .... Y
Kuiperstr. .... Z 12
Laarstr. .... YZ
Lange Hofstr. .... Z 13
Marspoortstr. .... Y 15
Martinetsingel .... Z
Molengracht .... Y
Nieuwstad .... Y
Oude Wand .... Y
Overwelving .... Y 16
Paardenwal .... Y 18
Rijkenhage .... Y 19
Spittaalstr. .... Z
Stationsplein .... Y
Tadamasingel .... Z
Vispoortstr. .... Z
Waterstraat .... YZ

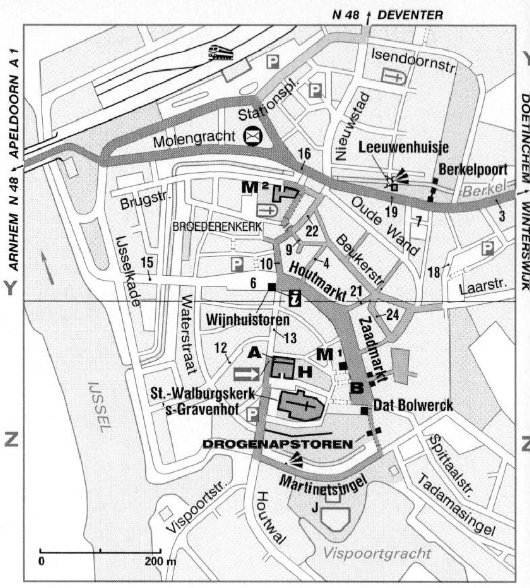

The exterior of the church is particularly attractive for the decorative roofscape above the trimming of balustrade and pinnacles and for the variety of building materials used.

On the north side the 15C **Doorway to the Virgin** was rebuilt between 1890 and 1925. Inside the vaulting is covered with 14C and 15C frescoes. The chancel has an extremely elaborate 15C ironwork **chandelier**. The plainer pulpit is 17C, like the organ case with its rich ornamentation. The **baptismal font** is a triumphant piece of copperwork cast in Mechelen, Belgium in 1527. It is decorated with the figures of the evangelists and saints with a pelican at the summit. The **library★** dates from 1564 when it was built onto the ambulatory. The original aspect of the interior remains unchanged with low pointed vaulting and the supporting columns. The ribs descend to sculpted consoles and below in the place of capitals are numerous small figures. The library houses around 700 titles, including 8 manuscripts and 80 incunabula; about one hundred books are displayed on wooden stands: illuminated missals, anthologies of texts written by St Thomas Aquinas and Luther. It is one of the few libraries in Europe which has retained its original appearance and furnishings.

Stadhuis (Z H) – This 15C building was considerably altered in 1716 and again 1729. It adjoins the former **meat market** (Z A) and its 15C frontage is best admired from Lange Hofstraat. Inside the great hall, **Burgerzaal**, has a lovely wooden ceiling;

Return south past the church to reach Martinetsingel passing on the way a section of the old town walls.

Martinetsingel – From this street there is an attractive **view★** of the town wall with gardens sloping down to the green waters of the canal; of the pointed towers of the Drogenapstoren away to the right and St.-Walburgskerk with its truncated tower in the background.

★ **Drogenapstoren** – This splendid gateway dates from 1444-46. The change from square to octogonal is marked by crenellations and four octagonal turrets with pointed roofs. The tower itself is crowned by an even taller pointed roof.

Dat Bolwerck – This attractive Gothic house (1549) is surmounted by pinnacles. Next door are the 1639 cavalry barracks, **Ruiter Kortegaard**, with an attractive scrolled gable.

Zaadmarkt – This was the site of the grain market. On the right at no 101 is the doorway of an **almshouse** (Z **B**) dating from 1723.

Museum Henriette Polak (Z **M¹**) ⏲ – The impressive **De Wildeman** mansion was altered in the 19C and today houses an interesting collection of paintings, sculpture and graphic arts by contemporary Dutch artists. Of particular interest are the portraits of *Queen Wilhelmina aged 10* by Mari Andriessen and *A Child* by T Sondaar-Dobbelmann.

The secret chapel (1628) on the second floor was a refuge for Catholics. *The Adoration of the Magi* is by the studio of Jan van Scorel (16C).

Houtmarkt (Y) – The lovely 17C Renaissance tower, the **Wijnhuistoren**, stands on the site of the former timber market. Its **carillon** ⏲ was made by the Hemony brothers. A market is held here every Thursday.

Stedelijk Museum (Y **M²**) ⏲ – The desecularised Dominican convent is now the home of the municipal museum. The convent church stands to the south of a lovely garden.

The exhibits on the ground floor include sections on clocks and watches, glasswork, gold and silver work as well as some paintings. Look for Barent Avercamp's *View of Zutphen* and the IJssel. Barent worked in the same style as his more famous uncle, Hendrick Avercamp.

The first floor is reserved for temporary exhibitions. The local collections on the second floor cover Zutphen and its immediate region.

Archaeological finds and pottery are exhibited in the basement.

ADDITIONAL SIGHT

Berkelpoort – This 15C brick-built water gate spans the Berkel with three arches. The entrances are flanked by watch turrets.
There is a good **view** ot the gateway from the footbridge to the west. Overlooking the footbridge is the **Leeuwenhuisje** with an overhang supported by lion-headed brackets.

EXCURSIONS

Achterhoek – *44km - 27 miles to the southeast by the Winterswijk road.*
Now known as Achterhoek, the area from Zutphen to the German border was originally the county of Zutphen. It is an area of woodland (conifers, oaks and beeches) and pastures criss crossed by quiet country roads and forest rides.

Vorden – Pop 8 315. This town has two 19C **windmills** with hand-rails. Vorden lies at the heart of a region where **eight castles** nestle in the surrounding woodlands: Vorden, Hackfort, Kiefskamp, Wildenborch, Bramel, Onstein, Medler and Wiersse. There are in actual fact 12 castles or small brick-built manor houses in all. Many were rebuit in the 18C in a quite plain style. The nobility, attracted by the good hunting provided by the local forests, elected to build seats in the area. Some can only be reached on foot or by bicycle *(paths are signposted opengesteld).*
Kasteel Vorden has an L-shape with a slender octagonal tower in the angle. Today the castle serves as town hall. Note the shell ornamentation above the windows.
The most impressive castle is **Hackfort**, flanked by two great round towers. Next to it is a **water mill** dating from about 1700.

B & U International Picture Service Amsterdam/Loek Polders

Kasteel Vorden

Groenlo – Pop 8 982. The historic city of Groenlo stands on the banks of the Slinge and is still encircled by sections of its town walls. The town is famous for its beer. In 1627 Groenlo capitulated to Prince Frederick Henry following a month-long siege.
The small **Het Grolsch Museum** ⊙ occupies a farmhouse and presents displays of regional costumes, funerary urns, coins...

Winterswijk – Pop 27 954. This town is also on the Slinge and in the surrounding forested areas the solitary but impressive farmhouses resemble quite closely those of the Twente *(see Introduction: Farmhouses).*

ZWOLLE Overijssel Ⓟ

Pop 95 572

Michelin map 408 J4
Plan of the conurbation in the current Michelin Red Guide Benelux

Zwolle has kept its special character in the historic centre within the ring of canals.

HISTORICAL NOTES

It was a member of the Hanseatic League *(qv)* in the 13C, linked to the Zuiderzee by the Zwarte Water, and for a long time it remained the depot for traffic between the Netherlands and northern Germany.

After the Spaniards left in 1572, its 15C curtain wall was considerably strengthened due to its strategic position. The wall was destroyed in 1674 during the Third Dutch War and little remains apart from the Sassenpoort in the south and in the north Rode Tower, which was truncated in 1845.

Today the ditches still surround the town and the pleasant gardens on the south and east sides mark the course of the ramparts and bastions.

Zwolle was, from 1810 to 1814, the main town of the French *département* of the Bouches-de-l'Yssel.

Thomas à Kempis (1379/80-1741), who was a pupil at the School of the Brethren of the Common Life in Deventer, and to whom is attributed the *Imitatio Christi (Imitation of Christ)* lived in a convent to the north of the town (in Agnietenberg).

Gerard Terborch or Ter Borch (1617-81) was born in Zwolle. This painter, like his contemporary Gerrit Dou *(qv),* is above all the dignified and meticulous painter of refined and peaceful interior scenes where young women wear shiny satin dresses; he also made excellent portraits and miniatures of the local notables.

Zwolle's main commercial activities are wholesale trade and transport, as well as graphics and metallurgy.

The town's specialities are *zwolse balletjes,* sweets shaped like a small cushion with different flavours, and *blauwvingers,* shortbread in the form of fingers with chocolate tips.

ZWOLLE

Street	Grid
Diezerstr.	CY
Grote Kerkplein	BY12
Luttekestr.	BY19
Roggenstr.	BY30
Sassenstr.	BYZ31
Achter de Broeren	BCY3
Bagijnesingel	CY6
Buitenkant	BY7
Diezerpoortenplas	CY10
Harm Smeengekade	BZ15
Kamperstr.	BY18
Nieuwe Markt	CYZ24
Oude Vismarkt	BY25
Potgietersingel	BZ27
Ter Pelkwijkstr.	CY34
Thomas a Kempisstraat	CY36
Voorstr.	BY39
van Wevelink Hovenstraat	CY40

The numbers ①, ② etc indicate the main routes into and out of town They are numbered in this way on town plans and on Michelin Maps

SIGHTS

★ **Provinciaal Overijssels Museum** (BY M) ⊙ – The provincial museum has been set out in a 16C patrician residence where the roof is hidden behind an 18C balustrade, abundantly decorated with coats of arms and carved figures in the rococo style.
The refined interior with furniture from the 16 to 18C and well presented collections (ceramics, etc) is witness to the town's rich past. There is a remarkable collection of silverware from the Overijssel province.

Grote-of St.-Michaëlskerk (BY A) ⊙ – St Michael's is a hall-church with three naves, dating from the 14 and 15C, of Protestant worship. Unlike the neighbouring church of Our Lady, it does not possess the traditional great bell tower, which was the victim of successive disasters.
Inside note a remarkable early 17C carved pulpit and an organ loft of 1721. The organ is excellent. It was made by the **Schnitger** brothers *(qv)*, sons of a well-known German organ builder, who lived in Groningen; it has 4 000 pipes. There is also a small 17C clock with a statue of St Michael which makes a movement every half hour.
Attached to the left side of the fine 16C north portal there is a picturesque little building with a decorated pediment: the **Hoofdwacht** or guard room.

Stadhuis (BYZ H) ⊙ – Beside the old building (15 and 19C) which had become too small, a new one has been built by the architect J.J. Konijnenburg.
The façades are punctuated by types of concrete buttresses on top of which appear a series of pointed red roofs. Inside the play of volumes and materials, and the arrangement of furniture make for a functional as well as aesthetic use of space.
The old part on the left, covered with mustard-yellow roughcast contains the **Aldermen's Hall** (Schepenzaal) dating from 1448. This old court room, now used for marriages, has a ceiling whose beams are held by 14 corbels with **sculptures★** depicting grotesque figures. Legend has it that the artists of Zwolle, rival town of Kampen, carved these heads to hold the governors of Kampen up to ridicule.
Note the brass chandeliers, and the small cupboards with locks fixed in the wall. Above the 16C fireplace there is a picture of the *Last Judgment,* which is a reminder of the room's original use.
On the terrace in front of the town hall there is a statue of *Adam* by Rodin.

Karel V-huis (BYZ B) – A medallion of Charles V's head can be seen on the gable, giving his name to this house built in 1571, which has a fine Renaissance façade decorated with pilasters, carved friezes and a voluted gable above which are recumbent gods.

Sassenpoort (CZ) – Built *c*1406, the Saxon Gateway is the only one which still exists from the fortified town wall. Of red brick, it is flanked by four octagonal pointed turrets and topped by a spire.

T. Groves/PIX

Keukenhof

F. Chazot/EXPLORER

TRAVELLING TO THE NETHERLANDS

Formalities – Despite the new law which came into force on 1 January 1993 authorising the free flow of goods and people within the EU, it is nonetheless advisable that travellers should be equipped with some valid piece of identification such as a **passport**. Holders of British, Irish and US passports require no visa to enter the Netherlands, although visas may be necessary for visitors from some Commonwealth countries, and for those planning to stay for longer than 3 months. US citizens should obtain the booklet *Your Trip Abroad* ($1) which provides useful information on visa requirements, customs regulations, medical care, etc for international travellers. Apply to the Superintendent of Documents, Government Printing Office, Washington DC 20402-9325.

Customs Regulations – There are no customs formalities between the countries of Benelux (Netherlands, Belgium and the Grand Duchy of Luxembourg). Tax-free allowances for various commodities within the EU have increased with the birth of the Single European Market. The HM Customs and Excise Notice 1 *A Guide for Travellers* explains how recent changes affect travellers within the EU. The US Treasury Department (☎ 202 566 8195) offers a publication *Know Before You Go* for US citizens.

By air – Various international airlines operate regular services to the international airports in the Netherlands (Amsterdam's Schiphol airport, Rotterdam, Eindhoven and Maastricht). Contact airlines and travel agents for information and timetables.

By sea – There are several ferry services from the United Kingdom.
Hull to Rotterdam: night crossing 14 hours. **North Sea Ferries**, King George Dock, Hedon Road, Hull, Humberside, HU9 5QA, ☎ 0482 795141.
Hull to Zeebrugge: see North Sea Ferries above.
Harwich to Hoek van Holland: day crossing 6 3/4 hours; night 8 3/4 hours. **Stena Sealink Line**, Charter House, Park Street, Ashford, Kent TN24 8EX, ☎ 0233 647 047.
Sheerness to Vlissingen: day crossing 7 hours; night crossing 8 1/2 hours. **Olau Line (UK) Ltd**, Sheerness, Kent, ME12 1SN, ☎ 0795 666666.
Dover to Ostend and Zeebrugge: P & O European Ferries
Dover to Calais: there are numerous cross-Channel services (passenger and car ferries, hovercraft, SeaCat, Channel Tunnel) on this route

By rail: The Channel Tunnel – Two distinct forms of transport use the tunnel: the **"Eurostar" service** with direct high-speed French (SNCF), Belgian (SNCB) and British Rail passenger and goods trains; **"Le Shuttle" service** with cars, coaches and motorcycles on the passenger shuttles and heavy goods vehicles on freight shuttles. Journey time will be 35 minutes, 28 minutes of which are in the tunnel at a maximum speed of 130km - 80 miles per hour.
"Le Shuttle" operates 24 hours a day, throughout the year and the number of departures is determined by the volume of traffic. For information and advance tickets call Le Shuttle Passenger enquiries ☎ 0303 271100 or consult the French Telecom videotex service, Minitel 3615 under the access code LESHUTTLE.

By road – When driving to the continent the ideal ports of entry for the Netherlands are Vlissingen, Rotterdam and Hoek van Holland. Depending on the point of departure it may be more convenient to land at Hamburg (seasonal service from Harwich), Zeebrugge (from Felixstowe and Kingston-upon-Hull), Ostende or Calais (both from Dover) and then motor on to the Netherlands.
Calais to Rotterdam via Antwerp: 305 km - 3 hours 30 min.
Calais to Amsterdam via Antwerp and Rotterdam: 379km - 4 hours 30min
Hamburg to Amsterdam via Bremen: 472 km - 4 hours 50 min.

TRAVELLING IN THE NETHERLANDS

By car

Documents – Nationals of EU countries require a national driving licence; nationals of non-EU countries require an **international driving licence** (obtainable in the US from the American Automobile Club). Third party insurance is the minimum cover required by insurance legislation in the Netherlands, but it is advisable to take out additional insurance for fully comprehensive cover (the Green Card). Special breakdown and get-you-home packages are a good idea (AA, Five Star RAC, National Breakdown, Europ-Assistance....

Motorways – The 905km - 1 189 miles of motorways *(autosnelweg)* are toll-free. There are however tolls for certain bridges and tunnels (Zeeland Brug, Kiltunnel and Prins Willem Alexander Brug).

Overtaking and priority – Do not forget to drive on the right! The minimum age for driving is 18 for cars and motor-cycles and 16 for mopeds. Children under 12 should travel in the back. Seatbelts are compulsory in the back as well as the front of the car.
Priority must be given to cars coming from the right at junctions and on roundabouts, unless shown otherwise. Give way also to trams, passengers boarding or alighting from trams, and pedestrians crossing the road into which you are just turning. Only pass trams on the right unless there is insufficient room. Trams generally have priority. Cyclists will pass on the right and have priority over motorists when the latter want to turn off the road.
The regulation **red warning triangle** must be carried, and displayed in the event of a breakdown.

Speed limits – Maximum speed limits are 120kph - 75mph on motorways (100kph - 62mph in the vicinity of large towns); 80kph - 50mph on other roads and 50kph - 31mph in built-up areas.

Breakdown service – The main organisation is the ANWB (Koninklijke Nederlandsche Toeristenbend) or Royal Dutch Touring Club which operates road patrols *(wegenwacht)* on main roads. If no patrol happens to pass then phone from one of the roadside telephones to the nearest ANWB office *(alarmcentrale)* ☎ 06 08 88. This breakdown service operates 24h/24h. The receptionist usually speaks several languages. Non-members have to pay 160fl (1993) for a two-month membership card. Foreign motorists will be asked to provide evidence of affiliated club membership.

Petrol – The following kinds of petrol are on sale in the Netherlands

Super	Super gelood
Super (unleaded, only 95 octane)	Super (loodvrij)
Diesel	diesel
Euro (unleaded, only 95 octane)	euroloodvrij
LPG	gas

Credit cards are accepted in most petrol stations but visitors are strongly advise to have other means of payment with them.

Car hire – Cars can be hired in most major towns and resorts. The minimum age is 21 although some companies maintain a minimum age of 23 and possession of a valid licence for a minimum of one year. A valid national licence is required. It is cheaper to reserve in advance rather than to pay on the spot. All the major companies (Avis, Hertz, Budget Europcar) are to be found in the main Dutch cities as well as local companies.

Signposts - In the Netherlands the names of certain foreign towns are often signposted in Dutch:
Belgium: Luik for Liège.
France: Parijs for Paris; Rijsel for Lille.
Germany: Aken for Aachen.
For useful terms when motoring see the phrasebook.

Road maps – The Michelin map **407** covers all the Benelux countries at a scale of 1:400 000 while map **408** covers the Netherlands. Map **408** has an index and enlarged inset maps of the conurbations of Amsterdam and Rotterdam. Michelin is to publish two new maps on the Netherlands at a scale of 1:200 000.

36 15 MICHELIN Minitel Service – Michelin Travel Assistance (AMI) is a computerised route-finding system offering integrated information on roads, tourist sights, hotels and restaurants. 36 15 MICHELIN is one of the French Telecom videotex services. Foreign subscribers can access the service. For route planning give your point of departure and destination, stipulate your preference for motorways or local roads, indicate the sights to see along the way and it will do the rest. The same applies when looking for that special restaurant, secluded country hotel or pleasant camp site along the chosen route.

Tourist routes – The ANWB has organised and signposted about 40 itineraries ranging in distance from 80 to 150km - 50 to 94 miles. These routes have hexagonal signposts and take in the most picturesque regions and interesting towns. Leaflets showing the routes and main points of interest are available from the ANWB offices. Other tourist and heritage trails are organised by local authorities.

By train

Netherlands Railways – The Netherlands has an extensive and efficient railway network. There is an inter-city network of express trains linking major cities. It is not possible to reserve seats on national train services. There are two classes (first and second). A day return is cheaper than two singles. There are numerous organised day trips and Rover tickets (multi, family and teenager) at reduced rates. The Euro Domino Card (Freedom Pass) offers unlimited travel throughout the Netherlands for a 3, 5 or 10-day period in any one month.

GENERAL INFORMATION

Currency – The Dutch unit of currency is the guilder (abbreviated to fl) comprising 100 cents. Approximate exchange rate £1 = 2.80fl.
Money can be changed at post offices, banks and GWK offices (exchange) and in some coastal VVV offices. Commissions vary so check before cashing. For an indication of hotel and restaurant prices consult the Michelin Red Guide Benelux.

Credit cards – All major credit cards (American Express, Diners Club, Eurocard, Visacard, Access and MasterCard) are accepted but always check in advance.

Tips – The bill is usually inclusive of service charge and VAT. An extra tip can be left for special service. The price shown on the taxi meter includes service charge although it is customary to give an extra tip.

Opening hours –
Banks open Mondays to Fridays from 0900 to 1600 (until 1700 some days).
Post offices open from 0900 to 1700 (or 1800) and close at weekends. In some larger towns they are open on Saturday mornings.
Shops open Tuesdays to Saturdays from 0900 to 1800 (they tend to close earlier on Saturdays 1600 or 1700). Closed on Sundays and Mondays, sometimes only Monday mornings.
GWK offices open Mondays to Saturdays from 0800 to 2000, Sundays 1000 to 1600.
Restaurants open for lunch from 1100 to 1430 or 1500 and for dinner from 1730 to 2200 or 2300. There are some late-opening restaurants in the larger cities.

Telephones – To phone abroad from the Netherlands dial
GB: 00 44; USA: 00 1; Canada: 00 1; Australia: 00 61: Eire: 00 353 followed by the trunk code and subscriber's number.
Dutch dialling codes are given in the Michelin Red Guide Benelux. Amsterdam (020); The Hague (070); Rotterdam (010); Utrecht (030) and Maastricht (043).
In the Netherlands the phone boxes are green. The grey telephones take coins (25cent, 1fl and 2.50fl pieces) while the blue phones accept pre-paid phonecards. Phonecards, in five different units, are available from railway stations and post offices.

Public Holidays – 1 January, Easter Monday, 30 April (Queen's official Birthday or National Day), Ascension Day, Whit Monday, 5 May (Liberation Day), 25 and 26 December.
Remembrance Day, 4 May, is not a public holiday.

Embassies and Consulates

Australia:	Embassy	Carnegielaan 4, 2517 KH Den Haag, ☎ (070) 310 8200.
Canada:	Embassy	Sophialaan 7, 2514 JP Den Haag, ☎ (070) 361 4111.
Eire:	Embassy	Dr. Kuyperstraat 9, 2514 BA Den Haag, ☎ (070) 363 0993.
UK:	Embassy	Lange Voorhout 10, 2514 ED Den Haag, ☎ (070) 364 5800.
USA:	Embassy	Lange Voorhout 102, 2514 EJ Den Haag, ☎ (070) 310 9209.

ACCOMMODATION

Hotels and restaurants – For choosing a stopover for a few hours or a few days, the current Michelin Red Guide Benelux is an indispensible complement to this guide. It is updated every year and offers a range of hotels and restaurants with an indication of their standard of service and comfort, their location, their degree of pleasantness and their prices.
It is strongly advised to reserve hotel rooms in advance, especially for a weekend break, when visiting Amsterdam, or any area where there is a local festival taking place.

Netherlands Reservation Centre (NRC) – This national reservation centre not only books a hotel room but also bungalows and apartments and is generally geared to those booking from outside the country. Netherlands Reservation Centre, PO Box 404, 2260 AK Leidschendam, Netherlands, ☎ (070) 320 26 00; Fax 70 320 26 11. Once in the Netherlands call on a VVV office which also offers an accommodation service.

Bed and Breakfast – The VVV offices have listings of families offering bed and breakfast style accommodation. Although it is quite cheap there are not a large number of B & Bs. Price range including breakfast is 17.50 - 50fl per person.
Reservations are also possible through Bed and Breakfast Holland, Warmondstraat 129/1, 1058 KV Amsterdam, ☎ (020) 615 75 27, Fax 020 669 1573.

Youth hostels - Nederlandse Jengdherberg Centrale (NJHC), Prof Tulpplein 4, 1018 GX Amsterdam ☎ (020) 55 13 133.
The Dutch youth hostels (40) are open to young and old who are members of their own national youth organisation or have an international card. The rates are from 20fl per person for bed and breakfast. Some hostels offer family facilities. Reservations are possible.

Rented accommodation – A wide range of accommodation (bungalows, log cabins, holiday cottages, flats and apartments) from the luxurious to simple is available for visitors. These can also be booked through the Netherlands Reservation Centre.

Camping – The Michelin map 408 shows a large selection of camping sites with the symbol ⛺. The Netherlands Tourism Board, the VVV and ANWB offices also have guides or lists of camp sites. The ANWB classification awards stars for the standard of sanitary installations and flags for the recreational facilities. Some form of identity is required when checking into a camping site. Independent camping outside official sites is not allowed in the Netherlands.
Many camping sites in the Netherlands have **hikers' cabins** *(trekkershut).* Normally for four people these offer rudimentary facilities (beds, table and chairs, cooking facilities and electricity; sanitary facilities are on camp site) and are ideal for those on the move on cycling, hiking or canoeing holidays. A maximum of three nights can be spent in any one cabin. It is necessary to book ahead through the NRC. Both the VVV and ANWB offices have lists of camp sites which have hikkers' cabins.

Down on the farm – If you are interested in staying on a farm or pitching your tent on one, contact the SVR (Stichting Vrije Recreatie) which has a list of 1 200 mini-campings. Dutch law limits the number of tents per farm to five.
Stichting Vrije Recreatie, ☎ 01837 2741.

Holiday villages – The Netherlands has a wide choice of holiday parks where you can rent accommodation (bungalows or apartments) on a weekly basis. The accent is usually on sports and leisure facilities and the villages have the same classification criteria as the camping sites *(see above)*. The Netherlands Reservation Centre can help you with the choice of park and then make the reservation.

EATING OUT

Although the Dutch have a hearty breakfast, lunch is a light meal served around 1230. Their meal is in the evening between 1800 and 1900. For restaurant opening times see under General Information.
The **Michelin Red Guide Benelux** offers a wide selection of restaurants of varying price. There are also suggestions concerning local specialities.

Neerlands Dis – The 110 restaurants of this nationwide chain, are easily recognisable by their red, white and blue soup tureen emblem. They offer a selection of traditional Dutch dishes. See the Food and Drink chapter in the Introduction for a description of some Dutch specialities.

Tourist Menu – The restaurants displaying a blue wall plaque with a white fork serve a three course meal (starter, main course and desert) at a reasonable price (25fl in 1994). A booklet is available from VVV offices.

Brown Cafés (Bruin café) – These traditional dark panelled bars are famous for their atmosphere, conviviality and their comfort more typical of a cosy sitting room. These are in sharp contrast to the chrome and glass designer bars popular with the trendy set.
The **cafés** of Amsterdam and other large towns are known for the friendly atmosphere of their cocktail hour when drinks are accompanied by small cubes of cheese and the famous Bitterballen (small hot meatballs).
Choose your **coffee shop** with care, as many specialise in the sale and consumption of soft drugs. The non-smoking establishments often call themselves tearooms.

TOURIST INFORMATION

Netherlands Boards of Tourism (NBT)

London: NBT, PO Box 523, London SW1E 6NT, ☎ (0891) 200 277.

USA: East Coast, 355 Lexington Avenue, 21st floor, New York NY 10017, ☎ (212) 370 7367.
West Coast, 9841 Airport Boulevard, 10th floor, Los Angeles, CA 90045, ☎ (310) 348 9333.
Middle West, 225 Michigan Avenue, Suite 326, Chicago, IL 60601, ☎ (312) 819 0300.

Canada: NBT, 25 Adelaide Street East, Suite 710, Toronto, Ont M5C 1Y2, ☎ (416) 363 1577.

Australia: NBT, 5 Elizabeth Street, 6th floor, Sydney, NSW 2000, ☎ 2 247 6921.

VVV – In The Netherlands the **tourist information centres** are indicated by **i** or **VVV** (Verenining voor Vreemdelingenverkeer), three blue v's on a white triangle. These offices supply information on a wide range of subjects: hotels, restaurants, camping sites, rented accommodation, youth hostels, local events, bicycling, sailing, sightseeing, opening hours and entertainment. They also sell tourist, cycling and walking maps and provide exchange facilities as well as a nationwide hotel reservation service. The addresses and phone numbers of the VVV offices in the main towns are given in the listing of times and charges at the end of this guide and they are located on all town plans by the symbol **i**.

ANWB – The **ANWB** (Koninklijke Nederlandse Toeristenbond) Royal Dutch Touring Club has offices throughout the country. ANWB, Wassenaarseweg 220, PO Box 93200, 2596 EC Den Haag, ☎ (070) 314 71 47.

GWK offices – These offer banking (exchange facilities, cash cheques or credit cards) and tourist services and are to be found at airports, railway stations, border crossing points, on motorways and in tourist resorts.

Museum Year Pass – The holder of this card is entitled to free entry or reduced rates to 400 museums. Price in 1994: 120fl adult; 50fl for children under 18; OAP's 25fl. Extra charges are made for special exhibitions.
The card can be bought at most affiliated museums, VVV offices and all Netherlands Boards of Tourism.

Under 26 – This European cultural pass gives reduced rates for museums, theatres, concerts... For further information apply to Under 26, 52 Grosvenor Gardens, London, ☎ (071) 823 53 63.

Tourism for the disabled – The Netherlands provides good facilities for the handicapped and all hotels, motels, guest houses, youth hostels, holiday bungalows and cottages, camping sites accessible to the handicapped carry the international symbol ♿. The NBT offers a special brochure for the physically handicapped. The Michelin Red Guide Benelux indicates rooms and facilities suitable for physically handicapped people.
The Netherlands Railways offer a comprehensive service for the disabled traveller which includes a free escort service. The train timetables are available in braille.
Access to the Channel Ports is a guide for the disabled and those who have problems getting around. This carefully researched guide gives information on the following Dutch ports: Hook of Holland, Rotterdam and Vlissingen. *Access in the Channel Ports* (Disabled Tourists' Guide) is obtainable from Access Project (PHSP), 39 Bradley Gardens, London W13 8HE.

DISCOVERING THE NETHERLANDS

Which is the best time of year to visit?

The Netherlands is a land for all seasons and although the country is uniformly flat it is never dull as there is a constantly changing play of light between sea and sky.

Spring – Without doubt the outstanding attractions are the bulbfields, a kaleidoscope of dazzling colours *(from mid-April to end of May)*. The main bulb growing areas are between Haarlem and Leyden and in the vicinity of Alkmaar. Spring is the season when the foliage of the countryside is a tender green and in town the canalside trees add a splash of fresh colour.
The Betuwe region is a delight when the cherry orchards are in blossom *(from mid-April to end of May)* and the bright yellow of the fields of oil seed rape make a colourful splash in the provinces of Friesland, Groningen, Overijssel and Flevoland *(from mid-May to early June)*.

Summer – The great stretches of sandy beach along the North Sea coast are popular with holidaymakers and locals alike. Here as in other popular resorts and holiday areas (Drenthe and Southern Limburg) it is always wise to book in advance as accommodation is scarce during the summer season.
The many lakes, reservoirs, canals and waterways make this ideal sailing country and good for water sports.
Throughout spring and summer flowers are everywhere: towns and villages are bright with well-tended public gardens and parks and cheerful flower boxes and window displays enhance even the plainest façades.

Autumn – By late August and early September the dunes and heathlands are bright with the purple tints of heather in bloom. The forests like those of the Veluwe start to sport their autumn tints.

Winter – The frozen landscapes have a charm of their own so well portrayed by Dutch artists in the past and even the towns take on an uncanny stillness as they lie muffled under their first mantle of snow. In the Netherlands frozen lakes and canals are an invitation to skate and children are not the only ones to take it up.

Cycling

The Netherlands is traditionally the land of the bicycle and there is no better way of discovering the country at a leisurely pace than by bicycle.
There are approximately 14 million bicyles in the country which works out at virtually one for every inhabitant. Bicycles are everywhere, especially during the rush hour.

Cycling lanes and paths – The Netherlands has many special lanes and paths for cyclists (about 15 000km - 9 320 miles). Follow the special lanes - marked by a white bicycle on a blue sign - to be found in both towns and the countryside and you won't be bothered by other traffic.
Normally cyclists are not allowed on footpaths.

Special signs – The Netherlands is generally well-signposted and is it important for cyclists to be able to recognise the main ones.
– blue circular sign with a white bicycle: bicycles *(fietsen)* and mopeds *(bromfietsen)* must use this lane which usually runs parallel to the road.
– rectangular sign with the mention **Fietspad**: an optional cycling lane for cyclists but mopeds are prohibited.
– sign with **Fietsers oversteken**: yield crossing for bicycles and mopeds. Care is required as motorists may be surprised to suddenly see cyclists emerging onto a road which had no cycling lane.

Cycling rules – Keep to the right and overtake other bicycles on the left. Never overtake cars on the left even when turning left. Only proceed two abreast if this does not hinder others.
Bicycles and mopeds are not allowed on motorways. All bicycles must have lights that work.
Children under 10 must use a special safety seat. Use clear hand signs to indicate a change of direction.

Hiring a bicycle – It is possible to hire a bicycle almost anywhere in the Netherlands. Over 100 railway stations have bicycles for hire, look for the blue and white square sign. Rate: 2.75fl for 2 hours or 7.50fl per day. In towns there are numerous bicycle hire firms but cycle dealers and repair shops also have bicycles for hire *(fietsverhuur)*. A deposit and proof of identity are required.
Gears are not always considered necessary in a flat country like the Netherlands so do not be surprised if your bike has none! Many bicycles have the traditional braking system where you have to back-pedal. You push backwards on pedals to stop the back wheel. This often surprises foreigners and practise is necessary.

Parking – Especially in towns it is advisable to lock your bike and it is preferable to leave it in a guarded park.

Cycling routes – The ANWB has marked out about 250 tours with an average length of 40km - 25 miles for bicycles and mopeds. These routes are waymarked by blue rectangular roadsigns which have a white hexagonal sign with a bicycle or by hexagonal white signs with indications in red. Descriptive leaflets are available for the different routes.
The Stichting Landelijk Fietsplatform has waymarked over 6 000km - 3 730 miles of national cycling routes (LF-routes). These numbered routes follow cycling paths or quieter local roads. The association also publishes several guides for these routes. Stichting Landelijk Fietsplatform, PO Box 846, Bergstraat 6, 3800 AV Amersfoort, ☎ (033) 65 36 56.
The VVV's will also provide information on local cycling routes.
A good map is a must. The small mushroom-shaped signposts waymarking the cycling paths are numbered and indicated on the maps.

Water sports

Sailing – The Netherlands, with its rivers, canals, waterways, broads, lakes, reservoirs and the sea, provides ample opportunities for water sports and the Dutch with their tradition of a seafaring nation are enthusiastic sailors. There are over 300 000 boat owners ie one boat per 47 inhabitants and there are at least 950 marinas or pleasure boat harbours throughout the country.
Being so geared to sailing there is no shortage of good facilities (marinas, moorings, repair yards, fuel and water points, shops, restaurants and cafés) for the visiting sailor.
Few places are far from a navigable waterway and one of the unexpected charms of sailing in Holland is that it is possible to sail into or through many of the town centres with their networks of canals.
The most popular sailing areas are IJsselmeer (high seas possible), the lakes bordering the IJsselmeer polders (calmer waters), the Lakes of Zuid-Holland, the Utrecht Lake District (Loosdrechtse and Vinkeveense) and the Frisian Lakes.
Further information can be obtained from Koninklijk Nederlands Watersport Verbond, (Watersports Federation), Runneburg 12, PO Box 87, 3980 CB Bunnik, ☎ (03405) 71 325 or the ANWB vakgroep Watersport (Watersports Section), Wassenaarseweg 220, 2596 EC Den Haag, ☎ (070) 314 7720.

Customs formalities – On arrival and departure visiting sailors with boats over 5.4m - 18ft must report to the nearest customs harbour office which will issue the necessary sailing certificate. Boats capable of travelling at more than 16 km/h should be registered at a post office and the licence costs 47.50fl. Insurance cover is compulsory with a legal liability of a minimum of 250 000fl. To use a sea-scooter you must be over 18 and have a Dutch licence to navigate.

Restrictions – There are **speed limits** on certain canals especially urban ones, but also on some of the busier waterways. For other regulations consult the *Almanac for Water Tourism* (I for general shipping rules and regulations and II for tide timetables, opening times of bridges and locks and facilities offered by the various marinas). These almanacs have introductions in English and are available from the ANWB and some specialised bookshops.
Yachts with high fixed masts must look out for fixed bridges with a limited headroom and remember that some bridges only open at certain hours. At movable bridges there is often a fee to pay, usually well indicated, and the bridgekeeper will lower a clog *(klomp)* for you to put the fee into.

Hiring a sailing or motor boat – In the high season it is best to book in advance. For lists of companies chartering boats apply to the Netherlands Tourist Board, ANWB, VVV offices or Top of Holland Yachtcharter, Stationsplein 1, 8911 AC Leewarden, ☎ (058) 13 6691.
Both the ANWB and the Netherlands Hydrographic Services publish **hydrographic charts** which can be purchased from ANWB offices, water sports shops or good bookshops.

Canoeing – The calm waterways of the Netherlands provide ideal conditions for this sport. The VVV offices can provide more information on request.

Surfing – Again the opportunities are varied. Experienced surfers will enjoy the rougher waters of the IJsselmeer or the North Sea waves. The inland waters of the Utrecht Lakes and the lakes bordering the polders are also suitable for surfing.

Historic ships – Some companies offer for charter historic canal and sea going vessels: flat-bottomed boats *(tjalken)*, fishing smacks *(botters)* and clippers. Skipper and crew are provided in most cases.

Boat trips – For those who prefer to take it easy there are numerous boat trips to choose from. For towns with a good canal network this is a relaxing way to sightsee and ideal for admiring all those canal houses . The following towns offer boat trips on the canals: Alkmaar, Amsterdam, Delft, Groningen, Leyden and Utrecht. Others such as Enkhuizen, Harderwijk, Kampen and Urk organise trips on the IJsselmeer while Leyden (Rhine), Maastricht (Meuse to the Belgian border), Nijmegen (Waal), Rotterdam (Rhine), Venlo (Meuse) and Zierikzee (Eastern Scheldt) propose river excursions.

Water skiing – This sport is subject to quite strict regulations and it can only be practised in authorised areas. In some cases it is necessary to obtain an authorisation from the local authorities.

Fishing – Two documents are necessary: a fishing licence *(sportvisakte)* and a permit *(vergunning)*. The first is on sale in post offices while the second can be obtained from the local Angling Associations (Hengelsportverenigingen).

Rambling

The Staatsbosbeheer (SBB symbol right) and the ANWB edit a series of eight rambling maps (Welkom bij de boswachter) indicating footpaths and their characteristics. These can be obtained from the ANWB.
Rambling is popular in the Netherlands and there are numerous annual meetings. The Four-Day Walk takes place in Apeldoorn and Nijmegen and the Tour of the Eleven Towns of Friesland leaves from Leeuwarden.
Most of the forests and woods are State owned and are administered by the Staatsbosbeheer *(see above)*. the recreational facilities provided usually include cycling paths, picnic areas and footpaths. Many trails are waymarked and differentiated by colour. Signs give the time required for each tour.

Other activities

Steam trains – Tourist trains are operated between Apeldoorn and Dieren, Hoorn and Medemblik as well as Goes and Oudeland.

Skating – When snow lies thick on the ground and frost has set in, the many waterways and lakes are ideal for skating.

Bird watching – The wetlands (Biesbosch National Park, the Frisian Lakes), the Wadden Islands, the many low-tide mudflats and the polderlands provide a variety of ecological habitats rich in birdlife, ideal for the amateur bird-watcher. For those interested in bird watching the address to contact locally is Vogelbescherming Nederland, Driebergseweg 16c, 3708 JB Zeist, ☎ (03404) 37700.

Golf – The Michelin map **408** locates the country's golf courses, many of which welcome visitors. The Dutch Golf Federation's headquarters are at: Nederlandse Golf Federatie, Rijnzathe 8, 3454 PV De Meern, ☎ (03406) 2 18 88.

Entertainment

In the larger cities – Amsterdam, the Hague and Rotterdam – the wide choice of entertainment caters for every taste: ballet, music, theatre, opera, discos, night clubs. The performances range from top-class (reservations necessary) to avant garde. In these towns the tourist information centres publish fortnightly English-language magazines *What's on in...*

Theatre, Dance and Music – The title of cultural capital goes to **Amsterdam** with its 62 museums, 60 art galleries, 32 theatres and 12 concert halls. The 1986 Muziektheater, part of the modern Stopera development in its attractive riverside setting, provides state-of-the-art facilities for the **Nederlandse Opera** and the **Nationale Ballet**. The vitality of the ballet company owes much to its founder, the Russian choreographer Sonia Gaskall, and the choreographer Hans van Manen and its repertoire consists of traditional, classical and romantic ballets. In summer musicians from the two orchestras give free lunchtime concerts. Since its resplendent refurbishment the 100-year old Concertgebouw is the perfect setting for the performances of the famous **Koninklijk Concertgebouworkest** under the baton of Riccardo Chailly. Berlage's famous Beurs building has been refurbished to serve as a cultural centre and provides a home to the **Netherlands Philharmonic** and **Chamber Orchestras**. In summer, the open-air theatre in Vondelpark is the venue for free concerts.
The Hague is home to the more contemporary culture of the **Nederlands Dans Theater** acclaimed for its adventurous performances in modern dance under the Czech-born artistic director, Jiri Kylián. The Anton Philipszaal is home to the city's **Residentie Orkest**. The refurbished Circustheater (1904) in Scheveningen now serves as a venue for musical extravaganzas while the redecorated Schouwburg Theatre concentrates on drama. The North Sea Jazz Festival is a well known international event and welcomes as many as 1 000 musicians.
Rotterdam boasts the **Scapino Ballet** with its narrative ballet repertoire while the **Rotterdam Philharmonic** plays at the Doelen.

Casinos – The eight official gambling palaces (Holland casinos) offer an afternoon or evening of gambling where you can try your hand at Blackjack, Punto Banco, American or French Roulette or the jackpot machines in pleasant surroundings. These include ones at Breda, Groningen, Nijmegen, Rotterdam, Scheveningen, Valkenburg and Zandvoort. They are open from 1400 to 0200 and guests have to be 18 years of age and have valid identity with them.

Cinemas – Most films are shown in the original version with Dutch sub-titles. In larger towns there are usually two performances (1845 and 2130).

PHRASEBOOK

Common words

NB for restaurant terminology, consult the current Michelin Red Guide Benelux.

U	you
Mijnheer	Mr
mevrouw	Mrs, Ms
juffrouw	Miss
rechts	right
links	left
ja	yes
nee	no
goedemorgen	good morning
goedemiddag	good afternoon
goedeavond	good evening
tot ziens	goodbye
alstublieft	please
dank u (wel)	thank you (very much)
hoeveel?	how much?
zegel	stamp

Tourist vocabulary

abdij	abbey
begraafplaats	cemetery
berg	mountain, hill
beurs	stock exchange
bezienswaardigheid	sight
bezoek	visit
boerderij	farm
boot	boat
brug	bridge
dam	dam
dierenpark	zoo
dijk	dike
duin	dune
eiland	island
gasthuis	hospice, old hospital
gemeentehuis	town hall
gracht	canal (in town)
groot, grote	great
grot	grotto, cave
gulden	florin
haven	harbour, port
heilige	saint
heuvel	hill
hof	court, palace
hofje	almshouse
ingang, toegang	entrance
jachthaven	pleasure boat harbour
kaai, kade	quay
kasteel	castle
kerk	church
kerkhof	churchyard
kerkschat	treasury
klooster	convent
koninklijk	royal
markt	market, main square
meer	lake
molen	(wind)mill
museum	museum
natuurreservaat	nature reserve
noord	north
Onze Lieve Vrouwe	Our Lady
oost	east
open	open
opengesteld	open, accessible
orgel	organ
oud	old
oudheidkamer	antiquities (museum)
paleis	palace
plas	lake
plein	square
poort	gate (to town)
raadhuis	town hall
rederij	shipping company
Rijks-	of the State
rondvaart	boat trip
scheepvaart	navigation
schilderij	painting, picture
schouwburg	theatre
singel	ring canal
slot	castle, fortress
sluis	lock
stad	town
stadhuis	town hall
state	castle (in Friesland)
stedelijk	municipal
straat	street
tegel	earthenware tile
tentoonstelling	exhibition
tuin	garden
uitgang	exit
veer	ferryboat
vest	rampart
vogel	bird
vuurtoren	lighthouse
waag	weigh house
wal	rampart
wandeling	walking tour
weg	path, road
west	west
zee	sea
zuid	south

This guide, which is revised regularly, incorporates tourist information provided at the time of going to press Changes are however inevitable owing to improved facilities and fluctuations in the cost of living

Road vocabulary

autosnelweg	motorway	parkeerschijf verplicht	parking disk obligatory
doorgaand verkeer	through traffic	richting	direction
eenrichtings-verkeer	one-way street	uitrit	exit
inhaalverbod	no overtaking	verboden	prohibited
knooppunt	junction	verboden toegang	no entry
let op! gevaar!	caution! danger!	voorrang geven	give way
niet parkeren	no parking	werk in uit-voering	roadworks
omleiding	diversion	zachte berm	soft shoulder
overstekende wielrijders	cyclists path crossing		

Provinces

Noord-Brabant	North Brabant	Zuid-Holland	South Holland
Noord-Holland	North Holland		

Towns

s-Gravenhage; Den Haag	The Hague	Leiden	Leyden
		Vlissingen	Flushing

SOME BOOKS TO READ

Of Dutch Ways H Colijn (Harper & Row)
Holland A Hopkins (Faber & Faber)
The British and the Dutch K H D Haley (George Philip)
Mondrian John Milner (Phaidon Press)
Vincent van Gogh: Paintings, Drawings (two volumes) Louis van Tiborg and Evert van Uitert (Thames and Hudson)
Rembrandt The Master and his Workshop Paintings, Drawings and Etchings (two volumes) (Yale University Press)
Rembrandt Annemarie Vels Heijn (Sotheby's Publications)
Rembrandt M Kitson (Phaidon)
The Paintings of the Willem van de Veldes M S Robinson
Jacob van Ruisdael: The Perception of landscape E J Walford (Yale University Press)
Dutch and Flemish Painting: Art in the Netherlands in the 17C C Brown (Phaidon)
Dutch Painting R H Fuchs (Thames and Hudson)
Dawn of the Golden Age, North Netherlandish Art, 1580-1620 Kloek et al (Yale University Press)
Dutch Art and Architecture: 1600-1800 J Rosenberg, S Slive and E H ter Kuile (Pelican History of Art)
Dutch Houses and Castles J Guillermo (Tauris Parke Books)
Dutch Arts (Ministry of Cultural Affairs)
Guide to Dutch Art (Ministry of Education, Arts and Sciences)
The Gardens of William and Mary D Jacques and A J van der Horst (Christopher Helm)
The Black Tulip Alexandre Dumas, edited by David Covard (Oxford University press)
Through the Dutch and Belgian Canals P Bristow (A & C Black)
The Diary of a Young Girl Anne Frank (Pan)
The Dutch Revolt Geoffrey Parker (Penguin)
The Revolt of the Netherlands 1555-1609 Pieter Geyl (Cassell)
The Netherlands in the 17th Century 1609-1648 Pieter Geyl (Cassell)
A Bridge Too Far Cornelius Ryan
The Sorrow of Belgium Hugo Claus
Max Havelaar Multatuli (Penguin)
The Assault H Mulisch(Penguin)
Toothless Tiger A F T van der Heijden
Mystic Body F Kellendonk
In a Dark Wood Wandering: A Novel of the Middle Ages Hella S Haasse

For historical information on the region consult the table and notes in the Introduction

CALENDAR OF EVENTS

Listed below are the most important festivals; others will be found, under the locality (see index).
A detailed calendar of festivals appears in leaflets produced annually by the VVV (tourist information centre).

In February or March during Lent

Breda .... **Carnival★**
Bergen op Zoom .... Carnival
Eindhoven .... Carnival
Venlo .... Carnival
's-Hertogenbosch ...... Carnival
Maastricht .... **Carnival★**
Sittard .... Carnival

1 week in March

Maastricht .... The European Fine Art Fair ☎ (073) 14 51 65

Late March to mid or late May

Keukenhof .... **National Floral Exhibition★★★**

1 April (Saturday before if the 1st is a Sunday)

Brielle .... Historical Festival

Mid-April to mid-September, Fridays

Alkmaar .... **Cheese Market★★**

Last (second last) Saturday in April

Haarlem-Noordwijk ..... Procession of floral floats

Early May to late September, Thursdays

The Hague .... Antiques Market

Saturday before Whitsun

Exloo .... Shepherds' Feast

June

Amsterdam .... **Holland Festival★** (concerts, opera, ballet, theatre). To reserve apply to: Holland Festival, Kleine Gartmanplantsoen 21, 1071 RP Amsterdam; ☎ (020) 627 65 66 or to large travel agencies abroad

Early June

Dokkum .... St Boniface Pilgrimage

Early June to late September

Tegelen .... Passion Plays *(1995; every 5 years)*

Late June to late August, Thursdays

Schagen .... Market: Westfriese Markt

July

Haarlem .... International Organ Festival (with an Improvisation Competition) (even years only: 1st week in July) ☎ (023) 16 05 74
Kerkrade .... International Music Competition (1997: every 4 years)

Second weekend in July

The Hague .... North Sea Jazz Festival ☎ (070) 354 29 59

Third Sunday in July

Exloo .... Ancient Handicrafts Festival

July or August (2 weeks)

Frisian Lakes .... Regattas: *Skûtsjesilen*

July, August evenings

Maastricht .... Carillon Concerts in Town Hall

July, August Wednesdays

Edam .... Cheese Market

Early July to early August, Thursdays

Barneveld 408 H5 *(1)* .... Old Veluwe Market

July, August, Saturday afternoons

Kinderdijk .... Windmill Days

Late July - early August, Wednesday evenings

Markelo .... Country wedding

Early August

Sneek .... Sneekweek Regattas

1st Saturday in August

Rijnsburg **408** E5 - **Noordwijk** Procession of floral floats

Late August

Breda .... Taptoe: Military Music Festival

Late August - early September

Utrecht .... Holland Festival of Ancient Music. Further info ☎ (030) 36 22 36

Harlingen .... Fishing Days

1st Saturday in September

Aalsmeer-Amsterdam ... Procession of floral floats *(approximately 0900 to 1600)*

1st Sunday in September

Zundert **408** E7 .... Procession of floral floats

2nd Saturday in September

Tiel .... Harvest Fruit Parade *(1400)*

3rd Tuesday in September

The Hague .... State Opening of Parliament: the Queen arrives in a golden coach

4th Wednesday in September

Odoorn .... Sheep market

3 October (following Monday if the 3rd is a Sunday)

Leyden .... Leidens Ontzet: historical procession

1st Wednesday in October

Leeuwarden .... Show of prize Frisian bulls

Mid-October

Delft .... Antiques Fair

3rd Saturday after 5 December

Amsterdam .... St Nicholas' official entrance *(Prins Hendrikkade)*

From 1st Sunday of Advent to 1st January

Denekamp .... Blowing of *midwinterhorens*

---

(1) The Michelin map **408** *is given for all places listed above not mentioned in this guide.*

Sports Competitions

Automobile and motorcycle races – The Grand Prix of the Netherlands Formula 1 is the most famous automobile competition in the country.
In Assen, during the last weekend in June, the Motorcycle Dutch Grand Prix is held. Cross-country motorcycling is very popular and races on ice are held in ice skating rinks.

Cycling Events – The National Bicycle Day is held every year in May. The tour of 11 Friesland towns (depart from Bolsward) is held Whit Monday; Drenthe's 4 Days is held in late July and Nijmegen's 4 Days (Fietsvierdaagse) is held in late July.

Water sports competition – Throughout the country different water sports activities are held. The most spectacular are the **skûtsjesilen**, *skûtsjes* regattas on the Frisian Lakes *(qv)*. Among the other activities are Delta Week (Zierikzee) in early July and Sneekweek in early August.

Walking – The 4-Day Walking Tour takes place in Apeldoorn (mid-July) and in Nijmegen (3rd or 4th week in July). The Frisian 11 Town Walking Tour lasts 5 days (depart from Leeuwarden) between mid-May and early June.

Traditional sports – Archers Processions *(boogschieten)* are held from mid-May to late August in the Limburg.
Those who like ball games can watch **kaatsen** held in Frisian villages (early May - mid September; important meets in August).
The annual pole vaulting *(polsstokspringen)* is held in Winsum (10km - 6 miles southwest of Leeuwarden) in August.

ADMISSION TIMES AND CHARGES

As admission times and charges are subject to modification due to increase in the cost of living, the information printed below is for guidance only.

The following list details the opening times and charges (if any) and other relevant information concerning all sights in the descriptive part of this Guide accompanied by the symbol ⏲. The entries given below are listed in the same order as in the alphabetical section of the Guide.

The prices quoted apply to individual adults but many places offer reduced rates for children, OAPs and some a family discount. Prices are given in florins (abbreviated to fl).

The times are those of opening and closure but remember that some places do not admit visitors during the last hour or half hour.

Most tours are conducted by Dutch-speaking guides but in some cases the term "guided tours" may cover groups visiting with recorded commentaries. Some of the larger and more popular sights may offer guided tours in other languages. Enquire at the ticket desk or book stall.

For most towns the address and/or telephone number of the local Tourist Information Centre (VVV), indicated by the symbol ℹ, is given below. Generally most efficient, these organisations are able to help passing tourists find accommodation (hotel, guest house, camp site, youth hostel, etc) as well as providing information on exhibitions, performances, guided tours, market days and other items of interest locally.

City tours are given regularly during the tourist season in Amsterdam, Breda, Groningen, The Hague, Leeuwarden, Leyden, Maastricht, Rotterdam and Utrecht. Apply to the Tourist Information Centre.

A

AALSMEER

ℹ Drie Kolommenplein 1, 1431 LA, ☎ (02977) 2 53 74

Bloemenveiling – Open mornings from 0730. Closed Saturdays, Sundays and public holidays. 4fl. ☎ (02977) 3 45 67.

ALKMAAR

ℹ Waagplein 3, 1811 JP, ☎ (072) 1 43 00

Boat trips – Apply to Rederij Woltheus, Ark (boat) "d'Elmare", Kanaalkade, opposite no 60. ☎ (072) 11 48 40.

Kaasmarkt – Open mid-April to mid-September Fridays from 1000 to 1200. ☎ (072) 11 42 84.

Hollands Kaasmuseum – Open April to October from 1000 (0900 Fridays) to 1600. Closed Sundays and public holidays. 2fl. ☎ (072) 11 42 84.

Stadhuis – Guided tours by appointment. ☎ (072) 14 23 23.

St.-Laurenskerk – The church is presently undergoing restoration work. ☎ (072) 11 33 78.

Stedelijk Museum – Open from 1000 to 1700 (1300 to 1700 Saturdays, Sundays and public holidays). Closed Mondays and on 1 January and 25 December. 3fl. ☎ (072) 11 07 37.

Excursions

Bergen: Noordhollands Duinreservaat (Nature Reserve) – Open from sunrise to sunset. 1.80fl. ☎ (02518) 6 29 11.

Bergen aan Zee: Zee-Aquarium – Open April to October from 1000 to 1800; the rest of the year Saturdays, Sundays, public holidays and school holidays from 1100 to 1700. 5fl. ☎ 02208) 1 29 28.

Graft-De Rijp: Hervormde Kerk – Open early June to mid-September from 1300 to 1700; guided tours the rest of the year. Closed Mondays. ☎ (02997) 19 79.

AMELAND See Waddeneilanden

AMERSFOORT

ℹ Stationsplein 9, 3818 LE, ☎ (033) 63 51 51

Onze Lieve Vrouwe Toren – Closed for restoration work. ☎ (033) 63 51 51.

St.-Joriskerk – Open late June to early September from 1400 to 1630. Closed Sundays and public holidays. 1fl. ☎ (033) 61 61 78.

AMERSFOORT

Groenmarkt: Antiques Market – Open the first Saturday of each month (except in January) from 1000 to 1600.

Tinnegieterij – Open Thursdays to Saturdays from 1000 to 1700. Closed in August. ☎ (033) 63 51 51.

Koppelpoort – Guided tours for groups of ten people minimum; apply to VVV. ☎ (033) 63 51 51. The visit is included in a guided tour leaving from the Hof at 1100 Tuesdays and Thursdays. 3.50fl.

Poppentheater: Puppet Theatre – Open Wednesdays and Saturdays at 1430. 7.50fl. For reservations call ☎ (033) 61 96 29.

Museum Flehite – Open from 1000 (1400 Saturdays and Sundays) to 1700. Closed Mondays, Good Friday, Easter Sunday, Ascension Day, 30 April, Whit Sunday and on 25 and 26 December. 4fl. ☎ (033) 61 99 87.

Excursions

Wijk bij Duurstede: Kantonnaal en Stedelijk Museum – Open from 1330 to 1700. Closed Mondays, on 1 January, Easter Sunday, Whit Sunday and 25 December. 2fl. ☎ (03435) 71448.

Kasteel Amerongen – Open April to October Tuesdays to Fridays from 1000 to 1700; open Saturdays, Sundays and public holidays from 1300 to 1700. Closed Mondays. 5fl. ☎ (03434) 54212.

Leersumse Plassen: nature reserve – Open mid-July to mid-March. Guided tours on request May to July. 2.50fl.☎(03434) 54777.

AMSTERDAM

🅸 Stationsplein 10, 1012 AB, ☎ (06) 34 03 40 66

Illuminations – In the high season many of the historic buildings and bridges are illuminated.

Taxi-boats – ☎ (020) 622 21 81.

Bicycle hire – Amstelstation, Pieter Jacobz. Dwarsstraat 11, Nieuw Uilenburgstraat 116, Centraal Station, Damrak 247, Marnixstraat 220, St-Nicolaasstraat 1b. ☎ (06) 34 03 40 66.

Diamond Cutting Workshops – Around fifteen workshops are open to the public. Apply to VVV. ☎ (06) 34 03 40 66.

Boat trips – Landing stages are indicated on the town plans. The boat trips last 1 hour to 1 1/2 hours. Prices range from 10 to 40 fl. The night excursion is strongly recommended. For information apply to VVV. ☎ (06) 34 03 40 66.

Koninklijk Paleis – Open June to August daily from 1230 to 1700; the rest of the year Tuesdays to Thursdays from 1300 to 1600. The palace is of course closed when the royal family is in residence. 5fl. There are free guided tours on Wednesdays at 1400 (guided tours in English are available). ☎ (020) 624 86 98.

Nieuwe Kerk – Open from 1100 to 1700 (with all reserve). Enter from Dam square. ☎ (020) 638 69 09.

Madame Tussaud Scenerama – Open from 1000 to 1800. Closed on 30 April and 25 December. 17fl. (12fl for children). ☎ (020) 622 99 49.

Amsterdams Historisch Museum – Open from 1000 (1100 Saturdays and Sundays) to 1700. Closed on 1 January. 7.50fl. ☎ (020) 523 18 22.

Munttoren: Carillon Concerts – On Fridays June to September at 1200.

Bloemenmarkt – Open from 0900 to 1700. Closed Sundays and on 1 January, Easter Monday, Whit Monday, Ascension Day, and 25 and 26 December.

Rijksmuseum – Open from 1000 (1300 Sundays and public holidays) to 1700. Closed Mondays and on 1 January. 10fl. ☎ (020) 673 21 21.

Van Gogh Museum – Open from 1000 to 1700. Closed on 1 January. 10fl. ☎ (020) 570 62 00.

Stedelijk Museum – Open from 1100 to 1700. Closed on 1 January. 7.50fl. ☎ (020) 573 27 37.

B. Lipnitzki/EXPLORER

Façade stone
Beguinage, Amsterdam

Museum Amstelkring Ons' Lieve Heer op Solder – Open from 1000 (1300 Sundays and public holidays) to 1700. Closed on 1 January. 4.50fl. ☎ (020) 624 66 04.

Oude Kerk – Open mid-April to Mid-October from 1100 (1300 Sundays) to 1700; mid-October to mid-April Fridays, Saturdays and Sundays from 1300 to 1700. 3.50fl. ☎ (020) 624 91 83.

Museum Het Rembrandthuis – Open from 1000 (1300 Sundays and public holidays) to 1700. Closed on 1 January. 5fl. ☎ (020) 624 94 86.

Flea Market – Open to the public from 1000 to 1600. Closed Sundays and on 1 January, Easter Monday, Whit Monday, Ascension Day, 25 and 26 December.

Antiques Market – Open to the public from 1000 to 1600 Sundays May to September.

Joods Historisch Museum – Open daily from 1100 to 1700. Closed on Yom Kippur. 7fl. ☎ (020) 626 99 45.

Portugese Synagoge – Open from 1000 to 1230 and from 1300 to 1600; November to March Sundays from 1000 to 1200. Closed Saturdays and on Jewish and Christian holidays. 2.50fl. ☎ (020) 624 53 51.

Zuiderkerk: Tower – Open from 1200 to 1700 (2000 Thursdays). Closed Saturdays, Sundays and public holidays. ☎ (020) 623 58 23.

Allard Pierson Museum – Open from 1000 (1300 Saturdays, Sundays and public holidays) to 1700. Closed Mondays and on 1 January, Easter Sunday, Ascension Day, 30 April, 25 and 26 December. 3.50fl. ☎ (020) 525 25 56.

Anne Frank Huis – Open June, July and August from 0900 (1000 Sundays and public holidays) to 1900; the rest of the year from 0900 (1000 Sundays and public holidays) to 1700. Closed on 1 January, 25 December and Yom Kippur. 8fl. ☎ (020) 5 56 71 00.

Westerkerk – Open April to September from 1000 to 1600. Closed Sundays and public holidays. ☎ (020) 624 77 66.

Theatermuseum – Open from 1100 to 1700. Closed Mondays and on 1 January, 30 April and 25 December. 5fl. ☎ (020) 623 51 04.

Museum Willet-Holthuysen – Open from 1000 (1100 Saturdays and Sundays) to 1700. Closed on 1 January. 5fl. ☎ (020) 523 18 22.

Museum Van Loon – Open from 1000 (1300 Sundays) to 1700. 5fl. ☎ (020) 624 52 55.

Kattenkabinet – Temporary exhibitions only. For information about opening hours call ☎ (090) 696 53 78.

Bijbels Museum – Open from 1000 (1300 Sundays and public holidays) to 1700. Closed Mondays and on 1 January and 30 April. 3fl. ☎ (020) 624 24 36.

Nieuwe of Ronde Lutherse Kerk: Concerts – The church is presently undergoing restoration work. For information apply to ☎ (020) 621 22 23.

Fruit and Vegetable Market – Open Mondays and Saturdays from 1000 to 1700.

Artis – Open daily from 0900 to 1800.
Zeiss Planetarium Artis – Open from 0900 (1230 Mondays) to 1700. 18.50fl (11fl for children, including Planetarium). ☎ (020) 523 34 00.

Tropenmuseum – Open from 1000 (1200 Saturdays, Sundays and public holidays) to 1700. Closed on 1 January, 30 April, 5 May and 25 December. 12.50fl. ☎ (020) 568 82 00.

Nederlands Scheepvaart Museum – Open from 1000 (1200 Sundays and public holidays) to 1700. Closed Mondays (except from 15 June to 18 September), on 1 January and 30 April. 10fl. ☎ (020) 523 22 22.

Excursions

Schiphol: Aviodome – Open April to September from 1000 to 1700; the rest of the year open from 1000 (1200 Saturdays, Sundays and public holidays) to 1700. Closed on 1 January, 25 and 31 December. 7.50fl. ☎ (020) 604 16 21.

Broek in Waterland: Kerk – For information call ☎ (02903) 12 35 or 36 09.

Kaasmakerij – Open Tuesdays to Saturdays from 0900 to 1230 and 1330 to 1700. ☎ (02903) 14 54.

APELDOORN

i Stationsplein 6, 7311 NZ, ☎ (055) 78 84 21

Steam Train – Departures daily mid-July to late August (except Saturdays and Sundays). Single ticket 12fl. Rtn ticket 18fl. ☎ (055) 78 84 21.

Historisch Museum Marialust – Temporarily closed; reopening scheduled for 1995. The new address is Raadhuisplein 8. For opening times ☎ (055) 21 61 29.

ARNHEM

i Stationsplein 45, 6811 KL, ☎ (085) 42 03 30

Boat Trips – Departures 5 July to 20 August from 1000 to 1600. Apply to Rederij Heymen, Kantoorschip (boat) Rijnkade. ☎ (085) 51 51 81.

Het Nederlands Openluchtmuseum – Open from 0930 (1000 Saturdays, Sundays and public holidays) to 1700 April to October. 11.50fl. ☎ (085) 57 61 11.

Grote- of Eusebiuskerk – Open late June to mid-September from 1200 to 1700. Closed Mondays, Sundays and public holidays. 1.50fl. ☎ (085) 43 13 97.

Gemeentemuseum – Open Tuesdays to Thursdays from 1000 (1100 Sundays and public holidays) to 1700. Closed on 1 January. ☎ (085) 51 24 31.

Burgers' Zoo, Bush en Safaripark – Open from 0900 to 1900 in summer, from 0900 to sunset in winter. 20fl. (15fl for children). ☎ (085) 42 45 34.

Excursions

Kasteel Rosendael – Guided tours (1 hour) from 1000 (1300 Sundays) to 1600 April to October. Closed Mondays. 6fl. (3fl for children).
Park – Open May to October from 1000 (1100 Sundays) to 1700. 4fl. (1.50fl for children). Combined ticket 9fl. (4fl for children). ☎ (085) 64 46 45.

Nationaal Park Veluwezoom: Visitor Centre – Open from 1000 to 1700. Closed Mondays. ☎ (08309) 5 10 23.

De Steeg: Kasteel Middachten – The castle and its grounds are open to the public in July Tuesdays to Sundays from 1300 to 1600; the grounds are open mid-May to mid-September from 1030 to 1630. 12fl (castle and grounds). ☎ (08309) 5 21 86.

Oosterbeek: Airborne Museum – Open from 1100 (1200 Sundays and public holidays) to 1700. Closed on 1 January and 25 December. 4fl. ☎ (085) 33 77 10.

Kasteel Doorwerth: Nederlands Jachtmuseum – Open April to October from 1000 (1300 Saturdays and Sundays) to 1700; the rest of the year Saturdays and Sundays only from 1300 to 1700 . Closed on 1 January and 25 December. 6.50fl. ☎ (085) 33 53 75.

Rhenen:

Ouwehands Dierenpark (Zoological Garden) – Open from 0900 to 1800 (1700 October to March). 17.50fl (children under 3 free). ☎ (08376) 1 91 10.

Cunerakerk – Open late June to Memorial Day in September Tuesdays to Fridays from 1400 to 1530. 1fl. ☎ (08376) 1 40 93.

ASSEN

i Brink 42, 9401 HV, ☎ (05920) 1 73 06

Drents Museum – Open from 1100 to 1700. Closed Mondays (except during summer holidays) and on 1 January and 25 December. 5fl. ☎ (05920) 1 27 41.

Excursions

Leek: Nationaal Rijtuigmuseum – Open from 0900 (1300 Sundays) to 1700. 4.50fl. ☎ (05945) 1 22 60.

Midwolde: Kerk – Open from 1100 to 1230 and from 1400 to 1700 Easter to September; Sundays open from 1300 to 1700. Closed Mondays. 1fl. ☎ (05945) 1 30 80.

B

BERGEN OP ZOOM

i Beursplein 7, 4611 JG, ☎ (01640) 6 60 00

Stadhuis – Open from 0830 to 1230 and from 1330 to 1700. Closed Saturdays, Sundays and public holidays. ☎ (01640) 6 60 00.

Markiezenhof – Open June, July and August from 1100 (1400 Saturdays and Sundays) to 1700; the rest of the year Tuesdays to Sundays from 1400 to 1700. Closed Mondays and on 1 January, Easter Sunday and 25 December. 5fl. ☎ (01640) 42930.

Excursions

Wouw: Kerk – For opening times apply to VVV, ☎ (01658) 52 02.

Roosendaal: Streekmuseum De Ghulden Roos – Open from 1400 to 1700. Closed Mondays (except on public holidays), during Carnival, on Easter Sunday, Whit Sunday and 25 December. 2.25fl. ☎ (01650) 3 69 16.

BOLSWARD

i Broereplein 1, 8701 JC, ☎ (05157) 27 27

Stadhuis – Open July to mid-August Mondays to Saturdays from 1000 to 1700; April to June and mid-August to late October Mondays to Fridays from 0900 to 1200 and 1400 to 1600. Closed public holidays. 2fl. ☎ (05157) 32 44.

Martinikerk – Open from 0900 to 1200 and from 1330 to 1700. Closed Saturdays and Sundays. 2fl. ☎ (05157) 22 74.

Excursion

Witmarsum: Menno-Simonskerkje – Apply to Arumerweg 36. ☎ (05175) 31959.

BREDA

i Willemstraat 17, 4811 AJ, ☎ (076) 22 24 44

Onze Lieve Vrouwekerk – Open May to November from 1000 (1300 Sundays and public holidays) to 1700; the rest of the year Mondays to Fridays from 1000 to 1200 and 1400 to 1700 . 2fl.
Organ concerts: Apply to VVV. ☎ (076) 22 24 44.

Kasteel – Guided tours on request (included in the guided tour of the town). Apply to VVV. ☎ (076) 22 24 44.

Stadhuis – Open from 0900 to 1700. Closed Saturdays, Sundays and public holidays. ☎ (076) 29 40 55.

Breda's Museum – Open from 1030 (1300 Tuesdays, Sundays and public holidays) to 1700. Closed on 1 January and 25 December. 1.50fl. ☎ (076) 22 31 10.

De Beyerd – Open from 1000 (1300 Saturdays, Sundays and public holidays) to 1700. Closed on 1 January, during Carnival, Easter Sunday, Whit Sunday and 25 December. 3fl. ☎ (076) 22 50 25.

Kasteel Bouvigne – The castle is not open to the public; the grounds are open Mondays to Fridays from 0900 to 1600. Closed public holidays. 0.75fl. For information apply to VVV. ☎ (076) 22 24 44.

Hoeven: Volkssterrenwacht Simon Stevin – Guided tours all year at 1330 and 1500 Sundays and at 1930 Wednesdays and Saturdays. Additionally, guided tours at 1500 Wednesdays May and June, and at 1500 every day July and August (except Saturdays). Closed on 1 January, Easter Sunday, Whit Sunday, 25 and 26 December. 7.50fl. ☎ (01659) 24 39.

Oudenbosch: Nederlands Zouavenmuseum – Open Tuesdays, Thursdays and the 1st and 3rd Sunday of the month May to September from 1400 to 1700. 2fl. ☎ (01652) 1 34 48.

Willemstad: Mauritshuis – Open from 0830 to 1200 and from 1300 to 1630. Closed Saturdays, Sundays, Wednesday afternoons and public holidays. ☎ (01687) 23 50.

Raamsdonksveer: Nationaal Automobielmuseum – Open from 1000 (1100 Sundays and public holidays) to 1700. 16fl. (8fl for children). ☎ (01621) 8 54 00.

Biesbosch: Boat Trips – Apply in Drimmelen to [Rederij de Zilvermeeuw (016) 26 82 609, Avontuur (016) 96 74 196 or De Branding (016) 26 87 121]; in Lage Zwaluwe to [Rederij Biesboschtours (016) 84 22 50] and in Geertruidenberg to [Rederij De Stad Geertruidenberg (016) 21 15 184].

BRIELLE

ℹ Trompmuseum, Venkelstraat 3, 3231 XT, ☎ (01810) 1 33 33

Trompmuseum – Open from 0900 to 1230 and from 1330 to 1600. Closed Sundays and public holidays. 2fl. ☎ (01810) 1 33 33.

Grote- of St.-Catharijnekerk – Open June, July and August from 1000 (1330 Saturdays) to 1600; the two last weeks in May and September (except Wednesdays) from 1330 to 1600. Closed Sundays and public holidays.

BULBFIELDS See Keukenhof

D

DELFT

ℹ Markt 85, 2611 GS, ☎ (015) 12 61 00

Boat Trips on the Canals – April to Mid-October departure every hour (time: 3/4 hour) from 1100 to 1800. 7fl. (5fl for children). ☎ (015) 12 63 85.

Nieuwe Kerk – Open April to October from 0900 to 1700; the rest of the year from 1100 to 1600. Closed Sundays. 2.50fl.

Access to the Tower – From April to August 1000 to 1630. Closed Mondays. 3.25fl. ☎ (015) 60 29 60.

Koninklijk Nederlands Leger- en Wapenmuseum – Open from 1000 (1300 Sundays and public holidays) to 1700. Closed Mondays and on 1 January, Easter Sunday, Whit Sunday, Ascension Day and 25 December. 3.50fl. ☎ (015) 15 05 00.

Prinsenhof – Open from 1000 (1300 Sundays and public holidays) to 1700. Closed Mondays and on 1 January and 25 December. 3.50fl. (ticket giving access to Museum Lambert van Meerten and Volkenkundig Museum Nusantara). ☎ (015) 60 23 58.

Oude Kerk – Open April to October from 1000 to 1700. Closed Sundays. 2.50fl. ☎ (015) 12 30 15.

Museum Lambert van Meerten – Same times and charges as for Prinsenhof. ☎ (015) 60 23 58.

Volkenkundig Museum Nusantara – Same times and charges as for the Museum Lambert van Meerten. ☎ (015) 60 23 58.

R. Mazin/TOP

Delftware

Museum Paul Tetar van Elven – Open May to mid-October from 1300 to 1700. Closed Mondays, Sundays and public holidays. 3.50fl. ☎ (015) 12 42 06.

DELTA

Boat Trips in the Delta – See under Rotterdam and Zierikzee.

Renesse: Slot Moermond – Guided tours (1 1/2 hours) by appointment mid-June to early September at 1900 Thursdays and at 1430 Saturdays. 1.50fl. ☎ (01116) 17 88.

Brouwershaven: St.-Nicolaaskerk – For opening times apply to the VVV, ☎ (01119) 19 40.

Delta Expo – Open daily from April to October 1000 to 1700; open Wednesdays to Sundays only November to March. Closed on 25 December. April to October (ticket includes boat trip) 15fl; children 10fl. November to March (not including boat trip) 13fl; children 7.50fl. ☎ (01115) 27 02.

DEVENTER

ℹ Brink 55, 7411 BV, ☎ (05700) 1 62 00

Boat Trips – During the summer season only. Apply to Rederij Scheers, Worp 39. ☎ (05700) 1 32 54 and Rederij Eureka, Bolwerksweg 1. ☎ (05700) 1 59 14.

Museum De Waag – Open from 1000 (1400 Sundays and public holidays) to 1700. Closed Mondays and on 1 January, Easter Sunday, Whit Sunday and 25 December. 5fl. ☎ (05700) 9 37 80.

Speelgoed- en Blikmuseum – Same times and charges as for Museum De Waag. ☎ (05700) 9 37 86.

Stadhuis – Open from 0830 to 1715. Closed Saturdays, Sundays and public holidays. ☎ (05700) 9 33 11.

St.-Lebuïnuskerk – Open from 1100 to 1700. Closed Sundays, and on Easter Monday, Whit Monday and Ascension Day.
Carillon and Organ Concerts: For information apply to ☎ (05700) 1 25 48.
Access to the Tower: From 1300 to 1700 July to August. 2 fl.

Buiskensklooster: Library – Open Tuesdays to Fridays from 0900 to 1230 and 1330 to 1700. Closed public holidays. ☎ (05700) 9 37 13.

Excursion

Holten: Bos Museum – Open Easter to October from 0900 (1200 Sundays and public holidays) to 1800. Closed Easter Sunday and Whit Sunday. 5fl. ☎ (05483) 6 15 33.

DOESBURG

ℹ Kerkstraat 16, 6981 CM, ☎ (08334) 79088

Boat Trips – Departures July and August. Apply to Rederij Scheers. ☎ (05700) 1 32 54.

Martinikerk – Open April to September, during the autumn holidays and on Easter Monday from 1400 to 1700. Closed Sundays.
Access to the Tower: Apply to VVV.

Museum De Roode Tooren – Open Tuesdays to Fridays from 1000 to 1200 and 1330 to 1630; June, July and August Saturdays and Sundays from 1330 to 1630. Closed Mondays, Sundays (except June to August) and on 1 January, Easter Sunday, Whit Sunday and 25 December. 2.50fl. ☎ (08334) 7 42 65.

Doesburgsche Mosterdfabriek – Open from 1000 to 1700 (1100 to 1600 Saturdays and Easter Monday). Closed Sundays and public holidays. 2fl.

Excursion

's-Heerenberg: Huis Bergh – Guided tours (1 1/4 hours) July and August from 1100 to 1600; June and September Mondays to Fridays at 1400 and 1500; April, May and October Saturdays and Sundays at 1400 and 1500; the rest of the year Sundays at 1400 and 1500. Closed on 25 December. 7.50fl. ☎ (08346) 6 12 81.

DOKKUM

Museum Het Admiraliteitshuis – Open April to September Mondays to Saturdays from 1000 to 1700, some Sundays and public holidays 1400 to 1700; the rest of the year Mondays to Saturdays from 1400 to 1700. 2.50fl. ☎ (05190) 9 31 34.

St.-Martinuskerk – If closed, apply to the sacristan (Koster).

DOORN

ℹ Dorpsstraat 4, 3941, ☎ (03430) 1 20 15

Huis Doorn – Guided tours from 1000 to 1600 (open to the public Sundays). Closed Mondays. 7.50fl. ☎ (03430) 1 22 44.

DORDRECHT

ℹ Stationsweg 1, 3311 JW, ☎ (078) 13 28 00

Boat Trips – For information and reservations, apply to Biesbosch Bezoekerscentrum, Baanhoekweg 53, 3313 LP Dordrecht. ☎ (078) 21 13 11.

Onze Lieve Vrouwekerk – Open April to October from 1030 (1200 Sundays) to 1600; additionally, open the 1st and 3rd Saturday in November and December from 1400 to 1600. ☎ (01823) 14 46 60.
Carillon Concerts: 1100 to 1200 Fridays, 1400 to 1500 Saturdays and public holidays during the summer season.
Organ Concerts: during the summer season. ☎ (078) 13 28 00.
Access to the Tower: April to October 1030 (1200 Sundays) to 1600; July and August Mondays 1200 to 1600; the rest of the year closed Mondays. Additionally, Saturdays November to March and Sundays when the weather is fine from 1300 to 1600. 2fl. ☎ (01823) 31 04 13.

Museum Mr. Simon van Gijn – Open from 1000 (1300 Sundays and public holidays) to 1700. Closed Mondays and on 1 January and 25 December. 5fl. ☎ (078) 13 37 93.

Dordrechts Museum – Same times and charges as for Museum Mr. Simon van Gijn. 6.25fl. ☎ (078) 13 41 00.

This guide, which is revised regularly,
incorporates tourist information provided at the time of going to press
Changes are however inevitable owing to improved facilities and fluctuations in the cost of living

E

EDAM

🅸 Damplein 1, 1135 BK, ☎ (02993) 7 17 27

Edams Museum – Open from 1000 (1330 Sundays and public holidays) to 1630 Good Friday to October. 2fl. ☎ (02993) 7 13 74.

Kaaswaag: Exhibition – Open April to October from 1000 to 1700. ☎ (02993) 7 18 61.

St.-Nicolaaskerk – Open April to September from 1400 to 1630. ☎ (02993) 7 16 87.

EINDHOVEN

🅸 Sationsplein 17, 5611 AC, ☎ (040) 44 92 31

Stedelijk Van Abbemuseum – Open from 1100 to 1700. Closed Mondays (except public holidays) and on 1 January and 25 December. 5fl. ☎ (040) 38 97 30.

Animali – Open from 0900 to 1800. 6fl. (4.75fl. for children). ☎ (040) 11 37 38.

Museum Kempenland – Open from 1300 to 1700. Closed Mondays and on 1 January, Easter Sunday and 25 December. 3fl. ☎ (040) 52 90 93.

Excursions

Kasteel Helmond: Museum – Open from 1000 to 1700, Sundays and public holidays from 1400 to 1700. 2.50fl. Closed 1 January, during carnival time and 25 December. ☎ (04920) 4 74 75.

Asten: Nationaal Beiaardmuseum – Open from 0930 (1300 Mondays, Saturdays, Sundays and public holidays) to 1700. Closed on 1 January, during Carnival and 25 December. 6fl. (ticket giving access to the Natuurstudiecentrum en Museum Jan Vriends). ☎ (04936) 18 65.

Asten: Natuurstudiecentrum en Museum Jan Vriends – Same times and charges as for the Nationaal Beiaardmuseum.

De Groote Peel National Park – Open from sunrise to sunset.
Bezoekerscentrum Mijl op Zeven – Open April to October, during the autumn holidays and at Christmas from 0900 (1000 Saturdays and Sundays) to 1700. Closed on 1 January and 25 December. ☎ (04951) 4 14 97.

EMMEN

🅸 Marktplein 17, 7811 AM, ☎ (05910) 1 30 00

Noorder Dierenpark – Open from 0900 to 1630 (November to February) or 1700 (October and March to May) or 1750 (September). 19fl. (15fl for children). ☎ (05910) 1 88 00.

Excursion

Coevorden: Museum "Drenthe's Veste" – Open from 1000 to 1230 and 1330 to 1700. Closed Saturdays, Sundays, public holidays and the 1st Monday of the month. 1.25fl. ☎ (05240) 1 62 25.

ENKHUIZEN

🅸 Tussen Twee Havens 1, 1601 EM, ☎ (02280) 1 31 64

Boat Trips – Towards Stavoren (1 1/4 hours). Three daily departures May to mid-September. 9.50fl. (return ticket 15fl). For information apply to Rederij NACO. ☎ (020) 62 62 466. Boat trips to Medemblik: apply to Rederij de Jonge. ☎ (02280) 1 79 71.

Westerkerk – Apply to VVV. ☎ (02280) 1 31 64.

Dromedaris – Open from 1400 to 2200. ☎ (02280) 1 20 76.

Zuiderzeemuseum – Indoor Museum: Open from 1000 to 1700. Closed 1 January, 25 and 26 December. Outdoor Museum: Open April to October from 1000 to 1700. 5fl. (Indoor Museum). 14fl. (Indoor and Outdoor Museums). ☎ (02280) 1 01 22.

Stedelijk Waagmuseum – Closed, for further information apply to the VVV.

Zuiderkerk – For information apply to VVV. ☎ (02280) 1 31 64.

Summer Garden – Open from 0900 (1300 Sundays) to 1700 July and August. ☎ (02280) 1 31 64.

ENSCHEDE

🅸 Oude Markt 31, 7511 GB, ☎ (053) 32 32 00

Rijksmuseum Twenthe – Open from 1000 (1300 Saturdays, Sundays and public holidays) to 1700. Closed on 1 January. ☎ (053) 35 86 75.

Museum Jannink – Open from 1000 (1300 Saturdays, Sundays and public holidays) to 1700. Closed Mondays and on 1 January, Easter Sunday and 25 December. 3fl. ☎ (053) 31 90 93.

Natuurmuseum – Open from 1000 (1300 Sundays and public holidays) to 1700. Closed Mondays and on 1 January, Easter Sunday, Whit Sunday and 25 December. 2.50fl. ☎ (053) 32 34 09.

Excursions

Oldenzaal

St.-Plechelmusbasiliek – Open June to September Tuesdays and Thursdays from 1400 to 1500 (1600 Wednesdays). Closed public holidays. ☎ (05410) 1 28 08.

Museum Het Palthe Huis – Open from 1000 to 1200 and from 1400 to 1700 (afternoons only Saturdays, Sundays and public holidays). Closed on 1 January, during Carnival, Easter Sunday, Ascension Day, Whit Sunday and 25 December. 3.50fl. ☎ (05410) 1 34 82.

Denekamp

Kasteel Singraven – Guided tours (1 hour) mid-April to October Tuesdays to Fridays at 1100, 1400, 1500 and 1600; guided tours Saturdays at 1100, 1200, 1400 and 1500. Closed Mondays, Sundays and public holidays. 9fl. (4.50fl. for children). ☎ (05413) 5 19 86 (temporary no).

Watermolen van Singraven – Open mid-April to October Tuesdays to Fridays at 1100, 1400, 1500 and 1600. 9fl. ☎ (05413) 5 13 72.

Ootmarsum

Kerk van de H. H. Simon en Judas – Open mid-May to October Mondays to Fridays from 1000 to 1200 and from 1430 to 1600; open Sundays and public holidays from 1500 to 1600. Closed Saturdays. ☎ (05419) 9 18 34.

Delden

Kasteel Twickel: Gardens – Open mid-May to mid-October Wednesdays and Saturdays from 1330 to 1700. Closed public holidays. 3fl. ☎ (05407) 6 13 00.

Het Zoutmuseum – Open May to August Mondays to Fridays from 1000 to 1700, weekends 1400 to 1700; the rest of the year Tuesdays to Fridays and Sundays 1400 to 1700. Closed Easter Sunday, Whit Sunday and 25 December. 4fl. ☎ (05407) 6 45 46.

F

FLEVOLAND

Ketelhaven: Museum voor Scheepsarcheologie – Open from 0900 (1000 Saturdays and Sundays April to September, 1100 Saturdays and Sundays October to March) to 1700. Closed on 1 January and 25 December. 3.50fl. ☎ (03210) 1 32 87.

Walibi-Flevo: Amusement Park – Open mid-May to October, daily 1000 to 1800; 28fl, children under 4 free: ☎ (03211) 15 14.

Lelystad: Informatiecentrum Nieuw Land (Visitor Centre) – Open from 1000 (1130 Saturdays, Sundays and public holidays) to 1700. Closed on 1 January and 25 December. 7fl. ☎ (03200) 6 07 99.

Batavia – Open daily from 1000 to 1700. Closed on 1 January and 25 December. 15fl. (5fl for children). ☎ (03200) 6 14 09.

FLUSHING See Vlissingen

FRANEKER

Stadhuis – Open from 0900 to 1200 and 1400 to 1600. Closed Saturdays, Sundays and public holidays. ☎ (05170) 9 83 83.

Planetarium – Open May to August weekdays from 1000 to 1230 and 1330 to 1700; Sundays from 1300 to 1700; the rest of the year open Tuesdays to Saturdays from 1000 to 1230 and 1330 to 1700. 4fl. ☎ (05170) 9 30 70.

Museum 't Coopmanshûs – Open Tuesdays to Saturdays from 1000 to 1700; open Sundays April to September from 1300 to 1700. 2.75fl. ☎ (05170) 9 21 92.

G

GIETHOORN

ℹ Beulakerweg, 8355 AM, ☎ (05216) 12 48

Tour of the Village – Guided tours with a helmsman (1 hour): 7fl. per person. Dinghy rentals: 12.50fl. an hour, 40fl. a day. Launch rentals: 17.50-20fl. an hour, 85-90 fl. a day. ☎ (05216) 12 48.

GOES

ℹ Stationsplein 3, 4461 HP, ☎ (01100) 2 05 77

Steam Tramway – Daily departures at 1400 during the summer season (except Saturdays). Sundays only in spring and autumn. 18fl (1st class) or 14fl (2nd class). ☎ (01100) 2 83 07.

Maria Magdalenakerk – Open July and August from 1000 to 1600. Closed Saturdays, Sundays and Tuesday mornings. ☎ (01100) 1 67 68.
Organ Concerts: For information apply to VVV. ☎ (01100) 2 05 77.

Excursion

Kapelle: Hervormde Kerk – Open from 0900 to 1130 and 1230 to 1730. Closed Sundays and public holidays. ☎ (01102) 4 29 38.

GORINCHEM

ℹ Zusterhuis 6, 4201 EH, ☎ (01830) 3 15 25

St.-Maartenskerk: Access to St.-Janstoren – Open July and August Mondays from 1000 to 1200 and Saturdays from 1400 to 1600; open Easter Monday and Whit Monday from 1000 to 1200. 1fl. ☎ (01830) 3 15 25.

Museum "Dit is in Bethlehem" – Open from 1400 to 1700. Closed Mondays, Tuesdays and on 1 January and 25 December. 3fl. ☎ (01830) 3 28 21.

Excursions

Leerdam: Nationaal Glasmuseum – Open Tuesdays to Fridays from 1000 to 1300 and 1400 to 1700; open April to October Saturdays, Sundays and public holidays from 1300 to 1700. Closed Mondays and on 1 January, 25 and 26 December. 5fl. ☎ (03451) 1 31 41.

Slot Loevestein – Guided tours (50 min) April to October from 1000 (1300 Saturdays, Sundays and public holidays) to 1700 . Last guided tour at 1600. 6fl. ☎ (01832) 13 75.

GOUDA

Markt 27, 2801 JJ, ☎ (01820) 1 36 66

Boat Trips – Departure from Bleekersingel. Apply to Rederij 't Groene Hart. ☎ (01820) 2 59 28.

Cheese Market and Handicraft Market – Open late June to late August Thursdays from 0930 to 1200. ☎ (01820) 1 36 66.

Stadhuis – Open Mondays to Fridays from 0900 to 1700 (1100 to 1500 Saturdays); open late June to early September Sundays from 1030 to 1600. Closed public holidays. 0.25 fl. ☎ (01820) 1 38 00.

St.-Janskerk – Open March to October from 0900 (1300 public holidays) to 1700; the rest of the year from 1000 to 1600. Closed Sundays and on 1 January, 25 and 26 December. 2.50fl. ☎ (01820) 1 26 84.

Stedelijk Museum Het Catharina Gasthuis – Open from 1000 (1200 Sundays and public holidays) to 1700. Closed on 1 January and 25 December. 3.50fl. (ticket gives access to Stedelijk Museum De Moriaan). ☎ (01820) 8 84 40.

Stedelijk Museum De Moriaan – Same times and charges as for Stedelijk Museum Het Catharina Gasthuis.

Excursions

Woerden: Stadsmuseum – Open from 1400 to 1700. Closed public holidays. 1fl. ☎ (03480) 2 84 15.

Oudewater: Heksenwaag – Open April to October from 1000 (1200 Sundays and public holidays) to 1700. 2.50fl. ☎ (03486) 34 00.

Schoonhoven: Nederlands Goud-, Zilver- en Klokkenmuseum – Open from 1200 to 1700. Closed Mondays and on 1 January and 25 December. 4fl. ☎ (01823) 8 56 12.

's-GRAVENHAGE See Den Haag

GRONINGEN

Gedempte Kattendiep 6, ☎ (050) 13 97 00

Boat Trips on the Canals – Allow 1 1/4 hours. June to August daily departures (except Sundays) at 1115, 1345, 1530 and 1715. 9fl. (5fl. for children). ☎ (050) 12 83 79.

Flea Market – Open Tuesdays and Saturdays from 0900 to 1600 (1700 in summer). ☎ (050) 13 97 00.

Martinikerk – Open late May to early September from 1200 to 1700. Closed Sundays and Mondays. 8fl. ☎ (050) 18 36 36.
Access to the Tower: Apply to VVV.

Noordelijk Scheepvaart Museum – Open from 1000 (1300 Sundays and public holidays) to 1700. Closed Mondays and on 1 January, 30 April, 28 August and 25 December. 5fl. ☎ (050) 12 22 02.

Niemeyer Tabaksmuseum – Same times and charges as for Noordelijk Scheepvaart Museum.

Groninger Museum – The museum is now in new premises opposite the railway station. Apply to the VVV for the opening times and charges.

Excursions

Aduard: Hervormde Kerk – Open March to September Mondays to Fridays (by appointment Saturdays) from 0900 to 1200. Closed Sundays and public holidays. 1.50fl. ☎ (05903) 17 24.

Leens: Petruskerk: Organ Concerts – May to August Saturdays at 2015. ☎ (05957) 16 77.

Lauwersoog Expozee – Open from 1400 to 1700. Closed Mondays and on 1 January and 25, 26 and 31 December. 3fl. ☎ (05193) 4 90 45.

Garmerwolde: Kerk – For information apply to the sacristan Harm Winters, Dorpsweg 62. ☎ (050) 41 30 63.

Loppersum: Kerk – For information apply to Mr L. Aslander, Nieuwstraat 4. ☎ (05967) 15 73.

Zeerijp: Kerk – For information call ☎ (05967) 18 26.

Krewerd: Kerk – For information call ☎ (05960) 2 23 47.

Appingedam: Nicolaikerk – Open mid-June to mid-September Tuesdays to Saturdays from 1400 to 1700; the rest of the year open by appointment. ☎ (05960) 2 29 92.

Delfzijl: Boat Trips – By appointment only. For information apply to Mr P. Bakker. ☎ (05962) 13 48.

Bierum: Kerkje – Guided tours March to mid-July and August to November from 1230 to 1730. Closed Sundays. ☎ (05969) 15 39.

Uithuizermeeden: Kerk – To visit the church and tower, read the notice board at the entrance of the tower.

Stichting Museum 1939-1945 – Open from 0900 to 1800. Closed early October to late March. 6fl.

H

DEN HAAG (The HAGUE)

Kon. Julianaplein 30, 2595 AA, ☎ (070) 06 34 50 51

Ridderzaal: Upper Chamber and Lower Chamber – This information is for guidance only. The visiting possibilities for individuals are very limited: usually around 1200 and 1400. Guided tours (3/4 hour) Mondays to Saturdays from 1015 to 1545. Closed Sundays and public holidays. 5fl. (ticket includes audio-visual presentation, Ridderzaal, Upper or Lower Chamber when not in session). The Upper Chamber is temporarily closed. Apply to 8A Binnenhof. It is recommended that you book in advance. ☎ (070) 364 61 44.

Exhibition: Same opening times as Ridderzaal, admission free. The Balzaal (ballroom) is presently undergoing restoration work.

Mauritshuis – Open from Tuesdays to Saturdays 1000 (1100 Sundays and public holidays) to 1700. Closed Mondays and on 1 January and 25 December. 7.50fl. ☎ (070) 365 47 79.

Haags Historisch Museum – Open from 1100 (1200 Saturdays, Sundays and public holidays) to 1700. Closed Mondays and on 1 January and 25 December. 5fl. ☎ (070) 364 69 40.

Museum Bredius – Open from 1200 to 1700. Closed Mondays and on 1 January and 25 December. 4fl. ☎ (070) 362 07 29.

Antiques Market – Open mid-May to late September Thursdays from 0900 to 2100 and Sundays from 1100 to 1700.

Paleis Lange Voorhout – For further details on temporary exhibitions phone (070) 338 11 11.

Waals-Hervormde Kerk – The church is not open to the public.

Gevangenpoort – Guided tours every hour from 1000 (1300 Sundays) to 1700 (last tour at 1600). Closed Saturdays and on 1 January and 25 and 26 December. 5fl. ☎ (070) 346 08 61.

Schilderijengalerij Prins Willem V – Open from 1100 to 1600. Closed Mondays and on 1 January and 25 December. 2.50fl. ☎ (070) 318 24 86.

St.-Jacobskerk – Open mid-May to late August from 1100 to 1600. Closed Sundays and public holidays. ☎ (070) 365 86 65.

Panorama Mesdag – Open from 1000 (1200 Sundays and public holidays) to 1700. Closed on 25 December. 4fl. ☎ (070) 364 25 63.

Museum Mesdag – Temporarily closed; reopening scheduled for 1996.

Vredespaleis (Peace Palace) – Guided tours (3/4 hour) at 1000, 1100, 1400 and 1500; additional guided tour at 1600 May to August. Closed Saturdays, Sundays and public holidays. 5fl. ☎ (070) 346 96 80.

Haags Gemeentemuseum – Open from 1100 to 1700. Closed Mondays (except public holidays). 8fl. ☎ (070) 338 11 11.

Museon – Open from 1000 (1200 Saturdays, Sundays and public holidays) to 1700. Closed Mondays and on 1 January and 25 December. 5fl. ☎ (070) 338 13 38.

Omniversum – Films every hour from 1100 to 1600; from 1100 to 2100 Fridays, Saturdays, Sundays, public holidays and during school holidays. 16fl. (13fl. for children). For reservations call ☎ (070) 354 54 54. Headphones with an English commentary can be hired for certain films.

Madurodam – Open June, July and August from 0900 to 2300; March, April and May 0900 to 2230; September 0900 to 2130; October to early January 0900 to 1800. Closed the rest of the year. 14fl. (8.50fl. for children). ☎ (070) 355 39 00.

Rijksmuseum Meermanno-Westreenianum – Open from 1300 to 1700. Closed Sundays and public holidays. ☎ (070) 346 27 00.

Scheveningen Pier – Open from 0900 to 2100. 1fl. ☎ (070) 354 36 77.
Boat Trips – Apply to Rederij Vrolijk, Doorniksestraat 7. ☎ (070) 351 40 21.

Excursions

Voorburg: Huygensmuseum – Open from 1400 to 1700. Closed Mondays, Tuesdays, Fridays and on 1 January, Easter Sunday, 30 April and 5, 25, 26 and 31 December. 2.50fl. ☎ (070) 387 23 11.

Naaldwijk: Flower and Plant Auctions – Open Mondays to Fridays from 0800 to 1200. For a guided tour apply to ☎ (01740) 3 21 58.

HAARLEM

ℹ Stationsplein 1, 2011 LR, ☎ (023) 31 90 59

St.-Bavokerk – Open from 1000 to 1600. Closed Sundays and public holidays. 2fl. ☎ (023) 32 43 99.
Organ Concerts: At 2000 mid-May to mid-October Tuesdays and July and August Thursdays at 1500.

Stadhuis – Guided tours by appointment from 0900 to 1700 Mondays to Fridays. ☎ (023) 17 12 98.

Vleeshal – Same times and charges as for Frans Halsmuseum. 3fl. (ticket giving access to the Vishal).

Vishal – Same times and charges as for Frans Hals Museum. 3fl. (ticket giving access to the Vleeshal).

Frans Halsmuseum – Open from 1100 (1300 Sundays and public holidays) to 1700. Closed on 1 January and 25 December. 6.25fl. ☎ (023) 16 42 00.

Teylers Museum – Open from 1000 (1300 Sundays and public holidays) to 1700. Closed Mondays and on 1 January and 25 December. 6.50fl. ☎ (023) 31 90 10.

Kathedrale Basiliek St.-Bavo – Open May to September from 1000 to 1200 and from 1400 to 1630. Closed Sunday mornings.

Outskirts

Museum De Cruquius – Open March to September Mondays to Thursdays from 1000 to 1700, Saturdays, Sundays and public holidays 1100 to 1700; October Mondays to Thursdays from 1000 to 1600, Saturdays and public holidays 1100 to 1600. Closed Fridays. 4fl. ☎ (023) 28 57 04.

Excursions

De Kennemerduinen Nationaal Park – Open from sunrise to sunset. 1.75fl.
Visitor Centre: Open mid-April to mid-September from 0900 to 1630; the rest of the year open Sundays, public holidays and during school holidays. ☎ (023) 25 76 53.

THE HAGUE See Den Haag

HARDERWIJK

ℹ Havendam 58, 3841 AA, ☎ (03410) 2 66 66

Boat Trips – Departures from 1100 mid-June to August. The boats leave from Strandboulevard, near the port.

Dolfinarium – Open late February to October from 1000 to 1800 (last ticket sold 1600). 20.50fl. (17.50fl for children). ☎ (03410) 1 60 41.

Veluws Museum – Open Mondays to Fridays from 1000 to 1700; additionally, May to September Saturdays from 1300 to 1600. Closed Sundays and public holidays. 2.50fl. ☎ (03410) 1 44 68.

Grote Kerk – Open mid-May to mid-September Mondays and Thursdays from 1330 to 1630 and Tuesdays and Wednesdays 1100 to 1630. Closed public holidays. ☎ (03410) 2 66 66.

Excursions

Elburg

Vischpoort – Open June to August Mondays from 1400 to 1630, Tuesdays to Fridays from 0930 to 1200 and 1400 to 1630. Closed Saturdays, Sundays and public holidays. 2.75fl (ticket gives access to Gemeentemuseum).

Gemeentemuseum – Open in summer from 1000 (1400 Mondays) to 1700; the rest of the year from 0900 to 1200 and 1400 to 1700 (closed Monday mornings). Closed Saturdays, Sundays and public holidays. 2.75fl. ☎ (05250) 13 41.

St.-Nicolaaskerk – Open in summer from 1000 to 1200 and 1400 to 1630 in summer; the rest of the year open by appointment. Closed Saturdays, Sundays and public holidays. ☎ (05250) 15 20.

Boat Trips – For information apply to VVV, Jufferenstraat 9. ☎ (05250) 15 20.

HARLINGEN

ℹ Voorstraat 34, 8861 BL, ☎ (05178) 1 72 22

Gemeentemuseum Hannemahuis – Open 5 April to 25 June and 20 September to 29 October Mondays to Fridays from 1330 to 1700; open 29 June to 18 September Tuesdays to Saturdays from 1000 to 1700; Sundays from 1330 to 1700. 2.50fl. ☎ (5178) 1 36 58.

HEERENVEEN

Oranjewoud and Oranjestein – For information apply to VVV. ☎ (05130) 2 55 55.

HEERLEN

ℹ Honigmanstraat 100, 6411 LM, ☎ (045) 71 62 00

Thermenmuseum – Open from 1000 (1400 Saturdays, Sundays and public holidays) to 1700. Closed Mondays and on 1 January, during Carnival, Easter Sunday, 30 April, Whit Sunday and 25 December. 3fl. ☎ (045) 76 45 81.

Excursions

Kerkrade

Abdij Rolduc – Guided tours by appointment. ☎ (045) 46 68 88.

Mijnmuseum – Open from 0900 (1300 Sundays) to 1700; open Saturdays in July and August. Closed Mondays, Saturdays (except in July and August) and public holidays. 3.50fl. ☎ (045) 45 71 38.

DEN HELDER

Julianaplein 30, 1781 HC, ☎ (02230) 2 55 44

Helders Marinemuseum – Open mid-January to late November Mondays to Fridays from 1000 (1300 Mondays June to August) to 1645 ; Saturdays, Sundays and public holidays from 1300 to 1630 . 2.50fl. ☎ (02230) 5 71 37.

Excursion

Callantsoog

Het Zwanenwater Nature Reserve – Open mid-March to July from 0700 to 2100; the rest of the year open from sunrise to sunset. 1fl.

's-HERTOGENBOSCH

Markt 77, 5211 JX, ☎ (073) 12 30 71

St.-Janskathedraal – Open Mondays to Fridaysfrom 1000 to 1630; Saturdays, Sundays and public holidays from 1300 to 1700.
Organ Concerts: early July to late September at 1530 Saturdays; also early June to late September Tuesday evenings; for information apply to VVV. ☎ (073) 12 30 71.

Stadhuis: Carillon – At 1000 Wednesdays.

Noordbrabants Museum – Open from 1000 (1200 Saturdays, Sundays and public holidays) to 1700. Closed Mondays and on 1 January, during Carnival and 25 December. 7.50fl. ☎ (073) 13 96 64.

Museum Slager – Open from 1400 to 1700. Closed Mondays, Saturdays and on 1 January, Easter Sunday, Whit Sunday and 25 December. ☎ (073) 13 32 16.

Museum Het Kruithuis – Open from 1100 (1300 Sundays and public holidays) to 1700. Closed Mondays, during Carnival, on Easter Sunday, Whit Sunday and 25 December. 3fl. ☎ (073) 12 21 88.

Boat Trips on the Binnendieze – Early April to late October (except Mondays) departure every hour from 1100 to 1700. Time: 50 min. 6fl. It is recommended that you book in advance. ☎ (073) 12 23 34.

Excursions

Heeswijk-Dinther

Kasteel Heeswijk – Temporarily closed.

De Meierijsche Museumboerderij – Open May to September Wednesdays, Saturdays and Sundays from 1400 to 1700. Closed on Easter Sunday and Whit Sunday. 2fl. ☎ (04139) 15 46.

Waalwijk: Nederlands Leder en Schoenenmuseum – Open from 1000 to 1700 (1200 to 1600 Saturdays, Sundays and public holidays). Closed Mondays and on 1 January, Easter Sunday, Whit Sunday and 25 December. 5fl. ☎ (04160) 3 27 38.

De Efteling: Recreatiepark (Theme Park) – Open Good Thursday to late October from 1000 to 1800 . 30fl (children under 3 are free). ☎ (04167) 8 81 11.

Zaltbommel: Streekmuseum – Open from 1000 to 1230 and from 1330 to 1630 (1400 to 1630 Saturdays and Sundays). Closed Mondays and on 1 January, Easter Sunday, Whit Sunday and 25 December. 2.50fl. ☎ (04180) 1 26 17.

Heusden: Stadhuis – Carillon concerts in summer. For information call ☎ (04162) 22 34.

Rosmalen

Autotron – Open early April to late October from 1000 to 1700 (1800 July and August). 17.50fl. (14.50fl for children). ☎ (04192) 1 90 50.

Huis van de Toekomst – Same admission times as for Autotron.

HET LOO

Park – Open from 0900 to 1800 (1600 in winter). 2fl. (1fl for children).

Palace, Stables and Gardens – Open from 1000 to 1700. Closed Mondays (except public holidays) and on 25 December. 10fl. ☎ (055) 21 22 44. Concerts on the last Friday of the month. To book call ☎ (055) 21 22 44.

HILVERSUM

Emmastraat 2, 1211 NG, ☎ (035) 21 16 51

Gooi

Laren: Singermuseum – Open from 1100 (1200 Sundays and public holidays) to 1700. Closed Mondays and on 1 January, 30 April and 25 December. 8.50fl. ☎ (02153) 1 56 56.

Muiden

Muiderslot – Guided tours (1 hour) April to September from 1000 (1300 Saturdays, Sundays and public holidays) to 1700; the rest of the year from 1000 (1300 Sundays and public holidays) to 1600. Last guided tour one hour before closing time. Closed Saturdays October to March and on 1 January, 25 and 26 December. 5fl. ☎ (02942) 6 13 25.

HINDELOOPEN

Museum Hidde Nijland Stichting – Open from 1000 (1330 Sundays and public holidays) to 1700. 3.50fl. ☎ (05142) 14 20.

For historical information on the region consult the table and notes in the ***Introduction***

DE HOGE VELUWE

National Park – Open early March to October from 0800 to sunset; the rest of the year from 0900 to sunset. 7.50fl per automobile plus 7.50fl per passenger (3.75fl per child). The ticket includes admission to all the sites in the park.

Rijksmuseum Kröller-Müller – Open from 1000 to 1700. Closed Mondays, except holiday Mondays, and 1 January. ☎ (08382) 10 41.

Beeldenpark (Sculpture Garden) – Open April to October from 1000 to 1630. Closed Mondays, except holiday Mondays, and 1 January. ☎ (08382) 10 41.

Bezoekerscentrum De Aanschouw (Visitor Centre) – Open from 0900 (1000 November to March) to 1700. ☎ (05768) 14 41 or (08382) 16 27.

Jachtslot St.-Hubertus – Open May to October from 1000 to 1130 and 1400 to 1630. ☎ (05768) 12 37.

Excursion

Otterlo: Nederlands Tegelmuseum – Open from 1000 to 1200 and 1400 to 1700 (1400 to 1600 Sundays and public holidays). Closed Mondays and on 1 January and 25 December. 3fl. ☎ (08382) 15 19.

HOORN

🅸 Statenpoort, Nieuwstraat 23, 1621 EA, ☎ (02290) 06-34 03 10 55

Tourist Train – Ride: 1 hour. Two daily departures in July and August; one daily departure mid-April to June and in September and October Tuesdays to Sundays . Rtn 19fl, single 12fl. ☎ (02290) 1 48 62.

J.S.R./PIX

Façade stone, Hoorn

Westfries Museum – Open from 1100 (1400 Saturdays, Sundays and public holidays) to 1700. Closed on 1 January, the 3rd Monday in August and 25 December. 5fl. ☎ (02290) 1 57 83.

HULST

Streekmuseum – Open May to early September from 1400 to 1700. Closed Sundays except in July and August. 1.25fl. ☎ (01140) 1 23 11.

HUNEBEDDEN

Borger: Nationaal Hunebedden Informatiecentrum (Visitor Centre) – Open from 1000 (1300 Saturdays, Sundays and public holidays) to 1700. 3fl. ☎ (05998) 3 63 74.

K

KAMPEN

🅸 Botermarkt 5, 8261 GR, ☎ (05202) 1 35 00

Boat Trips – Departures early June to mid-September Sundays and Wednesdays to Fridays at 1100, 1300 and 1530 ; return trip leaving at 1200, 1430 and 1630. 6fl. For information apply to VVV. ☎ (05202) 1 35 00.

Oude Raadhuis – Guided tours (1/2 hour) Mondays to Thursdays from 1100 to 1200 and from 1400 to 1600; additionally, open Saturdays May to October from 1400 to 1700. Closed Sundays and public holidays. 1fl. ☎ (05202) 9 29 99.

Nieuwe Toren – Open May to October Wednesdays and Saturdays from 1400 to 1700. Closed public holidays. 1fl. ☎ (05202) 9 29 99.

Stedelijk Museum – Open February to December, Tuesdays to Saturdays from 1100 to 1230 and 1330 to 1700; mid-June to mid-December, Tuesdays to Saturdays, 1100 to 1700, Sundays 1300 to 1700. Closed Whit Sunday, 25, 26 and 31 December. 2fl. ☎ (05202) 1 73 61.

St.-Nicolaaskerk – Open mid-April to early September Mondays and Tuesdays from 1300 to 1700, Wednesdays to Fridays from 1000 to 1700; closed at 1600 during the autumn holidays. Closed Saturdays and Sundays.
Organ Concerts: Thursday evenings and at 1500 Saturdays in summer.

KEUKENHOF

Flight over the Bulbfields – Apply to Luchtvaartmij, Kroonduif, Rotterdam. ☎ (010) 415 78 55.

Keukenhof – Open late March to mid-May or late May from 0800 to 1930 (last admission 1800). On certain days the park is open at 0600. 15fl. ☎ (02521) 1 91 44 or 1 90 34.

Tulipshow – Open late March to late May from 0800 to 1800. ☎ (02521) 1 90 34.

L

LEEUWARDEN

i Stationsplein 1, 8911 AC, ☎ (058) 13 22 24

Fries Museum – Open from 1000 (1300 Sundays and public holidays) to 1700. Closed Mondays and on 1 January, 30 April and 25 December.

Jacobijnerkerk – Open June to September Tuesdays to Fridays from 1400 to 1600. ☎ (058) 12 83 13.
Organ Concerts: July and August Wednesdays at 2000 and Fridays at 1230.

Museum het Princessehof, Nederlands Keramiek Museum – Open from 1000 (1400 Sundays and public holidays) to 1700. Closed on 1 January and 25 December. 5fl. ☎ (058) 12 74 38.

Oldehove – Open mid-May to September Tuesdays to Saturdays from 0930 to 1230 and 1330 to 1630 . 2fl. ☎ (058) 13 22 24.

Excursions

Marssum: Poptaslot – April to September Mondays to Fridays guided tours (1 hour) at 1100, 1400 and 1500. 4fl. ☎ (05107) 4 12 31.

Rinsumageest: Kerk – Open from 0900 to 1200 and from 1300 to 1800. Closed Sundays and public holidays. ☎ (05111) 33 99.

Veenklooster: Fogelsangh State – Open May to September from 1000 to 1200 and from 1300 to 1700. Closed Mondays and Sundays (open from 1300 to 1700 Sundays mid-June to September). 2fl. ☎ (05113) 19 70.

Kollum: Kerk – For information apply to Madame Bijlsma, Bernhardlaan 4, Kollum.

Hoogebeintum: Kerk – Guided tours from 1000 (1200 Sundays and public holidays) to 1700. Closed Mondays. 4fl. ☎ (05181) 17 83.

LEIDEN

i Stationsplein 210, 2312 AR, ☎ (071) 14 68 46

Boat Trips – Canal rides April to Whitsun at 1200, 1400 and 1600 , Whitsun to early September at 1100, 1200, 1330, 1445, 1600 and 1700 . 8fl. ☎ (071) 13 49 38. For a boat trip along the Oude Rijn up to Avifauna, apply to Avifauna. ☎ (01720) 8 75 01.

Rijksmuseum voor Volkenkunde – Temporary exhibitions only during restoration work, which is scheduled to finish in 1998. Open from 1000 (1200 Saturdays and Sundays) to 1700. Closed Mondays and on 1 January and 3 October. 5fl. ☎ (071) 16 88 00.

Molen De Valk – Open from 1000 (1300 Sundays and public holidays) to 1700. Closed Mondays and on 1 January, 3 October and 25 December.

Stedelijk Museum De Lakenhal – Open from 1000 (1200 Saturdays and Sundays) to 1700. Open 3 October, local holiday from 1000 to 1200. Closed Mondays (except public holidays) and on 1 January and 25 December. 5fl. ☎ (071) 16 53 60.

Rijksmuseum van Oudheden – Open from 1000 (1200 Sundays and public holidays) to 1700. Closed Mondays and on 1 January, 3 October and 25 December. 5fl. ☎ (071) 16 31 63.

Hortus Botanicus (Botanical Garden) – Open from 0900 (1000 Sundays and public holidays) to 1700. Closed Saturdays (except April to September), on 3 October and the week between Christmas and New Year. 3.50fl. ☎ (071) 27 72 49.

Pieterskerk – Open from 1330 to 1600. ☎ (071) 12 43 19.

Museum Boerhaave – Open from 1000 (1200 Sundays) to 1700. Closed Mondays and on 1 January and 3 October. 3.50fl. ☎ (071) 21 42 24.

Pilgrim Fathers Documentatiecentrum – Open Mondays to Fridays from 0930 to 1630. Closed public holidays and on 3 October. ☎ (071) 12 01 91.

Excursions

Alphen aan den Rijn: Avifauna – Open daily. 7.50 fl. **Boat trips** (1 1/2 hours) from 1000 Easter to late September. 6fl. For reservations call ☎ (01720) 8 75 01.

AMELAND See Waddeneilanden

M

MAASTRICHT

i Het Dinghuis, Kleine Staat 1, 6211 ED, ☎ (043) 25 21 21.

Mastreechter Staar – The public may attend rehearsals of the choir at 2000 and 2200 Mondays and Thursdays during the summer season (Kesselkade 43, in the old Augustinian Church).

Boat Trips – Apply to Rederij Stiphout, Maaspromenade 27, 6211 HS Maastricht. ☎ (043) 25 41 51.

St.-Servaasbasiliek: Treasure – Enter through Vrijthof; open July and August from 1000 to 1800 and December to March 1000 to 1600; the rest of the year from 1000 to 1700. Closed on 1 January, during Carnival and 25 December. 3.50fl. ☎ (043) 21 04 90.

BENELUX PRESS B.V.

Carnival time, Maastricht

Onze Lieve Vrouwebasiliek – Open from 0730 to 1530. ☎ (043) 25 18 51.
Treasure: Open from 1030 (1230 Sundays) to 1700 Easter to December. 3.50fl.

Stadhuis: Carillon – Concerts at 1130 Fridays and on summer evenings.

Bonnefantenmuseum – New address as of March 1995 is Avenue Céramique 250. For the opening times and charges apply to the VVV.

Kazematten – Guided tours (1 hour) the first fortnight in July and 23 August to 5 September at 1400; mid-July to 22 August also at 1230. 5fl. ☎ (043) 25 21 21.

Outskirts

Fort St.-Pieter – Guided tours (1 hour) July, August and during school holidays at 1515. 5 fl. For information apply to VVV. ☎ (043) 25 21 21.

Mergelgrotten (Marl Caves): North Gallery – Guided tours (1 hour) April to September daily; the rest of the year Wednesdays, Saturdays and Sundays only. 5fl. Apply to VVV. ☎ (043) 25 21 21.

Gangenstelsel Zonneberg – Guided tours (1 hour) May to mid-September every hour from 1045 (1345 Sundays) to 1545; the rest of the year Sundays only around 1430. 5fl. ☎ (043) 25 21 21.

Excursions

Cadier en Keer: Afrika-Centrum – Open from 1330 (1400 Sundays and public holidays) to 1700; November to March Sundays only from 1400 to 1700. Closed Saturdays and on 1 January, during Carnival, Easter Sunday, Whit Sunday, 25 and 26 December. 5fl. ☎ (04407) 12 26.

Stein: Archeologisch Reservaat – Open May to September from 1400 to 1700. 1fl. ☎ (046) 33 18 43.

Sittard: St.-Petruskerk – Guided tours (1 1/2 hours, including St Michael's and the Basilica) early May to early September Tuesdays to Saturdays at 1400. 1fl. Departure from Kritzraedhuis, Rosmalenstraat.

Susteren: St.-Amelbergakerk – Open by appointment. Apply to Mr L.M.G. Pesgens, Pasteur Tijssenstraat 5. 1.75fl. ☎ (04499) 14 73.

MARKEN

The Village – Interiors: A few on the port can be visited.

MEDEMBLIK

i Stationsgebouw, Dam 2, 1671 AW, ☎ (02274) 28 52

Kasteel Radboud – Open from 1000 (1400 Sundays and public holidays) to 1700; the rest of the year open Sundays only. 3.50fl. ☎ (02274) 19 60.

MENKEMABORG

Kasteel – Open April to October from 1000 to 1200 and from 1300 to 1700; the rest of the year 1000 to 1200 and 1300 to 1600. Closed all January. 5fl. ☎ (05953) 19 70.

MIDDELBURG

i Markt 65a, 4331 LL, ☎ (01180) 1 68 51

Stadhuis – Guided tours (3/4 hour) July and August from 1100 to 1600, April to June and September and October, from 1030 to 1125 and 1330 to 1600. Closed Saturdays, Sundays and public holidays. 3fl. ☎ (01180) 7 54 43.

Abdijkerken (Abbey Churches) – Open May to the autumn holidays Tuesdays to Fridays from 1000 to 1700; Mondays 1000 to 1200 and 1300 to 1700. ☎ (01180) 1 68 51.

Lange Jan Toren – Open April to October from 1000 to 1700. Closed Sundays. 2.25fl. ☎ (01180) 1 68 51.

Zeeuws Museum – Open from 1000 (1330 Saturdays to Mondays) to 1700. Closed Mondays November to March. 4fl. ☎ (01180) 2 66 55.

Miniatuur Walcheren – Open from 0930 to 1900 (2000 July and August). 7fl. ☎ (01180) 1 25 25.

*Consult the **Index** to find an individual town or sight*

N

NAARDEN

i Dorstmanplein 1b, 1411 RC, ☎ (02159) 4 28 36

Stadhuis – Open April to September from 1330 to 1630. Closed Sundays and public holidays. ☎ (02159) 5 78 11.

Comeniusmuseum – Open Easter to September from 1000 (1200 Sundays) to 1700; the rest of the year open from 1400 to 1700. 2.50fl. ☎ (02159) 4 30 45.

Waalse Kerk – Open mid-January to mid-December 1600 to 1700. ☎ (02159) 4 30 45

Vestingmuseum – Open from 1000 to 1630 (1200 to 1700 Saturdays and Sundays). 5fl. ☎ (02159) 4 54 59.

NIJMEGEN

i St.-Jorisstraat 72, 6511 TD, ☎ (080) 22 54 40

Boat Trips – Departures July and August. Apply to Rederij Tonissen, Waalkade. 7.50fl. or 12fl. ☎ (080) 23 32 85.

St.-Stevenskerk – Open mid-May to September Mondays to Fridays from 1000 to 1700 (closed from 1230 to 1300 mid-May to mid-June and mid-August to late September) and from 1000 to 1300 Saturdays; additionally, open mid-June to mid-August Sundays and public holidays from 1400 to 1700. 1fl.
Organ and Carillon Concerts: Apply to VVV. ☎ (080) 22 554 40.

Nijmeegs Museum – Open from 1000 (1300 Sundays and public holidays) to 1700. Closed on 25 December. 2.50fl. ☎ (080) 22 91 93.

Stadhuis – Guided tours by appointment. ☎ (080) 29 24 03.

Provinciaal Museum G.M.Kam – Open from 1000 (1300 Saturdays, Sundays and public holidays) to 1700. Closed Mondays and on 25 December. 3fl. ☎ (080) 22 06 19.

Excursions

Heilig Land Stichting: Open-air Bible Museum – Open Easter to October daily from 0900 to 1800; the rest of the year for exhibitions only 8fl, children 5fl. ☎ (080) 22 98 29.

Berg en Dal: Afrika Museum – Open from 1000 (1100 Saturdays, Sundays and public holidays) to 1700; the rest of the year Tuesdays and Fridays from 1000 to 1700, Sundays and public holidays (during this period the open-air section is closed) from 1300 to 1700 . Closed on 1 January and 25 December. 7.50fl. ☎ (08895) 4 20 44.

Doornenburg Kasteel – Guided tours July and August Tuesdays to Thursdays at 1100, 1400 and 1530 (1400 and 1530 Fridays, Saturdays and Sundays); April to June and in September Sundays only at 1400 and 1530 . 5fl. ☎ (08812) 14 56.

NOORDOOSTPOLDER

Emmeloord: Watertoren – For information apply to VVV. ☎ (05270) 1 20 00.

Museum Schokland – Open from 1000 to 1700. Closed on 1 January and 25 December. 3fl. ☎ (05275) 13 96.

Urk to Enkhuizen by boat – May to late September, daily except Sundays, departures at 0900 and 1430; return boats from Enkhuizen leave at 1100 and 1530. The boat takes foot passengers and bicycles only. Day Rtn ticket 18fl; bicycle 6.50fl. ☎ (020) 626 24 66.

NUENEN

Van Gogh Documentatiecentrum – Open from 0900 to 1200 and from 1400 to 1600. Closed Saturdays, Sundays and public holidays. 1fl. ☎ (040) 63 16 68.

R

ROERMOND

ℹ Markt 24, 6041 EM, ☎ (04750) 3 32 05

Onze Lieve Vrouwe or Munsterkerk – Open from 1000 to 1200 and 1400 to 1800 Fridays (1000 to 1630 Saturdays). ☎ (04750) 3 32 05.

Kathedrale Kerk – Open April to October Saturdays from 1400 to 1700. ☎ (04750) 3 32 05.

Excursion

Thorn: Abdijkerk (Church) – Open April to October from 0930 to 1700. 2fl. ☎ (04750) 13 73.

ROTTERDAM

ℹ Centraal Station, Spoorsingel 10, 3033 GK,☎ (010) 413 60 06

Boat Trips – Excursion (9 hours) in the Delta July and August Wednesdays and Thursdays at 1000. 42.50fl. (21.50fl for children). Apply to Spido ☎ (010) 413 54 00.

Stadhuis – Guided tours by appointment. ☎ (010) 417 24 59.
Carillon Concerts: ☎ (010) 417 23 16.

St.-Laurenskerk – Open Tuesdays to Fridays from 1000 to 1600 (1200 to 1400 Thursdays mid-October to mid-May). Closed public holidays. ☎ (010) 413 14 94.

Historisch Museum Het Schielandshuis – Open from 1000 (1300 Sundays and public holidays) to 1700. Closed Mondays and on 1 January and 30 April. 6fl. ☎ (010) 433 41 88.

Museum Boymans-van Beuningen – Open from 1000 (1100 Sundays and public holidays) to 1700. Closed Mondays and on 1 January and 30 April. 6fl. ☎ (010) 441 94 00.

Museum De Dubbelde Palmboom – Same times and charges as for Historisch Museum Het Schielandshuis.

Zakkendragershuisje – Same times and charges as for Historisch Museum Het Schielandshuis.

Euromast – Open July and August from 1000 to 2300; April to June 1000 to 1900; the rest of the year 1000 to 1700; Space Tower open from 1000 to 1800. 14.50fl. (9fl for children). ☎ (010) 436 48 11.

Maritiem Museum "Prins Hendrik" – Open from 1000 (1100 Sundays and public holidays) to 1700. Closed Mondays and on 1 January and 30 April. 6fl. ☎ (010) 413 26 80.

IMAX – Showings Tuesdays to Fridays at 1400, 1500, 1930 and 2030; weekends, holidays and school holidays 1300, 1400, 1500, 1600, 1930 and 2030; 14fl, children 11fl. It is strongly advisable to book in advance, ☎ (010) 404 88 44 between 0900 and 1200.

Museum voor Volkenkunde – Same times and charges as for Maritiem Museum Prins Hendrik. ☎ (010) 411 10 55.

Diergaarde Blijdorp (Zoo) – Open from 0900 to 1800 (in summer) or 1700 (in winter). 17.50fl. (12.50fl for children). ☎ (010) 44 31 495.

Molen De Ster – Open April to November Tuesdays and Wednesdays from 0900 to 1600; the rest of the year open Wednesdays only. ☎ (010) 452 62 87.

Short Boat Trip – Duration of tour 1 1/4 hours. Departures every 45 min April to September from 0930 to 1530 and at 1700; departures March and October at 1000, 1130, 1300 and 1430; the rest of the year departures at 1100 and 1400. 12fl. (6fl for children). For information apply to Spido. ☎ (010) 413 54 00.

Long Boat Trip – Duration of tour: 2 1/4 hours. Departures June to August at 1000 and 1230. 20fl. (10fl for children). For information apply to Spido. ☎ (010) 413 54 00.

Boat Trip: Europoort – Duration of tour: 6 hours. Departure July and August at 1000. 35 fl. (17.50fl for children). For information apply to Spido. ☎ (010) 413 54 00.

Excursions

Kinderdijk

Molen – The windmills are illuminated at night during the 2nd week in September.

Boat Trips – Daily departures every 30 min May to September and during the school holidays. 2.50fl. ☎ (01859) 1 24 82.

Molen – Open April to September and during the school holidays from 0930 to 1730. 2.50 fl.

The chapter on art and architecture in this guide gives an outline of artistic achievement in the region providing the context of the buildings and works of art described in the ***Sights*** *section*

This chapter may also provide ideas for touring
It is advisable to read it at leisure

S

SCHIEDAM

Buitenhavenweg 9, 3113 BC, ☎ (010) 4 73 30 00

Stedelijk Museum – Open from 1000 (1230 Sundays and public holidays) to 1700. Closed Mondays and on 1 January, 5 May and 25 December. 3fl. ☎ (010) 426 90 67.

SCHIERMONNIKOOG See Waddeneilanden

SLUIS

St-Annastraat 15, 4524 JB, ☎ (01178) 6 17 00

Stadhuis – Open July and August and some days in April, May and June from 1000 to 1200 and 1300 to 1500. 2fl. ☎ (01178) 17 00.

Molen De Brak – Open from 1000 to 1700 Easter to October. 2.25fl. ☎ (01178) 18 10.

Aardenburg: St.-Bavokerk – Open May to September from 1000 to 1200 and from 1400 to 1630; the rest of the year by appointment. ☎ (01177) 17 34.

IJzendijke: Streekmuseum West-Zeeuws-Vlaanderen – Open Mondays to Fridays from 1000 to 1200 and 1300 to 1700; Saturdays, Sundays and public holidays from 1400 to 1700 . 2fl. ☎ (01176) 12 00.

Breskens: Vlissingen/Flushing Ferry – Departures every 30 min October to May, every hour Sundays. 11 fl. for a car and its passengers (8.25fl. out of season). Pedestrians: single ticket 1fl. ☎ (01172) 16 63.

SNEEK

Marktstraat 18, 8601 CV, ☎ (05150) 1 40 96

Stadhuis – Guided tours July to mid-August from 1400 to 1600. Closed Saturdays, Sundays, public holidays and on 11 August. ☎ (05150) 8 53 73.

Fries Scheepvaart Museum en Sneker Oudheidkamer – Open from 1000 (1200 Sundays) to 1700. Closed public holidays. 2fl. ☎ (05150) 1 40 57.

Friese Meren (Frisian Lakes)

Exmorra: Museum – Open April to October from 1000 to 1700. 3.50fl. ☎ (05157) 56 81.

Allingawier: Oude Boerderij (Farmhouse) – Open April to October from 1000 to 1700. 3fl. ☎ (05157) 56 81.

Makkum

Fries Aardewerkmuseum De Waag – Open April to October from 1000 (1330 Sundays and public holidays) to 1700. 2.50fl. ☎ (05158) 3 14 22.

Tichelaar's Aardewerk- en Tegelfabriek – Guided tours (45 min) Mondays to Fridays from 1000 to 1130 and 1300 to 1600 (1500 Fridays). The exhibition rooms are open Mondays to Fridays from 0900 to 1730 and Saturdays and public holidays 1000 to 1700. Closed on 1 January, 25 and 26 December. 4fl. ☎ (05158) 3 13 41.

Ferwoude: Boerderij (Farmhouse) – Open April to October from 1000 to 1700. 3 fl. ☎ (05157) 56 81.

Wieuwerd: Kerk – Open April to October from 0900 to 1200 and 1300 to 1630. Closed Sundays. 2fl. ☎ (05104) 12 26.

Bozum: Kerk – Open April to October from 1000 to 1800. Closed Sundays and public holidays. ☎ (05152) 383

STADSKANAAL

Excursion

Ter Apel: Oud Klooster (Convent) – Open from 1000 (1330 Sundays) to 1700. Closed Mondays. 4.50fl. ☎ (05995) 13 70.

T

TERSCHELLING See Waddeneilanden

TEXEL See Waddeneilanden

TIEL

Korenbeursplein 4, 4001 KX, ☎ (03440) 1 64 41

Excursion

Buren

Museum der Koninklijke Marechaussee – Open mid-April to September from 1000 to 1600 (1330 to 1700 Saturdays, Sundays and public holidays) . Closed Mondays. 3.50fl. ☎ (03447) 12 56.

Boerenwagenmuseum – Open May to September from 1300 to 1700. Closed Mondays. 3.50fl. ☎ (03447) 14 31.

TILBURG

Stadhuisplein 128, 5038 TC, ☎ (013) 35 11 35

Nederlands Textielmuseum – Open from 1000 (1200 Saturdays, Sundays and public holidays) to 1700. Closed Mondays and on 1 January, Easter Sunday, 30 April, 5 May, Whit Sunday and 24, 25 and 31 December. 7.50fl. ☎ (013) 36 74 75.

Excursions

Beekse Bergen: Safari-park – Open from 1000 to 1730 (July and August) or 1630 (March to June and in September) or 1600 (February, October and November) or 1530 (January and December). 16fl per person (with car), 10fl in winter, 18.50fl (with safari-car). **Strandpark (Amusement Park):** Open May to early September from 1000 to 1800. ☎ (013) 36 00 32.

Oisterwijk: Vogelpark (Bird Garden) – Open April to October from 0900 to 1800. 6fl. ☎ (04242) 8 34 49.

U

UTRECHT

🅸 Vredenburg 90, 3511 BD, ☎ (030) 06 34 40 85

Boat Trips – Boat rides on the canals (1 hour) are available all year, on the Vecht (8 1/2 hours) Tuesdays to Sundays late May to September, and on the Kromme Rijn (1 1/2 hours) Wednesdays and Sundays late May to September. Apply to Utrechts Rondvaartbedrijf. ☎ (030) 31 93 77. For information concerning boat trips on Loosdrecht Lakes apply to Watersportbedrijf Wolfrat. Landing stage: Oudegracht. To book call ☎ (030) 72 01 11. ☎ (02158) 2 33 09.

Nationaal Museum van Speelklok tot Pierement – Open from 1000 (1300 Sundays and public holidays) to 1700. Closed Mondays and on 1 January, 30 April, Easter Sunday, Whit Sunday and 25 December. 7.50fl. ☎ (030) 31 27 89. Guided tours are available in English.

Domtoren – Guided tours April to October Mondays to Fridays from 1000 to 1700; the rest of the year from 1200 to 1700 Saturdays, Sundays and public holidays. 3.50fl. ☎ (030) 91 95 40.

Domkerk – Open May to September Mondays to Fridays from 1000 to 1700 (1400 to 1600 Sundays); the rest of the year Mondays to Fridays from 1100 to 1600 (1400 to 1600 Sundays). ☎ (030) 31 04 03.

Rijksuniversiteit – Open Mondays to Fridays. ☎ (030) 53 91 11.

Pieterskerk – Open mid-July to mid-September Tuesdays to Fridays from 1100 to 1700 (1000 to 1500 Saturdays); the rest of the year by appointment. 1fl. ☎ (030) 31 14 85. **Organ Concerts:** At 1245 and 1330 Fridays in winter.

Centraal Museum – Open from 1000 (1200 Sundays and public holidays) to 1700. Closed Mondays and on 1 January and 25 December. 5fl. ☎ (030) 36 23 62.

Rijksmuseum Het Catharijneconvent – Open from 1000 (1100 Saturdays, Sundays and public holidays) to 1700. Closed Mondays and on 1 January. 5fl. ☎ (030) 31 38 35.

Nederlands Spoorwegmuseum – Open from 1000 (1300 Sundays and public holidays) to 1700. Closed Mondays and on 1 January, Easter Sunday, Whit Sunday and 25 December. 8.50fl. ☎ (030) 30 62 06.

Universiteitsmuseum – Open from 1000 (1300 Saturdays and Sundays) to 1700. Closed Mondays, on Easter Sunday and 30 April. ☎ (030) 73 13 05.

Rietveld Schröderhuis – Guided tours by appointment only Wednesdays to Sundays and on public holidays from 1100 to 1530. Closed Mondays, Tuesdays and on 1 January and 25 December. 9fl. ☎ (030) 36 23 10.

Excursions

Nieuw-Loosdrecht: Kasteel Sypesteyn – Guided tours (1 hour) Easter to the autumn holidays from 1100 (1300 Sundays and public holidays) to 1600. 6fl. ☎ (02158) 2 32 08.

Haarzuilens: Kasteel De Haar – Guided tours (1 hour) March to mid-August and mid-October to mid-November from 1100 (1300 Saturdays, Sundays and public holidays) to 1600. 10fl. ☎ (03407) 12 75.

Oud-Zuilen: Slot Zuylen – Guided tours (1 hour) from 1000 to 1600 Tuesdays to Thursdays mid-March to mid-September; from 1400 to 1600 Saturdays (1300 to 1600 Sundays) mid-September to mid-November. 6fl. ☎ (030) 44 02 55.

V

VALKENBURG

🅸 Th. Dorrenplein 5, 6301 DV, ☎ (04406) 1 33 64

Kasteel Ruïne (Castle Ruins) – Open Easter to the end of the autumn holidays from 1000 to 1700. 5fl. ☎ (04406) 1 63 55.

Steenkolenmijn Valkenburg – Guided tours (1 1/4 hours) Easter to October from 1000 to 1700; the rest of the year Saturdays and Sundays only at 1400 and 1500. Closed on 1 January, during Carnival and 25 December. 8.50fl. ☎ (04406) 1 24 91.

Gemeentegrot (Municipal Caves) – Guided tours (1 hour) April to October from 0900 to 1700; the rest of the year from 1030 to 1600. Closed on 1 January, during Carnival and 25 December. ☎ (04406) 1 22 71.

Fluwelengrot (Caves) – Guided tours (50 min) Easter to the end of the autumn holidays from 1000 to 1700. 4fl. ☎ (04406) 1 63 55.

Wilhelminatoren – Open from March to November 0800 to 2000. 2fl. ☎ (04454) 6 16 64.

Romeinse Katakomben (Catacombs) – Guided tours (45 min) April to September from 1000 to 1600; the rest of the year at 1400 Saturdays, Sundays and during the school holidays. Closed on 1 January, during Carnival and 25 December. 5fl. ☎ (04406) 1 25 54.

Streekmuseum – Open from 1000 to 1700. Closed Mondays and on 1 January and 25 December. 2.50fl. ☎ (04406) 1 30 64.

Zuid-Limburg (Southern Limburg)

Drielandenpunt: Boudewijntoren – Open from 1000 to 1700 March to October (0900 to 1900 in summer). 2fl. ☎ (04454) 6 10 19.

VEERE

ℹ Oudestraat 28, 4351 AV, ☎ (01181) 13 65

Schotse Huizen – Open mid-April to October from 1000 (1300 Mondays) to 1700. Closed Sundays. 2fl. ☎ (01181) 17 44.

Oude Stadhuis – Open June to September from 1200 to 1700. Closed Sundays and occasionally Fridays. 2fl. ☎ (01181) 19 51.
Carillon Concerts: June to September Thursdays at 1500 and 1600 and Saturdays at 1900 and 2000.

Onze Lieve Vrouwekerk – Open mid-April to October from 1000 (1400 Sundays) to 1700. 2.25fl. ☎ (01181) 18 29.

VENLO

ℹ Koninginneplein 2, 5911 KK, ☎ (077) 54 38 00

Boat Trips – Departures July and August. For information apply to VVV ☎. (077) 54 38 00 or Rederij 't Veerhuis ☎ (04759) 13 18.

St.-Martinuskerk – Open 1000 to 1200 and 1400 to 1600; afternoons only on Sundays and holidays. ☎ (077) 51 23 94.

Goltziusmuseum – Open from 1000 to 1630 (1400 to 1700 Saturdays, Sundays and public holidays). Closed Mondays, during Carnival, on Easter Sunday, 30 April and 25 December. 2.50fl. ☎ (077) 59 67 62.

Museum van Bommel-van Dam – Open from 1000 to 1630 (1400 to 1700 Saturdays, Sundays and public holidays). Closed Mondays and on 1 January, during Carnival, Good Friday, Easter Sunday, 30 April and 25 December. 2.50fl. ☎ (077) 51 34 57.

Excursions

Tegelen

Museum Steyl – Open 21 March to 20 October and during the Christmas holidays from 1000 to 1700; the rest of the year Sundays and public holidays from 1300 to 1700. Closed Mondays 20 October to 20 March and on 1 January, Good Friday and 25 December. 3fl. ☎ (077) 76 82 94.

Botanische Tuin Jochum-Hof – Open Easter to October from 1100 to 1700. 4fl. ☎ (077) 73 30 20.

VENRAY

ℹ Grote Markt 23, 5801 BL, ☎ (04780) 1 05 05

St.-Petrus Bandenkerk – Open Mondays to Saturdays from 1400 to 1600. ☎ (04780) 1 05 05.

Excursion

Overloon: Nederlands Nationaal Oorlogs- en Verzetsmuseum – Open June to August from 0930 to 1800; the rest of the year from 1000 to 1700. Closed on 24 and 25 December. 8fl. ☎ (04781) 41820.

VLIELAND See Waddeneilanden

VLISSINGEN

ℹ Nieuwendijk 15, 4381 BV, ☎ (01184) 1 23 45

Vlissingen/Flushing: Boat Trips – Departures in July and August. Apply to VVV. ☎ (01184) 1 92 75.

W

WADDENEILANDEN

Crossing the mud-flats – Walking tours are conducted daily April to October (weather permitting). 10-28 fl. To obtain a brochure (in English) and to book, apply to Dijkstra's Wadlooptochten, Hoofdstraat 118, 9968 AM Pieterburen. ☎ (05952) 345.

Ameland

ℹ Rixt van Doniaweg 2, Nes 9163 GR, ☎ (05191) 4 25 25

Access – Reservations needed for cars: Wagenborg's Passagiersdiensten, Reeweg 4, 9163 ZM Nes, Ameland. ☎ (05191) 4 61 11. Bicycles for hire in each locality. Access to the main beach (Badstrand) by bus from the landing stage.

Hollum: Sorgdragermuseum – Open April to October Mondays, Saturdays and Sunday afternoons from 0930 to 1230 and 1400 to 1630; November to March Tuesdays to Fridays from 1400 to 1630. Closed public holidays. 3.25fl. ☎ (05191) 5 44 77.

Reddingsmuseum Abraham Fock – Open April to late September, Mondays to Fridays, 0930 to 1230 and 1400 to 1630; weekends and holidays 1400 to 1630; the rest of the year, Mondays to Saturdays, 1400 to 1600; 3fl; ☎ (05191) 5 42 43.
Reddingboot (Lifeboat) – 7 to 8 demonstrations a year; phone VVV ☎ (05191) 4 20 20.

Schiermonnikoog

ℹ Reeweg 5, 9166 PW, ☎ (05195) 3 12 33

Access – Crossing takes approximately 45 min. 14.80fl Rtn. No cars allowed on the island. Bicycles for hire at Schiermonnikoog.

Bezoekerscentrum en Natuurhistorisch Museum – Open April to October and during the school holidays from 1330 to 1700; additionally, June to August Mondays, Wednesdays and Fridays from 1900 to 2100; the rest of the year apply to the Visitor Centre and VVV. Closed Sundays. ☎ (05195) 3 16 41.

Terschelling

ℹ Willem Barentskade 19a, West-Terschelling 8881 EC, ☎ (05620) 30 00

Access – Crossing takes 1 1/2 hours, 2 to 3 times a day. 37.65fl. For cars (average price 19.40fl per 0.50m length) it is necessary to book with Rederij Doeksen. ☎ (05620) 61 11. For crossings between Vlieland and Terschelling see at Vlieland. Bicycles for hire in most localities. For car rentals apply to Autoverhuur Visser, Westerburen 15, Midsland. ☎ (05620) 89 66.

Gemeentemuseum 't Behouden Huys – Open April to October Mondays to Fridays from 1000 to 1700; open mid-June to August and Sundays July and August from 1300 to 1700 Saturdays. 5fl. ☎ (05620) 23 89.

De Boschplaat – To tour in a wagon apply to Hoorn (Terpstra, Dorpsstraat 20). 20-25fl. For guided tours apply to VVV, West-Terschelling. ☎ (05620) 30 00.

Texel

ℹ Emmalaan 66, Den Burg 1791 AV, ☎ (02220) 1 47 41

Access – Crossing takes approximately 20 min. No reservations taken for cars. 11.15fl. per person Rtn, 49.25fl. per car.

Natuurreservaten – Guided tours: Slufter Reserve at 1100 April to August; Muy and Geul Reserves at 1100 April to August; Westerduinen Reserve at 1100 May to mid-July. For reservations apply to ☎ (02220) 1 77 41 between 0900 and 1700 (except Sundays November to March). Boots and binoculars recommended.

Eco Mare – Open from 0900 to 1700. Closed Sundays November to March and on 1 January and 25 December. 8fl. ☎ (02220) 1 77 41. **Seals** are fed at 1100 and 1500.

Oudheidkamer – Open from 1000 to 1230 and from 1330 to 1500 April to October. Closed Saturdays and Sundays. 3fl. ☎ (02220) 1 31 35.

Agrarisch en Wagenmuseum – Open Easter to the autumn holidays Mondays from 1300 to 1700, Tuesdays to Saturdays from 1000 to 1700 and Sundays 1400 to 1600. 3.50fl. ☎ (02220) 1 86 22.

Vlieland

ℹ Havenweg 10, 8899 BB, ☎ (05621) 11 11

Access – From Harlingen (crossing: 1 1/2 hours) 2 or 3 times a day. From Terschelling: daily May to September except on Sundays and the 1st Tuesday of each month. From Texel: mid-May to September. No cars allowed on the island. Bicycles for hire at Dorpsstraat 2, 8, 17 and 113 or Havenweg 7.

Tromp's Huys – Open May to September from 1000 to 1200 and from 1400 to 1700 (1400 to 1700 Saturdays); October and April daily from 1400 to 1700; open November to March Wednesdays and Saturdays from 1400 to 1700. 3fl. ☎ (05621) 16 00.

Bezoekerscentrum (Visitor Centre) – Open May to September from 1000 to 1200 and 1400 to 1700; from October and April 1400 to 1600; November to March Wednesdays and Saturdays only from 1400 to 1600. Closed Sundays. 3fl. ☎ (05621) 1700.

Kerk – Apply to VVV. ☎ (05621) 11 11.

WORKUM

ℹ Waaggebouw, Merk 4, 8711 CL, ☎ (05151) 4 13 00

St.-Gertrudiskerk – Open March Tuesdays, Thursdays and Saturdays from 1300 to 1700 (Mondays to Saturdays in April); May to September Mondays to Saturdays from 1100 to 1700. 1.50fl. ☎ 05151) 4 19 76.

Museum Warkums Erfskip – Open March to October Mondays and Saturdays from 1300 to 1700 and Tuesdays to Fridays from 1000 to 1700; open April to October Sundays from 1300 to 1700. 2.50fl. ☎ (05151) 4 31 55.

Z

ZAANSTREEK

Boat Trips – 50 min. Departures every hour April to September from 1000 to 1700. 7fl.

Klompenmakerij – Open from 0900 to 1730. ☎ (075) 17 71 21.

Bakkerijmuseum – Open July and August daily from 1000 to 1700; April, May, June, September and October Tuesdays to Sundays; November to February Saturdays and Sundays only. 1.50fl. ☎ (075) 17 35 22.

ZAANSTREEK

Kaasmakerij Catharina Hoeve – Open from 0900 to 1800. ☎ (075) 21 58 20.

Tinnegieterij – Open March to December from 1000 to 1700; the rest of the year Saturdays, Sundays and public holidays. ☎ (075) 17 62 04.

Uurwerkenmuseum – Open March to October from 1000 to 1300 and 1400 to 1700; the rest of the year Saturdays, Sundays and public holidays from 1200 to 1700. 2.50 fl. ☎ (075) 17 97 69.

Museum Kruidenierswinkel Albert Heijn – Open March to October from 1000 to 1300 and from 1400 to 1700. ☎ (075) 16 96 19.

Het Noorderhuis – Open July and August daily from 1000 to 1700; March to October Tuesdays to Sundays; the rest of the year Saturdays, Sundays and public holidays only. 1.50 fl. ☎ (075) 17 32 37.

De Poelenburg – Open the 2nd Saturday of the month from 1400 to 1700. 3.50fl. ☎ (075) 21 02 08.

De Kat – Open April to October from 0900 to 1700; the rest of the year Saturdays and Sundays only. Closed Mondays. 3.50fl. ☎ (075) 21 04 77.

De Zoeker – Open March to October Mondays from 1030 to 1600 (1045 to 1145 Tuesdays to Fridays). 3.50fl. ☎ (075) 28 58 22.

Additional sights

Zaandijk: Zaanlandse Oudheidkamer – Open from 1000 to 1200 and 1400 to 1600 (afternoons only Sundays and public holidays). Closed Mondays, Saturdays and on 1 January, Easter Sunday and Whit Sunday. 2.50fl. ☎ (075) 21 76 26.

Koog aan de Zaan: Molenmuseum – Open Tuesdays to Fridays from 1000 to 1200 and 1300 to 1700; Saturdays from 1400 to 1700 and Sundays and public holidays from 1300 to 1700; additionally, open April to September Mondays from 1300 to 1700. ☎ (075) 28 89 68.

ZIERIKZEE — **i** Havenpark 29, 4301 JG, ☎ (01110) 1 24 50

Boat Trips – Departures Easter to September. For information apply to Rederij den Breejen, Mantelmeeuwstraat 13, 4301 WT Zierikzee. ☎ (01110) 1 49 95.

Maritiem Museum – Open April to October and during the school holidays from 1000 (1200 Sundays and public holidays) to 1700. Closed on 1 January and 25 December. 2 fl. ☎ (01110) 1 31 51.

Stadhuis: Carillon Concerts – At 1030 Thursdays.
Stadhuismuseum: Open May to October from 1000 to 1700. Closed Saturdays and Sundays. 2 fl.☎(01110) 1 31 51.

St.-Lievensmonstertoren – Open April to mid-September from 1100 (1200 Sundays and public holidays) to 1600; the rest of the year open during school holidays only (same times). 2 fl. ☎ (01110) 1 59 38.

ZUTPHEN — **i** Wijnhuis, Groenmarkt 40, 7201 HZ, ☎ (05750) 1 93 55

St.-Walburgskerk – Open late June to mid-September from 1030 (1330 Mondays) to 1600; guided tours May and June and 13 to 25 September at 1100 (except Mondays), 1400 and 1500. Closed Sundays. 2.50 fl. ☎ (05750) 1 93 55.

Museum Henriette Polak – Open from 1100 to 1700 (1330 to 1700 Saturdays, Sundays and public holidays). Closed Mondays and on 1 January, Easter Sunday, Whit Sunday and 25 December. 3fl. ☎ (05750) 1 68 78.

Wijnhuistoren: Carillon – Thursdays and Saturdays at 1100.

Stedelijk Museum – Same times and charges as for Museum Henriette Polak.

Excursion

Groenlo: Het Grolsch Museum – Open April to September from 1000 to 1200 and 1400 to 1700. Closed Saturdays, Sundays and over Easter. 2 fl. ☎ (05440) 6 36 18.

ZWOLLE — **i** Grote Kerkplein 14, 8011 PK, ☎ (038) 21 39 00

Provinciaal Overijssels Museum – Open from 1000 (1400 Sundays and public holidays) to 1700. Closed Mondays and on 1 January, Easter Sunday, Whit Sunday and 25 December. 2.50 fl. ☎ (038) 21 46 50.

St.-Michaëlskerk – The church was closed for restoration work, for opening times apply to the VVV, ☎ (038) 21 39 00.

Stadhuis – Open from 0900 to 1600. Closed Saturdays, Sundays and public holidays. ☎ (038) 98 21 58.

Join us in our constant task of keeping up-to-date
Please send us your comments and suggestions

Michelin Tyre PLC
Tourism Department
The Edward Hyde Building
38 Clarendon Road
WATFORD - Herts WD1 1SX
Tel: (0923) 41 50 00

INDEX

Haarlem N.-Holland	**Towns, sights and tourist regions followed by name of the province.**
Rembrandt	**People, historical events, artistic styles and local terms explained in the text.**
Mauritshuis	**Sights in important towns.**

A

B

C

D

I - IJ

J - K

L

M

N

O

P - Q

R

S

T

U

V

W

Y - Z

MANUFACTURE FRANÇAISE DES PNEUMATIQUES MICHELIN

Société en commandite par actions au capital de 2 000 000 000 de francs

Place des Carmes-Déchaux - 63 Clermont-Ferrand (France)

R.C.S. Clermont-Fd B 855 200 507

Dépôt légal octobre 94 – ISBN 2-06-157401-7 – ISSN 0763-1383

Printed in the EC 09-94-28

Photocomposition : TALLON Type, Bruxelles
Impression et Brochage : MAME Imprimeurs, Tours